Also by Fox Butterfield

The Pentagon Papers *(with Neil Sheehan, Hedrick Smith, and E. W. Kenworthy)*
American Missionaries in China *(edited by Kwang-Ching Liu)*

CHINA

ALIVE
IN
THE
BITTER
SEA

<small>REVISED AND UPDATED</small>

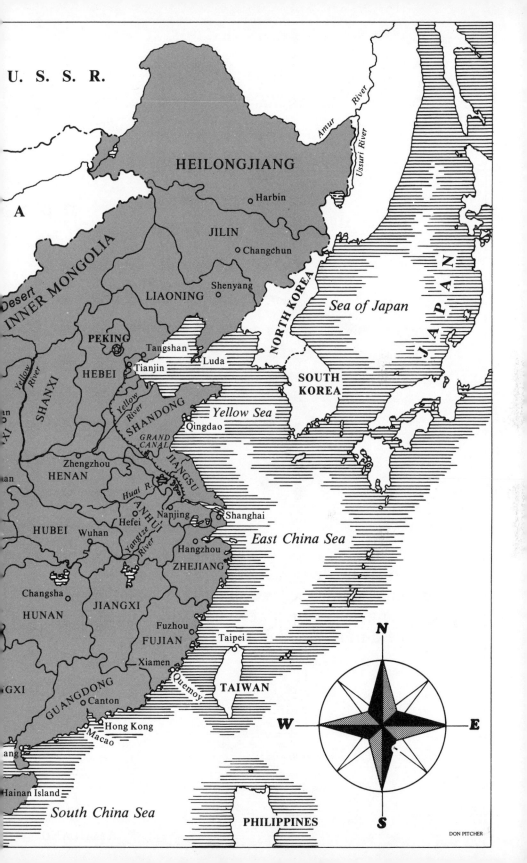

"Alive in the bitter sea," *Ku-hai yu-sheng,* is an ancient Buddhist adage about survival in a world of suffering that Chinese revived to describe their experience during the Cultural Revolution.

CHINA

ALIVE
IN
THE
BITTER
SEA

Revised and Updated

Fox Butterfield

TIMES BOOKS

RANDOM HOUSE

This book was originally published in different form
by Times Books, a division of Quadrangle/The New
York Times Book Co., Inc., in 1982.

Calligraphy by Charles Chu

Library of Congress Cataloging-in-Publication Data

Butterfield, Fox.
    China, alive in the bitter sea / by Fox Butterfield. — Updated
and rev. ed.
        p.   cm.
    ISBN 0-394-91865-7
    1. China. I. Title.
    DS706.B79   1990
    098—dc20
    [951]   89-40791

Manufactured in the United States of America

9   8   7   6   5   4   3   2

Random House, Inc. 1990 Edition

To the memory of my mother and father:
Elizabeth Eaton Butterfield
and
Lyman Henry Butterfield

CONTENTS

Preface   xiii

Preface to the Revised Edition   xvii

Introduction: Clawed by the Tiger   3

*Part One: Connections

1. Foreign Devils—Hostmanship   23

2. "Where Are You, Comrade?"—Identity   39

3. The Giant Flight of Stairs—
   Rank But Not Class   64

4. The Back Door—Getting Along   89

5. Eating Bitterness—Lihua   113

*Part Two: Passages

6. Sex Without Joy—Love and Marriage   129

7. Holding Up Half the Sky—Women   162

8. No Road Out—Youth   179

9. Growing Up Guai—
   The Chinese Passages   203

10. Report in the Evening—Bing   221

*Part Three: Systems

11. A Pig Under the Roof—Peasants   235

12. The Iron Rice Bowl—Industry   258
13. Follow the Leader—The Organization   280
14. A World Turned Upside Down—
Hong and Weidong   305

*Part Four: Persuasions
15. Soldiers in the Grass—
The Control Apparatus   319
16. *Lao Gai*—The Chinese Gulag   342
17. The American Agent—Dr. Bill Gao   370

*Part Five: Messages
18. Little Road News—Information   383
19. To Rebel Is Justified—Dissent   406
20. Serving the Workers and Peasants—
Wang Keping   435

Epilogue: Still Alive in
the Bitter Sea   446
Index   481

Illustrations follow page 236.

PREFACE

If, as the Chinese say, a journey of a thousand miles begins with a single step, this book had its origin in the now dimly remembered crisis over the islands of Quemoy and Matsu in 1958. In August of that year Mao Zedong had ordered the bombardment of these two outposts occupied by the Chinese Nationalists, and there was fear the Eisenhower administration might be drawn into war with Peking because of the Mutual Security Treaty between Taiwan and the United States. I was about to begin my sophomore year at Harvard, and the controversy over the "offshore islands" impelled me to attend a lecture by Professor John K. Fairbank. Fairbank, a tall, spare man with a passionate commitment to the study of China and a dry, ironic wit, told the audience that China had 800 million people and an ancient history— and therefore it was a country to be taken seriously.

On the surface this seemed a simplistic thesis, but as Fairbank expounded it, I began to appreciate that here was the oldest nation on earth, with the largest number of people, and I knew nothing about it. I decided to sit in on Social Sciences 111, an introduction to the history of China, Japan, and Southeast Asia then taught by Fairbank and Edwin O. Reischauer (three years later, President Kennedy named Reischauer as his ambassador to Tokyo). It turned out to be the beginning of a romance that has lasted over two decades; I was infatuated with China. I still couldn't pronounce Chinese names correctly. But when we read Edgar Snow's account of the Communists' epic Long March in the 1930s, *Red Star Over China,* I instinctively felt attracted to Mao and his followers for the hope and idealism they offered China after the misery and corruption of the Kuomintang period.

The next spring, when final exam time came, I enclosed a stamped, self-addressed postcard with my blue test booklet, in keeping with Harvard practice. The card came back with a summons to report to Fairbank's office. What had I done wrong? I wondered as I walked to Widener Library at the appointed hour.

"You wrote a wonderful exam," Fairbank said, to my relief. "Have you considered Chinese studies as a career? You ought to begin studying Chinese."

I was flattered. I didn't yet know that Fairbank, the proselytizer, tried this routine out on almost anyone eccentric enough to show an interest in his field. And so that summer I did start studying Chinese. It was still such an obscure subject that the next fall when I asked for Chinese tapes at the Harvard languages laboratory the matronly looking woman behind the desk peered at me over the top of her glasses as if I had stumbled into the wrong church. "Chinese? Chinese?" she repeated. "Isn't Chinese a dead language?"

But each new course I took drew me deeper. I wrote my senior thesis on an unlikely group of American missionaries in north China who at the beginning of World War Two cooperated with the Communists, also attracted by their ideals and reform-minded policies. When I graduated in 1961, I journeyed to Taiwan on a Fulbright Fellowship to try to improve my spoken Chinese. There I lived with a Chinese family, discovered the joys of real Chinese food, and began to learn about how the Chinese social universe differs from ours. Later I went back to Harvard for five years for graduate work in Chinese history and then returned to Taiwan again in 1967 to do research on my doctoral dissertation.

By now, however, it was the height of the American war in Vietnam, and a life spent re-creating the past in musty library stacks had come to seem irrelevant. I wanted to get to China, to experience it first hand. So when I was offered a job as a stringer, or part-time reporter, in Taiwan for *The New York Times,* I happily accepted. I dreamed of being the first American correspondent to live in Peking after 1949.

It took me ten years to get there. There were two mandatory years learning the craft of journalism at *The Times* in New York and then a series of assignments in Asia—in Vietnam, Japan, and Hong Kong—waiting for China to open its doors to U.S. news organizations. When Jimmy Carter finally normalized U.S. relations with China in December 1978, I was ready to go to Peking, though unfortunately it meant leaving my wife, Barbara, who was pregnant, and our three-year-old son, Ethan, in Hong Kong. Peking had an acute housing shortage, and the government warned me that the only accommodation they could offer for at least the next year was a single hotel room, hardly enough space to both live in with my family and do my work.

As a police state, China poses special problems for a journalist. Many of the most significant insights I gained, or the most poignant anecdotes I heard, came from people I cannot name or portray in detail because of the reprisals they would face. Wherever possible, I have identified the people I knew, and wherever a full three-syllable Chinese name appears, like that of the sculptor Wang Keping, it is the name of the actual person. But where I felt it necessary to camouflage identities, I have either left my informants anonymous or given them only a fictional first or last name, like Lihua, the young petitioner in Chapter 5, or Bing, in Chapter 10. In several cases, I have altered minor details of my friends' lives to protect them—placing them in a different city or giving them a new occupation. But all their comments and quotations are genuine, and none of the characters are composites.

This book is intended for general readers, and I hope that specialists will forgive a few conventions I have chosen to make it easier for the ordinary reader. Instead of the usual Chinese nomenclature for their education system—junior middle school and senior middle school—I have opted for the more familiar terms junior and senior high school. I have followed *The New York Times*'s policy of adopting the Communists' *pinyin* system for transcribing Chinese names except for a few well-known places. The capital of China thus remains Peking, rather than the *pinyin* version, Beijing. Similarly, in keeping with *The Times*'s format, I have retained the traditional spelling for places and people outside the mainland, like Hong Kong (which would become Xiang Gang in *pinyin*), and the Nationalist leaders like Chiang Kai-shek and his son, Chiang Ching-kuo. The *pinyin* system presents a few special tasks for the English-speaking reader: Q is pronounced like the ch in chicken, x like the s in she, zh like the j in Joe, and c is like the ts in hats.

I alone am responsible for the judgments in this book, but my obligations to others who helped me on my journey are manifold. I owe a primary debt to Jan Wong, my assistant in Peking, for her guidance, enthusiasm, and generous introductions to her Chinese friends. Jan appears by name on a number of pages, but her real contributions are immeasurable. I am deeply grateful to my editors at *The New York Times,* A. M. Rosenthal and Seymour Topping, who encouraged and sustained this enterprise. John Fairbank at Harvard, who introduced me to China, has been a wise counselor for many years. To him and to several other academic specialists I am indebted for their useful suggestions: Merle Goldman at Boston University, Nicholas Lardy at Yale, and Jerome Alan Cohen, formerly of the Harvard Law School and now of New York. I want to express thanks to two sage Chinese friends in Hong Kong who instructed me in the arcane art of China-watching, Vincent Lo and Sydney Liu; to my journalistic colleagues in Peking, Michael Parks, Victoria Graham, and Liu Heunghsing, for their timely assistance; to friends in the diplomatic corps who shared their knowledge and time, Roger Garside of the British Embassy, and Charles Sylvester, Christopher Szymanski, and William McCahill of the U.S. mission; to the research staff of *The New York Times* for their prompt and resourceful aid, Barbara Oliver, Donna Anderson, and Judith Greenfeld; to others in Peking who contributed generously, Eileen Wu and Janet Yang; and not least to Charles Chu of Connecticut College, who graciously provided the handsome calligraphy that decorates the book.

Roger Jellinek, my main editor, has been an imaginative, patient, and invaluable guide. I also want to express special acknowledgment to my other editor, Fredrica S. Friedman, for her constant encouragement and judicious improvements. And I have a particular debt to those Chinese who cannot be named but who made this book possible.

F.B.
Wellesley, Massachusetts
February 1, 1982

PREFACE
TO THE REVISED EDITION

One day in late May, 1989, with up to a million Chinese joyously gathering in Tiananmen Square to call for greater democracy, I received a letter from a student at People's University in Peking. He said a group of professors and students at his school, which had been founded to produce future leaders of the Communist Party, had translated this book into Chinese. The translators were members of the Chinese Communist Party History Department, the only such department allowed in China, where heroes are often transmogrified into villains and villains into heroes within the course of a semester. The student explained that he and his colleagues wanted to publish my book in Chinese because they felt it was the most accurate depiction of contemporary Chinese society. Would I assent to the publication and would I write a new preface, he asked?

Naturally, I was enormously flattered. I also took it as a good omen for China. For I knew China's rulers had reacted angrily when the book was first published in 1982. There were reports that senior officials in the Foreign Ministry had complained to the American embassy about the book, and even inquired about whether Washington could stop its publication. The Party Central Committee issued a lengthy confidential document designed to rebut much of what I had written. Some American tourists said Chinese customs officials had confiscated their copies of the book. But other tourists wrote to tell me that their guides, from the China Travel Service, had eagerly asked to borrow the book and then devoured it. And many individual Chinese who had come to the United States to study wrote to say that the book correctly portrayed their own lives.

So I was delighted with the student's request to write a new preface for the Chinese edition. I was especially pleased because I learned through an American scholar who had been doing research at People's University, Lee Feighon, a professor of history at Colby College, that members of the Communist Party History Department were among the earliest and most active leaders of the pro-democracy demonstrations. On April 15, after the death of Hu Yaobang, the former party General Secretary who had been ousted after being blamed for a series of student protests two years earlier, a group of undergraduates and graduate students from the Party History Department went to Tiananmen Square. There they layed wreaths in honor of Hu, whom they cherished as the patron of liberalization. This was the action that sparked the student demonstrations. Significantly, these early protestors from the Party History Department were not radicals attacking the Communist Party; instead they saw themselves as future leaders of the Party and were upset by all the corruption and bureaucratism besetting the regime. They wanted reform from within, not revolution to overthrow the Party, as the authorities would eventually charge.

Two days later, on April 17, the students in the Party History Department began a boycott of classes, demanding a reappraisal of Hu's career—this was the first student demand of the spring. The same group of students also formed a militia to enforce the strike throughout People's University, and the idea soon spread to other schools in the city, including nearby Peking University. On April 17, Professor Feighon told me, it was again students from the Party History Department who formulated plans for a large march into Tiananmen Square on the day of Mr. Hu's funeral, the initial large student foray into central Peking. And most important, on April 27, after Deng Xiaoping, China's senior leader, had secretly called for a crackdown on any further student activities, it was students from People's University who led a procession into downtown Peking, pushing past police lines for the first time. The die was now cast.

Tragically, before I could respond to the request to write a preface for the Chinese edition, China's aging oligarchs called in the People's Liberation Army on the evening of June 3 to put an end to the greatest effort to introduce democracy in China since the Communists' triumph in 1949. Several hundred, perhaps several thousand Chinese civilians were killed in the resulting massacre. Without a full accounting by the Chinese government, no one will ever know the exact number. (Amnesty International estimates that at least 1,000 people were killed in Peking alone; the Chinese Red Cross in a preliminary unofficial count said 2,600.) Thousands more were arrested throughout China and an unknown number executed. At the order of Deng, to avoid further adverse publicity overseas, Peking simply stopped announcing arrests and executions after the first few days.

Nevertheless, the crackdown continued, albeit quietly. At People's University, students were ordered to attend daily political study sessions. A few of the most active protestors were forced to write lengthy confessions detailing their actions during the Peking spring. The confession of one young professor, who was kept under house arrest, was said to have reached more than 3,000 pages. He and others faced the loss of their jobs and the likelihood of being transferred to a distant province, away from their families.

In June, shortly after the massacre, *The New York Times* asked me to go to Hong Kong and then on to China to help with the paper's coverage. The month-long assignment gave me a rare chance, a special privilege for an author, to test my earlier judgments in this book against what has happened in China since I had left there in 1981. There were some things I had not foreseen, mainly the rapid economic changes that flowed from Deng's decade of reforms. These include a cornucopia of new consumer goods, miles of new housing, a profusion of privately owned restaurants and shops, and a vastly greater variety in dress. But most of my original assessments, harsh as they may have been, remained valid: that the Communists had created an extraordinarily repressive control system, that the Communist Party had become a privileged elite, and that the cruelties of the Cultural Revolution had fostered widespread disillusionment with the Communists. In the original edition, I had written that China had become an authoritarian country with an authority crisis. That conclusion seems even more true today. Indeed, most Chinese I talked with were, if anything, more cynical now than at the beginning of the decade.

In an epilogue, which forms the final chapter of this new edition, I try to take account of the economic changes of recent years and show how the enduring problems of repression, privilege and disenchantment have continued. In a very real sense, they form the background to the democracy movement and then the government's brutal crackdown. I have not, however, sought to write a complete history of these stunning events in April, May, and June of 1989; I leave that in the capable hands of Chinese and foreigners who participated in or observed firsthand what took place.

Except for the epilogue, the book remains substantially unchanged. To avoid confusion in the body of the book, I have left virtually all statistics, dates, and official titles as they were when the book was published in 1982. These include the exchange rate between China's currency, the renmenbi, and the dollar, and the post of Deng Xiaoping, who at the time was deputy Party chairman. Then, as now, Deng's titular position carried little clue to his real power. I have also retained the spelling of China's capital as Peking, which was what almost everyone I knew in 1981 called it. Many old China hands still do. The reader, however, should be aware of several changes. China's population has increased to 1.1 billion, Peking's residents have exploded from 4 million to 9.7 million and the number of members of the Communist Party has climbed from 38 million to 47 million. There is another change—I am no longer married to Barbara, my wife at the time I lived in China. But all the experiences described in the book were genuinely shared.

I offer the epilogue as a poor substitute for the new chapter I happily would have written for the Chinese translation.

CHINA

ALIVE
IN
THE
BITTER
SEA

REVISED AND UPDATED

Clawed by the Tiger

虎 口 逃 生

INTRODUCTION

It was a cold, overcast day in January 1980 when I arrived at the cavernous Shanghai railroad station for the overnight express train to Peking. A blue-uniformed woman conductor with short pigtails poking out from under her round cap was waiting beside the door to my car. In what had seemed a routine transaction, I had purchased my ticket the day before in an office of the China Travel Service, the state-run tourist agency. At least the middle-aged clerk at the counter had not evinced any particular interest in me—I just presented my green travel pass from the Public Security Bureau, China's police, and paid for my passage. That struck me as a good omen. I had chosen to make the trip by train, a twenty-hour ride, rather than by plane, a mere two hours' flight, in hopes of encountering some Chinese who might be willing to ignore the official regulations against talking to a foreigner away from the prying eyes of neighbors or office mates. It was a tactic other Westerners in China had sometimes used with success.

But when I approached the green and yellow train, the conductor's broad face broke into an immense smile. "Welcome to our train," she said almost too eagerly. "You are the American reporter, are you not?"

It was more a statement of fact than a question. As I stood with my suitcase in my hand, I might as well have been naked. My hopes continued to fade as the conductor, a stocky woman in her late twenties, whose bulk was magnified by the layers of sweaters and padded underwear she had stuffed under her uniform, began walking down the car corridor. Through a crack in my compartment door, I could hear her stopping to announce to the other passengers in her booming voice:

"We have a foreigner on board. He is an American journalist. He speaks Chinese. He speaks very good Chinese." That was the alert, I calculated.

Then she returned to minister to me. "Please let me know if there is

3

anything I can do to serve you. My name is Ding." An appropriate appellation, for in Chinese *ding* means solid, like nails, and she struck me as a rare cross between a Marine drill sergeant and a cheerful, overweight waitress.

Mustering the remains of my courage, I asked Ding how she was so well informed about me. "The responsible comrades notify us who the passengers are, so we can make preparations," she replied.

Ding's preparations included making sure that I had the four-berth compartment all to myself, a comfortable but to me disappointing way to travel. Still, I thought, I might meet someone in the dining car. What time was lunch? I asked Ding.

"I will call you after the other passengers are finished," she answered. "It will be more convenient for you, it won't be so crowded."

Indeed, when she finally did summon me, there were only two Chinese left in the dining car, and they were finishing their soup, the last course in a Chinese meal. When they saw me, they hastily gulped down the final sips and departed. I felt like the plague. As the train crossed the rice fields of the Yangtze River Valley, dry and brown in the weak winter afternoon, the long trip appeared a mistake.

Several hours later when we stopped in Nanjing, the old capital of Chiang Kai-shek's Nationalists, I got out to stretch my legs. Ding was already on the platform, a bucket and mop in her hands, to wash down the outside of our car. She was the model of discipline. Another passenger, a dignified man with only a thin patch of white hair left on his head, who appeared to be in his seventies, was also taking some exercise. In the most innocent gambit I could think of, I asked if he was going to Peking.

The answer came back in flawless English. "Yes, are you?" Again I was caught off guard. "Where did you learn such good English?" I continued, growing bolder.

"At Harvard. I went to Harvard Medical School and lived in Cambridge, before Liberation in 1949," the stranger explained. By chance, I went to Harvard also, and Cambridge is my hometown. When the time came to reboard the train, the doctor volunteered to sit with me.

"You are the first American I have talked to since 1949," he said. He had tucked his hands up inside the long sleeves of his padded brown jacket with a high mandarin collar against the cold, an old Chinese gesture. "Until recently I wouldn't have dared to be seen with you, but I think it may be all right now," he said. Then, as afternoon turned into evening, he recounted the story of his past thirty years.

Like many of his friends studying abroad, he had returned to China in 1949 because he felt himself a patriot and wanted to take part in rebuilding China. "I was not a Communist," the doctor said, "but I admired what they were trying to do. Old China was so backward, so poor, and so corrupt, there were beggars who starved to death in the streets every day." The early 1950s were a time of optimism—under Communist guidance, new factories were built, land in the countryside was collectivized, and China proved its strength by fighting the United States to a standstill in Korea.

But the doctor's life changed in 1957 with the Hundred Flowers campaign, the time when Mao Zedong encouraged greater freedom of expression and invited intellectuals like him to criticize the Party's shortcomings in the belief that the overwhelming majority of Chinese now accepted Communist rule.

"I took Mao at his word, I thought he was sincere," the physician recalled. When the Shanghai city government asked him to a large meeting to express his views, he recommended that the Communists ought to remove the largely uneducated former peasants turned guerrilla warriors whom they had installed as Party secretaries to run the country's hospitals. Instead, he urged, hospitals should be left to the charge of professional doctors. But a few weeks later Mao reversed his policy and instituted the Anti-Rightist campaign.

"They did what they call 'putting a cap' on me, I was labeled a rightist." The doctor was taken to a struggle session, a mass meeting where the victim is shouted at, insulted, and often beaten by dozens of people until he finally confesses his supposed crimes. "They called it a 'self-help meeting,' to help me improve my attitude," he continued in a simple matter-of-fact tone devoid of self-pity. After a month of this treatment, he was arrested, imprisoned, and eventually sent to a labor reform camp in the mountains several days' bus ride from Shanghai, where he worked breaking rocks in a quarry.

He got out of the labor camp just in time to be assailed again in the Cultural Revolution. Mao launched this adventure in 1966 both to oust his adversaries in the Party hierarchy and to prevent the country from slipping back into what the Great Helmsman feared were the soft, corrupt ways of pre-1949 China. The doctor was arrested once more—his old label of rightist made him a handy target for eager radicals in his hospital. They incarcerated him in a basement room in the hospital where autopsies were performed and beat him with wooden boards every day for several months. This time his label was also extended to his family. His wife, a doctor herself, was prohibited from practicing medicine and made to sweep the floors and clean the toilets in her clinic. His son, a brilliant medical school student who had passed the college entrance exams with nearly the highest marks in China, was shipped off to labor as a peasant in a village in the far northeast. His teen-age daughter was expelled from her junior high school, since she was the offspring of a reactionary, and assigned to work in an automobile garage.

After Mao's death and the overthrow of the radical Gang of Four, including Mao's termagant widow, Jiang Qing, in 1976, the doctor had been restored to a position of authority in his hospital. But he was still surrounded by his former tormentors, with whom he had to work daily. "It's funny, some of them now fall asleep at political study sessions from boredom," he said of his accusers. "For all of us, the revolution is over. What is left is cynicism. It is very sad for China."

This episode on the train was typical of my experience in China. There seemed to be two Chinas: one the official version, with a cast of people like the conductor, cardboard cutouts from the *People's Daily,* the Communist Party newspaper, always smiling, selfless, and dedicated to the cause. The other China was partially hidden, an inner universe whose one billion inhabitants had gone through three decades of cataclysmic change, sometimes for the better, but often, like the doctor's trauma, involving brutality, waste, and terrible personal suffering. The tragic concatenation of one political campaign after another—land reform in the early 1950s, the Hundred Flowers Campaign, the Great Leap Forward in 1958 with its resulting food shortages, the Cultural Revolution in the late 1960s, and the continued factional battles in the 1970s—had left a legacy of popular apathy and disillusionment. Gone were the idealism, the drive, the almost religious fervor which marked the Communists' early years.

The official China was the one I had read about in the often breathless accounts of Western visitors who had spent a few weeks in China. Traveling on the invisible dotted line of a few dozen cities and communes that is the authorized itinerary for almost all foreigners in China, they had returned to assure the world that China had really ended crime, inflation, and unemployment. China was the country where a tourist who left a used razor blade or an expended ball-point pen in his wastebasket would have it miraculously returned to him at the next city he visited. China was also the remarkable land where millions of urban high school graduates, following Chairman Mao Zedong's call, happily went off to work for the rest of their lives as peasants in the villages, like Boy Scouts, some Americans said. I remembered Jerry Rubin stopping in my office in Hong Kong, where I reported on China for four years for *The New York Times* before American news organizations were permitted to open bureaus in Peking in 1979, after the normalization of Sino–American relations. The former Yippie leader had just spent several weeks touring China and he enthused over what he said was "the spirit of real love the people all have for each other. You can see it in their eyes." They weren't concerned for themselves or money, like materialistic Americans. I asked him if he had any doubts about what he had seen. Yes, he admitted, he had wondered, briefly. "One day as I was riding on a bus, I said to myself, either everyone is telling the truth or everyone is pulling my leg. It came to me that everyone must be telling the truth."

Americans would not suspend their critical judgment like this in analyzing the Soviet Union—we had learned what Stalin was like; we had read Solzhe-

6

nitsyn. But we gave China the benefit of the doubt. It seemed to me that China cast a kind of magic spell over Americans and other Westerners. There was nothing new in this. It had been going on since the French Philosophes of the eighteenth century, who imagined that the ancient sage Confucius had created a perfectly harmonious government which China was still following. In the late nineteenth century, when a current of missionary zeal swept churches and college campuses in the United States, Americans dreamed of converting China to Christianity and "saving" China in a single generation. At the turn of the century, as Americans became terrified by the specter of what was then called overproduction, a new image arose—that of the fabulous China market, the 400 million customers who would buy up the excess of American manufacturers. During World War Two, when we were fighting Japan, we looked to Chiang Kai-shek as a valiant democrat leading China into the free world. All these images were more the projection of our own myths than a hard look at reality. Indeed, they contained a measure of cultural condescension, an unwillingness to look at things from the Chinese perspective.

But the longer I lived in Peking, the more the other dimension came into view—the hardships, the absurdities, the stratagems of daily life. Gradually over the twenty months I lived there, I formed genuine friendships with a number of Chinese and they initiated me into this human quotient, the myriad ways Chinese had invented to ignore, evade, resist, or confound the revolution that Mao had thrust on them. In short, to survive.

In the process, I had to unlearn many of what I took to be facts about China. The 38 million members of the Communist Party, I had presumed, must be stalwart adherents of the revolution. So I was not prepared for an energetic, candid, middle-aged Party member who was chairman of her local street committee, the lowest level of government organization. One evening when I stopped by her fifth-floor walk-up apartment, I found she was reading the Bible. I was incredulous. By its own regulations, the Communist Party is devoted to atheism, at least when it was not worshiping Mao. When I asked if she was not afraid of getting in trouble, she laughed and awkwardly practiced crossing herself. She explained that recently a forty-five-year-old man had knocked on her door, claiming to be a friend of a woman she knew. He wondered if she believed in God or had read the Bible. It was a very dangerous act, but she was impressed with his sincerity and intrigued by what he had to say. He had spent ten years in prison because of his Christian belief and was unable to get a job.

"If there is a god, why has he let you be treated so cruelly?" she asked.

"You don't understand," he replied. Actually, he claimed, he had been very lucky. "God gave me a wonderful wife. When I was in prison, the police demanded that she divorce me to show she did not share my ideas, but she refused. Now I can't get a job, but though she is only a factory worker, she supports both of us."

In the end, my friend accepted his offering of a Chinese-language Bible that had been printed in Hong Kong and smuggled into the mainland. She was reading it with evident interest. "You don't know it," she advised me. "But Christianity is spreading rapidly in China because people are so disillusioned with communism." If she had been a political dissident, I would have been doubtful. But she was the neighborhood Party boss.

With Mao's commitment to revolution, I had assumed China would offer great social mobility, the chance for people to get ahead. But in many ways, I discovered, China was more conservative and hierarchical than the United States, Japan, or Western Europe. Only 3 percent of China's young people can go to college, one of the major routes to success. By comparison, 35 percent of Americans go to university. Chinese can't pick their own job, they must wait till they are assigned work by the state, and once given a job, it is very difficult to arrange a transfer. China's peasants probably have less chance to escape their bondage to toil than their ancestors did before 1949 because of the restrictions the Communists have erected against people leaving the countryside.

A hustling, fast-talking youthful official in a foreign trade corporation who had recently returned from his first trip to the United States said the most impressive thing in America to him was its sense of opportunity.

"Even an elevator operator can start his own business and become a millionaire if he works hard and saves his money," the official commented over lunch in the Peking Hotel where I lived and worked for the first year I was in China.

In a joking riposte, I suggested the opposite might happen in China—the ex-millionaire capitalist would be turned into an elevator operator. For a moment my companion stared at me in silence and I was afraid he had construed my remark as a slur on China.

"No," he finally said. "In China they wouldn't let a millionaire be an elevator operator. That is a job for someone who works for the Public Security Ministry, to keep track of who goes in and out of buildings. The millionaire would be forced to clean toilets."

Mao demanded a strong belief in equality. So I was surprised to find that the Party itself is divided into twenty-four grades, and that in a supposedly classless society the children and grandchildren of people who were branded as landlords in 1949 are still stuck with the stigma, barring them from joining the Party or the army, or sharing in benefits like cooperative health insurance in the countryside. I was also startled to discover that some of my new Chinese friends had servants, affectionately and euphemistically dubbed

8

"aunties." I hadn't realized that Party officials have their own exclusive network of markets, bookshops, hospitals, and resorts which provides them with food and services unavailable to the "masses." Many of these privileges are carefully sheltered behind official secrecy to preserve the appearance of equality. Only at the end of my tour in China was I able to find out where Hua Guofeng, then still Chairman of the Communist Party, lived. A friend whose father was a general in the People's Liberation Army volunteered to drive with me there. Hua's residence turned out to be a large, forbidding compound in the northwest section of the city, measuring four hundred yards long by three hundred yards wide, set behind twenty-five-foot-high gray concrete walls that were topped with slits for guns. Chinese called it simply "Building Number Eight," since they said it had cost eight million yuan, or $5.3 million, to construct, an extraordinary sum of money for China.*

Chinese industry has grown at the impressive pace of almost 10 percent a year since 1950, I knew from reading Peking's statistical claims, so I was constantly struck by reports of bungling and incompetence by the country's economic managers. In 1981, the New China News Agency disclosed, the Ministry of Petroleum had wasted several billion dollars on building a cross-country pipeline for natural gas from Sichuan province to the industrialized region of China along the middle and lower reaches of the Yangtze River. Senior officials of the ministry had deliberately inflated Sichuan's gas reserves, ignoring protests from lower-level technicians, in order to get the appropriations to build the pipeline. Then when the promised gas failed to materialize, the project had to be scrapped.

That Peking maintained its control through a large police ministry, supported by a sophisticated system of agencies like the street committees, was no secret. But it took a personal encounter to learn just how pervasive the police could be. One evening when I went out for a walk from the Peking Hotel, I noticed a tiny figure of a woman in the shadows. It was a bitterly cold February night, and she was bundled in a black overcoat, with a yellow scarf over her head and a cotton surgical mask covering her face, the kind many Chinese wear to help keep out Peking's cold and dust. As I walked, I sensed she was keeping pace with me and, after fifty feet, was approaching me.

"Where are you going?" she asked. It was an unexpectedly bold opening for a Chinese.

"For a walk," I replied.

*At the official exchange rate set by Peking in 1981 $1 is worth 1.50 yuan. But most diplomats and foreign businessmen calculate that the real value of the Chinese currency is only about half that. Peking has conceded as much by allowing Chinese factories which export their goods to sell them at a lower exchange rate; otherwise they would be priced too high for the world market. In the interest of simplicity, I have stuck with the official rate.

"May I walk with you?"

"Yes," I replied, "but aren't you afraid of being seen with a foreigner?"

No, she responded. Then, through her mask, with only her small eyes showing, she began pouring out a tale of trouble which was only half comprehensible. She seemed nervous, or feverish, it was impossible to tell which.

She was twenty-three years old, she related, and had been sent to work in the countryside after she finished junior high school as part of Mao's utopian program to rusticate urban youth. Life had proved harsh in the village where she had been settled, and she had finally resolved to come back, illegally, to Peking. Her father was retired, and the family had little money. She couldn't get a job, because she was in the city without proper identification papers. As she talked, she took my hand, another unlikely gesture for a Chinese. Was she a prostitute? I began to wonder. It was then that I realized someone else was following us, a young man in a blue jacket, with crew-cut hair and sunglasses, though the night was dark and there were only a few faint street-lights. Ostentatiously, he would walk a few steps behind us, then trot to the front, then back again. Finally he pushed directly in front, blocking our path on the sidewalk. Were they working as a team? the thought flashed through my head; had I been set up in a Chinese gang mugging?

"Who are you?" he demanded of me.

I returned the question.

"What are you doing with her, what is your relationship?" he continued, without identifying himself. We were friends, I told him. By now two more men, in their forties, had joined us, one of them in the blue uniform of the Public Security Bureau, China's police, with a high fur cap on his head. My anxieties about being robbed vanished, but other fears took their place.

The uniformed policeman grabbed my new acquaintance by the arm and shoved her up against a storefront wall. "How did you meet?" he began interrogating her. "What is your work unit?" By then half a dozen more police, some in uniform, some in plainclothes, had appeared out of the night and surrounded me. "Go home, get out of there," they ordered me.

A typical American, I felt compelled to try to protect the woman, whoever she was, and the journalist in me wanted to know exactly who she was. So when the police began marching her back down the street toward the Peking Hotel, I followed to see where they would go. This time two police pushed me against the wall.

"What did we do wrong?" I asked. "Can't a foreigner talk to a Chinese?"

At first they just glowered at me, the interfering foreigner. Finally the younger of the pair, who was in his early twenties and had a strong smell of garlic on his breath, answered with bureaucratic ambiguity. "It is okay to talk in the daytime, but not at night," he said. By then, the woman had been led around a corner and was out of sight. I had to admit defeat.

Despite the pervasiveness of the police network, however, I also learned it had its holes. In Zhengzhou, the nondescript capital of Henan province, on the north China plain, a group of robbers armed with AK-47 automatic rifles held up the main office of the People's Bank, killing one of the guards and escaping with the equivalent of more than $150,000. An American married to a Chinese woman from Henan told me that the thieves had become local folk heroes for their daring. Defying an intense police search for them, they put up wall posters around the city on black paper: "You can dig up all of Henan province to a depth of three feet, but you will never find us."

In the aftermath of the Cultural Revolution, there was a growth of white-collar crime, too, corruption in the ranks of the Party. A fifty-eight-year-old woman cashier in a county coal company in the far northeast of China, named Wang Shouxin, was accused in the press of being the ringleader in a syndicate of officials which embezzled $320,000. Wang was said to have lavished furs, television sets, record players, tape recorders, electric fans, and eiderdown quilts on more than two hundred people who participated in the scheme.

When I tried to puzzle out how such anomalies as crime and corruption could exist, given the size of China's police apparatus and the earlier reputation of the Party for selflessness, a graduate student friend laughed at my naïveté. In China, she said, everyone had to devise his own method for dealing with the omnipresence of authority. Her technique was daydreaming. That was how she had learned to speak almost flawless English. Because her father was condemned as a counterrevolutionary during the Cultural Revolution, she had been forced to drop out of school and never went beyond the sixth grade.

"But I got an English textbook and went through it in two months on my own," she said as we drove around Peking in *The Times*'s office car, a tan Honda, one of the best ways to talk to a Chinese without being observed. "Then I just daydreamed long conversations in English with myself. I could even speak it out loud, no one else understood." Eventually, in 1978, after the radicals' downfall, her father was rehabilitated and she was able to use her ability in English to win admission to a graduate school.

This penchant for inventiveness, born of necessity, had spawned an entire counter economy, what the Chinese call "going through the back door." They used the back door to break through the restraints placed on them by the cranky bureaucracy and the cumbersome centrally planned economy. A young journalist at the New China News Agency who favored well-tailored Mao suits explained how this worked. When his neighborhood market ran out of bean curd, a cheese-like food rich in protein made from pressed soybeans, his parents sent his sister to shop. She had former schoolmates who worked in the market and would pull out reserves they had hidden under the counter. That was her back door. He himself would have been shipped off to the countryside after he finished high school as part of Mao's rustication program except that his father, a general, had a former comrade-in-arms from the Communists' guerrilla days who had become a senior official in the press agency. The colleague arranged a job for him there. Later, in exchange, his father was able to secure a comfortable post in the army for the official's daughter. One day my friend pulled back the sleeve on his blue jacket to show me a new Chinese-made wristwatch. His father had been given it by the factory as a so-called trial product, a disguised way of distributing scarce items to favored officials or relatives. His family also had a trial television set and refrigerator at home, two real luxuries in China. The system of trial goods had become so widespread, he added, that some people jokingly wondered if they could get trial cremations, since China's cemeteries and crematoria have long waiting lists. My friend had applied to get an exit visa and passport so he could go abroad to study in the United States. He didn't expect any trouble getting them; he had a back door in the Public Security Ministry, his uncle.

This counterpoint of the two Chinas, the formal system and the eccentric, often-anguished human dimension, was much like what my colleague on *The New York Times,* Hedrick Smith, had found in the Soviet Union and portrayed brilliantly in his book, *The Russians.* That was not a coincidence, the doctor on the train from Shanghai suggested. He had read Smith's book in Chinese translation. Peking had printed it in installments in one of the confidential bulletins circulated to officials and then often illegally passed on to their friends. The government presumably calculated it would show how bad conditions were in the Soviet Union. But the doctor had another perspective. Actually, he said, much the same book could be written about China. Nothing he read had surprised him. It was all too familiar. Both countries were run by powerful bureaucracies that stifled individual initiative and often gummed up the economy. But there was a significant difference between Russia and China, he pointed out—it lies in the history of the two peoples. China was the only survivor of the world's great early civilizations: Egypt, Mesopotamia, Greece, and Rome. That gives China a language, culture, and state structure that date back over two thousand years. It also makes history a palpable force, not just something written down in textbooks for schoolboys to read about. Mao often liked to compare himself to the first Emperor of the Chin dynasty, Chin Shi Huang, who unified China in 221 B.C., built the Great Wall, and ruthlessly burned all heterodox books. Ronald Reagan thinks his style of government compares with that of Eisenhower. But no American President would be likely to reach back to Julius Caesar or Hannibal for inspiration. The very Chinese name for their country, Zhong Guo, is redolent of the antiquity and the pride Chinese feel about themselves.

It means "central country," the seat of civilization at the middle of the known world.

Customs spawned over these two millennia have not easily withered with the advent of communism, an import from the West. When the doctor and I went to the dining car for supper, ignoring a look of displeasure from the conductor, he noted one simple but profound difference between Chinese and Westerners. We order our own separate food from the menu and eat from our own individual plates. Chinese order their meals together and then share the dishes, each person eating with chopsticks from the same plates and bowls in the middle of the table. We are oriented to the individual, to satisfying and gratifying his needs, catering to his tastes, and we feel this is legitimate. But the Chinese has his center of gravity in his group or his family. A Chinese scientist who visited the United States and stayed with an American family told me afterward that he had been surprised to find the children all had their own rooms. He felt it was unnatural sleeping in a bed by himself, so accustomed was he to having his entire family together. To spend the night in a room alone actually made him nervous. He could not imagine how some Americans managed to live in a whole house by themselves.

The primacy of the group in China has political repercussions. It makes it easier for Chinese to adjust to pressures to conform and to accept authority —"The tall tree is crushed by the wind" is an old proverb. But many Chinese still try to develop their own personal lives free from the official trammels, I found. The government is puritanical and frowns on even kissing and dancing. But most young people I met admitted they had slept with their spouses before getting married. A nurse told me that her hospital made money by quietly performing abortions on unmarried women without reporting them to their work units, as many clinics would. That would have ruined the women's reputations. Chinese go through many of the same life crises as Americans. A precocious teen-age girl complained bitterly to me that her parents didn't understand her. A thirty-year-old woman charged that her husband was interested only in his career and was insensitive to her. When he came home at night, all he wanted was for her to cook for him and make love with him before he fell asleep. She wanted to grow, to expand, to travel abroad if possible, to go back to graduate school. It was like a classic thirties passage in Gail Sheehy's popular book *Passages.* She ended up having an affair with another man.

The Chinese preference for the group over the individual may have grown out of the country's economic conditions. From early times the Chinese planted rice in irrigated fields, a type of agriculture which calls for intensive cultivation by large numbers of strong backs and in turn produces high yields that can support a bigger population than Western farming did until the last century. The result is everywhere visible. As our train crossed the flat countryside north of Nanjing, we could see whole villages of small mud-walled houses at half-mile intervals. In the American Middle West there would be only the farmstead and clump of trees of a single family in the same area. This density of people on the land has subtly conditioned the minds of centuries of Chinese.

Geography and history have also left a legacy of harsh facts for China. In total area China is only slightly larger than the United States (3.7 million square miles to 3.6 million square miles), stretching 2,500 miles from the Pamir Mountains in the west to the Pacific Ocean in the east, and 2,000 miles from the Amur River in the north, on the border of the Soviet Far East, to Vietnam in the south. But much of this territory, particularly around the periphery, is uninhabitable mountains and desert, like the vast 10,000-foot Tibetan plateau and the Taklamakan desert in Xinjiang, the most utterly desolate region in the world. Only one tenth of China's land, in fact, is cultivable, a scant quarter of an acre per person. On this, China must feed a population of one billion people, almost a fourth of the world's total, more than the total number of inhabitants of the United States, the Soviet Union, and Western Europe combined.

These bare statements of geography and demography do not really convey the sense of crowding, the ubiquitous swarm of people that overwhelms a Westerner on his first exposure to China, what the Communists with simple truth call "the masses." Invariably, Chinese who travel to the United States have the opposite impression. "The first thing I noticed about New York," a Chinese journalist told me, "was that there never seem to be any people on the street." For whoever governs China, this sheer bulk of population makes the country almost unmanageable.

Traditionally, the Chinese themselves were confined to a square-shaped segment in the east and central part of the country, roughly half the size of the continental United States. The vast outer zone was sparsely populated by separate ethnic groups who today have come under Chinese Communist rule: the Manchus in the northeast, the Mongols, the Moslem Uighurs in Xinjiang, the Tibetans, the Zhuang, and the Dai, cousins of the natives of Thailand, in the south. Climatically, the great divide in China was between the cold, dry wheat-growing north and the moist rice land of the south. These regions separated at a line halfway between the Yellow River and the Yangtze, on the 33rd parallel. In comparative terms, China lies somewhat south of both the United States and Europe. Peking, in north China, just inside the Great Wall, is on the same latitude as Philadelphia and Madrid; Shanghai, in central China, corresponds to New Orleans and Suez; Canton, in the south, to Havana and Calcutta.

With hard work and improved organization, the Communists have succeeded in doubling China's grain production since 1949. But with peace and good public health work, the population has also nearly doubled at the same time. It took over 4,000 years of recorded history for China to reach its first 500 million people, but a mere three decades more to swell to one billion. In the 1950s and 1960s, as China experienced a baby boom, Mao dismissed warnings about the danger of overpopulation as bourgeois claptrap and purged China's most respected economist for his temerity in urging the necessity of birth control. The more people, the greater the value of production, Mao argued, following Marxist orthodoxy. In the long run, that miscalculation may prove the Communists' most calamitous error. For recent Western studies show that food consumption per capita is actually only about what it was in the mid-1950s and, more surprisingly, no better than in the 1930s, before World War Two. These studies suggest that the average daily calorie supply in China is between 2,000 and 2,100 per person. Two thousand calories a day is the level of India, 2,100 is the norm in Pakistan. Americans eat an average of 3,240 calories a day. But what makes these figures worse is that three fourths of the protein in the Chinese diet and five sixths of the calories are derived from food grains like rice, wheat, and corn, rather than from other richer and more varied sources like meat, fish, eggs, vegetables, or sugar. In Asia only Bangladesh and Laos approach these proportions. Uneven distribution has compounded this shortage of food. A Communist periodical in Hong Kong disclosed in 1978, while I was based there, that the annual grain ration of 200 million Chinese peasants was less than 330 pounds a year. "That is to say," the journal said, "they are living in a state of semistarvation."

Here was another of those paradoxes, or to use one of Mao's favorite terms, contradictions. Because China has launched an intercontinental ballistic missile and exploded hydrogen bombs, because it has a sophisticated art and literature, it is easy to forget that China is still a poor country, that in some ways it belongs to the third world, not to the superpower category. I was constantly struck by these contrasts. Chinese industry now turns out over two million television sets a year; but in Sichuan province, in the southwest, I saw four teen-age girls hitched to a cart, like oxen, pulling hundreds of pounds of steel reinforcing rods up a steep hill. I had dinner one night with a Chinese pilot who had trained to be an astronaut. But his family lived in a house without a toilet or running water. They had to use a public lavatory, with an open hole to squat over, that was a hundred feet from their house. The stench instinctively made me hold my nose. Peking University is one of China's two most prestigious colleges. But because of the penurious budget for education, the school cafeteria has no tables, chairs, or even bowls or chopsticks. The students must bring their own utensils and then take the food back to their dormitories to eat, a situation that has led to occasional campus protests.

The most important contrast is that between the large cities and the countryside, where live 800 million Chinese, one third of all the world's farmers. Parts of rural China seem stuck in another century. A Chinese professor who at the end of the Cultural Revolution was sent to Anhui province, in central China, not far from where we saw the mud-walled villages from the train, described what it was like to live there. Everything was made from mud, he recalled: the floors, the walls, even the beds and the stools the peasants sat on were constructed from pounded earth. The villagers had no wood for fuel —all the trees in the region had long ago been chopped down—so the women and children gathered grass and wheat stalks, depriving the earth of valuable natural nutrients. During the year the professor was there, he ate no meat, and the family he was quartered with had no matches, no soap, and most of the time no cooking oil, an essential part of the Chinese diet. A wrinkled seventy-year-old woman neighbor said to him admiringly one day, "Even the hair on your legs is bigger than the hair raised on ours."

The Communists have largely abolished the brutal poverty and starvation which afflicted China before 1949, a significant achievement. The clearest indication is that the average life expectancy has jumped from thirty-two years before Liberation in 1949 to sixty-four years now, a phenomenal improvement matched by only a few other developing countries. But there is still great disparity, though it is often obscured from foreigners in comparatively comfortable Peking.

My wife, Barbara, discovered this when she went on a visit with an Australian friend, Sue Walker, to Xian, 600 miles southwest of Peking, once the ancient capital of China in the Han and Tang dynasties when it was known as Changan. At the recommendation of their guide from the China Travel Service, they went out to dinner to the May First Restaurant, one of the city's main eateries. From the time they sat down on low stools at a plain wooden table covered with dirty dishes, leftover scraps of food, and puddles of grease, the atmosphere made them uneasy. There were flies buzzing around the table, and the concrete floor was littered with bits of bone and gristle shoved off the table by previous customers who had cleared a space for themselves at which to dine. A waitress wearing a dirty white smock and cap informed them brusquely that the only thing left to eat was *baozi,* a kind of steamed roll filled with chopped cabbage and bits of meat. As they waited for the food to arrive, eight other customers, all men dressed in patched and faded blue clothes, pulled up their stools in a semicircle around their table to watch. Some of them were picking their teeth. "We got the feeling we were the nightly entertainment," Barbara said after she came back to Peking.

Finally the food came, along with a bowl of greasy chicken broth with small pieces of coriander floating in it, the only thing the restaurant had to drink. After the two women ate all they could and were about to leave, "suddenly a dirty, weathered hand appeared on the table, palm up. Almost before we realized that the hand belonged to a disheveled old beggar dressed in rags, a waitress spotted him and shooed him away." He moved a few paces off, then squatted down on his haunches to watch for another opportunity.

It soon came. Barbara's friend decided it was best to leave and went over to the cashier's table to pay but left her silk Chinese-style jacket draped over her stool. As she got up, the beggar who had been eying them leapt onto the table, while another beggar, just as dirty and ragged, appeared from the opposite direction.

"They began fighting over what was left of the food," Barbara related. "The first man grabbed three of the steamed rolls, clenching them so tightly the juice ran down his sleeve. The other grabbed for a bowl of soup, splashing it all over Sue's jacket. The whole time they were yelling and flailing at each other. Finally the waitresses and some of the other customers managed to pull them apart. But they kept their loot."

As the restaurant staff urged Barbara and her friend to leave, out of evident embarrassment, they saw the two beggars jump for another table that had just been vacated by a Chinese.

None of these experiences moved me as deeply, however, as did the accounts our Chinese friends told about the persecution they had undergone during the political campaigns of the past thirty years, particularly the most tumultuous of all, the Cultural Revolution. A young girl recounted how her family was banished from their home in Peking to a remote mountain village and she had to watch as her mother was clubbed to death with iron bars and her father beaten senseless because they were accused of being reactionaries. A woman in her twenties recalled how she felt when as a teen-ager in 1966 she willingly denounced her father as a counterrevolutionary at a mass meeting in front of her parents—it was all for the glory of Chairman Mao, she believed at the time. A Chinese surgeon told me how his father, a respected engineer, and his mother had been tortured to death and he himself exiled to a kind of Chinese Siberia in Xinjiang province in the far northwest, all on suspicion they were American spies.

The official Chinese press itself has limned the dimensions of the disaster brought on by the Cultural Revolution. According to the *People's Daily*, 100 million people suffered from political harassment during the decade from 1966 to Mao's death in 1976. Three reporters from the New China News Agency recounted an incident in Shanghai that more than any other episode illustrates to me the brutalization of the spirit at the time. On May 1, 1968, by their account, a contingent of government officials went to the Shanghai home of the mother of a young woman named Lin Zhao, who had been jailed for keeping a diary critical of the Party. The officials told Lin's mother that her daughter had been executed three days earlier as a counterrevolutionary.

But the money spent on the execution had been a waste, the officials added sardonically, and they demanded that the mother pay five fen—a little more than three cents—to cover the cost of the bullet they had put through the back of her daughter's head.

Almost all the Chinese I met had been compelled to throw away valued books, records, or paintings to placate bands of fanatic Red Guards who ransacked their homes looking for decadent "bourgeois" or "feudal" culture. Most of China's leading writers, musicians, and artists were imprisoned or forced to stop their creative work for over a decade. For some it was worse. Lao She, the brilliant author of the poignant novel known as *Rickshaw Boy* in the West, about the tragic life of a rickshaw puller in Peking before 1949, was forced head-down into the bottom of a muddy lake by a band of Red Guards till he drowned.

Looking back on the Cultural Revolution, Liao Mosha, a distinguished seventy-five-year-old Communist Party writer who himself had his teeth knocked out by Red Guards and was imprisoned for thirteen years, wrote in 1981, "When we old comrades get together we often talk about the books we miss, books that have been forbidden, books that have been destroyed, books, carefully collected in libraries, that have been stolen, books that have perished. The 'Great Cultural Revolution' was the great revolution that sent culture to its death."

Ironically, the Cultural Revolution was also a disaster for the Red Guards themselves, for young people between the ages of fifteen and thirty-five. Many were thrown out of school as Mao ordered the nation's colleges closed and the curriculum shortened and simplified. Standards slipped when tests were abolished. Eighteen million urban teen-agers, one out of every ten people in the cities, were shipped off to the countryside in another of Mao's experiments. All of these changes resulted in over 100 million young people, by government count, ending up illiterate and many jobs being filled with people who had little or no training because of Mao's disdain for expertise. An architect pointed with shame to the Telecommunications Building, a hulking, Soviet-style edifice topped by a pointed tower at the western end of the Avenue of Eternal Tranquility in Peking. From the street it seemed to have no front door. The reason, my friend explained, was that young, untrained architectural students had been used to design the building at a time when older, more qualified builders were under political attack and by mistake they put the door at the rear of the building. A surgeon told me with anguish that most of the younger doctors on his staff couldn't be trusted to operate because they barely knew the difference between a vein and an artery. A first-year student at the Peking Foreign Languages Institute complained that his English teacher, who graduated from the same school in 1976, when Mao's Cultural Revolution reforms were in effect, didn't know as much English as he did. The legacy of Mao's utopian venture was a generation of lost and frustrated youth.

But ultimately the most corrosive effect was on the Communist Party itself. In the 1950s, Chinese friends assured me, most people had a genuine enthusiasm for the Communists. They had stamped out inflation and corruption and helped China "stand up," in Mao's phrase, for the first time in over one hundred years. No more. A middle-aged Party member, a short combative man with a square jaw, recalled how when he first joined the Party as a twenty-year-old he had written many letters volunteering to be sent to work in Hainan, the backward, jungle-covered island in the South China Sea. "I wanted to go to the poorest, hardest area to build a new China. My friends all had the same ideals," he said. "Now, no one would write such a letter."

One of the most chilling comments I heard came from a sixteen-year-old high school student, a lithe, intelligent girl who had a secret passion for trying on makeup and fashionable clothes when she wasn't in school.

"The Cultural Revolution actually was a good thing," she told me one day during a walk around the North Ocean Park in Peking, where China's emperors and their consorts used to stroll. "In the 1950s the Chinese were very naïve. They believed in the Communists, like my mother. Whatever the Communists said, she thought, that's great." Her mother is a high school teacher.

"Then in the Cultural Revolution, they locked her up for a year and a half because her father was a well-known scholar, what they derided as a 'bourgeois authority.' Some Red Guards in her school made her kneel on broken glass in front of all the students. For an intellectual, it was the worst thing that can happen—humiliation. She was disillusioned. With the Cultural Revolution, she saw through the Communists."

A balding archaeologist tried to put China's experience in perspective: "It may be presumptuous to say it, but what China has been through is like the holocaust," he remarked. There were no gas ovens, of course, no genocidal plan to eliminate an entire race. But there are horrifying parallels. Many people, like the doctor on the train or the teacher, were persecuted, arrested, tortured, or killed because of their class background, not for what they did, but for what they were said to be. Moreover, the destruction in lives, in lost education, in ruined books and art, in mismanaged factories and wasted resources as the country's population spiraled out of control was so staggering that it defies the Western imagination. What made it even more painful was that it began with a noble purpose—Mao launched his campaigns to eliminate poverty, bureaucracy, and class differences. But enthrall to his vision, his great if not final solution, he lost sight of the people who were forced to implement his dictates.

There was another similarity to the holocaust. Chinese who came through the cataclysms of the past thirty years seemed to me like survivors; they were chastened and cynical and numb. When I asked friends how they had coped with their personal tragedies, they often answered, *"Ma-mu-le"* (I was numbed). "Surviving" was also a word they frequently used. It reminded me of a passage in the most daring and dramatic of all the posters that have been affixed to China's walls in recent years, an epic 20,000 word broadside written on sixty-seven sheets of newsprint strung out for one hundred yards in downtown Canton in 1974. It was penned by three former Red Guards who combined their surnames into a single pen name, Li Yizhe. The Communist regime had degenerated into a "feudal fascist autocracy," they charged. They were soon arrested, then released after the downfall of the radicals in 1976 when Deng Xiaoping, Mao's successor as China's paramount leader, offered what seemed like greater freedom of expression. But in late 1980, shortly before I left China, they were rearrested as Peking clamped down again.

"We are survivors," the three men had written. "We were once bitten by the tiger but it failed to grind us small enough to swallow. Its claws left scars on our faces, so we are not handsome." They spoke for the many Chinese I met who had all been clawed by the tiger.

PART

1

CONNECTIONS

—

I. Foreign Devils

洋 鬼 子

HOSTMANSHIP

"Is it not a pleasure to have friends come from afar?"
Confucius, in the opening passage of the Analects

My four-year-old son, Ethan, and I were walking down the Avenue of Eternal Tranquility outside the Peking Hotel on a blustery fall afternoon when I noticed a bespectacled man in his fifties, dressed in a shabby gray overcoat, staring at us. I had long since become accustomed to the Chinese habit of gawking at foreigners. They gathered in front of the Peking Hotel, where I lived and worked for the first year I was stationed in China, and surrounded any Westerner who emerged. It was always friendly, simple curiosity, never menacing. And Ethan was a special marvel, with long blond hair trimmed in a Buster Brown cut and the build of a miniature fullback.

This spectator was so intense that he began to follow us, a few steps off to the left, never taking his eyes off us. He was still staring at us when, with a loud thwack, he walked straight into a tree. His horn-rimmed glasses split neatly in two over the bridge of his nose, the two halves dropping to the pavement and smashing. He was stunned by the blow, bouncing off a few feet before falling to the ground. A trickle of blood flowed from a gash on his forehead. I went over to try to help him, but he looked up at me and smiled. Where an American would have cursed or cried out in anger, he smiled.

As much as any other during my twenty months in China, this tragicomic encounter illustrated how bizarre foreigners seem to Chinese, how exotic Westerners are in Chinese eyes. For in a land of people who all have straight dark hair, our hair is not hair color at all, but yellow, brown, even red, curly, not straight, like old Chinese paintings of demons. Our bodies are too fat and covered with horrible fuzz, like animals; Chinese have smooth, hairless skin.

In a country where history weighs heavily, we foreigners have too much bouncing vitality and always try to get things accomplished too quickly. Perhaps because of our richer diet, we have energy to waste that Chinese prefer to conserve for the long haul. If we move in allegro, Chinese are keyed in adagio. We are too frank; we can quarrel in public and then make up later without fear of losing face and causing permanent enmity.

The gap between Chinese and foreigners is almost unbridgeable. Every Monday through Saturday I sat in *The Times*'s office—an ordinary hotel room supplemented by three filing cabinets, a bookcase, and a typewriter—with my Chinese assistant, Wu Qianwei. Lanky and angular, with an incorrigible cowlick and heavy Coke-bottle glasses, he was assigned to me by the Diplomatic Services Bureau, the government agency which provides foreign diplomats and journalists with everything from housing to maids and chauffeurs. But despite our constant physical proximity and a certain slow warmth that developed between us, Wu still referred to me, when he was talking to other Chinese in the room or over the phone, as the *wai-guo-ren,* literally, the "external country person," the foreigner. When I lived in Taiwan for three years as a graduate student and later as a part-time correspondent for *The Times,* the neighborhood children always shouted, *"Yang-gui-zi"* (Foreign devil), when I walked in and out of the house.

China's greatest twentieth-century writer, Lu Xun, observed, "Throughout the ages, the Chinese have had only two ways of looking at foreigners, up to them as superior beings or down on them as wild animals. They have never been able to treat them as friends, to consider them as people like themselves."

This sense of separateness has a long history. For 4,000 years, the Chinese rested secure in their superiority. The Chinese empire was unquestionably the greatest in the world, the "Central Kingdom," its boundaries coterminous with civilization. Outside it were only barbarians. The Chinese Emperor was the "Son of Heaven," mediator between heaven and earth; China had invented paper, gunpowder, and the compass; its poetry and art neared the sublime; its system of government by an elite of ethical bureaucrats had achieved perfect equipoise. Not even famines, floods, or conquest by alien nomads disturbed its serenity for long. In the early legends of the origin of the universe in China, there is an odd omission. There is no hint of any hero who led the Chinese to China from elsewhere. It was assumed that the Chinese originated in China.

The pride all this inspired among the Chinese is something beyond Western experience and comprehension. "Nationalism" is too paltry a word to describe it, for to the Chinese, China was a synthesis of people, territory, language, history, art, and philosophy, more like a religion than simply another nation state. In the twentieth century Chinese xenophobia became a potent force contributing to the Communists' victory, as many frustrated middle-class Chinese intellectuals and hungry peasants threw in their lot with Mao when they came to believe that only the Communists could expel the Japanese and make China strong again.

If nationalism has now gone out of style for many people in Europe and America, it has not for Chinese. At a banquet my wife, Barbara, and I attended in the immense East Room of the Great Hall of the People given by Pan American World Airlines to mark the beginning of its flights from New York to Peking, several Chinese officials were discussing the news they had just heard that John Lennon had been shot in New York. The menu that evening included sharks' fin soup with crab meat, roast goose with plum sauce, candied white fungus, and giant sliced prawns with chillies. Pan Am had added to the festivities by giving each guest a battery-operated quartz alarm clock, a trinket the Chinese at our table had never seen before. But they were concerned about Lennon. He was a famous singer, wasn't he, with some British musical group? a stern-faced cadre in a black Mao suit asked. Yes, said another, he had been honored by the Queen for his services to England. The shooting was a real tragedy, the second man added.

"Lennon certainly earned a lot of foreign exchange for his country." For the Chinese, that was John Lennon's epitaph; not the member of the Beatles, or the singer who pioneered a new musical idiom, or the pacifist, but the patriot.

History gave Chinese a unique sense of pride, and it also left them with an unusual style of dealing with foreigners. For several millennia foreigners who came to China were fitted into the tribute system—if they recognized China's superiority by bringing presents to the Emperor, they were allowed limited rights to live and trade in one of the ports farthest from Peking. In the seventeenth, eighteenth, and nineteenth centuries, as Europeans and then Americans began to buy Chinese tea and silk in exchange for silver and opium, they were added to the other barbarians, the Japanese, the Vietnamese, the traders from the petty states of the Malay Peninsula and the coasts of India. British and American merchants were confined to the "Thirteen Factories" outside the walls of Canton, a tiny area under a quarter of a mile long and two hundred yards wide. There, in the distant tropical south, they operated under irksome restrictions: they could not bring their wives with them, ride in sedan chairs, row on the river, or enter Canton city.

In 1793, peeved by these rules, an expansive British government sent an emissary, the Earl of Macartney, to the court of the Emperor Qian-long in Peking. His mission was to seek permission to open other ports for trade and an island depot where British goods could be stored and ships refitted. Macartney also brought magnificent gifts: 600 packages transported through the city walls by 90 wagons, 40 barrows, 200 horses, and 3,000 coolies. The Chinese instantly labeled these "tribute presents," confirming Britain's subservient position. The Emperor would not alter the traditional system. He issued an edict thanking King George III for his "respectful spirit of submission." But he pointed out, "The virtue and prestige of the Celestial Dynasty having spread far and wide, the kings of the myriad nations come by land and sea with all sorts of precious things. Consequently there is nothing we lack, as your principal envoy and others have themselves observed. We have never set much store on strange or ingenious objects, nor do we need any more of your country's manufactures."

In the end, the British broke down their confinement at Canton only with the Opium War of 1839–42, when British gunboats and soldiers forced a weak and reluctant Qing government to accept the import of opium from British India and the opening of a series of "treaty ports" to foreigners. There followed a century of humiliating Chinese decay and impotence. But in 1949 when a powerful Chinese government was finally reestablished once more, by the Communists, it moved to re-create some of the glory of the old empire, if in modern guise.

I was constantly struck by how much time and effort the Communist hierarchy devoted to receiving endless streams of foreign visitors in the Great Hall of the People, just across the street from the palace of the Ming and Qing emperors. It was a solemn quotidian ritual, the African colonels, the French bankers, the Japanese industrialists, the American congressmen, the heads of the Marxist splinter parties who came to pay court on the aging Chinese leaders in their new marble throne room. Once, when I accompanied the U.S. Defense Secretary, Harold Brown, on a courtesy call on Party Chairman Hua Guofeng, Deng was just emerging from another room next door where he had received the head of the lower house of the Japanese Diet. All these audiences were recorded on television and shown that night on the news. In no Western country would most of these visitors be newsworthy; certainly in no Western capital would senior officials devote so much time to greeting foreigners, however humble. But in China it was a signal to the Chinese people that their country was again the epicenter of the world, a strong nation that respectful foreigners came to pay homage to.

Since Confucius, Chinese have made a priority of entertaining visitors, making a good impression on them, and they have raised hostmanship into an art form. It is one of the most delightful aspects of Chinese society, and accounts in large measure for the vastly different perceptions Westerners have of China and the Soviet Union, even though their Communist systems have much in common.

I was often both flattered and amused by the efforts made on my behalf during my stay in China. Whenever I took a bus, invariably jammed, Chinese men and women both would insist on giving me their seats, just because I was a foreign guest. At first I tried to refuse, but that only made me more embarrassed because the Chinese passenger would get up from his or her seat and stay standing until I finally acquiesced and sat down. I remember going to a department store in Urumqi, the capital of Xinjiang, shortly before 7 P.M. as it was about to close for the day. I was with Wu, my government-assigned assistant, whom I called simply Lao Wu in the old Chinese informal style which the Communists have adopted. (*Lao* means old, and since he was forty-two, a year older than I, he became Lao Wu. Anyone younger than I, I addressed with the prefix *xiao,* "Little.") We needed to buy some of the string mesh bags Chinese use to carry their groceries in, for we had just purchased half a dozen succulent Hami melons, the sugary orange fruit that barbarians from Central Asia used to bring by camel caravan as presents to the Emperor. A sullen clerk behind the counter pointed to her watch.

"Too late, it's seven P.M., the store is closed," she said triumphantly.

But Lao Wu acted decisively, scoring the ultimate debating point in China. "But this is a foreign guest. He needs a shopping bag." The clerk looked at me, grunted with resignation, and then reached down and produced the bags we needed.

On another trip, in the northwest city of Lanzhou, it appeared Lao Wu and I would be stuck for several days longer than we wanted to because the once-a-day airplane flights to Peking were fully booked. "It's no big problem," my guide from the local foreign affairs office said with a self-confident smile. "I will use my connections to get you a seat." A prim, slender woman in her late twenties, she was as good as her word. A few hours later she reported success.

"I had to ask them to bump two Chinese passengers off the plane for a foreigner," she recounted. "The cadre in charge was reluctant to do it because he had already taken two other Chinese off for a foreign technician and his interpreter. But when I told him you are a journalist, he finally agreed. We can always do it for foreigners," the guide concluded.

Careful preparation and a dash of deception are other ingredients in the treatment for visiting foreigners. When I first took up residence in China in June 1979, I remember a trip to the Yiliu people's commune on the mile-high Yunnan plateau in the southwestern part of the country near the city of Kunming. It may be the only commune in China with its own parking lot, a big, paved empty space in front of the main administration building. Most of the peasants there still walk or ride in horse carts, so the parking lot is for visitors. At least that was my guess when I arrived for a tour in a snaking convoy of thirty cars and buses with the U.S. Secretary of Health, Education and Welfare, Joseph A. Califano. This was one of the obligatory stops on any visitor's itinerary of China, be he private tourist or foreign dignitary, an hour at a commune, a little look at how well agriculture has done since Liberation. Califano, an intelligent, energetic, and forceful man, a lawyer by training, asked if the commune was average for China. Yes, the local authorities assured him. Had other foreign visitors been here before? he pressed further, hinting the commune might be a showpiece. No, the officials responded, he was the first foreigner to be brought here.

But there were small telltale signs which suggested that the commune was not just average. The building where Califano was greeted and given a briefing on the commune's grain output had just been whitewashed—some of the paint had splashed on the dirt floor. In the back there were toilets thoughtfully differentiated by painted profiles of men and women, their large sharp-pointed noses and curly hair decidedly un-Chinese. Outside, I noticed, the dirt path leading toward a village of mud-brick houses, our next destination, had just been swept. The trace marks of the wicker brooms in the dust were still visible. At an outdoor public privy on our path, lime had been generously spread to dampen the usual rich, nauseous aroma. There were lines of peasant women in broad, flat bamboo hats weeding the knee-high fields of ripening green rice. Bent double at the waist, they were performing China's most ancient ritual. But on each narrow dike that led from the village to the fields, between the American visitors and the natives, there were young cadres in blue Mao tunics, just to avoid any untoward incident. It was easy to tell they weren't peasants themselves, for they bore the special insignia of those who have made it in Communist China, a fountain pen in their left-hand breast pocket.

Califano must have had his doubts about what he was shown, because that afternoon, driving back to Kunming, he suddenly asked his host, a deputy governor of Yunnan province, to stop as they passed through another village. Their long black Red Flag limousine screeched to a halt at the head of the long caravan of vehicles. To the consternation of the Chinese, Califano got out and tried to walk around the village. But there had been no official preparation here, and the peasants, caught by surprise, fled like chickens, scattering in all directions. So thorough was the panic that Califano couldn't find anyone to talk to.

When I recounted the episode later to a friend in Peking who worked for a government diplomatic agency, she snickered at my naïveté. Such precautions are typical of the lengths Chinese go to to entertain, please, beguile, and often manipulate foreigners, she said. A vivacious, winsome woman with large sparkling eyes and the standard short, bowl-cut hair, it was her job to escort state guests around Peking. One place she often took them was the big Chaoyang market in the northeast part of the city to show how well the Chinese are fed. When an important visitor was scheduled to arrive, the market would be given a "visiting task," she told me. Trucks would be sent to the market early that morning with extra supplies of live chickens and frozen fish, two delicacies often unavailable. The visitors were always impressed, she recalled. What they didn't know was that, though the Chinese customers could buy the goods on display, the fish would be counted against their monthly ration and most of the special fish were so large they were over people's quota of one pound a month. So all they could do was look.

Another key part of the treatment for visiting politicians, cultural luminaries, and assorted bigwigs is the airport reception by hundreds of clapping, singing schoolchildren, their cheeks rouged and their eyebrows blackened for the occasion, followed by a twelve-course epicurean banquet in the Great Hall of the People, complete with endless libations of fiery *maotai* liquor and toasts to friendship. The total effect of this hostmanship is like a powerful tranquilizer, enough to make otherwise rational and intelligent people suspend disbelief. I remember Mayor Ed Koch of New York, normally canny, self-assured, and unflappable, accepting a cigarette from the Party boss of Xian, the old capital in the west, and then lighting up. His aides were stunned. Koch never smokes and hates people to smoke in his presence.

"I didn't want to offend these people, they have been so nice to us," Koch said afterward. "It's the first cigarette I've smoked in twenty years, and I shall not take another for twenty more years."

Then there was Shirley MacLaine at the White House banquet for Deng Xiaoping in 1979. President Carter had invited her to sit at the head table with him and the diminutive Chinese leader since she had been one of the first Americans to visit China after Ping-Pong diplomacy began in 1971 and had both written a book—*You Can Get There From Here*—and made a movie extolling the benefits Mao's Cultural Revolution reforms had brought to a happy and prosperous China. At the White House dinner, Miss MacLaine enthusiastically recounted to Deng a meeting she had with a Chinese nuclear physicist who had been sent to a commune to grow tomatoes. The scientist had assured her he felt much happier and more productive on the farm than in his lab, Miss MacLaine said. "He lied," Deng cut her off. "That was what he had to say at the time." To her credit, Miss MacLaine told the story on herself on television the next day.

But there was also a less congenial, more sinister side to hostmanship as practiced by the Communists. Along with restoring the grandeur of imperial audiences for visitors, the Communists also reimposed the traditional hermetic restrictions on foreigners in China, both to buffer the outsiders from the less pleasant realities of Chinese life and to prevent any bourgeois contagion from infecting China. Just as in imperial times foreigners were confined to a small ghetto, so today virtually all foreigners in China must live in specially designated housing: diplomats and journalists in three-walled compounds of modern high-rise apartment buildings guarded by army sentries on the northeast edge of Peking, teachers in the isolated, rambling Friendship Hotel (originally built for Soviet advisers) to the northwest, and students in reserved quarters in the university dormitories.

Any Chinese who wanted to visit my office in the Peking Hotel had to register his or her name and work unit with the Public Security Ministry guards at the front desk; then the next day their office would receive a slip reporting their contact with a foreigner. I learned this when an earnest young Chinese journalist from Peking television daringly, but foolishly, it turned out, insisted on coming to see me in the hotel. Deng had said the officials should "emancipate their minds," and she took him seriously. But a few days later three policemen went to call on her Party secretary, who in turn summoned her to the meeting. "Why did you go to see Butterfield, what information did you give him?" they demanded. She was ordered to write a self-criticism and barred from seeing me again, she told me in one last rendezvous.

"We are supposed to be a socialist country, that means relying on the people," she said with disappointment. "But our government doesn't trust the people. What is there so secret that we can't talk with foreigners? This is no different from the Gang of Four." Several times later I ran into her at press conferences, but she cautiously turned her head so she wouldn't have to see me.

Another acquaintance, a college English teacher, reported that at a weekly political study session their Party leader had read out a new directive from the Peking city government prohibiting Chinese from meeting foreigners unless they first received clearance from their workplace. Afterward they were to make a full report of everything that was said. (Several other Chinese recounted being given the same instructions.) The regulation angered the teacher, and she insisted on inviting me to visit her apartment one Sunday afternoon on the school campus. I tried to decline, but she said I would be rude to refuse her hospitality. At her direction, we drove up to the front door of her building in *The Times*'s car, clearly marked by my foreigner's license plate, the usual 31 prefix denoting Peking but colored in red.

A plain, stocky woman whose passion in life was improving her already fluent English and going abroad to study, she lived with her retired parents. Her father, tall, stooped, and balding, a former government clerk, was clearly unsettled by my arrival. He understood the risks and saw little to gain from my visit. He called her into the bedroom and upbraided her. "You shouldn't have brought him here," he said, loud enough for me to hear through the thin walls.

I felt I should leave, but her mother, a round, kindly, former kindergarten teacher with short gray hair held firmly in place with bobby pins, blocked the door. "It's nothing, you must stay, besides I have already started cooking dinner," she said affably. I was caught in a dilemma. It would be an offense against Chinese manners to go, but a political offense to stay. Her mother sensed my unease. She took my arm gently and led me to a red plastic-covered armchair. "Just sit there till dinner is ready," she counseled.

Unfortunately, the next day the family received a visit from two neighbors, both Party members and administrators in the college. "We saw you had a foreign visitor, that was a mistake," they rebuked her. A few weeks later she took an English test for teachers in her school to decide who would win three coveted scholarships to spend a year studying in the United States. She got the highest mark, she claimed, but was turned down "for political reasons."

"For a Chinese to become friendly with a foreigner is like the old saying about a silk worm—you are just spinning a cocoon around yourself, ensnaring yourself in a web," she added. I felt guilty, as if I were radioactive and contaminated any Chinese I came in contact with. The government's restrictions were in hypocritical contrast to the large red illuminated sign in Chinese and English in the lobby of the Peking Hotel that I passed several times a day: "We have friends all over the world." Friendship to the government meant those carefully controlled tours of China for foreigners who came away full of sympathy for the People's Republic, or giving foreigners special privileges like access to the Friendship Store—the department and grocery store reserved for foreigners—where they could buy more goods than are available to ordinary Chinese. But friendship did not include intimacy with individual Chinese.

Many Chinese themselves resent the government's rules barring them from the hotels where foreigners stay and the Friendship Store. They see the regulations as discrimination by the regime against its own people. A doctor in Shanghai recalled the infamous sign that before 1949 blocked a small park by the city's waterfront: "No dogs or Chinese allowed." The Communists often dredged it up as an example of imperialist perfidy. But when the physician tried to visit me in the Jinjiang Hotel in Shanghai, the police guard at the gate wouldn't let him in without registering. "Nowadays dogs can go into the hotel, but Chinese still can't," he said with uncharacteristic animus.

The government is particularly sensitive about any romantic involvement between Chinese and foreigners, regarding it virtually as a form of national dishonor. When a precocious, outspoken high school student I knew began dating a European exchange student at Peking University, two agents from the Public Security Ministry paid a call on her parents, they told me later.

"What is the relationship between your daughter and this foreigner?" the police quizzed them. "Why has she been seeing him? You should educate her not to go out with foreigners, it is a shameful thing for China. Foreigners are always trying to ferret out our secrets and destroy the revolution. If your daughter loves her country, she will break off this relationship."

The student had met her European boy friend at a dance at the Nationalities Palace, a cavernous theater and office building where the government had opened an incongruous three-times-a-week discotheque in 1979 complete with flashing colored lights and Chinese beer and orange soda. The move was part of Mao's successors' gradual liberalization, "to satisfy the requests of our foreign friends," as one official said to me, for more to do on Saturday nights. The dances were supposed to be strictly segregated—foreigners only. But occasionally a few venturesome Chinese would sneak in, like the high school student, after dressing themselves up in tight-fitting trousers or putting on lipstick and eye shadow to try to confound the guards. What most Westerners didn't realize, she said, was that while the disco for foreigners occupied the first floor and the basement, there were also dances for Chinese on the second floor, no foreigners admitted.

For a Chinese woman to be caught sleeping with a foreign man is a serious offense. An acquaintance in the army related that a popular and attractive female singer in an air force music troupe had been arrested after spending the night with several Japanese diplomats and businessmen. He found out about the affair because the army mounted a confidential exhibit in Peking to display the tainted loot she had supposedly received for her promiscuity: a Japanese-made television set, a refrigerator, a tape recorder, and some clothes. The show hinted the police even had videotapes of some of the bedroom scenes.

Some love stories between Chinese and foreigners have a happier ending. Susan Wilf, a bright, outgoing graduate student from Harvard with curly brown hair and a voluptuous figure, managed to become the first American to marry a Chinese since the Cultural Revolution. She met her future spouse, a strikingly handsome accordion player in a Chinese band, Chen Daying, when a mutual friend arranged for her to tutor Chen in English. Government regulations required that they get permission to marry from their respective work units—for Susan, it was the Peking Second Foreign Languages Institute, where she was teaching. She wasn't sure what to expect. The couple had not even been able to buy an engagement ring until Susan pretended to the guard at the Friendship Store that Chen was already her husband. For ordinary Chinese are not allowed in the store, and it is the only place in Peking where precious stones are sold. But after a wait of six weeks, the minimum in a case of such magnitude, their union was approved by the State Council itself, China's cabinet, she was told.

At their wedding party, the couple opened the occasion by bowing four times to the one hundred guests, once for each of the directions of the compass, a Chinese custom. Then they startled the assemblage by kissing, for a full thirty seconds. In revolutionary China, kissing in public is still bourgeois.

A tiny pigtailed sixteen-year-old girl with rosy cheeks sitting in the rear of the room took it philosophically. "Each nationality has its own habits," she whispered to me. "It's all right for foreigners to kiss. Chinese might normally shake hands or something."

But the government also took steps to limit marriage between Chinese and foreigners as the number of foreign students, teachers, and tourists mushroomed in the late 1970s.* In 1980, Peking put out a decree prohibiting four categories of Chinese from marrying foreigners under any circumstances: all those in the armed forces, anyone in the political departments of the Party who handled personnel matters, those who worked with state secrets, and everyone in what was termed foreign affairs work, including diplomats, guides for the China Travel Service, and interpreters, like my assistant Lao Wu.

Chinese in this last group, who deal with foreigners on a daily basis, are selected for their jobs with extra prudence and kept under a number of special constraints. Over my twenty months in Peking, I gradually developed a genuine fondness for Lao Wu. Although he kept a discreet silence whenever I tried to discuss politics with him, I appreciated his conscientious work in the office. Without a complaint, he turned out reams of translations from the Chinese press and sparred on my behalf with the bureaucracy. But a friend whose father was a general cautioned me not to become too close to him.

"You know, every Saturday afternoon he and your driver have to make a full report about what you do and say during the week at their political study session in the Diplomatic Services Bureau," the general's son confided. He himself had a friend who was an interpreter for a European embassy, so he knew the drill. "They are told to draw a very clear line with you, they will never tell you anything, and it is part of their job to investigate you."

It was an unsettling sensation to know you lived with a spy, with yourself as the object of attention, and I sometimes tended to dismiss the notion as unthinkable. But one Friday afternoon when Lao Wu was out of the office running an errand, the Diplomatic Services Bureau rang for him on the phone. My other assistant, Jan Wong, answered. Jan is a Canadian-Chinese whose father runs a Chinese restaurant in Montreal and who had come to China to study at Peking University in the early 1970s. Because of Lao Wu's official role, I had hired Jan to help when I wanted to interview political dissidents or broaden my contacts among ordinary Chinese. At this, she was marvelous and soon became indispensable. Short, energetic, and engaging,

*The number of American students in China jumped from zero in 1978, before the normalization of Sino–U.S. relations, to 300 in 1981. In 1978, when China first opened its doors to regular tourism, the number of visitors reached 125,000, more than in all the previous years since 1949. In 1981, the number of tourists increased further to 218,000.

with a round, girlish face, Jan wore her hair in pigtails and dressed in plain, baggy proletarian blue like her former schoolmates. She had also learned to speak Chinese without a trace of a foreign accent. So she passed as a native. On that Friday afternoon when she took the call for Lao Wu, the woman at the Diplomatic Services Bureau assumed she was Chinese.

"Tell Wu he doesn't have to make his report tomorrow, the meeting is canceled," the caller said.

After the Chinese finally gave me an apartment and my family was able to move to Peking in September 1980, we had a similar problem with the woman the Diplomatic Services Bureau assigned to us as a maid, Wang *a-yi*, or "Auntie" Wang. Squat and expansive, with a full round face, she had the cherubic smile of a middle-aged Buddha. But she too reported on us each week, I was told, and she proved extraordinarily reticent about divulging even the most trivial personal information. When my wife asked her what her husband did, she replied, "He works." Several times when we asked her to stay late and baby-sit—you can't just call up a Chinese girl and ask her to watch your children for the evening—I was concerned that she would have difficulty getting home. She lived more than a half-hour bicycle ride from our apartment and the weather was very cold, so I offered to drive her home. But each time she refused. If she appeared in her neighborhood in *The Times*'s car, it would be reported and she might be accused of forming too close a relationship with us, we surmised. Another journalist, Tony Walker of the *Melbourne Age,* did manage to become friendly with his *a-yi.* Before her son got married, she extended an invitation to the Walkers, a great honor they thought. But a few days later she apologized with great embarrassment. The Diplomatic Services Bureau had found out about the invitation and ordered her to rescind it.

As a further precaution against foreigners, the general's son told me, there was a list of foreign diplomats who were regarded as intelligence agents. One copy was kept in the office at Peking University that handles foreign students, he added. That way the cadres who monitored the activities of the overseas students could check if they were in contact with the presumed spies. Among the names on the sheet he mentioned to me was that of a close friend, Roger Garside, a career diplomat in the British Foreign Office who has since written an informative book about contemporary Chinese politics, *Coming Alive, China After Mao.* I suspected his worst crime was that he spoke Chinese too well and had too many Chinese acquaintances. There was also a list giving the government's opinion about each foreign correspondent, a disaffected young journalist told me. Whenever I had an interview or took a trip, the officials involved were briefed on my rating. My name had an asterisk next to it, the journalist said. That meant I was considered *fan-hua,* "Anti-China," a particularly odorous label. He advised me not to be offended, it only meant the government was disturbed by my reporting. But it did warrant the Public Security Ministry giving me special attention.

Only occasionally was I aware of this vigilance. One fall afternoon when I carelessly arranged to meet a young unemployed high school graduate outside the Peking Hotel and got directly in *The Times*'s car from the hotel parking lot, I noticed a shiny black Mercedes 280 behind us—no underpowered Chinese-made cars for the police. My acquaintance was a tall, stocky young woman with a set of toothpaste-fresh white teeth. We were driving straight west on the Avenue of Eternal Tranquility, and the Mercedes stayed close behind, speeding up when I drove faster, slowing down when I tried a more leisurely pace. Finally, at the far western edge of the city, I suddenly cut across the middle lane and did a U-turn. The Mercedes, filled with four men, I noted, followed suit. We continued driving for an hour, till it grew dark, both of us increasingly nervous. Then, in hopes of shaking our pursuers, I turned into the side road next to the Friendship Store. It was filled with other foreign cars and a swarm of Chinese waiting for a bus. The police calculated we were going into the store and stopped a few yards back. In the protection of the darkness and the crowd, my friend jumped out and joined the straggling queue for the bus.

Of all the forms of control and discrimination involving foreigners, the one that most nettled Westerners was the government's double-price standard, one set for foreigners, another for Chinese. When I took a trip to Sichuan with Lao Wu, for example, my airplane ticket cost 200 yuan ($133), his only 85 yuan ($57). In the hotel in Chengdu, the provincial capital, I was charged 100 yuan ($67) a night for my room, food, and use of a car, Lao Wu only 40 ($27). The authorities presented both bills to me to pay, since I was Lao Wu's employer, so there was no attempt to hide the price differential.

This system was designed to extract badly needed foreign currency for China, so it could import more U.S. grain, West German coal-mining technology, and Japanese steel mills. Rich capitalists could afford to pay, this theory holds. But only in a country with China's heritage of superiority would the government be so blatant about overcharging, I felt, so contemptuous of standards of fair play. One evening I invited a scholarly editor to the Xinjiang Restaurant in Peking, which was famous for its spicy mutton shashlik and its fried bread, Chinese food with a Middle Eastern flavor. The editor knew the manager of the restaurant and volunteered to make the reservation to save me the trouble. After we finished, I went to the counter to pay the bill. The waitress looked confused and annoyed.

"If you pay, then we have to charge a different price," she announced. "We calculated the bill for a Chinese, because it was a Chinese who made the reservation." When I still insisted on paying, she carefully crossed out each price on the check and entered a new one, twice or more the original amount.

Sometimes this double-price policy turns into sheer greed. When a delegation from the American public television network, PBS, came to Peking to discuss filming a series of seven one-hour documentaries on China, the Chinese television authorities said it would cost them $1.5 million for local assistance. That was ten times what it would cost in other countries and what the Americans were prepared to pay, an outraged New York producer said afterward.

"But the Japanese have already paid four million dollars to make a documentary on the Yellow River," the Chinese countered.

From another foreign television crew that had shot a historical documentary in China, the PBS delegation heard how the costs mounted up. The crew was filming a scene involving a warrior. The Chinese first asked that the crew pay for the rent of the costume, which was reasonable. Then the Chinese demanded that the foreign company pay for the horse on which the warrior would sit; that was also fair. Next the Chinese asked for money for the actor who would sit on the horse; agreed, said the crew. After the scene was completed, the Chinese had another charge—the crew had to pay for the cancellation of the Chinese opera performance in which the actor was to have played that night.

When the Japanese filmed a movie about the Yangtze River, the PBS delegation heard, they needed a boat. The Chinese said they would have to rent it for a month, though they used it for only a few days. After the Japanese finished shooting, the Chinese presented another bill—they would also have to pay for all the passengers who didn't ride on the boat for the month it would be out of service.

But the most bizarre story of price discrimination was a simple one told by an American woman married to an American-Chinese who had come to Peking to teach. When they took a train trip to Loyang, in central China, she was charged double what her husband was for the ride, since he counted as an overseas Chinese. Then when they spent the night in a hotel, in the same double bed, her bill was triple that of her husband.

Despite China's self-assurance and xenophobia, there is a radical ambivalence about how China should deal with the West and its technological and economic superiority. Since China's ignominious defeat in the Opium War a century ago, this has been the pivotal issue for Chinese, how to make China "rich and strong" again, and the country's policy has swung back and forth like a pendulum. Some Chinese statesmen, like Mao, have preached self-reliance and shutting out the world, the nativist approach. Others, like Deng, who himself spent six years in France as a worker and student in the 1920s, have held that salvation lies in copying the secrets of Western science and opening China to expanded foreign trade. Deng's epochal trip to the United States in 1979 was designed to underscore the correctness of his plan, but it also helped stimulate an insatiable new appetite for the bounties of capitalism as Chinese television beamed back pictures of American suburban living, the split-level ranch-style home with two cars in the garage, and a color television set in every living room. When the Communists, partially as a result, then saw young Chinese letting their hair grow long and listening to Hong Kong rock music and putting up posters on Democracy Wall calling for freedom of speech, it made them nervous. A backlash set in. Deng muttered darkly about creeping "bourgeois liberalism" and the press tried to counteract the glamor of the West by painting it in unfavorable terms. American workers eat meat and draw high salaries, the *People's Daily* sermonized, but the United States is beset by inflation, crime, unemployment, racial conflict, and a collapsing family system.

I recall one especially venomous speech by Zhang Guangdou, a vice chairman of Qinghua University, China's equivalent of the Massachusetts Institute of Technology. People should not be misled by the material prosperity of capitalist countries but look to the nature of the system, asserted Zhang, a hydroelectric expert who had studied in the United States before World War Two and had recently returned from a two-month visit to America.

"Our revolutionary teachers have all said that capitalism must collapse and socialism must replace capitalism," Zhang declared. It is important to remember that America's wealth was based on a long history of exploitation, Zhang charged, of the Indians, of the blacks, of Chinese immigrant laborers, of the whole continent of Latin America, which the United States had converted into a colony. In recent years, "even second world countries, such as Japan, Germany, and England are victims of its bullying.

"The United States did not participate in the two world wars. You fight, and they come in near the end. They did not fight on their own territory, the battles were mainly fought in Europe and Asia. As a consequence they grabbed up many resources, many things, it is an imperialist country." After World War Two, Zhang continued, the United States "enlisted the service of many German scientists. So all of the scientists and technicians are foreigners."

In China, he said, "After our victory over Japan, the Americans came in. American soldiers pushed their way around, doing whatever they pleased, raping women. They did every bad thing possible. At the time our country was very poor and productivity was low. Everything bought on the streets was American, toilet paper, milk powder, etc." This explained why America is rich and China poor, Zhang argued. But young Chinese should also be aware of the troubles Americans face in their own daily lives.

"Americans are always figuring and figuring, worrying that there won't be enough money. My standard of living is low, but I am not anxious. If a son in America goes to his mother's home to eat, he must pay money. If the mother goes to the son's house to eat, she must also give money. I'm not joking in the least. I'll give you an example. A family invited me to eat dinner. Four of them invited me, and after eating, and in front of me, they took out a calculator and calculated who owed what."

But in a society already made cynical by the constant din of propaganda, the stridency of attacks like Zhang's are counterproductive, too exaggerated to be credible. Perhaps nothing illustrates the Communists' ambivalence toward the West better than the steady stream of children of the Party elite who have gone to the United States since the normalization of relations in 1979. One of Deng's sons, a physicist, is a graduate student at the University of Rochester; Deng's daughter lives in the Chinese Embassy in Washington, where her husband is a military attaché. A son of the Foreign Minister, Huang Hua, is an undergraduate at Harvard; a daughter of Liu Shaoqi, the late head of state, is enrolled at Boston University. From Chinese friends, I heard of over a dozen offspring of Politburo members and cabinet ministers now in the United States. There has been no comparable exodus from the elite of the Soviet Union. For the Chinese Communists, this represents a tangible investment, a belief that China can usefully learn from America and that Peking's relations with Washington will continue to improve. Otherwise these children could be a liability in a future internal Chinese power struggle.

2. "Where Are You, Comrade?"

你那几同志

IDENTITY

"If language is incorrect, then what is said does not concord with what was meant; and if what is said does not concord with what was meant, what is to be done cannot be effected."

Confucius, in the Analects

The new wing of the Peking Hotel is a handsome, seventeen-story concrete and glass edifice in the modern international mode. It could have been built in Chicago, Nairobi, or Istanbul. The front is graced with rows of recessed balconies climbing to flag poles on the flat roof, very different from the gentle curve of traditional Chinese tiled eaves. An elevated driveway leads visitors to a set of high glass doors that automatically glide open and closed each time a guest steps on a sensitized metal grille. Inside the entrance there is a marble-topped reservations desk, and in the rear of the vast high-ceilinged lobby, padded by yards of plush red carpeting, an electronic panel that controls twin banks of eight elevators flickers with red, yellow, and blue lights like a computer console. Off to one side is the main dining room, to the other a shopping arcade that offers, along with postcards and maps of the capital, Chinese elixirs for long life and flagging virility: powdered rhinoceros horn, deer's tail, and ginseng root. When I first arrived in June 1979 to set up *The New York Times* bureau, I took these merely as pleasant exotica. I was not prepared for what came next.

A balding, slightly stooped clerk in a loose-fitting brownish-gray tunic stood behind the reservations desk, which was identified by a sign in English that said, "Accommodation Center."

"Do you have a room?" I asked in my best Chinese.

After examining me for what seemed several minutes, he replied, "Where are you?" or *"Ni nar"* in Chinese.

Thinking I had heard wrong, I repeated my question. But he answered again, "Where are you?"

Finally, sensing my confusion, he amplified. "We only give rooms to units, not to individuals," he said, using the Chinese word *danwei. Danwei,* I knew, meant a person's workplace, their office, factory, school, or commune. "Where are you?" therefore meant "What is your unit?" But I had just arrived in China as a U.S. journalist; I didn't have a *danwei.*

"Everyone in China has a *danwei,*" the clerk said definitively. "You must find your *danwei,* or we can't give you a room."

Thus began my first task in China, to find my *danwei.* The Information Department, which had granted me my visa, disclaimed responsibility. The China Travel Service said they couldn't help because I was a resident in China and not a tourist. The Diplomatic Services Bureau, which arranges housing for foreigners in Peking, turned down my request because they said they gave out only apartments, which they didn't have, and not hotel rooms. The American Embassy was reluctant to become involved because the press and the government in the United States are supposed to keep their distance from each other. Eventually, I did appeal to the American ambassador, Leonard Woodcock, who wrote to the Foreign Ministry suggesting they should take the awful responsibility and adopt me as part of their *danwei.*

This adventure was a useful lesson. *Danwei,* I quickly discovered, are the basic building blocks of Chinese society, almost a second citizenship for most Chinese. A Chinese is more likely to be asked his *danwei* than his name when he goes someplace new. Chinese telephone conversations usually begin "Where are you?" not "Who is this?" When I stopped for a night in the remote industrial city of Qiqihar in the far northeastern corner of China, the first question on the registration form of the local hotel asked for the guest's unit. Only the second line inquired about his name.

At the entrance to the Peking Hotel the Public Security Bureau stations two guards in plainclothes. One day soon after my arrival I stood outside the door to observe their ritual. They automatically let in all foreigners, Chinese they recognize as hotel employees, and Party officials who arrive in prestigious chauffeur-driven sedans. But any other Chinese they pull over and challenge, "Where are you, comrade?" On one occasion Martin King Whyte, a sociologist from the University of Michigan who was in Peking on an academic exchange program, invited a deputy mayor of the capital to lunch in the hotel. This official, Lei Jieqiong, was actually a distinguished seventy-four-year-old sociologist herself, a graduate of the University of California, who had only recently been appointed to the city post even though she was not a Party member. Since she did not arrive in the requisite limousine which transports most officials, the police guards didn't recognize her importance. "Where are you?" they snarled. When she answered that she was a deputy mayor of the city, they laughed and forced her to go to the security desk and show her work pass. Only then did they realize their mistake. The irony of the story, Miss Lei pointed out later, was that the Peking Hotel actually as a unit belongs to the Peking city government.

The reason for this stress on *danwei* is that a *danwei* to a Chinese is far more than just his workplace. A tall thirty-five-year-old woman who worked in the semisecret Fourth Ministry of Machine Building, which produces electronics for China's defense industry, explained how the system works. She lived in an apartment in a vast compound of five-story gray-brick buildings managed by her ministry. All her neighbors were also employed by the ministry. To go in or out of the one entrance, she had to walk past an army guard in uniform, and if she brought any visitors into the compound, they had to register in the sentry box. The woman's nine-year-old son went to school in another building inside the compound; she shopped for groceries in the compound store; when the family was sick there was a clinic in the compound. The ministry also issued her her ration cards for rice, cooking oil, cloth, and what the Chinese call "industrial goods," including radios, watches, sewing machines, or bicycles.

But the *danwei*'s authority over her went even deeper, as she related one summer afternoon when we drove by her compound. It would have been impossible for me to go in past the sentry, she apologized. When she wanted to get married a decade ago, she recalled, she had been required to apply to the Party secretary of her *danwei* for permission, a standard procedure. Her *danwei* then ran a security check with her boy friend's unit, and only after both *danwei* approved, could they wed. If she wanted to try to transfer to another job, her unit had to agree. When an elderly neighbor died recently, she added, the *danwei* had arranged for his funeral and cremation. To talk to me, a foreigner, she was supposed to receive permission from her *danwei* beforehand, and she was to report back on whatever we discussed.

Not every *danwei* in China is so well equipped that it can provide this full range of cradle-to-grave services. Some units don't have their own housing; only the largest have both their own schools and hospitals. But for the government the *danwei* structure means that society is organized as much as a security system as it is as a social or economic system. If the hallmark of the feudal system in medieval Europe and Japan was the peasant's inescapable bondage to the land, the essence of the Chinese system, I sometimes thought, was the individual's ties to his *danwei,* a kind of industrial feudalism.

There was no exact counterpart for the *danwei* in traditional China. Earlier dynasties did practice a mutual guarantee organization called the *bao-jia* system: families were organized in groups of tens and hundreds with each unit responsible for the acts of all the others. But the real antecedent probably lies simply in the Chinese penchant for bonding the individual to his group.

41

Chinese are more naturally comfortable with their group than by themselves. We say "everyone"; the Chinese equivalent is *da-jia,* "the great family." We select our own separate food from the menu, then eat from our own dishes. Chinese order their meals together and then eat from common plates, sharing the food. When Chinese drink alcohol at a meal, they never drink by themselves. They first lift their glass to a companion and offer a small toast, looking their dinner partner in the eye. To drink by oneself would be rude and selfish.

One Easter Sunday I found myself in Shanghai. I had been assigned to cover the China tour of a delegation from the U.S. Senate Foreign Relations Committee, and we were quartered in the Jinjiang Hotel, an elegant collection of dark-stone gothic buildings erected in the 1930s by some of the city's wealthiest Chinese and European residents. Somehow the Jinjiang has preserved that era—its rich mahogany floors and the brass fixtures on its doors are still polished every day. Richard Nixon stayed in the Jinjiang during his trip to China in 1972, and he signed the Shanghai Communiqué restoring ties between the United States and China after a hiatus of over two decades in a suite in the hotel. The hotel's roomboys, in crisp white uniforms, show an awareness of this tradition. Hence when I went to bed at 2 A.M. the night before, after filing a story to New York, I counted on a peaceful night's sleep.

But at 7 A.M. precisely I was awakened by a young roomboy carrying a large red thermos of hot tea which he proceeded to place on my bedside table. From years of habit, I don't wear pajamas when I sleep, and I can vaguely recall trying to gather the sheets around me.

"It's very early, would you mind leaving so I can sleep?" I ventured, probably with anger. "You might at least have knocked on the door."

But he was neither embarrassed nor daunted by my command.

"It's not important, please go ahead and sleep," he replied with a smile.

After he accomplished his errand, I was considering trying to go back to sleep when I heard his footsteps again. This time he had another thermos, for cold water. Five minutes later he was back for a third time, with a change of towels.

It was an experience that I was to have over and over again in China, as do other foreigners—roomboys who don't knock before entering and pay no heed to "Do Not Disturb" signs on doors. Chinese simply do not recognize privacy; indeed, there is no word for privacy in the 50,000 characters of the Chinese language. Life in China is so crowded and clamorous, privacy is normally impossible except by the hazard of circumstance.

Even in hospitals, patients often wait in the doctor's examining room while he is tending to another case. When I went to the Institute of Traditional Medicine to have a master in the art of Chinese massage see if he could repair the ravages of too much tennis in my shoulder, I shared the doctor's room and services with half a dozen patients. They nodded appreciatively as he discussed how my meridians had become inflamed and watched with interest as he pummeled and flexed my shoulder. David Eisenberg, a student from the Harvard Medical School who was the first American allowed to actually work in a Chinese hospital, said he had seen one case where the patient was dying of cancer and the other patients all sat there listening to the doctor's diagnosis.

Nor is there a word for intimacy in Chinese. In the summer of 1972, shortly after President Nixon's China trip, while I was stationed in Vietnam as a correspondent, *The Times* asked me to come back to New York to help act as guide and interpreter for the first group of reporters from the New China News Agency who wanted to tour the United States. For two weeks, in a rented car, we crossed Pennsylvania, West Virginia, Ohio, Michigan, Wisconsin, Illinois, New York, and Massachusetts, visiting a coal mine, a Ford automobile assembly plant, a dairy farm, and Niagara Falls. Some nights I had arranged for the Chinese journalists to stay with American families, but other evenings we ended up in roadside motels, like Holiday Inn. The dining rooms in these establishments all seemed to have been designed from a common plan: the atmosphere was subdued, the light was dim, some had artificial electric candles on the tables. It was suburban elegance. But one of the Chinese reporters, Ye Xiangzhi, a short, wiry man with a quick mind, was disturbed.

"Why do Americans like to eat in the dark?" he asked. "They can't even read the menu."

It was hard to answer him, for the Chinese have a value that is the flip side of privacy and intimacy—*renao,* for which there is no word in English or any European language. Literally it means "hot and noisy," suggesting the pleasure and excitement of a large group of friends and relatives who get together for a meal, with everyone talking and plenty of lights in the room. Anyone who has been to an ordinary restaurant in one of America's Chinatowns can get a hint of this, with the chopsticks clicking, the guests shouting out their orders, the waiters banging the dishes on the table without ceremony, and perhaps a game of Mah-jongg in a back room, the ivory tiles grating like the sound of surf withdrawing on a shale beach.

But the Chinese preference for the group does not mean any group; they are not indiscriminately gregarious. Walking down Peking's streets, as crowded as taking a subway in New York or Tokyo, it is almost impossible not to bump into someone, and at first when I did make contact I tried to preserve my American manners. "Excuse me, I'm sorry," I would say.

But Chinese friends laughed at my ignorance. I didn't even know the person, why should I apologize to him? I recalled an incident that happened when I first lived in Taiwan as a graduate student in 1961. I was coming back on my bicycle from a language class and watched with horror as a pedicab, a three-wheeled bicycle-powered taxi, ran over an infant about a year old who had just learned to toddle. The child was covered with blood and screaming, but the pedicab driver kept on pedaling without slowing down and none of the many passersby in the street went to help. I tried to comfort the baby until its mother finally appeared. Later when I repeated the story to the Chinese family I was living with, they did not find it as outrageous as I did.

This is perhaps an extreme example, but I began to appreciate how differently Chinese order their mental universe than do Westerners. We tend to see people as individuals; we make some distinctions, of course, between those we know and those we don't. But basically we have one code of manners for all. Chinese, on the other hand, instinctively divide people into those with whom they already have a fixed relationship, a connection, what the Chinese call *guan-xi,* and those they don't. These connections operate like a series of invisible threads, tying Chinese to each other with far greater tensile strength than mere friendship in the West would do. *Guan-xi* have created a social magnetic field in which all Chinese move, keenly aware of those people with whom they have connections and those they don't. They explain why the Communist leadership, which was so grateful to Richard Nixon for helping make the breakthrough in Sino–American relations, could never understand Watergate and why Peking even sent a special plane to bring Nixon back to China for a visit after his disgrace. In a broader sense, *guan-xi* also help explain how a nation of one billion people coheres.

Take our friendship with the Wang family. Li, the husband, was an industrial engineer, a tall, reserved, aristocratic man with a high forehead and long swept-back hair. Xiao Miao, "Little Sprout," his wife, was a piano teacher with a quick wit and a pretty face that must once have been coquettish. We met at another Chinese friend's wedding. I gave the Wangs my card and they promised to get in touch. But I knew that only a tiny fraction of the Chinese I talked with once would dare to meet me again.

So I was surprised several months later, after my wife and children had moved to Peking, to hear Li's voice on the phone. Did I remember him? he asked. Yes, I said. Would I come to dinner at their apartment? Of course, I said instantly. To avoid arousing suspicion, we agreed to meet at the Telegraph Office, an easy landmark where both foreigners and Chinese went, and then drove with Li to his apartment inside the institute where his wife worked. There was a guard in the gatehouse, but to my relief he did not try to stop us, and we drove in past a tall white statue of Mao. The Great Helmsman was standing and staring expressionlessly into the distance, his long overcoat blown open by an unfelt breeze.

By the time we arrived it was dark. There were no streetlights, nor any lights at the front door or in the hallway; China is too poor to waste electricity in public places. Li picked up Ethan, our four-year-old, and began carrying him up the four flights to their apartment in the toal darkness. I could hear Ethan groan; he had been in China only a few weeks and was scared. I asked him to be quiet, we didn't want to alert the neighbors there were foreigners in the building and get the Wangs in trouble. Barbara carried Sarah, our one-year-old, and I took the baby stroller and the bag with Sarah's food. In the gloom of the stairs I could make out piles of cabbage left to dry for the winter—Chinese have no refrigerators—and bicycles chained to the railings.

When we reached the fourth floor, the door flew open and Yuanyuan, the Wangs' ten-year-old daughter, bounced out. "Uncle, Auntie," she chorused. "Welcome, welcome." Then she took Ethan by the hand, pulling him inside and simultaneously thrusting an enormous five-pound stuffed panda into his unprepared arms. It was the first of many gifts. Sensing his unease, she began tickling him in the ribs and taunting him to chase her through their tiny two-room home. Ethan still didn't speak more than a dozen words of Chinese, but he understood the challenge and was off with a whoop.

I looked at Yuanyuan with admiration. She was only ten, but already her instincts for playing the proper host were perfect. Her hair was cut in bangs, short on the sides, and her eyes were narrow slits, like a Japanese doll, her father said. She had on a new white blouse with a pair of well-tailored rust-colored corduroy slacks.

The Wangs' apartment was spartan by Western standards, but very much middle-class for a Chinese. Yuanyuan occupied one room about six feet long and six feet wide; the family used the other for eating, living, and sleeping. A double bed took up one corner, with four bright-green, orange, blue, and red quilts piled neatly on top of it. There was a small green plastic-covered sofa where we were directed to sit, and a folding card table the Wangs took out to eat on. On a small desk in another corner was a portrait of the late Prime Minister Zhou Enlai, almost everyone's popular hero, and on the wall a calendar supplied by Japan Air Lines with bathing beauties from all the countries the airline services. They had a squat-style toilet in a separate tiny cubicle, where they kept their supply of rice in a crockery pot, but no bathtub. The floors were bare concrete, with no rugs. The concrete walls could have used a coat of whitewash.

Dinner started with cold dishes, as good Chinese meals do: there were plates of chewy jellyfish and sliced cucumbers in a mustard sauce, tiny whole birds fried in a brown sauce which you ate bones and all, a cold noodle dish made from bean curd, preserved eggs with their distinctive brown and yellow color, sugared crab apples, and Chinese sausages. Yuanyuan kept piling Ethan's plate with the tiny birds and crab apples till I thought it would tip over. She would not accept Ethan's loud protestations.

45

Then came the hot dishes: first, dozens of spring rolls, vegetables and meat wrapped in crispy fried dough, then a spicy Sichuan-style pork with peanuts, a sweet and sour pork with honey, northern Chinese style, an omelette with tomatoes, and taro cooked in boiling sugar so that it had caramelized. Li's wife would appear for the presentation of each dish, then disappear back into their tiny kitchen, the size of a small closet, to prepare the next one. Her only equipment was a blackened metal wok, or Chinese deep-bottomed frying pan, which she heated over a coal-burning brazier. They also had a small sink with a single spigot for cold water. Both Miao and Li had taken the day off from work to shop and cook for us. I didn't realize it then, but to cook the spring rolls alone consumed their entire month's ration of one pound of peanut oil. When we finally were ready to leave, they piled us with large red apples, hard to find in the local market, and several bottles of special Chinese grape wine.

Barbara and I went home exhausted and ecstatic. Despite all the government's efforts to restrict contact between Chinese and foreigners, we had formed a friendship. The next week we invited the Wangs to our new apartment, on the eleventh floor of one of the high-rise buildings reserved for foreign diplomats and journalists. To us, it always seemed cramped, a mere six hundred square feet, with two tiny bedrooms, just big enough to squeeze in the beds, a modest combination living–dining room, a bathroom with shower, and a surprisingly large kitchen that occupied half the space of the overall apartment—the result of earlier complaints by Westerners that the Chinese made their kitchens too small. There were no closets. But after seeing the Wangs' dingy, poorly lit, and utilitarian quarters, we felt we were reveling in luxury. We had wall-to-wall carpeting and an American-made refrigerator, stove, and washing machine, all imported from Hong Kong.

Before Mao's death, it would have been impossible for a Chinese to enter our forbidden zone. But by 1980 the government had relaxed its rules enough that any Chinese with sufficient bravura could get in. All it required was that I pick the Wangs up in our car and drive them past the guard from the People's Liberation Army who stood outside our compound gate. Li covered his face with his hand as we passed the sentry, pretending to be rubbing his eyes. Then they had to accept the stares of the middle-aged women who operated the elevators in our building and reported to the Public Security Bureau on all visitors. For the Wangs, accepting our invitation was a risk. I often wondered about their motives; I sensed a mixture of curiosity, the thrill of the illicit, a practical eye for gain, and real friendship.

Miao had dressed for the occasion in a *qipao*, or *cheongsam*, the old Chinese dress with a high mandarin collar, side fastenings, a tight waist, and a slit up the side. She had kept it hidden when Red Guards searched their home during the Cultural Revolution. "I haven't worn it in years," she confided.

"It was too dangerous to dress up. To be beautiful or fashionable was bourgeois and could get you in trouble."

Miao had also uncovered a lacquer box with several exquisite jade hairpins and carved jade belt buckles which she presented to Barbara. It was an extravagant but delightful gift, for Barbara loves old Chinese jewelry and is a belt designer by profession. For me there was a Qing dynasty blue and white vase.

When we showed the Wangs around the apartment, Miao begged to peek in Barbara's clothes closet, a wardrobe we had also shipped up from Hong Kong. Miao giggled with embarrassment at several dresses with low-cut necklines, but she exclaimed with pleasure at a more chaste loose-fitting burgundy-red Calvin Klein dress with an ascot at the collar. She asked Barbara to try it on for her.

"You don't look like most foreigners," Miao observed after Barbara had disrobed. "They are so hideous, very big and fat, with huge noses. You are more petite." It was a high compliment.

Afterward Miao wanted to try the dress on herself but, with Chinese modesty, slipped it on over her dress. Luckily Barbara had a collection of magazines—*Harper's Bazaar, Vogue,* and fashion supplements from *The New York Times*—along with several sets of French pantyhose to give Miao and her daughter. But we clearly were getting in deeper than we had anticipated, for we soon began to sense that friendship to the Wangs, and to other Chinese, carries obligations that it doesn't to a Westerner. The next week we were back at the Wangs for dinner. This time Miao explained, with cautious circumlocutions at first, that cooking the spring rolls had consumed their entire month's ration of one pound of oil. Would we be willing to go to the Friendship Store, the large grocery and department store near our apartment, reserved in theory for foreigners only, and, at their expense, to buy them more? There is no limit on the amount of cooking oil foreigners can buy, she pointed out. When I assented she immediately produced a large plastic container like those we use to carry gasoline. It could hold ten pounds. We felt set up. Then she brought out another plastic bottle for me to buy four pounds of sesame oil. The Wangs' monthly ration was only two ounces. Li wondered if we might consider buying them a television set in the Friendship Store. A thirteen-inch Japanese-made black and white set cost only about $200 in the Friendship Store but $700 in a regular Chinese store. Moreover, a customer had to have the proper ration coupons and a letter from his unit saying that he was the person in the unit entitled to buy a television set that year. The wait could be a long one. Again we agreed, but we felt we were being subjected to a pressure that wouldn't have existed in the West. Barbara described it as claustrophobia. But I thought it was something more. Friendship in China offered assurances and an intimacy that we have abandoned in

America; it gave the Chinese psychic as well as material rewards that we have lost. We ourselves did feel close to the Wangs, but as Westerners the constant gift-giving and obligations left us uneasy.

Several weeks before we left China we had dinner with the Wangs in a restaurant. Ethan and Yuanyuan played hide and seek under the table; Li suggested we might let Yuanyuan come and live with us in the United States so she could learn English and go to better schools. It was a stunning proposal, that the Wangs would trust their only daughter's education to a foreigner.

"We feel you are really our friends now," Li explained, offering a toast of beer. "Our *guan-xi* are very close. We don't think of you as foreigners anymore."

From our friendships with the Wangs and other Chinese we came to realize that *guan-xi* provide the lubricant for Chinese to get through life. In a society which for millennia had no public law as we know it in the West to enforce impartial justice, people depended on their *guan-xi,* their personal relationships, particularly their contacts with those in power, to get things done. It was a form of social investment. Developing, cultivating, and expanding one's *guan-xi* became a common preoccupation. The advent of the Communists has not fundamentally changed that. As a result, the Chinese have turned the art of personal relations into a carefully calculated science. There are even people who live entirely on their *guan-xi,* or *guan-xi-hu,* as the Chinese term them, like a friend who returned to China in 1950 after studying political science in graduate school in the United States. This put him under immediate suspicion in the eyes of the Communists, though his motive in coming back had been patriotic, and he found himself without a job. But his English was excellent and he had read widely in Western books about China. Soon he discovered that many of the elderly Communist veterans, none of whom could read a foreign language, were curious as to what was being written about them abroad. It was the only place they could relive the glories of their past, because the Communists had banned all historical accounts about themselves in Chinese lest one faction get a better treatment than the others. Over a period of time my friend built up a circle of powerful acquaintances who asked him to come and read to them. In exchange he managed to get a comfortable apartment and access to special stores reserved for high-level officials by borrowing their identification cards. Eventually he parlayed his contacts into an exit visa for Hong Kong. There in turn he convinced some overseas Chinese businessmen that he knew Peking's leaders. The last time I saw him he was back in China, still with a Chinese passport but operating as a representative for a group of Hong Kong companies.

The importance Chinese attach to the distinction between people with whom they have *guan-xi* and those they don't is reflected in an idiosyncrasy of the Chinese language. There are a number of words that begin either with *nei,* meaning "inner," or *wai,* "external." A foreigner in Chinese is a *wai-guo-ren,* an "external country person." Any Chinese who isn't a native of Peking comes from *wai-di,* "an external region." An expert is *nei-hang,* someone who is "inside the profession," while a novice is a *wai-hang,* "outside the profession." Classified information in China, which can include even weather forecasts, is called *nei-bu,* "internal." Your father's parents are your grandparents, *zu-fu,* but your mother's parents are your "external" grandparents, or *wai-zu-fu.*

The family is the foundation of the Chinese social universe and the training ground for the proper application of *guan-xi.* In the past the function of the family was to raise filial sons who would become loyal subjects to the Emperor, a tradition the Communists have made their own use of. The father was a supreme autocrat, with power even to sell his children into slavery. Status in Chinese society was codified in the famous three bonds: the loyalty of subject to ruler, filial obedience of son to father, and fidelity of the wife to her husband (though not the other way around). Traditional Chinese homes had high walls around the outside, often topped with cut glass, emphasizing the family's distance from the rest of the community. But within the house the family lived and slept in the same rooms with much less sense of individual space than Westerners have.

"We grew up in a very complex world where you learned your proper place early," Mrs. Wang told me one evening as I drove her back home from our apartment. "I had two older brothers, an older sister, and two younger sisters, and we also had my grandfather and three aunts and uncles who lived next to us."

In Chinese, however, these relationships are much more carefully spelled out. An uncle is not just an uncle, but either a "father's older brother," a "father's younger brother," or a "mother's older brother," or "mother's younger brother." There is a separate term for each. Similarly, there are more than a dozen different terms for cousin to distinguish the exact form of relationship.

Foreigners have a difficult time appreciating the strength of the Chinese family, but I did get occasional glimpses of what it looks like from the Chinese side. When Deng Xiaoping, China's energetic, diminutive Deputy Party Chairman visited the United States in 1979, one of the stops he wanted to make was Houston. He was interested in the Johnson Space Center, the headquarters of the American space effort, and in talking with oil-drilling companies. But local boosters decided Deng should get a real Texas welcome and arranged a full-blown rodeo in the little town of Simonton, an hour's drive across the flat Texas range. Simonton consists of a liquor store, a post office, a general store, a pecan warehouse, and a huge enclosure for the dirt-floored indoor rodeo. In the parking lot outside a peeling sign proclaimed, "Simonton Rodeo Roundup, Where East Meets West." When Deng unexpectedly was whisked into an old-fashioned stagecoach and driven around the arena, I stationed myself behind two reporters from the New China News Agency. They were holding paper plates with slabs of barbecue and potato salad on their laps, uncertain how to attack the giant hunks of meat. Chinese are accustomed to eating their meat finely sliced into bite-size pieces—anything else is barbarian, reminiscent of the way the Mongols consumed their food.

At that moment, a tall slender blonde, with her honey-colored long hair combed so that it fell over one side of her face, sat down on the wooden plank next to one of the Chinese. She was dressed in skin-tight blue jeans and high leather boots; her face was made up for going on a movie set—and she had on more perfume than the Chinese had probably ever smelled before in their lives.

"Howdy, how y'all doing?" she inquired, giving the Chinese a broad wink. She introduced herself as Joan Shephard and said she had broken a Friday-night date to come out to help entertain the Chinese at the request of a White House advance man she knew vaguely.

After a moment's hesitation, the reporter asked shyly, "Are you a student?"

"No," she said.

"Then you live with your family?" he added, making an assumption natural for a Chinese that a young woman who wasn't married would live with her parents.

"No, I live by myself," she responded. The newsman's face fell. "Oh, I am so sorry," he said, as if in sympathy. He could only assume that her parents must be dead or that the American system had forced her to take a job far away from them. Her explanation that she had moved out of her parents' home because she wanted more freedom only left him perplexed.

A pert twenty-seven-year-old woman with a tiny turned-up nose who worked in Peking Radio related an encounter she once had in a department store in the city of Tianjin, China's third largest metropolis, which illustrated the depth of Chinese family feeling in a different way. She and her husband were shopping when suddenly a young man about twenty years old ordered them to give him 10 yuan, about $6.50. It was very crowded in the store, so the other customers couldn't see that he had taken a knife out from under his blue worker's jacket. My friend's husband was angry and didn't want to pay. Ten yuan was a quarter of his month's wages. But she was scared and handed over the money.

Then the robber apologized. "I am sorry to do this," he said softly, his head bowed in shame. "But I am unemployed and am too embarrassed to ask my parents for any more money."

Some foreigners who have visited China, particularly those who went during the Great Leap Forward in 1958 when Mao was experimenting with communal mess halls, have concluded that the Communists set out to destroy the family. Paradoxically, the opposite has happened. Xiao Yan, "Little Bird," a twenty-seven-year-old teacher, with the high cheekbones and broad face of a northern Chinese, explained how this occurred in her own case. Her father had been born a poor peasant and joined the Red Army as a teen-ager, rising to become a senior Communist officer. But he had died prematurely in 1960, and in the Cultural Revolution the family had been separated. Yan had been sent to work on a state farm on the frozen Soviet border in far northern Heilongjiang (Black Dragon River) province; her older sister had been ordered to move to a remote valley in Sichuan in the southwest when the defense factory where she worked was relocated there for security reasons; a younger sister was rusticated to a commune in Shandong, in east China, and her brother was sent to work in a factory in Shanxi province in the northwest. Their situation appeared hopeless, but eventually, Yan said, she won permission to move back to Peking after she was selected the best worker on her farm. Recently her younger sister has also moved back to the small apartment they share with their aged mother. Her older sister cannot move back to the capital, but she has sent her six-year-old daughter to Yan to enroll in school in Peking and get a city education. Yan also mails 10 yuan a month from the 43 yuan she earns to her brother since he makes only 23 yuan a month in his factory, "not enough to pay for his food," she told me. The family remained a magnet.

I wondered if Yan had any plans to get married. She had a lively mind, an infectious smile, and was pretty enough that a girl friend said, "Men would melt to look at her."

But Yan herself saw little chance of a wedding. "My first duty is to my mother and brother and sisters. Besides, I could never apply for and get more housing from the government. So there would be no place to live with a husband."

On one of the evenings we invited the Wang family to dinner at our apartment, Li arrived two hours late because he had to sing in a concert and we had already finished eating by the time he came. I explained to Li that since he was in an American's home he must now follow our customs. In Chinese, there is an expression, "When you cross the border, obey the local custom." In this case, I added, that meant he must be frank. If you want something, you must say yes. If you say no when you are offered something, we foreigners will take it as a refusal. I knew Chinese are trained to say no as a sign of good manners whenever they are offered food or a gift, no matter how much they want it. Li agreed he would comply.

So I asked him the question "Are you hungry?" By then it was after 8:30, and I was sure he had not had a chance to eat during his concert. But with a solemn look on his face he replied, "No, thank you, I am not hungry."

Guessing that he was still being Chinese, I went to the kitchen and brought out a platter of roast chicken with gravy and stuffing, some homemade bread Barbara had baked, and a dish of broiled tomatoes, onions, peppers, and carrots, all the vegetables then available in the market. I also put a large helping of crepes stuffed with an orange sauce on another plate. He devoured it all.

Li had been acting according to the traditional Confucian code which underlies Chinese character today much as *guan-xi* are the invisible threads that hold society together. It provides the public identity, the mask, the persona which enable Chinese to deal with the world with the least friction. In essence, Confucianism was the broad rules of conduct evolved for the relations of Chinese with each other. Confucius was a teacher and a gentleman, a very great if at times a pedantic gentleman, who with pious reverence had assembled all the details of etiquette practiced at the courts of the feudal lords of his day. (He was born in 551 B.C., a generation before the Buddha in India, and died in 479, a decade before the birth of Socrates in Greece.)

Fundamentally, Confucius wanted to establish the gentleman, or the princely man, as the ruler of the state. For Confucius, good was good and bad was bad, just as in a John Wayne movie. The princely man always knew where rectitude lay—in those rules of decorum, the *li,* which we translate variously as the rites or etiquette. Originally these abstruse rules may have grown out of a primitive animism in which the spirits of land, wind, and water played an active role in man's affairs. By Confucius' time this had congealed into a belief that improper conduct by man could throw the world of nature out of joint. A correct observance of the rites was a sign of perfect social order, and to abuse the rites must therefore indicate deeper decay. Confucius was particularly insistent that to neglect the outer form of the rites was to abuse the reality, the moral order, they represented.

To us the *li* may seem rather formalistic: where to stand in the presence of superiors, where to sit (a guest should face the door), how far to go in seeing off a visitor. A good Chinese host still walks his guest not only to the front door but out to his car and stands and waves till the visitor is out of sight. After I became accustomed to this elegant treatment, I have always felt somewhat cheated when leaving a Western friend's house to be shown just to the door and left standing there. The *li* dictated there should never be a touching of persons (a Chinese formerly shook his own hand, not yours, and Chinese officials still seem reluctant to grasp an extended hand). A slap on the back is more than indelicate, though American businessmen visiting Peking today insist on putting their arms around their Chinese hosts in picture-taking sessions. Nor should there be any immature enthusiasm. Western musicians, actors, and athletes visiting Peking are often puzzled by the lack of audience reaction to their performances. After a brilliant display of ice skating one November evening by the American star Peggy Fleming, the crowd of over 10,000 in the Capital Gymnasium offered a modest round of applause. Fleming, an Olympic champion, was genuinely hurt. She asked me afterward, "Why didn't the Chinese like me, what did I do wrong?" I had to try to explain that she got what amounted to a standing ovation for the Chinese. Confucius' ideal was to maintain composure at all times. Characteristically, his golden rule was phrased in the negative: "Don't do to others what you yourself would not like." The Western version—"Do unto others . . ."—might have seemed overly aggressive to him.

The influence of the rites, for doing things according to the correct form, created a fondness for ritual which has persisted under the Communists. At an important Party congress in 1977, foreign diplomats and newsmen were enchanted to watch the voting for the top leadership, which for the first time was shown on Chinese television. The officials marched up to the ballot box in the ornate Great Hall of the People in the exact order in which it was later announced they had been elected. First came Hua Guofeng, who at the time was Party Chairman, followed by Ye Jianying, the first deputy chairman, and then the other men who would win the post of deputy chairman, Deng Xiaoping, Chen Yun, Li Xiannian, and Wang Dongxing. It was as if at a bitterly contested Democratic or Republican convention the winning candidates for President and Vice President posed for their traditional victory celebration on the rostrum before any votes had been cast by the state delegates. When I asked a Chinese journalist why the Party leaders had acted this way, he insisted it was natural. Of course, he said, they would vote according to their rank in the hierarchy, and the new, forthcoming hierarchy was more important than the old, outgoing one.

The consummate ritual, I thought, was the series of toasts delivered at formal state banquets for visiting dignitaries. Most foreigners, delighted or dazed by the amount of food thrust on them at these twelve- or fifteen-course gastronomical extravaganzas, tended to miss the subtlety of the toasts, the host's well-turned knack of seeming to convey great warmth and friendship without ever revealing a personal feeling. To have been personal would have been to violate the *li*. The following is taken from my notes at a banquet given by a deputy mayor of Shanghai, Yan Youmin, for Senator Frank Church of the U.S. Senate Foreign Relations Committee, though it could have been delivered at many other such festivities.

"I am extremely glad to welcome you," Yan began, speaking through an

53

interpreter. Senator Church did not know that the phrase Yan actually used was a stock expression, "I am ten parts happy," which showed up in virtually every toast I heard in China.

"You have come a long way from across the ocean and we are delighted you have chosen to honor us," Yan went on, another expression drawn from the standard phrase book. "Your journey has been hard."

How to end a party is often awkward for Westerners, but the *li* provide for that too. When the last course was served and consumed, Yan rose to speak again:

"Please forgive us, we didn't entertain you very well. Your stay in our city has been too short. Next time you must stay longer." (This is invariably taken by the visitors as an invitation to return to China, though it is just another of those stock polite expressions.)

"Tomorrow you have to set out early," Yan went on, speaking to Senator Church. "Everybody should go and get some rest now."

With these words, all the Chinese around the room rose and made for the door, knowing the banquet was concluded. It took the Americans a few minutes to realize what had happened.

To a Westerner, the Chinese penchant for ritual sometimes turns into a pattern of public make-believe. It is almost as if the Chinese live by the Stanislavski method, in which actors' words and actions imitate the correct outside gestures while downplaying their inner feelings. I think it is this quality which often makes frustrated foreigners feel the Chinese are inscrutable, and I remember an incident which drove me to the brink of apoplexy.

I was flying back with a group of Western and Japanese journalists after an exhilarating trip to Tibet. We were one of the first groups of reporters allowed into Tibet since 1949, and we were anxious to get back to file our stories. Since Lhasa, the small provincial town that serves as Tibet's capital, had only one telegraph line and a dubious phone connection to the outside world, we had agreed among ourselves not to send our material till we were back in Peking. Normally, at least one reporter would have tried to sneak his copy through, but perhaps because we were all delighted just to be in Tibet, no one broke the embargo.

On the last day we took off at 6 A.M. from Lhasa's airstrip, in a dry, brown valley at 10,000 feet, and headed over "the roof of the world" back to China proper in Sichuan. The four-hour flight is an endless succession of jagged granite peaks, covered with snow even in the middle of the summer, before touching down in the emerald-green paddy fields around Chengdu that simmered in the tropical sun like soup on a stove. Qi Mingzong, one of our escorts from the Information Department, explained that we would have an hour for lunch while our chartered plane, a Russian-built Ilyushin-18, a four-engine turboprop that belonged to the Chinese Air Force, was refueled and the crew had lunch. Mr. Qi, a slender man with a pinched face and an extraordinary, clipped upper-class British accent, was proud that the chief pilot had flown Chairman Hua to Lhasa when he visited Tibet the year before. We were scheduled to take off at 12:30 P.M. for Peking.

But just as we finished eating, Mr. Qi came over to our table. "I'm so sorry," he said with all the polish he could muster, "but there is a thunderstorm in Peking and we can't fly. We must wait."

Such delays are common in China—many planes and airports are not equipped with modern radar or instrument landing systems, and the Chinese are intelligently conservative about not flying when they risk danger.

But a few minutes later the public-address system crackled out an announcement that the regular afternoon plane for Peking, flight 622, was now boarding. It was a British-built Trident jet belonging to CAAC, or the Civil Aviation Administration of China (in Chinese the name is easier, simply People's Aviation). We looked at Mr. Qi, whose face grew tighter than usual. After watching it board and depart, we demanded an explanation.

"It will have to turn back, don't worry," Mr. Qi assured us. He suggested we sit down in the airport lounge and wait. With both the temperature and the humidity close to 100 degrees, we began to imagine arcane political reasons why the government would try to keep us out of Peking, or from filing our stories on Tibet. A coup perhaps had taken place.

Finally, three hours later, Mr. Qi emerged after another conference with the airport control tower and the air force to say that the weather in Peking had grown so bad that all flights into the capital for the day had been canceled.

"You will have to go into downtown Chengdu and stay in a hotel overnight, till the weather breaks," he insisted.

Only a vulgar foreigner would have questioned this story. Mr. Qi was obviously trying to preserve a correct appearance and the *li*. But we were vulgar foreigners.

When we got to the hotel, a run-down Soviet monstrosity of endless corridors that lacked both running water and electricity that afternoon, several of the newsmen phoned their wives in Peking. The weather there was beautiful, they said, the first day in a week it had not rained. Flight 622 from Chengdu had already landed on schedule. But a representative from the Information Department in the capital had called them a few minutes earlier to report that there was a terrible storm in Chengdu, so sadly our plane couldn't take off.

At dinner we tracked down Mr. Qi and confronted him again. There was no storm in Peking, we could say with assurance, and no storm here in Chengdu. Why were we being held hostage in a hot, miserable hotel in Chengdu?

But Mr. Qi was prepared. "Actually, I have checked and the storm was halfway between Peking and Chengdu, in Shijiazhuang," he said. That might have settled the affair, but on the drive into town I had seen that the local meteorological station was just down the street from the hotel, so we went there to check. There was no major storm that day anywhere in China.

It would have been easy to dismiss our hosts' explanations as just make-believe, and at the time I was angry enough to do so. But that would be missing an important distinction, I later came to realize. Mr. Qi was not being deliberately cynical, at least from his point of view. There was probably a real mechanical failure on the plane, or a problem with a crew member, and the Chinese felt it would have been embarrassing to tell us. Instead, they created the polite fiction about the storm, a happy pretense any Chinese would knowingly have accepted.

This same capacity for make-believe underlies the conventions of Chinese opera, where a headdress with long feathers signifies a general, flicking a whip indicates a man on horseback, and pacing about the stage means taking a journey. It is evident in a number of popular proverbs and historical incidents. In the third century B.C., a scheming prime minister of the Chin dynasty wished to determine who among his courtiers were really faithful to him. When a deer was presented in court, he pretended it was a horse. All those who insisted it was a deer were executed. In more modern times, the ambassadors from England and France considered it a triumph when in 1873, after fighting three wars with China, they were finally granted an audience with the Emperor. What they did not know at the time was that they had been taken into the palace reserved for tribute missions from smaller states. This preserved China's conceit that the Europeans were still loyal vassals.

This Chinese penchant for playacting stems from a different appreciation of appearance and reality. To the Chinese words are accorded a power of their own—they are power. As the American scholar of Chinese Buddhism, Holmes Welch, has pointed out, when a man died, his coffin would be decorated with the word "Longevity." It was not put there to celebrate the great age he had reached, since he may have died young, but to assert the immortality of the body. The Chinese language, in fact, is full of euphemisms to circumvent the ugly facts of life. When a poor family drowned an un-wanted girl child, since she could not bring in any income, they called it "bathing the infant." Two thousand years before modern communications and Marshall McLuhan, the Chinese had discovered the principle that the medium is the message.

The Chinese system of writing in ideograms may have contributed to the weight given words. Chinese characters have no innate phonetic value; but because they are often pictographic and the written language was held in almost religious esteem, each character has a life of its own, a magical potency. Confucius was deeply concerned with the problem of words—if the name, or the form, was correct, he asserted, things would follow their proper course. This Chinese belief in the power of language underlies the Communists' fondness for slogans. Walk into an office and you are likely to be greeted by large red letters on the wall proclaiming, "Serve the People," an apothegm of Mao. During the Cultural Revolution, friends said, they often felt it safest to begin conversations with a quotation from the Chairman like, "Good morning, Grasp Revolution." There is nothing new in this. In the Qing dynasty emperors instructed local officials to post villages with hortatory decrees for the edification of the peasantry. The Nationalists on Taiwan also cover walls with official sentiment; but in Taipei they are more likely to say, "Counterattack the mainland."

By make-believe we usually envision child's play. But there is nothing childish about the way Chinese can conjure reality out of illusion with the right words. When Chiang Kai-shek fled to Taiwan in 1949 after his ignominious defeat, he insisted that he was still the leader of "Free China" and that henceforth Taipei would be the capital of the Republic of China. Both Washington and the United Nations accepted this fiction for over two decades, keeping the Communists from what they felt was their rightful recognition. It is still a serious political crime in both China and Taiwan to suggest that Taiwan in any way is really separate from the mainland, whatever foreigners may think.

This same faith in the power of words has governed how Chinese name their children. In the past, girls were fitted with fanciful two-character given names like Jingxian, meaning "Quiet and Virtuous," or Yushuang, "Jade Frost." (In Chinese, the surname comes first, the given name after, so a woman whose family name was Li and who was called Yushuang, would be known as Li Yushuang.) These feminine names were to suggest the grace of birds, the delicacy of flowers, or the proper womanly attributes. Little boys were given names to develop their will or courage.

But after 1949 parents wanted to show their loyalty to the new Communist regime and they adopted a different nomenclature. One of the most common names, given to both boys and girls, was Hong, "Red." I had one friend whose name was Wang Xiaohong, "Wang Little Red," a common diminutive. Another was called Wang Yaohong, "Wang Who Wants to Be Red," and a third Wang Yonghong, "Wang Forever Red." Many parents picked the name Weidong, meaning "Protect Mao," *dong* being the last character in Mao's name. In the 1950s, in the era of good feelings between Peking and Moscow, some young Chinese ended up being called Xiaolin, "Little Stalin." A young high school teacher I met had been named Kangmei, "Resist America," because he was born during the Korean War.

With changes in political power, however, some names became bad magic. The daughter of a Chinese diplomat recalled that when she was in high school there were three sisters named Li. Their father was a former general in the Red Army, a genuine patriot, and so he called his first daughter Li Aiguo, "Li Who Loves Her Country," the second Li Aimin, "Li Who Loves the People," and the third, Li Aidang, "Li Who Loves the Party." But in the Cultural Revolution an earnest Red Guard noted that if you lined up the last syllables of each of their names, Guo, Min, and Dang, they came out, "Li Who Loves the Guomindang," the Nationalists. The father was clapped in prison.

During the Cultural Revolution, Red Guards also changed the name of the street that ran through the old foreign legation quarter to "Anti-Imperialism Street" and the narrow alley that leads to the Soviet Embassy to "Anti-Revisionism Street." Some radicals even proposed switching the colors of the city traffic lights because red was the symbol of revolution and ought to mean go, not stop.

In the last few years, as disillusionment with the Communists has spread, Chinese have stopped giving their children "revolutionary" names. A peasant woman I encountered had reverted to an old tradition and called her daughter, her first child, Zhaodi. The name means "Call in Younger Brothers," signifying her wish for a son. A young city couple named their daughter DoDo, not a Chinese name at all but the first two syllables from the musical scale made famous in China by Julie Andrews's song "Do, Re, Mi," in the movie *The Sound of Music.* She said that if she had another child she and her husband planned to call it ReRe, the next two syllables.

The Chinese belief in the importance of titles, of ensuring that the name fits the subject, may underlie one of the least attractive Communist practices, that of labeling people. Like the doctor I met on the train from Shanghai to Peking who had been stigmatized as a "Rightist" in 1957 and then attacked again in the Cultural Revolution because of his earlier label, millions of Chinese have had what the Communists call "caps" put on them. The term *dai-mao-zi,* to put a political hat on someone, is one of the cruelest in the current Chinese lexicon. The custom began on a large scale with the land reform campaign in the late 1940s as the Communists swept toward victory and won control in village after village. Detailed rules were drawn up for classifying everyone according to his economic, political, and social background. At the bottom of the scale the Communists eventually devised came the "five black elements": landlords, rich peasants, counterrevolutionaries, bad elements, and rightists. Officially Peking always describes these groups as a small minority, 5 percent of the population. But with a billion people in China, that would mean 50 million outcasts, about the same number of people that live in France or Great Britain.

Under a 1950 law, landlords were supposed to be able to shed their labels if they worked hard for five years and showed they had reformed. But as time passed, the classifications stuck and hardened into a permanent form of discrimination. Huang San, a short, intense man whose grandfather had been tarred with the label of rich peasant, related how serious a liability it could be. His grandfather had owned three acres of wheat fields in Hebei province near Peking, he said, along with a cart, a horse, and a small house. His grandfather had worked some of the land himself and rented out the remainder. After Liberation, his property had been divided up by what the Communists called the village's poor and middle peasants. Although Huang was not born until 1955, well after the family lost all its land, he found he too was labeled a rich peasant; whenever he filled in an official form, he had to give that degrading status as his *cheng-fen,* or "family origin." It meant that while he was one of the smartest students in his local primary school, he was not allowed to go beyond the fifth grade. His application to join the Communist Youth League branch in his village was rejected, and he was turned down later when he volunteered for the army, one of the few routes to upward mobility for rural youth. Huang's family was also excluded from their commune's cooperative medical insurance program. When his mother needed an operation for gallstones, they had to pay the full cost themselves, a charge of 45 yuan ($30), a year's income for Huang. Their neighbors with a better class origin had their medical care covered by a small monthly premium.

Moreover, Huang complained when I met him during a visit to some of his relatives in Peking, he, his father, and his older brother received less income for the same amount of work in the fields than the other peasants. As one of the bad classes, they were ordered to perform "duty labor," a kind of corvée duty, on the communal fields, and at the end of the year, when the village's harvest was added up and everyone's share was portioned out, half of their income was deducted for the "duty labor."

"What is left over is not enough to support our family," Huang charged. The family was constantly in debt to the production team (the lowest level of the commune) for which they worked, and his older brother, now thirty-three years old, had not been able to get married because of the family's status and low income. No peasant woman would want him.

In 1979 the Communists announced they had finally rescinded these class labels. But Huang said the officials in his village simply ignored Peking's order. "If they took away our labels, someone might look for a new exploiting class," Huang suggested. "That might lead to the Communist Party."

The road from the city of Lanzhou in northwest China to the Kushui, or "Bitterwater" commune, runs through endless small fields of sere brown earth, each carefully terraced upward toward the surrounding barren hills. Not a tree grows anywhere in sight. The land is as dry as desert, and it is hard to remember that millions of peasants make their existence in soil like this. Suddenly, as I was contemplating the peasants' hardihood, the Shanghai-model sedan I was driving in almost crashed into a man and his wife on the back of a bicycle. They were dressed in the faded and patched gray garb of farmers. The wife was holding a bundle of big green cabbages on her lap. Her husband obviously was not used to cars on his village road and he had wobbled out into the middle of the track without looking behind. Luckily, our driver pushed his brakes to the floor and our car swerved off onto the shoulder of the road. The two peasants toppled off their bike from fright, the cabbages spilling across the road.

When I retrieved my head from the windshield, I noticed the husband and wife were smiling and laughing as they picked themselves up. Our driver, hired from the Lanzhou Foreign Affairs Office, was also grinning, ear-to-ear. In the United States or Europe there would have been shouted imprecations, or worse. Death had been close. But this was another of those Chinese characteristics so baffling to foreigners—they laugh at adversity.

For "face" was involved here. If either party had gotten angry, face would have been forfeited, and the ancient *li* would have been violated. Face is an outgrowth of the extreme sensitivity Chinese have about personal dignity; it colors all personal relations. George Kates, in his charming, evocative portrait of life in Peking in the 1930s, *The Years That Were Fat,* suggests that it was so easy to wound this Chinese sense of dignity and so difficult for the wounds to heal that the condition might be called "spiritual hemophilia."

To salve relations between two Chinese, a middleman is often necessary. Not long after I returned to the United States, I invited a prominent Chinese editor to dinner at our home. He was studying at Harvard, spoke impeccable English, and seemed in every way Westernized. Professor John Fairbank and his wife, Wilma, also happened to be at the party. A few days later the editor called to thank me for the dinner and wondered if I would come to his place for a return meal. When I agreed, he inquired if I would call Professor Fairbank and ask him to come along also. As accustomed to the West as he was, he still needed a go-between to assure that he would not lose face if the famous professor declined his invitation.

This sensitivity has created a special reflex in the Chinese, an instinct to flee any situation where they might risk face. "Of the thirty-six ways of handling a situation, running away is the best," goes an old adage.

My Chinese assistant Lao Wu was a constant lesson to me in the importance of sensitivity; he was an expert at avoidance. On the first day we met, I tried to ease into our new relationship with what I thought were standard and innocuous Chinese questions. How many children do you have? I asked him.

After looking at me for a moment, he replied, "One or two." Here was a man who would never expose himself. The most I could learn was that he had previously worked at the Yugoslav Embassy as an English interpreter.

Gradually, over a period of time, I came to appreciate what in an earlier era would have been called his Confucian rectitude. He always arrived for work at 9 A.M. precisely, never a minute late. He never let slip an angry word, no matter how much I shouted at him. His sternest rebuff in a touchy situation would be a suggestion that my anger did not help get the job done. Lao Wu also endeavored to carry out all my requests: securing permission from the Information Department for a trip out of Peking, arranging interviews with a government official, reserving a table in a restaurant for lunch. But if I wanted him to plead my cause with a sticky bureaucrat, Lao Wu would seek shelter in his shell. These tests often came over my efforts to outwit the Peking Hotel. Among its rules that I felt were illogical was one that I could not let anyone else spend the night in either of the two rooms which I, or rather *The Times,* rented. One room was officially our office, where Lao Wu sat during the day, though because of another hotel rule about not moving furniture, the two beds remained. The second room I used for sleeping until I got an apartment in September 1980. On one occasion, our Tokyo correspondent, Henry Scott-Stokes, came through Peking on his way to North Korea and needed a hotel room. I asked Lao Wu to inform the hotel that another employee of *The Times* would be using the office overnight. With only a perfunctory check, Lao Wu said the answer was no, Scott-Stokes could not use a bed in the office. When I asked him to press harder, he looked at me and said, "You are making me feel like a sandwich."

Then I heard him mutter, *"Pa Ma-fan,"* an expression which literally means "to fear trouble" but which conveys centuries of wisdom about avoiding entanglements.

For all the pitfalls of face for the unsuspecting foreigner, there is one charming variation—a person must always express his abilities and even his name as being of less value than those of the person being addressed. Some of this formality has lapsed under the Communists, but much has survived. When a Chinese asked my name, they would preface it by saying, *"Nin gui xing?"* (What is your precious name?) In reply, I had to answer, "My humble name is . . ." The same formula is employed when asking a foreigner what country he comes from, though no Chinese seriously doubts that China is superior. If a Chinese compliments you on your appearance or your ability to speak Chinese, the *li* require that you must immediately decline the praise. "No, I speak very badly," which of course is nearer the truth. At dinner a Chinese host will invariably apologize after the tenth delicious dish has been served, "I am sorry, we had nothing to feed you tonight."

Sinologists love to dispute whether China today is more Chinese or more Communist. To me, it is like arguing about the number of angels that can dance on the head of a pin. The question is inherently unanswerable, since there are so many factors involved. But the longer I stayed in China the more

I was struck by the number of strong resonances to the past, if not exact similarities. It was not an accident that the Communists had made their Party headquarters in Zhongnanhai, a compound of lakes, palaces, and temples that was once part of the quarter in the old Imperial City reserved for the Emperors and their families. It was more than a coincidence that the Communist officials' claim to rule included their possession of the correct doctrine, Marxism, just as the mandarins in the past won their position by their superior knowledge of the Confucian classics. When I arrived in Peking, the first action Lao Wu counseled me in was to acquire a chop, or seal, with my name and position as *New York Times* bureau chief inscribed on it. Later, every time I wrote a letter, paid a bill, or sent in a request to the government, I affixed my chop to the document, tangible proof of my authority. It was a tradition carried on from the mandarins who served the dragon throne. In the Cultural Revolution, friends told me, Red Guards attacking an official they considered reactionary celebrated in triumph when they seized his seal of office. It was only then that they toppled him.

But most of all, I felt, the specific gravity of China's past came through in the patterns of personal relations in daily life, like *guan-xi* and the *li,* the importance of connections, names, and face. These shape the Chinese identity now much as they have for thousands of years. Even the trauma of the Communists' political campaigns have not shaken the Chinese people's unique consciousness of their own history and all that went with it. An American scholar, John Dolfin, who was married to a Chinese, once recounted an experience that befell him when he visited the village in northern China where his wife had been born. The hamlet lay in Henan province, just south of the Yellow River, the area where Chinese civilization began 3,000 years ago. It was unusual for the Communists to let a foreigner visit the village, Dolfin said, since it was far from the accepted tourist track and very poor. One afternoon, Dolfin, a tall, kindly man who speaks excellent Chinese, found himself in conversation with a group of elderly peasants who had gathered around his in-laws mud-walled house.

Had they ever seen a foreigner in their village before? he asked.

Yes, said several of the men, gnarled and browned from their years of labor in the fields. Was it a Russian? Dolfin suggested, thinking that a Soviet adviser might have happened through the area during the 1950s when relations between China and Russia were still good.

No, the peasants replied. Then could it have been a Japanese during Tokyo's long invasion of China from 1937 to 1945 in World War Two? The Japanese had come close, a talkative peasant said: "They reached a neighboring village and we buried all our valuables to hide from them. But we never actually saw a Japanese."

Perhaps it was a Western missionary in the late nineteenth or early twentieth century? Dolfin then asked. No, again, said the peasants. One mission-ary had worked his way into the region in the 1930s, but the people had driven him away after he spent one night there, assuming he was a spy.

Finally Dolfin had to give up.

"It was the Yuan dynasty," said another man with a white beard like a patriarch, referring to the period from 1264 to 1368 when the Mongols under Kublai Khan ruled China. "Some Mongol troops came through the village."

3. The Giant Flight of Stairs

等 級 无 边

RANK BUT NOT CLASS

"If a man becomes an official, even his chickens and dogs will ascend to heaven."

An old Chinese proverb

Under the shadow of the madder rose-stained west wall of the Forbidden City, the old sacred residence of China's emperors, is a large Chinese-style courtyard home with a sloping tiled roof. The house is invisible to passersby, hidden from the street by a gray-brick fence. But one afternoon a young Chinese graduate student acquaintance pointed out the location of the house as we drove by. It is the residence of a deputy chief of staff of the People's Liberation Army, she said, and contains the ultimate luxury in China—space. In a teeming city of four million people, where the average allotment of housing space is only a little over three square yards per person, the size of a dining-room table, and most families live squeezed in one- or two-room apartments, the general occupied a compound with two separate houses, a garden, and access to a small lake for swimming in the summer.

The general's family has four bedrooms, a living room with a piano and a large new Japanese-made color television set, and a commodious kitchen equipped with an American refrigerator. Unlike most Chinese houses today, which have plain concrete floors, the general's rooms are tastefully covered with polished wood. The general's family also has three modern bathrooms, each with flush toilets and bathtubs and regular running hot water, amenities Westerners take for granted but which the average Chinese can only dream about. Most Chinese still use public latrines and make do with cold water from a sink, if they have that. The house and its furnishings are all supplied by the army, free of charge, my friend confided. She knew one of the general's two children and so was a frequent guest in the residence.

Equally impressive, she said, was the general's retinue of servants, also supplied gratis by the military high command. There was an *a-yi,* or maid, to do the cooking, a driver for the general's army car, and an orderly who helped with the cleaning and errands. In addition, the general had two soldiers for bodyguards; they accompanied him whenever he left the house. All the help lived in a room attached to the smaller of the two buildings in the compound. The cook sometimes went out to buy food in a regular market, my friend added, but much of the time army trucks delivered special shipments of meat, rice, vegetables, and fruit from farms run by the military. In a society of constant food shortages, where grocery shopping consumes as much as two hours a day for most people (and seven days a week because there are few refrigerators), this service, too, was a "breathtaking" luxury, as my friend described it.

The general's main trouble was that despite the high front fence and the lack of any identifying name or number on his gate, some ordinary Chinese had discovered an important official was living there. In keeping with an old Chinese tradition, these people came to plead with the general for favors. "If you are poor, even if you live in the noisiest neighborhood, no one will ask about you," the general lamented, quoting a proverb. "But if you are rich, even if you live in the most remote mountains, people will seek you out."

In one case, my student friend related, a woman who had undergone an eye operation that left scars on her face repeatedly left letters on the general's doorstep asking for help in getting better medical treatment. She was in her late twenties and worried that her physical defect would prevent her from finding a husband.

"Please do something," she begged. "If you don't, I will commit suicide." The woman didn't address the general by name; in fact, she didn't know his name. She simply wrote, "To whoever lives here, I know you are someone important."

In another instance, a young man had deposited a package of liquor, cigarettes, and food in front of the house with a note asking for the general's daughter in marriage. A few days later the suitor dropped off a gift of 300 yuan ($200), half a year's salary for an average urban Chinese. He, too, wrote, "If you don't let me marry your daughter, I will kill myself."

The general, an aging veteran of the Communists' Long March in the 1930s, was disturbed. His two children are both young men. Clearly the letter writer was only surmising that whoever lived in such a house must be a senior official and therefore worth cultivating. The general turned all these letters and the money over to the police, but they couldn't catch the supplicants.

The story about the general's luxurious standard of living and the awe in which he was held by ordinary Chinese surprised me. For foreigners have long accepted as an article of faith that Mao Zedong had worked hard to create an egalitarian society—that was what the Communist revolution was about, putting an end to the excruciating injustices of the Nationalist era, the beggars, the opium addicts, the wealthy landlords, and the bloated warlords. Most Western visitors to China have reported that Mao succeeded. They have tended to see the uniformity of dress and the millions of Chinese pedaling their bicycles silently to work; they have been impressed by briefings from their China Travel Service guides on the low-cost housing and the inexpensive medical care, and they have believed the Maoist rhetoric about egalitarianism. But beneath this facade of the classless society, I gradually learned, some people are much more equal than others.

An American diplomat who traveled with Henry Kissinger on one of his first visits to China in the early 1970s recalled his own shock introduction to the subtle though significant differences between Chinese. It was the Foreign Service Officer's task to arrange the obligatory return banquet, the meal given by the visiting dignitary at the end of his journey to repay his Chinese hosts for their feast on his arrival. As it happened, China's Foreign Minister had entertained Kissinger in the Great Hall of the People, so under the adamantine rules of Chinese protocol, Kissinger would invite the Foreign Minister for the return banquet. When the diplomat came to the question of price with his Chinese counterpart, he suggested that 10 yuan a person might be a good figure. (Chinese arrange dinners by the cost per head, what they call the "standard," rather than by the price per dish.)

But the Chinese official looked troubled by the amount, in those days a handsome sum to pay for a meal in that country. That was much too low, the Chinese advised. The American should remember that the Foreign Minister himself would be coming. To which the American rejoined, with an attempt at humor, "I thought you had abolished class in China?"

"Yes," the Chinese said. "We have abolished class. But not rank."

A Chinese physicist I got to know, a specialist on lasers, put it another way. "All people in China may look alike, but they are not. The differences are narrow, but for that reason are keenly felt, and vitally important to us." He talked as we strolled around one of the unexcavated tombs of the Ming dynasty emperors in a broad valley north of Peking, just inside the Great Wall. It was one of the first warm days of spring, and the scientist, who had an unusual sartorial flair, took off his expensively tailored Mao jacket.

"You should imagine China as a giant flight of stairs," he continued. "There is a person on each step. Each person knows only what is on his step. No one sees the whole stairway from top to bottom. It is too vast."

The stairs begin with a labyrinthine system of grades and ranks, like a Chinese puzzle, into which each occupation has been divided by the Communists. First, there are twenty-four separate grades for the country's 20 million cadres. The Chinese term cadre, or *ganbu*, requires some explanation, for Chinese use it in two different though overlapping senses. Sometimes it refers to anyone with a position of leadership, from Deng Xiaoping on down to the heads of the village production teams. But Chinese also use it to cover all state functionaries, including a number of white-collar workers in the bureaucracy, like clerks and accountants, without any leadership role. A cadre may or may not be a member of the Communist Party. By Peking's count, there are 38 million Party members. At the bottom of the stairs on which the cadres are ranked are the ordinary clerks, grade twenty-four. Then come the section chiefs and department heads, grades fourteen to eighteen, bureau chiefs, grade thirteen, deputy ministers, grade eight, governors of the provinces, grades six and seven, and cabinet ministers, grades four and five. At the top of the pyramid only the late Chairman Mao, Premier Zhou Enlai, and Marshal Zhu De, the former head of the National People's Congress, were grade one, Chinese friends said. They were not sure, but they believed Deng Xiaoping and the former Party Chairman, Hua Guofeng, were only grade two or three. The reason, my friends insisted, was that the Communists, once in power in the 1950s, became very conservative and grades tended to become fixed. People were promoted very slowly, if at all.

Each rank has its corresponding salary: 40 yuan a month for grade twenty-four, rising to 190 yuan a month for grade thirteen, 280 yuan a month for grade eight, and then 400 yuan for grade one, ten times the lowest level. Office workers can tell a cadre's rank instantly by the type of chair he uses, a graying newspaper editor told me. Only cadres above grade thirteen are allowed a leather swivel chair, like those used by Western executives. Officials in the grades thirteen to sixteen range get a soft upholstered chair with springs and a velvet-covered seat. Grade seventeen cadres are entitled to a wooden chair with a cushion; those below that, only a plain wooden seat.

In determining an official's real authority, it is equally important to know the time and place a man joined the Communist movement, friends explained. Was it before or after the Long March, the epochal two-year trek across China in 1935 and 1936 that both saved and shaped the Communists? Did the cadre serve in Yanan, the Communists' wartime cave headquarters in the northwest, or did he work as an undercover agent in the Kuomintang, or "white" areas, a less prestigious assignment, at least in retrospect? Was he a member of the Red Army, or just a civilian party official? Such distinctions serve as pedigree and diploma to the Communists, like a family coat of arms, a place in the social register, or the name of the prep school one attended in some other societies.

The system of grades is virtually never mentioned in the official Chinese press, perhaps to help preserve the illusion of egalitarianism; but I gradually came to learn about a range of other hierarchies too. In China's universities, professors are factored into twelve ranks, with salaries ranging from 56 yuan a month to 360 yuan, more than a six to one differential. Actors, stars of Chinese opera, and musicians have their own scale of grades one to sixteen. Artists and writers have been classified by the government along another index, and are paid, in addition to a regular monthly salary, a fee for their output calculated at so much per square foot of canvas or so much per 1,000 words of written text, depending on their ranking. I discovered at a cooking school in Chungqing, in Sichuan, where future experts in preparing the peppery cuisine of that province are trained, that Chinese chefs are graded from one to four, with master chef the highest encomium.

Technicians and engineers in factories have been placed on still another scale of eighteen grades, with a wage differential of ten to one; and factory workers are divided into eight grades, with wages ranging from about 34 yuan a month to 110 yuan. This spread of three to one is roughly equal to the wage differential in American and West European industry. The Communists' rationale for maintaining these differences is also similar to capitalist practice—to keep up motivation. Only Peking refers to the idea by the Marxist principle of "to each according to his work." This elaborate structure of ranks and wages has proven one of the most resilient of the Communists' accomplishments. Although it was originally established in the 1950s, it has remained largely unchanged, even in the face of repeated attacks on its inequalities during the Cultural Revolution. In fact, the laser scientist recalled his own experience in that tumultuous period when he was sent down to a May Seventh Cadre School for two years, supposedly to "be educated" by the local peasants. Here he helped plant rice and pulled carts loaded with hundreds of pounds of bricks. But he continued to draw his regular salary of 280 yuan a month—with one condition: he was ordered not to disclose how much he received to the peasants, for their total income per capita, for an entire year, at that time, the scientist said, was less than 40 yuan. Other city officials sent down to the countryside also continued to receive their normal pay, he added.

The physicist related another story to demonstrate how rigidly Chinese can adhere to the rank system. At an international conference on lasers in Peking, which he helped organize, the Chinese professors of grades one through four and the foreign scientists invited to attend sat in the first six rows of the conference hall. In front of each place was a white porcelain mug with scalding hot tea. One morning he arrived late for the symposium, because of some administrative details he had to clear up, and took a seat in a back row, assigned to professors of lesser standing. There he found the same white porcelain mug. But inside was only hot water, no tea leaves, to save money. Unless he had sat there, or one of the junior scientists had tried to grab a place in one of the front rows, no one would know the difference. The appearance of equality had been preserved.

This penchant for hierarchy is rooted in China's past, at least from the time when Confucius decreed that men who labor with their minds are destined to rule those who merely grovel with their hands. "The gentleman's part is like that of the wind; the smaller man's part is like that of the grass," Confucius said. "When the wind blows, he cannot chose but bend." In Confucian doctrine, each person's status was codified along the "Three Bonds," the loyalty of subject to ruler, filial obedience of son to father, and fidelity of wife to husband. Each of these was between superior and subordinate; none were between equals. The result was that each Chinese was enmeshed in a highly ordered system of kinship relations, with elder brothers, younger brothers, sisters, maternal aunts, paternal elder brothers' wives, all spelled out in a complex vocabulary which does not even exist in English or European languages. Each relationship also carried with it a corresponding set of rights and duties. Given this system within the family, Chinese were habituated to accept a similar pattern of authority and ranks in their government. It served to tell a man, or woman, where they stood automatically, providing a kind of security. If you fulfilled your prescribed role, you didn't need to worry about what others would do.

The Communists, of course, came to power dedicated to overthrowing China's past, the old love of hierarchy, cursed as feudalism, finding in it an explanation why the country that had invented gunpowder, the compass, and paper failed to keep pace with the West after the Industrial Revolution. While still guerrillas the Communists banned the old polite forms of address in Chinese for Mr., Mrs., and Miss: *xiansheng,* literally, "elder born," *taitai,* "great one," and *xiaojie,* "little miss." These smacked of feudalism, the Communists charged, and they replaced them with the simple Marxist term "comrade," *tongzhi.* They also adopted the old peasant convention of referring to other people, regardless of gender, simply as "Little Wang" or "Old Fung," depending on whether the person was younger or older than the speaker.

Yet somewhere along the way the Communists' Chinese heritage began to catch up with them. When I first arrived in Peking, I was very careful to avoid using the proper old-fashioned Chinese I had learned at Harvard and on Taiwan, and called people "comrade." But I noticed that almost no Chinese used it among themselves. Instead, I found, they often employed the same formal way of speaking that the Nationalists did, addressing people by their titles: Deputy Section Chief Wu, School President Mai, on up to Chairman Hua, never just Hua. I myself was addressed as Reporter Butterfield, or sometimes archaically as Mr. Butterfield.

As the Communists fell back into some of the old terminology of the mandarin class, they also worked out a system of perquisites to go with each rank, much like that established by the emperors for their retainers. Indeed, Chinese explained to me, you couldn't really measure a person's status by his salary alone, for many of the amenities of the good life, which in the West are acquired with money, in China can be gotten only through political position—better housing, cars, vacation trips, plane and train tickets.

"In China today it's not money but power that people want," said a tall, lean, crew-cut thirty-year-old son of an army general. "Money is very limited in what it can buy, you need connections and rank." On a hot July morning with the temperature in the nineties, he took me on a tour of some of the facilities which provide the politically annointed in China with what the Chinese call *te-quan*, "special privileges." These prerogatives had existed ever since 1949, he said, but with the breakdown in Party authority and public morality in the Cultural Revolution, they had become far more widespread and blatant. The constant political buffeting, the persecutions, and the economic dislocations of recent years had undermined people's devotion to the revolution and led to more self-seeking.

Our first stop was a few blocks east of the Forbidden City, Number 53 Dong Hua Men Street, a modern five-story concrete building with large plate-glass windows on the ground floor. Their curtains are perpetually drawn, so a passerby cannot peer inside. The only identifying clue to the structure was a small plaque, nailed to a post across a driveway, which described it modestly as the "Peking City Food Supply Place."

Yet it did not resemble any of Peking's ordinary markets, with their long patient queues of housewives and, occasionally, husbands, plastic airline-style bags in hand, waiting for the daily ration of whatever fresh vegetable or cut of meat happened to be available. Instead, there was a covey of vehicles drawn up outside, parked on a ramp leading to the entrance and cluttering the sidewalk, illegally. Among them were several Shanghai sedans, like a 1950s Packard, a few jeeps, a new imported Japanese panel van, a freezer truck, and a small three-wheeled truck that looked like an oversized motorcycle. Several chauffeurs squatted idly under the shade of a locust tree. Stacked in the back of the three-wheeler were a dozen chickens, two sides of pork, a crate full of large yellow croaker fish, each big enough to feed a Chinese banquet table of twelve, and packages of frozen giant prawns from the Bohai Gulf. My Chinese acquaintance was stunned by the abundance of meat, the proportions of the fish, the biggest he had ever seen, he said, and the number of prawns, an item that ordinary Chinese cannot buy except at the New Year's holiday.

The store, he explained, is for China's highest ranking officials only— members of the Communist Party Central Committee, the heads of the eleven large military regions into which command of the army is divided, and a few nationally prominent non-Communists who had collaborated with Peking. A number of aged Party veterans had also been given the "special purchase cards" required for admission. In addition, the store provided daily supplies to the capital's top restaurants and hotels patronized by China's leaders and foreigners.

A few blocks farther east, on the ground floor of a dark-brown, granite-faced apartment building, was a shop identified only by its address, Number 83, Chao Yang Men Street. The store's windows had been shuttered up with red-painted boards. Just inside the door sat a fat, middle-aged woman attendant with short hair trimmed in the shape of a bowl. When I tried to walk in, she demanded, "Have you got a card?" When in turn I asked, "What is this place?" she responded, "You're in the wrong place." I tried the question again, but got the same answer. Inside, a large screen shielded the contents from view. Only a large portrait of Chairman Mao was visible.

According to my companion, it was a special bookstore for high cadres only. Occasionally, he said, he borrowed his father's "special purchase card," which allowed him to go inside. Unlike the regular bookshops, which are always jammed with customers clamoring for attention from rude salesclerks, the officials' bookstore had banks of easy chairs for the cadres to sit in while they decided on their selection. Most of the volumes for sale were marked *Nei-bu*, "for internal distribution only," or classified. They included translations of popular foreign novels which the Party authorities deemed unfit for ordinary Chinese to read, like *Love Story*. There were also Western political tracts, including former President Nixon's memoirs, *RN*, and his earlier book, *My Six Crises*, which are not available to the public. But the most important service of the special bookstore, my friend explained, was simply that it had books. Chinese have long loved to read, given the value tradition-ally placed on the written word and education. But because of the vast size of China's population and the country's scant forest cover, denuded centuries ago by peasants who needed wood for fuel, there is a terrible shortage of paper. It had been aggravated during the Cultural Revolution by the deluge of propaganda materials, notably the hundreds of millions of copies of the little red plastic-covered edition of Mao's quotations venerated by the Red Guards as their bible. Hence most books today are issued in small editions of perhaps 10,000 to 20,000 copies, hardly enough for a country of a billion people. Popular works, like English-language textbooks or a Chinese–English dictionary, are sold out in a few hours. Not so in the special book-store, which keeps adequate reserves. The most eagerly sought-after book, my friend confided, was a recent photo-offset edition of a sixteenth-century copy of the *Golden Lotus,* China's classic of pornography. It has been banned in ordinary bookshops since the Communists' victory in 1949.

Continuing our drive, opposite the northern wall of the Forbidden City, across from the old moat, my guide pointed to an unmarked edifice built in imitation of a Chinese temple. The roof was set with mustard-yellow tiles, and the front was decorated with a series of red-painted columns and three tall red doors. Two army sentries stood stiffly beside a driveway lined with pine trees that led to the rear of the building. It is the Three Gates Theater, my friend said, where high cadres can see current American, European, and Japanese hit movies not otherwise shown in China. From 1966 to 1972, under the cultural despotism of Jiang Qing, no movies at all were produced in China, and only ten were filmed in the next four years up to Mao's death and the overthrow of the radicals. Even today the offerings of the Chinese film industry tend to be hackneyed and bombastic, avoiding sex or politically sensitive plots. So watching foreign movies has become something of a passion for those lucky enough to have the proper political credentials.

Two blocks away, also facing the northern wall of the Forbidden City, is a two-story gray-brick house with a sloping tile roof partially hidden behind a ten-foot-high wall. From the outside the building is unpretentious, but my friend identified it as the home of Deng Xiaoping, the vice chairman of the Party, who is China's most powerful leader. Rumor has it that the gray steel gates to the house are equipped with an electronic device to let Deng's car in without stopping, a common gadget in America, though still rare in China. But Deng now spends most of his time in a more spacious villa in the Western Hills outside Peking, a quiet wooded neighborhood off limits to foreigners and ordinary Chinese. In imperial times the area where he lives, known as Jade Spring Mountain, was reserved for the Emperor's pleasure during the summer months.

My friend was especially proud to be able to show me Deng's in-town residence, because only a few high ranking Chinese know where their country's leaders live. The locations are a state secret. He found it difficult to believe that Americans not only know where their President lives but can visit the White House as tourists. This Chinese penchant for secrecy stems partly from the Communists' mania for security, born of their guerrilla days, but it also follows an old imperial tradition under which dignitaries sought to maintain their exalted status by aloofness from the public. The greater their distance from the people, the higher their prestige. In his later years, Mao almost never appeared in public, with the exception of the monster rallies of hundreds of thousands of Red Guards during the Cultural Revolution, and even then he stood atop the tower of the Gate of Heavenly Peace, with no personal contact with the worshipful masses below. Mao's successors also tend to appear only on ceremonial occasions, like China's National Day on October 1 or at Party congresses. Members of the Politburo, the inner sanctum of power, do not hold press conferences for Chinese journalists or work crowds at airports or kiss babies.

Other officials below the highest rung on the ladder also are assigned cloistered and special housing according to their rank, I learned. One new development in the western part of Peking, across the street from the State Guesthouse, where former President Nixon stayed in 1972, has been sardonically dubbed *Fu-pi-lou,* roughly translatable as the "Capitalist Restoration Building," since many of its residents are officials who were purged as capitalist roaders during the Cultural Revolution but have since been rehabilitated. It is actually two separate sets of buildings divided by a black-topped driveway. On one side is a series of three-story red-brick residences with ample balconies, large picture windows, and grassy yards planted with small pine trees, a rarity in a city so sere and dusty that grass does not seem to grow. The apartments on this side are reserved for cadres of grade eight and above, like the Minister of Education, Zhang Nanxiang. But after the many stories I had heard about how luxurious the *Fu-pi-lou* was from Chinese, I was surprised that the apartments were comparable only to a lower-middle-class housing project in an American city.

On the other side of the driveway is a group of more modest six-story gray-concrete apartment buildings. Among the residents are the son of Fang Yi, a Politburo member who is head of the State Science and Technology Commission, a daughter of Ulanhu, another Politburo member, several prominent movie stars, and the artist Huang Zhou, popular in China for his ink wash paintings of donkeys. But even here the quarters are spacious by Chinese standards. One senior scholar I met who lived there had three bedrooms, a living room, a kitchen, a toilet with a bathtub, and even a telephone, still a novelty for the average Chinese, for they cost 1,900 yuan ($1,267) to install, over three years wages for an urban Chinese, and the telephone company can take years to act unless a person has the right political connections.

I did manage to visit the home of one senior Chinese, Madame Sun Yat-sen, the widow of the leader of the 1911 revolution that overthrew the Manchu Qing dynasty and herself a deputy head of the National People's Congress, the nominal legislature. Madame Sun, who was born Soong Ching-ling and was an elder sister of Madame Chiang Kai-shek, was in frail health at the time and died in May 1981, a few months after I left China, of leukemia. Her position in Peking was largely symbolic, representing the tradition of her husband and other non-Communist patriotic Chinese, and she had little real power. But her regal life-style resembled that of an American millionaire. She lived in an extraordinary house built by a Manchu prince in the late nineteenth century where the last Emperor of the Qing dynasty, Henry Pu Yi, was born. It is located on a quiet street on the north side of the Back Lake, one of the man-made imperial lakes which stretch out behind the Forbidden City. Today the house is hidden by a fifteen-foot-high gray-brick wall.

When I drove up at 6:20 P.M. precisely, as called for in the letter of invitation sent by Madame Sun's personal secretary, three sentries of the People's Liberation Army, in green fatigues, emerged and checked my name against a master list. Then they swung open a high red iron gate topped by a ceremonial Chinese tile arch. I had wangled the invitation because for years *The New York Times* had been sending Madame Sun free copies of the Sunday paper, at her request.

The broad driveway led through several acres of parklike grounds set with pines and willows, a large pond, and several gardens. The house itself appeared only after the visitor navigates a sweeping curve. The roof was sloped and finished in tile, Chinese-style. But the proportions were Western, three stories high, and the floors were covered with thick carpets spread from wall to wall.

Madame Sun was waiting in an anteroom, a tiny woman of ninety-two, with a round, cherub face, her long hair, still black, pulled back in a bun. She was dressed in a simple though elegant blue silk jacket with high mandarin collar and Chinese cloth fastenings. A woman aide and one of her foster daughters supported Madame Sun when we went into dinner.

The dining room suggested a Chinese re-creation of a European château, a long rectangular room, decorated with portraits of Mao and Hua at one end, and a huge piece of Mao's calligraphy, a gift to Madame Sun, hung on the other. The table was set with antique Chinese blue and white porcelain, and silver knives and forks, along with chopsticks. Servants in white livery produced a meal, part Chinese, part Western, unobtainable in any Peking restaurant, that reflected Madame Sun's own mixed upbringing. Although she was born in Shanghai, to a wealthy business family, she was educated in Macon, Georgia, and spoke English with an American accent.

The meal began with a Chinese hot and sour soup, strips of pork and bean curd in a broth laced with pepper and vinegar. Then came a Shanghai roast duck, rich with tender meat, and served cold. There followed a cold chicken dish, a grilled white fish, Western-style, a curried beef, stewed cucumber in brown sauce, and what Madame Sun announced as "the house specialty," macaroni with cheese, American-style. Dessert was cold almond-paste soup, a Chinese delicacy made from real almonds in the old-fashioned way, by crushing them between two stones, she said. "In the restaurants they don't use real almonds anymore," she insisted. Here again was a true luxury well beyond the means of normal Chinese.

After dinner, Madame Sun's personal doctor appeared at the door, made a signal to her secretary, who gave a sign to her woman assistant seated next to her. "It is time for you to rest," the aide declared.

As she was led upstairs for the night, I was taken on a tour of the rest of the house, which included her private movie theater. It was another long room with high ceilings, large glass windows facing the gardens, and ten rows of stuffed easy chairs covered with brown and gray slip covers. The room was equipped with two projectors and a screen that stretched full across it. When she was in good health, Madame Sun was famous for her screenings of the latest American films, often double features, and sometimes, I was told, triple features. The shows could last till the middle of the night, and it was considered rude to leave before they were over. Under the protocol of privileges for the elite, only members of the Politburo were supposed to be able to show movies at home, but Madame Sun was granted an exception because of her advanced age, Chinese said.

In the gravel driveway of Madame Sun's house stood another of the perquisites that go with being a member of the elite, a long black Hong Qi, or Red Flag limousine. There are no private cars in China; all automobiles are assigned by the state, usually with a chauffeur. Technically the vehicles belong to the government office, school, or factory which allocates them, rather than to the official, and the *People's Daily* periodically admonished against personal use of cars, meaning cadres should not let their wives take them for shopping or sending the children to school. Yet pick any day to visit one of Peking's major department stores or first-class restaurants and you will see fleets of these cars, disgorging families, lined up outside.

"I used to worry about my wife using the office car," a graying engineer in Shanghai told me, "since the car belongs to the people. But then we talked about it, and she pointed out that we are the people, too. I couldn't argue with her," and he laughed. Many people seem to share in this joke.

In a country where most people must still rely on bicycles for transportation, the Red Flag is a special wonder, a hand-tooled luxury car designed in the 1950s, with the interior modeled after the Mercedes and the rear end copied from the Cadillac. The inside sparkles with polished wood; there are jump seats for extra passengers, like the stretch version of the Cadillac; a lace antimacassar is spread over the rear upholstery, and brown curtains shield passengers in the back from public scrutiny. Only two hundred Red Flags are produced a year, at a truck factory in Changchun, in the northeast, so they are alloted only to the highest officials.

When traffic policemen spot a Red Flag on the road, they will often push other cars, trucks, or bicyclists aside. And Red Flags are excluded by special right from having to brake to a sudden stop if confronted with an unexpected pedestrian or bicyclist, constant hazards in Peking. I discovered this when a friend who worked in the computer center of the Academy of Sciences reported that a man in his office who had recently learned how to ride a bike made an abrupt turn without signaling. A Red Flag behind him smashed into the man, braking only slightly. He lay in a coma for a week, then died. Ordinarily, the family of a victim in an accident would receive a substantial settlement under the system of strict accountability in Chinese law. But his family got nothing, the office mate said. For Red Flags, they learned, are exempted from these regulations for fear that if they brake to a sudden stop they might injure a high cadre riding in the back seat. Ironically, this Red Flag had been loaded with foreigners, businessmen who can now rent the prestige cars to help China earn foreign exchange.

Driving a Red Flag, I saw on other occasions, gives its passengers a license to go almost anywhere. One fall afternoon when I was playing tennis with an Australian diplomat on the bumpy, leaf-strewn courts of the International Club—supposedly reserved for foreigners only—I watched as the familiar long black shape of a Red Flag pulled up and an elderly, white-haired man in an air force uniform disembarked. One aide carried two new American-made graphite tennis rackets, worth over $200 apiece; another aide brought out a thermos and cups for tea. When I quizzed the aides about the identity of their boss, they shook their heads and replied, "I'm not too clear." But a Chinese attendant who looks after the courts told me later that the mystery player was a general in the air force.

When I repeated the incident to my friend whose father was a general and who had given me the tour of the special facilities for the elite, he nodded in recognition.

"The real power in China is in the military," he said, with more than a touch of pride. Indeed, as he explained it, the military in China is a state within the state. His own father, who held a rank equivalent to lieutenant general, got a salary of 400 yuan ($267) a month, higher than any civilian except Mao. But the figure was meaningless, because his father, like the deputy chief of staff who lived under the shadow of the Forbidden City, also got a free house, car, and food from the army. In addition, his father had access to a store in the Western suburbs of Peking that sells cheap consumer goods made by the nation's huge network of defense industries, like the post exchange, or PX, system in the United States. That was how he and some of his friends had bought motorcycles, an item not available in regular stores.

Privilege in the military is not only for high-ranking officers; ordinary soldiers in China's 4.5 million-man armed forces are also better off than their civilian counterparts. While only 3.8 percent of China's population as a whole are members of the Communist Party, 35 percent of the military have been accepted into the Party, an important route to the better life in China. When soldiers are demobilized, they are often given important leadership posts in factories or communes, despite their lack of training, because of their presumed political loyalty. Families of soldiers in the villages have traditionally been given an extra share of the harvest at the end of the year. During the Cultural Revolution, Mao called in the army to take over many universities and factories riven by factional battles. The military units were supposed to go back to their barracks in the early 1970s, but some found their new quarters so comfortable that they have stayed on despite repeated orders from the State Council. The Ministry of Education reported while I was in Peking that the army still occupied 20 million square yards of school land, more than the government could build in several years. In Peking, when students and faculty at People's University organized a protest march in 1979 over the continued occupation of two thirds of their campus by the Second Artillery, a missile command, the leaders of the demonstration were expelled from school. The students had no classrooms or cafeteria because of the soldiers' presence.

But the most surprising feature of army life to me, in a Communist state, was the amplitude of servants allotted to officers. Every officer, from company commander up, is assigned an orderly, my friend said. His father's orderly did everything from shining shoes and sweeping the floor in their house to setting out his father's toothbrush and putting toothpaste on it. One former army general, Wang Meng, now head of the Sports Commission, took his orderly on a trip to Mexico with him. Later I learned that all civilian officials of grade eight and above, from Deputy Minister up, receive allowances of 50 yuan ($33) a month to hire maids. Many of these servants in Peking come from Anhui, a province in central China that is one of the poorest in the country, a kind of Chinese Appalachia, other friends related. They had come to the capital in search of a better life and managed to stay on, without the necessary legal identification papers, because of their employment.

And yet, for all this consciousness of rank, all the privileges and prerogatives, the Communists have made efforts to reduce the gap between the top and the bottom. The distinctive feature of the Chinese system has not been to eliminate all the differences but to try to mute them. People in high positions are entitled to their rewards, but they should not flaunt them.

This strange sweet and sour, elitist–egalitarian ambivalence comes out in the way Chinese handle their chauffeurs. On the one hand, officials shouldn't labor with their hands, and therefore don't drive. But on the other hand, chauffeurs are a living reminder they are not practicing socialist equality. So when cadres go out for dinner they have worked out an ingenious compromise to resolve this dilemma. The first time I invited some Chinese to a banquet, a group of journalists from the New China News Agency, I thought I had made all the necessary arrangements. I had called the restaurant and negotiated the price per head, the number of guests, and the date. But then the man on duty at the restaurant caught me off guard.

"What is the standard for the chauffeurs?" he asked.

It took me a minute to realize that I had to buy dinner for the newsmen's drivers as well. For of course they would come in chauffeured cars, their drivers would wait, and would expect to be fed.

But I did not have to pay as much for the chauffeurs' meals, the clerk in the restaurant assured me. I had agreed to pay 20 yuan apiece for the journalists. Five yuan would be more than sufficient for the drivers, and would include beer and cigarettes, he said.

The most obvious way in which the Chinese have sought to minimize or blur the distinctions between people is by the uniformity of dress. Proletarian blue and peasant black, like the baggy pants and formless jackets, are a defense against charges of trying to be better than one's neighbors, of being too interested in fashion and therefore bourgeois. The degree of shabbiness and shapelessness varies with the political season.

"When a major campaign develops, like the Cultural Revolution, we bring out all our oldest, most tattered clothes," an English teacher related. "My family still keeps our patched pants and jackets, like peasants' clothes, in the bottom of a trunk, just in case."

But with China's more relaxed mood since Mao's death and the downfall of the radicals in 1976, style consciousness has made a comeback. Most Chinese feel they can now judge a cadre's rank by the cut of his tunic—the higher his status, the finer the fabric, the better the fit, and the neater the crease in his trousers. Cadres still have their own tailor shops. In Peking it's the Hung Bin, near the old foreign legation quarter. In Shanghai it's the Paramount, on Nanking Road, the main shopping street. When I stopped in there, drawn by a tuxedo displayed in the window, an elderly white-haired salesman assured me all their products were hand-stitched. "We make suits for the senior cadres," he went on. "They appreciate our workmanship."

In an effort to reduce inequality in the army, Peking abolished formal ranks in 1965. To foreigners the results are impressive. Members of China's armed forces wear no epaulets, no insignia of rank. But the difference may be more cosmetic than real. It does not mean that privates can give orders to generals, or that their pay is the same. Enlisted men still know who their officers are and salute them. The head of a company, instead of being called a captain, is merely identified as company commander. Everyone wears baggy green fatigues. But officers' jackets have four pockets, enlisted men's only two.

The government has also taken a number of deliberate steps to try to equalize social and economic differences. To ensure that in a country of one billion people with limited resources everyone gets a minimal supply of food and consumer goods, the Communists have strictly rationed key items like rice, cooking oil, and cloth. Housing may be scarce, and often shabby by Western standards, but the government has held rents to the very low level of three or four yuan a month, affordable by all. Salaries are low—the average urban worker earns 64 yuan ($42) a month—but there are no income taxes and over one quarter of the gross national product has gone to investment. Much of this is in industry, but Peking has also devoted it to expanding education and health care, which benefit the public. Each occupation has its scale of ranks and corresponding salaries, but they are virtually identical all across China. To try to make up for the higher cost and scarcity of goods in remote areas, like Xinjiang and Tibet, or the higher cost of living in the most expensive cities, like Peking and Shanghai, the government employs an eleven grade cost-of-living index. On this scale, a small town in Anhui, where meat and vegetables are cheap, is pegged at four, the provincial capital of Hefei at five, Peking six, and Shanghai eight. Tibet is at the top, eleven. All state employees are given minor adjustments in their salaries to reflect whether they live in a cheap or expensive area. Nobody, I learned, has to suffer by being classed as being in a one, two, or three region, which would cut their incomes. The lowest is a four.

One of the best examples of how Peking has attempted to mute differences is in its policy toward athletes. For a long time I found it difficult to learn about how China trains its sports stars. I knew there was a system of state support for sports, based on that in the Soviet Union, organized under the State Physical Culture and Sports Commission, a cabinet-level agency with a large headquarters in Peking. It is public knowledge that China is dotted with what are called spare-time sports schools, after-school gyms, and swimming pools where promising youngsters are sent; and it is an open secret that members of the national teams draw government salaries. But even my best Chinese friends, including one who worked in the Sports Commission and lived near the special dormitories for members of the national teams on Sports Street, refused to discuss the system.

"It's supposed to be a secret that Chinese athletes are professionals," he said, and indicated he would rather express his disillusionment about Marxism than discuss the nurture of athletes. This clandestine atmosphere suggested a massive, richly endowed program, like that in Russia or East Germany, where athletes are pampered and have the chance to become millionaires.

But when an acquaintance whose daughter was a fast-rising young swimmer finally broke this code of silence, her revelations seemed tame. Her daughter had begun swimming when she was five years old, the woman said, after being discovered by a coach from their neighborhood spare-time sports school. She used to work out four or five hours a day in the school's pool. Then at eleven she was picked for the Peking city team, and to help her train full-time, her mother enrolled her in what is called a "training camp." The daughter attended regular classes only in the morning, with a reduced academic load, mathematics, Chinese language, and politics, the three R's for Chinese. "Then she has all afternoon and evening to practice, swimming laps, jogging, doing flexibility exercises, and lifting weights," her mother said. Her daughter now comes home only on Sunday afternoons.

Thanks to this regimen, her daughter has won a national championship meet in her event, freestyle, and has been awarded the honor of being named a first-grade athlete, one short of the top, master of sports. The lowest is third-grade athlete.

But the rewards for such achievement are slight by American or Soviet standards. In fact, the mother is worried about her daughter's future, for Chinese athletes don't draw any salary until they are seventeen years old. Then they get only the wage of a beginning factory worker, about 40 yuan a month. Promotion comes slowly, as it does for other Chinese, and even China's world champion Ping-Pong player, Zhuang Zedong, who won favor with Jiang Qing and was named head of the Sports Commission, earned only 80 yuan a month. For a period before the Cultural Revolution any Chinese star who placed in the top three in an international meet received a bonus of 100 yuan, but that has been scrapped as too bourgeois. Moreover, the mother pointed out, her daughter will have nothing to fall back on when she finishes high school, for she has sacrificed her education and won't be able to go to college. She might be sent to work in a factory or, if she is lucky, be named a coach.

Still, her mother admitted, there are rewards that set her daughter apart. She gets a food "supplement" of 60 yuan a month, more than an average worker's salary, which is paid to the training camp for more nourishing meals. She gets all her uniforms free; she will get a bonus of six yuan a month if she becomes a master of sports, and there is frequent travel around China, a privilege few Chinese enjoy in a country where transportation is inadequate and buying tickets takes official approval. Besides, her mother observed, "athletes have more fun." In China, then, even the smallest difference looms large, magnified by the very ordinariness of most people's lives.

The same system of small gradations, minor to an outsider, but of real significance to a Chinese, applies to other occupations. Peking's supporters often note that China has not allowed its favored writers, movie stars, or nuclear physicists, those who have contributed to the glory of the state, to become millionaires, as the Soviet Union has. Many of them do, however, live very comfortably, practicing discreet rather than conspicuous consumption. Perhaps the wealthiest writer is Ba Jin, a left-wing novelist whose semiautobiographical trilogy, *Family,* made him China's most popular writer before 1949. Today he still lives in a large Western-style house he purchased in the 1950s, secluded behind a wrought-iron gate and a long driveway. He doesn't draw a state salary, he said in an interview, he doesn't need to.

During the Cultural Revolution, Red Guard pamphlets estimated his fortune, derived from his royalties, at 200,000 yuan ($133,000). Like other cultural figures, he was attacked by the Red Guards and his property confiscated, but he has since been rehabilitated and his house returned.

There are many ways those with the proper rank and credentials can beat the asperities of life without being too conspicuous about it. If they are ill, there are special hospitals. In the capital, it's the Peking Hospital, a modern tree-shaded complex around the corner from the Xinqiao Hotel, where Prime Minister Zhou Enlai was treated for cancer till his death in 1976. A Chinese scientist who visited a high-ranking relative there was amazed at all the latest American, West European, and Japanese medical technology he found, including a large computer that was not in operation, apparently because no one knew how to run it. He contrasted the equipment with that in his neighborhood clinic, which did not have a working X-ray machine. In Kunming, in Yunnan, a doctor told me, he worked in a special wing of a hospital reserved for high-level cadres who got the small supplies of foreign drugs when they were available. During the Cultural Revolution the doctor came under attack for being a Christian and was forced to clean the lavatories. But when one of these ranking patients arrived, the doctor was called back for consultation.

Cadres get the same ration coupons as ordinary Chinese. But officials get extra allowances for entertainment and, friends related, often spend up to twenty days a month engaged in meetings where they will be well fed, largely at state expense.

Some special consumer goods are available only to the favored. Panda brand filter cigarettes, which are made with imported tobacco, cannot be purchased in any store. But a number of leaders smoke them, and once during a press conference given by Deng, in the Great Hall of the People, I found a blue packet of Pandas, decorated with its namesake, on a desk in front of my chair, along with a pad of paper and pencil.

The Peking Hotel is strictly off limits to Chinese, and gray-uniformed security guards rigorously question anyone they don't recognize as working there. But I was charmed one fall afternoon to watch a Red Flag pull up to the entrance and observe an orderly in military uniform jump out to help the passenger in the back seat open the door. Slowly a portly white-haired gentleman in his seventies emerged, accompanied by his wife. Without a word from the guards, they trundled in, took the elevator to the mezzanine floor, and went to the hotel barbershop. I discovered later that cabinet ministers, generals, and their sons and daughters are regular patrons of the men's and women's hairdressers, theoretically reserved for foreigners. The daughter of one senior general, now an army officer herself, said she had been coming there to get her hair cut since she was a girl.

Similarly, only ranking cadres, army officers, and others with special status can buy tickets for China's limited number of daily airplane flights or purchase "soft seat," first-class accommodations on the nation's railroad network. ("Soft-seat" means literally that, plushy stuffed chairs, windows shaded by lace curtains, no extra passengers pushing in the aisles. "Hard-seat," or second-class, means flat wooden or wicker-framed seats, and usually more passengers than seats.)

Passengers going "soft-seat" or "soft-berth" usually board their train through a special entrance, set off to the side of the main railroad station for discretion. In the old lakeside city of Hangzhou, China's capital during the Sung dynasty, the first-class waiting room is in a small building hidden behind a closed iron gate and up a gravel drive. It is furnished with easy chairs and carpeted with soft rugs. From there passengers enter the far end of the platform, undisturbed by the crush of people pushing through in the main station, which has only hard wooden benches to sit on. I came to be familiar with many of these first-class waiting rooms, because they are also where foreigners are taken.

China does not have private dachas, the country retreats available to the privileged in the Soviet Union as a reward for service to the state. But cadres on trips have access to well-appointed "guesthouses," *zhao-dai-suo.* In Hefei, the capital of Anhui, I accidentally got a glimpse of the style to which China's most senior leaders are accustomed. I was traveling with Governor Harry Hughes of Maryland, who had come to sign a sister-state agreement with Anhui, and was housed in a villa built for a visit by Mao in 1958. The villa lay in a sprawling compound of guesthouses set on a hilly park overlooking a lake. Mao's residence was a modernistic brick and glass structure, with something of early Frank Lloyd Wright in its lines, though it was trimmed in a dubious shade of pea-soup green, perhaps to match the surrounding pine trees. Next door was a small power station to ensure electricity for important visitors, presumably a reflection on the city's wavering supply. The power station included a building where an attendant lived, and on a hot June evening he was sitting on a chair on the roof. The door to his own room was thrown open, revealing a bed under a tangle of wires.

The entrance to Mao's bungalow was gained by a fifty-foot-long corridor carpeted in red. The entire suite of eight rooms was finished with dark wood paneling, a rarity in China, where wood is in short supply, and it had a somber, Victorian feeling. The master bedroom contained a full-length double mirror, a voluminous wardrobe, and a dark rosewood four-poster double bed hung with a mosquito net. The windows were covered with light-brown patterned-silk curtains. Off to one side was a small sitting room with a sunken leather sofa built into three of its walls. Two other bedrooms also came equipped with four-posters and their own private sitting rooms. The combination living–dining room was furnished with three heavy sofas, large porcelain vases, and a color television set.

The most luxurious feature, however, by Chinese standards, was the enormous bathroom. The bathtub was formed in the shape of an L, five feet to the side, with a short set of steps leading up to it. The stairs were topped with steel handrails, to assist the elderly or infirm bather. The bathroom contained a choice of a Western flush toilet, a Chinese-style seatless squat toilet, and a urinal. It was also furnished with a reclining leather couch beside the tub, so a guest could be given a rubdown after his bath. The villa was staffed by twenty attendants.

The Communists have also set aside a number of villas and hotels for the faithful at China's favorite resorts like Beidaihe, the old summer colony for European businessmen, diplomats, and missionaries on the Yellow Sea coast east of Peking, Huang Shan, or Yellow Mountain in Anhui, and West Lake in Hangzhou. At Qingdao, another resort and port on the Yellow Sea which also produces China's most famous beer, Robert Piccus, an American businessman, recalled his difficulty in penetrating the secrecy which surrounds the occupants of the seaside villas. Before coming to Qingdao, Piccus had arranged to meet a Danish executive whose company was negotiating a deal to improve the harbor. Piccus was put up in the regular city hotel, but the Dane was quartered in a special guest house and Piccus couldn't find him. Finally the Dane managed to call Piccus to explain.

"I can't tell you where I am, since the people in charge of the guesthouse say they don't know the name of the building or our address," the Dane said, suppressing a laugh. "I also can't tell you how to call me, since they say they don't know the phone number here."

Although the elite have veiled many of their privileges behind this kind of secrecy, ordinary Chinese are still aware they are not equal and often bitter about it. Mao's impassioned pleas for revolutionary egalitarianism made a deep impression on both urban and rural Chinese, though the Great Helmsman may not have been an exemplar of his idealistic doctine.

At Fudan University in Shanghai, one of the three most prestigious colleges in China, a group of journalism majors conducted a daring public opinion poll in which they asked other students what they thought China's most serious problem was. The pollsters went to the school library, locked its doors, and passed out their questionnaires. Of the several hundred students who responded, 60 percent listed *te-quan,* special privileges, an American exchange student at Fudan said.

From time to time a member of the leadership does get into political trouble because of overstepping the fine line between legitimate enjoyment of the spoils of office and arrogance. Chen Muhua, the tall, formidable woman who is an alternate member of the Politburo and a deputy premier, came under attack after a trip to Rumania. She was about to fly back to Peking when a group of Chinese students studying in Rumania who were sick arranged through the Chinese ambassador in Bucharest to return with her on her special plane. The ambassador thought it would help the students and save the government some money. But when he informed Chen at the airport, she was piqued. According to an account published in a Communist magazine in Hong Kong, she declared:

"Since you have arranged to have so many students board the plane, I will let them return home first. I will not leave for the time being." The ambassador was forced to reverse his plan and take the students off the plane.

Not long afterward the *People's Daily* observed that such abuses have helped undermine the prestige of the Party. "Why is it that in the early days of the present regime we could discard the dirt of the old society without delay and establish a new spirit?" the paper asked. "One of the main reasons is that the spirit was sound then and the Communist Party enjoyed high prestige among the masses."

But now, the paper added, Party members and cadres "are demanding special privileges not only for themselves but also for their children. They let them enter the Party, get them back from the villages to the cities, put them into schools, and get permits for them to go abroad. They treat their children as their private property. . . . Such behavior in cadres can seriously damage the Party among the masses." The paper blamed this decline in idealism and rise in selfishness on the Gang of Four, a euphemism, most Chinese knew, for the whole Cultural Revolution decade.

Indeed, the abuses that have aroused the most resentment are those involving the children of high cadres. The most notorious case of nepotism—or "the shade of the Emperor's favor" in Chinese—is that of the family of Ye Jianying, the pudgy, balding eighty-four-year-old vice chairman of the Party, marshal of the People's Liberation Army and head of the National People's Congress. Ye is so frail that in his rare public appearances he often has to be propped up by a bevy of nurses. But Chinese friends reported that on his eightieth birthday he had staged a party for himself that cost 300,000 yuan ($200,000), and whether or not the story was true, it received wide credence. To honor him, his children had approached a number of China's most famous artists and hinted that papa, an avid art collector, would appreciate a gift for the occasion, one of the painters told me.

Ye's eldest son, a man in his forties, is married to the daughter of a senior navy officer in Canton in the south, my friends related. But Ye's son had lost interest in her and, while she lived with her father, he courted other women in Peking. The roommate of a Chinese woman I knew who worked for Peking television was dating the son. She was slender, attractive, a stylish dresser who got her clothes from relatives in Hong Kong and had learned all the latest Western dance steps. The son usually appeared in a Red Flag to collect her and carried a wad of 10-yuan bills, the largest denomination in which China's currency is minted, that was as thick as you could hold in your hand, the woman boasted. Ye's son actually held a senior command post in the air force, she added, though it was not public knowledge, and with this job was able to travel abroad frequently, a much-coveted privilege. Another son had been appointed deputy mayor of Canton, a job which gave him the chance for frequent trips to Hong Kong.

One of Ye's daughters, Ye Xiangzhen, had been a leader of a virulent Red Guard faction during the Cultural Revolution. She had personally taken part in harassing Peng Zhen, then the mayor of Peking, now rehabilitated and restored to the Politburo. But Ye's prestige had protected her from retribution. In school she had first studied art, lost interest in that, then somehow gone to medical school, the kind of switch ordinary Chinese could not make. Recently she has formed a movie company of her own, an improbable achievement in a country where all film studios are owned by the state; but an American businessman reported talking with her about distributing one of her films in the United States. She is married to China's most famous pianist, Liu Shikun, a tall, gaunt, crew-cut man. But their relationship turned sour and Liu often showed up at the bar in the Peking Hotel with other fashionably dressed young women, I noticed during the year I lived there.

Ye's younger brother, I also learned, who was a businessman in their hometown in Guangdong province before 1949, is now manager of the large Xinqiao Hotel in Peking where I often ate dinner. But the most talked-about member of the clan is one of Ye's grandsons. In 1980 the Peking police caught him when they set a trap for a group of Chinese smuggling gold out of the country in exchange for Japanese tape recorders and digital watches. The grandson arrived at the supposed site for the smuggling operation in one of his family's Red Flags and proved to be the ringleader of the gang. But once the embarrassed Public Security Bureau realized his identity, he was set free, several Chinese related.

Another member of the capital's fast set is Yolanda Sui, one of the two foster daughters of Madame Sun Yat-sen. The first time I encountered her was in the dining room of the Peking Hotel. She was dressed in a short, hip-hugging wool skirt, high brown-leather boots, and a bright-orange blouse. Yolanda was in her mid-twenties, slender, and very tall for a Chinese, about five feet eight. She had on heavy eye shadow and lipstick; not pretty, but haughty, striking, and sexy. She looked like a movie star from Taiwan or Hong Kong.

Later a mutual acquaintance introduced us and I asked what she did. "I'm in movies," she replied, saying she had just returned from shooting a film with an army movie production studio on location in Hunan. I noticed her often after that, on her way to the beauty parlor in the hotel or driving in her Red Flag to the evening movies at the International Club, reserved for foreigners. When I was at Madame Sun's house for dinner, I asked her about Yolanda's background. Madame Sun explained that she had adopted Yolanda after her father, who was one of her bodyguards, had become paralyzed from drinking too much.

On the night the head of the Party Propaganda Department bestowed China's version of the Academy Awards for the best movie of the year and the most popular actor and actress, I spotted Yolanda sitting at a table with Li Rentang, the man who had just won the best actor trophy. The ceremony was held in a ballroom of the Peking Hotel and was televised around China. Yolanda was outfitted in a red silk blouse and a long, embroidered red-print skirt, a dazzle of color and style in a forest of baggy blue. She was also smoking a cigarette, something very few young Chinese women do in public. When a Canadian television crew also noticed her, she pulled a compact out of her handbag and checked to see if her nose was shiny. Inside her bag, I saw, was a packet of Marlboros; foreign cigarettes are not available in regular Chinese stores. A middle-aged Chinese woman who works in the movie industry and witnessed the scene commented later, "She will be a movie star until Madame Sun dies. Then it's all over." Shortly before Madame Sun did die in 1981, Yolanda married a dashingly handsome movie actor. I often wondered what her final fate was.

Not all children of high cadres slip into such a free-wheeling life-style. The leading dissident in Peking's short-lived democracy movement in 1978 and 1979 was Wei Jingsheng, whose father was a senior economic official and Party veteran. Several other Chinese I met whose parents were ranking Party or army officials accepted the benefits of their parents' positions, though tried to be more discreet about it. Little Liu, a tiny, twenty-eight-year-old woman with a small, up-turned nose and a Doris Day smile, admitted that she had managed to get out of the village where she had been sent after high school because her father was a provincial leader. Both her father and mother had been born into poor peasant families, she said. As a teen-ager her father had run away to join the Red Army guerrillas, and in retaliation the Nationalists had executed his parents. That gave her an outstanding class background, an asset that was useful in getting transferred out of the village and gaining admission to Peking University at the end of the Cultural Revolution. After graduation her father had secured a plum job for her in the Central Broadcasting Station in Peking, where she screened Western movies. Half of her colleagues there were sons or daughters of cadres, she said. But Little Liu dressed in plain blues and grays and didn't brag about her father's rank.

Her admission to college, making use of her father's position, was not unusual. The New China News Agency once admitted in a candid report that

39 percent of the freshman class at Peking University were offspring of cadres or army men. Since cadres and soldiers make up only about 2 percent of the total population, that suggests that an official parentage is a clear advantage in education, much as being from a well-to-do upper-middle-class family in the United States is.

But Little Liu turned down an offer from some of her father's friends in Peking to help her join the Communist Party. "I don't believe in turning black into white, and white into black, the kind of things you have to do to curry favor and get ahead in the Party," she explained. "When I told my father my decision, he was very upset, but in his heart he knows too that the Party is not like it was before Liberation or in the 1950s. It has changed."

Her refusal to join the Party despite its promise of added privileges and a better life raises a question about how successful the Communists have been in passing on their real power, their political positions, to their children.

"This worries them a lot, they talk about it with their families," said a thoughtful, taciturn economist who was trained in America. "The best the old man can do is to arrange a good education and job for his kids before he dies." This was largely true, I found. With a few exceptions, like the sons of Marshal Ye, children of Politburo members have not risen to important Party or army posts. Instead, most of the elite's offspring have sought, or been guided into, careers elsewhere, as scientists, like Deng's son who is studying physics in the United States, or movie stars, guides for the China Travel Service, or doctors. Perhaps these are safer from the vicissitudes of the constantly shifting political line and the frequent purges in Peking. Perhaps the younger generation, spoiled by growing up comfortably, lack their parents' ambition, as happened in imperial times to the spoiled sons of the court mandarins. Unlike Europe, China has never had a hereditary aristocracy that managed to survive over a period of generations.

When the patriarch does die, my economist acquaintance explained, there is a gentle process of diminution. After a Central Committee member whom he knew passed away, his wife and children were asked to move out of their spacious, sun-lit old Chinese courtyard-style home. They were given a grace period of six months, however, and furnished with a handsome apartment. Then when the mother died, the children were requested to move again, to somewhat smaller quarters, all arranged by the Party. They were stepping down the stairs.

"This illustrates something about the Communists," the economist said. "They can be brutal. But they can also do things in the old humane Chinese way."

China's apologists have argued over the years that Peking has created a model revolutionary society, one that has gone a long way toward eliminating inequality. In the Communists' cave headquarters in Yanan in the 1930s and 1940s and in the early days after Liberation in the 1950s there was some truth to this. But the endless political campaigns of the past three decades combined with the shortages of food, consumer goods, housing, and jobs have weakened the Communists' revolutionary fiber. The cadres have become protective of their positions and their families and hungry for the better material life.

In purely monetary terms, it is true, the Communists still maintain the appearance of their old egalitarianism. All salaries are limited. But money by itself is not a good measure; the real differences are the hidden privileges, prerogatives, and perquisites that go with political status: the better housing, the chauffeur-driven cars, the special food stores, and the ability to travel. It seemed to me that the Chinese obsession with rank is at least as blatant as the snobbery of New York debutante society. The life-style of high cadres, with their lavish guesthouses, home movie theaters, and imported tobacco is as far beyond the grasp of the peasant in his rice paddy as the doings of a successful Hollywood rock-music impresario or a wealthy Wall Street lawyer billing $200,000 a year are from the life of a West Virginia coal miner or a black dropout in Harlem.

Attention to rank in China does not end even with death. At the Babaoshan Cemetery in Peking, where many of China's Communist leaders are buried, there are several different funeral halls for mourners and a number of separate vaults where the ashes are kept. By law everyone in the cities now must be cremated, to save land for productive agriculture, and the fee of 20 yuan is automatically paid for all state employees by their workplaces. But vaults are numbered, and the number one room is for the highest cadres only, the number two room for the next rung on the ladder, and so on, a Chinese whose mother was cremated there told me. The result is often fights over which vault a person's remains will rest in.

In the past the ashes could stay forever. But with China's population squeeze, there is now a time limit of five years for ordinary Chinese. After that, their families must come and move their remains elsewhere. High cadres' ashes may still stay indefinitely.

4.   The Back Door

GETTING ALONG

"Our minds are on the left, but our pockets are on the right."
A current Chinese saying

I had never had a crank phone call in China before, but one Saturday morning shortly before I was scheduled to leave Peking, I received a call that I was certain was either a friend playing a practical joke or a daft Chinese. The caller identified himself as an employee of the restaurant in the Peking Exhibition Hall, a huge Stalinesque confection built during the halcyon days of Chinese–Russian relations in the 1950s. The caller asked if I was the American correspondent Bao Defu. That was the Chinese name a teacher had given me years before in Taiwan—it was as close as one could get in Chinese to the English pronunciation of Butterfield while retaining the sound and meaning of a real Chinese name.

Why hadn't I come last night to eat the dinner I had ordered and the restaurant had prepared? he demanded.

I was mystified. I had never been to the restaurant, and I certainly had not ordered a meal there. Perhaps he had the wrong name, I suggested.

But the caller was insistent. "You came here two days ago with your name card and ordered a banquet for forty guests. You must pay." His voice was edged with anger.

It is common practice in China's better restaurants to order ahead of time, and for foreigners, it is almost mandatory. That way, you will be seated in a special reserved room at the back, or upstairs, and charged double, triple, or quadruple the price. The cost of a meal is fixed by the "standard," the amount you set per head, not by the price per dish, as in Western restaurants. If a guest fails to appear, and the number of people is fewer than you ordered, the host must pay anyway. I was familiar with all these rules. How much was the price for each of the forty guests I supposedly had ordered for? I asked the caller. Forty yuan each, he said, about $27, a mere total of $1,080 for dinner.

That convinced me he must be a crank and I slammed down the phone.

But the next day the phone rang again. This time it was the Dong Lai Shun restaurant, an eatery popular for its Mongolian hot pot, strips of thinly sliced lamb which diners cook for themselves in a Chinese chafing dish. The caller had the same question for me: why had I failed to show up and pay for a dinner I had ordered for the previous evening? After all, he said, encouraging me to confess, "your own secretary came here to place the order."

My secretary? I said. I don't have a secretary. Was it a woman? Yes, he assented, a woman with your name card. That offered a new view—someone was impersonating me. Was this woman Chinese or foreign? I inquired. Chinese, was the answer.

Over the next two weeks, the calls kept coming, almost every day. The Peking Vegetarian restaurant claimed I had ordered a banquet for sixty people and twelve chauffeurs at 60 yuan a head for the guests and five yuan for the drivers. That was a mere $2,440. A large department store phoned to say that four hundred pounds of wool thread I had ordered was now ready to be picked up. The odd thing was, no one ever appeared to eat those lavish meals or pick up the material that had been ordered.

Finally, one morning, I received a call from the police. An officer of the Public Security Bureau began with the usual routine—was I the American correspondent named Bao? When I replied yes, he said he wanted to check some details about the complaint I had lodged the day before at a local police station in the northern part of Peking. I had stopped in to report that a man named Chen from the Central Philharmonic Orchestra had swindled me in a business transaction, the officer continued. I was tempted to interrupt and protest the story was fraudulent. But here was a glimpse at how real Chinese life might work. I was fascinated and let him go on. This fellow Chen had supposedly asked me to buy him a bicycle, liquor, and cigarettes in the Friendship Store, using my foreign currency. After I bought the goods for him, Chen absconded without paying, and now I wanted the police to catch him, or so the officer said.

This added a new twist. Now the imposter was brazen enough even to walk into a police station using her false identity. I thought it would be easy to persuade the policeman that it wasn't me. Was the person who went to your station yesterday Chinese? I asked. Yes, he said.

"I am not Chinese," I said, springing my trap.

"But you are speaking Chinese," the policeman responded.

I had underestimated the situation again. There was only one more thing

I could think of to do. I offered to go to the police station to show them that I was not Chinese.

"But how will we know you are not Chinese?" the officer asked. I was flattered that anyone would be so impressed by my ability to speak Chinese, but was rapidly losing patience.

Eventually, I persuaded the policeman to let me come down to the Foreign Affairs Section of the Public Security Bureau that afternoon to give my evidence. This agency for dealing with foreigners is housed in a lovely old Chinese-style courtyard building, set behind a circular moon gate, that must once have belonged to a wealthy capitalist. The office has bright-red wooden pillars and a sloping roof covered with green and blue tiles. Five policemen were waiting for me, including a tall handsome man with long gray hair, a Chinese Cary Grant, a woman stenographer who kept laughing at my story, and a lean, crew-cut man whose sober face never betrayed any expression. He was the only Chinese I met during my time in China who still wore a Mao button. "I like Chairman Mao," he said when I asked why he kept what had become an anachronism, something like an American wearing a Nixon campaign button. He asked if I would please supply a list of all my Chinese friends to help the police track down the culprit. I politely declined. That seemed too obvious a subterfuge.

Soon after, the police did catch the impersonator. The *Peking Evening News,* China's closest thing to a spicy Western tabloid, disclosed that she was Cui Xinfeng, a twenty-three-year-old worker in a Peking phonograph-needle factory. Cui had also claimed to be a Hong Kong businesswoman called Su Lina, whose calling card she showed when she arrived in restaurants and shops. That was how I had originally met her. One night when I was filing a story at the high-vaulted Peking Telegraph office, I had encountered a woman standing at the counter arguing with the clerk over the address on her cable. She wanted to send it to the Kowloon Trading Company of Hong Kong, but she had no other address for the firm and the clerk would not accept the message.

I noticed that she was dressed like an ordinary Peking resident, with a wool scarf over her head and a short, bulky black coat. She also suffered from acne. But her accent sounded Cantonese, the dialect of south China that is spoken in Hong Kong, as thick in its way as a Georgia drawl in America. Finally, after she stepped aside, the clerk began reading my cable, and she asked me who I was. I gave her one of my name cards, a common practice among foreign correspondents in Peking, like a fisherman putting out a line, hoping for a new Chinese acquaintance and possible source. She volunteered that she worked for the Kowloon Company and lived in the Overseas Chinese Hotel in Peking. Only later did it occur to me that both her accent and her identity might be false.

I was intrigued and at first baffled by the incident. Only once had Cui actually gotten any material benefit by her impersonation—the manager of the Mongolian hot-pot restaurant was so impressed by the size of her banquet order that he invited her to stay for a sumptuous lunch, free of charge. But Chinese friends instinctively understood and helped explain her bizarre behavior. In China, they said, the bureaucracy is so clumsy and rigid that there are constant shortages of food, housing, and consumer goods. Communist Party cadres avoid the problem because of their privileges: the special food shops, the bookstores, the hospitals, and resorts. But "the masses," ordinary people, must be more inventive. To survive, they have created a nationwide system of informal exchange; more than a black market, it is a second, or countereconomy, that exists in tandem with the regular state-planned economy and helps it function. Chinese call it "taking the back door," *zou-hou-men.*

The ultimate back-door ploy was to impersonate a Party official or foreigner, someone who had regular access to luxuries most Chinese could only dream about. I heard of a number of other cases of imposters. In Shanghai, the local paper, the *Wenhuibao,* reported in tantalizing detail the exploits of a Chinese pauper turned prince, a peasant who masqueraded as the son of a deputy chief of staff of the army. The trickster, Zhang Longqian, a twenty-five-year-old farmer of no distinction, began his adventures during a visit to Shanghai when he wanted to see a performance of Shakespeare's *Much Ado About Nothing* but found, as often in China, that all the tickets were reserved for distribution to special *danwei.* So Zhang rang up the theater, using the name of a department head of the city Communist Party committee, and said in an authoritative manner that a friend of his, a deputy chief of staff of the army, had a son who wanted to watch the play. The theater director who took the call was flattered, and soon Zhang not only had a ticket, he was also introduced to a pretty young actress whose affections were easily won by the son of such a prominent official. One deceit led to another, and Zhang found himself with gifts of new clothes, a watch, a house to live in, and a car, loaned by the Communist boss of Fudan University. Zhang's fairy-tale life ended only when a member of the street committee where he was living developed scruples about a demand Zhang had made to have his new girl friend promoted to a more prestigious theater company. The transfer required permission from the street committee, and the local cadre didn't approve of such back-door deals done on the request of high officials. He launched an investigation, and Zhang's real identity was uncovered.

The woman who impersonated me was less successful; she never showed up to collect. Perhaps she was a trifle zany, perhaps for her it was just acting out a fantasy, the psychic thrill of using a foreigner's name to order what she could never get on her own. Sometimes madness is a more accurate mirror of reality.

Most examples of the back door are more mundane, simple everyday arrangements by which individuals as well as factories, communes, and offices cope with the centrally planned economy, using their ingenuity to coax, wheedle, or procure items and services that are normally unavailable or may require months of waiting. It may be extra food for a wedding, a coveted job assignment, or a ticket on an airplane—plane travel is normally reserved for officials.

I recall one afternoon, when I was trying to finish a story for *The Times,* a Peking journalist I knew called to invite me to the movies. When I asked her what the name of the film was, Ling said she didn't know. All she could tell me was that a friend of hers, who had given her the tickets, promised it was an American movie. It would also be a *neibu,* literally "an internal," or restricted, show not intended for the public. In Peking, where screenings of foreign movies are rare and tickets to such events are a highly sought-after commodity, it hadn't occurred to her to find out the title.

The theater itself was a small private screening room inside a hulking brick office building. There was no sign outside advertising the showing. I noticed that in contrast to the usual concrete floor and hardwood folding seats in Peking's commercial theaters, it had a plush blue carpet and stuffed armchairs covered with gray cloth. We had agreed to arrive separately because of the regulations against Chinese having contact with foreigners, but Ling contrived to sit next to me just before the lights went out. It was a bold gesture on her part; she delighted in challenging the authorities, savoring the thrill of the illicit. She whispered that she had recognized several other members of the audience: in front of us was the wife of a deputy foreign minister, herself an official in the ministry, while behind us sat the son of a member of the Politburo. When the projector began to roll, the movie turned out to be *Patton.* I was bemused by the choice of the film, but Ling and the other members of the audience enjoyed Patton's unconcealed patriotism and the scene at the end when he snubs a group of Russian generals as American and Soviet troops meet to celebrate their victory over the Germans.

Afterward I asked Ling, a brusque, determined, middle-aged woman who had recently treated herself to a permanent in a beauty shop, how she had gotten the tickets. "Through the back door," she replied. A man she knew who worked for Peking Television desperately wanted to find a new apartment since he lived a fifty-minute bicycle ride away from work, and Ling had introduced him to one of her relatives who was an official in the city housing office. In return, from time to time he gave her tickets to private movies. Another evening, she recalled with a chuckle, the film was *The Red Nuptials,* a French soft-porn movie. Later she discovered that it had been borrowed from a French diplomat by a so-called foreign expert, a foreigner who taught French under contract to the Chinese government. The movie had then been enthusiastically traded from *danwei* to *danwei;* it finally ended up being shown at the Peking Exhibition Hall to a large audience, including senior officials, most of whom were caught unaware and were embarrassed.

Ling's tickets to these movies were classic back-door deals. As Chinese friends described the workings of the back door, these exchanges usually do not involve money. That would be considered bribery and therefore illegal. Instead they are based on the traditional use of *guan-xi,* the cultivation of contacts and connections among friends, relatives, and colleagues. The longer I stayed in Peking, the more I sensed that almost anything that got done went through the back door. A nurse in Peking recalled that during the Cultural Revolution, when teen-agers were shipped off to resettle in the countryside, she wanted her son to have a special skill that might help him avoid being rusticated. So she asked a neighbor, a famous pianist, to give him lessons. There are no private music schools or lessons, but the neighbor, out of long-standing friendship, consented. Later, when the pianist's mother fell ill, the nurse arranged for her admission to a good hospital. The piano lessons also did their trick—the nurse's son was kept in Peking and not sent to the countryside.

"No money changed hands, for that would have been condescending in China today," the nurse said. "It was just friendship. Even the Communists can't replace friendship with class struggle."

But I was puzzled why the pianist's mother couldn't get into the hospital on her own. The Communists have greatly expanded medical care in China since 1949 and made much of it free; it was one of their greatest accomplishments. The nurse shook her head at my naïveté. Yes, that was true, she admitted. But the hospitals were still terribly overcrowded—in part because medical care was so cheap—and doctors had to see an average of ten to fifteen patients an hour, like an assembly line. Western drugs were also in short supply because they were given low priority in the state plan.

"Patients in my hospital have to line up three times," said a balding, gregarious physician who had been trained by American missionaries. "First they have to queue at the registration desk, then at the doctor's office, and finally at the pharmacy counter for their prescriptions. You can spend the whole morning just waiting.

"Many doctors are so busy they just make a casual examination of the patient and then scribble something out. It's not good medicine and the patients know it.

"So many of the patients use the back door," the doctor added. "If you know a doctor, you don't have to line up for him but just walk right into his room. He will give you better attention.

"Patients who have an even closer relationship with a doctor will go see him at home, after hours. That's where the best care is.

"Of course, in exchange, the patients must give presents to the doctors. At the New Year's holiday, they will bring around good cuts of meat, or a fish, or some fruit.

"That's why we say being a doctor in China is a 'fat job,' " he continued. "There is a joke that doctors, drivers, and shop clerks are the 'three treasures,' because they have more access to things that can be traded through the back door." He himself admitted that it was easier for him to get clothes made at one of the good tailor shops on Wangfujing Street, which often turn down customers, because the tailors knew him. And it was simple for him to get a table in the popular Mongolian hot-pot restaurant, where other diners had to buy tickets a day or more in advance, because the manager was his patient.

Drivers of trucks, buses, and cars are valued, I learned, because there are virtually no privately owned motor vehicles, and drivers therefore have an unusual ability to move around the country. Once in a noisy restaurant that stays open late and is frequented by drivers, I met a swarthy man in his late twenties who said he drove a truck for a farm machinery factory in Shandong province, east of Peking. After we exchanged a few toasts of beer and cheap white grain alcohol that stung my throat, he began recalling his adventures. It seemed that his factory often had slack periods, when there weren't enough raw materials or there was a shortage of electricity. When these occurred, he would take off in his truck to haul coal from another province. The scheme worked well, with him splitting the profits with the factory Party secretary, until one evening he fell asleep at the wheel and crashed into another vehicle, wrecking his truck.

"It was too bad," the driver said wistfully, pouring both of us some more beer. "On Sundays I used to be able to use the truck to take my girl friend and some of our other friends on picnics."

On another occasion, I went with a student acquaintance to a small, crowded eatery that served peppery Sichuan-style cooking. The tables were full, but we finally found two empty stools and squeezed down. The previous customers' dishes and chopsticks still lay scattered on the table, along with small piles of chicken bones picked clean of their meat. My friend often patronized the restaurant and recommended its "home style" bean curd, cooked with fried red chili peppers and another form of pulverized pepper powder.

But when the waitress arrived, she said she was sorry the bean curd was sold out. My friend then casually took out a pack of China brand cigarettes, one of the more expensive varieties, and placed it on a corner of the table. If I hadn't been watching closely, I might not have seen that she scooped up the cigarettes along with some of the used dishes. My friend, a bright, outgoing fellow who liked to practice his English on me, smiled at the transaction. She was an old classmate of his from junior high school, and she saved bean curd, a Chinese favorite, for her friends, he explained. A few minutes later she came back from the kitchen with a steaming bowl heaped full of chunks of the soft brownish delicacy.

In China's rigid system of state job assignments, where an impersonal government agency determines a person's career, getting a favored job or a transfer requires even more artifice and use of the back door. The same college student had an older sister who had been sent to Tibet as part of Mao's utopian program to resettle city high school graduates in the country-side. She had been there ten years already; she was thirty years old, and, from her family's point of view, was in critical danger both of becoming an old maid, since almost all Chinese women get married before they are twenty-nine, and being stuck forever on the remote, backward, 10,000-foot-high plateau of Tibet, which most Chinese abominate. Something had to be done fast.

"So my parents looked around very carefully," the student told me. "They knew that few men would marry a thirty-year-old woman. But my father located a very ambitious junior clerk, only twenty-seven, who worked in his office. Then they sounded him out through an intermediary. If he would agree to marry my sister, he could use his Peking household registration certificate to apply to bring my sister back to the city. In return, my father found him a much better job, with a promotion to be a cadre, in one of the hot, new, state import and export corporations that do a lot of business with foreigners. My father had an old comrade-in-arms from Red Army days in the trade corporation. It was all a matter of connections."

The arrival of large numbers of foreign businessmen, after Mao's successors moved to expand foreign trade as part of their modernization program, provided new opportunities for the back door. A Texan in the oil equipment business recalled that during a banquet hosted by the Ministry of Metallurgy his Chinese dinner partner became very expansive.

"You Americans just don't know how to do business," the Chinese official said. "Look at all the new Mercedes we are driving in our ministry. Where do you suppose they come from?" Then he laughed and waved his hands. "From our good friends in West Germany."

Another time, said the Texan, a short, stocky man who spent much of his time traveling in China, he had been in the final stages of negotiations with the Machinery Import–Export Corporation for the sale of some American oil-drilling parts.

"There is just one more thing we will need," one of the officials told him. "The deal will cost you two percent of the value of the sale. If you agree, the money should be deposited in a bank account in Switzerland whose number I will give you."

The Texan was stunned. It was the kind of pitch he expected in Indonesia or the Philippines, not in socialist China. As they talked further, the American added, the Chinese insisted that the money was not for his personal use, but for his corporation. Normally, as a state agency, they had to turn over all the foreign exchange they earned to the government. But this way they would have a special discretionary fund for their own use, outside the state plan, to buy equipment not allocated to them in the budget process. Still, it was illegal.

What astounded me was not such tales of misdoings—every country has its corruption—but that factories and communes in China routinely had to depend on the counter economy just as individuals did. A letter to the *People's Daily* from a county in Jiangxi province in central China disclosed that communes in the area had to buy 60 to 70 percent of their chemical fertilizer through the back door since the amount of fertilizer allocated to them by the central plan fell far short of what they had to have for their crops. The communes actually signed private contracts with the fertilizer factories, the letter writer charged, paying the plants with their produce: pork, peanuts, soybeans, melon seeds, or timber. To conclude such deals, he added, the commune officials also had to treat the factory cadres and their drivers to banquets and ply them with liquor and cigarettes.

Chinese factories have a whole category of employees just to help them cope when they can't get what they need from the plan. They are called *cai gou yuan,* literally, "purchasing agents" or "buyers," though the way Chinese described their functions they might better have been termed "fixers." Another article in the *People's Daily* estimated that every day 50,000 to 60,000 buyers arrive in Peking and Shanghai on urgent errands for their factories.

I got to know one of these agents, a husky, full-faced, energetic man in his mid-thirties who by sheer artfulness and use of *guan-xi* had worked his way up from being an orphan son of poor peasants to travel abroad as a private agent for a senior government official. At the outset his good class background, "poor peasant," had enabled him to wangle a job in an electronics factory in Peking and escape his village origins. From there his acumen quickly got him a job as the factory's buyer. Then, by chance, when he was sent to work on a so-called May Seventh School in the countryside where cadres were supposed to be purified by farm labor, he met a deputy mayor of the capital. The official sensed something special in him and assigned him as fixer to a new high-powered agency Peking set up to handle foreign trade in the city.

By the time I encountered him he was operating out of his own room in the Peking Hotel, one of the very few Chinese permitted to live there. He proved endlessly useful to his business associates. If a foreign businessman needed a room in the hotel and it was full—it always was—he could arrange it. If you needed a seat on the CAAC flight to Tokyo or Canton—they were always booked too—he could take care of that. If the hotel itself needed customs clearance for a new shipment of imported Japanese television sets, he knew how to handle it, no matter that the ultimate recipient of the TV sets might be a cadre outside the hotel who used the hotel's involvement in the tourist trade as a cover for a private back-door transaction.

One day when I went to his room he had on a new gold Seiko quartz watch. It was a present given him during a month's trip to Hong Kong and Tokyo which was paid for by grateful foreign firms.

The phone rang. It was a friend advising him that the manager of the hotel was in the hospital. He picked out a Japanese calculator from his desk and prepared to pay a solicitous visit to the sick man.

Later his contacts paid off further. He was able to arrange a trip to the United States, a feat in itself, requiring clearance from the Public Security Ministry and the Foreign Ministry. When he came back, he was wearing a Western-style blue pinstripe suit. He had also had business cards printed up identifying him as president of a newly formed import–export company in New York that would trade with China. Before I left China, an American businessman who worked closely with him said they had gone together one day to the office of a cabinet minister. The official had briefed them on the latest shift in economic policy, which industries were being cut back in a new retrenchment, and which factories would get special subsidies. It was classic inside information. The purpose of the leak, the American surmised, was that the fixer was acting as an agent, buying Chinese commodities for the official which they then sold overseas.

Even policemen participated in the back door, I discovered. During the fall of 1980, I noticed that more and more Chinese were gaining access to the Friendship Store. To use the store, you had to pay in special script issued only to foreigners in exchange for dollars, marks, or yen. And to get into the marble entranceway, you had to pass several guards in gray Mao tunics from the Public Security Bureau. They lounged around the door, letting anyone with a foreign face pass but questioning Chinese.

One morning, as I was sitting in our car outside waiting for Barbara to finish some shopping, I saw an unusually pretty girl, with red cheeks and hair worn loose to her shoulders, in a black wool coat, pacing up and down in front of the store. She looked anxious. After a few minutes one of the younger guards came out to talk to her, and I wondered if she would be in trouble for loitering. But they smiled at each other, he took her hand, and then he led her into the store. The other guards looked on benevolently as they went in, boy friend and girl friend apparently.

When Barbara came out, she said she had seen a Chinese family of father, mother, and two children on a wild buying spree. First they had bought three suitcases in the store, then they began stuffing them as fast as they could, as if time might run out on them or the back-door connection they used to gain entrance might be detected. Barbara was standing at the woolen-goods counter when they came by and ordered a half-dozen scarves, five cashmere sweaters, a dozen pairs of socks, and ten pairs of gloves. The items they bought, she observed, were all of a much better quality than what was available in regular Chinese stores.

Another time I came across a Chinese friend in the store. I was curious how he had gotten in.

"It was simple," he replied. "What you need is a letter of introduction from your *danwei* saying that you are going on an official mission abroad or that the *danwei* needs certain goods for an official purpose." It was a stratagem cadres sometimes used to buy things for themselves.

What he had done, he confessed, was to forge a letter. Then he persuaded a friend who had access to the *danwei*'s seal to chop the letter for him, making it look correct. A friend who worked in the People's Bank had arranged to get some of the foreign script for him. Properly prepared, he bought three television sets in the Friendship Store, one for each of them.

Before 1949 the Chinese had long practiced a form of petty corruption that foreigners call "squeeze," demanding a little extra money or a cut of any deal before it is consummated. The Communists claimed with pride they had eradicated such malfeasance. But the very nature of the Chinese Communist economy and its inefficiencies—the shortages, the endless waits in line, the shoddy quality of goods—reproduced "squeeze" in a new guise, the back door. In 1957, when the population of China stood at 600 million, the *People's Daily* reported, there were about one million stores in China, grocery shops, bicycle repair shops, laundries, barbers, cobblers. But by 1981 the population had swollen to one billion, an increase of 400 million, almost equal to the total of the United States and Western Europe combined, yet the number of stores had shrunk to only 190,000. The rest had fallen victim to the Communists' distaste for private enterprise and zeal for unified central control. In Peking alone the number of restaurants plummeted from 10,200 in 1949 to 679 in 1981. Mao had proclaimed, "Serve the People," a slogan emblazoned on the walls of thousands of offices and stores. But less than 10 percent of the Chinese work force are employed in the service industry compared to 48 percent in the United States and 42 percent in France and Japan. For Peking had decided to copy the Soviet model of industrialization and put emphasis on the expansion of heavy industry, like steel, rather than on agriculture, consumer goods, and housing. This produced glamorous annual statistics of growth in the gross national product and added to the leaders' sense that China was becoming a modern industrial power. But it did

99

not keep up with the needs of a swiftly growing population. It was a costly mistake in priorities avoided by other nations in the region, including Japan, South Korea, and Taiwan.

To cope with the resulting shortages, the Communists have devised a rationing system so Byzantine in its complexity that many Chinese themselves are at a loss to understand it. In Peking people have to carry as many as seven or eight different types of coupons and ration booklets, explained Fuli, a soft-spoken woman factory worker with a weathered face and prominent teeth. First, she said, is your grain ration book, in a red plastic cover; new pages for it are issued each month by your local government grain store, if you are a legal resident of the neighborhood and have a valid household registration. The Communists have added to the intricacy of the rationing system by an egalitarian attempt to tie a person's food allotment to the energy they expend in their work. Fuli herself, as a worker in a musical instrument factory, got thirty-five catties a month (a catty is 1.1 pounds, or half a kilogram). Her father, a cadre, got thirty-one catties, since his work is less physically taxing; her younger brother, a construction worker, got forty catties. Infants get six catties a month, she said, with the maximum of sixty catties for men tending blast furnaces in steel plants. In Peking, she added, people get 50 percent of their grain ration in wheat flour (northern Chinese prefer noodles and steamed bread to rice), 20 percent in rice, and 30 percent in coupons good for buying bowls of rice or noodles in restaurants. The first time I went out to eat with Chinese I was surprised when the waiter asked them for their grain coupons before accepting their orders. As a foreigner, I was exempt. If a Chinese cadre is sent on a business trip, there are special national grain tickets which he has to use on trains or in restaurants outside his hometown.

In effect, the system means that any time you go out and get hungry, you have to have your grain coupons with you as well as cash. When Judy McCahill, the wife of an American diplomat, was on the operating table in the Capital Hospital in Peking, about to have a baby, one of the doctors suddenly announced he was hungry.

"Should we get some doughnuts?" a nurse suggested.

"I don't have any grain coupons," the doctor said.

"That's all right," another nurse cut in. "There are some in a drawer in the office."

Next come a series of separate coupons: for cooking oil (a catty a month in Peking, but as little as two ounces a month in Yunnan), for cotton cloth (sixteen feet seven inches a year, in Peking), for coal, and for cooking gas. Since 1979 meat has not been rationed in Peking, but in some other provinces the allowance is as little as a pound or two a month.

In addition, each neighborhood state grocery shop issues another type of ration booklet. It includes monthly allotments of soap, sugar, bean curd, corn starch, some types of fish, and several Chinese delicacies like sesame paste and vermicelli noodles made from green beans.

Finally, Fuli explained, her factory gave each worker four industrial coupons each January good for purchasing manufactured products. Two or three of these coupons could buy enough wool to knit a sweater; half a coupon was necessary for some brands of tea. Ten industrial coupons, two and a half years' worth, were required to make the most important purchase of all, a bicycle, as indispensable to a Chinese as a car to twentieth-century Americans. But that was not all. To buy a bike you also had to have a special bike purchase coupon. In her factory, Fuli said, out of every one hundred workers, only two were given these treasured certificates each year.

"The chance to buy a bike is so important to us," she said, "that when a new worker is assigned to the factory, the first thing they do is go to the quartermaster to put their name on the bike list. Some of my friends who already have bikes of their own register their names on the list again when they have a baby. That way, by the time their kids are in their teens and old enough to need a bike, they will be able to get one.

"If you lose your coupons, it is a real disaster," Fuli continued, contorting her face into a grimace. Once a friend of hers had all the family's coupons in an envelope and his wife threw them out by accident. The government wouldn't replace some of them till the next year; but in Chinese fashion, their friends and colleagues chipped in and shared some of their own coupons. It was the kind of generosity I was to witness several times.

An astonishing example of the rationing system is that to buy a light bulb a Chinese has to turn in his old one. Each bulb bears a serial number—those used in factories are different from those intended for home use, and those sold in Peking are marked with a different sequence from those in other places. That way, you can't cheat and bring in a light bulb from anyplace but your home. If your bulb is stolen, you have to get a letter from the police before you can replace it.

In a developing country like China with a population of one billion, some rationing may be essential to prevent inequalities, Chinese I knew conceded. But Fuli saw another purpose to the government's program. "It's really a way to control you," Fuli remarked. "If you don't have the proper residence certificate, you can't get your ration cards, and, without them, you can't live."

With Mao's death and the ascension of Deng Xiaoping, Peking recognized that its stress on heavy industry had been a strategic mistake. The *People's Daily* reported that heavy industry had actually grown ninety-fold between 1949 and 1980, while light industry, which turns out consumer goods like shoes, textiles, bicycles, radios, and television sets, increased only nineteen-fold. Deng and his practical-minded colleagues understood better than Mao that centuries of living with scarcity had bred a strong strain of materialism in Chinese, a craving only intensified by the shortages of recent years. When Chinese friends came over to our apartment, they often began by walking around and asking how much the television set, the refrigerator, or the furniture had cost. In elevators, when I was able to overhear conversations, much of the talk was about where a person had bought something or what he had paid for it. In 1972, when one of the first groups of Chinese journalists came to the United States and I was asked to help escort them around the country, they confounded a vice president of the Ford Motor Company by asking him what his salary was in front of other employees. To a Chinese, it was as normal as asking an American his name or where he went to school.

To satisfy the pent-up desire for a better standard of living, Deng gave Chinese their first wage raises in twenty years; he restored bonuses, which had been banned as capitalistic, and he openly encouraged a new consumerism by ordering factories to expand their production of goods like television sets and allowing advertising on television and street billboards. The results were immediately apparent. I remember on a chilly January afternoon, under a dull gray sky, I came across a crowd of twenty people jammed around the entrance to an old, unmarked brick building on East Single Arch Street, not far from the Peking Hotel. The fading-red wooden door was closed, but the group stood there patiently, stamping their feet against the cold and chatting with an air of excitement. Eventually, the door opened and a man came out clutching his prize, a carton containing a new twelve-inch Sony black and white television set made in Japan. He and his wife, who had waited outside, strapped it to the back of their bicycle and walked off with care.

I was curious at what was happening. A middle-aged woman standing in line, her shape lost in a heavy blue overcoat, explained. They had drawn lots in their offices, she said, and the lucky winners got coupons to buy the TV sets. They let only one customer at a time into the store to prevent a crush, she added, and no one was permitted to take the sets out of their cardboard cartons to examine them before buying. They cost 600 yuan ($400), over ten months' salary for an average urban Chinese. Americans would have been outraged by the price; the government was exacting more than a 100 percent sales tax on the sets. But the woman didn't mind. She said she hadn't had any luxury goods to buy for many years, so she had accumulated a substantial savings account, and she and her husband's brothers had pooled their money for the purchase.

"We're happy to buy them, whatever the price," the woman said after I told her I was a foreign correspondent. "Tell them to send us more."

But I wondered whether the government, having unleashed this new consumerism, would be able to satisfy it. To appreciate what daily life really meant, despite the regime's new policy, Chinese friends suggested I should go grocery shopping, for that was where the continued shortages and rude service hit hardest. So on a cold, crisp December morning I went with our friends the Wangs, Li and Miao, to the Chong Wen Men market, a cavernous building shaped like an airplane hangar, with a rounded roof and skylights to let in shafts of sunshine. It is considered one of the biggest and best-supplied markets in Peking, and on the day we went was jammed with several thousand people. Unlike Western supermarkets, where the shoppers pick out their own food and then pay at the check-out counter, the Chinese customers had to line up separately for each item: vegetables, fruit, pork, chicken, fish, bean curd, and canned goods. Inefficient as it might be, that was the rule, and there was no changing it.

We joined the line for live chickens, the way Chinese prefer to buy their fowl. There were twenty-seven people in front of us, I counted, and it took almost half an hour to get to the clerk who was pulling the birds out of their metal cages. Because of lines like this, the Wangs calculated, it took them two hours a day to shop for food, about average among Chinese I knew. And since refrigerators have made their appearance only in the homes of top officials, grocery shopping means a seven-day-a-week chore for Chinese. One way to cut down on the time, Miao said, was pooling. She and her friends often went shopping in teams—one woman bought the chickens, another the vegetables, and so forth.

Most of the salesclerks, or "service personnel," as they are known in Chinese, were young men and women in their late teens or early twenties dressed in long white or blue smocks over their blue trousers. They wore high rubber boots since they were constantly washing down the brown marble floor with buckets of water to keep it clean. The walls of the market were covered with large red characters urging them to "raise higher the level of service" or "work hard to serve the people." But it didn't do for a customer to get too picky. At the chicken counter, a short, elderly man with a heavily wrinkled face upbraided a woman clerk with long pigtails for waiting on another shopper who had pushed his way into the line. The queue jumper had on a well-tailored black-wool overcoat and a Mao cap; "a cadre," Miao remarked under her breath.

When the older man's turn finally came, he complained that the chicken the clerk handed him was a cock rather than a hen. "Too tough and lean, give me a fatter one," he said.

The clerk responded by walking to the other end of the counter where there was another line of people waiting to have the chickens they had already bought killed and their feathers plucked. The customer tried to entice her back with several calls, but she ignored him. Finally he left in defeat, empty-handed.

Salespeople, Li explained, are among the lowest paid in China, and get few of the benefits of factory workers like free medical care and large pensions. In a state that equates heavy industry with socialism and commerce with capitalism, salesclerks are generally looked down on and their only revenge is to give customers a hard time. Once when the Wangs and I went to a restaurant to eat, the waitress forgot to bring half our order. I tried to get her attention by waving, and then by shouting, but the Wangs looked at me as if I were a madman.

"We try to be as polite and nice as possible to get them to wait on us," Li said. "They are used to shouting at the customers, not the customers shouting at them."

When we moved on to the market's fish counter, where there were forty people waiting in line, there was only one variety for sale, a small, thin, silver-skinned fish with a sharp snout. They were frozen and imported from North Korea. The Wangs had never seen them before and didn't know the name. Two clerks were taking clumps of the icy fish off a steel dolly, throwing them on the floor, then beating them with long-handled wooden mallets to separate them before selling. During the 1950s and early 1960s, before the Cultural Revolution, Li commented, it was easy to buy fish; but now it had become increasingly difficult, and the most popular variety in Peking, the yellow croaker, had disappeared entirely, unless you had a friend with access to the special food shop for high cadres. I noted in the *People's Daily* that China's total catch of fish had remained stagnant since the 1950s, while the population had soared, and that the intake of freshwater fish had dropped from 600,000 tons a year two decades ago to 300,000 tons now, because of overfishing, reclamation of land for planting grain, and pollution.

On our way out of the market, we passed a green metal stand with a sign: "Please Raise Your Precious Ideas." It was supposed to hold a "comment book" for customers. But someone had taken the book away. Next to it was a blue-painted wooden stand labeled "Public Scales," a thoughtful device so shoppers could weigh their purchases and ensure they had not been cheated. But the scale was missing too. The absent book and scale were an ironic reminder of the gap between Mao's call to "serve the people" and the everyday neglect of consumers.

As we walked a few blocks down the street, we came across several peasants in from the countryside squatting on the sidewalk and offering some of their produce for sale. There were live chickens trussed up in the small, black-plastic airline-style bags that many Chinese like to carry, piles of dried watermelon seeds, and candied crab apples on skewers. Knots of people had gathered around two of the hawkers; we pushed closer to look. A middle-aged man in a heavy, faded blue overcoat was holding out mimeographed papers. I couldn't see what they were, but Li laughed. They were crib sheets for the college entrance exam in math. A younger man with a mustache and hair down to his collar—a small sign of rebellion—had a stack of women's shoes. The Wangs explained that he had probably bought up all the popular styles and sizes when they came on sale in one of the few government shoe stores. Now he was reselling them at a markup of 20 percent. All these forms of private enterprise had been prohibited during the decade from 1966 to Mao's death and the overthrow of the radicals in 1976 as a "tail of capitalism." But Deng had decreed that China still needed some free markets to supplement the state-planned economy. The trouble was, the government never clearly defined how much private commerce was permitted, so selling chickens or reselling shoes was always risky and remained part of the quasilegal back-door system.

The practice of "taking the back door" had begun on a small scale in the 1950s, the Wangs and other Chinese said. But with the breakdown of governmental authority in the Cultural Revolution and a stagnant economy, the back door had really blossomed in the 1970s into a major nationwide phenomenon. It had become so widespread, the Wangs told me, that it had spawned its own jokes. Peking residents liked to tell the story of the old woman who waited in line all day at the market to buy a fish. After hours of queueing in vain, she spotted several well-dressed customers walk past with large fresh fish in their straw baskets.

"Comrade, where did you get the fish?" she inquired.

"Through the back door," was their reply.

But when the woman went around behind the market to look, all she found was a locked gate.

"There is a back door," another elderly bystander told her, sensing her plight. "But it is closed to you and me."

The Wangs, however, like other Chinese, did not find anything amusing about their difficulty in buying food. For to Chinese, food is an obsession. When Chinese greet each other, they don't say, "Hello, how are you?" but "Have you eaten or not?" When Chinese measure population, they don't count heads, as Westerners do, but *kou,* or "mouths." The word for population is *ren-kou,* "people mouths." When Chinese want to express appreciation, I found, they don't give flowers; that would be too ephemeral and is reserved for funerals. Instead they bring fruit, something to eat. To entertain, Chinese don't host cocktail parties, they put on lavish banquets, sometimes costing several months' salary. Then as soon as the eating is over, the guests depart. The food is the thing, not the talk.

I remember a spectacular nine-course luncheon in an unpretentious little restaurant in the Nine Dragons Slope district of Chongqing, the city in Sichuan that was Chiang Kai-shek's wartime capital. Cooking in Sichuan is a serious business, dating back two thousand years to the legendary Three

Kingdoms period, and the head chef in the restaurant, Zhang Kaichi, was one of only eight men in the city of six million people to earn the title of master chef. In the kitchen, a dark smoky chamber warmed by a bank of six open coal stoves, Zhang explained that the essence of Sichuan cuisine is *ma-la-tang,* or numbing, spicy, and scalding hot. The numbing taste derives from tiny Sichuan peppercorns, which actually left my lips insensate. His own favorite dish, Zhang said, was an explosively hot concoction with the misleading name of "meat slices cooked in water." I had never seen it on the menu of the burgeoning number of Sichuan restaurants in the United States; when it arrived, I understood why. It was a formidable sight; an almost inch-thick reddish-brown sauce laced with ground fried chilies and crushed pepper-corns was still bubbling on its surface, hiding strips of pork and vegetables beneath. Although long an aficionado of Sichuan cooking, I hesitated before digging my chopsticks into the dish. The meat, prepared with egg whites, was tender, but the spice was ferocious. Sensing my plight, a waitress immediately proferred a hot towel to wipe my forehead.

Other dishes that followed included a salty duck smoked with camphor and tea, a Sichuan specialty, a chicken with peanut granules, spiced with garlic, ginger, and pickles, a peppery bean-curd treat, and a clear—and blessedly mild—fish-ball soup. Then came a delicate velvet chicken, Sichuan-style, chicken breasts pounded to a gossamer texture and served with fresh mush-rooms, bamboo shoots, and spinach, with just a hint of chili. The meal was completed with another Sichuan favorite, "fish fragrance meat shreds." The name, Zhang explained, does not mean fish is used in the cooking, but simply that it is prepared in the same fashion as any sensible Sichuanese would serve a fish—with a blend of ginger, onions, garlic, vinegar, and chilies.

The Chinese preoccupation with food grows out of the country's condi-tion. For three millennia, though China's chefs had unlocked the secrets of sauce and spice, millions of Chinese have not been sure where their next meal was coming from. The Communists ended the tragic famines of the past, an important accomplishment, and have doubled grain output since 1949. But I was surprised how meager the diet of many Chinese remains. The *People's Daily* reported that Chinese eat only fourteen pounds of meat a year, thirteen pounds of fruit, twelve pounds of fish. Chinese consumption of sugar is only one tenth the world average. Consequently most of the protein and calories Chinese get—and they get an average of only 2,000 to 2,100 calories a day, far below the U.S. figure of 3,200—come from rice, wheat, corn, or other grains. This takes its toll on energy levels.

In the industrial city of Shenyang, in the northeast, I met a crew-cut twenty-seven-year-old student who used the English name of John. Tall, self-confident, and outspoken, he had worked for five years in a factory before being admitted to college and, under the Chinese system, continued to receive his full salary of 40 yuan ($26) a month while in school. That was lucky, he calculated, because he spent almost the entire amount to supplement the university cafeteria diet so he would have enough stamina to study.

"Some of my friends, if they jog in the morning, the way the university president tells us to, get drowsy and doze off in class," John said. They had to live on the regular government subsidy for college students of only 19 yuan ($12.60) a month. Their daily diet, as John described it, was a breakfast of steamed bread and salted vegetables; a dish of vegetables and some fatty pork for lunch—which by itself cost 50 fen (Chinese cents), a total of 15 yuan a month—and more steamed bread with some cold vegetables for dinner. On Sundays the school cafeteria served only two meals, at 10 A.M. and 3 P.M. "Sundays, we often end up hungry," John said.

Although at first I was inclined to dismiss his account as too bleak to be true, I found that students at other colleges across China ate roughly the same way. At Yunnan University, in the southwest, an American woman teaching there, Elizabeth Booz, told me her students got meat only three times a week, and it was usually just fat. Even so, their government allowances tended to run out before the end of the month, so some of the students would pool their resources. The girls, being smaller, tended to eat less rice than the boys, Mrs. Booz said, and so again they would share their grain ration coupons with their male classmates. At Peking University, some American exchange students studying there said they felt their own energy slipping when they ate only in the university dining room for more than a few days at a time.

"Because of the constant shortage of food, your mind isn't on your work a lot of the time," a reserved, courteous, but intense archaeologist said. "People are always thinking and scheming how to get some food for their next meal. It is one of the greatest causes of inefficiency in China.

"The cadres are not aware of the problem because they don't have to go through it," he went on. "They have maids to do their shopping, or special purchase cards to get into the shops for cadres only, and they have more opportunities for back-door trade-offs.

"But it affects people's working habits. In my office, you are supposed to be at work at eight A.M. But many people are not there till eight fifteen or eight thirty. What they are doing is shopping.

"Then at ten, when we get our fifteen-minute morning break, some people take off for half an hour, forty minutes, or even longer in search of food. When lunchtime comes, people break at eleven thirty instead of twelve to make sure they get the daily dish in the cafeteria with meat in it. If they are late, the meat will be all gone."

This propensity of Chinese to bolt their offices at 11:30 sometimes baffles and frustrates foreigners, who put it down, mistakenly, to laziness. Not long after I arrived in China, John Rich, a former NBC television correspondent who now represents RCA in Asia, checked into the Peking Hotel with a team of RCA specialists to present a seminar to the Chinese on satellite communications. They had flown to China at their own expense, and they were enthused that they were offering the Chinese their first chance at some highly advanced technical information. But on the first day, with the Americans in the midst of their talks, their Chinese host suddenly asked them to stop. It was 11:30, he said, all the Chinese scientists present had to leave for lunch. The Americans were stunned; couldn't lunch wait a few minutes? No, said the Chinese official. And the Chinese walked out.

If getting enough to eat remains an obsession for Chinese, other routines of daily life which Westerners take for granted—buying furniture, taking a bath, finding a house—require all the connections, luck, and artifice that Chinese can muster. When Jan Wong, my Canadian-Chinese assistant, and her husband, Norman Shulman, wanted to buy furniture for their apartment, they quickly discovered that to purchase three of the most essential items, a double bed, a folding dinner table, and a dresser-cabinet, you had to have a special ration coupon issued only to newly married couples. To prevent cheating, you also had to present your marriage certificate, which the furniture shop stamped on the back. Even so, it took a six-month wait to get a bed, the *People's Daily* once disclosed.

There was a terrible shortage of wood. In a scathing article, the *Workers' Daily* reported that in 1957, when the population was only 600 million, four million cubic meters of timber were allotted for carpentry in the state plan and 40 million articles of furniture were produced. But because of lack of concern with the consumer, in 1979, with close to a billion people, only two million cubic meters of timber were designated for carpentry and only 20 million pieces of furniture were turned out, half the production of two decades earlier. And 50 percent of that lumber went to government offices, the paper added.

When Norman, an American from New York who had lived in China since 1965 and worked as a computer technician for the Academy of Sciences, investigated the state shops that sold new furniture, he learned that you had to line up by 6 A.M. on a day when the stores expected a shipment of new goods. Otherwise, within a few hours, everything would be sold out and the shops would close up for the day, leaving only a blackboard outside with the date of the next arrival. One back-door alternative was to hire a group of unemployed young men who had set themselves up in business and for a fee would take your place in line, starting as early as 3 A.M.

Given these difficulties, what most Chinese did, I learned, was to become amateur carpenters. Soon after arriving in China I visited the apartment of a man whose father was a general in the People's Liberation Army. From upstairs came a constant sound of hammering, shaking the room and making conversation difficult.

"They are building the Four Modernizations," my friend said sarcastically, referring to the government's program to develop farming, industry, science, and national defense. "They start at seven A.M. and then after work they go at it again, making their own furniture."

His wife, a slender woman with long hair and a finely shaped up-turned nose, laughed at his complaint. She pointed to the small two-seat sofa I was sitting on. She called it a *shafa,* one of the few foreign words to make its way into Chinese, by nature an exclusive, xenophobic tongue that rejects imports. They had built the sofa themselves, she said, from metal springs they had bought in a store and pieces of wood scavenged from a nearby apartment under construction. Since lumber and other building materials are in such short supply, pilfering had become a major business, other Chinese said. I noticed that at night, though cars in China are forbidden to drive with their headlights on, evidently to save energy, and many streets and buildings are not lit, construction sites usually basked in floodlit splendor as a precaution.

In the building where Jan and Norman lived when she first began working for me, Jan had to share a shower with the other women. They got hot water three times a week in the summer, twice a week in the winter, for one hour at a time. It was from 5 to 6 P.M., the hour before people got out of work, so they took their baths on office time, just as many Chinese did their grocery shopping. The odd bath times of different *danwei* were a frequent topic of conversation among Chinese, I noticed. At the Second Foreign Languages Institute, located in farmland east of Peking, the students and faculty got their showers two afternoons a week, from noon all the way to 6 P.M. But the two afternoons were Wednesday and Thursday. The reason, a teacher explained, was that the workers who ran the bathhouse wanted to work only two consecutive days and took the rest of the week off. "There has been criticism from the students and teachers, but there is nothing we can do about it," my friend said.

The short hours for bathing were presumably also designed by the government as an economy measure to conserve scarce fuel. But Chinese I knew regarded the situation as a serious inconvenience because most were fastidious about keeping themselves clean. This led to still another set of stratagems. Jan used to take baths in our office in the Peking Hotel, which had hot water twenty-four hours a day, a royal privilege. Lao Wu didn't have hot water or a bathtub in his apartment either. Sometimes, he said, on his way home from work he would stop at the headquarters of his *danwei,* where they had showers for their employees. Other times he would bathe in *The Times*'s office.

Equally inconvenient and uncomfortable was the government's strict policy of not turning on the heat in buildings until November 15, no matter what the weather. My first year in Peking, winter arrived early. By the first few days of November the lakes in the North Ocean Park behind the Forbidden City were frozen, a bitter, dry wind blew down across the Gobi Desert from Siberia, and the temperature fell to 10 degrees fahrenheit (− 10 degrees centigrade). But Chinese who lived in apartments or worked in offices with central heating still had to wait till the magic date of November 15. The only remedy was to pile on layers of undergarments, sometimes as many as four or five—long, knitted woolen pants called *maoku,* silk-padded long underwear, sweaters and more sweaters, till people moved with the grace of penguins. Americans who balked at turning down their thermostats to 65 degrees or even 68 degrees because of the oil shortage could hardly imagine what it is like to live in a house that is close to freezing inside. At the Second Foreign Languages Institute, some of the classrooms had no heat all winter. To make matters worse, a teacher told me, his room had many empty windowpanes, the result of fighting during the Cultural Revolution over ten years before. Students had to stamp their feet during class and wear gloves in order not to get frostbite.

One afternoon when I was walking around an old section of Peking, down a series of narrow alleys fronted with anonymous gray-brick walls, I was intrigued by a series of small handwritten signs affixed to a lamppost. Several were written on bright, eye-catching red and yellow paper, the others merely on sheets torn from a school notebook. They all involved one subject— housing. "Wanted to exchange," one of these notices read, "a two-room apartment at 125 Andingmen Street, of 11.8 square meters, for a home nearer to Qianmen or the Number 7 trolley bus route." The author, whose name was Huang, went on to explain in cursive but plaintive form that he needed to be closer to his job and that he had been looking for a new place for two years.

Unlike the United States or Europe, where there are classified ads in the newspapers or real estate agents to help you find housing, in China most people have only one choice—to apply to a government housing office. Only 10 percent of the housing in China's cities is still privately owned; the rest is allocated either by city housing departments or by some of the larger factories, offices, and schools that have their own buildings.

"When you register for a new apartment," said a translator who worked in the Academy of Social Sciences, a government think-tank, "the first thing they do is measure your current housing. If you have more than three square meters per person, forget it. They won't consider you. You will have to find something on your own, through the back door or by putting up a sign and hoping." She herself had been married for three years, but still lived with her husband's parents and his brother in their old Chinese-style courtyard house, a low, one-story structure with a tile roof. It had three small rooms, one of which she and her husband had built themselves so they could have a room of their own. It was just large enough for their bed and a tall wooden cabinet. They shared a kitchen and toilet with neighbors in a surrounding compound that had once belonged to a wealthy merchant.

She and her husband were victims of the acute housing shortage that has hit China's cities. The Communists have pointed proudly to their record of keeping the cost of housing low and affordable to all. Most Chinese I knew paid only two or three dollars a month in rent, a fabulous bargain compared to the $1,000 a month it can cost for an apartment in New York or Tokyo and the $500,000 it takes to buy a fashionable house in Los Angeles. But the other side of the coin has been that the average allotment of housing space per person in China's cities is only 3.6 square yards, about the size of a large dining-room table. That is less than half the average amount in the Soviet Union, which itself has long had a serious housing problem. I noted once that the New China News Agency reported that 35 percent of all urban families in China had a "housing problem" and "5 to 6 percent of them do not have proper housing at all." A forty-five-year-old schoolteacher I met slept on the desk in his classroom because he did not have an apartment. His housing had been confiscated in the Cultural Revolution when he was declared a capitalist roader, and the government had not found him new quarters since.

The major cause of the shortage has been that the government, following Stalin's lead, treated housing as an item of consumption and therefore saw it as having less legitimate claim on the country's scarce resources than construction for factories or office buildings. This was another of those strategic errors which Mao's successors belatedly recognized and tried to correct, with a burst of new housing projects in the late 1970s. In 1979 alone the government put up 118 million square yards of housing, one sixth of the total built nationwide since 1949. But even this figure is less impressive than it sounds. In the United States in the same year, 267 million square yards of housing were built, for a population that is only one quarter of China's and was already far better housed.

Even after people finally are assigned a new apartment, their troubles aren't necessarily over. Jan and Norman were told by the Academy of Sciences that they would soon be given a new apartment in a series of luxury buildings being put up for high-level officials of the academy, senior scientists, and overseas Chinese researchers who had volunteered to come back to the motherland. They waited expectantly for word to move, but a year elapsed before they were allowed to occupy their new quarters. Part of the delay, they discovered later, was that the construction workers objected that the interior of the apartments was too bourgeois—they had terrazzo floors, wallpaper, and a frosted-glass partition between the living room and the dining area, all unheard of in Peking. So the workers had gone on strike.

When they actually did move in, Jan and Norman found other reminders of the shoddy workmanship that often gives Chinese buildings a predilapidated look. Plaster was falling from the ceiling, the bathtub was cracked in two places, the closet door was too big to close, and a pile of lime lay frozen on the kitchen floor.

The lime got hacked away when fellow workers in Norman's *danwei,* including his unit's Party secretary, volunteered to come over to help. But Jan then discovered that the telephone company would not install a phone and the local government grain shop would not sell them rice or wheat.

"We were baffled at first," said Jan. But later they learned that their trouble was just part of another back-door practice. "Some friends told us that the telephone company was negotiating with the Academy of Sciences to try to get a share of the new apartments for itself before it would put in any phones. It was extortion."

Still, she considered herself lucky. The *People's Daily* reported that in some new buildings there was no running water or electricity because the city water and electric power agencies had demanded a number of the apartments for themselves from the *danwei* that put them up. Jan's aunt, a ranking intellectual in Tianjin, China's third largest city, was assigned an apartment in a special new project for high-level officials. The post office used a similar ploy. It would not recognize the existence of her building, so every day her aunt had to go back across the city to her old apartment to fetch her mail.

5. Eating Bitterness

吃 苦

LIHUA

"Everyone is given a difficult sutra to read."
                                    A Chinese proverb

She was only six years old when it happened.

Until then, Lihua ("Strength for China") had lived in a spacious apartment in Peking with her three older brothers, a younger sister, her father, who was a scientist, and her mother, a nurse. They thought of themselves with pride as what the Chinese call intellectuals, the carriers of the great tradition. Her mother used to tell the children about her own grandfather, who had passed one of the imperial exams under the Qing dynasty before the turn of the century and had held a sinecure job in the court in Peking.

But they had a neighbor who was jealous of them. He was a worker and a Communist Party member, in Chinese terms a good class status. But he drank and smoked a lot, his wife was unemployed, and he had a hard time supporting their five children. In 1966, at the start of the Cultural Revolution, the neighbor moved quickly to organize a radical faction in their apartment building in support of Mao. His new position enabled him to examine Lihua's father's confidential dossier in the Party's files; in it he found her father had once been briefly a member of the Kuomintang before 1949 when he was a student. That was enough to convict him. A rally was held, Lihua's father was judged a "hidden counterrevolutionary," and he was stripped of his teaching post.

"Red Guards came to search our house, they confiscated everything," she recalled. "They took my father's books, my mother's jewelry, her college photo albums, our furniture. Then they built a bonfire in the yard outside and burned everything.

"That was the end of my childhood," Lihua said.

Afterward, the Public Security Bureau ordered her entire family to move to a village in a remote part of Hunan province, eight hundred miles south of Peking. It was punishment for her father's supposed past sins. Lihua's ancestors had come from the village, Gold Mountain, but neither her mother nor father had ever lived there, and no one in the family knew how to farm. Six teen-age Red Guards accompanied the family on the three-day train trip to make sure they got there.

"When we arrived, the local cadres took away the few things we had left, our clothes and our bedding. They left us only what we had on our backs." The family was put in the village schoolhouse, a small one-room building with holes in the walls where the windows should have been and a roof that leaked. There was no furniture. Lihua had to learn to sleep on the mud floor. The school had already been closed by the Cultural Revolution. The teacher had been arrested as a reactionary.

"The peasants and the cadres made my parents parade through the streets every day for several weeks," she related. "They hung a placard around my father's neck, they made him kneel down to confess his crimes, and they beat both my father and mother with iron bars.

"A person is made of flesh. If you beat them long enough, they will die." Within a month her mother was dead and her father was left deaf and unable to use his right arm.

"My mouth is very stupid because I didn't go to school, but these are a few of the facts."

Lihua recounted this story the first time we met in September 1979 on the steps of the Peking Municipal Party Committee Headquarters, a functional gray-concrete building. I had gone there when I heard there were a number of petitioners from the countryside standing outside the Party office trying to present their grievances to the city authorities. It was one of those periods when China's leaders temporarily relaxed their control. Some young factory workers and students took advantage of the slack to put up wall posters or print unofficial journals criticizing the regime, what we foreign correspondents came to call the "democracy movement." Thousands of other people materialized from the countryside asking to have their own personal cases reexamined. The Chinese referred to them as *shang-fang,* meaning they were "entreating a higher level for help." Lihua was one of these.

I didn't notice her at first. I was interviewing an eighteen-year-old man, dressed in a faded, soiled pair of loose blue trousers, who said he had been sold by his father for a pig after the family had been forced out of Peking during the Cultural Revolution. Lihua had come over and stood quietly by my side, waiting for me to finish asking the other man questions. She didn't look like a petitioner. She was wearing a neat tomato-red cotton jacket, with a blue- and white-striped shirt underneath. Her long hair, worn in braids to her waist, was carefully combed; her skin was creamy, unlike most peasants, who have been burned brown by years in the sun; and her teeth were straight and white. Above all, it was the easy smile on her broad face—she didn't look angry. She talked in a calm, dispassionate voice, almost as if all this had happened to someone else, but her story soon gathered a crowd.

After her mother died and her father became an invalid, she had to find a way to earn a living, for the cadres in charge of the village retroactively labeled her family "landlords" and at first wouldn't let her brothers take part in working in the collective fields or have their own small private plot for raising vegetables. The one thing she found she could do as a six-year-old was to go out to the mountains around the village to collect firewood to sell to a brick kiln nearby.

"I would walk thirty li [ten miles] up to the hills at sunrise every day, then back that evening. Sometimes I had to carry a hundred pounds, almost twice my weight. But I was inexperienced and often cut myself with the ax," she said. When I looked down at her hands, there were long scars on the backs of both hands and a gash down the middle finger of her left hand from the tip of the nail to the first joint. "We didn't have enough money to pay for a doctor to stitch it," she explained. The village, as part of a commune, had a cooperative medical program, but families of landlords were not eligible to join.

"In that first year, our clothes soon became like tattered pieces of paper. I had to teach myself how to sew for the family by taking apart our old clothes and then putting them back together.

"I was born into the new society," she went on, using a Chinese expression for the years after the Communists' victory in 1949. "I grew up under the Red flag and at first I didn't understand how such things could happen. But gradually I came to realize that I represent many thousands of people. It is just like in the old feudal society before Liberation. We Chinese must still *chi-ku,* 'eat bitterness.' Nothing has really changed.

"As humans, we should have rights, the right to a job, to get an education, but the cadres often treat us like dogs and pigs," she said, still speaking in her level, matter-of-fact tone, addressing both me and the crowd around her.

I broke off our talk here. It was as much as I could listen to that morning, and I was getting nervous about the size of the crowd, now over a hundred people. It was noontime, and a number of Party officials were coming out of their offices. A cadre in his fifties, gray-haired and dressed in a well-tailored Mao tunic, walked down the steps and into a chauffeur-driven black Mercedes that was waiting. He did not stop to talk to any of the petitioners. I was with Jan Wong, my assistant, who dressed and looked like a Peking college student, a useful disguise. Jan wrote out *The Times*'s office phone number, and Lihua agreed to meet us again.

I felt depressed by Lihua's story, but euphoric about meeting her. Confined to Peking, it was rare for me to encounter someone from the countryside. Most Chinese I knew were city people, and the Information Department had rebuffed all my requests to live even for a few days in a village. Yet four fifths of China's one billion people were peasants, and perhaps 200 million of them still lived in isolated areas in conditions that the government itself described as verging on poverty. By chance, Lihua's village was in one of the most remote and poorest regions, the Jinggangshan, a legendary belt of forested mountains on the border of Hunan and Jiangxi provinces. Mao had taken advantage of its isolation and backwardness to set up his first guerrilla base there in 1928. At our next meeting, I asked Lihua if she would describe life in Gold Mountain. I didn't have to put another question to her—she was a born raconteur, like one of the traditional storytellers who recited picaresque sagas of adventure and misfortune at rural fairs.

Evidently little had changed since Mao's Red Army days in the Jinggang-shan in the 1930s, she indicated. From her village it was still a half day's walk to the nearest road. There was no electricity—most villages now do have electric power, the government claims—and no running water. The peasants used ponds and irrigation ditches to wash their clothes. Gold Mountain had seven hundred inhabitants, in one hundred families, larger than the average village because the government had formed it by consolidating four separate hamlets scattered across a mountain during the Great Leap Forward in 1958. Officially it was designated as a production team, the lowest of the three tiers that make up a commune, but in size it was more like a brigade, the middle level.

"Our village used to be in an area the people called the land of rice and fish," Lihua said. "The land was fertile, rainfall was plentiful, rice grew in the paddies, and the peasants had to work only half the year to survive."

But the Great Leap Forward in 1958, when Mao ordered the formation of the communes, altered all that, she asserted. Mao had calculated that China could be transformed almost overnight from a poor agricultural country to a modern industrial power if the peasants labored hard enough in the fields and began enough small-scale rural factories. In Gold Mountain, the cadres tried to produce Mao's miracle. Some officials in Peking believed there was coal in the area, so the peasants were told to dig tunnels in all their fields. The rice and sweet potato crops were left to rot in the rush, though no coal was found. Some other ministry determined that the peasants could increase their supply of fertilizer by cutting down all the trees around the village, and spreading the ashes on the fields. That left them without fuel for cooking and heating their homes.

When Lihua's family arrived in the village a few years later, it had still not recovered. They found themselves constantly short of food. "We had to borrow or beg a few ounces of rice or sweet potatoes from the other peasants," she remembered. "My brothers didn't know how to cook, so I had to learn that also. I would put the rice in a pot, with too much water for it, to make a thin gruel, then add in whatever vegetables we could scavenge, maybe some cabbage, turnips, scallions, wild herbs, or mushrooms from the mountains. The peasants say, 'There are poor people, but no poor mountains.' You couldn't cut down the mountains."

Her hunts in the mountains were not always successful. "I was still very young, and I didn't know what I could pick and eat. One day I was poisoned by something I had gathered. My face turned purple, I vomited, and was delirious. An old woman saved me with some herbal medicine she had.

"Sometimes we were so short of food we had to eat the husks of the rice too. I would make them into pancakes. But they were so hard, I couldn't swallow them unless I was very hungry. I would carry one up to the mountains and eat it when I was cutting firewood.

"For years we couldn't get cooking oil," she said, meaning vegetable oils like peanut or rapeseed oil that the Chinese use for frying their food. "There was so little oil our cooking pot got rusty."

Lihua blamed this diet for her current health problems. Her hair was falling out in clumps when she brushed it, she said; her eyes hurt when she read, and she often felt weak or dizzy. I noticed that at lunch she ate only two or three mouthfuls of rice and some chicken soup. She had no appetite for more, she insisted. Over the next few months, as we met several dozen times, I never saw her eat a normal meal.

Lihua's family faced other shortages too. They couldn't buy soap or matches. Each peasant family was supposed to get a pack of 1,000 matches a year, but the cadres in Gold Mountain took that ration away from Lihua's brothers and sisters, as they had been labeled landlords. "We had to take a bundle of loose straw to a neighbor's house to borrow fire," she recalled. "They took pity on us." Soap simply wasn't available.

The peasants in Gold Mountain ate meat only five or six times a year, on the traditional festival days like the lunar New Year, she said. Before 1949 the peasants never had much meat either, but the problem had been compounded by the Communists' limits on the number of chickens and pigs each family could raise. Mao had been afraid that a family that grew more than a few animals would turn into capitalists. So each household in Gold Mountain, Lihua related, had been restricted to raising one pig and two chickens. They had to be sold to the state, at the state's low, fixed price.

"If you slaughtered them yourself, the cadres would ask for a piece," she said. "Once at New Year's, they asked us for a whole pig. If they were being polite, the cadres would say, 'Such and such a cadre is coming down for a visit from a higher level for a visit and we need some money for his food.

It is your duty to give it.' Sometimes they would just get people to write a slip to the production team to borrow money from the collective account. Then they took the money for themselves. It was up to you to repay it." Lihua claimed her family had lost about $600 this way, counting chickens, pigs, and cash.

"We called the head of the production team the local emperor. He was master of all. They weren't any different from the landlords in the old society."

The man who was head of the production team when she first arrived in Gold Mountain was a veteran of the Red Army who had gained local prestige by fighting in the Korean war with China's troops. He had now retired and his son had taken over the post. Although China's official policy is that the heads of production teams are to be elected, Lihua said she had never heard of any vote in her village. As far as she knew, the cadres were all appointed by some higher authority.

The team leaders were faced with the problem of trying to make Gold Mountain's production figures look better. The average distribution to able-bodied male peasants at the end of the year in the village, when the harvest of all the crops was added up and state taxes were deducted, came out to 550 pounds of unhusked rice or its equivalent in sweet potatoes, Lihua recalled. That works out to about 380 pounds of edible rice. When she said that, Jan Wong, who was helping me interpret, was shocked. Jan calculated that she, herself, consumed 350 pounds of rice a year in Peking, but that was in addition to the generous amounts of meat, fish, and vegetables she ate every day. Published Chinese government figures suggest that 330 pounds of rice a year is semistarvation rations. Moreover, Lihua added, unlike better-off teams, Gold Mountain had no cash to divide at year's end because the village had no sideline occupations, like growing oranges or silkworms, and no local factories.

One year the cadres decided they could raise production by introducing a new high-yield variety of rice with short stalks they had heard about. But it required extra amounts of fertilizer, which they didn't have, and, as the peasants soon discovered, it was susceptible to insects. To try to overcome the pest problem, the cadres bought new chemical sprays; the pesticides soon killed most of the fish in the village ponds. In the end the crop failed, and the peasants had to go for a year without rice, begging from a nearby village. Even the stalks left in the fields weren't as good for fuel as the old long-stemmed strain.

But the team leader reported an increase in output anyway, Lihua charged, and consequently had to deliver a larger amount to the state. "To cover up what had happened, he ordered us to put what good grain we had on the tops of the rice sacks, to put stalks at the bottom, and rocks in the middle.

"This was our education from the Cultural Revolution.

"Before, the peasants were very *lao shi,*" a Chinese virtue that translates as "honest and upright." "Afterward they became evil. People began to steal from each other's private plots. You had to watch out your neighbors didn't take your chickens or pig. People's philosophy became *guo yi tian, suan yi tian* [get through the day and forget it]. Everyone was very pessimistic."

Lihua herself was growing up in these years. At the early summer and fall harvests (they grew two crops a year), she made her way to a state farm fifteen miles away where they paid 50 cents for every bag of 110 pounds of husked rice she brought in. They also gave her eight pounds of rice to eat.

"That was my best chance of the year. I would work day and night till I couldn't bend from the waist. Then I would lie down and crawl to harvest the rice. In the war the soldiers used to sleep while they marched. I used to sleep while I worked, I was so tired."

Some of the other workers on the state farm were young people who had been sent to resettle in the countryside from their homes in Shanghai. They were part of the 18 million urban Chinese school graduates rusticated on Mao's order after the start of the Cultural Revolution. "When they first arrived, their heads were full of beautiful ideas about the villages," Lihua remembered. "They believed what they had heard, that the land was rich, that the peasants were revolutionary." But once they found how hard life was, they changed. Many of the city youth couldn't work hard enough to support themselves and had to depend on money sent by their parents. Some of the men took to carrying knives and going around in gangs.

"When they showed up in Gold Mountain, it was just like a scene in a movie about bandits. The people all scattered and ran indoors. The chickens flew in the air."

One afternoon when she was thirteen, Lihua recalled, she set out for a small rural market with eggs from their chicken to sell. Her family didn't eat the eggs themselves, they were too valuable. She was walking through a sugar cane field, the maturing cane over her head, and had just crossed a small stream when she saw a man in his early twenties in front of her. He was wearing a watch and glasses, and his clothes were clean, not like a peasant. He asked her to sit down and talk with him.

"I was afraid, my heart was beating fast," Lihua told me. Then he produced a knife from under his shirt. He ordered her to take off her clothes.

"I don't know why I thought of it, but I said, 'You take off your clothes first.'"

The man agreed and, in a bout of modesty, turned his back before loosening his pants. He also put the knife down on the ground.

"When he did, I rushed forward and grabbed it and began stabbing him. Blood spurted all over the place. He fell to the ground, and I kept stabbing him until I thought he was dead. Then I fainted, I can't remember exactly."

When she awoke, it was dark, and she washed herself off in the stream. On her way home she came across the graveyard where her mother was buried. "I dug at her grave with my hands. I wanted to crawl inside." Then she passed out again. The next morning an old man on his way to the mountains to gather wood found her and notified one of her brothers, who came to get her.

"He thought I was overtired. I didn't tell him what had happened." After the incident, she went on, she didn't feel like living anymore. "But I had responsibilities. My little sister was four years younger than me, my father was weak. I decided I would never get married and just devote my life to taking care of them. Men are a bad thing."

There never was an investigation, she said. At the time, with the large number of discontent rusticated students in their area, violence was not uncommon and there had been a number of violent fights and murders in the village.

It was at this period in her life, in her early teens, that Lihua began to listen to the stories of other peasant women about spirits, demons, and ghosts. "I wondered how life could be so cruel. Sometimes at night, when I had gone out to wash our clothes after my day's work was done and hadn't had anything to eat, I would look up at the moon and wish some fairy would come down and save me. I began to burn incense, and I thought that I must have been a criminal in an earlier life. When I walked down the road, I imagined that every plant, every tree, was cursing me for my previous life."

There had been a Buddhist temple with a priest in the village before Red Guards destroyed it in the Cultural Revolution, she said. "Some of the peasants said that was the reason the era was so poor." But many of the villagers continued to practice their old rites at home. On the first and fifteenth day of each month they burned incense and put a bowl of rice in front of a picture of the kitchen god, which they kept on an altar. "You were supposed to put meat or fruit in front of the god, but they were too poor," she said.

Lihua's description was the first authentic account I had heard of continued folk religion in the countryside. In theory China's constitution guarantees freedom of religion; but in practice the Communists have tended to see religion as a rival claim to Marxism and have imposed tight restrictions on most religious rituals and beliefs. I was curious, therefore, if other traditional ideas that the Communists had derided as superstition and tried to eradicate had survived. Yes, she said.

"There was a witch in our village. The authorities couldn't do anything about her because she was protected by the *lao bai xing*," literally, the "old hundred names," the Chinese word for common people. "She and the witches in some other villages were really mad, so they weren't treated as commune members by the cadres. They didn't work in the fields. But the people gave them food for their services, like curing illnesses. For example, they will place a bowl of clear water on the altar table in the former temple. That night, the person who was sick would drink it, believing that in the meantime the gods have added some medicine to it."

The peasants in Gold Mountain also practiced a Chinese form of voodoo, she said. "If someone you hate is very sick and you want them to die, to speed up the process you must find out the exact date of their birth. Then you learn some chants for that date, make a wooden doll, and stick it with seven pins. Finally, you burn it at night. The person is guaranteed to die by morning."

Somehow during all these years Lihua managed to educate herself. Her only formal schooling was part of a year in first grade before the family was forced out of Peking. "But I wanted so much to learn," she explained. "My language teacher was a dictionary. Everyone I met was a teacher to me, I could ask them questions. I got a copy of the *Three Character Classic,*" the Confucian moral primer and grammar that generations of Chinese school-boys had to master. It contained short homilies that rhymed in Chinese and could easily be memorized: "At men's beginning their nature is fundamentally good, by nature they are similar but in practice they grow apart." This appealed to Lihua. "Even though the government said it was decadent, I thought it had a lot to teach," she said.

One of her older brothers also tried to continue his education. He had managed to save an English and a Russian dictionary when the family was exiled and he took them with him to the fields during the day. When the peasants took a break from their labor, he would go to a corner of the field to study.

"The peasants didn't understand foreign languages and didn't know what he was doing," Lihua told me later. "They accused him of maintaining illicit relations with foreign countries and being an American spy." She laughed at the memory, her large almond eyes wrinkling up and almost disappearing in the folds of her heavy eyelids. But it wasn't funny at the time. "The peasants took him to a struggle session. They beat him and took away all his notes. But they couldn't find anyone else who could read them to tell them what the notes said." After that, her brother gave up studying.

By now we were meeting once every two or three weeks. I would write her a letter setting the time, and Lihua's short, solid figure would appear at the magazine kiosk across the street from the Peking Hotel. Chinese are always punctual; it is a mark of respect and character to be on time. But Lihua was inevitably late, the only Chinese I knew who was less punctual than I. I finally realized why. She lived on the outskirts of Peking and it took her over an hour's ride on the city's crowded bus system, with three transfers, to get into the center of town. Each ride was an adventure because she didn't have any money, and when the conductor asked for her fare, Lihua would plead that she was in Peking as a petitioner. Lihua also did not have a watch. When I discovered this, the next time I went to Hong Kong on vacation to visit my family, I bought her an inexpensive Japanese wristwatch.

Each time we met we would go for lunch in a different restaurant, hoping to avoid suspicion. Lihua would start talking, and if we managed to get a table in a quiet corner, I would scribble notes as fast as I could, holding my notebook in my lap against the waiters' prying eyes. Some days I had to wait till I got back to my office to type up my recollections. Lihua didn't mind my writing about her; in fact, she said she had kept a diary herself but her father had found it and burned it. He was worried about further retribution. But Lihua seemed to have an endless supply of grit and courage; she was already taking a giant risk by coming to Peking as a petitioner; and she wanted her story to be told. "I want people outside China to know what the Cultural Revolution was like and what the Chinese have been through," she said during one lunch.

I was curious how she had managed to get back from her village to Peking. Her father had made the first effort, she said, in 1969, three years after they had been sent out of the city. He had written to his old institute in Peking appealing for reconsideration. But the school sent his letter back to the village and the cadres had him dragged through the streets and beaten again. He himself never sought redress after that.

"People like him have ink in their stomachs," Lihua remarked. "They are learned, but have no courage."

In 1976, after Mao died and Jiang Qing, his widow, was arrested, Lihua wrote an appeal. But she discovered that the institute had by then been converted into a factory, not an ususual fate for schools during the Cultural Revolution. The officials in charge of the factory didn't recall her father's case, but they were considerate enough to dispatch two men to the village to investigate her charges. Several months later she got the reply. Her father had indeed been wronged. He would be rehabilitated. But he was now so old and weak—he was fifty-eight years old, two years short of normal retirement—that he should retire. There would be a small pension, but no financial compensation for all the years lost. Nor would the factory consider letting the family back into Peking. They had too many members for that. Government policy was to keep the size of the cities down. Therefore the officials would not give Lihua what she most wanted, a change in her *hu-kou,* the household registration certificate that is a key form of identification in China. It specified whether a person lived in the countryside or a city, and which city. A peasant could not get a job or an apartment in the cities without an urban *hu-kou,* nor could he buy grain, oil, or cloth in the cities, since these depended on city ration cards. For Lihua, a Peking household registration certificate was to become the magic talisman, "like a fortune-teller's card in the old society," she remarked. "It held your fate in its hands."

By the summer of 1979 Lihua had turned twenty and was impatient. She had heard about the petitioners coming to Peking and she decided to try herself. Her oldest brother, now thirty-three, had managed to move back to the capital because he had been sent down to the countryside separately, in a different campaign, just before the beginning of the Cultural Revolution. He was working for a construction company and lived in a tiny dormitory room. She could stay with him there temporarily. But this risked a neighbor turning her in to the police. So she developed the first of a series of stratagems, creating good, new *guan-xi.* She discovered that the neighbors needed clothes—the ready-made clothes in the stores fit poorly and Peking's few tailor shops were always busy. Lihua knew how to sew. It was a natural way to ingratiate herself.

"These days you have to do things to buy a person's humanity," Lihua commented.

Then she began making the rounds of all the government offices she thought might help: her father's old school (which had now been converted back to its original teaching function), the Public Security Bureau, the State Council, or cabinet, the High Court, and the Peking city Party Committee, where we met. I asked if she wasn't afraid of being picked up as a troublemaker and put in jail, as I knew some petitioners were.

"No," she replied. "I have no future anyway."

At her father's former institute, an official assigned to deal with petitioners invited her in to talk. They spent two hours each morning for several weeks discussing the case and drinking tea, but an investigation the official promised into her plight never took place. "To the Communists we are just like noodles in the hands of a noodle-maker, something to shape as you like," she said afterward.

One day during her rounds she met another woman petitioner. The woman had a neighbor who had a relative who knew someone in the police. "It was very roundabout, but I began going to the police officer's house. I found they needed clothes for their children, so I began to sew for them, too. They would give me the material, since I couldn't buy any myself."

There was one problem with all this sewing, however. Lihua did not have her own sewing machine. By this time Jan and I felt as caught up in her tale as she was, so we went out and bought her a Chinese copy of an early Singer.

Four months after her initial meeting with the policeman, he also felt sorry enough for her to invite her to write out her story so he might submit it for official consideration.

"I had to be very careful not to complain in explaining how my mother had been killed," she told me a few days later. "I couldn't blame the police. But who do I say is responsible? Even though nobody had done anything, I had to say I was grateful to the Party for its help." She was smiling her girlish smile again. I thought she showed a tenaciousness and sense of strategy beyond her twenty years. She was a gentle diplomat; her only resource was the sympathy she could evoke. "I hate them, but I never let it show," she once explained.

By now it was winter in Peking, and one day I dropped in to see her in the room, thirty feet square, she shared with her brother, his wife, and her younger sister and father, whom she had recently brought up from Gold Mountain. She had sent for her sister so she could get an education, but Lihua had had to use all her negotiating skills to get her into a school because of that missing household registration. Lihua also attended the parent–teacher meetings, since her father remained an invalid. Their room faced north, the undesirable vantage in Peking, letting in the cold and the wind but little light. The room was heated only by a small coal-burning stove, though to save money they didn't use it during the day and my breath showed in little puffs. It might have been forty degrees in the room. Lihua had freshly whitewashed the walls, and even the bare concrete floor she kept spotless—not a speck of dust in a city where most people seemed resigned to the daily damage visited by the dust storms from the Gobi Desert.

Their only furniture was two wide wooden planks planted on sawhorses and covered with cotton pallets the entire family used as its bed. A short wire strung along the wall near the stove was hung with newly washed laundry. On the window sill were twenty bottles of medicine and traditional Chinese tonics, testimony to Lihua's chronic ailments.

After a day's sewing, Lihua got out a low stool, spread a newspaper over the spotless sheet, and used the bed for a desk on which to study. She was trying to learn English.

Finally, the next July, a year after she had come to Peking, she received a notice from the police reporting her family could get its household registration transferred to the capital. But there was a catch. The permission would expire in three weeks and within that time she had to show they had permanent housing in Peking. That was the law: without a city household registration, you couldn't get an apartment; but without an apartment, you couldn't get a household registration.

"I am frantic," Lihua told me the next day. "China is too hopeless." She was wearing her summer costume, a white cotton blouse and yellow flowered skirt she had made herself. (After Mao's death, such departures from orthodox blue were allowable.) In the winter she had one set of clothes she wore every day, in the summer another one. That was all she could afford.

She had gone to the construction company where her brother worked and asked them to write a letter saying she and her father were entitled to live in the company's housing. She promised to move out as soon as she found her own quarters. But the company refused. They were afraid she would stay, like many people in Peking. Eventually, I learned, she got a letter from her father's former school saying they would find housing for him within two months. It was a fib, but with that note she got the construction company to write to the police certifying her residence in their dormitory.

Lihua felt triumphant, but the saga was not over. The cadres in Gold Mountain wouldn't let her two remaining brothers leave. The family still owed the production team $300, they claimed. In Lihua's view, it was a debtor's trap. Because the family had long ago been labeled as landlords, half of all the work points they earned for their daily labor in the fields were deducted as "duty points." As a result, they got only half as much grain at the year-end distribution as other peasants and had to borrow money to live on. Her brothers also had to spend time cultivating land assigned to the team cadres as so-called duty labor. She deduced that the cadres didn't want to lose this form of free serf labor.

"They treated my family as criminals," she complained. In 1979, Peking had announced that the stigma of the landlord class label would be removed, but she claimed it had not been in their village. That left the cadres free to do what they liked with her family. One time she had mailed a packet of shirts and pants she had made for her brothers to Gold Mountain, but they never received the clothes. When Lihua visited the village later, she said the team leader was wearing some of her handiwork.

The situation now appeared hopeless; the three-week deadline was approaching and her brothers were still down in the village. They had to arrive in Peking before the end of July or the permit for them to live in the city would expire. Lihua made one last appeal to her father's old school. They agreed to send an official on the three-day train trip to Gold Mountain to talk with the cadres there. Finally, the team leader consented; he would reschedule the debt. The family could repay from Peking. The two missing brothers appeared a day before the deadline.

I saw Lihua a few more times after that. She was busy studying. She had spotted an advertisement for a new school set up by the city for unemployed young people. It would train them to be primary school teachers. Admission required a high school education, but Lihua spun her usual story and the head of the school agreed to let her take a test to see if she had taught herself as well as a regular school would have. She passed.

After my wife moved to Peking and we had our own apartment, Lihua came over for lunch one day. It meant walking past the two middle-aged women who operated the elevator in our building. But that was easy for her.

When the elevator women stared at her on the way up to the eleventh floor, trying to fix her description for their report to the Public Security Bureau, she smiled back and asked the polite Chinese question, "Have you eaten or not?"

She had brought a pair of tiny cotton shoes she had sewn for our baby, Sarah, and a piece of lace she had made for Barbara.

I noticed she was not wearing the watch I had given her. Now that her brothers had come, she explained with embarrassment, she was worried that they would be jealous about such an expensive item, so she had hidden it. "I don't want to cause a contradiction in my family. We have managed so far to stay together despite our problems. I don't want to spoil that."

In her modest way, she had the virtues Chinese have always prized: devotion to her family, carefully controlled emotions, a willingness to work hard, and a passion for knowledge. At the same time, she also had that ability to use people and situations, *guan-xi,* to her own advantage. In others it might have seemed manipulation; in Lihua it grew out of desperation and added to her attraction. To me she was the quintessential Chinese, proof that the Confucian character had not been wiped out.

There was another Chinese trait too—her righteous anger. Confucius taught moderation and never losing one's temper, but China did not have the moral of turning the other cheek. The last time we met I asked Lihua if, now that her family was safely in Peking, her unhappiness with the Communists had abated. No, she replied.

"People say that now that I've got my household registration, I should be happy. But I won't be happy till I die. I've never lived a good day in my life. My mother was beaten to death, my father was left senseless, and I still have to beg for everything.

"That is what the Cultural Revolution did. It is unfixable. My scars will never heal."

PART
2

PASSAGES

—

6. Sex Without Joy

爱情与婚姻

LOVE AND MARRIAGE

"To die over an unhappy love affair is absolutely worthless. You should plunge yourself into the hot struggle for production and gradually your wounds will be healed."
Advice from the editors of **China Youth News** *to a lovelorn young man jilted by his girl friend*

Lili was an exceptionally pretty teen-ager, with smooth white skin, shiny black hair, and delicately carved features. Her father was a senior general in the People's Liberation Army, and she had always led a comfortable life. She went to a special school for children of high cadres, her family had a spacious house, and there was a maid to help with the chores. Until the Cultural Revolution in 1967. Then her father was arrested on trumped-up charges of being a capitalist roader. He was taken to a struggle session where he was shouted at, insulted, and spit on, and then dragged off to prison where he was tortured to death. Lili's mother, the daughter of a former landlord and a woman unaccustomed to hardship, went mad and died. Because her father had been branded a traitor, the family's house was confiscated and Lili was expelled from high school. At the age of seventeen Lili was left alone to fend for herself and her younger sister, who was twelve.

A mutual friend who recounted Lili's adventures said that her only recourse was to become a beggar, for her only other resources, her clothes, a silk bedspread, her cello, were soon sold off for food. Her younger sister fell ill, probably from eating nothing but boiled cabbage leavings from the market in the city of Hangzhou, where they lived. Lili was desperate.

That was when the envelopes began to arrive every month with 50 yuan ($33) inside and no return address. It was more than an average month's wage at the time. At first Lili could not believe it and put the money aside.

"But," she said, "when no one came around knocking at the door, I decided to use the money for my sister." The money continued to come until two years later when Lili made it into the army. Because of her good looks and her musical talent, she was put into a military song and dance troupe that traveled around the country entertaining high-level officers.

It was only then, during a visit to Peking, that she discovered who her mysterious benefactor was. He was an old friend of her father's, a general himself, named Cao, who had found out where Lili was and sent the money. Naturally Lili felt an enormous debt to him and went to see him whenever her ensemble performed in Peking.

There was one slight problem. Cao had a son who was also an army officer, stationed in Sichuan, in the southwest, and Cao very much wanted Lili to marry him. Cao brought the subject up many times, but Lili had never met the son and she always put Cao off good-naturedly, pleading that she was too young to get married. In fact, Lili did not like the old-fashioned idea of an arranged marriage, which the Communists had formally declared illegal with their progressive family law of 1950, one of their first pieces of legislation after Liberation. But Cao persisted. He got his son transferred up from Sichuan to Peking so Lili could meet him—that only increased the trouble. She didn't like him at all. He was "empty-headed and interested in nothing but his own pleasure," she found.

Then old Cao fell ill and Lili got a leave of absence to rush to Peking to be with him in the hospital. On his deathbed he pleaded with her to marry his son and let him die a happy man. Lili was distraught. She not only felt a great sense of obligation to Cao, but she was an orphan and had no relatives who could act as go-betweens in the traditional Chinese way to argue her case. Finally she spoke with the son, striking a deal. They would agree in front of Cao to be married, so he could die happily, but she would not marry him.

But as soon as Cao was dead, the son "rushed all around Peking," Lili related, telling his relatives and friends that they were engaged. Lili ignored him, but he increased the pressure. He tried to kill himself, citing his loss of face when Lili reneged on her pledge. Cao's widow then went to the Party secretary of Lili's army *danwei,* charging her with improper conduct. She had agreed to the marriage, now she was backing out. Lili's Party leader called her in for investigation and "advised" her—it was tantamount to an order in the army—to marry the son since she had already committed herself.

The son proposed what looked like a happy solution. "I'm losing too much face with things as they are," he said. Why not just go with him to the local civil affairs office and register their marriage—the official process for getting married in China today—and then they could forget it. She believed him and went to register. But that night he broke into the house where she was staying and, in her view, raped her, since she was unwilling. "I left a nice scar bite on his shoulder as evidence," she recalled.

The friend who told me about Lili's quiet tragedy did not do so to titillate me. She meant only to offer a personal insight into one of the most secretive aspects of life in China, sexual mores. Peking publishes a cornucopia of data on everything from the production of pigs and wristwatches to hydroelectric power. Since Mao's death it has sanctioned the press to write about crime and investigate corruption in the Party. It has even disclosed an official figure for the percentage of the national budget devoted to defense. But sex has usually been treated as if it didn't exist. Indeed, for more than a decade after the start of the Cultural Revolution, love was denounced as a sensual, unnecessary, and decadent bourgeois conceit and banished from public discussion. The Communists themselves came to power as Marxist revolutionaries dedicated to reordering what they decried as the backwardness and injustices of China's feudal society. But their revolution stopped at the bedroom door. Instead, in a state which has "put politics in command," in Mao's phrase, sex and love have become entangled with politics too. Much as the government impinges on the individual through controls over jobs and housing, by restricting travel, and by grouping people into *danwei,* so, too, Peking has helped shape the sex lives of millions of Chinese. Romance, marriage, the number of children a couple can have, divorce, even intercourse, are all subject in one way or another to Communist Party dictates. The result is a mixture our grandparents would be more familiar with than we are. On the surface China seems remarkably chaste and moralistic, Victorian, to borrow a Western term; but behind this apparent primness often lie frustrations and problems of sexual repression.

It is the outer modesty which charms and intrigues foreign visitors. Women eschew makeup, and even after the downfall of the radicals, the majority still dress in formless Mao jackets and baggy trousers that discourage a young man's fancy. Shirts on men and women should always be buttoned up to the top. When I first took up residence in Peking and was still infected with the macho Western custom of leaving my top shirt button undone, a roomboy in the Peking Hotel where I was staying kept reminding me to close it. He thought I had simply forgotten and would be embarrassed when I discovered my omission. In the summertime, a woman with her blouse open, even one button, is considered lewd, and in some cities, Chinese say, her affectation will be taken as a sign she is a prostitute.

In the winter, women are always expected to wear jackets in public. My assistant Jan Wong recalled that, when she was a student at Peking University, her Chinese roommate would always pause to put on her jacket before going to answer a knock at the door, even if she was already wearing a sweater.

But when Chinese women are alone among themselves, without men around, they are not shy about their bodies the way Western women often are. Jan remembers the first time she went to a public bathhouse—many Chinese must use them because of the lack of modern plumbing—and found small groups of naked women happily scrubbing each other's backs with soap and towels. Men do the same thing; in fact, part of the pleasure of going to the bathhouses is to go with a friend or two. There is no implication of homosexuality in this.

In high school and college boys and girls still sit separately, as they did in schools in the United States until a generation or two ago. Female students blush and giggle if asked whether they have a boy friend; few would admit it. Indeed, Chinese themselves usually use the circumlocution "Do you have a friend?" without any romatic overtone, to spare a person embarrassment. During a visit to an English-language class at Yunnan University in Kunming, I tried to coax an admission that the students sometimes thought about members of the opposite sex. "We'd rather study," they chorused in response.

Art Buchwald, the columnist, who was along on the trip, tried to press the question further. "But what do you dream about?" he asked. They only giggled.

It is not unusual to find people in their mid-twenties who have never been on dates, much less have steady boy friends or girl friends. In Shanghai once I quizzed my guide from China Travel Service, a pert twenty-seven-year-old woman with jaunty short pigtails named Yang Guidi, on what she wanted in a husband. "I haven't thought about that," she replied, covering her mouth with her hand in an old Chinese gesture of shyness. "I'm conservative. I have never been out with a boy. I don't like to watch television or dance. Some young people get so excited by such things they forget to study or work. I prefer to read at home, to improve myself, before I go to bed. Then I get up every morning at six thirty and go for a jog." On Sundays, insisted Miss Yang, who is a Party member, she stays home with her father and mother.

For a man to kiss a woman, many Chinese feel, is tantamount to a proposal of marriage, or should swiftly lead to it. A foreign woman who is married to a Chinese and has lived in China for many years recalled an episode when her twenty-eight-year-old daughter came to her in outrage. The daughter was deeply in love with a young Chinese man and was scheduled to marry him the next week. But then her fiancé tried to kiss her. "It's disgusting," the daughter complained. She argued vehemently that she wanted to call off the wedding until her mother explained the facts of life to her. "The average twenty-year-old Chinese woman knows as much about sex as our grandmothers did a hundred years ago," the woman later told me.

According to the Chinese press, kissing is not only in questionable moral taste, it is also downright unhealthy. The *Workers' Daily,* a paper published for factory workers, warned in one memorable article that kissing helps transmit the hepatitis B virus, which is found in 6 to 10 percent of all people, even those in good health. "That's a terrible figure," the paper cautioned. "You could say that these people are dangerous people who could at any moment contaminate their loved ones," since the virus is contained in saliva and works its way from there to the bloodstream. "So one can see that kissing is really dangerous behavior. Adults and children, we must all rid ourselves of this kissing habit," the paper concluded.

Jokes with sexual innuendos are not told in public. Once during a banquet for a delegation of foreign journalists hosted by the deputy governor of Fujian, the province opposite Taiwan, a Yugoslav correspondent was commenting on what China might want from the United States. America is already exporting its technological revolution, the Yugoslav said, raising his glass of *maotai,* the fiery clear liquor. "And now the Americans are trying to export their sexual revolution too." At this, the official interpreter, a pleasant middle-aged man with an excellent command of English, suddenly turned silent and looked at me.

"I think, if you don't mind," he said in English, "it's better not to translate that."

Foreigners, coming from our own overly sex-conscious societies, often applaud this innocence and the downplaying of the erotic in China as a healthy sign—the absence of sex on television, the clothes that aren't designed to reveal every curve of the body. Some visitors have even hypothesized that the Chinese have somehow conquered their libidos by making sex invisible or thinking the good thoughts of Chairman Mao. An earnest Harvard undergraduate who spent the summer working on a commune in China confided afterward that the experience had provided him an unexpected benefit. "Back in Cambridge, I'm always obsessed with sex, I'm always thinking about making it with some girl," he told me. But on the commune, where the women dressed without a thought to sexual attraction and conversation did not turn to boy friends and girl friends, "I just stopped thinking about sex. It wasn't in the air."

No doubt most Chinese are more straitlaced than Westerners today, less sexually flamboyant and promiscuous. We were too, a generation or two back. But the Chinese are not made of plastic either, and the notion that they have learned to surmount their sexual appetites without any consequences is another of those home-grown perceptions which foreigners have projected on China.

To some extent, China's prudish attitude toward sex is an inheritance from the Confucian past. The notion of romantic love was never a respectable one in China. The very term for love between men and women, *lian ai,* is a modern linguistic creation designed to meet the need for an equivalent to the Western expression. In classical Chinese the two components of *lian ai* appeared separately, each meaning love or affection, but in connection with the concept of loyalty between emperor and subject or father and son. Western-style dating, dancing, and necking, any public display of affection, were regarded as licentious by the Chinese. Chinese women could not, as Americans and Europeans do, justify intercourse by invoking a claim to be in love. Since ancient times, relations between men and women had a more serious purpose, marriage. And marriage meant a careful arrangement between two families, to ensure their prosperity and provide for progeny. It was too important a business to be left to the young people themselves. Love came second to parental wishes and was not a reason for acting impetuously. Often the first sight the bride and groom had of each other was when she was brought to her new in-laws' house for the wedding in a covered sedan chair. All this worked in a society where the individual had his center of gravity more in his social relations than in himself and was willing to give first place to the feelings of others.

At the same time, however, Chinese were not burdened by the Western notion that sex itself was sinful. There was no Chinese counterpart to the Christian dogma of immaculate conception and the virgin birth, or the biblical injunction that got Jimmy Carter into trouble in his first campaign: "But I say to you that everyone who looks at a woman lustfully has already committed adultery in his heart." Sex was simply a natural urge, like eating, sleeping, or moving the bowels, to which, said Mencius, the great early expounder of Confucianism, expression should be given in the right time and place. Chinese did not need to feel guilty when making love, as long as they did it with the proper party.

This traditional Chinese view of love and sex is reflected in the country's literature. Chinese novels did not turn on romance, the great theme of Western writing, since romantic love did not play such an instrumental role in Chinese life and thought. But pornography was a highly developed genre, and though Confucian literati might not admit it, few had qualms about viewing the most graphic pictures in private with their spouses or teahouse girls. One of the greatest Chinese novels, *The Golden Lotus,* widely printed before 1949, recounts in salacious detail the roisterous doings of a rich, wastrel merchant named Hsi-men Ching, his relations with his wives and concubines, and his affairs with his neighbors' wives, maids, and prostitutes. The novel, by an unknown sixteenth-century author, was condemned by outraged Western missionaries, but to the Chinese it had artistic appeal. It was the earliest Chinese book about the personal lives of believable, middle-class characters and the first to deal with women as individual personalities. Western writers of erotica did not match it in candor till very recent years.

In the first tryst between Hsi-men Ching and Golden Lotus, one of the heroines of the story who later becomes his concubine, the author sets the scene thus:

> In the days when Golden Lotus had performed the act of darkness with Chan [an earlier lover], that miserable old man had never been able to offer any substantial contribution to the proceedings, and not once had she been satisfied. Then she married Wu Ta. You may imagine the prowess which might be expected from Master Tom Thumb. It could hardly be described as heroic. Now she met Hsi-men Ching, whose capacity in such matters was unlimited and whose skill was exceptionally refined and cunning.
>
> Soon they had drunk as much as they desired, and a fit of passion swept over them. Hsi-men Ching's desire could no longer be restrained; he disclosed the treasure which sprang from his loins, and made the woman touch it with her delicate fingers. Upstanding it was, and flushed with pride, the black hair strong and bristling. A mighty warrior in very truth.
>
> Then Golden Lotus took off her clothes. Hsi-men Ching fondled the fragrant blossom. No down concealed it. It had all the fragrance and tenderness of fresh-made pastry, the softness and the appearance of a new-made pie. It was a thing so exquisite all the world would have desired it.*

In the traditional Chinese view, both prostitution and concubinage were part of nature, not subject to moral denunciation. Much the same casual attitude still prevails in Taiwan today. Once, when I lived in Taipei, I reported to the local police substation for our annual neighborhood security registration, a kind of census. At the head of a line of people stood two women—one, grown into comfortable middle age, with a plump figure and nondescript clothes; the other, ten years her junior, still slender and well made up. When queried by a policeman, they both gave their surname as Huang and listed the same address and apartment number.

"But you can't both be Mrs. Huang," the policeman objected. From the middle of the queue came a voice of explanation. "One's the wife, the other is the concubine." The crowd chuckled at the information, but the two women did not appear embarrassed and the police officer dutifully recorded their names, though taking a concubine is theoretically illegal in Taiwan.

From this traditional approach to sex, the Communists have adopted the first half—that the needs of society should take preference over an individual's pursuit of love—but they have reversed the second half—that sex itself is not sinful. Instead, as part of their effort to control society, the Communists have substituted something new, a rigid puritanism that does lead to guilt and repression. Peking's view comes through in the current vocabulary. There is no widely accepted polite expression in China today for "making love,"

*The Golden Lotus, translated by Clement Egerton (London: Routledge and Kegan Paul, 1939), Vol. I, p. 67.

though the term exists in Taiwan and Hong Kong, probably adopted from the West. When intercourse is mentioned in the Communist press, it always turns out to be lewd, deviant, described by phrases like "improper relations between men and women" or "relations between men and women done in a messy way." Even the vernacular term, "having relations," now has a sordid ring to Chinese.*

"You shouldn't talk about such things," Yang Wanhua, one of my closest friends, chided me when I asked for her reaction to the word. "It is a very dirty thing."

Slim and short, with a pixie turned-up nose, freckles, high, prominent cheekbones, and a forward, direct manner for a Chinese, Hua, as I called her, looked much younger than her age of forty. Her hair was cut very short, in boyish fashion, and her face was unlined. She kept herself in good physical condition by jogging three miles every morning at 5:30 on a track near the Physical Culture and Sports Commission where she worked. She was a re-porter for the sports agency's English-language magazine, *Sports of China.* Hua was also, I came to learn, a Party member and cadre who had enjoyed a brief meteoric promotion during the Cultural Revolution when the radicals who took over the Sports Commission needed a token woman to show they were adhering to Mao's ideas.

Hua had been born to a family of schoolteachers in a small town near Canton. Soon after the Communists came to power and then the Korean War broke out in 1950, she dropped out of primary school. "It was the time of the revolutionary high tide," she explained. "I was very young and innocent and believed everything the Party said. I was an activist, so I joined the revolution at the age of twelve." Translated, it meant she went to work as a clerk in a Canton Party office. At night she continued to study on her own and practiced swimming with the local city team where she was a champion backstroker. She still moves gracefully, with the gait of an athlete, her legs springing rather than walking.

By the time Hua was nineteen, she had already been selected as a Party member, a very early age for the honor. She also had a boy friend. "He was the captain of the city soccer team," Hua told me with a hint of pride not long after we first met while we were both looking at rugs in the Friendship Store. She was acting as guide and interpreter for a group of visiting Aus-tralian sports coaches.

For a year, Hua and her boy friend used to go for walks in one of Canton's parks. Parks are one of the few places where young Chinese couples can find

*There is, however, a substantial lexicon of vulgar slang terms men use to describe sexual activity. "Give her a blast" is a street term meaning to screw. One ingenious Chinese ideogram is composed of two characters—one for the word enter, the other for flesh. It, too, means to fuck someone.

privacy, since there are almost no automobiles and unmarried people can't get their own housing. "It was very serious, almost like getting married, we were very much in love," Hua recalled. "We kissed a lot, but we never did more than that, there was no way." Her boy friend lived in a dormitory run by the Sports Commission where Chinese athletes stay with all their expenses paid. "Every day he had practice, and when he wasn't practicing, he had games to play," Hua continued. "So mostly I just went to watch him practice or play. On the night before a game, they wouldn't let the players out of the training camp."

But then something went wrong. "He came from a very bad class background," Hua related. "His father had been an officer in the Kuomintang, his older brother had been labeled a rightist in 1957. It didn't matter to me, but it did to him. He worried that I was too good for him, since I was a Party member and an activist. Later, when we broke up, he said it was because he didn't want me to have trouble because of him. He was the only person I ever loved."

Not long afterward, Hua's boss, a ranking city official, decided to send her to Peking to college, though she had only five years of formal education. Most of the other students were children of ranking cadres, diplomats, or army officers from Peking and on Sundays would go home, leaving her with only a few other male students on campus.

"Sundays were the worst days," Hua said. "The boys tried to flirt with me, and even though I used to lock my door, some of them would manage to get in." Her rebuffs angered her would-be suitors, who accused her of being unfriendly, a serious charge against a rising young Party member who should always be convivial and outgoing, a paragon of Communist rectitude.

"One boy in particular chased after me," Hua went on. "He told me he loved me and threatened to commit suicide if I didn't marry him. We had just had a student who killed himself by jumping in the furnace, so it worried me."

One day the Party secretary of her class, a man who could play an important role in her later life by what he wrote in her personal dossier, and a man she recollects as a good person, asked her for a talk. He counseled her to accept the boys more, and if the one student wanted to marry her, she should consent. The young man was already an officer in the People's Liberation Army, it would be a fine match. As happened to Lili, Hua was at the mercy of her Party leader, even in her most private life.

"I was afraid of getting in trouble. When that boy kept after me, finally I said yes, but on one condition. We had to have separate beds and he had to leave me alone. We were not to sleep together. I had been taught that sex was very dirty. It was all we ever heard in study classes and read in the papers."

This prudishness was also to be the seed of years of unhappiness. Hua unfolded her story gradually over a period of months, as we got to know each other better, each time stripping away another of the protective shells she had constructed to shield her psyche. I wondered if she wasn't taking a great risk, meeting me, a foreign journalist, and offering such a personal tale. But she usually took the initiative herself, calling me to arrange a meeting somewhere circumspect, on a street corner or in a bookshop. "I never tell any of my friends, or anyone in my office, about my life. It would be too dangerous. Even if they didn't report me, the next time there is a campaign, they would be forced to speak out," she said. "With a job like mine and a husband who is an army officer, I am supposed to be very happy." So ironically she found she could confide to a foreigner what she dared not say to another Chinese.

There was another reason for her friendship with me. She had once been a determined activist, throwing all of her considerable energy into working for the Party. But her sudden promotion in the Cultural Revolution and then demotion after it, all because of factional quarrels, had soured her on the Party. Now she found a new, illicit pleasure in defying the system—meeting with a foreigner, practicing her English, sometimes even affecting Western dress with a pair of tight-fitting slacks she had made at home from material a relative had sent her from Hong Kong. It was in this way she eventually came to the heart of her story.

It was an unhappy marriage from the start, Hua insisted. She and her husband soon had a baby girl, but she tried to resist him whenever he wanted to make love.

"We would get into terrible arguments about it. He was away most of the time, the army separated us, but when he came home, about once a month, he would look at me and I could tell what he wanted. How I hated it. He would take off his pants, and it made me so angry, sick, and tired. He kept trying to touch me, to caress my breast, but I wouldn't let him touch me, not even my hand. I was disgusted."

In the end, though, Hua said, her husband was stronger than she was and would overpower her. "It was always very painful. I didn't get wet, so he had a hard time getting inside me. It hurt me, and it hurt him too."

Eventually she developed a better defense mechanism. "Later, when he came after me and began to play with me, I felt like I was having a heart attack. My chest grew tight and I couldn't breathe. I would cry out. He would get afraid and leave me alone." Sometimes after they had intercourse, Hua recalled, she would rush to the toilet down the hallway to throw up.

"I went to the doctor many times for a check-up," Hua told me one day during a walk through the Forbidden City. "I was worried about my heart. He examined me very carefully. He did an electrocardiogram test, and made me run on one of those machines. But, of course, I was an athlete and still jog for an hour every morning, so there wasn't anything wrong with my heart."

I asked if she had told the doctor what brought on her symptoms. "No, I never told the doctor what caused it. That would be too terrible." Hua said she had never heard of Freud, but the Viennese psychiatrist would have recognized her symptoms, so much like those of nineteenth-century hysterical women he saw.

When I asked if she had ever experienced an orgasm, Hua's face furrowed into a frown. Just to make sure, I used a slang expression common in Taiwan and Hong Kong, and one some Chinese on the mainland I have talked to do know, *gao-chao,* literally, "high tide." "What is that?" she asked in reply. She had never had any such sensation. Intercourse, as she knew it, consumed three or four minutes and ended when her husband withdrew. The only position they had tried, she said, was for her to lie flat on her back and her husband to climb on top of her.

Had she ever tried oral sex then? I asked. "What is that, kissing?" she responded.

She was incredulous when I tried, with considerable embarrassment, to explain that in the United States and Europe fellatio and cunnilingus had become an accepted part of sexual conduct between men and women. "How could people do that, it's disgusting." When informed of the plot of the movie *Deep Throat,* she commented, "People in China would not watch such dirty things."

Despite our conversations, Hua did not feel she had missed anything sexually. "I am very strong. I never had such desires. I never think about doing such kinds of things. We are not like you people in the West, you kiss a girl and then you are changeable as the wind." Still, Hua liked to describe herself as a romantic. She said she had enjoyed watching the film *The Way We Were,* with Robert Redford and Barbra Streisand, which she had seen at an unofficial showing in a small theater, courtesy of a friend who had given her a coveted ticket. Hua could even sing the theme song from the movie, though in a hoarse, infelicitous voice. Once in a rare admission, she said, "Sometimes when I wake up at night, I dream about meeting a man who will really love me and make me happy. But I think that will never happen to me."

Hua was skeptical about the suggestion that she might be frigid and that the cause was psychological. She had not heard of the term. When told that in the United States some doctors and social scientists, like Alfred Kinsey and the team of Masters and Johnson, had spent years studying human sexual response and that books on the subject usually could be found on the bestseller list, she laughed. "What a waste of time for a doctor."

By this time I had grown increasingly nervous about the frequency of our contact—we saw each other about once a week—and over Hua's habit of phoning me in the Peking Hotel. Sooner or later, I suggested, the Public Security Bureau would get curious. It might be safer if we didn't see each other for a few weeks, I ventured. But Hua remained insistent on keeping up our meetings. "China is a socialist state, a people's state, we should have the right to pick our own friends," she contended. Then one evening she called to say she had been asked to accompany an official delegation to Shenyang, in the northeast, to examine some new sports facilities and would be gone for a week or two. She was surprised by the order to go, it was out of her usual line of work, but there was no hint of suspicion or foreboding in her voice.

A month later, when I hadn't heard from her, I became worried. I decided to risk calling her office from a pay phone. The man who answered wouldn't say where she was and demanded to know, "Where are you?" or what my *danwei* was. I hung up, thoroughly alarmed. I decided to ask Jan Wong to call Hua's office and pretend to be a relative visiting from Canton. This time the man in her office said, "She's away on business." How long would Hua be gone? Jan inquired. "A very long time," he replied. When would Hua return? Jan pressed him. "I don't know," he said with finality. Jan agreed it sounded very bad.

But it was not until a few months later when I met another person who worked in the Sports Commission that I found out what had happened. Hua had been arrested and sent to a labor reform camp for talking to me about her sex life. I had written an article about sex in China for the Sunday *New York Times Magazine* and, without mentioning any names, referred to some unhappy marriages in the Sports Commission. Unfortunately, the article had been reprinted in a classified bulletin that was circulated to members of the Party Central Committee. Evidently some official had taken offense at the revelation of such intimacies to a foreigner and ordered the police to investigate. Eventually, Hua was tracked down. Talking about sex in China, it turned out, was a crime. I was appalled, both at this realization and by my culpability in Hua's fate. Later another Chinese friend who had read a secret Central Committee document on Hua's case said I should not blame myself completely—there were other factors. But I never found out what they were.

China has not put out any statistics on the incidence of frigidity among women, or what percentage reach orgasm, so any conclusions on the subject must be fragmentary. But the more Chinese I talked with, the more it seemed that Hua was not unusual: that many Chinese women do not enjoy sex, or feel they shouldn't, that a number of Chinese men do not know how to satisfy their partners, and that there is widespread ignorance about sexual performance and fulfillment in China.

Susan Wilf, a Harvard graduate student who taught English in Peking and married a Chinese, recalled her amusement at the reaction of a fellow Chinese teacher when he heard her tape of the Donna Summer song "Love to Love Ya." The teacher, a happily married forty-year-old man with two children, whom Susan recalled as being very smart and a Party member, was puzzled at the recording. In it, the "Queen of Disco" moans, sighs, and pants as she sings, suggesting a woman reaching climax. But the teacher asked Susan, "What is she doing? Having a baby?"

Soon after my arrival in Peking, I witnessed an incident which suggested how people felt they had to mask their sexual feelings. I had gone to the large drugstore on Wangfujing Street to buy some medicine. As I was standing at the counter, a matronly looking woman in her early forties came in and asked a salesgirl for a packet of birth-control pills. These are dispensed free to all Chinese, either by pharmacies or a person's local street committee, as part of the government's ambitious program to cut the population growth rate to zero by the year 2000. So the transaction should have been perfectly natural.

But when the salesgirl, a young woman in her early twenties, with braids to her waist and wearing a white sanitary smock, noticed the customer's age, she raised an eyebrow.

"For you?" she inquired of the woman, whose salt and pepper hair was cropped in a severe, short bowl cut and firmly anchored with bobby pins.

"Oh no, for my daughter," the customer replied.

It seemed an obvious subterfuge. For given the woman's own age, her daughter was probably not old enough to get married in China. Legally, women in the cities must wait till they are at least twenty-five years old, men till they are twenty-seven or twenty-eight, depending on the location. This provision for delayed marriage is another part of Peking's birth-control plan to cut down on the number of offspring by requiring people to put off wedlock until they have fewer childbearing years left. Delayed marriage is even enshrined in China's 1978 constitution, like other rights and duties of individuals. So it seemed likely that the customer in the drugstore was too embarrassed to admit that she and her husband still made love.

"Most Chinese women I know treat sex as a duty to be performed and complain when their husbands want too much," the American woman who is married to a Chinese related. "After forty, they feel they have completed their duty and can stop it altogether." Her own husband, who is fifty years old, gets ribbed when he goes to pick up his monthly allotment of condoms because people think that by that age "neither he nor I should be interested anymore."

Another woman I got to know, a schoolteacher named Li Mei, did have a serious complaint against her husband. When we were walking in the park behind the Temple of the Sleeping Buddha, in the Fragrant Hills area to the west of Peking, she recounted why she wanted a divorce. Her words came in a rush, blunt for a Chinese, and seemed out of character for a plain-looking thirty-six-year-old woman who had been raised by a grandmother so strict that when she was six years old she was not allowed to play in a neighbor's house because they had a little boy. "Grandmother thought it was bad for a girl to do that. She was very feudal, a real Qing dynasty lady.

"I never refused my husband's demands to do it," Li Mei explained of her own troubles. "I had never been to bed with a man before we were married, so I didn't know anything about it. But he had a disease. He came too quickly, as soon as he penetrated me.

"Then he would fall asleep immediately. After the first year of marriage I developed insomnia. My husband would lie there and snore. At first I would just lie awake and think. But then I began to weep. I have cried a lot. For twelve years."

Both Hua and Li Mei said they had never had any sex education in school, or advice from friends. The closest Hua came to such instruction was a birth-control lecture given in her office, but she had not listened carefully. "It was too dirty." Their experience in this is typical—counseling in sex therapy, either in schoolroom courses or private consultation with doctors, simply does not exist, according to every Chinese I queried.

Much of this ignorance about sex and official puritanism prevail in the Soviet Union, too. For love and sex are usually equated with being cheap and bourgeois, with promiscuity; they are unrevolutionary, not worthy of brave hearts that should be beating with thoughts of building a new socialist nation. It is not so much that the Chinese Communists borrowed their sexual mores from the Russians, along with their ideology and Party apparatus, but that revolutionaries traditionally see themselves as dedicated, ascetic souls, and sex as a libertine sideshow that detracts from the more important tasks of economic development and preserving Party discipline. When the Chinese press, in a rare sensual moment, does offer advice on sexual matters, it is usually to urge that people sublimate their improper passions into more constructive work or study for the benefit of the nation, like the following exchange between a high school student and the paper *China Youth News:*

> *Comrade Editor:*
> *I've already fallen in love with a girl student. But I don't have the courage to break off relations. What shall I do?*
> *Tao Jie*

The response was written by a man who identified himself as a high school teacher.

"You have fallen in love with each other and it is not easy to break up," the teacher wrote. "But you have to make a decision. High school is a time of high aspiration. If you fall in love now, you will lose precious time. Your generation will play a vital role in modernizing China. You should concentrate on training yourself to be useful to the motherland. Love at your age is too soon. Besides, it will lead to a neglect of your studies. It takes will power to give up bad habits and will power to control emotions. You can keep your friendship with the girl, but avoid intimacy. See more of your classmates."

Peking's view that proper thinking can overcome biological imperatives was also reflected in another delicate colloquy between a youthful letter writer and the *China Youth News* on the subject of masturbation. The paper translated it as "hand lewdness."

Comrade Editor:

I have a problem which I am embarrassed to talk about, that is, masturbation. For over a year now I've wanted to change but I can't. I feel my strength draining from me, and want to see a doctor, but I'm afraid of being laughed at. What should I do?

Xiao Li, Henan province

The answer was provided by a professor at the Peking Medical College:

After reading your letter, I feel it necessary to talk a bit about some facts of biology and hygiene.

At first, many young people are simply curious and use masturbation to satisfy their sexual needs. But gradually it becomes a bad habit. While young people are developing, if they lack correct understanding of sex or are influenced by pornographic reading materials, they will masturbate. Done once in a while, it will have no harmful effect on one's health. But if it is done regularly, it will stimulate sex nerves to a certain degree which will produce fatigue, dizziness, listlessness, bad memory, and other phenomena which will hamper work and study. In more serious cases, it will lead to nervous breakdowns. After marriage, many disorders and premature ejaculation are very much related to masturbation.

Second, what should you do about masturbating? I can tell you with confidence that this problem can be completely overcome and that it will not leave any aftereffects. You must put your main energy into study and work, and arrange your extra time to take part in cultural and sports activities in order to have a regulated life.

Before sleeping at night, go jogging, wash your feet in warm water, and try to fall asleep immediately upon getting into bed. In the morning when you wake up, don't lie around. When sleeping, be careful not to sleep on your

stomach, and don't use covers that are too heavy. Don't wear underpants that
are too tight, and maintain cleanliness of the penis.

Will masturbation affect sex life after marriage? If your health is normal
it generally won't be a problem. If your health is poor and you commit
masturbation, then there may be some adverse effects.

Some people say that one drop of sperm is equal to many drops of blood,
but there is no basis for this. Sperm is mainly made of protein, and the more
you lose, the more you can produce. However, it causes wear and tear on the
body. Therefore, young people already married should restrict themselves
somewhat in terms of sex.

A pocket-sized pamphlet written by two other professors entitled *Sexual
Knowledge,* the only sex manual I ever saw in China, took an even stricter view
of the need to limit the frequency of intercourse. "Newlyweds will have
very, very frequent sex right after marriage: that is, once every three to seven
days," the professors postulated. As passions cool, they went on, married
couples can expect a more normal routine of "once every week or two." But
the guidebook, which was sold out within hours after it went on sale in the
New China Bookstore near the Peking Hotel, suggested that individuals
should make their own choices based on how they feel the morning after they
have intercourse.

"When the frequency is balanced, they will not feel tired the day after. In
fact, quite the opposite, their whole bodies are light and loose and relaxed
and their temperaments are happy."

A sure sign of overindulgence, the professors caution, is if the sexual
partners "feel tired, heavy-headed, if their legs are tingly and ticklish, if their
heart beats rapidly, and they're short of breath or lose their appetite."

The good professors' view that sexual activity causes bodily deterioration
and therefore should be conducted with moderation might spring straight
out of a nineteenth-century tract inveighing against the evils of fornication.
But they do not deal with a major conundrum for all Chinese young people. What are they supposed to do if by law women in the cities cannot
legally marry till they are twenty-five and men twenty-seven or twenty-
eight, for premarital sex is also taboo, if not actually illegal, and the penal-
ties for being caught are often harsh. When Jan Wong was at Peking University, one of her friends, a very bright and attractive young man, passed
the tough exams for entrance to a graduate school of engineering. But only
a few weeks after the semester started, the school authorities received a
letter signed by three women all claiming that he had "tricked" them into
sleeping with him on the promise of marriage. Such a scoundrel, they
charged, should not be allowed to have a chance at graduate school, a very
prestigious opportunity since there are only about 8,000 places for all of

China's one billion people. The school agreed, and he was kicked out, a serious blow to his career.

When A. M. Rosenthal, the Executive Editor of *The New York Times,* visited China in 1981, he was taken to a reformatory for teen-agers in Shanghai. In the girls' wing he walked into a room where a dozen youths were fixing boxes. Rosenthal asked one of the girls why she was there. She stood up immediately, looked him straight in the eye, and said with pain, "My name is Ma Xiulan. I am eighteen years old. I am here because I had affairs with boys." In another room where a group of girls were working on sewing machines, Rosenthal repeated the question and got the same answer. Later the principal explained that most of the girls were in the reformatory for having affairs with boys—not prostitution, but the crime of sex without sanction.

If masturbation can be dangerous to your health and making love must await marriage, homosexuality is truly *terra incognita* in China. I have never seen a reference to it in the Chinese press—it is too deviant even to mention. Classical Chinese literature contains a number of examples of homosexual lovers, but most Chinese today seem to have only a vague idea of what this means. A twenty-eight-year-old man who had special access to American newspapers and magazines and had read about Gay Liberation once asked me how two men could possibly mate. He was genuinely puzzled. When John Roderick, the veteran correspondent of the Associated Press, arrived in Peking to open his agency's bureau in early 1979, his government-assigned interpreter startled him with a seemingly irrelevant question soon after they met. "Do you know what we do with homosexuals here in China?" he asked. No, replied Roderick, he didn't know. "We shoot them," the interpreter said.

On the other hand, it is also true that Chinese, like other Asians, accept certain forms of behavior as natural that Westerners have tended to see in homosexual terms, like men walking down the street holding hands, or helping each other scrub down in public bathhouses. When I was studying Chinese in Taiwan, it took me some time to get accustomed to a Chinese male student friend taking me by the arm when we went downtown. I was also surprised later when another acquaintance put his hand on my thigh as we drove in a taxi and kept it there for much of the ride. It was only a gesture of companionship. Foreign tourists in China often misunderstand when they see two People's Liberation Army soldiers in uniform locked hand in hand.

Nevertheless there do seem to be a few, a tiny handful, of homosexuals in China, tucked away deep in the closet, and they face a real threat of social ostracism and political reprisal. A middle-aged Chinese intellectual told me of an instance of which he knew. In a Peking factory there was an older worker who was a homosexual and who knew that one of the younger workers had not confessed he had a close relative who was a former landlord. The older man used this knowledge to blackmail the junior man into engaging in sex with him. Finally the younger worker calculated that the political charge against him was the lesser of two evils and reported the affair. Both men were heavily criticized in meetings in the factory.

A friend of Jan's told her about a distant relative who has been a lesbian for years. She and her partner, both nurses, have been together since the 1940s. They sleep together on the same bed and make no secret of their relationship. All the neighbors know, but have not interfered, partly because the two women haven't caused any trouble, and partly because the neighbors feel the women's only problem is that they haven't found a man to straighten them out. Both men and women normally come under enormous pressure from relatives to get married, so there are few "old maids" in China.

The two nurses did get in trouble during the Cultural Revolution, however. They had adopted a young girl, a relative of one of them. The daughter hated them for the unusual situation in which she was raised. After the Cultural Revolution began the girl became a Red Guard and one day led her faction to the women's home and exposed them. She also pointed out where they had buried their savings under the floor. Jan's friend speculated that establishing such a lesbian union today would be impossible. "You couldn't apply for housing, like other newlyweds," she explained, laughing with a mixture of shock and amusement. Even straight couples often have to wait for several years for an apartment, given China's housing shortage.

Still, the strict puritanical morality prescribed by Peking is beginning to give way, eroded by the troubles of the Cultural Revolution just as education, factory production, and Communist Party discipline have been undermined. When Mao encouraged gangs of youthful Red Guards to traverse the country, going from city to city to batter Party cadres, they often ended up sleeping together, regardless of sex, in railroad trains, crowded barracks, or whatever shelter they could find. The old barriers against intimacy began to tumble. When Mao also shipped millions of city school graduates off to the countryside, supposedly to toughen their revolutionary fiber, they again found themselves thrown together, away from parental authority. The commune authorities often housed them together for convenience, and the young city men and women discovered the best solace against the rigors of village life lay in companionships they could not have formed at home.

As a result, I found, while many young men may still want their wives to be virgins, fewer are. A radar technician in the air force whom I met in a small restaurant when I sat down at a table where he was dining confessed later that he himself was still a virgin. "But I'm almost the only one of my friends who is," he explained. It was hard to tell whether he was boasting or complaining.

"My father is a high-ranking cadre," he said, "and I'm afraid to have relations with a woman. If I did, and I didn't like her and didn't want to marry her, she might charge me with rape," the same problem which got the student expelled from Peking University. Most women, he seemed convinced, were interested in him only because of his family's standing.

A tall, good-looking lathe operator in a Peking machinery factory said that premarital sex was definitely on the increase among his friends in the past few years. "It started in the Cultural Revolution when there was no law," he observed. "But the real problem is, the government says we can't get married till we are twenty-eight. How can anyone wait that long to have relations?" He also blamed China's housing shortage. "Even when I got to be twenty-eight and my girl friend was twenty-five, we still couldn't get our own apartment. We had to wait three more years for it. Both of us were afraid that if we waited till we finally had our own housing to make love, we would be too old." So he and his girl friend, a fellow factory worker, started sleeping together in his parents' apartment. There is a term for this arrangement, he said, a pun, *zhu-li.* It means "assistant," but also "live-in." Among his friends, he said, almost everyone now has been a "live-in" before they get married. "My parents understood, I just didn't tell my *danwei,*" the worker related. He was then thirty-three years old and happily married, with a two-year-old daughter.

Another indication of the changing morality is that despite all the official pressure, some Chinese women now do get pregnant before marriage, even teen-agers. David Eisenberg, a graduate of the Harvard Medical School who spent a year working in the Institute for Traditional Chinese Medicine in Peking, said that when a European doctor there had the rare chance to observe the institute's gynecology ward, he saw twelve pregnant and unmarried women come in for abortions during a two-week period. They ranged in age from seventeen to twenty-four, Dr. Eisenberg said. One, who was twenty-two, had come in for the second time. She was with her boy friend and was weeping.

In the countryside, where the government's hand sits more lightly, premarital sex may be easier than in the cities even though rural life is supposed to be more conservative. Maggie Mosher, an American-Chinese woman who spent a year with her sociologist husband conducting interviews in her ancestral village in Guangdong province, near Hong Kong, calculated that 70 percent of the young women she talked to had been pregnant before getting married. This was not true of women above thirty, she said, so it seemed to be a new development. That so many young people ignored the regime's official policy suggested how deeply cynicism has spread.

Maggie remembered an incident when a neighbor of hers, already six months pregnant, was collected by her new in-laws and driven to their house on the back of a bike (bicycles have replaced sedan chairs in the contemporary wedding party). "It was a wonderful sight, sitting on the bike with her belly sticking out."

In the cities, women in the past few years have started to complain about men pinching their bottoms or slipping hands inside their clothes while riding on the tightly packed buses. On a December afternoon, after I boarded the number 1 bus near the old Democracy Wall on Changan Boulevard, I noticed a comely woman in her late twenties berating a man squeezed next to her. He had his hand pressed firmly between her legs, though she was still well protected by layers of winter cotton-paded pants.

"If you touch me again, I'll hit you," she warned loud enough for most of us passengers to hear. People stared. A minute later, making good her threat, she cracked him in the chest with her elbow. She was still muttering when she pushed her way to the door and got off at the Square of the Gate of Heavenly Peace.

The women's dormitory at the Foreign Languages Institute has occasionally been troubled by flashers. An American student related an incident that happened to her as she was reading one evening in her room. A man in his early twenties she had seen hanging around campus, dressed in a Western-style jacket belted at the waist, walked in and took down his pants. She had to scream to get him to leave. The woman suspected he was a factory worker rather than a student, but he managed to get into the dorm more than once.

The same things happen in New York and Tokyo; but that's the point. Chinese are like other people. They get hungry, sleepy, and feel the tug of sexual desire. The Communists in the end have not been able to legislate sexuality. Paradoxically, it's easier for Chinese to break the rules when they are in a crowd. At home, or in their unit, they would be subject to the usual pressures and likely to be detected. Perhaps that's why young men in China's cities have become increasingly brazen in trying to pick up girls on the street, something unheard of until the past few years.

Xiaopei, a translator at Peking Radio with large almond eyes and a button nose, said it happened a number of times to her as she was riding her bicycle downtown. "The surprising thing was, they were rather cultured types, well-dressed, not like those punks you see with mustaches and foreign-style sunglasses," she recalled.

"One day when I was riding along, I heard a voice behind me call, 'Miss, let's go to the movies. I have lots of tickets.'

"I suppose he meant to impress me, that he was the son of a high cadre with all those tickets, so I told him to get lost. I said I was already old and married. But he laughed. 'You look only like a sixth grader.'

"Eventually we were approaching the Peking Hotel and I told him I had to go in on business," also an an impressive remark for a Chinese, indicating that she must hold an important post necessitating contact with foreigners. "But not to be outdone, he retorted, 'What's so great about that? I often go in there to eat.'" But when she pedaled into the hotel parking lot, he couldn't follow her and had to ride off.

To the Chinese this increase in attempted pickups is one of the clearest indications of the general breakdown in authority and morality that accompanied the Cultural Revolution. For most Chinese have always felt awkward just striking up friendships in the office or during chance encounters on a train or in a restaurant. They are much more comfortable waiting to be introduced by a friend or relative, in the traditional style. Connections, *guan-xi,* in China are not formed haphazardly and on individual whim, as in the West, but are built up guardedly over a long period. It is the opposite of the American craze for singles bars. A Chinese depends on his group and uses a go-between to deal with strangers.

Our friend Miao, Mrs. Wang, sometimes acted as a matchmaker, she told me one evening at dinner. She usually became involved because she knew either the young man or woman and their families asked her to help locate a suitable partner. Her first step, she explained, was to study details of any prospective candidate's class background, his or her family's income, the education record of each, job, and physical appearance. Cadres looked for other cadres, she said, intellectuals were picky about wanting to marry only intellectuals, and workers preferred other workers.

The other main principle she noticed was that "boys want a girl who is good-looking, while girls want a boy with a good job and money."

In the past few years, she added, young women had become almost obsessed with money in deciding on a potential husband. "It's a bad thing, but they are all doing it," Miao commented. In her view, it was again a result of the Cultural Revolution, for with the Communists' denunciation of love as vulgar, cheap, and bourgeois, ironically what took its place was the very unrevolutionary notion that a woman should make a good match in material terms.

In fact, she related, there is a popular saying that a bridegroom in the cities must be able to supply "the ten musts for marriage." Number one is one set of furniture. Two is both of the husband's parents out of the way or a separate apartment. Three stands for the "three things that go around," a wristwatch, sewing machine, and bicycle. Four is "four seasons all wearing fine material," or to have good clothes. Five is "the five extremities in good shape," or be in good health and handsome. Six is "the six relations not concerned," or no poor relatives to take care of. Seven, a 70-yuan-a-month salary, well above average. Eight, "eight ways flexible," someone who is smooth and slick in social relations. Nine, a pun on avoiding liquor, which rhymes with the word for nine in Chinese. Ten, "ten parts," or completely obedient to one's wife.

The Communists actually outlawed the old practice of bride price in their progressive family law of 1950. But the New China News Agency admitted that during 1980 newlyweds in Peking spent an average of 1,554 yuan ($1,036) on purchases connected with their marriage, the great bulk of it by the groom and his family. The figure represents more than a year's salary for both bride and groom.

Miao said that after she located someone whom she thought would make a good partner for her own young man or woman, normally through another go-between, she fixed a day for the couple to meet. Her preference was for a neutral location away from both sets of parents. That way, if either party didn't like the prospective mate, there would be no need to go through with the marriage and no loss of face. Miao always consulted an old family book of Chinese astrology in picking the day for the first meeting.

It was on a propitious Sunday afternoon in September that I followed Miao and one of her young men to the Sun Yat-sen Park at the side of the Forbidden City. The park, set with potted plants tended by gardeners, had stone paths for walking and rows of cypress trees and gnarled pines. It is also dotted with old pavilions dating from the time when it was part of the Imperial City. The young woman Miao had chosen showed up dressed in a neatly pressed white blouse and gray slacks, her hair in two long braids. While Miao and her counterpart chatted for fifteen minutes, sitting on a wooden bench, the new couple eyed each other gingerly, exchanging a few sentences. Later, the young man expressed his general satisfaction, though he felt the girl's neck was too short and her skin too dark. The first criterion of beauty, and sex appeal, to most Chinese men, is white skin, a heritage perhaps of feudal days when proper upper-class ladies stayed indoors and protected their delicate bodies from the sun, unlike peasant girls. For her part in the affair, Miao was rewarded with presents of cloth, some extra grain coupons, and a second-hand bicycle.

One time, Miao confessed, she had great trouble finding a suitable match —it was for a thirty-one-year-old woman who hadn't gotten married because she had been sent to work as a teacher in a village several hours' bus ride from Peking. The woman was a university graduate and, as an intellectual, in Chinese terms, was not interested in any man on the local commune. "She also wasn't exactly good-looking," Miao added with a wink. Few Chinese men want to marry a woman over thirty, the year is a kind of magic cut-off date, the difference between being eligible and being a spinster. But Miao finally, after interviewing twenty-four candidates, found a scientist in his fifties who had been trained in the United States and then attacked as a rightist because of his American education. His political label had prevented him from finding a wife before.

Not all couples go through formal matchmakers. Miao and Li had met while they were both in the army. He was a dashing actor in a theater troupe, and she spotted him when he came to her company to perform. She knew a friend of his in the troupe and boldly asked for an introduction after the show. "It was she who chased after me," Li recalled. "She kept asking me to the movies or to go for walks in the park." She even took the initiative in kissing him, he claimed, over Miao's mock protest. He still remembered the place—it was in her barracks. Her roommates had all arranged to go out and leave them alone for a few hours, the only way for them to get privacy. But it had taken him four years to make up his mind, a decision he reached only when he was about to be sent off to labor in the countryside late in the Cultural Revolution. Their wedding was simple; they registered at the local civil affairs office, then he hosted a small dinner party with beer and *maotai* in his quarters. His commanding officer came and made a speech urging them to contribute to the Cultural Revolution. Then they had to bow from the waist three times to a statue of Chairman Mao. There was no honeymoon. Like many Chinese, they had neither the money to afford one nor were they given any time off by their *danwei*.

The most startling of all the changes in sexual mores that have come with the breakdown in the Communists' authority after the Cultural Revolution has been a small revival of prostitution. It is a very sensitive subject to Peking, for in the early 1950s, when the Communists were at the zenith of their zeal and power, they moved forcefully to eradicate the world's oldest profession, condemning it as a scourge of the old feudal society. The brothels were closed and the whores rehabilitated, an accomplishment of which they often boasted.

While reporting on China from Hong Kong, I heard rumors that street-walkers had reappeared in some cities. A construction worker from Canton, who escaped to Hong Kong, claimed he had paid two yuan ($1.33) to procure a woman he met on a busy street near the Pearl River in the downtown part of the city. Such women, he said, were called "roadside chickens," after the name of a Cantonese dish, and were easy to spot if you knew the signals. Some left the top two buttons on their shirts undone; some kept a handkerchief sticking halfway out of a pocket; others combed their hair so it covered one eye in an alluring fashion.

Still, I was skeptical about such stories. So many visiting foreigners for years had said China had abolished prostitution, it was an accepted fact. Hence I was not prepared for what I found at the Peace Cafe in Peking. It was a ten-minute walk from the Peking Hotel, past the sycamore trees on

Wangfujing Street, the darkened headquarters of the *People's Daily* and the bustling Peking Number One Department Store, or "One Hundred Goods Big Building" in Chinese. Turning right at the Four Unities Hair Salon, now decorated with photos of Western models, you enter Goldfish Alley, one of the thousands of narrow streets, or *hutongs,* which make up the heart of old Peking. The darkened alley was jammed with bicyclists, all clanging their tinny horns in the shadows—Chinese bikes don't have lights. On the outside the Peace Cafe was a nondescript gray-brick edifice with two small carved-stone lions guarding the Chinese-style red doors. A drunk had vomited neatly in the doorway. Inside, a heavy cloud of cigarette smoke hung in the glare of the bare fluorescent lights, mixed with the smell of stale beer. The cafe was made up of two rooms, each jammed with customers seated on folding chairs at tables covered with dirty plastic cloths. By the door was a small fishpond with several orange carp floating lazily in it. Despite its lack of decor, for six months during 1979, before the police cracked down, it became a hangout for Peking's trendy young set, the scene—in American terms a cross between the old neighborhood drugstore and a seedy Eighth Avenue bar in New York. Some of the patrons—factory workers, soldiers, unemployed high school graduates waiting for their job assignments, children of high-ranking cadres—went only to drink beer or indulge in the Peace Cafe's special, a chocolate sundae complete with whipped cream and nuts. They were there to see and be seen. Others went to make assignations.

One of the first nights I went, a group of four soldiers in uniform were sitting near the entrance transfixed by the blare of a large, shiny, new Japanese cassette tape recorder with twin speakers. It was playing the beat of a pop recording star from Hong Kong, and on the table in front of them they had strewn a collection of other cassettes, emblazoned with pictures of crooning female vocalists from Taiwan and Hong Kong. The tapes were a boast of the connections which had enabled them to purchase such forbidden material, and a challenge to the authorities.

At another table a woman in her twenties, dressed in a bright-blue sweater, with a metal chain around her neck and blue pants that had been cut several inches closer to her hips than normal, jumped up and embraced a man who had just strutted in. She had brightened her mouth with lipstick, and her hair had been curled by one of those machines used in Chinese beauty parlors that look like a relic from the set of a Frankenstein movie, all wires and tubes designed to electrocute rather than coif the hair. The effect was disastrous. But it was evidently the effort and daring that went into it, rather than the aesthetic result, that counted. When the man and woman sat down, he thrust his hand into her lap and began rubbing between her legs.

Later, outside, as I was walking home, I was approached by a short, wiry, crew-cut young Chinese who had also just left the Peace Cafe. He was dressed in the green garb of the People's Liberation Army, minus the red tags on his collar, which are worn to denote a soldier on active service. Many soldiers after they are demobilized continue to wear their old uniforms, but strip the red tags off. It saves money on clothes and carries extra prestige.

"I'm in the army, but I take my tags off so no one will know," the man explained, as if by way of introduction. "My name is Wang Wei," "Benefit the People" Wang. He spit the words out staccato, like the sound of a machine gun. "My father is a general. I've got a lot of foreign friends," and he mentioned the Dutch ambassador.

"I can fix you up with a young girl, if you want," he went on, with hardly a pause or a connecting link. "She's fourteen, very cute. You can take her home. But you'd better show up if I get her. The other day I got one for a foreign friend and then he didn't come. She was very mad."

I wasn't sure if he could really be what he sounded, a pimp, or whether this was just braggadocio. To find out, I arranged to go back the next evening with Orville Schell, the writer, and an old Harvard classmate, who was visiting Peking.

But Wang Wei was there, sitting in the back of the Peace Cafe with three women. They looked to be in their twenties, not fourteen, but he assured us they were, in fact, *yeh ji*, "wild pheasants," the Peking slang for a strumpet. Did we want to take them out? One was a square, solidly built woman of twenty-three clad in a faded gray jacket and baggy pants. Her figure and clothes matched her daytime job as a steelworker in Peking's Capital Iron and Steel Plant. But she had put on lipstick and cut her hair in the China-doll style, with long bangs over her eyes. To a foreigner that might not make much of a difference in her overall appearance. But in China, nuance can be everything. She was also smoking a cigarette, another tip-off. Almost no young women smoke in public in China.

"How about it?" Wang Wei asked us. After some shuffling, Orville and I decided that if we wanted to see how the operation worked, and if we were going to talk with the women themselves, we should go outside with them. Wang Wei followed. From somewhere he had acquired a trench coat and an old battered felt hat, the kind worn in China in the 1930s during the Nationalist period. We stood in a dark corner of the alley, under a stone wall, where the dim streetlights did not reach. The sharp stench of urine from a public toilet nearby carried to us. The whole scene conjured up a Chinese gangster film, the kind the Communists like to make about the bad old days before Liberation.

When we asked how much, Wang Wei suggested 200 or 300 yuan, or $133 to $200. We laughed. The price for Chinese is $2.78 I replied, repeating what other Chinese had told me. Fifty-three dollars then, he retorted.

Eventually we agreed on $20 for the two of us. The price for foreigners is always higher—in restaurants, museums, even for underground journals or prostitutes.

Wang Wei turned over a share to one of the women, named Wu Yao, who had been selected to go with us. We only wanted to talk, we told her. She looked puzzled but, having been paid, wanted to get whatever it was over with quickly.

"I have to get home," she advised, placing her hands on her broad hips and staring at us. She, too, had put on lipstick and blackened her eyebrows, but there was little alluring about her, except her availability. "My parents try to keep tight control over me. They want me back home by nine o'clock every night," she told us in a hard voice. Then how did she manage to go to the Peace Cafe? "I fool them. I tell them I am going over to a friend's house."

She was a nurse, she continued, and earned 22 yuan ($15) a month, less than half what Peking officially calls an average salary. She began making love when she was seventeen, in high school, she said. "It's pretty common now in school." Where could people go to do it, we asked, given the absence of privacy? "It's not so hard. You can use someone's house when their parents or brothers and sisters are at work."

She had been to bed with a large number of men, including overseas Chinese, Pakistanis, and Africans. She didn't think it was too risky. "You can get an abortion if you need it. Take the back door. Pay the doctor some money, there's no problem."

A group of men walked by where we were still standing. One called to her. It was her brother, she said. Her parents were looking for her. She had to go.

A few months later, after a number of foreign correspondents had written about the Peace Cafe, Wu was arrested. She and the pimps "corrupted the reputation of China and detracted from the fame of our country," the *People's Daily* charged.

If the Cultural Revolution had unintentionally contributed to a breakdown in sexual mores, the Communists had very deliberately set about politicizing marriage. Since 1949 any couple that wants to get married must first receive clearance from the Party secretary of their *danwei*. Only then can they legally register their marriage. For many people, those with "clean" class backgrounds, this is routine. But for Communist Party members and army officers, who carry extra responsibility, a more thorough investigation is made of their intended mate's political record. The higher the rank, the more careful the scrutiny, Chinese say.

And some couples with political blemishes are denied permission, evidently to preserve public security. Yang Fuguo, a clerk in a hospital in Canton, was turned down when he applied to marry a petite, pretty nurse.

"They didn't have to tell me the reason, only the verdict—no," said Yang, a short, direct man in his late thirties with wiry hair and crooked teeth.

"I never found out why, but eventually we began to piece things together, from hints. Apparently someone had branded her a spy risk during the Cultural Revolution because she had a sister in the United States and other relatives in Hong Kong. This was put in her dossier. Of course, we never saw the dossier, that was impossible. And they wouldn't confirm it."

Yang kept on seeing the nurse, however, and was ordered not to talk to her anymore. When he still refused to give her up, he was transferred to a remote state farm in the mountains. Only six years later, after the downfall of Lin Biao, the former Defense Minister, when the political leadership in the hospital changed, were they allowed to marry.

The Communists' strict regulation of marriage and their puritanical sexual code have not deterred China's leaders from enjoying active sex lives themselves. High political position, if not an aphrodisiac, has proved a definite advantage in romantic conquests, much as it does in securing such privileges as better housing, chauffeured cars, and good jobs for one's children. Mao married four times. His first marriage was arranged by his father when he was only thirteen to a local peasant girl and was never consummated. His second wife, Yang Kaihui, was the daughter of a favorite professor. What began as an intellectual affair, however, led to her pregnancy and then a swift wedding. Today the official interpretation of Mao holds that Yang was the Chairman's favorite, but he had left her before she was picked up by the Kuomintang and beheaded.

By this time, in fact, Mao was already living with a Communist woman partisan, He Zizhen, who accompanied him on the Long March despite being wounded badly enough to require being carried on a stretcher. In the caves of Yanan, the Communists' wartime headquarters in the northwest, this relationship, too, deteriorated. Mao's fancy was caught by a comely, aggressive young actress from Shanghai who ventured to Yanan and made herself conspicuous by sitting in the front row at one of his lectures. He Zizhen was packed off to the Soviet Union for medical care—on her return to China she was confined to a mental hospital from about 1939 until recently—and Mao married the actress, who took the name of Jiang Qing.

"Sex is engaging in the first rounds, but what sustains interest in the long run is power," Jiang Qing later told her American biographer, Roxanne Witke. The Great Helmsman put it somewhat differently: "Political power grows out of the barrel of a gun," he said in his most widely quoted aphorism.

Before the Cultural Revolution, China's Party leaders used to hold dances to which attractive and politically reliable young women were invited. A middle-aged woman cadre who worked for a film studio recalled she often had been escorted to these dances on Saturday nights in the Peking Hotel in the early 1960s, when she was a college student in the capital, by a deputy mayor. On several other occasions she was invited to a special guesthouse behind the Forbidden City, where a number of senior officials lived, for dances given by Foreign Minister Chen Yi, a veteran military officer. Twice she found herself included in parties for Mao and Premier Zhou and ended up dancing with them. "Zhou was very light on his feet," she recalled. "Mao just asked me questions like, 'Where do you work, what is your parents' background?' I was too nervous to really talk to them." From the outset of the Cultural Revolution in 1966, of course, dancing was proscribed as a decadent bourgeois diversion, and even today, despite a certain revival, it can lead to political trouble for those who dare take the floor.

Even in Mao's later years he seems to have sustained a fondness for the opposite sex and surrounded himself with young women, like the Brooklyn-born Nancy Tang, his English interpreter, and Wang Hairong, the daughter of a distant relative, whose job was to put his Delphic utterances into more comprehensible Chinese. Peking gossip holds that Mao also had a final mistress, a very pretty woman named Zhang Yufeng, whom he appointed his personal secretary. To pacify her husband, Mao awarded him a handsome post as deputy chief in a Central Committee office. But Jiang Qing hated her, the story goes, and, when Mao died in September 1976, had her arrested. A month later, with Jiang Qing's own downfall, Zhang was ordered to write a confession detailing her knowledge of the Gang of Four's conspiracies, which was then used in compiling the official dossier against them.

The story did not end there, however. Hua Guofeng, then the newly appointed Party Chairman, is said to have feared Zhang because of all she knew about Mao's last years (the basis of Hua's claim to legitimacy was that Mao personally selected him as his successor). So Hua, too, had her locked up in a house outside Peking until she eventually committed suicide by slashing her wrists with glass from a bathroom window.

Several Chinese acquaintances regaled me with accounts of the adventures of Lin Like, the son of the late Defense Minister Lin Biao who reportedly died in an airplane crash after trying to assassinate Mao. The younger Lin, a ranking air force officer, had looked at nearly 10,000 photographs of young women in search of the most beautiful wife in China, they said. The wives of two senior Party officials also cruised Wangfujing, Peking's Fifth Avenue, looking for candidates. Eventually, using the pretext of a hunt for actresses and dancers, ten semifinalists were selected, my friends said they had read in a Central Committee document on Lin. Lin then picked three—one a Chinese, one a member of the Bai minority, and the third a member of the Miao minority in southwest China. (China, too, has its myths that ethnic minorities somehow are sexier or enjoy more sexual prowess.) But Lin died in the plane crash with his father before he finally got married.

On a more mundane level, there is evidence that local party officials and army officers have more than occasionally utilized their ranks for sexual favors. Once on a train from Hangzhou to Shanghai I was seated behind three elderly navy officers who looked to be in their sixties. Each was accompanied by an aide. Only, unlike in the United States, the aides were all women, in their early twenties, and pretty. The car was hot from the steam radiators, and the three women had taken off their blue uniform jackets. Underneath, each had on a matching outfit, with a round-collared blouse, sweater, and socks, one in blue, one in pink, and the other in yellow. Few ordinary Chinese could indulge such tastes.

The most flagrant abuses, however, cropped up in Mao's idealistic program to resettle young school graduates from the cities in the countryside. Rusticated in villages far from home, these young women had no relatives to protect them and were at the mercy of the local officials for food, work points, and housing. The *China Youth News* once printed a letter accusing the head of a state farm in Heilongjiang province, a certain Yan Ziyang, of raping or "behaving indecently" toward eight of the eleven rusticated women stationed there. The letter was signed "Families of the Victims." In response, an investigation was carried out and the paper published the findings in the form of a letter to the families:

"The facts in your letter are basically true. Yan raped two female, educated youths [the term for people resettled in the countryside], and had indecent behavior toward five others. This is very bad."

Yan was dismissed from the Party and arrested, though the paper never reported what further punishment he suffered.

A number of Chinese I knew told similar tales of advances by superiors, sometimes ending in rape, but the most poignant story came from an accountant. He had a girl friend who was a nurse in an army hospital in Chanjiang, a port in southern China near Hainan island. She was very idealistic, always kind and sympathetic to her patients, and they adored her, the accountant recalled.

During the Cultural Revolution, the political commissar of the local garrison took a fancy to her and began coming around to her apartment, first asking, then demanding, that she sleep with him. She was unusually pretty and delicate and had little defense. She told her boy friend that the officer had threatened her with a pistol to coerce her. But the accountant suspected the intimidation was more political—a suggestion that she might be sent to a labor camp.

So she gave in—not once, but many times over a period of several months. And she was not the only victim on the base. The officer also raped twenty other women, the accountant charged. Several years later, when the Cultural Revolution was over, he persuaded her to press a complaint against the officer.

"It was a daring and foolhardy thing to do," the accountant recalled. They took the case to a military tribunal in Canton, but after a cursory hearing, the court dismissed her charges, for the officer argued that he was a veteran guerrilla fighter; she was from a bad class background with relatives overseas. How could he have raped her? It was she who had seduced him, he asserted.

"He turned the dead cat toward her," the accountant commented, a Chinese phrase equivalent to turning the tables on someone.

Now the officer really had her at his mercy. First she was put on half pay. Later all her income was stopped. Next he ordered her transferred to a remote state farm in the mountains where she was made a cattle herder. Unable to endure the hardships, she finally ran away, back to her family home in Canton. Her sister, who was also a friend of mine, was shocked by her appearance, emaciated, with large welts from insect bites that had not been treated, because she was denied medicine.

Unfortunately, her mother was not sympathetic. "Mother said she was a fool for trying to get justice," her sister related. "Mother's view was, you have to live with the system." Because she had absconded, she did not have a valid household registration certificate for Canton and therefore no ration cards for food and no hope of getting a job.

Finally, driven by her family's rejection, she committed suicide. By Chinese practice, that sealed her guilt. At the state farm, when her sister went to claim her belongings, she found her dormitory window had been painted black and her name on the local records was marked with a black cross.

In the aftermath, her mother was officially accused of driving her to suicide, for their neighbors in Canton had overheard a family quarrel the day before her death.

China does not release nationwide figures on crime, so it is difficult to judge the incidence of rape. But during a visit to the main Shanghai municipal prison, a somber compound of concrete buildings stained dark gray by the years, the political commissar told me that rape was the second most common crime for which his prisoners had been convicted, trailing only robbery. Indeed, in the prison infirmary, of the three inmates I talked to, one had been convicted for rape, another for robbery, and a third for being a Kuomintang spy.

The impression that rape is a widespread problem is confirmed by other pieces of evidence. Many of the posters I have seen outside courthouses around China, detailing the misdeeds of recently convicted criminals, are for rape. Then there was the story of Lihua, the young petitioner I saw many times in Peking, who killed a youth after he tried to rape her in the countryside. Lihua also told me about the case of a sixteen-year-old high school student in her dorm. The girl had trouble with her homework, Lihua said, but her father and mother, illiterate construction workers, were of little help. Hence, she often went across the hall to a thirty-year-old Communist party member and technician for assistance. Their relationship was so close she even called him "Uncle." One day, however, when her mother came home she noticed the girl was distraught. When her mother asked why, she cried but would not explain. So her mother took out a large kitchen chopper, like an American butcher's knife, and threatened her. "Uncle" had raped her, the girl confessed. He was arrested by the Public Security Bureau.

American psychiatrists now generally believe that rape is less a sexual crime, less an overwhelming need for sexual gratification, than an act brought on by "uncontrolled hostility, a sense of inadequacy or a quest for power," as Dr. Carol C. Nadelson, a specialist on rape, put it.* Whether this finding applies equally in China remains a matter of speculation, for no Chinese I talked with ever heard of a study of rape. Indeed, they were not aware of any counseling for rape victims either. Rape remains off limits, a subject too sensitive for discussion.

Yet the evidence for an interconnection in China between the urge for power and rape, and between politics and sex, is there. The most spectacular case that occurred during my stay in Peking was that of the Xiong twins, a pair of twenty-seven-year-old brothers in the lakeside city of Hangzhou whose father was an army general. The brothers, Xiong Beiping and Xiong Zhiping, developed a bad reputation from an early age. In school they refused to study, often were truant, and beat up their seventy-year-old principal when he tried to discipline them, according to later accounts in the Chinese press. After they were admitted to the army, they would not take part in physical training. Returned to civilian life and given jobs in a factory, they failed to show up for work. They lived in a large house, walled off from the street, with their own garden, a "pleasure nest," the *China Youth News* later called it. From here they sallied forth to a nearby park to lure young women with blandishments like tickets to concerts, the chance to watch television (a novelty in China), or the promise of love and marriage. Over a period of four years, from 1974 to 1978, they and a gang of their friends, nicknamed "Rotten Eggplant," "Big Head," and "the Nun," raped 106 women. On occasion they also held kangaroo court in their house, forcing women they had brought in to kneel on the floor and be tried. Their neighbors and the police were aware of the twins' activities but did nothing.

One day the twins' younger sister invited a classmate to spend the night at their house. Beiping entered the room where the girl was sleeping and

*Dr. Carol C. Nadelson, "Rapist and Victim," *The New England Journal of Medicine,* Vol. 297, No. 14, Oct. 6, 1977, p. 784.

raped her at knifepoint. The twins' mother heard the girl's cries but pretended nothing had happened. "Don't tell anyone," she advised the girl the next morning. "If you do, no one will believe you."

The explanation for this extraordinary episode was that the twins' father held what the Chinese press referred to without elaboration as "a leading post." In fact, diplomats concluded after consulting their files, he was a major general and a former commander of the local military district. When the twins were eventually arrested and brought to trial as part of a general crackdown on juvenile crime, one brother was sentenced to death and executed immediately—with the shooting shown on national television; the other, because he showed some repentance in court, was given a two-year stay of execution to test his behavior. What the press did not say, however, was that the brothers' father had himself been purged in 1971, as a follower of Lin Biao, several years before their crimes began. That suggested just how great the power of senior army commanders was, some Chinese acquaintances said—enough to intimidate the police and the civilian authorities even from jail.

For all China's strict official puritanism, adultery is hardly unknown, though less widespread than in Europe or the United States. Jan Wong related with amusement her discovery of a triangle of a husband, wife, and her lover, all of whom worked in the Foreign Languages Press, China's large publisher of foreign-language books and magazines such as *Peking Review* and *China Reconstructs*. The wife, whom Jan called Ping, was a slim and attractive thirty-two-year-old with a penchant for well-cut jackets and blouses that gave more than the usual hint of her figure. She met her boy friend, Jan learned, after she returned from a sojourn at a May Seventh Cadre School in the countryside at the end of the Cultural Revolution when her husband was still sequestered in the village. Chen, the lover, is a good-looking, dark, strong man, a photographer a few years younger than Ping. He is married to a factory worker and has a son, as do Ping and her husband, Song. But even after Song discovered their affair, he did not take any action. Indeed, the three often ate in the Foreign Languages Press dining room and went to the movies together.

The reason, Jan finally learned, is that Chen is only half Chinese and therefore has access to the Friendship Store, normally open only to foreigners. Chen used this privilege to buy goods Song never could: better meat and vegetables, high-grade Chinese cigarettes, electrical appliances. Then the three of them shared the bounty.

In the countryside also there is considerable sexual promiscuity, friends who have lived there assured me. A Harvard-educated professor who worked for a year in a village in Shanxi province, in the northwest, during the Socialist Education Campaign in 1964, just before the Cultural Revolution, remembered the chagrin of the Communist Party cadres on his work team when they tried to get the local peasants to meetings in the evenings. "The peasants were too busy with their mistresses," he told me. "They called it hiding in small rooms." Some of the women were single, some married. It usually occurred among the men who earned a better than average income and could treat the women to gifts, the professor explained. One shepherd, a job considered taxing and therefore well paid, actually had ten mistresses.

But legally the government views adultery, like premarital sex, as a crime, disruptive of social order. A hotel roomboy I knew in Peking, who was married, was sentenced to three years in prison for sleeping with a waitress who also worked in the hotel.

My unlucky friend Hua told me about a well-respected Party member and middle-ranking cadre in the Sports Commission who on the surface seemed a happily married man with two children. But then one day he was discovered having an affair with another woman in their *danwei* who was also married. In the United States, their infidelity might have been passed over by their colleagues; their spouses perhaps would have filed for divorce. But sex in China is not a private matter between individuals. Under the Communists it has become a highly politicized act which the regime regards as part of its legitimate area of control. To get a divorce, the lovers had to apply to the *danwei* for permission. It was refused. The cadre, mortified by being found out and unable to resolve the situation legally, tried to save his family further embarrassment. He walked to the railroad line that runs behind the Sports Commission headquarters and waited till a train approached. Then he lay down on the tracks and let himself be run over.

Yet his final act failed. In keeping with regulations, the Sports Commission drew up a detailed document on their indiscretion and circulated it around the *danwei*. His lover was ordered before a public rally and criticized for several hours. For good measure, her husband was forced to attend.

7. Holding Up Half the Sky

WOMEN

"If a woman marries a chicken, she should act like a chicken; if she marries a dog, she should act like a dog."
Old Chinese proverb

The Peking First Infectious Diseases Hospital is a forbidding complex of gray-brick buildings set incongruously inside what remains of the ancient Altar of the Earth Park. In Ming and Qing times, this was where the Emperor came at the summer solstice to offer sacrifices to the earth, rising an hour before sunup from the Hall of Abstinence to present the meat of a yellow bull, a cup of wine, a bolt of silk, and then prostrate himself nine times. Neither the hospital—which now largely houses victims of tuberculosis and hepatitis—nor the Altar of the Earth are on the usual tourist itinerary, and I might never have visited the area except that my wife, Barbara, developed a serious bout of what was diagnosed as bacillary dysentery. It was so serious, with a temperature of 104° and constant vomiting and diarrhea, that the doctor at the Capital Hospital, where foreigners are normally treated, ordered me to take her immediately to the Infectious Diseases Hospital so she could be quarantined.

When we tried to drive into the hospital, I saw what quarantine meant. The high green-painted steel front gate was bolted shut, and after we finally were able to summon a guard to admit us, we found the door to the second-floor ward where Barbara was to be ensconced was padlocked both on the inside and outside. Eventually, after pounding on the door for several minutes, a petite nurse, her face hidden by a surgical mask, materialized to usher us shyly into a large private room with its own toilet and the usual concrete floor. Our anxiety did not subside when one of the nurse's first acts was to bring Barbara a large dusty apple to eat. From a decade in Asia, we at least knew that the first remedy for stomach ailments is a rigorously bland diet, excluding fruit. Our trepidations increased further when the nurse reappeared with an apparatus to feed Barbara intravenously. The old bottle on top had an open mouth, with a black rubber stopper hanging beside it and a piece of worn, frayed cotton bandage to bind it closed. Next she brought in another bottle, filled with an unidentified solution, which she poured into the one that would trickle into Barbara's veins. Barbara said she felt too weak to argue about American notions of sterility. Outside we could see a number of the other patients, clad in striped blue and white pajamas and brown robes, convulsively clearing their throats and then spitting in the courtyard below. We looked at each other, thinking that many of them had TB.

Finally the doctor arrived, Wang Chaoqi, a plump, jolly, benign woman of forty-five. Calm and self-confident, with straight black hair cut short, proletarian style, at the nape of her neck, she brought Barbara back to health over the next week despite our initial doubts about the quality of the medical care. To Barbara's further surprise, she discovered that the entire hospital staff of over two hundred doctors and nurses was women. During Barbara's week there, she never encountered a male physician. Even the hospital director, who came solicitously to call on her foreign patient, was a woman.

I was intrigued by this plentitude of women. Like other foreigners who have traveled in China, I had been introduced to a number of Chinese women who had achieved prominence—the director of a submarine shipyard in the industrial city of Wuhan, a lawyer who was head of the China Democratic League, one of the tiny non-Communist parties permitted to survive. Most of them were really examples of Chinese tokenism, women who held figurehead positions. But Dr. Wang and the staff at the Infectious Diseases Hospital had achieved genuine responsibility. When I asked Dr. Wang if she had ever felt any discrimination as a woman, she smiled, showing two rows of perfect white teeth.

"No, why should I?" she replied. She said she had graduated from the Peking Medical College, the best in the city, which before 1949 had been the Peking Union Medical College, built early in the century by the Rockefeller Foundation. She was married to a doctor, and they drew equal salaries, she said.

"I have read that some American women's groups are disappointed when they come to China and Chinese women they meet tell them everything is good," she added with another smile. "Don't you think I am telling the truth?"

Dr. Wang and the staff at the Infectious Diseases Hospital were not a showpiece; they were too far off the beaten track. But they were the best example I encountered of the great leap forward in human dignity that Chinese women have made since 1949. In the past, women's subservience to men was summed up in the injunction in the *Classic for Girls:* "If the wife does not serve her husband, the rules of propriety will be broken." Every Chinese grew up knowing the ancient adages, "An ignorant woman is virtuous" and "A woman should be a virtuous wife and a good mother." Chinese baby girls were more likely than boys to suffer infanticide in poor families. A daughter was referred to as an "outsider" because she would eventually be given away in marriage and no longer bring any economic benefit to her family, "like spilled water," the proverb decreed. After the wedding the new bride fell under the tyranny of her husband's mother. In a wealthy family, she might have to suffer the indignity of a second wife or concubine being brought into the household, especially if she was childless. Her husband could repudiate her; but if he died, she could not easily remarry.

Women were expected to stay secluded inside the home and never venture out. Before 1949 the very word for wife was *neiren,* "inside person." As the classic *The Book of Rites* put it, "A man does not talk about affairs inside" the household, "a woman does not talk about affairs outside" the home. The Chinese ideogram for peace and harmony is a woman under a roof: 安. In this scheme, a woman's labor was absorbed within the home and brought in no income. Women were largely illiterate and could not inherit property.

This traditional inferiority was given philosophical legitimacy in an elaborate cosmological explanation which held that the world is divided into two interacting elements: yin, the attribute of all things female, which was dark, weak, and passive, and yang, the male characteristic, bright, strong, and active.

Until well into the twentieth century women's subordination was reinforced by the crippling practice of foot-binding. From the age of about five to fifteen, a young girl's feet were tightly wrapped, with the arch broken and the toes curled under, to produce the "lily foot." Men's interest in these small sensitive objects made them genuinely erogenous but a terrible pain for women. Even today it is not unusual in Peking to see elderly women with short, stumpy feet hobbling across the roads, trying to dodge the rivers of bicycles coming toward them. In all this, women were supposed to be tolerant. "Obey heaven and follow fate," counseled another saying.

When the Communists came to make their revolution, women represented easily the largest disinherited group in China—in Mao's phrase, they "held up half the sky"—and the Communists moved quickly to tap this latent force with favorable policies. Their main line of attack was to break down the barriers to women working, for Marxists have argued since Engels that the key to women's subservience is their exclusion from the marketplace. Articulate Chinese women I talked with quoted Lenin's comment that to assure woman's "complete emancipation and make her the equal of man . . . it is necessary for women to participate in common productive labor."

On paper, Chinese women today have made far more gains in this way than their American sisters. While American women are still struggling to get the Equal Rights Amendment into the Constitution, China's constitution, in Article 53, proclaims, "Women enjoy equal rights with men in all spheres of political, economic, cultural, social, and family life. Men and women enjoy equal pay for equal work." Elsewhere, the Chinese constitution guarantees everyone's right to work. In practice this means women must work; they no longer have the choice between career or family. A liberal 1950 family law, the first law passed by the Communists, provided for freedom of choice in marriage, abolished concubinage, and gave women the right to own property, use their own names, and sue for divorce. In recent years the Communists have also legalized abortion and made it free on demand. Women in the cities get a minimum of fifty-six days paid maternity leave, six months if they sign the pledge to have only one child. The government has set up a network of child-care centers. Many Chinese women now go to college, and one third of all scientists and engineers are women.

Yet despite these achievements, China is still a man's world; Chinese women may be liberated but they are still not equal. On every plane ride I took on the Chinese airlines, CAAC, almost all the passengers were men; only the stewardesses were female. In the small provincial city of Foshan, outside Canton, in the south, I stopped to eat lunch in a nondescript three-story concrete restaurant. There were hundreds of male patrons busy gobbling down bowls of fried noodles, dishes of pork and mustard greens, and tureens of soup—young factory workers in their undershirts and old peasants in their traditional black pajamas. But I didn't see a single woman except for the waitresses. When I remarked on the absence of female customers, my guide, a cheerful, rosy-cheeked woman in her late twenties, responded, "the men don't have housework to do." Jan Wong reported that when she traveled "soft-berth" class on the trains, she often drew suspicious looks, for none of the other passengers, all men, could figure out how a woman, and such a young one at that, got access to this privileged status. Most of the men, she learned, were on business trips, or "missions," as the Chinese termed them.

In the countryside, I noticed, women now work in the fields, giving them new economic independence, especially important for young wives who can begin to prove themselves to their mothers-in-law before they give birth to a son. In the past that was the critical test—providing a male heir to continue the family line. But today women are usually assigned the most backbreaking labor, transplanting rice or picking beans while many of their menfolk are off driving tractors or acting as cadres. Steven Butler, an American sociologist who lived on a commune in Hebei province, in north China, calculated that women actually did 80 percent of all the fieldwork. And while in theory pay is supposed to be equal, I found on visits to over a dozen communes that men normally were awarded about ten work points per day while women got only seven or eight for much the same labor. (Work points are the system of remuneration for peasants. Each person is given a certain number for his day's work, and at the end of the year, after the harvest is in, the total number of work points is added up and the peasants are paid according to their share of the overall output.) Cadres at the communes I toured explained that the discrepancy in awarding work points was the result of the natural physiological difference between the sexes—men are stronger and should be paid more for doing harder work. Similarly, in industry, women tend to be shunted into light industry like textiles, electronics, and neighborhood cooperative handicraft factories making embroidery, lacquerware, paper boxes, toys, and silk flowers. These are the most repetitive jobs, which draw the lowest pay and other benefits.

In education, a nationwide survey by the Ministry of Education found that girls make up 50 percent of all the pupils in primary schools. But by high school the number has shrunk to 40 percent of the total student body and by college only 30 percent. At Peking University, according to the New China News Agency, the entering class in 1980 had only 23 percent women. Kang Keqing, the septuagenarian president of the All-China Women's Federation, the largely toothless official government women's organization, complained in a meeting once that women account for 80 percent of the illiterates in China today. Females, she added, in an unusual burst of candor, also make up 60 to 70 percent of the young people in the cities who have not yet been assigned jobs after finishing school. And, she charged, "pass grades for recruiting workers in factories and enrolling students are arbitrarily raised for women." It was the only time I heard a Chinese leader admit to continuing inequality.

One reason for these statistics is that, contrary to Marxist expectations, mass access to the job market has not proved a panacea because the old assumptions of male superiority and female subservience endure. I was surprised one evening when our friend Miao commented on the natural difference between our son and her daughter.

"Boys are more inclined to rough sports, they are more naughty, and they will do better in science and math," she said over dinner. "Girls are better-behaved, more partial to music and dance, and they are better in school in languages. It is their nature."

These stereotypes remain even stronger in the countryside, where the level of education is lower. Lihua, my petitioner friend, recalled that in her village girls were not sent to school at all, for their parents still regard them as "outsiders" in whom such an investment is really being made for another family, she explained. At marriage, they will move away. Girl babies in her village are called "a thousand ounces of gold"; but a boy child is called "ten thousand ounces of gold."

A confidential study on the status of women and marriage prepared by a team of investigators for the Women's Federation in 1980 discovered the persistence of other old customs which the Communists claimed to have eliminated. (I was given a copy of the document by a woman student at Peking University.) In one commune in Shanxi, there were 146 girls under the age of five who were betrothed, accounting for 43 percent of their age group, the investigators found. Among those five to ten years old, 81 percent were engaged. In a county in Fujian, on the southeast coast, the investigators said that, because of the continued selling of child brides, parental interference in their daughters' marriages, and ill treatment of new brides there were four suicides by poisoning, four cases of nervous breakdown, and two attempted murders, all within the first five months of 1980. In the Tungfang commune of the county, three women and one young man left home to join Buddhist nunneries and a monastery because of marriage problems. The report described these troubles as a "feudal remnant."

The report also uncovered a new problem, one caused by modernization —"the abandonment of wives is on the rise," it said. This occurred largely among men who were promoted to be cadres and were then transferred to urban areas or among young men who got into college. The investigators cited the case of a teacher at Guizhou University, in the southwest, Zhang Guangxi. He had originally married a peasant woman in his native village, but after he was appointed a professor in the university he divorced her to marry an elementary school teacher. Later, however, he fell in love with a student in his school. To complicate matters, his second wife was pregnant and Zhang pushed her into getting abortions, twice. In the meantime, without bothering to get a second divorce, he went to register his marriage to the student at the local civil affairs office. The pair were convicted of bigamy.

The investigators also turned up evidence of battered wives. "The major reasons for maltreatment of wives are male chauvinism and a desire to force the wife into divorce," the authors of the report stated. Of the 2,128 letters the Women's Federation received in 1979 about marriage problems, evidently from women who had no other outlet for their grievances, 436 of them, 20 percent, concerned physical abuse. The report related the gruesome example of a former peasant turned soldier, Qiu Haichi, in Henan province, in central China. Qiu was engaged to a local peasant woman before entering the army, and even after he suffered severe burns, which covered much of his face, his fiancée went through with the wedding. But after Qiu's scars healed, the report found, he had an affair with another woman and pressed his wife for a divorce. She refused. Their quarrels then worsened, and "on January 3, 1980, he attacked her with a knife, slicing off both her arms and digging out her eyes. After this, he trampled her eyeballs underfoot. Neighbors heard and rushed to save her, but she was on her last breath," the report concluded.

Within the Communist Party itself, despite its lip service to equality, Chinese women have fared no better, and perhaps not as well, as American women in gaining access to political power. Women now make up 4.7 million of the 20 million Chinese cadres, 24 percent of the total, it is true. But there is only one woman among the twenty-four regular members of the ruling Politburo, which makes the key decisions, and she is the widow of Zhou Enlai, Deng Yingchao. Although Madame Deng herself is regarded with saintly affection, she was selected for the post only after her husband's death as part of respect for his legacy. There are no women among the eleven members of the Party Secretariat, the powerful organization that runs the Party on a daily basis. And while several American women have been elected governors of their states, none of the first Party secretaries and governors of China's twenty-nine provincial level units are women. One woman, Chen Muhua, a tall, robust, former engineering student, has become one of the two alternate members of the Politburo. She is also the only woman among the dozen deputy prime ministers who administer the government apparatus. But Chinese friends cautioned against looking to her as a future national leader. They noted that her areas of responsibility—family planning, day-care centers, and China's economic aid program to Third World nations—are not the portfolios given to members of the inner circle. They also said her career had been blunted by charges of corruption and arrogance, including an incident, as mentioned earlier, when she refused to give a ride on her special plane to a group of sick Chinese athletes when she was returning from a trip to Rumania. Instead, she brought back a load of West German furniture for herself.

Virtually all the other women who have risen to prominence in Communist China have done so by marrying well—Jiang Qing, Mao's widow, Soong Qing Ling, the widow of Sun Yat-sen, who was a deputy chairman of the National People's Congress until her death in 1981, and Miss Kang, the head of the Women's Federation. Her late husband was Zhu De, the leader of the Red Army and a revered military hero. The Women's Federation, despite some activities like the confidential study of women's status, devotes much of its energy to urging women to support the current Party line. I was amused at the opening ceremony of the fourth, and most recent, national women's congress in 1978 when the welcoming speech was delivered by a man, Wang Dongxing, the former head of Mao's bodyguards who has since been purged. In her own address, Miss Kang declared that "the major task for the new period" set by the Party "was also the task for Chinese women." That is, she said, "To steadfastly continue the revolution under the dictatorship of the proletariat, deepen the three great revolutionary movements of class struggle, the struggle for production and scientific experiment, and transform China into a great and powerful socialist country with modern agriculture, industry, national defense, and science and technology by the end of the century." Stern rhetoric, but not what American feminists would applaud. In China, class struggle comes before the battle between the sexes.

Perhaps because of the tradition of women shunning involvement outside the home, the wives of Chinese leaders do not play a regular ceremonial role accompanying their husbands on trips abroad or appearing with them on podiums as do the spouses of American presidents and astronauts. In fact, while Hua Guofeng was Party Chairman and Prime Minister, the Chinese press never even disclosed the name of his wife. But, Chinese friends advised, senior officials ensured good jobs for their wives in keeping with another tradition, family solidarity. Hua's wife, they said, had been a political commissar in the Light Industry Bureau before his selection as Party Chairman, when she was given a plum post inside Zhongnanhai, the Communist headquarters. Deng's wife, Cho Lin, a short, round-faced woman who did travel with her husband on his epochal trip to the United States in 1979, is said to be head of the General Office of the Party Military Affairs Commission. That innocuous-sounding title would put her in charge of communications between the Party and the army, a critical post from which she can help Deng exert authority over the armed forces.

"Wives may not play an important role in public," the daughter of an army general said. "But as we say, a lot of decisions are made by whispering in the ear on the pillow, especially when the family may benefit in some way."

If wives of the leaders share their husbands' rise to fame, they also share their ignominy. Wang Guangmei, the sophisticated, articulate, attractive wife of the former head of state, Liu Shaoqi, was dragged before mass rallies and imprisoned for a decade after her husband was denounced as China's leading capitalist roader in the Cultural Revolution. Now that Liu has been posthumously rehabilitated—he died in 1969 in prison—she has been released from jail and given a new job. The most famous downfall, of course, was that of Jiang Qing, who was arrested less than a month after Mao died in 1976. But to me an equally telling example of how wives are tied to their husbands involved Cao Yiou. She was the widow of Kang Sheng, a Politburo member who was a close supporter of Mao and for many years the dreaded head of China's secret police. Cao was a deputy to the National People's Congress. But when Kang was posthumously criticized for his role in the Cultural Revolution and then expelled from the Party in 1980, four years after his death, she suddenly lost her legislative seat. Cao herself was not attacked.

In the countryside also women's entry into the job market has not translated into greater political power. Whenever I visited a commune I made it a practice to ask how many of the local cadres were women. The answer at the Bitter Water commune in Gansu, in the northwest, was typical. Of the thirty-three cadres in the commune and its composite brigades and production teams, only two were women. One of these was Deng Meisheng, the deputy commune chairman. Tall and lithe, with short straight hair, a strong flat nose, and broad cheekbones, she bore a striking resemblance to an American Indian. During an interview with commune officials in a peasant's mud-walled house, she sat on a low stool in a corner. I noticed she was not dressed like a peasant—under her regulation blue-cotton cadre's tunic she had on a tan cardigan sweater and a pale-blue flower-printed blouse with a high round collar. When I asked what her duties were, the commune chairman replied for her. She was in charge of work with women, youth, family planning, public health, education, and culture, the chairman said. In other words, everything excluding actual farm production and its financing, the critical sectors for the peasants. In the communes I was taken to, the women cadres I encountered almost always were responsible for what the Chinese call "women's work," meaning family planning and encouraging women to work in the fields, not the consciousness-raising activity Western feminists think of by the same term.

There are several reasons why women's increased work in the fields has not had the effect the Communists, and some American women's groups, expected. For one thing, in a traditional Chinese way, the payment of work points at the end of the year is handed over to the family head, usually a man, not to an individual, since the income is regarded as the earnings of the whole family. Because women still move to their husband's family at marriage, they aren't able to build up the network of *guan-xi* necessary to be selected for leadership posts. And equally important, women are still expected to do the household chores, which gives them less time than men for cadre duties.

It is this wearisome double burden, of trying to juggle the conflicting demands of a job and a family, which seems to press hardest on Chinese women today, both in the cities and villages. Unlike American women, many of whom feel torn about embarking on a career, Chinese women have no choice—by law, they must work. When we went to the Wangs' house for dinner, Miao had to shop and do the cooking. Li was the polite host, keeping us company, pouring us beer, and filling our bowls with the latest dish of hot food, which Li would bring from their tiny kitchen with its cold-water sink and coal brazier for cooking. Only at the end of the meal, after she had finished all the cooking, did she come in and sit down to eat herself. Giving a dinner party is particularly hard for a Chinese wife, Barbara pointed out, because none of the food can be cooked ahead of time and must be served immediately after each dish is individually fried. Like most other Chinese, the Wangs did not have a refrigerator and Miao had to shop seven days a week.

When we were together with the Wangs, they seemed a happy couple. But once when I was driving Li home alone in the car he complained that his wife was too involved in her work and too tired and moody at the end of the day. Miao, on the other hand, confessed in private that she felt like the character in a popular new novel, *At Middle Age,* about a hardworking, middle-aged eye surgeon who finds herself exhausted after a day's work in the hospital, which may include performing several operations. Gradually, she realizes, she is neglecting her husband and children.

American women who have children and also work can sympathize with Miao's plight. But even the most energetic Western woman would find it difficult to cope with life in China, for many of the labor-saving devices she takes for granted simply don't exist there. There are no vacuum cleaners to do the cleaning. Nor has Chinese industry yet produced dishwashers, clothes washers, or dryers. Chinese workmen are so unfamiliar with these appliances that when my colleague Michael Parks of *The Los Angeles Times* moved into his apartment, he discovered the technician assigned to help him had connected his American-made clothes washer to the sink to bring water into it. But he had not attached the hose in the back of the machine to drain the water out. When Parks suggested politely the washer might not work that way, the worker assured him that was how he always installed them for diplomats. Some Chinese who can afford it take their clothes to a neighborhood laundry; others do them in buckets at home, often using cold water. But whatever that ingredient is, advertised in American television commercials, that gets clothes "whiter than white," Chinese soap doesn't have it; it leaves them gray.

China has not yet developed a tampon either. During their menstrual period, Chinese women make do with a roll of coarse grayish toilet paper which they form into pads; then, if they have enough money, they buy some cotton to wad around the paper pad. All this fits into a belt that is made of reddish rubber on one side and flowered cotton on the other. Peasant women use rags which they must wash over and over, since it is impossible to buy paper or cotton in the countryside, friends told me. Before the influx of tourists in the late 1970s, a customs official confiscated a box of tampons from an American woman who had planned a lengthy stay in Peking. He didn't believe her explanation of what they were for and evidently thought they were a new smuggling technique. The proper Chinese word for menstruation is *yue-jing,* "monthly passing." But the colloquial term is *dao-mei,* "rotten luck," reflecting Chinese attitudes toward the problem.

The double burden of worker and wife is especially difficult for mothers with infants. Although China has sired more babies than any nation on earth, there are no disposable diapers yet, only the old cloth variety which must be washed by hand and hung to dry in people's small apartments. Nor has Chinese industry manufactured any canned baby food or even maternity clothes for pregnant women.

China is still a developing country, of course, and it would be wrong to expect it to reach the same level of creature comforts as the United States, Japan, or Western Europe. But given the Communists' proclaimed devotion to equality for women, I was surprised that there are still far from enough nursery schools and kindergartens. Mao once told André Malraux, the French writer, that "to liberate women is not to manufacture sewing machines." In his cryptic way, the Chairman was suggesting that the real path to emancipating women from household drudgery lay in providing collective social services like day-care centers and communal dining facilities. But despite the fanfare with which Chinese display their nurseries to foreign visitors, Miss Chen, the Deputy Prime Minister, admitted in 1980 that only 28 percent of China's babies and young children are in nurseries and a slightly smaller number in kindergartens. The majority of mothers, even though they work, still have to fend for themselves. By comparison, 53 percent of Americans' three-, four-, and five-year-olds were in some kind of day-care center, nursery school, or kindergarten in 1980.

The most common solution for Chinese families, said Lao Wu, my Chinese assistant, was to call for grandmother to come and live with the family until the child reached school age. He had brought his own mother from their native town in Fujian, as far south of Peking as Miami is from New York, and a four-day journey by train. Some parents whose apartments were too small to accommodate a visiting relative farmed their children out to grandparents in the countryside, as did a woman I knew in the Foreign Ministry. But her four-year-old daughter, after a year in the village, refused to call her mother. Those who could afford it, high cadres, some army officers, and well-paid technicians, hired maids.

All this work, managing a family as well as a job, takes its toll on Chinese women. "Women have a harder life than men," observed an astute woman professor at Peking University who was married herself. "Have you noticed," she asked me, "how women in China age faster than men? By their early thirties they look like they are forty, heavier around the middle, the jowls, and with lines showing in their faces. Our husbands stay slimmer and younger-looking." She, at thirty-five, had become very conscious of her diet and was fighting a battle with her waistline and hips. To me, her husband did look ten years younger.

The imperative for women to work in China, ironically, has created a strong countercurrent of anti-women's liberation feeling among some educated Chinese women, much the same segment of well-educated, affluent women who in America have been the most active feminists and for whom a career is the panacea. Where the Americans are rebelling against having to be housewives, the Chinese are unhappy about having to be breadwinners. Having a career, once it becomes a necessity, can be transformed from a means to self-fulfillment and independence into drudgery.

The professor at Peking University complained that what she really wanted to do was to stay home and raise her son and daughter, who currently live in a government kindergarten from Monday morning till the parents pick them up after work on Saturday. Their only real chance to be with the children is on Sundays.

"If I had my choice," she said, "I would devote my time to tutoring my son, to make sure he gets into the best school." Surprisingly, she was less concerned about her daughter's education. "It is our boy who must make a career," the professor explained, reflecting the persistence of the traditional attitude.

But it is the difficulty women often have in getting a divorce which more than anything else illustrates the ambivalent position Chinese women have reached—freed from some of the old fetters, yet not fully equal. In theory, divorce in China should be easy. The Communist family law, specifically amended in 1980 to make it more progressive, provides that "in cases of complete alienation of mutual affection, and when mediation has failed, divorce should be granted." The language is clear and simple. But a number of Chinese women I met complained more bitterly about their trouble in getting a divorce than about anything else.

Take the case of Guiying, a slight, cheerful worker in a battery factory with tiny eyes and short pigtails. She recalled that she and her husband, another worker, had been married only a few months when they began quarreling about the money she spent on clothes and he consumed on cigarettes and alcohol. Soon, she said, he had turned violent and she moved back into her old cubicle in the factory dormitory. Three years after they separated, she felt sanguine about applying for a divorce, particularly since her husband had found a new girl friend and agreed to apply, too. But when she went to her factory Party committee, in accordance with proper procedure, they told her it would take time to investigate. Six months later, she asked what had happened. Her application had been handed over to the security section, she was told. Finally, a full year later, she was notified—the request was turned down.

"The Party secretary said it would be better if we got together again," Guiying told me during a meal in a small restaurant near the Peking Hotel. "He wouldn't say why we had been refused, but I think personally it is a matter of face. The authorities are very feudal. They want it to look as if everyone is happily married. Divorce to them is still immoral."

Guiying then quoted another proverb: "A good horse won't accept two saddles; a good wife doesn't marry twice."

I wondered why she didn't apply to the court directly.

"If your *danwei* doesn't agree, there's no hope," she explained. "The court will always come back and ask your *danwei* before looking into the case. Marriage is for life."

Just how sternly many Chinese still feel about divorce I discovered when I had the rare chance to attend a divorce trial in Shanghai. It might have been a tale out of an old Chinese novel. The wife, Wei Jingfeng, who was the plaintiff, charged that her "contradictions," or troubles with her husband, began because he was too filial to his mother. A dour, round-faced, thirty-five-year-old worker in a meteorological instruments factory, she testified that her husband had insisted they live with his mother and grandparents. Then when she gave birth to her first child, her in-laws were unhappy. It was a girl, not a boy.

"They had very feudal ideas," Wei recalled in the makeshift courtroom, the headquarters of her neighborhood committee. The building was an old Chinese-style structure with a sloping tile roof; inside, the only adornments on the high yellow walls were color portraits of Mao and Hua.

"After I was discharged from the hospital, when I entered our house, my mother-in-law followed an old custom," Wei continued. "She took a young boy in her arms, meaning she wanted a grandson next time.

"I was very unhappy when I saw this. My husband's grandmother is over eighty. She told me, 'You had flowers, now the next time bear fruit.' "

Later, Wei said, she and her mother-in-law quarreled over the number of eggs she ate; her husband's family thought she was wasting money. Things reached a crisis when Wei had an abortion without consulting the family rather than risk giving birth to another girl. Finally, she moved out with her daughter to a small apartment of her own, she related, but it was an impossible situation because her husband kept all their ration cards.

As she recounted her story, the couple's now five-year-old daughter wandered around the packed room, seemingly oblivious to the family tragedy. But when her mother concluded her testimony, she suddenly came up to her mother's side and put her straw sun hat, with a red ribbon, on her mother's head. Then she climbed on her mother's lap.

The estranged husband, Hong Songdao, thirty-nine, a tall, slim and solemn man who worked as a cadre in a machine exporting agency, told the story differently. He claimed that, when his wife came back from the hospital, one of his nephews happened to be visiting and his mother had picked the boy up to look at the new baby. In his view, the trouble was that his wife had shown no respect for his mother; she had smashed much of his family's furniture in fits of anger, and she had ripped his clothes one day when she encountered him on the street. She had also gone to his office "over 140 times" to complain about his behavior, causing him serious embarrassment.

"Because of her shrewish temperament, we're incompatible," Hong testified. "But because of my daughter, I felt contradictions in my heart and don't want to be divorced."

My Chinese guide, a cherubic woman with graying hair from the Chinese People's Association for Friendship with Foreign Countries, looked at me knowledgeably. Most men oppose divorce, she whispered, and most divorce cases are now instituted by women, one mark of their progress. In the past, men could discard their wives, while women had virtually no right to seek divorce. But my guide hinted she already knew what the court would decide. It was composed of a male judge and two so-called lay assessors, one each from the husband's and wife's *danweis.*

"Our duty is to educate people, not to attack them," the judge began. "You should both be more patient. Our country needs stability and unity and families need stability and unity." It was a Confucian plea for social harmony. Then, the judge counseled the wife, she should withdraw her petition for divorce. It would be economically wasteful, he implied. Two apartments and two sets of ration tickets for one couple were more than a crowded city could afford.

To the judge's opinion, the lay assessors added the weight of community pressure, always strong in China. "I think it's not a case where divorce is necessary," a middle-aged male worker from the husband's office interjected. "It is only a problem of some lingering feudal ideas by the mother-in-law."

He turned to the wife. "You should tell your mother-in-law that today in our society there are women airplane pilots, like men, so girls are not less valuable than boys. Both you and your husband should carry out more ideological work to reeducate her." Here again was a Confucian idea, that people are inherently maleable, that had made its way into Chinese Communist practice.

A woman worker from the wife's factory, with a broad, full face and blue tunic, also chastised the plaintiff. "You should know it is not a happy result to get divorced," she said to Wei. "You must consider your daughter's happiness as well as your own. My suggestion is, the wife should show more respect for the old generation. Otherwise, in the future, how would you feel if your child did not respect you?"

This was not exactly sisterly solidarity, and it was more pressure than the wife could bear. She assented to a reconciliation. It was their sixth, she said as she left the courtroom.

Still, the Chinese press often reported that divorce was on the increase, as in other countries undergoing modernization. Some articles applauded the trend as a sign of liberation for women; others railed that this was degeneration into capitalist licentiousness. The confidential investigation prepared for the Women's Federation on the status of marriage charged, "Under the influence of bourgeois attitudes toward matters of love and marriage, ethics are sliding. Some young women think that women's liberation means sexual freedom.

"Some young people think of marrying as a sort of game, marry carelessly and divorce lightly. They choose a partner only on the basis of family background, how good their job is, or how good-looking they are. As a result, they don't get along and fight right up to divorce."

The report found that in the city of Wuhan, in central China, in one recent year there were 110 cases of divorce, five of them within six months of marriage, 60 percent within three years. In Peking, the investigators said, there was even a case where a couple went to register their marriage in the morning, in the afternoon when they went to buy furniture, began to argue, and by late in the day were back at the local government office to try to get their marriage annulled.

One woman I met had succeeded in getting divorced, Limei, a plain-looking schoolteacher who felt sexually unfulfilled with her husband. The divorce had actually been her husband's idea, she insisted, but she now regarded it as a disaster.

"My friends and people at school treat me like a strange animal," she lamented. "At school they talk about me behind my back, and in person my friends pretend they don't know I'm divorced. It's as if there was something evil about it."

She had become depressed. She would call me one day on the phone in high spirits just to say hello; then the next day she would upbraid me morosely for not inviting her over to our house more often. I came to dread her calls, not knowing how to respond and feeling guilty when I took refuge in saying I was too busy working to talk.

The situation was awkward for her, because she and her ex-husband taught in the same school and they were constantly bumping into each other. Neither had yet been able to get a transfer, or to get separate housing, though he had finally moved out and slept in his classroom.

I learned just how correct Limei's complaint about gossip was from another teacher in her school who didn't realize we were friends. One day the other teacher recounted the story of her divorce as if it were the school scandal. "She dresses fashionably, she likes to sing and dance," he said of Limei, "and she got divorced." It was as close as Chinese come in polite conversation to saying that someone is loose and fooled around.

And yet, for all Limei's troubles, when I once asked her if she felt women in China had achieved equality, she looked at me as if I had said something foolish. "Certainly," she answered. "A lot of work has been done for women since Liberation." Her response was typical. Most Chinese women simply did not seem concerned with the issues that agitate American feminists: equal pay, promotions, exclusion from political power, sexism in the office.

Jan Wong came to the office angry one day. She said a notice had just been put up on the bulletin board of the *danwei* where she then lived, the Foreign Languages Press. It announced the summer schedule for use of the communal shower room. Women would get three hours per week, men nine. She had scrawled a sarcastic comment using a thick red-felt pen: "What kind of male-female equality is this?" The next morning someone had retorted, "This is a scientific arrangement." Another person wrote, "This is equality." Jan could not induce any mutters of protest from other women in the building, though, as she pointed out, they were equal in number to the men.

At first I was baffled by this lack of feminine consciousness. But the woman professor at Peking University who wanted to stay home to tutor her son helped put it in perspective. At her college, she said, if a husband and wife were both teaching in the same department and they came up for a raise at the same time, the husband would get the money first. She knew, because that was what had happened to her and her husband.

"You may say that's unequal. It is. But that is not important. It doesn't matter who gets the raise as long as one of us does."

For, she went on to explain, "in China we still operate on the family system. Everything still goes to the family. What is important to me is to see that my children get properly cared for and get ahead." She did not see women as a separate category.

Another woman, a slender, graceful Chinese-American architect who was born in China, summarized the crux of the issue. "Part of the story is that Chinese women have made real progress," she said. "But you must also remember China's level of economic development. Chinese women can't afford to be interested in feminist issues. They focus on the things that are important to them—getting a decent apartment with a toilet of its own, buying groceries, figuring out who will take care of the children while they work. They don't yet identify with their jobs or careers. Fulfillment for them comes at home with the family."

But it was an incident that happened during Deng Xiaoping's tour of the United States in 1979 which helped me realize Chinese men and women have not yet gone through the arguments feminists in the West advance. Among the large contingent of Chinese correspondents covering the trip was Deng Qin, a short, wiry, nervous, and very aggressive television camera woman, no relative of the Party leader. At the welcoming reception at the White House, she burst through the other reporters and a cordon of Secret Service guards to get close to Deng and President Carter. Later, at a formal state dinner in the White House, she again shoved past a line drawn by the Secret Service. But the third time she did it, one of the agents, a tall, heavyset, muscular man with a mustache and dressed in a brown three-piece suit, cuffed her hard on the shoulder and pushed her back behind the rope set up for the press.

Miss Deng was incensed. She complained, in tears, to her leader, an official of the Central Television Station, and he in turn demanded a formal apology from the U.S. government.

"It would have been okay if it had happened to a man, but she was a woman," the Chinese official said sternly to an American diplomat. "It shows a lack of manners." There was a scare that the episode might mar Deng's visit.

When told about her grievance, the Secret Service agent responded, "They may think that way in China, but in the United States now men and women get equal treatment. My job is to protect the President."

Later on in the trip, Miss Deng began to relax. Coached by an American interpreter, she sang a song to the Secret Service man, "Getting to Know You." He leaned down and kissed her on the forehead.

8.　No Road Out

没　出　路

YOUTH

"Youth must be put to the test."
  Mao Zedong to André Malraux, 1965, at the outset of the
  Cultural Revolution
"Don't read too much. Too much study can kill people."
  Mao to his niece, Wang Hairong, 1965

Lao San was tall and slim, with smoothly combed back hair and handsome, even features. Like many children of Party cadres, he was self-assured and gregarious—his friends said debonair. He never appeared in rumpled blues, like other Chinese; his pants were always well tailored and neatly pressed. The last night I saw Lao San (the name means "Number Three," as in third-born son), he was wearing a Western-style dark-gray dacron and wool suit, an expensive and daring affectation in proletarian Peking. Lao San, who was in his late twenties, was a reporter for the English-language magazine *China Reconstructs,* and that evening had been assigned to cover a press conference at the Peking Hotel given by the World Wildlife Fund to announce its plans to help save China's giant pandas. There wasn't anything unusual in his behavior. He sat next to Sir Peter Scott, the chairman of the Wildlife Fund, taking notes. After the press conference, an office car took him home to the one-room apartment he shared with his slender, pretty wife and eighteen-month-old son.

Two plainclothes detectives from the Public Security Bureau were waiting outside in the mild spring air to arrest him. Later that evening other policemen searched his home and found five stolen tape recorders and a typewriter, only a fraction of the loot he had purloined over the past few years from his office. For Lao San, it turned out, had been the leader of a juvenile gang since his high school days over a decade before.

I was intrigued by his story, which was pieced together by my assistant Jan Wong. He had first been caught stealing as a teen-ager when he lived across the street from the Foreign Languages Press, which housed *China Reconstructs* and where his father was an official. But because of his father's position, his peccadillos were covered up. He was able first to join the Communist Party and then to be "recommended by the masses" for admission to college as one of what were called the worker-peasant-soldier students. At the time, during the Cultural Revolution, Mao had abolished the regular college entrance exams—he felt they discriminated against peasants and workers—and replaced the tests with a system of admission by recommendation according to a candidate's political background. In college, Lao San was again charged with theft, but he made a public self-criticism and his father's friends managed to get his wrongdoing expunged from his dossier, a difficult trick.

After graduation, when he was assigned to *China Reconstructs,* things began to be missing from the office. First there was one comrade's copies of *National Geographic,* a treasured item since at the time foreign magazines were contraband. Next it was a typewriter; then an English dictionary (they were unavailable in stores). The office owned a collective bicycle, ostensibly for the proofreaders to use when they had to travel to the printing factory; but most of them were lethargic, middle-aged women who preferred knitting and grocery shopping. When Lao San discovered no one used it, he asked if he could keep it for riding to work. Shortly after he was given the key, he reported the chain had been stolen. The office had no choice but to give him money to replace it. A few days later he announced the tires had been snatched.

Still, Lao San hadn't been caught in the act, and government policy was to try to "reform" errant Party members like him, not arrest them. Besides, he proved useful. The Foreign Languages Press often screened "internal" movies in its auditorium. The neighborhood kids inevitably learned about the showings, though they weren't advertised, and would storm the doors if they weren't let in. Officials at the press discovered that Lao San was the only person who could control them, friends recalled. He would go to the front gate and say, "Humph, don't you recognize me?"

They were immediately respectful. "Oh, it's you, Lao San."

Lao San's downfall came when he broke into the apartment of a fellow employee whose boy friend had just been to Japan and brought her back an expensive stereo tape recorder. After stuffing the recorder in his satchel, he arrived at the office late to find a meeting in progress in the hallway. Everyone noticed the large bag on his shoulder. During the morning break, still cool, he laid the satchel on a radiator and played Ping-Pong with a friend on the office table. But the victim happened to go home and found a window smashed and her apartment in disorder. The cadres immediately suspected

Lao San and, while he was engrossed in his game, peeked in his bag. They hesitated to arrest him on the spot, afraid he might have accomplices.

Shortly after he was detained, I asked Jan to interview his wife. She had permed hair and a reputation as a fashion plate. On the day of the last robbery, she had created a sensation in the collective cafeteria when she appeared in a fake leopard-skin coat.

"I am a person who cares a lot about face," she told Jan. "When all this happened, I felt extremely depressed." Jan noticed there were dirty clothes soaking in the sink, dirty dishes on the small stove, and garbage in the pan on the floor.

"It was society that made him do it," his wife complained. His father had been an important cadre in the Foreign Languages Press, had led delegations abroad—a mark of authority—and his mother was also a Party member, his wife related. But in the Cultural Revolution his parents were attacked and sent to prison. "The big character posters against his parents were even pasted up outside their front door. He began to get disillusioned." She sighed. "Some people say that the old cadres suffered during the Cultural Revolution, but in fact an entire generation was destroyed, the young people."

His wife also lashed out at all the campaigns of the past three decades and all the changes in political line.

"One day our big brother, the Soviet Union, becomes our revisionist enemy. Then, overnight, our staunch and loyal ally, Albania, is wrong and always has been wrong. Next it is our lips and teeth neighbor, Vietnam, who attacks us. What are we supposed to believe?

"In the 1950s morality was taught in class. It was the new Communist morality, but there was a definite sense of right and wrong. Now right and wrong is simply a matter of the current line; it depends on who is in power. So people care only about themselves and getting ahead. Everyone does it."

Whether one agreed with all his wife's claims or not, Lao San did seem to me a casualty of the Cultural Revolution, one of those young people under thirty whom the Chinese now call "the lost generation." Mao had always looked on youth as the bearers of the new society. It was young people who had fueled the May Fourth movement of 1919 which rekindled Chinese nationalism and led to the founding of the Chinese Communist Party in 1921. Mao himself was only twenty-eight years old when he took part in the Party's first session. But the Cultural Revolution had turned China's younger generation into a social and economic problem. The problem is particularly serious because 65 percent of China's population is under thirty, or 650 million people. There are over 200 million teen-agers, almost as many as the entire population of the United States.

Generalizing about Chinese youth is as impossible as generalizing about young people in America. In sophistication and life-style, the brilliant son of Foreign Minister Huang Hua, who won a scholarship to Harvard and lives in a dormitory with friends who smoke pot, is a world apart from a young factory worker in Peking, not to mention the youthful peasant in tropical Sichuan who may have had five years of primary school before he took his place behind a water buffalo tilling the fields the way his ancestors did.

But the predominant mood of all these young people when I was in Peking —from 1979 to 1981—was cynicism, apathy, and indifference. The first political joke I heard in China came from a crew-cut twenty-seven-year-old graduate student at People's University in Peking, a school that trains cadres.

"Do you know about the son who asked his father what communism is like?" he asked me.

" 'Well, son,' the father explained. 'Communism is like the horizon. The more you approach it, the farther it recedes.' "

My first winter in Peking, the *People's Daily* reported with outrage that a group of youths had stood and jeered when three soldiers attempted to rescue a young boy who fell through a lake in Peking while skating. "Run, soldiers, you want to join the Party," the crowd was said to have shouted, alluding to the Party's reputation for trying to recruit activists who are always the first to volunteer.

In the southern port city of Xiamen, I watched with fascination from my hotel-room window as a small teen-age boy across the street let the air out of the tires of an olive-drab People's Liberation Army truck. Each time, before bending down to his task, he looked around carefully to see if anyone was watching. Ironically, on the wall behind him was a red-painted poster extolling China's young people to copy the heroic deeds of a model soldier named Lei Feng, who has long been held up an an exemplar of Communist rectitude. Earlier that day, I had heard children in a local school reciting a ditty about Lei Feng, who had died in 1962, the victim of a prosaic automobile accident:

"In the winter Lei Feng repairs cars regardless of the cold.
Lei Feng walks a thousand miles and does 10,000 good things.
Working for the Party and the people, his heart is red
and never changes."

But such Communist pieties about him had spent their force, as witnessed by the boy deflating the tires of the army truck. The cynicism of young people was the flip side of the earnest idealism of the early years of the People's Republic, the Boy Scout enthusiasm which showed in all the pictures of innocent, rosy-cheeked city youngsters going off to be resettled in the countryside "in accordance with Chairman Mao's great call," as the Chinese press liked to say. Some of this may always have been a sham. But for a foreigner conditioned by years of reading official propaganda and listening to glowing accounts from tourists, it came as a shock to meet some of these rusticated youth.

Lu Hong could have been a model for a propaganda poster—she had a beautiful, round, open face with high cheekbones, a vivacious smile, and those perpetually pink cheeks. Her shiny black hair was cut short on the sides and back and fell over her eyes in thick bangs. She was thirty years old, born in the same year as the People's Republic.

"I was very young when the Cultural Revolution began," she told me over a meal of *guo-tieh*, fried dumplings stuffed with cabbage and pork. "My schoolmates and I were among the first in Peking to become Red Guards, we believed deeply in Chairman Mao. I could recite the entire book of the Chairman's quotations backward and forward, we spent hours just shouting the slogans at our teachers."

Hong remembered in particular a winter day, with the temperature below freezing, when she and her faction of Red Guards put on their red armbands and made three of the teachers from their high school kneel on the ground outside without their coats or gloves. "We had gone to their houses to conduct an investigation, to search them, and we found some English-language books. They were probably only textbooks, but to us it was proof they were worshiping foreign things and were slaves to the foreigners. We held a bonfire and burned everything we had found."

After that, she recalled, the leader of her group, a tall, charismatic eighteen-year-old boy, the son of an army general, whose nickname was "Old Dog," ordered them to beat the teachers. He produced some wooden boards, and the students starting hitting the teachers on their bodies. "We kept on till one of the teachers starting coughing blood," Hong said. "Then Old Dog told us to stop. We felt very proud of ourselves. It seemed very revolutionary."

Two years later, Hong went on, she was one of the first to volunteer when Mao proclaimed, "It is very necessary for educated young people to go to the countryside to be reeducated by the poor and lower-middle peasants."

"They put me on a train to the northeast. There were two thousand four hundred other high school students in the cars. We were traveling for four days and didn't know what our destination was until they let us off at a state farm near the Soviet border. At the time, I was full of patriotism and wanted to protect the motherland.

"Then they put us in a dormitory made of mud, with mud walls and mud floors," she continued. "Sixty people slept in one room on two *kangs*, made of mud, straw, and manure." (A *kang* is a raised platform heated by flues running underneath which northern Chinese use for sitting on during the day and sleeping on at night to keep warm.) "At night, if you came in late, all you could see were sixty heads sticking out of the covers, down a narrow aisle."

The only way for her to bathe, Hong said, was in a small enamel basin. In the entire eight years she spent on the farm, she never got to take a bath or shower.

But the worst problem was boredom. The nearest town was a three-hour walk. That was where she had to go to see a movie. But in the first five years on the farm, she saw only three movies, all of which she had seen before in Peking. There were no books or magazines for sale, and many of her friends had not brought any with them.

"After getting up at five A.M. to work in the fields, you were too tired to read at night anyway, so some of the young people forgot how to read and write."

Still, Hong was lucky. Her father was a cadre and eventually arranged through the back door to get her transferred back to Peking.

"I spent eight years fanning the flames of revolution; it was like losing a big chunk out of your life. Now I would like to contribute to the motherland, but what do I have? I never finished high school. It's like my friends say, the Chinese people don't live, they just exist."

Hong was one of 17 million city youngsters sent down to the villages, nearly one in every ten urban residents. There were over one million from Shanghai, 620,000 from Peking, the greatest forced movement of population in history. Mao's purpose was threefold: to narrow the gap between the cities and the villages, to revive the young generation's flagging revolutionary spirit, and to relieve some of the excess population pressure on the urban areas. But these high-minded goals were lost on the young people themselves. What they found were the hardships, the boredom, and the frustration of rural life, and it sapped their revolutionary zeal.

Song Mingchao, a wiry, emphatic man who smoked constantly, said he had been revolted at first when he had to carry night soil—human excrement saved from the common privies around the village—and spread it on the fields by hand. Song was a southerner, from Canton, who was sent to Hainan Island, then still a remote backward area covered with jungle and inhabited by ethnic minorities.

But far worse, he said, was that he could never earn enough to support himself. The local male peasants, accustomed to the hard labor, drew ten work points a day, the women eight; but he never could get more than six or seven. "So we were always hungry. We scrounged in the fields, looking for sweet potatoes, roots, wild herbs, whatever we could find.

"Chairman Mao said we were supposed to learn from the peasants, but the peasants didn't want anything to do with us. We couldn't understand their dialect. And they said we were lazy; they blamed us for consuming their food without earning our share.

"The boys had another problem," Song added. "We couldn't find girl friends because the peasants wanted to marry someone who was a good worker and could earn lots of money. Once three of my friends shaved their heads. The cadres were angry and asked why. 'We might as well become monks,' they answered."

Eventually, Song decided, "There is no future for me in China." He and some friends forged travel documents and made their way to Canton. There he lived for six months illegally. He had no household registration and no ration coupons, so he joined an underground gang of other young people like himself. Some of the boys became pickpockets, hanging around the markets and movie theaters; a few of the girls acted as prostitutes. Whenever he had a chance, he practiced swimming in a park. After two attempts, he escaped to Hong Kong, swimming three hours across a bay where other refugees often drowned or were bitten by sharks. In 1980 the number of illegal refugees who managed to make it to Hong Kong reached as many as five hundred a night.

It was in the British colony where I talked with Song. He still read the Communist press, and he noted that after Mao's death the government largely abandoned the rustication program. Only five million of the seventeen million youth sent down to the villages were still there; the others had found their way back legally or illegally to add to the pressures on the cities. Song also liked to recite from Chairman Mao. He wondered if I knew what Mao had said in a talk at the caves in Yanan in 1939:

"How should we judge if a youth is revolutionary? There can be only one criterion, namely whether or not he is willing to integrate himself with the broad masses of the workers and peasants and does so in practice."

By that test, Song said, the revolution had failed.

It sometimes seemed as if young people had now deliberately inverted Mao's values, creating their own counterculture. Instead of calling each other "comrade," in good Communist fashion, I noticed, they addressed people as *shi-fu,* or "master," a traditional term for skilled craftsmen or experts. At the Peace Cafe, the restaurant and bar on Goldfish Alley where I encountered prostitutes, one of the customers was a tall, swaggering twenty-year-old who dressed in what looked like a zoot suit—a Western suit jacket with broad lapels, high padded shoulders, and gray bell-bottom pants, or "trumpet trousers," in the Chinese vernacular. He had teased up his hair and greased it into a pompadour, like a Chinese John Travolta.

When we met, he grabbed my hand in a gesture of bravado, identifying himself as Liu Guanghua, or "Liu Glory to China." (When he was later arrested for procuring, the *People's Daily* delicately changed his name to Liu Xiaohua, Liu Little Flower.)

"Do I look like a Chinese?" he asked proudly. "Not many Chinese can dress this way; but I do." When I told him he looked like a Hong Kong Chinese, he beamed.

"When I was a boy, I was very bad," he went on, his conversation and manners a parody of all the Maoist virtues. "You know what I liked to do? Fight. Every day I would have fistfights. Not just one on one, but gang fights, twenty at a time. I was the best." He gestured with his thumbs up to show he was tops. He also pointed to his nose. It looked like it had been broken half a dozen times.

"I studied Russian in school, but I never learned any. I could write only one letter, R. I didn't learn many Chinese characters either. I was a really bad student."

Liu had to go, some business with women, he said. I was curious to learn more about him and asked for his address. He hesitated. At first I thought he was nervous about having a foreigner visit his house. But then another friend of his explained, "He really doesn't write well." When he scribbled down the address, his calligraphy was almost as bad, I thought, as my own misshapen Chinese handwriting.

The younger generation's reversal of Maoist values also showed in their music. Chinese young people, unlike Russian youth, have not shown much interest in American rock music or jazz, perhaps because the sounds are too foreign and harsh. But while I was in Peking, people in their teens and twenties were swept by a craze for soft, wistful love songs from Taiwan and Hong Kong, many of them set to the music of Hawaiian guitars and electric organs. To Western ears, they sound old-fashioned, like a Chinese version of the Andrews Sisters from the 1940s. But to Chinese, who for years have been able to hear only the drumbeating ditties cranked out by the People's Liberation Army band like "The Night Soil Collectors Are Coming Down the Mountain," the new songs had a strong emotional appeal. The music made its way quickly around the cities as Chinese who began traveling abroad in the late 1970s or overseas Chinese coming back to visit relatives brought in cassette tapes. I found one of the most valued presents I could give young Chinese friends was a handful of Hong Kong cassettes; every time I returned from a trip to the British colony the roomboys in the Peking Hotel would stop by to see which new tapes I had brought.

An eminent Chinese journalist told me with a wry grin that the official Chinese Music Association had gotten itself into a dilemma over a contest it sponsored in the spring of 1980 to pick the fifteen most popular songs. It was the first such competition since 1949, and the association received over a million letters. The trouble was, the writers voted overwhelmingly for Teresa Teng, a glamorous, svelte chanteuse from Taiwan who had never been to the mainland, and Li Guyi, a petite, controversial soprano who imitated the beat of the Taiwan hits. Li had divorced her husband—on the grounds that he was sterile—to marry the son of the commander of the navy, shocking the Communist hierarchy. While the Music Association tried to figure out what to do about the results of its contest, the press fulminated against "bourgeois, decadent" songs. A paper in Tianjin declared that Teng's songs "are either too bitter or sentimental and should be resolutely resisted because they can only impair our physical and mental health and corrupt our revolutionary will." Finally the Music Association decided to manufacture its own list of the fifteen winners, all what the government called "militant" songs, including "Good-bye Mother," about a soldier going off to fight in the 1979 border war with Vietnam, and "Our Lives Are Full of Sunshine," about the Four Modernizations.

But people were not so easily hoodwinked. Several weeks after the official results were announced, the League of Left-Wing Writers held a large party to mark the fiftieth anniversary of its founding in Shanghai, well before Liberation. Li Guyi was one of the singers. After she performed, the audience gave her a standing ovation, unusual in China, but when she did not come back for an encore and was followed by an army chorus, half the people at the party walked out, the journalist later said. The event was being shown on live television, and a microphone picked up shouts of, "If Li Guyi isn't going to sing anymore, let's go home." The situation was doubly embarrassing because one of the participants was the deputy head of the Party Propaganda Department, Zhou Yang, who for years has been the Communists' cultural czar.

Just as the sudden availability of cassette recorders helped spread the rage for Hong Kong music, they also fueled a new passion for dancing. Before the Cultural Revolution some Party leaders had held sedate dances in the Peking Hotel on Saturday nights; but from 1966 to 1979 dancing was banned as a corrupt capitalist pastime. As a result, Barbara and I were not prepared for what happened the second night we went to our friends the Wangs for dinner. After the meal was finished, they folded up the table, stowed it in a corner, and turned on their new Japanese recorder, a present from a relative in Hong Kong. The first song was by Donna Summer. Miao and Li began clapping for Barbara and me to demonstrate the disco for them. Neither of us is a good dancer, but there was no choice, and soon we found ourselves on their tiny living-room floor switching partners not only with the Wangs but with several neighbors and relatives who had been alerted to the arrival of the hip foreigners. Somehow the Wangs had taught themselves a stiff facsimile of disco, and they had not forgotten the fox-trot, waltz, and tango they had learned before the Cultural Revolution.

"Life in China is dull, so dull," Mrs. Wang exclaimed. "It's why young people get in trouble." It was a comment I heard repeated often.

Another evening a young friend in his twenties, Yining, who worked for Peking Television, called to say he had tickets to a dance in the Great Hall of the People. I was incredulous. I was accustomed to thinking of the Great Hall as the holy sepulcher, the mother church of Chinese communism. In my mind its polished marble steps and hushed grand meeting rooms, always guarded by soldiers at attention with bayonet-tipped rifles, recalled the late Zhou Enlai feting Richard Nixon. But in 1980, in keeping with the government's new stress on profits to spur economic development, the Party began renting out some of the rooms in the Great Hall on a commercial basis. The dance that evening began early, at 6:30, in a huge room on the third floor with giant pillars and a green marble floor. Two bands played a medley of approved tunes, including several Western songs that have become part of the Chinese repertoire: "Red River Valley," "Auld Lang Syne," and "Do Re Mi" from the movie *The Sound of Music.* The lights had been left on bright; intimacy was impossible; but that didn't bother the dancers—they had come to dance, not hold hands or embrace in a dark corner. There were men dancing with men, women with women, even a mother essaying a new step with her small daughter. Several times an announcer warned over the loudspeaker, "It is forbidden to do rock and roll," but a number of young couples ground away anyway, behind a high lacquer screen. The illicit dancers were wearing sunglasses with the price tag and made in Hong Kong sticker still on them, a kind of magic talisman assuring their modernity. One of the women swung to the beat with her long waist-length hair loosed from its usual braids. She was tall for a Chinese, and had on a fur coat, tight red sweater, and hip-hugging bell-bottom slacks.

"The daughter of a high cadre," Yining said, pointing to her. "Only cadres' kids are well fed on milk and meat, and it shows."

At 9:30 the announcer abruptly declared the party over and the guests immediately streamed out, docile and obedient, without a pause. Americans would have hung around, hoping for another dance, I said to my host as we walked down the majestic steps looking toward the Gate of Heavenly Peace.

"We may be compliant on the surface," he replied. "We are conditioned to accepting authority. It is just like in *1984* by George Orwell," he said, adding that he had recently read the book. "It is an exact description of the Cultural Revolution; I loved it. But something else happened in the Cultural Revolution which Orwell didn't foresee—many people became disillusioned. Mao sent us out as Red Guards to topple the capitalist roaders. 'To rebel is justified,' he told us and we believed him. We pulled down the power holders. But then Mao said stop, and he called in the army to get rid of us and packed many of us off to the countryside. All he really wanted was for us to get rid of his enemies in the Party. We felt manipulated and betrayed." It was a widely shared sentiment among young Chinese I met.

He himself had spent three years on a commune planting rice before his father, a county official, had used a back-door connection to have him "recommended" by the peasants for admission to university under one of Mao's reforms. "It wasn't the peasants who picked me, it was the commune Party secretary," my acquaintance recalled. "You were supposed to be selected on the basis of your political background. Actually, my father was born into a poor peasant family, ran away to join the Red Army as a boy, and his parents were executed by the Kuomintang, so I did have a clean class record. But that wasn't what Mao intended."

After he graduated, his father again used his influence to have him assigned to the television station, a prestigious and easy job. But even this presumably fortunate young man was now disgruntled. For all Chinese who had entered college when the "recommendation" system was in effect, from 1970 to 1976, were stigmatized as "worker-peasant-soldier students." They hadn't had to pass the old exams to get into college—many had only a few years of primary school education before being selected—and while they were in university the classrooms were in chaos. Yining said he had never had to take a test during his college career. Mao's successors had taken their revenge on the worker-peasant-soldier students by excluding them from several national wage raises after 1976 and putting them in a separate category outside the regular salary grades. Yining was paid only 43 yuan a month ($28.67), less than the average factory worker's income of 58 yuan ($38.67).

"We're not all stupid, it isn't our fault we didn't learn anything in those days," Yining lamented.

In some ways the worker-peasant-soldier students are the most tangible result of the Cultural Revolution. Almost a million of them are spread throughout the country—in research laboratories under the Academy of Sciences and in far off Tibet, where some volunteered to go. But Yining sees little future for them.

"Now people discriminate against us everywhere, they look down on us as the afterbirth of the Cultural Revolution. We just missed getting thrown out with the Gang of Four."

For all the difficulties of the worker-peasant-soldier students, they were not as bad off as another even larger group of young people who began to surface after I arrived in China. The Chinese called them *dai-ye,* "waiting for work"; it was a euphemism for unemployed. One of the Communists' great accomplishments in the 1950s was that in a poor, overcrowded country they had given everyone a job—indeed, most Chinese had come to look on their jobs as having a lifetime guarantee. The system was administered by labor agencies which coordinated among factories, schools, and neighborhoods; students finishing school didn't have to go out to look for a job, they were assigned one. But in 1979 the government suddenly discovered it had a major unemployment problem. The trouble had actually been building for several years because of the effect of the great baby boom in the 1950s and 1960s, after the return of peace and stability; but it had been obscured by Mao's down-to-the-countryside program, which siphoned off excess city youth to the villages. With Mao's death, his successors recognized that the policy had become unpopular and unworkable and millions of discontented people flooded back to their homes, some legally and some without permission. The seriousness of the situation was brought home to the Communist hierarchy at New Year's in 1979 when youths returning to Shanghai to spend the holiday with their families extended their stay to demonstrate against their continued rustication. Westerners in the city reported that tens of thousands of these young people had looted shops, blockaded the railway station, tying up trains, and marched on the city Party headquarters along the waterfront. To compound the employment problem, there are an estimated four million Chinese coming on the job market in the cities each year after finishing school. Government officials indicated there were anywhere from 10 to 20 million young people in the cities "waiting for work." That does not sound like a large figure in a country of one billion, but what it meant in human terms was revealed in a New China News Agency story claiming that 70.4 percent of all urban young people now had jobs. Looked at in reverse, that also showed that 29.6 percent did not—almost as high unemployment as black youth suffered in America.

Because the government could not create new jobs fast enough in state-run factories, the coveted sector of the economy, Mao's successors reversed the Great Helmsman's contempt for small private and cooperative enterprises as a "tail of capitalism" and encouraged youngsters to work in them. Some of these proved a minor success—I visited a small hotel with 110 beds started by a group of unemployed young people in an underground bomb shelter in the capital, and a three-table restaurant in a family home. But this kind of enterprise didn't resolve the problem.

On a crisp November day I encountered a twenty-one-year-old woman, Kang Keli, who had been given one of these new and often makeshift jobs as an attendant in a small bicycle parking lot near the Forbidden City. It was the best weather of the year in Peking; the persimmons had ripened into bright-orange spheres on the gray branches of the trees inside the emperors' old residence; the high sky was an azure blue and free of pollution for a day. Keli said she had graduated from high school two years before but only in the past month had been assigned her first work, guarding the bikes. Her pay was only 24 yuan ($16), less than half the average for a factory worker, and she got none of the usual benefits in China—a bonus, free medical care, housing, or a pension.

"It's better than sitting at home doing nothing," said Keli, who had short braids and large round eyes. Her younger sister had just graduated from high school the previous July and also still hadn't been assigned work. A younger brother would finish school next spring.

"For us young people, there is no road out," she said, using a phrase I heard often. "There is no future." Keli smiled when she said it, as Chinese do when confronted with an unkind fate, but her words conveyed a finality. In the 1950s, when the Communists' triumph was still fresh, a surge of optimism had swept China—there was hope that the country could finally be transformed from its backwardness and poverty. But now the mood was pessimistic again. It was partly an indictment of the Communists, of their wasted opportunity, and partly a reflection of the intractability of poverty in a country with a quarter of the world's population.

Not long before I had come across a lanky teen-ager with horn-rimmed glasses hawking copies of a four-page newspaper called *The Torch,* a daily bulletin put out to publicize the results of the then ongoing national games, a Chinese olympics. He was carrying the papers in a bag around his neck, but unlike newspaper boys elsewhere wasn't shouting the headlines to attract customers.

"I don't want to cheat people," he explained. "It's bad enough if they buy it on their own because there's nothing in it, but I'm not going to encourage them."

He said his neighborhood committee had given him the job a few days ago, but it would end when the games were over. Then he would just have to wait for another assignment. Suddenly he shoved the papers in his hand into the bag and began to run. "Bottle caps," he whispered, teen-age slang for the police, because of the round red national emblem they wear on their hats.

"Isn't it legal for you to sell papers?" I half shouted at him, assuming that his neighborhood committee must have cleared the job with the police.

"Not in this place," he shouted back ambiguously before he was out of sight.

I never discovered whether he was violating the law; but I did learn during my stay in Peking that juvenile delinquency and crime among young people had become a serious problem in China. Here was another of those shibboleths. The Chinese had long boasted that they had virtually eliminated crime. Yet a radio station in Changchun, an industrial center in the northeast, reported an incident that sounded like a scene from the movie *Blackboard Jungle.* At the city's Number 9 High School, the broadcast charged, two "gangster students," miffed that one of their classmates had been chastised by a teacher, broke into the teacher's room and "violently attacked him with sticks and stones.

"When the teacher ran to the teachers' office on the second floor," the radio went on, one of the students "caught him from behind and shot him with a zip gun, shooting a nail in his back."

The *Southern Daily* in Canton once reported that a twenty-one-year-old rural youth went on a thirteen-day joyride across Guangdong province in which he stole two bicycles, two cars, and four trucks and hit and killed two cyclists. The young man, Wang Yonghe, began his adventure when he was caught stealing peanut oil that belonged to his production team. Looking for a means to escape, he spied a truck belonging to a local cigarette factory. The door was not locked, so he loaded the bike he was riding in the back and took off. But because he had learned how to drive only on a tractor, the paper said, "the truck ran like a mad horse. In less than two hundred meters, he hit and damaged a cart, a bamboo fence, and a bike repair shop." Eventually, after a chase through the Canton airport and a swim across the Pearl River in Canton to avoid his pursuers, Wang was captured when he tried to steal some clothes from a theatrical troupe performing in a park. The *Southern Daily* noted with dissatisfaction that Wang's father was Party secretary of his production brigade and should have disciplined him more as a boy.

People like Wang and the students who shot the teacher were what the Chinese had come to call *liu-mang,* an old term that originally meant vagabond but had been appropriated to connote hoodlums. A number of Chinese I knew showed the same anxiety about meeting *liu-mang* on the street as New Yorkers do about being mugged on the subway. One evening when I invited a Chinese teacher to a play in a workers' club away from the center of the city, she was visibly upset when she arrived at the theater. She had come by herself on her bicycle to avoid arousing suspicion. Halfway through the performance, she whispered that she wanted to leave early before the crowd got out. I couldn't figure out what was bothering her, but the next day she called to explain.

"That is a very bad section of town," she said. "You shouldn't have asked me there. The streets are very dark and there are lots of *liu-mang.* You never know what could happen."

How can you tell a *liu-mang?* I asked. "They have long hair and mustaches, and they smoke a lot on the street," she answered. "Sometimes they drink too much in the restaurants and then they throw up on the floor. It's terrible. It never happened before the Cultural Revolution." She almost sounded like an outraged American parent describing hippies in the late 1960s.

Like other journalists and diplomats in Peking, I wondered whether juvenile crime had really grown or whether with the greater openness of the Chinese press and the freer contact between Chinese and foreigners after

1976 we had just become more aware of what had been going on all along. Both explanations probably had a measure of truth. But Chinese officials insisted the increase was dramatic. The president of the Supreme People's Court, Jiang Hua, said in a speech that juvenile delinquency was ten times higher in 1980 than in the early 1960s. A professor of law at Peking University, Shen Zhongling, stated in an interview that young people now commit 60 percent of all crimes in China. That is about the same proportion as in the United States, where people under twenty-five accounted for 57 percent of all arrests in 1980, according to the FBI. A leftist magazine in Hong Kong, *Tunghsiang,* reported that one district of Shanghai registered 1,042 thefts and burglaries in 1978, 87 percent of them committed by young people. In compliance with a new national policy, the district subsequently set up a reform school to "reeducate" juvenile offenders. In its first year it took in 104 students.

The growing alienation of young people baffled the older generation of Chinese. Many times I heard Party cadres wonder why young people were not more grateful for what the Communists had done for China. But they had forgotten that the majority of people were born after 1949 and didn't remember what the bad old days were like. The most noticeable improvements in the conditions of life took place in the 1950s—the more equitable and secure supply of food, the new security of employment, the increased availability of education and medical care. These were impressive changes, but young people now took them for granted. There had not been similar gains in the 1960s or 1970s and the major event in the lives of everyone under thirty was the Cultural Revolution.

Perplexed by young people's attitudes, the government was tempted to see the handiwork of the devil—in their case, capitalism, just as rightists in America often blame rising crime rates and drug addiction on the Communists.

"A few young people are deluded by the temporary prosperity of the capitalist countries," the *People's Daily* fulminated in an editorial. "They see the prosperity and technological advances of the capitalist nations and the backwardness of the socialist states and conclude that capitalism is better than socialism. This leads them astray. But this is completely wrong. Only socialism can save China."

A conscientious, hardworking high school teacher offered a more subtle but similar interpretation of what troubled young people. "What is happening is that the government now says it wants to learn from the West. By that it means Western science and technology and the rule of law.

"But when young people see it is fashionable to copy the West, what they imitate is all the superficial things, sunglasses, long hair, bell-bottom pants, dating in high school."

We were on a picnic at the tombs of the Ming emperors, northwest of Peking, with the teacher's husband, a scientist, and the couple's sixteen-year-old daughter. As we sat on the grass under a cluster of pine trees facing a three-arched gate, the sound of a woman singing drifted across the broad, grassy valley from a loudspeaker at another of the tombs a mile away. It was Li Guyi, the pop star.

"I hate to say it, but students today are not as good as those before the Cultural Revolution," the teacher continued. She had on a mannish pants suit made from a check material and spoke with a quiet intensity and sense of uprightness I noticed in many Chinese.

"There are a few good students, of course, but most don't have the habit of hard study. When they were young all they read were the thoughts of Chairman Mao. Worse, they don't believe anything you tell them. They argue with you about everything. After all the changes in the Party's line, they have seen through things." She used the same phrase, *kan to le,* that young people used themselves.

Her own teen-age daughter, Lingling, in some ways bore out her lament. The first time I met Lingling, when we were both reading a poster on Peking's now defunct Democracy Wall, she confided her cynicism.

"I am afraid China is going to end up just like the Soviet Union, with a powerful army, lots of factories, and no freedom," she said in her soft, girlish voice. "I don't like to go to the zoo, all those animals locked up in cages. It reminds me of how we Chinese are trapped."

That sounded precocious coming from a sixteen-year-old, I suggested.

"I'm almost seventeen," she said at first, defensively. Then she added, "I had to learn early. I was only three years old when the Cultural Revolution hit us. My father and mother were both criticized and taken away—they said she was a Kuomintang agent. By the time she came home, all her hair had turned white."

Lingling had a willowy figure and a perfect oval face, but she was mortified that she suffered from acne and so wore a *koujiao,* a white cotton surgical mask that many Chinese use against the cold and dust of Peking's winter. On the first day we met, she had on an ordinary blue worker's jacket, but she had left the top two buttons undone in a gesture of daring. Under it she wore a tight-fitting turquoise T-shirt, with a matching turquoise scarf around her neck. Her pants were made of blue denim, cut tight at the hips, a Chinese version of blue jeans. To complete her outfit, she had on open sandals with two-inch heels, very high for China, and black patterned stockings which showed through her shoes. Her father had bought them in Shanghai, China's center of fashion. When I commented that she was unusually well dressed for China, she smiled with pleasure.

"Most people just like those fatty pants, they're so ugly, but they are afraid of being stared at."

Lingling had tried wearing her tight pants to school, but her homeroom teacher stood in the door with a ruler and measured to see if the students' trousers were either too tight at the hips or too wide at the cuff. Another time, she recalled, she was taking her noon nap in school when she heard an announcement over the loudspeaker.

"It was a new government directive. Students must no longer wear foreign sunglasses, boys can't have long hair, girls can't get their hair permed or wear makeup, and no more listening to love songs from Hong Kong.

"So I will be careful about what I wear in school, but I'll do what I like at home. Life in China is a big play. We are all actors." Then she paused for a moment. "But I don't like to think about this too often. One has to have some illusions to live."

For all Lingling's cynicism, however, she was actually a bright, diligent youngster who was determined to get high grades and pass the college entrance exams, which had been restored in 1977. In this she was like many other young Chinese—their disillusionment was real, but presented with an opportunity to get ahead, they were still capable of hard work. The trick for Peking lay in providing them more hope to advance within the restricted, conservative confines of Chinese society. Once when Lingling opened her school notebook, I saw that inside the front cover she had written out her daily schedule. It began with getting up at 5:30 every day for half an hour of exercise, then fifteen minutes for breakfast, and an hour of study before classes started. Every subsequent quarter of an hour during the day was accounted for, till lights out at 10 P.M.

Lingling's mother had used her connections to get her into one of the better high schools and, because their apartment was over an hour's bus ride from the school, had also gotten permission for both mother and daughter to sleep in the teachers' room at night so Lingling wouldn't waste valuable study time commuting. In the evenings her mother tutored her in Chinese, her mother's own subject, and had other teachers give her extra help in math. Lingling's father lived by himself at home during the week, cooking his own meals.

"I don't mind," he said when we were on the picnic. "We just hope Lingling will be able to pass the exams and someday be able to go abroad to study." This dream of getting into college and ultimately going overseas to study was the last great motivation for young people and kept many of them from falling into the apathy that had overtaken the country's bureaucrats, factory workers, and less-talented youngsters.

Even during the Cultural Revolution when the universities were shuttered, the traditional Chinese passion for study did not slacken. At the University of Science and Technology in Hefei, in central China, a tall, gangly physicist in his early thirties named Chen Ping recalled how he had been assigned to work as an electrician in a small railroad station in a remote part of the country after his school was closed in 1968.

"I didn't have much work to do," he remembered, fingering his wispy mustache. "Maybe two or two and a half hours a day. There weren't many trains. They were stopped by all the factional fighting."

But during a trip to the local provincial capital, he found a 1947 edition of the Encyclopedia Britannica gathering dust on the shelves of the railroad office. It had been bequeathed to the railway by an old employee, but no one knew what the books were. Chen asked to buy them.

"At first they said no, but then they said I could borrow the books."

So with the help of his girl friend, a conductor on a train that passed through his lonely station, he began to read. She brought him one volume at a time, until he finished all twenty-eight. He might have gotten into political trouble, given the radical temper of the time, but his fellow workers were tolerant.

"They said, 'Why don't you tell us a story each day from what you read?' "

After the Cultural Revolution, Chen returned to his university as a teacher. He had mastered English. And he married his railroad conductor.

This reverence for education, which dated to Confucius, made Mao's reforms of the school system one of the most contentious issues in China. Like some progressive American educators in the 1960s, Mao felt the schools had become too elitist, that they discriminated against children from less-advantaged families like those of peasants and workers. That was why he had abolished the college entrance exams and simplified the curriculum in the schools. To lessen the traditional authority of the teachers, which Mao also believed was elitist, he had encouraged student attacks on teachers. And to make education more practical, he called for combining study with work in the fields and factories.

But since his death, most Chinese agree Mao's experiments only ended up lowering standards. The New China News Agency stated in one sensational report that China now has 140 million illiterates, 120 million of them under forty-five. In another article, the *People's Daily* revealed that while 95 percent of Chinese children do start out attending primary school, as the government has long claimed, "in reality only 60 percent finish their five years of primary school and only 30 percent can be said to have reached the five-year primary school standard." The problem lies with the poor quality of rural schools, the severe shortage of government funds for them, and the continued belief among many peasants that it is more useful for their children to work in the fields than go to school. As a result, the Chinese school system, like many American schools, is turning out functional illiterates.

Education is also an emotional subject in China because along with membership in the Communist Party and promotion to the officer corps in the armed forces, it is one of the three main avenues for moving up in society. Competition for survival starts early. The Communists have rapidly expanded the number of schools—there are 210 million Chinese in school today. But 12 percent of those who finish primary school are unable to go on to junior high, and there is no room in high school for 50 percent of the students who complete junior high. At the top of this pyramid, only 3 percent of the college-age population in China, about a million students, can get into university. In the United States, by comparison, 35 percent of the population between eighteen and twenty-one are in college; 23 percent of young people in the Soviet Union go to college, and even in the Philippines, which has a total of 40 million people, there are 1.27 million college students, more than in all of China. The *Guangming Daily* groused that China ranked 113 out of a list of 141 countries in the world in percentage of its young people who get a post-secondary education.

This figure startled me, given the value Chinese place on schooling. The major reason is money. Peking has not released exact data for its expenditure on education, but some rough calculations can be made. The 1980 national budget for education, plus health, culture, and science, of which over half went to scientific research, was 14.8 billion yuan ($9.87 billion), or about $10 per person. The real total would be somewhat higher, since Peking requires the villages to finance their own schools out of local revenue. But another article in the *Guangming Daily* disclosed that in the late 1970s, after the downfall of the Gang of Four, the government invested only 1.12 percent of China's gross national product in education. That would put China about 110th on the United Nations list of spending for education, after such countries as Somalia, 2.7 percent, Guatemala, 1.7 percent, and Bangladesh, 1.2 percent. The United States invests 6.4 percent of its GNP in education, the Soviet Union, 7.6 percent. Chinese friends traced Peking's miserly appropriations to Mao's contempt for expertise and the Communists' failure to understand the role of technology in the modern world. Mao had derided intellectuals as "the stinking ninth category," after landlords, capitalists, and assorted other bad elements. The Chairman's view became national policy. "For quite some time," the *People's Daily* said in a revealing 1980 article, "some people considered education as an item of consumption that had no connection with production. When they thought of expanding production, they considered building factories, buying machines, constructing irrigation works. They seldom considered, or simply did not consider, the question of training people."

For the lucky few who do get into college, the rewards are immense. Unlike those young people who finish only junior or senior high school and may have to wait a year or two before being assigned to work in a neighborhood cooperative or at best a factory, they are assured some of the most prestigious jobs in China: as scientists, engineers, interpreters for the China Travel Service. "It is a lifetime meal ticket," said an affable professor at Fudan University in Shanghai who had been trained in the United States. "You have to realize that under our system, almost no one flunks out once they get into college. Professors just don't fail students. It would go against the idea of a guaranteed lifetime position once they make it into college."

The key to success, since Mao's death, is passing the national university entrance exams, twelve and a half hours of tests in six subjects spread over three days. In 1980, of the 3.3 million students who qualified through a preliminary screening process to sit for the tests, only 285,000 were admitted to college. Most were high school seniors, seventeen, eighteen, or nineteen years old, though there were a few people in their mid- or late twenties whose schooling had been disrupted by the Cultural Revolution or who had flunked earlier exams. Americans are familiar with the ordeal of taking the college boards—the competition, the preparation, the anxiety; but the Chinese exams involve even more tension. The very word for test in Chinese, *kao-shi*, resonates with a hallowed significance, evoking memories of the old imperial exam system where thousands of scholar-candidates steeped in years of study of the Confucian classics were locked in cubicles for several days at a time. Those who succeeded became the Emperor's mandarins. Exams to Chinese are almost a religious ritual, admitting priests to a cult, a kind of theocracy.

For the current college exams, the teachers who have been picked to prepare the questions are kept incommunicado in a secret mountain resort for two months before the test date in July. They are not allowed to make phone calls, write letters, or send telegrams, to prevent cheating. Parents become as involved as their children in preparing for the exams. A teen-age acquaintance told me that for a month before he took the exams, his father and mother wouldn't let him have any friends over to his house, though they did excuse him from his household chores. For an entire year in advance, he said, he studied six hours a day in addition to his regular homework, studying texts of earlier exams. After he passed, his parents threw a large dinner party that cost several months of their salaries. His homeroom teacher wrote an inscription in an album he bought for the occasion: "Now you will be a success for life."

The pressure to succeed is intense. Each summer the Chinese press reports several cases of suicide among students who fail. Many students who do not succeed are unwilling to accept their defeat and try again the next year. The Ministry of Education once arranged for me to visit the Number 35 High School in Peking which was being used as a test site and talk with a group of fourteen students who had just finished their three days of tests. When I asked what they would do if they didn't pass, all fourteen said they would study on their own for a year and take the exam again.

Another young woman, a lathe operator in a Peking factory who had not been able to finish high school because of the Cultural Revolution, recounted her attempts to take the exams on her own. She had already tried twice. Why, I asked, was she not satisfied with being a worker in a socialist state?

"In the early years of the People's Republic, many people were very happy to be workers," she replied, arching her thick black eyebrows. "The pay was good, welfare was guaranteed, and it gave you a Red status," meaning you were politically safe. "But now people want to be intellectuals. There's a lot of prestige being a scientist. It may be a workers' state, but workers have a poor position. There is no equality between us and the cadres."

One of the consequences of the return to a conventional exam system has been the open creation of the kind of elite that Mao abhorred. Just as in America, children from families with a higher standard of living and better educational backgrounds now have an advantage in getting into college. The New China News Agency conceded that of the entering class of 2,000 students at Peking University in 1979, 39 percent came from families of cadres and soldiers, though these two groups make up only 2.2 percent of the overall population. Another 11 percent of the freshmen were offspring of intellectuals, who constitute perhaps 2.5 percent of the population. Friends who taught at Peking University, however, cautioned that the situation was not really that different while Mao's reforms were in effect—the only change was that his successors were more candid about the figures.

The government also returned to the pre-1966 system of "key schools" in which it could concentrate its scarce resources on the individuals with the greatest intellectual potential to provide the economy with talent in the speediest, most efficient fashion. At one of these favored institutions, the Fuzhou Number 1 High School on the southeast coast, the principal, Zhang Junshi, said 37 percent of his senior class had gotten into college the previous summer. Before the Cultural Revolution, when he was beaten by some of his students and packed off to work in a factory, the school had achieved the stunning record of placing 90 percent of its graduates in college, Zhang recalled. A tall, erect, courteous man with a high forehead, Zhang took obvious pride in his work. As a key school, the Fuzhou high school got an extra subsidy from the city government for each student, and admission was by exam only, as for college.

Walking through the high-ceilinged, whitewashed corridors of the school, I was struck by how different it was from an American high school. Chinese complain about how unruly their teen-agers have become, but the students in Fuzhou seemed serious, disciplined, dedicated, like my teen-age friend Lingling. These youngsters knew they had a chance to succeed within the system and reap its rewards. So no one ran in the hallways, there was no talking in class, the students stood when the teacher entered, they folded their hands behind their backs and recited in unison when the teacher read a lesson. Rote memory is still the main instructional technique just as it has been for over 2,000 years—Mao's strictures to the contrary. There were no frills—no audio-visual aids, no student cars in the parking lot, and no drugs. It was the kind of school in which my grandfather, who started out as a teacher in a one-room village schoolhouse in upstate New York at the turn of the century, might have felt comfortable.

The Chinese school system is designed to inculcate technical skills rather than teach students to think or develop their capacity for creativity, the goals of an American liberal arts education. The curriculum in the Fuzhou school, like those elsewhere in China, is largely determined in Peking. Electives are few. There are no music or fine arts appreciation courses, no homemaking, and no economics, sociology, or psychology—all regarded as too frivolous or too politically sensitive. Classes in Chinese history are carefully circumscribed. Even students majoring in history in the universities study events only up to 1949, the founding of the People's Republic. There is only one authorized textbook on the history of the Chinese Communist Party from its founding in 1921 to 1949, and none for the period since then, for with the incessant political purges and shifts in the Party line, the Communists have had difficulty deciding what the correct version of history is. Was Mao good or bad? In what degree? Why was Liu Shaoqi, the head of state until the Cultural Revolution, denounced as a capitalist roader and jailed only to be posthumously rehabilitated? Examined too carefully, these questions might threaten to unravel the whole fabric of the state. Students in high school and college are given compulsory political education, and politics is one of the six subjects tested on the college entrance exams.* But the courses stay away from sensitive issues like the roles of Mao and Liu and students say the content of the politics courses consists of dull memorization of the current Party line. On the 1980 politics test, the major essay question, worth twenty of a possible one hundred points on the whole exam, was "Why do we have to strengthen the leadership of the Communist Party in order to realize the Four Modernizations?" Under fill-in-the-blanks, students were asked, "What is the root cause of the inevitable crisis of capitalism?" The correct answer, the lathe operator in the Peking factory told me, was private property. She had no difficulty with the politics test because all the questions and answers

*The others are Chinese language, math, and a foreign language, mandatory for all candidates. Those concentrating in science must also take tests in physics and chemistry; those in the humanities and social sciences, tests in history and geography.

were provided in a review outline which she had purchased several months beforehand at the night school she was attending.

As another measure to try to assure conformity, the Ministry of Education admits it takes a student's political attitude into consideration along with his test scores in deciding who gains admission to college.

"What this means is that you have to join the China Youth League if you want to go to college," said Lingling. The Youth League, modeled on the Soviet Komsomol, is the training organization for Party members. "I didn't want to join, but my teacher and mother insisted. They said that if you apply for college and two students have the same grades, the one who is a Youth League member will get preference.

"So my mother wrote my application for me. I didn't know what to put down. She made up a wonderful essay, that the Youth League is important for China's future and only with the Communist Party can China achieve the Four Modernizations.

"Then when the day came we were to be sworn in, luckily I was sick. I don't know if I could have taken the oath with a straight face."

Only 20 to 30 percent of the students in her class belong to the Youth League, Lingling calculated, a sharp drop-off from the early years of the People's Republic when membership was usually over 50 percent. The league members' main activity is to stay at school on Saturday afternoons—most Chinese go to school regularly for half a day on Saturday mornings—and either do extra political study or voluntary labor, like planting trees or digging in the school garden.

"When it's time for the league members to perform labor, the rest of the students laugh at us and say, 'Bye, we're going home,' " Lingling concluded.

This cynicism makes today's Chinese young people hard to predict. The Communist Party was founded on idealism and willingness to sacrifice. It was the Communists' belief in their cause which enabled the older generation to accept privation and tight political controls during the revolution and up to the 1960s. But in the Cultural Revolution something snapped. The Communists lost popular confidence, a critical ingredient to ruling such a vast country as China, like the mandate of heaven, the traditional principle that gave legitimacy to China's emperors. Today, if China is to meet its goal of becoming a modern industrial power, it needs productive factory workers and creative scientists, not semieducated malcontents and frustrated cynics. I was surprised how disillusionment has spread even to the best universities, where the students have the most to gain from the system. At Fudan University in Shanghai, a group of journalism students decided to take a poll to find out what their colleagues believed in, a graduate student there told me. One afternoon they went to the library, locked the doors, and daringly passed out questionnaires. Only a third of those who responded said they believed in Marxism; nearly a quarter said fate; a few replied Christianity, and 25 percent said "nothing at all." In a similar unofficial sounding at the Peking University library, a friend told me, 95 percent of the students said they doubted China could achieve the government's modernization program.

But it was a compulsory freshman class on Marxism at Peking University that really brought home to me how deep this alienation is. A nervous young woman teacher, standing on a raised platform at the front of the room, had just explained what she called the five basic principles of socialism. Then she scanned a roll of her students and called on one to repeat the cardinal points. The student was absent.

The professor read out another name, and again there was no response. This time an embarrassed giggle went around the large, sunny room, perhaps because an American was present.

Finally, with the sixth name, the professor found a student who was actually there. "Well?" she asked.

"I don't know," the student replied.

The teacher's inability to evoke an answer about a subject so sacred to the Communists and the absence of so many students from a required class summed up for me a conundrum Peking's leaders now face: China has become an authoritarian country with an authority crisis.

9. Growing Up *Guai*

THE CHINESE PASSAGES

"We wax happily, but wane with ineptitude. The last part of life we tend to abandon, even to despair, whereas for the Chinese it is a summit, for the very reason that it has been built by human wisdom alone upon a notoriously fragile and transitory base."
George Kates, The Years That Were Fat

In a large sunny room with a bare concrete floor, ten one-year-olds were squeezed next to each other on a tiny wooden bench, their backs against a wall. For minutes they sat motionless. None cried, pushed, or shoved.

Then a middle-aged woman attendant, with short salt and pepper hair, took a windup toy chicken out of its carton, turned the key, and let the metallic yellow bird strut across the floor past the infants' feet. Again, none of them moved or tried to grab the toy, as my two children would. They simply followed it with their eyes.

Finally, one boy, dressed in a red jacket and green padded trousers, with hair that stuck up straight in tufts, couldn't resist. He toddled over and pounced on the chicken. The attendant, clad in a full-length white nurse's smock, gently picked him up and deposited him back on the bench with the others.

The episode took place during a visit I made to the four-story gray-brick nursery school and kindergarten run by the Peking Printing and Dyeing Factory for 270 children of its workers. But it was similar to scenes I saw acted out in other nursery schools in a dozen Chinese cities. Like many American visitors to China, I was constantly struck by the almost universal good behavior of Chinese children, what some Westerners interpret as passivity. They are quiet, obedient, quick to follow their teachers' instructions, and they seldom exhibit the boisterous aggressiveness or selfishness of

American children. Nor do they cry, whine, throw tantrums, or suck their thumbs, some of the typical signs of anxiety and tension to which Western kids are prone.

In the Printing and Dyeing Factory's nursery, the attendants had already begun to toilet-train the one-year-olds. In a corner of the room there was a pile of white enamel spittoons. "As soon as the infants wake from their naps, we put them on the potties," Li Jianzhi, the head of the school said. "They stay there till they defecate. When they want to urinate, they have learned to go by themselves."

I was incredulous. Our daughter Sarah was one herself and nowhere near ready for such discipline, I felt. But just then a fourteen-month-old girl wearing a green apron with the factory's name stenciled on the front wandered off the communal bench and picked up a spittoon. Then she sat down and accomplished her mission. Her pants had a slit in the rear, as all Chinese children's do, to make the task easier.

Afterward she returned to the bench where several of the attendants had begun to feed the kids their lunch, rice porridge mixed with scrambled eggs. Each woman, perched on a low stool in front of the bench, held three metal cups and spoons, one for each of the children they were charged with helping eat. I watched with growing amazement as the attendants managed to give first one of the kids a spoonful and then moved on to another. None complained or grabbed for more, out of turn. They were learning to share and take their place in a group.

An American woman resident of Peking who enrolled her five-year-old son in the local Chinese kindergarten that accepts foreign children was crestfallen to be told that her child was the only member of his class who misbehaved.

"The teacher said that when they had visitors, my son refused to stop playing with a toy and return to his seat like the others," she recalled. "The teacher was disturbed that my son lay down on the floor and had a fit. She couldn't understand it."

How Chinese induce their children to be so well-behaved, in an age of rampant permissiveness and disobedience in the West, was one of the mysteries about China that fascinated me. One key, I found, was that Chinese parents strive to create a special sense of closeness with their offspring— Americans might call it smothering. At the same time, in order to build in discipline and self-control, Chinese fathers and mothers carefully restrain any restless moves toward what we would see as independent activity and self-expression.

At birth, many Chinese mothers still swaddle their babies, binding their legs and arms in blankets or cloth so they can't move. Laura Chandler, a ginger-haired American teaching in the provincial town of Hefei, discovered that when she had a baby daughter in the local hospital the nurses tied its hands to its sides with strings. They were afraid otherwise the baby would wake itself. A Chinese from Shandong said the peasants in her native village still practiced an old custom of putting their newborn babies inside a sack which they tied up to the infants' necks. Rather than using diapers, they then filled the sack with sand, which acts like cat litter. When Chinese parents take their infants out for a walk, they usually hold them in their arms or tie them to their backs rather than push them in a stroller or pram, out in front. Hence where Western infants get their own independent view of the world around them, Chinese children tend to see it through their parents' prism.

Chinese children sleep in the same room and often on the same bed with their parents till they are at least three or four years old. Chinese friends were invariably surprised to find that Sarah slept in her own room and managed to get through the night without waking.

"How can she go to sleep by herself?" our friend Mrs. Wang inquired. "When Yuanyuan was small, she always slept in our bed. She would wake up five or six times a night, to urinate or be fed. I had to be there." In part, this custom may grow out of the small, cramped apartments that Chinese must accept because of the housing shortage; but it also produces an intimacy American children don't get.

The Wangs were also aghast when they came to supper and found that we let Sarah play on the floor by herself. She was just learning to walk and was determined to crawl and toddle while Barbara cooked.

"You shouldn't let your baby play on the floor," Miao reproved us. She picked Sarah up and held her on her lap. "She could get cold or dirty." Again, this was partly testimony to the economic conditions of Chinese homes—the lack of adequate heating and bare concrete floors, which are hard to keep clean from all the dust in Peking.

But I could see Barbara bristle at someone else telling her how to raise her child. When she finished cooking, it was already eight o'clock, and she put Sarah to bed before serving the meal. The baby's room, however, was only ten feet from the dinner table, and she could hear the conversation. She stood in her crib and voiced her displeasure at being excluded. Miao looked uncomfortable. After taking a few bites of roast chicken, she rushed into Sarah's room to comfort her, despite Barbara's protests that crying wouldn't hurt her and she wouldn't go to sleep if someone kept picking her up.

"When my child cried, I cried even harder," Miao explained. "I had to go to her."

Later that night, after I had driven the Wangs home, Barbara observed that neither of them ever reprimanded or punished Yuanyuan, even when she and Ethan, our four-year-old, charged around the living room yelling and throwing pillows. This, too, is part of the closeness between Chinese parents and children. Chinese cherish harmony, one of the central Confucian virtues, and I noticed that Chinese are reluctant to use harsh words or physical punishment.

"It is no use to beat children, they don't understand," Lao Wu, my Chinese assistant, said once when we discussed Chinese child-rearing practices. "If my boy misbehaves, I try to persuade him to stop. For example, if there is a thermos of hot water on the table and he tries to climb up and get it so he could burn himself or break it, I move it away. If he still goes for it, I tell him a neighbor's boy would not do that." He was almost serene in his confidence, born of Chinese belief in the power of education, that his son of course would do what he was taught.

I was skeptical of such comments at first, but as we stayed in China I realized that no country has greater love for children. The word for "good" in Chinese is a pictograph of a woman next to a child (好). It was also apparent that after Ethan and Sarah joined me in Peking, the reaction I got in the dining room of the Peking Hotel changed dramatically—the waiters and waitresses I had jousted with for a year to get service suddenly began coming over to our table immediately. Everyone wanted to talk with Ethan and pinch Sarah's cheeks. *"Nemma bai, nemma pang,"* they exclaimed (So white, so fat), almost an insult in English but the ultimate compliment to a Chinese, signs of a healthy, well-fed baby.

On the day the family first flew up from Hong Kong to Peking, Ethan insisted on exploring the CAAC plane by himself. Soon he had locked himself inside the lavatory in the rear of the Russian-built Ilyushin jetliner. I didn't realize what had happened until I saw all the Chinese passengers turned in their seats staring aft. A muffled cry of "Daddy Fox," Ethan's appellation for me, was coming from the toilet. He had turned the heavy latch and it couldn't be released from the outside. But a young engineer with a pitted face who had been sitting across the aisle feeding Ethan a steady diet of candy and apples leapt from his seat faster than I could and rushed to the rescue. First he whipped out a penknife and tried to pry the lock open. When that didn't work, he slammed himself against the door like a detective in the movies. Soon several stewardesses and even the pilot arrived, all to no avail. But after thirty minutes of coaxing, Ethan finally got the inner knob to turn, and as the sign on the outside swung from "Occupied" to "Vacant," he emerged. The engineer grabbed him in his arms like his own son.

Some Western Sinologists have observed that Chinese tend to indulge or spoil their children (the word for "spoil" is *ni-ai,* literally, "drown with love"). It is true that they often save the best food, like meat or milk, for their children, when they must subsist on a tight budget. It is also true that while Chinese adults today stick to somber proletarian blue and unisex baggy Mao tunics, they dress their children in brilliant oranges, reds, and pinks, as if they reserved all their pent-up interest in fashion and individuality for their off-spring. The most beautiful piece of clothing we found made in China today —in contrast to the lovely embroidered robes and dresses sewn before 1949 and sold in antique shops to foreigners—was a pink satin cloak with hood for Sarah.

But Chinese parents don't glorify their offspring the way child-centered middle-class Americans do. The quality they prize in their children is *guai,* a word that means "well-behaved," but which also coveys the sense of submissive, quiet, and placid. I can recall dozens of times, both in Taiwan and on the mainland, when a child made too much noise or got out of line, their parents would cluck at them, *"Guai, guai, guai,"* using the term like "shush," or "shame," "behave yourself." Ethan, by contrast, was *tiao-pi,* "naughty." Once when Barbara was sick, we sent our *a-yi,* or "maid," to pick him up from the kindergarten he attended, run by the wife of a Filipino journalist. The *a-yi* arrived home livid. Ethan had slapped and kicked at her all the way home, she said. He was crying. When I asked him what happened, he said she had tried to hold him by the hand. To an American child it was confining; to a Chinese it was natural and necessary.

Chinese parents don't ask what they can do for their children—as American fathers and mothers do—but what their children can do for them. This is a carry-over of the old virtue of filial piety, which lay at the heart of Chinese personal relations. A professional couple we got to know, the Hu's, have a girl eight years old and a boy twelve. The children never called their parents by their first names, as some American kids do, only by their titles of mother and father. Each is assigned his or her chores: the daughter goes to fetch the milk every morning from the neighborhood collection point (there is no home delivery); the son washes the supper dishes without a whimper. The two children rise at 6 A.M., get dressed quietly, and go out jogging, then come back and heat the milk and slice some bread for their Western-style breakfast, all without waking their parents. The son and daughter share a tiny room, and at night they sit face to face at two small desks doing their homework under a single lamp. I never saw them fight or quarrel. The absence of sibling rivalry, given the predatory instincts Ethan and Sarah sometimes showed for each other, was remarkable. One day the son came home late for dinner; he claimed he had stayed late at school to study. When Mr. Hu, a pleasant, polite man with neatly combed short hair, later found out he had actually been out turning cartwheels with some friends, he made his son kneel for an hour for telling a fib.

Before 1949, the anthropologist Francis Hsu has observed, China "was a country where children came last."* Parents had a completely free hand with

*Francis L. K. Hsu, *Americans and Chinese* (New York: Doubleday & Co., 1970), pp. 76–77.

their progeny. Infanticide was not a common practice, Hsu wrote, but in times of poverty parents who did kill their children were seldom punished by law or publicly censured. Children may not fall into such a benighted position today—the Communists have banned infanticide. But I was intrigued that, unlike in the United States, there is no public debate over abortion, though under the government's stringent birth-control campaign some commune clinics I visited handle more abortions in a year than live births. Traditionally there was no specialty of pediatrics in China, and even now I could not find any books in bookstores on how to make Chinese better parents. There is no Chinese equivalent of Dr. Spock, or Piaget, and no widely published studies of how children learn or behave.

Instead, in the past at least, Chinese were raised on the classic *The Twenty-four Examples of Filial Piety,* from which three- and four-year-olds were told stories like that of the boy who allowed mosquitoes "to feed without restraint upon his blood until they were satisfied" in order to prevent them from biting his parents. The most impressive of all was the tale entitled "On Account of His Mother He Buried His Child":

> A poor man by the name of Kuo and his wife were confronted with a serious problem. His aged mother was sick in bed. She needed both medicine and nourishment which Kuo could ill afford. After consultation between themselves, Kuo and his wife decided that the only way out was to get rid of their three-year-old and only son. Kuo and his wife said to each other, "We have only one mother, but we can always get another child." Thereupon the two went out to the field to dig a pit to bury their child alive. But shortly after they started to dig, they struck gold. It transpired that the gods were moved by the spirit of their filial piety and this was their reward.*

Such stories are now condemned as a relic of the feudal past, but Chinese children still learn early to see the world in terms of a network of others. By design or not, it is in the government-run day-care centers where this social training and discipline are the most intense, as if the Communists had transmuted filial piety into acceptance of the authority of the state. Some working mothers bring their infants to nurseries as early as fifty-six days, the end of their paid maternity leave. At the Peking Printing and Dyeing Factory, children under one are placed in a "feeding station," a large poorly heated room dominated by a single collective crib. Ten infants, spaced at intervals of two feet, were lying immobile on their backs on a plastic sheet the day of my visit. They were so bundled in their three or four layers of padded winter clothing they could not roll over. Three mothers were feeding their own babies in an anteroom from large bottles.

"The mothers can come to feed their children twice a day, during their

*As translated in Hsu, *Americans and Chinese,* p. 78.

work breaks," explained Miss Li, the head of the school. "Otherwise, we have nurses to take care of the babies." There were no toys in the crib, and no mobiles strung over it, no indications that the attendants were concerned about stimulating their sensory perception or intellectual development. "If they cry, we comfort them," added Miss Li, a benign woman with a radiant smile and a green sweater under her blue jacket. She felt that infants under one year old are largely passive and helpless and likely to learn little.

Children in the nursery school and kindergarten are divided into age groups—the one-, two-, three-, four-, and five-year-olds each had separate rooms—but as they grow older every activity is still highly organized and, I noticed, initiated by adults. In the room for three-year-olds, the teacher was playing a small pump organ and teaching the class a new song. As I entered, the entire group of twenty-four children chorused, "Good morning, Uncle," as if there had been a cue. They were seated at three low tables; none was pushing or poking the other. The teacher, a robust woman in her early twenties, commanded, "Sing," and they divided into girls and boys.

The girls chanted first:

Little brother, where are your little hands?

My hands are here.
They can grasp guns, they can fire, pow, pow, pow.
Little sister, where are your little hands?

My hands are here. They can do physical labor.
When the kerchiefs are dirty, they can wash them.
Little brother, where are your feet?

My feet are here, they can play football.
Little sister, where are your feet?

My feet are here, they can dance.

In earlier years the song would have been a paean to Chairman Mao. The Great Helmsman is out of fashion, but the moral tone was still strong, if sexist by current Western standards. The girls all had red- or blue-velvet bows in their hair, held in place by a plastic strap that ran behind their ears.

It was a charming and impressive performance, far beyond anything Ethan could sing or memorize. He could never get beyond the first line of "Mary Had a Little Lamb" or "Silent Night." He didn't have the power of concentration or ability to follow the teacher's instructions that these Chinese children did. But there were no books on display in the classroom, and during my day's visit to the school I didn't see any attempt by the teachers to encourage individual play or improvisation. The songs and dances were all collective behavior, requiring only a memorized response. They bred conformity and role-playing.

Next door, in the class for four-year-olds, the teacher had drawn a handsome ocean liner on the blackboard, green for the ship, blue for the waves, red for fish in the ocean, and a pennant flying from the ship's mast. All the students had dutifully copied the outline, some with more skill than others, but all with little deviation. Again, Ethan would have been put to shame; the art work he did was primitive free-form finger painting. But unlike American teachers, the instructor had not festooned the walls with the students' handiwork. "We don't glorify the work of individual students," the teacher explained. The only decoration was somber color portraits of Mao and Hua and a copy of the week's schedule for the class. Each activity was listed in advance.

As a left-hander, I was curious if there were any left-handed pupils in the school. Chinese for centuries have forcibly converted their heathen southpaws; calligraphy written with the left hand is infelicitous, they say.

"We have only one left-handed student in the whole school, a girl," Miss Li responded. "She is very stubborn. We have gotten her to use her right hand to write, but it will take more time to make her use her right hand to eat."

Some Chinese parents, however, do worry that the tough regimen of nursery schools like this tends to make their children too placid and uncreative. A professor at Peking Normal University was concerned that his two-year-old son just sits quietly and doesn't speak when he comes home. Sometimes he doesn't move or make a noise for an hour at a time. "We worry whether the treatment in the nursery is destroying his intelligence," the professor said. Because the professor and his wife both work and because their jobs are over an hour's bus ride from their apartment, they board their son in the nursery. They drop him off on Monday mornings before going to work and don't see him again till they pick him up on Saturday afternoon. About a third of the children in Peking's nurseries and kindergartens are boarders like this.

Chinese parents and teachers also recognize that children who are raised at home tend to be less disciplined and more individualistic than those sent off early to nursery school. (Despite the impression given visiting foreigners, only about a quarter of Chinese youngsters are in nurseries or kindergartens, a much lower figure than in the United States.)

Niannian is a four-year-old daughter of parents who are technicians in a factory. Living with them are their old servant, from before Liberation, and the families of two relatives who lost their own homes in the Cultural Revolution. So Niannian has grown up at the small center of attention of an adult world peopled by assorted uncles, aunts, and a nanny. She was used to eating her meals with the family and took part in the grown-ups' conversation until her mother shushed her. She hadn't learned the skills of cooperation necessary to life in kindergarten—and Chinese society as a whole. When her parents finally did start her in their factory nursery, she cried and wouldn't let her mother leave her. Even when she came home for dinner she was so miserable she wouldn't eat for the first few weeks.

Once during a visit to their home, Niannian wanted to go to a nearby park where she liked to ride on the slide. There was a long line of patient children behind the ladder, standing quietly, without visible parental supervision. They climbed up and slid down without a sound, sometimes even without a smile. Niannian did not want to stand in line. She started to climb the most direct way—up the front of the chute, to the chagrin of her mother. And when her mother pulled her off, she hollered, as an American child would.

As Chinese grow up, they also trace a different set of passages from Westerners, making the transition to young adulthood more slowly and with less disruption, for they are still circumscribed, and sustained, by their network of mutual dependence, their *guan-xi,* and therefore feel less compulsion to assert their own independent development. In traditional China there was no recognized period of adolescence; even today there is no term for it in the language. The cult of youth has never existed in China. As the psychiatrist Robert Lifton has observed, "One's importance lay, not in the youth he was, but in the man he would become, and mainly in relationship to his family and his society. A Chinese youth became a man not by casting off his father's influence and control, but rather by adapting himself to them, by becoming like him."* Youthful rebelliousness was countered by stories from the *Twenty-four Examples of Filial Piety.* Today this sense of loyalty to one's parents and other superiors remains strong, despite the outburst of youthful rebellion encouraged by Mao in the Cultural Revolution and the growth of cynicism about Communist society. Martha Ritter, an actress from New York who taught English for a year at Peking Normal University, recalled that her students were deeply puzzled when she assigned them to read *The Catcher in the Rye,* J. D. Salinger's classic account of American teen-age restlessness.

"Why if Holden Caulfield is sent to the best school, if his parents are well-off, and his teacher is a good person, why does he hate all of them?" one of her pupils asked. "Why do young Americans like this book, why is it considered great literature?" others inquired.

"They have no sense of adolescent rebellion," Ritter concluded. "They are not burning with rage to find themselves, to distance themselves from the institutions they grew up with."

No matter how old, Chinese must still defer to their parents, at least on

*Robert Jay Lifton, *Thought Reform and the Psychology of Totalism* (New York: W. W. Norton and Co., 1961), p. 363.

the surface. A nineteen-year-old college student, a lively, inquisitive boy with a fondness for reading American novels, told me he took his parents to the movies every weekend, something American teen-agers would be mortified to do. Lihua, my twenty-year-old petitioner friend who had been sent to the countryside, devoted much of her time to caring for her invalid father and her sister and brothers. Jan Wong noticed that, among her friends and roommates when she was an undergraduate at Peking University, most matured later than Westerners because of the prolonged child-parent relationship.

"A twenty-one-year-old here is probably equivalent to a fourteen-year-old in America in terms of independence from his or her parents, economically, philosophically, and psychologically," Jan said. "I was astounded by the number of times my Chinese friends asked me if I was homesick—they always were. My roommate, who lived in Peking, went home every weekend." When she attended McGill University in Montreal, her own hometown, Jan recalled, "I went home only when I had to.

"Twenty-one-year-olds here tend to still be giggly, unthoughtful about their future, and childlike in behavior. They take delight in pranks that would amuse a junior high school student in America, like throwing water on each other when they are sent to a village for labor stints, hiding things from one another, or popping out from behind doors to scare someone."

But the political and social breakdown of the Cultural Revolution has produced something of a chasm between generations in China. The parents of Lingling, the precocious sixteen-year-old high school student, summoned me urgently to their apartment shortly before I left China. Lingling wasn't there, and her mother was agitated. She had found a diary Lingling had been secretly keeping and discovered her daughter was involved with a foreign student at Peking University. She was also concerned that Lingling was no longer maintaining her spartan study routine.

"We don't understand her anymore," her mother said, talking rapidly. "She has been affected by all the things young people are thinking and copying from the West. Her school is near where Democracy Wall was, and last year she read all those posters. Now she has those ideas."

"Maybe we are too old now," added her father, who had been sitting in a corner silently. "There is a generation gap emerging in China."

They wondered if I, as a Westerner, could persuade Lingling to concentrate on her studies. Later, when I next saw her, she had just been ice skating with her foreign boy friend. She had on a new purple knit sweater and matching scarf and had cut her hair very short, in pixie fashion, like an early Audrey Hepburn. There was a dash of red lipstick on her mouth. She looked very pretty. It was the kind of daring display of fashion some Chinese women had begun to try out in private after Mao's death, though, as Lingling had told me, she couldn't do it in school because it wasn't officially sanctioned.

"My parents don't understand me," Lingling protested. "Since I am an only child, I am spoiled. My parents do everything for me. To put it nicely, they love me very much. To put it more candidly, they insist I spend all my time with them. They don't like me going out of the house without them. If we go to the movies and there is a boy sitting in the same row, they make me sit between them.

"I like to be free. But the more innocent and stupid I act, the better they like it. So I don't show them I am sophisticated and can think for myself."

A thoughtful Chinese editor, with two teen-age daughters of his own, related that they had occasionally laughed at him as old-fashioned. "They say I am a person of the 1930s. There is a growing generation gap in China. But I think it is a political problem rather than a biological or cultural phenomenon as in the West. It is a result of the frustrations of the Cultural Revolution, not a permanent trend." He believed the traditional Chinese family was still intact.

There may be the makings of a generation gap in China, but as Chinese young people move into their twenties, they do not yet go through the trauma or triumph of an identity crisis, as Americans and other Westerners do. They don't have that luxury, for they are hemmed in by a society that offers them little choice or mobility, the prerequisites for the full-blown, do-your-own-thing individualistic life-style that Americans now take for granted. Indeed, there is no word in Chinese for either identity crisis or life-style. Instead, Chinese tend to follow a carefully prescribed pattern with little deviation or exploration of alternatives. By law, Chinese men must wait until they are at least twenty-two years old to get married, twenty-seven in the cities; women must be a minimum of twenty, twenty-five in the urban areas. Then when they reach the legal age, all Chinese seem to rush to get married in the next year or two.

Lan, a twenty-six-year-old scientist with an impish smile, lives in a dormitory with three roommates. She had started living in the dorm two years ago when she was twenty-four and her roommates were the same age. At twenty-five the other three all got married; within the next year they all had children. Now she has a second set of twenty-five-year-old roommates, and all of them have boy friends and plan to have weddings soon.

Lan is worried. There are no eligible men in the institute where she does research, and she has found it hard to meet anyone with the same high education level she has. As an intellectual, she wouldn't consider marrying a factory worker or peasant. And the pressure for her to get married is intense.

"There is a telephone operator in our institute who is thirty-five and not married," Lan told me one day as we drove to the Summer Palace in the northwestern suburbs of the city. "She lives in a tiny room with her switchboard and a bed. Everyone gossips about her and ridicules her because of her condition.

"You can be the dumbest person in the institute, do no work, and no one will laugh at you," she went on. "But if you aren't married by thirty, they will laugh."

David Eisenberg, the Harvard Medical School graduate who worked in the Institute of Traditional Chinese Medicine, related that Chinese physicians frequently encountered a complaint from women in their late twenties. When they came in for treatment, the women said they were suffering from stomach pains or other common ailments. But after the doctors examined them, they found nothing wrong. Then the patients admitted their real problem; the symptoms were only an excuse. They had been married for a year and hadn't yet gotten pregnant. They felt they had to produce on schedule.

To make this social straitjacket tighter, young Chinese are dependent on their parents for many of the necessities of life. Housing is so scarce that newly married couples must often live with their parents until well into their thirties. In her best seller, *Passages,* Gail Sheehy classifies people like these in America as white ethnics and comments that "having missed out on the experimental round trips that help middle-class youth to pull up roots," they maintain dependent ties to their families.* Sheehy adds, disparagingly, that the white ethnics often have no vision of themselves. When they marry, it is mainly to comply with what they believe they should do. The white ethnic "may do his time on earth making a living, rather than committed to a lifework." But Chinese have little choice. They often have to count on their parents to use their connections to secure them a job, and, once assigned employment, there is scant opportunity to change it. Women are not confronted with the dilemma of whether to pick career or motherhood—they must work. There is no equivalent in China to the old American admonition "Go west, young man." The only time Chinese are likely to move to another city is when their *danweis* order them to go, often against their wills, having to leave their wives, husbands, or children behind. The kind of mobility Americans are accustomed to is totally alien to Chinese. I remember in 1972, on my tour of the United States with a group of Chinese newsmen, they were mystified by the sight of cars on the New Jersey Turnpike pulling house trailers behind them. What are these strange contraptions? they asked. I saw looks of disbelief when I explained that some Americans actually moved their homes with them.

*Gail Sheehy, *Passages* (New York: E. P. Dutton, 1976), p. 256.

But where Americans might chafe at this lack of choice, it can also provide Chinese with a psychological security that rootless Americans lack. Chinese are so accustomed to having everything decided for them—to having their jobs, their housing, sometimes their marriage partners picked out by someone else—that they are baffled when confronted by the uncertainties of life in the United States. When two of the first Chinese scholars to study in America arrived at Boston in 1980, they expected officials from Harvard to meet them at the airport, as visiting foreigners always are met in China. But no one was there. Then when they managed to collect their baggage and take a taxi to Cambridge, they had no idea where to go. The driver deposited them at the Faculty Club, where they could spend the night. When a university administrator told them they would have to find their own apartment and arrange their own class schedule, they felt insulted.

In middle age, this same constricted mobility again dictates a different voyage for Chinese—not having been able to dream as grandiosely when they were young, they have fewer illusions to abandon as their physical powers begin to falter. In the United States, Gail Sheehy found that "the transition into middle life is as critical as adolescence and in some ways more harrowing."* As Americans realize they will not become president of the bank and time is running out, they can be tormented into depression, sexual promiscuity, power chasing, alcoholism, and violent swings of mood.

But Chinese in their middle years are less likely to press down on the career accelerator and more likely to try to build themselves a safe niche in their old *danwei,* immunizing themselves from the dangers of political campaigns. They have already crossed the critical divide. If they didn't show political activism when they were in their late teens and join the Youth League, they have been labeled passive and can't recover later and join the Party, the major path to success. Otherwise promotion is almost solely on the basis of seniority—the year a person began working in his *danwei*—and it is dangerous to appear too ambitious.

"People resent anyone who is better than they are," a soft-spoken forty-year-old clerk in the Academy of Sciences said. "It is part of our heritage from Mao. They instinctively feel everyone should be equal." Because her father had been labeled a rightist in 1957, she had not been able to go to college; but her parents, who had been educated at schools run by American missionaries before 1949, taught her English at home. "I am only a typist, the lowest grade, but my English is much better than anyone else's in the office, so I volunteered to do some translations we needed. But the other

*Sheehy, *Passages,* p. 360.

215

people in the office said I put on airs, they said I should be satisfied with what I am. They are always gossiping about me."

Finally she considered asking for a transfer, but that would mean going to the personnel section of her institute, which is run by an old Party cadre who formerly served as a political commissar in the army. "Then they would make an investigation, they would go to my dossier, and the old issue of my father being a rightist would come up again." So she dropped the idea as too dangerous.

Middle-aged Chinese are also trapped in a much slower pattern of career promotion than Westerners. In Communist China, people in their forties and fifties are often still on the lower and middle levels of the ladder of success where their counterparts in the West would already be in top executive positions. Senior posts in China today—in the Party, the army, factory management, science, medicine, and the arts—are all reserved for elderly veterans who have reached at least their sixties and more often their seventies or even eighties, the men who joined the Party long before 1949.

"Among my friends," observed a newspaper editor in his mid-fifties, "the great frustration is that they are still lowly paid and don't have important posts." He himself earns only 75 yuan ($50) a month, not as much as many factory workers, and has not been promoted in over twenty years, though he is intelligent, dedicated, and respected by his colleagues. The problem is that his superior at his paper joined the Party in Yanan in the late 1930s and, while approaching seventy, has no intention of retiring.

"This is a problem for all Chinese who went to university or started their careers in the 1950s," the editor added. "They are at the height of their mental and physical powers, but they have to accept being in a low or mediocre position."

Even those few middle-aged Chinese who are successful are cautious about pressing ahead too far or too fast. A diminutive actress with a sensitive face and tiny hands that she waves as she talks said she prefers staying home with her husband and two children to appearing on television.

"There is a saying in Chinese—'A person fears fame the way a pig is afraid of becoming fat.' "

A one-time teacher who was imprisoned in the Cultural Revolution, she worried that her former colleagues would become jealous of her current good fortune. "No one can tell what will happen when Deng Xiaoping dies, there could be another campaign," she said. "Now my motto is, I don't want fame or money, only to avoid making mistakes." She still lives in the same apartment building where she has for years, and every day passes the people who were responsible for her earlier incarceration.

"Before when I walked past them, I wouldn't say hello, nor would they.

Now sometimes we greet each other. But I haven't forgiven them, and I wonder how they feel."

The greatest contrast to the West comes with old age. To Americans, it means the lonely end of life, the loss of vitality, lowered income, insecurity, and perhaps a small retirement home in Sun City or a bed in a nursing home, far away from family. But as Chinese approach old age, they become more content. It is the summit of existence, honored as a minor form of immortality. To be called *lao*, "old," is a compliment to a Chinese of either sex. Traditionally, as a person's physical powers waned, he was thought to gain in wisdom. Confucius told his disciples: "At fifteen, I set my heart on learning. At thirty, I was firmly established. At forty, I had no more doubts. At fifty, I knew the will of heaven. At sixty, I was ready to listen to it. At seventy, I could follow my heart's desire without transgressing what was right."

The elderly were also compensated by an increase in respect in their family. This was where the web of mutual dependence really paid dividends. A Chinese retained the parent–child relationship as his fundamental social tie as he went through life, adding other relations to it, not moving from one family to another as Americans do, like a snake shedding skins. Social security for a Chinese was just that. I knew of a forty-five-year-old cadre with two children of his own who wanted to exchange his old, cramped, Chinese courtyard-style home for a modern apartment, with a toilet and kitchen, closer to his office. His *danwei* was willing to arrange the switch. But his mother, a crotchety, senile eighty-year-old, refused to move. She was used to her neighborhood, though she seldom went out anymore, and got around their home only by supporting herself from table to chair. The son felt obligated to honor her wish.

Far from undermining this chivalry of age, the Communists have reinforced it. China must be one of the few countries in the world where children are actually bound by law to take care of their parents. Article Fifteen of China's family law stipulates that "children have the duty to support and assist their parents. When children fail to perform the duty of supporting their parents," the law continues, their parents "have the right to demand that their children pay for their support." Article Twenty-two makes it mandatory for grandchildren to assist their grandparents, if their parents are deceased. The *People's Daily* once reported that three peasants in Shandong, two sons and a daughter-in-law, were sentenced to up to seven years in jail for neglecting their eighty-year-old parents.

The Communists have also instituted a munificent welfare plan that ensures financial security for the elderly. In the cities, men can retire at sixty, after twenty years of service, women at fifty if they worked in a factory, or fifty-five if they spent their career in an office. They then draw a pension of 75 percent of their preretirement wages, up to 90 percent if they were model workers or veteran Communists who joined the Party before 1949. By a quirk of history, older people who started working in the 1950s are usually paid much higher salaries than those who joined the labor force in more recent years. (For the Communists awarded bigger starting pay to people in the 1950s than they do today, and in addition in the 1960s and most of the 1970s there was a national wage freeze.) Moreover, some retired men can find second jobs, particularly if they are technicians or skilled workers. The result is a strong incentive to keep the old three-generation Chinese family still living under one roof. For in an urban household with a retiree and four working members (father, mother, son, and daughter-in-law), the retired person's income often accounts for half of the total. This is the conclusion of Deborah Davis-Friedman, a sociologist at Yale who is working on a book on the care of the elderly in China.

Unlike young people, who are angry and frustrated, the elderly in China are genuinely grateful for what the Communists have done for them. Pick any morning, if you rise at five-thirty or six o'clock, and go to the Altar of the Sun Park near our apartment. There will be two hundred to three hundred elderly men and women gliding through the movements of China's ancient form of calisthenics, *tai ji*, performing as if in slow motion. Now and then they pause to chat with a neighbor or acquaintance.

"We are very thankful to Chairman Mao and the Communist Party," a white-bearded patriarch with a deeply furrowed forehead told me one morning when I went to watch their ritual. "The young people today don't understand, but we remember how hard life was before Liberation. In those days, old people could starve to death." His own father, a day laborer, had died of malnutrition and disease at the age of thirty-two, he recalled.

There are other economic imperatives holding the extended family together. When a factory or office worker does retire, under a unique system the Communists have devised, they have the right to turn over their job to a son or daughter. Given the current employment problem, this is a significant benefit. At the giant Lanzhou Petrochemical works, a sprawling oil refinery and complex of chemical plants, with 36,000 workers, a factory official said that of the six hundred workers who retire a year virtually all are replaced by their own children.

An acquaintance who worked as an accountant for the People's Bank said he planned on taking advantage of a new government offer to retire early —for him at age fifty-eight—so his son could take over his job. His son had finished high school two years before but still hadn't been assigned a job by the local labor office, and the accountant was concerned he might become a delinquent, like other unemployed young Chinese. When combined with Peking's program of delayed marriage and single-child families, the system of inherited jobs almost guarantees that if parents follow the rules, their offspring will be employed by the time they reach maturity.

Elderly people have another advantage. They are often the only members of the family who have been assigned housing—the authorities don't consider a desire by young people to set up their own separate household adequate reason for granting a new apartment. The cost of housing and food is relatively cheap; but prized new consumer goods like television sets, wristwatches, and bicycles, by which Chinese measure the improvement in their living standard, are much more expensive and require the combined savings of several family members. Grandparents are also useful for looking after small children when day-care centers are far away or unavailable.

In the countryside, the financial motives for keeping families together are even more powerful. Only a few of the richest communes have established pension plans, so the elderly must depend on their grown children for support, as they always have. But the aged can still play an important economic role themselves. Most housing in the villages is privately owned, and to build a new house takes years of joint savings. Public child-care facilities are rare. Those peasants over fifty are allowed to stop working on the collective labor teams, but this frees elderly men and women to devote full time to private sideline occupations like their small family plots, raising pigs and chickens, or growing fruit trees. For many peasants, this sideline work may account for over 30 percent of their total family income, and almost all their cash, as opposed to their payments in grain or oil which they get from their work in the collective fields. As a consequence, having older people in a family can be an economic asset, not a liability.

The Communist Party leadership itself is a tribute to the Chinese veneration for age. The average age of the Standing Committee of the Politburo, the inner sanctum of power, is seventy-two. Perhaps the two most powerful figures in China are Deng Xiaoping, who was born in 1904, and Chen Yun, who was born in 1900. Chen spends much of his time in the hospital, friends said. There is no legal requirement for senior Party or army officials to retire; they have lifetime tenure, like justices of the U.S. Supreme Court. At the last national congress of China's leading writers, artists, musicians, and actors in 1979, two of the delegates died during the conference. The average age of the nine men selected as the new heads of the various cultural associations was seventy-three.

At a session of the National People's Congress in September 1980, Ye Jianying, the stooped, fragile eighty-three-year-old chairman, was chosen to give the closing report. The meeting took place in the main auditorium of the Great Hall of the People, a giant amphitheater with seats for 10,000 people on three levels, a red star in the ceiling surrounded by four circles of lights, and a rostrum flanked by huge portraits of Mao and Hua and rows of red flags. Some of the delegates hobbled in on crutches or had to be helped to their seats by nurses. When the time came for Ye to begin, he was so weak a woman radio announcer actually read most of his speech for him. But at the end of the talk, Ye took over himself. He said the delegates should congratulate several aging deputy prime ministers who had agreed to retire at the congress, thus "raising the efficiency of the leading apparatus of the state. . . . They have, through this deed of theirs, set a shining example.

"I hereby propose that we all rise and give a standing ovation as a sincere tribute to them," Ye added. As he spoke, a group of a dozen women nurses in white coats and male attendants rushed onto the stage to help Ye and several other aged leaders to their feet. When he had finished, four of the nurses escorted Ye off the stage.

But China's cult of longevity may eventually be affected by the very success of the Communists' policies. With life expectancy up from thirty-two years in 1949 to sixty-four years now, there are many more elderly people surviving. And if the Communists follow through on their stringent one-child-per-family program, that will mean that each young person may be forced to help support as many as four aged parents and parents-in-law. A number of Chinese worry privately that this will prove an excessive burden unless the state moves in with an even larger and more costly social security plan, something the government can't afford. "It is a social problem waiting to happen," said the newspaper editor whose own career is blocked by an elderly boss.

10. Report in the Evening

BING

"From the Red East rises the sun,
There appears a Mao Zedong."
　　　From "The East Is Red," China's revolutionary anthem
　　　during the Cultural Revolution

It was a large room, with hundreds of people sitting on wooden chairs and standing in the aisles, she remembers. Her mother had been ushered to a prominent seat in the front row, to watch. Her father, a veteran general of the People's Liberation Army, a wounded hero in the wars against the Nationalists and the Americans in Korea, was placed on the rostrum. Then several armed guards with red armbands forced him to kneel, made him bow his head, and thrust his arms up behind him and tied his hands. It was what the Red Guards called the jet position, from the victim's resemblance to a plane with swept-back wings. The time was 1967, early in the Cultural Revolution, and her father had the misfortune to be in an army faction that had come under attack by Lin Biao, the Minister of Defense and Mao's chief ally. He was accused of being a capitalist roader and traitor, and the army command had organized the meeting as a mass criticism session. With everything in readiness, Xiao Bing, "Little Soldier," his thirteen-year-old daughter, was marched onto the stage to testify against him. Given the ancient code of filial piety, for a Chinese to denounce her father was the ultimate symbolic act, a rejection of the old system of parental authority and an acceptance of the new Communist regime as its replacement.

"It sounds incredible now, you can't understand it unless you were brought up in the system," Bing told me after I had met her by chance at a restaurant in Peking. Following the Chinese practice, I had sat down at a table where there was an empty chair.

"I was very young and naïve at the time," Bing explained about her attack on her father. "I thought I was a child of the Revolution, not of my parents." She saw herself, as millions of young Chinese did in the 1950s and 1960s, as belonging to Mao and to communism and to China.

"That was the way my parents had brought me up—to be very disciplined. My father himself had betrayed his own brother in 1958 during the Anti-Rightist movement because he had said something in private about China being too reliant on the Soviet Union. To my father, that was the meaning of loyalty and honesty, to be devoted to the Party. My parents felt revolutionaries shouldn't show personal affection.

"I remember one day when I was nine, I was feeling very lonely. My parents both worked late. I wanted to do something to show them that I missed them. So after I came back from school, I made the bed and fixed some tea. When my father came home, he laughed at me. It was not a mean laugh, but it hurt. After that, I was determined to be a good revolutionary myself and not show my feelings either."

Bing learned her lesson in self-discipline well. When her father came under criticism, she was the first to denounce him. "I said I wouldn't be sacrificed for a capitalist roader." Thousands of other Chinese youngsters were caught in the same situation.

At the mass meeting to attack her father, a panel of military interrogators asked Bing to report any of her father's crimes she could recall. "I said he sometimes ate meat at home, something a reactionary like him shouldn't be allowed to do." To an outsider, this might seem a trivial charge, irrelevant to the heinous crime of counterrevolution. But in the arbitrary and hothouse atmosphere of the Cultural Revolution, it was the kind of evidence that zealous radical prosecutors took seriously. They encouraged her to go on.

"I also remembered that during a conversation at home with us he had told a story of how during the civil war with the Nationalists he had once temporarily lost contact with his company. I said there might be something suspicious in that." Pressed for more, she related that her father had urged her to drink milk to make her tall and healthy. "That was a bourgeois idea, I told them." Bing did not know how much her testimony counted—only later had she realized the verdict was predetermined—but her father ended up spending almost ten years years in an army detention center.

Bing has since grown into a lithe, twenty-eight-year-old woman with short, wiry hair and tiny, narrow eyes, triangular at the corners, the kind foreigners think of when they say Chinese have slanted eyes. She was not pretty in a conventional way, but she had a verve and directness and an engaging way with words that helped her charm friends. Whenever we met she first put on what she termed her "costume" to avoid recognition. On the outside she wore a full-length olive-drab army overcoat—unlike Chinese military coats, it had a hood and there was something about its color that looked familiar though wrong for China. "A souvenir," she said, crinkling up her eyes into even narrower slits, "from the U.S. Army in Korea. My father brought it home." Through other relatives in the Party who had made official trips abroad, she had acquired a pair of high brown-leather boots, tight green corduroy slacks, and a green ski parka, all foreign-made. It was enough of a disguise to deceive the guards at the Peking Hotel, who let her pass as an overseas Chinese.

One day, several weeks after we first met, she tried to explain more fully how she could have denounced her father.

"In those days, Mao was really like a god in my mind," she went on. During the Cultural Revolution, there had been a ritual everyone had to follow. Every household had a white plaster bust of Mao, and each day all the family members had to bow before it twice. "The saying was, 'In the morning ask for instructions; in the evening report back what you have done.'" It was an imitation of an old imperial practice, Bing noted.

"Suddenly one morning when I bowed to the statue, he looked like he was smiling at me. I got very angry with him. But then I was horrified at my reaction."

At the time, Bing added, the cadres were preaching the idea that people's lives were determined by a sudden flash, like a photographer's flash, which would leave an imprint on your mind. Whatever the flash was, it would decide whether you were a revolutionary or a reactionary.

"I was scared I was a reactionary, and they had told us we must report immediately any reactionary thoughts. I was afraid they would take me before a criticism session like my father and throw me into prison. I was only thirteen, and there was no one for me to turn to.

"Those were times when we kept personal feelings to ourselves. For months and years, I didn't have a real conversation with friends." She was living in a school dormitory. It was near her parents' apartment and she passed her mother every day on the street, but she couldn't talk with her. It was too awkward. She feared her mother was angry with her for her betrayal of her father; she was embarrassed, and she was also afraid to be seen with the wife of a known counterrevolutionary.

Despite her rigorous training in controlling her emotions, Bing admitted there were times she did get homesick. "Once I went home on a weekend —my mother was away, but my younger sister was there. She was only ten. She said, 'Big sister, we really miss you.' I broke down and cried." Bing lacked the support systems Westerners take for granted. She was cut off emotionally and politically from her parents. She didn't dare talk with friends. There were no guidance counselors at school or psychiatrists to turn to.

"For many weeks I was close to a nervous breakdown," she continued her story. "Each morning when we woke up, we heard the loudspeakers playing 'The East Is Red' and it set my mind going. I asked Chairman Mao to forgive me. I prayed to him. I kept reading as many of his books as I could, to keep the terrible thought of what I had seen out of my head.

"I got a Peking city map, with the bus routes on it, and I would recite, the Number Seven bus goes here, the Number Eight bus goes there. At night I would leave the radio on. I couldn't sleep unless I was distracted.

"I thought about jumping off a tall building. But if you commit suicide, they would automatically take it as proof you were a reactionary."

Finally, she said, she couldn't stand the pressure anymore. She wrote on a piece of paper what had happened and turned it in to the authorities. "They actually were very kind to me, because I was so young," Bing said. "They didn't handle me," she went on, using a Chinese term meaning to be punished. "They just assigned another girl to watch me twenty-four hours a day."

But Bing's troubles weren't over. Even though she had publicly denounced her father, under the Communists' bloodline theory of guilt, in which several generations are implicated in the sins of one member of the family, she was also labeled a reactionary by the officials at her school. They would not let her join the Communist Youth League; they expelled her from the city Ping-Pong team, where she was a rising star, and they banned her from meetings where Party documents were read out.

"Finally one day when they taunted me as a reactionary, I couldn't stand it any longer," Bing recalled. "I ran out of the building. I didn't know where I was going. I was in a daze."

She ended up at the Peking Railroad Station, a vast Stalinesque structure with marble floors. She sat there all afternoon and evening until eleven o'clock when the militia went through the station rounding up everyone without a proper residence certificate.

"I didn't have mine with me," Bing said. "They thought I was a prostitute and took me next door to a police station. They put me in a cell with a dozen other people—thieves, beggars, a crazy old man in rags who kept shouting to himself. It was horrible, like gong to hell and finding yourself alive. I refused to sit down on a bench with the others, they were so dirty, so I stood all night near the door."

The next morning at 5 A.M. a guard came to interrogate her. By chance she remembered that a friend of hers on the Ping-Pong team had a relative who worked in the police station and asked to see him. "Luckily I recalled a lot about the girl—that she had just been to Albania, that she had come back with a pair of sunglasses. Those were big things in those days." Finally he said she could leave.

But the episode meant the end of her formal education at the seventh grade; she was expelled from school and assigned to work in a factory. In 1976, when Mao died, Bing related, the Party leader of her factory called the workers together to watch a memorial service on television. "The Party secretary expected us to cry and show grief for Mao. There was a lot of pressure. I couldn't get a tear out. But my clothes were soaked with sweat."

Only later, after the Gang of Four were arrested, did she learn that some of her friends hadn't been able to cry either. "They just faced the wall, so no one could see."

It was a few months after Mao's death and the arrest of the radicals that her father finally was released from prison and rehabilitated. He did not blame Bing for what had happened it turned out, and the family was reconciled. "He understood, he knew I had been very young and that I didn't do it for myself but for the revolution. But still, it was very stupid of me to do it, it is not something I will ever forget."

There was a ceremony in the Great Hall of the People to honor her father, she told me, but she refused to go. "It was too late." Her father had been dishonored, attacked, imprisoned for a decade; she had been forced to stop school and was isolated emotionally and politically. Her faith in the Communist system had been shattered.

Still, she found irony in the situation. "For those of us who survived," she said, "the Cultural Revolution was a good thing. We learned a lot. I could never put another god in my heart like Mao." As it was for millions of other Chinese, the Cultural Revolution had been a watershed for Bing. She was no longer a revolutionary.

Bing was nervous about our meeting—she lived in dread of being spied on and criticized. "You learn to live with fear from the time you are born in China, it is the condition of our lives," she said. "At every door there is a policeman, every pair of eyes is watching you." We were eating lunch in the Russian Restaurant, a vestige of the days of better relations between Peking and Moscow, where you could still get a bowl of borscht and chicken fried with butter à la Kiev. The restaurant is next to the Peking zoo, but outside our window on a bitter January day, with patches of ice on the ground, stood an army sentry, his coat bulging with layers of padded undergarments. Was he protecting the restaurant or the zoo, I wondered? Neither, Bing said. Behind the restaurant is a theater, and theaters are considered important political institutions. She had telephoned to arrange the time for our rendezvous that day—we had already agreed on a place to meet at our last encounter—so she didn't have to identify herself or the location over the phone. With all the dangers a Chinese faced making friends with a foreigner,

I wondered why Bing was so willing to talk to me. I sensed it stemmed from the terrible isolation she had felt since childhood. Paradoxically, since she couldn't trust her family, friends, or colleagues, she felt safe telling her innermost thoughts only to a foreigner.

When she was twenty-two years old, Bing went on with the story of her life, she had attracted the eye of the son of another general, Guoqiang, "Strengthen the Nation." Her friends reckoned he was a prime catch. He was handsome, with smooth white skin and a flashing smile; he was a brilliant student in university, and his father was a deputy chief of staff of the army, an excellent family to marry into, a critical consideration to Chinese. He also liked Ping-Pong and was impressed by how well Bing played in a game he chanced to see.

"I didn't think he would like me, because I thought of myself as an ugly duckling, but I was very flattered. It was a low time in my life. My father was still in prison, and I didn't have much of a future."

Guoqiang began writing her letters, to court her, and she eventually agreed to go to the movies with him. She was startled when he kissed her at the end of their first date, unusually fast for a Chinese. It turned out he was very interested in sex, though Bing used a circumlocution in talking about making love.

"He put a lot of pressure on me to do it," she said. "I felt an obligation to him, he had been kind to me when I was in a precarious position and he helped me in my effort to study English on my own, since I wasn't allowed to go to school." One day he invited her over to his parents' house, a spacious home given his father by the army. It had its own garden, two servants, and separate rooms for each of the family's four grown children, one of whom had two infants of his own. There was even a guest room, where Bing was to spend the night. Late that evening, after Guoqiang thought his parents had gone to sleep, he called her to his room. He had asked a friend to secretly change the lock on his door, so his parents couldn't get in.

But after Bing entered and undressed, his mother became suspicious and knocked at the door. When she found it was bolted, she was even more upset and kept pounding until Guoqiang finally had to open up.

"There was some laundry drying on a line in the room," Bing recalled. "I hid behind it, feeling ashamed. His mother pretended she didn't see me, to save face. It was terrible. After that, I never enjoyed doing it. I just closed my eyes. I could go without it."

The experience of Bing and Guoqiang seemed typical of the shifting sexuality of the younger generation of Chinese. They were moving toward a freer standard of sexual behavior in the aftermath of the Cultural Revolution, though they still had to keep it secret, and they had not rid themselves entirely of the government's officially encouraged inhibitions.

A few months later Bing discovered she was pregnant. They were not married, and it presented a dangerous situation. "Any hint to my *danwei* that I was pregnant would ruin my reputation," Bing said. "The Party thinks women are supposed to be virgins till they are married, and it would go straight into my dossier. It is the worst thing that can happen to a woman." Fortunately, Guoqiang had an old high school classmate who was a nurse in a maternity hospital.

"When we went to her house to see her, we didn't have to say anything. She knew. She just said, 'How many months pregnant?' That was all. Then she made the arrangements with her hospital through the back door. She put me down as married, so there would be no questions and no report to my *danwei*.

"Guoqiang was supposed to come with me, but on that day he started making excuses. He said he had to go to work. I felt embarrassed. I was supposed to be married and my husband didn't even show up at the hospital. At first the doctors figured I was just being selfish and having an abortion without telling my husband. They asked if I had his permission."

Bing was put in a room with a dozen other women. When they called her name, she walked across the hall to the operating room. "They used a hose and pump to suck the fetus out," she recalled. "Afterward they pieced it together, the little bits they had, to make sure some of it wasn't left inside to cause bleeding." Then they told her to go back to the ward and rest for half an hour before going home.

There are usually taxis at the hospital, one of the rare places in Peking where Chinese can get cabs—they are normally reserved for foreigners, and are too expensive for Chinese anyway. But that day there weren't any taxis. Bing had to take a bus back to her parents' home, a crowded, jostling half-hour ride. The nurse had come to the hospital door with her.

"I am sorry I have to stay and work," she said to Bing.

"The look in her eyes said she knew how lonely I was.

"The next afternoon Guoqiang came over. He wanted to make love. I said, I can't, I've just had an abortion, I'm in pain. But he complained, 'I've ridden my bike all the way over from school.' "

Six months later, Bing was pregnant again; they were still not married. This time Bing was certain the hospital would criticize her, so she decided to claim that she was married and already had one baby and didn't want a second, in keeping with the Party's effort to limit families to one child. But the woman physician who came to examine her before the abortion saw right through her. The doctor had brought along three medical-school students for a class.

"She started talking to the students," Bing said. " 'Look at her abdomen, you see it is still tight. Notice her breasts, they don't sag. She's lying. Come on miss, confess.' "

This time, after the abortion was performed—without anesthetic as before —Bing fainted from the pain. She had to sit down on the steps leading downstairs not to pass out again when she left the hospital. By chance the doctor came by and saw her.

" 'I hate men,' " the doctor exclaimed. Actually, Bing said, the doctor was even younger than she was, but was very serious. " 'Men cause so much suffering. I see it all, and they never know what they do. I will never get married,' " she told Bing.

Bing had pedaled her bicycle to the hospital and rode it home.

With free contraceptives available under the government's birth-control program, why didn't she take some precautions against getting pregnant? I inquired. "It's just so humiliating to go in there and ask," Bing replied. Chinese prophylactics, she explained, come in three sizes. "You have to say, large, medium, or small. Guoqiang refused to go, he said it was my job."

Bing's parents never chastised her for her denunciation of her father, they understood it. But her parents were disappointed with her cynicism about the Communists. Despite his mistreatment, her father remained steadfast in his belief in the Party.

"He is an old-fashioned cadre, selfless and dedicated," she said. "Even my mother says his thinking is back in Yanan in the 1940s. After dinner he will still get up to sweep the floor and wash the dishes, though we have a servant and an army orderly to do that for us. Everyone else uses his office car for personal errands, but my father never lets me take it. He doesn't bring mother to official banquets to enjoy the food, even when other generals now routinely take their wives." Her father, she said, had grown up in poverty —his own father was a peddler, his mother was an opium addict. He had managed to attend a primary school only because of the indulgence of a local merchant family who sponsored a free school for the indigent. Ironically, one of his teachers was a radical and took him to join the Red Army guerrillas in the early 1930s.

"He doesn't like young people today," Bing said. Once, at a family meal, they were discussing a student protest demonstration in Hunan over Party interference in an experimental campus election. "My father was furious. 'These young people, all they do is make trouble, don't you join them,' " she quoted him as warning her.

"I said, 'What trouble? Student action is a good thing for democracy.'

"He only got madder. 'You should listen to me. My membership in the Party is fifty years, your mother has forty years. Between us, we have ninety years. You must believe what we tell you.'

"I couldn't stand it," Bing added. "I said, 'Look at the Soviet Union. It has an even longer history, and see where it has gotten.' There is a generation gap growing in China. My experience has made me a cynic. I believe nothing, like my friends. Recently I heard a joke people were telling about the Soviet Union, but I thought you could apply it to China as well. 'Adam and Eve were Russians. They were naked and had only an apple to eat between them, but they thought they were in paradise.' My parents are like them, they don't see," Bing said.

Bing's parents were also unhappy with her decision not to have children. She had finally married Guoqiang, her boy friend, when she was twenty-six. His father had pulled strings to get her admitted to a university, and her gratitude to him had increased. "But I made it an absolute with him that we would never have children," she said. "It is a growing trend among intellectuals. Our interests are changing," she explained. "If you have a child, it ties you down. You don't have the money to spend on new things like tape recorders, you don't have the time or the energy to continue your studies." Her reasoning was symptomatic of the new materialism in China, but her calculations were also much the same as those of young people in the West who are delaying marriage and deciding against having babies. There is a rise of concern with the self, with seeking one's own fulfillment, and less commitment to society or the state. Not long before, Bing said, one of her friends had a baby boy. The parents nicknamed him, in English, "Mistake." But Bing was aware of the hurt her position caused her parents, who thought along more traditional lines despite their Communist Party membership. Mencius, the great early expounder of Confucian doctrine, had said, "There are three unfilial acts, and of these, lack of progeny is the greatest."

Most of all, her parents were shocked to learn that she had recently had an affair with another man. He had been her first sweetheart when they were teen-agers during the Cultural Revolution, but then he got involved in a factional fight, was accused of being a counterrevolutionary, and had fled to Hong Kong. "I hated him for leaving the motherland, I thought he was a traitor," Bing told me, "but I loved him too." That was seven years ago. Now suddenly he had come back, on a business trip, with a Hong Kong passport, and he had looked her up. "It was as if the seven years never existed. I found I was still in love with him."

To make matters worse, she was having problems with her husband, troubles an American woman approaching thirty might recognize. "I discovered we were very different people," Bing said. "I began to realize I want to grow, to expand, to continue my studies and go to the United States, if I can. All he cares about is doing well in his job and that I be presentable to his friends." Guoqiang had gotten a coveted position with CAAC, the

Chinese airlines, thanks to his father's connections. "At night I have to get in bed first to warm it up, our room is so cold. Then after we do it, he just falls asleep." Their tastes varied also. Guoqiang liked to go to *gung-fu* movies starring Bruce Lee, which he could see in special "internal" film shows. Bing liked books about women. An American teacher at her college lent her a copy of the feminist novel *The Woman's Room*. She asked Guoqiang to read it; he refused. When he went on an official trip to Western Europe, she felt "liberated." "My schoolwork was better, my teacher gave me higher grades, even my roommate in the school dorm where I lived during the week noticed I was more relaxed."

Then the foreign professor also gave her a copy of Gail Sheehy's book *Passages*. "It was a revelation. I was really going through a crisis, and it showed me there are turning points in your life. I fit right in to what Sheehy called 'Catch 30.'" There was a restless new vitality inside Bing, a side of her that had been suppressed, and she felt a need to reappraise and reconstruct her life. Reading the book didn't make her problems go away, she said, but it helped her understand what was happening.

Bing was sitting on the couch in my apartment. It was late afternoon, the day before New Year's, and as we talked, the leaden winter sky grew dark. I didn't want to move to turn on a light and break her train of thought. Outside construction workers putting up another apartment building were shooting off fireworks, green and red rockets that burst in the air, casting flashes on the walls in the room. It should have been a time for celebration.

Bing, I realized, had come full cycle in a single generation, like China since 1949. She had been Chairman Mao's good little revolutionary as a girl, dedicated to the cause; then she was disillusioned by her experience in the Cultural Revolution; now as she approached thirty she had become, in Chinese terms, a postrevolutionary woman. Like women in the West, she was launched on a voyage of self-discovery, questioning the roles she was supposed to play. And for her, each step in this process had been a lonely one.

Picking up the thread of her story, Bing recalled that soon after her old boy friend came back to Peking he asked her to spend a week night with him in his hotel.

"I didn't really want to do that with him, but he said he had gone those seven years without caring for another woman, without ever touching another woman. I felt sorry for him."

But when they got in bed, she discovered he was an expert at making love and knew far more than she did. "I couldn't do the things he wanted me to, they were awful. I was surprised and upset. I also felt guilty about what I was doing to my husband. I couldn't sleep. I left very early in the morning and went home, but I was crying, so Guoqiang knew something was wrong. I told him what I had done."

That changed everything, Bing said. "He could never trust me after that. He isn't a bad man. He didn't deserve what happened. But I didn't love him anymore."

Her husband's first reaction, she said, was that he had failed. He had never failed before in his life, and he was afraid people would laugh at him. It was a severe loss of face. Then he threatened to go to the police to have her lover arrested for adultery, a punishable crime in China. He also accused her of a lack of gratitude, of not repaying all the *guan-xi,* the connections, his family had arranged for her when she was in political difficulty.

Bing had entreated her lover to leave Peking to avoid any trouble with the police and assumed he had gone. But a month later she got a call from him saying he was departing the next morning and couldn't forget her. She was touched and decided to risk a last visit to say good-bye, an inviolable Chinese custom.

But when she knocked on his hotel-room door, she found him in bed with one of her girl friends. She was surprised, embarrassed, and wounded, but he did not seem flustered. He asked her to go down to the dining room and wait to have breakfast with the two of them.

After this encounter, she was in a quandary. She couldn't bring herself to tell Guoqiang; he would only ridicule her. But every night he was keeping her awake till four or five o'clock, pressing to know if she really loved him. All she wanted was to go to sleep and blot it out. He demanded an answer. If she said no, she didn't love him, he would ask for a divorce. That would go into her dossier and probably scrap any chance she had to get a passport to study abroad. Guoqiang had already told her parents about the affair, as a form of revenge, and her father had counseled her, "A divorced woman is ruined. Everyone has arrows at your back, ready to shoot."

I wondered if many Chinese women go through such crises, as American women now do. Yes, Bing replied, two of her girl friends were having similar trouble with their husbands.

"There are turning points in our lives, too. The difference is, we have much less room to maneuver. We know what is expected of us more clearly than Americans do, the rules are much more strict. And we know we can't break the rules so easily. So usually we just drag along. We never resolve our crises."

When I left China, Bing and her husband were still quarreling. There were no marriage counselors for her to see, no psychiatrists to help her, no lawyers she could hire to defend her. She reminded me of a heroine in some tragic nineteenth-century novel, a woman trapped by the conventions of her time, unable to gain understanding or support. She had become deeply pessimistic. From a dinner conversation at her parents-in-laws' house, she had heard that Chen Yun, one of the Party's most respected elder statesman, had prophesied that China would soon suffer from one of three disasters: the economy would collapse, the army would stage a coup, or there would be a popular rebellion.

"We should lead our lives with the lights turned out," she told me the day I departed, "so we don't have to see too clearly where we are going."

PART

3

SYSTEMS

—

II.   A Pig Under the Roof

PEASANTS

"You may rob the Three Armies of their commander in chief, but you cannot deprive the humblest peasant of his opinion."
Confucius, the Analects

When William Hinton first visited Long Bow village in 1948, it was just starting to emerge from centuries of medieval poverty and ignorance. In the past, if the harvest was good, the peasants had to give much of their crop to rapacious landlords to repay debts. If the harvest was bad, some peasants had to sell their children to survive; others starved. Babies died screaming from tetanus after untutored midwives used rusty scissors to snip their umbilical cords. Hinton, an American writer and farmer, recorded this misery and then the impact of the arrival of the Communists in Long Bow in the classic account of revolution in a Chinese village, *Fanshen* * (*Fanshen* literally means to "turn over," or in Communist usage, to undergo a revolution). When Hinton left later in 1948, the Communists had just carried out a traumatic land-reform campaign which killed or dispossessed the landlords and enfranchised the poor.

In 1980, Hinton, a tall, jovial man of sixty-three, with a craggy face and thatch of snow-white hair, returned to Long Bow to work on a sequel to his original book and help the village with mechanizing its agriculture. It was like a journey to a different world, he told me later.

Where the mule-cart track used to run, linking Long Bow to other hamlets in Shanxi province in central western China, there is an asphalt highway now. And beyond, where there were only small fields of corn and millet, there is a main north–south railroad line now, a locomotive repair shop, a cement

*William Hinton, *Fanshen. A Documentary of Revolution in a Chinese Village* (New York: Random House, 1966).

235

mill, and a saw-blade works with 5,000 employees. Another 30,000 workers are constructing a new east–west railroad that will run through the Taihang Mountains, which had long isolated the region.

Long Bow itself really isn't a village anymore. It's an industrial suburb of the new city of Changzhi, which has a population of 300,000 people. When Hinton stayed in Long Bow in 1948, Changzhi was only a small, walled town where Long Bow's peasants went to market several times a week.

Some of these changes have come to other areas of China's countryside under three decades of Communist rule. But what really distinguishes Long Bow, Hinton said with avuncular affection, pushing back a lock of white hair, is its new success in mechanizing corn production. With his guidance, the village took a risky experiment. It laid off fifty peasants and formed a team of twelve young people who opened up one hundred acres, which they farmed entirely with mechanized means, from plowing and spreading manure to spraying with herbicides, planting, picking, and drying. Although elsewhere in China mechanization has proved more costly than traditional hand cultivation and local officials were skeptical, Long Bow proved them wrong.

"We doubled the yield, cut the costs in half, and raised the earnings of the peasants to the level of factory workers," Hinton said with a boyish grin. As he talked, he paced around my hotel room with a loping stride, as if he were measuring off another field to plant. In his enthusiasm and sympathy for the villagers, I sensed something of the old left-wing ideals of the 1930s in Hinton, a folksy man whose easygoing manner masks his keen intellect. Output on the mechanized fields in Long Bow, he said, averaged 112 bushels of corn per acre, far above China's norm, and well beyond the 89 bushels an acre he had been getting on his farm in Pennsylvania.

As a result, Hinton found when he returned to Long Bow the following spring, "there was corn hanging all over the village—from trees, all sorts of platforms and boards. They never had such a harvest. It's one of the few places in China where they have really done this complete mechanization." There were other bonuses too. The fifty people who had been displaced by the new machinery were put to work in the local factories.

"It's hard to believe, but they even said the corn tasted sweeter, too," Hinton related. "It could be, because for the first time they had a complete fertilizer." In the past the peasants had used only night soil, excrement from the public latrines and pig sties. Now they added potash, phosphorus, and nitrogen from small local factories they ran themselves. The new fertilizer also helped account for the high yield.

"It's not sweet corn like we have in the States. They just raise what we call field corn and feed it to the cattle." The Chinese plant this kind of corn because it is much higher-yielding than sweet corn, he explained, and they

Buddhist pilgrims pray at sunrise on Mount E-mei in Sichuan, one of five mountains traditionally considered sacred by Chinese. Religion was proscribed during the Cultural Revolution but has made a comeback since Mao Zedong's successors adopted a more tolerant attitude. *(Photo © 1981 Liu Heung Shing/Contact Press Images)*

Young dissidents sell transcripts of the trial of Wei Jingsheng at Peking's Democracy Wall shortly before the police arrested them. The leader of the group was sentenced to a labor reform camp. *(Photo © 1981 Liu Heung Shing/Contact Press Images)*

Getting a permanent in one of China's revived beauty parlors. *(Photo © 1981 Liu Heung Shing/Contact Press Images)*

Three young *liu-mang*, or toughs, sport the latest fashion — sunglasses. *(Photo © 1981 Liu Heung Shing / Contact Press Images)*

Courtship Chinese-style. In crowded Peking, privacy is where you can find it. *(Photo © 1981 Liu Heung Shing / Contact Press Images)*

Peasants load a truck with cabbages at harvest time near Peking. Many farm products are spoiled by poor handling, since the peasants, like factory workers, are rewarded for quantity, not quality. *(Photo © 1981 Liu Heung Shing/Contact Press Images)*

Commune members divide their potato harvest in Gansu. An accountant, squatting on the left, has an abacus and an official seal to certify each peasant's share. *(Photo by Fox Butterfield)*

Skating and taking a stroll on the frozen moat outside the wall of the Forbidden City. *(Photo © 1981 Liu Heung Shing / Contact Press Images)*

A cobbler in Sichuan eats his lunch. In the past few years the Communists have encouraged a limited revival of individual enterprise to soak up the unemployed and create more consumer goods and services. *(Photo © 1981 Liu Heung Shing/Contact Press Images)*

One-year-olds in the nursery school of a Peking factory drink their morning apple juice. None moved or jostled the others. *(Photo by Fox Butterfield)*

School children in Tibet recite in unison after their teacher, with their hands dutifully clasped behind their backs, in the old pedagogical fashion. *(Photo by Fox Butterfield)*

A Chinese guard from the Bureau for the Preservation of Cultural Relics keeps Tibetans out of the Jokhang, the seventh-century temple in Lhasa that is the holiest shrine of Tibetan Buddhism. He is in charge, not the monks. *(Photo by Fox Butterfield)*

A Tibetan waits outside the Jokhang. The temple was closed during the Cultural Revolution and now is open only three mornings a week to Tibetans, though they come from all over Chinese Central Asia to worship at it. *(Photo by Fox Butterfield)*

Sarah, Ethan, Barbara, and the author in front of the Gate of Heavenly
Peace. The man on the left is wearing a surgical mask against Peking's cold and
dust. *(Photo © 1981 Liu Heung Shing/Contact Press Images)*

Confession in the Roman Catholic cathedral in Peking. Since the Cultural
Revolution, Chinese have become hungry for something spiritual, Chinese
Christian leaders say. *(Photo © 1981 Liu Heung Shing/Contact Press Images)*

Tibetan women at a pastoral commune 14,500 feet above sea level, on the great Tibetan plateau. *(Photo by Fox Butterfield)*

A young porter carries a 130-pound load of cement up Huang Shan, or Yellow Mountain, in Anhui province. *(Photo by Fox Butterfield)*

Roller skating in Shanghai, one of the few pleasures for young people in China's largest city. *(Photo © 1981 Liu Heung Shing / Contact Press Images)*

At China's Academy Awards night. On the right is Yolanda Sui, the foster daughter of the late Madame Sun Yat-sen, a member of the pampered elite and an aspiring movie actress. On the left is the woman voted best actress. *(Photo by Francis Deron, Agence France Press)*

Wang Keping, the dissident sculptor, in his tiny studio apartment. The carving is Chairman Mao as Buddha, with one eye closed and the other slyly open to see who is praying to him, Wang says. *(Photo © 1981 Liu Heung Shing/Contact Press Images)*

A propaganda poster painter enjoys his *xiu-xi*, or siesta, a right enshrined in China's constitution. *(Photo © 1981 Liu Heung Shing/Contact Press Images)*

Left: Youthful peasants working on a treadmill to irrigate rice paddies, just as their ancestors did. *(Photo by Fox Butterfield)*

The author and Lao Wu, my government-assigned assistant, in *The New York Times*'s office in the Peking Hotel. *(Photo by Liu Heung Shing/The New York Times)*

must worry about getting the maximum possible return. For Long Bow, like many other rural areas in China, has lost some of its land to the new factories. And with peace and prosperity, its population has soared. So where in 1948 there were a thousand peasants farming a thousand acres, an acre per person, today there are 2,400 people living on only about 600 acres, a quarter of an acre per capita, about the national average.

To further increase their income, Long Bow's peasants now plant much of their acreage in vegetables, which they sell to the new industrial city nearby. In 1948, Hinton recalled, the only vegetables the peasants ate were wild herbs they picked in the mountains. Their diet in those days was corn cakes for breakfast, more corn cakes for lunch, and noodles made from wheat for dinner, if they were lucky. Today almost every family raises a pig and eats meat on occasion, unheard of before the Communists' arrival. But it is still not a mainstay of their cuisine, as Hinton discovered from the local cook assigned to feed him during his most recent visit. The cook did not know how to prepare meat dishes.

One key to Long Bow's success, Hinton felt, has been the brigade leader, Wang Jinhung, a brilliant thirty-nine-year-old man born to a poor peasant family. In the 1950s he was sent off as an apprentice with a construction gang working for Russian engineers. "He always carried a ruler, measured things, and kept a notebook," Hinton said. Consequently, as he served variously as a welder, crane operator, electrician, mechanic, and building designer, he kept picking up new skills. After the Sino–Soviet split in the early 1960s, Wang was sent back to Long Bow as an electrician and eventually made brigade head.

The other vital ingredient in Long Bow's success was Hinton himself. Because of his book and long-standing sympathy for China, Peking classified Hinton as a "friend" and allowed him to make several return trips to the village over the years, an unusual privilege for a foreigner. He helped Wang design a grain dryer, using local coal for fuel, and a center pivot irrigation system. Then, drawing on his good connections with China's leaders, he took Wang to the provincial capital of Taiyuan and "borrowed a lot of machinery we found sitting around with a half inch of dust on it in the local agricultural machinery institute." No one else was bothering to use it.

This year, Hinton said, Long Bow will double the acreage farmed mechanically and lay off more peasants, who will be absorbed in the brigade's factories, further stimulating the village's growth.

I was fascinated with Hinton's account. He was virtually the only Westerner allowed to observe intimately the development of a Chinese village from before 1949 to the present. Three quarters of the country's population, 800 million people, still live in the countryside, an almost unimaginably large

number; yet for most foreigners and even many Chinese it remains an unknown continent. After my arrival in Peking, I made repeated applications
to the Information Department to let me live and work in a village so I could
more accurately report on the peasants. I even received an invitation from
a Chinese-American who was doing sociological research for a year with her
husband in her home village in Guangdong province, near Hong Kong.
They had built their own house, where I could stay, and had purchased a car,
to drive me back and forth to the village, so I would not be a burden to the
local authorities. But this request, like all the others, was turned down as
"inconvenient." It was as if there was something secret about the peasants
that the government wanted to hide.

I did manage to visit a dozen communes for the usual two- or three-hour
inspections foreigners get, with briefings by the local officials and quick stops
at peasants' homes. But each time, the communes I toured turned out to be
well above average in their economic development. According to the State
Statistical Bureau, the average per capita income for peasants from work in
their collective fields was the equivalent of $57 in 1980. But of the twelve
communes I visited, the lowest per capita income was $87. Several had
earnings of over $200 a year, and one outside Shanghai claimed $540, almost
ten times the national average. To Westerners, accustomed to measuring
their salaries in the tens of thousands of dollars, these figures may all appear
small; but they have real significance to Chinese. They also meant that I was
seeing only the most prosperous segment of rural China. Less than one
quarter of China's production teams—the team is the lowest level of rural
organization, under the brigade and the commune—have an average per
capita income of over $67 like those I was shown. Half of the teams make
between $33 and $67. Another 27 percent get less than $33. At the bottom,
in Jingyuan county in Ningxia province, in the arid northwest, the Communist Party theoretical journal *Red Flag* reported, the peasants receive a mere
$10 a year. That is far below the level Peking itself has defined as the
minimum for subsistence, an income of $27 a year.

More important to the peasants themselves than these monetary figures is
the amount of grain they receive for their work, for on most production
teams the peasants actually get the bulk of their income directly in kind at
the end of the year when the harvest is added up and divided among the
laborers. They get cash only to the extent that their team is prosperous
enough to have surplus grain to sell to the state or has small industries like
brick kilns or fruit orchards. Hence the monetary figure that Peking uses to
measure peasant income, and gives out to foreigners, is somewhat misleading. It is based on an artificial conversion from farm production. If the
subsistence level is calculated in grain, Peking reckons that peasants must get
at least 330 pounds of wheat or rice a year. That works out to 1,500 calories

a day, 100 calories less than the critical limit of 1,600 used by the U.N. Food and Agricultural Organization to measure malnourishment. But the Communist-controlled periodical *Cheng Ming* in Hong Kong reported in 1979 that 200 million peasants, almost as many people as live in the United States, receive less than that 330 pounds ration a year. "That is to say," the magazine stated, "they are living in a state of semistarvation."

These figures suggest that there is not one vast uniform countryside, rural China, but a wildly variant patchwork pattern of emerging prosperity and continued poverty. China has its equivalents to the Imperial Valley of California, rich farming communities, like Long Bow, but also its Appalachias. In their excellent 1978 study, *Village and Family in Contemporary China,* William L. Parish and Martin King Whyte estimate that in Guangdong province, in south China, the richest fifth of the peasants receive about 36 percent of the total per capita income, and the poorest fifth, 9 percent.* These figures indicate less inequality than rural India, Honduras, or the Philippines, but more than Taiwan, South Korea, or Egypt. Living on a commune does not automatically guarantee equality.

The more affluent villages tend to be where the natural conditions favor them—where the land is flat and fertile, in river valleys where water is adequate, and in rings around the cities, which provide a lucrative market for the nearby peasants and in turn send back bounteous quantities of night soil to fertilize their fields. The latter factor contributed to Long Bow's growth. The poorer areas lie in the remote mountains and in the drought-prone north China plain and northwest. Several of the poorest pockets are still the old areas that in the 1930s furnished bases for the fledgling Red Guerrillas because of their backwardness, like Yanan and the Jinggangshan Mountains where Lihua lived.

It is difficult for Americans and Europeans, who are accustomed to relatively stable rainfall, to appreciate how capricious and destructive the weather in China can be. On my tour of the United States with Chinese journalists in 1972, they told me that the single most striking sight to them was hundreds of acres of corn growing near Ottawa, Illinois, on a farm owned by a heavyset, gregarious man named Adrian Pike. As we stood examining the ripening green stalks, higher than the heads of the Chinese, one of the reporters turned to Pike with a mystified expression.

"How do you irrigate your fields?" he asked. Pike replied good-naturedly that he just depended on rainfall. I could see the look of incredulity on the Chinese faces. Irrigation ditches for rice, wheat, corn, and cotton are the lifeblood of the Chinese peasantry.

*William L. Parish and Martin King Whyte, *Village and Family in Contemporary China* (Chicago: University of Chicago Press, 1978), p. 376, fn. 1.

Since I was not allowed to visit any of the less prosperous parts of the Chinese countryside, I had to depend on others for descriptions of them. A scholarly, bespectacled economist who was sent to labor in a cadre school for several years in the mid-1970s in southern Henan province, in the valley of the Huai River, said there had been a devastating flood while he was there in 1975. Not a word about it appeared in the Chinese press, but he later read in a confidential report that 360,000 people had died. Historically, the economist said, the region has always been one of China's poorest: "It was either drought or flood every year, as long as the peasants could remember. Everyone builds their houses of mud, so that if they get swept away, the loss will be less."

In Gold Mountain, the village in the mountains of Hunan in central southern China where my petitioner friend Lihua was sent in the Cultural Revolution, the nearest road is still a half day's walk away and the peasants still don't send their daughters to school. Until recently, she told me, the peasants had never seen a tractor. The first time the team leader brought in a small hand-operated tractor, not much bigger or more powerful than a lawn mower, the peasants were very excited. They called it the "iron ox." But after running it for an hour, they became anxious and then frustrated when it inexplicably stopped. "Some of the peasants got angry and began beating it with sticks," Lihua said. The next day a mechanic arrived from the commune center. The tractor had run out of gas.

In a few provinces, Chinese told me, some communes are so poor that in the slack season they give their peasants what amounts to a license to go off to beg in the cities. In Ningxia, the province with the county that had an average income of only $23 a year, a doctor who worked there said he regularly had beggars come to his house. "They were mostly women and children," the doctor said. "Their communes give them a slip of paper which says they are entitled to go out begging. That way they won't be picked up by the police. There simply is not enough food for them at home; some places I knew of were reduced to three ounces of grain a day. The teams give it all to the men, who need their energy to work in the fields."

Once the physician went on a medical inspection of a poor commune inhabited by the Moslem Hui minority in Ningxia. "The people stayed hidden inside their homes. At first I thought it was because they were afraid of us. But when I went inside, I saw they were filthy dirty and so poor they didn't have any clothes on."

Stories like these helped me realize that the government's sensitivity about letting foreigners visit the countryside was because it represented both the triumph and the tragedy of the Chinese revolution. Unlike the Bolsheviks in Russia, who won a quick victory in the cities, the Chinese Communists had to battle their way to power through years of organizing discontented peasants into a guerrilla army. After Liberation, Mao recognized his debt to the countryside, in theory at least, by proclaiming that agriculture was the "foundation" of China's economic development. But for every success the Communists have achieved since 1949 in the villages, there have also been stupid blunders in policy, surprising discrimination in favor of the cities over the countryside, and terrible neglect. Some regions have made enormous progress. But others, contrary to the impression of many foreigners, are no better off than they were in 1949 or have even slipped backward in comparison to the cities and more advanced rural areas. For them, Mao's revolution has not delivered.

The most obvious success is that in the past three decades, thanks to improved rural organization, increased irrigation, better seeds, and more use of chemical fertilizer, the Communists have managed to double China's grain output. But since the population has nearly doubled at the same time, the per capita consumption of grain has remained at roughly the same low level. Nicholas Lardy, a professor of economics at Yale, has calculated that at the end of the 1970s per capita farm output was actually no better than it was in the early 1930s, before World War Two.*

The Communists also brought new security and vastly improved public health care to the villages. They introduced large-scale immunization programs, persuaded the peasants to remove refuse from around their houses, and pushed campaigns in the 1950s to eliminate the "Four Pests," rats, flies, mosquitoes, and grain-eating sparrows. Before 1949, with wars, banditry, famine, and pestilence, the average peasant lived to be only twenty to twenty-five years old. By the mid-1970s the average life expectancy had risen to sixty-four, according to a careful study by two American specialists.** Hence China has gained over 1.5 years of life expectancy for each calendar year since Liberation. This is a far better record than the other large developing nations, including India and Brazil, and is matched only by a few smaller countries like Taiwan and Sri Lanka.

Infant mortality is another useful index of improved living conditions. Prior to 1949, there were about 200 deaths at birth for every 1,000 children. By 1955, the number had declined to 74 per 1,000, and by the mid 1970s to 35 or 40 per 1,000, a dramatic change.

But the same discipline and organizational genius that produced these advances could also prove destructive when the orders from Peking were poorly conceived. The worst example of what the Communists call "com-

---

*Nicholas Lardy, "Food Consumption in the People's Republic of China," 1980, an unpublished paper. In using these figures and those that follow, I am deeply endebted to Professor Lardy, who is writing a book on Chinese agriculture.
**Judith Banister and Samuel H. Preston, "Mortality in China," *Population and Development Review*, Vol. 7, No. 1 (March 1981), p. 107.

mandism" was the Great Leap Forward in 1958 when Mao sought to transform China overnight into a purer form of communism, pushed the consolidation of the communes, set up communal mess halls and backyard iron blast furnaces, confiscated all private property, and guaranteed food, clothing, and even haircuts to all. "I have witnessed the tremendous energy of the masses," Mao said after a rural inspection tour in September of that year. "On this foundation it is possible to accomplish any task whatsoever." The real extent of the disaster that followed has long been hidden from the outside world. But data released by Peking in 1980 indicate that about 16.5 million more people than normal died in the three years of food shortages caused by the Great Leap, probably from malnutrition and its effects.*

In the aftermath, Mao also had to retreat from the full-blown commune structure established in 1958. The commune became more an administrative apparatus of local government in the countryside than a way of life, as Mao intended. Instead, the real functioning farm unit became the production team, which was natural for the peasants, since most teams were based on the old pre-1949 villages. It is the team to which the peasants report for work and which keeps track of the peasants' work points. Today there are five million production teams in China, with an average of thirty to forty families, or about 150 to 200 people, farming anywhere from 15 to 100 acres. A brigade normally has about 450 households, or 2,000 people. There are 50,000 communes, with an average of 16,000 members, though the actual size varies greatly depending on local geography. For most peasants, the commune is a dim and distant organization. They normally visit the commune center, located in the old market towns, only if they need more medical attention than the barefoot doctor attached to their team can provide, or if their children are lucky enough to go to the commune high school, or perhaps to visit the barber or the carpenter. Over the years Mao tried repeatedly to increase the powers of the communes, arguing that they are a more advanced form of communism than the team. But he failed, and since his death Deng Xiaoping has pushed in the opposite direction, contending that even the teams are sometimes too large for efficiency and allowing some teams to subdivide into groups of families for farm work.

Given the Communists' success as guerrillas in the countryside and their accomplishments in the 1950s in agriculture, I was surprised by the number of stories Chinese told about the cadres' mismanagement. An American married to a Chinese woman from Henan on the north China plain recalled what happened in his wife's native village after an order came down from Chairman Hua Guofeng in Peking to level all the hilly land in the area during the winter slack season. The commune Party secretary had picked one person

*Ansley J. Coale, "Population Trends, Population Policy, and Population Studies in China," *Population and Development Review,* Vol. 7, No. 1 (March 1981), p. 89.

from each family to join work gangs to get the job done. At first they had worked carefully, removing the valuable topsoil, putting it in an adjacent field, then leveling the hilly ground and replacing the topsoil. But as spring approached, it became obvious they wouldn't finish the task on time so the cadres ordered everyone to speed up. The good topsoil was simply plowed under.

"That meant no good crops for four years," a local peasant told the American with bitterness. Then he paused and looked at the American. "Tell me," the peasant asked, "in the United States, how does the government organize agriculture?" He was incredulous when told that farming in America is up to the farmers.

The combined effect of such mismanagement over many years and a prolonged drought had produced a serious food shortage, and the peasants were hungry and hostile toward the cadres. When the American and his wife visited the village in 1976, they were surprised to be given an armed escort from the provincial capital of Zhengzhou. Two policemen with AK-47 assault rifles rode in a jeep in front of them. Asked why the guards were necessary, a local cadre explained that a few weeks earlier, at the junction of the main road and the path to the village, *tu-fei,* "bandits," had held up some peasants. "But the bandits are not as bad as a few years ago," the official added reassuringly.

The American discovered that the best-fed people in the village, the men who did the hardest labor and earned the most work points, ate a diet that consisted of only about two pounds of wheat flour a day. Once or twice a week they also got some pickled vegetables and perhaps an egg; once a month they might get a small piece of fatty pork. While he and his wife stayed in the village, the police brought in special food in a jeep for them every morning. As a gesture of courtesy, the American's in-laws held a banquet for the local cadres. Again, the police delivered extra rations. The meal was held in the family compound, with high mud walls around the house.

"The peasants were so curious and hungry, they climbed to the top and sat there watching, craning their necks for what must have been a marvel for them," the American recalled. "We had three kinds of dishes with fatty pork. I couldn't eat it, but the cadres slurped it down like a banana split."

The final and crowning course was a fish. The Yellow River was only two miles away, and many of the nearby fields had fishponds in them, but when the American later asked the peasants about the last time they had eaten fish, they shook their heads and said they couldn't remember. "Only the cadres are allowed to catch fish," one elderly man with a wispy goatee told him.

A professor of engineering from Peking who was dispatched with colleagues from his institute to work on a so-called May Seventh School for cadres in the early 1970s in another part of Henan remembered a deep chasm between the peasants and the officials. Although he and his fellow teachers and administrators were supposedly in the countryside to be "reeducated" by the peasants, the newcomers kept to themselves. "The peasants lived in their mud huts, we built ourselves brick dorms with concrete floors. We had meat and cooking oil, they had none.

"When we went out to work in the fields, if we didn't leave someone behind to guard the place, the peasant children would sneak in and steal things. One time I left my mud boots on the windowsill to dry, and when I came back they were gone."

At harvest time, he recalled, marauding bands of local women and children would steal the school's crops. Finally when the school was ordered closed down and the professor returned to Peking, the peasants invaded the compound and carried everything away—the bricks, the boards, even the light fixtures. "There was a platoon of soldiers left to guard the compound, but they were helpless to stop it without shooting everyone."

Paradoxically, another of the reasons for the Communists' failure to bring about more equality in the countryside was Mao's very demand for egalitarianism. In the periods when the Chairman and his radical supporters held sway—like the Great Leap Forward, the Cultural Revolution, and parts of the early and mid-1970s—they sought to abolish the last traces of individual enterprise in the villages, the peasants' private plots and the free markets where the peasants could sell their extra grain or pigs and chickens they raised themselves. Mao condemned them as a vestige of capitalism and feared they would increase differences in income among the peasants. But since Mao's death it is now clear that when the private plots and rural markets were closed, farm production declined and peasant income everywhere dropped. Equality and economic efficiency don't always mix.

Equally ironic was the effect of Mao's insistence on self-reliance, that each province should produce all its own grain and not depend on others for supplies of wheat or rice. This was an outgrowth of the Chairman's guerrilla experience in the 1930s, but with the deepening Sino–Soviet conflict in the 1960s, he saw it as part of a strategy to render China less vulnerable to Russian attack. In a speech to the Politburo in March 1966, he warned that it was "dangerous" for individual provinces to rely on the government to ship them grain to meet their basic needs. The trouble was, some regions were better suited to grazing cattle or growing commercial crops like cotton and sugar cane and had long been grain-deficit areas. But to enforce Mao's policy of regional self-sufficiency, Peking began procuring less grain and reduced its shipments to grain-poor areas. Hence by 1977, Professor Lardy estimates, the government was transferring less grain than it had twenty years before even though overall output had nearly doubled. As an example of what happened, Professor Lardy points to Hunan, a rice-rich province in central south China, which by the late 1970s was able to distribute two thirds more grain per capita to its peasants than arid, grassy Ningxia. Under Mao's policy of enforced grain planting, Ningxia's pasturelands turned into a dust bowl and the province as a whole averaged only 334 pounds of grain per person, scarcely above the subsistence level of 330 pounds.

To compound the problem, Mao became obsessed with grain production as the key measure of farm success, like the Russian fixation on steel output as an indicator of industrial might. "Take grain as the key link," Mao proclaimed, and all the provinces and teams, even those that had previously grown large amounts of other food crops that are important sources of protein in the Chinese diet, like soybeans and edible oils (peanuts and rapeseed), had to fall in line. As a consequence, Professor Lardy has found, the output of these valuable food sources declined in per capita terms as much as 30 to 50 percent from their high point in 1956, before the Great Leap Forward, to the late 1970s. This, too, added to the peasants' hunger.

But what is far more startling than these persistent differences between one rural area and another and the Communists' mistakes in farm policy is that the Communists, despite their rhetoric of putting the countryside first, have not done more to close the gap between the cities and the villages. From earliest times there have always been two Chinas, one urban, one rural. Ensconced in Peking, with its broad avenues, sophisticated bureaucrats, and crowded department stores, I tended to forget how the vast majority of Chinese lived. But I remember once stopping at a village in Fujian province, on the southeast coast, at planting time in the spring. The weather was already hot and humid, with banks of heavy white clouds hugging the low green mountains inland from the rice paddies along the shore. The noonday sun shimmered off the flooded fields like a mirror, the newly transplanted rice sprouts an emerald green. Young peasants, their backs hunched under swaying bamboo shoulder poles with buckets at each end, were walking along the narrow mud dikes between the paddies, ferrying loads of night soil. Then they waded barefoot into the unplanted fields, sinking ankle deep in the mud, and upturned their buckets of slop. The pungent, choking smell of excrement hung in the air for yards around, the most basic reality of village life. Part of the manure came from the local privy, a piece of granite with a circular cutout suspended over a small pond. The rest came from the village's pigs. The importance of the pig in rural life is reflected in the Chinese ideograph for home—it shows a pig under a roof. Out in the fields, other peasants, bent double at the waist, were moving backward step by step as they transplanted the rice seedlings, an operation that multiplied millions of times is the greatest expenditure of human energy in the world.

Four teen-age girls, their loose-fitting black pants rolled to their knees, were working on a long wooden treadmill to pump water into another field. When I approached and tried to talk with them, they smiled and giggled, but none spoke Mandarin, or "the common language," as it is now called, only the local Fujian dialect. It was a sign they had not gone far in school, since all education is now supposed to be in the unified language. During a full day's drive the length of Fujian, I saw only a handful of tractors, most of which were being used as trucks to pull loads of bricks, rice, or trussed pigs. Plowing was still the work of men hitched to lumbering water buffaloes. The pace of life was slower than in the cities, the work harder.

It is hard for Americans, accustomed to mechanized farming, to realize how primitive and backbreaking Chinese agriculture still is. But in a 1978 speech, Deng Xiaoping gave a neat vest-pocket guide. The average annual output of grain per farm worker in China is about 2,200 pounds, he said. In the United States, it is over 110,000 pounds, a disparity of "several dozen times," Deng noted.

In Anhui, in central China, another of the poorer provinces, I recall climbing Huang Shan, or Yellow Mountain, whose oddly shaped peaks, pines, and clouds traditionally make it one of the wonders of nature to Chinese. A pilgrimage to Huang Shan has been a goal of Chinese since the great eighth-century poet Li Bo celebrated its phantasmagoric beauties. To accommodate the thousands of Chinese and foreign tourists who now flock to its summit, the government is enlarging several mountaintop hotels and restaurants. But since there is no road, all the cement, timber, and prefabricated sections must be carried up the mountain on foot. On the thousands of steep stone steps cut into the mountain over the centuries by laborers, I passed convoys of porters. Most were teen-agers and young men and women in their twenties from villages hidden by mist in the valley below.

At one level spot, where I stopped to catch my breath, a girl of fifteen, less than five feet tall, vaulted past me. Her two long, thick black braids bobbed as she climbed with an eighty-pound basket of rice strapped to her back. The load must have been more than equal her weight. Beads of perspiration stood out on her forehead, and her blue plaid shirt was soaked through. She had begun her trek at 5 A.M., to avoid the noonday heat, she said.

In the past Chinese peasants faced the harsh reality that their labor was worth less than land; good muscles were more plentiful than good earth. The Communists have preserved this tradition in their own way, friends who had worked in the countryside said. In figuring the cost of farm production, commune accountants do not include human labor.

In the 1930s, surveys made at the time suggest, the ratio of urban to rural income was about two to one. But from reports of friends and data I was able to piece together, the gap today looms much larger. Exact comparisons are difficult because of the way the government furnishes data. In 1980 the average city worker, not counting dependents, earned the equivalent of $508. The average per capita income for peasants, including men, women, and children, was $57 from their collective labor and another $20 from sideline occupations like growing vegetables in their private plots, raising pigs, or weaving straw baskets, for a total of $77. Both of these figures must then be deflated, the urban one to allow for the number of dependents, the rural one because economists believe the government's use of grain prices in calculating peasants' income overstates the real value they receive.* When these deductions are made, urban per capita income was about $276 in 1980, peasant per capita earnings around $58. That would be a differential of nearly five to one in favor of the cities.

But the real difference between city and countryside goes beyond income figures. The peasants' livelihood is still at the mercy of the weather. With drought or flood, the team's harvest goes down and so does a peasant's income. City workers have fixed wages and guaranteed lifetime jobs. In 1981 international relief officials were invited for the first time by Peking to inspect the ravages of drought in Hebei, in north China, and a flood of the Yangtze River in Hubei, in central China. They estimated that up to 130 million people were facing food shortages in a total of nine provinces and reported widespread cases of rickets and anemia among children.

In the cities, the state provides free education, medical care, old-age pensions, and low-cost housing. By government count, its subsidies for these services total $351 a year for every urban resident, more than doubling city income. In the countryside the Communists have established a widespread network of schools and clinics; but unlike the cities, the local teams and brigades have been left largely to pay for them out of their own slender earnings. This happened because of a critical decision by Peking in the 1950s to concentrate its investment resources on building up industry and the cities to support it, despite the Communists' claim to give preference to agriculture.

Lihua recalled that in Gold Mountain the peasants had to pay tuition charges that amounted to the equivalent of $4 a year—calculated in work points—to send their children to the small one-room primary school. The rickety building, once a landlord's residence, had holes for windows, its roof leaked, and it had no desks or even stools, so the students had to squat on the mud floor or bring their own seats. The teacher was a young woman peasant from a neighboring village who had managed to get as far as junior

*Most peasants receive the bulk of their distributions from their teams in grain and oil, not in cash. But Peking, in converting their income to a cash figure for statistical purposes, uses grain prices, which have gone up several times in recent years. That of course does not change the amount of grain the peasants really receive. Professor Lardy suggests true peasant income from collective labor in 1980 should be about $38.

high school. There were no books, only some materials she prepared herself and sold to the students for the equivalent of another $2. These expenses might seem small, but the total cost for a year's education amounted to a quarter of a villager's annual income, and the high price kept attendance down. The only high school was in the commune center, a four-hour walk, and parents who wanted to send their children had to pay additional charges for room and board. Lihua's team had a rudimentary clinic staffed by a barefoot doctor, or paramedic, with a cooperative health insurance plan that cost another $2.67 a year. But Lihua's own family was excluded from the benefits of the insurance scheme since they were labeled landlords. They had to pay full cost if they used the clinic. The village had no pension plan, like city factories, and all housing was built at the peasants' expense.

Badly funded village schools like those in Gold Mountain are no match for government-supported city schools in getting their pupils into college. The *People's Daily* once conceded that there is only one person with a college-level education for every ten communes, or about one out of every 160,000 peasants and rural cadres.

The daughter of a county Party secretary who had been able to go to college and get a job in Peking told me that the brightest student in her primary school had been the son of a peasant. "He was fantastically intelligent," she said. "I was already in third grade. He had not been able to go to first or second grade because his parents were very poor and they held him out of school to help with work at home. But he jumped right into our class and learned to read and write. He always got the highest marks." His career ended in fifth grade, the final year of primary school. His parents could not afford to pay his school fees anymore.

There are other ways also in which the countryside is discriminated against. Under China's election law, the rural areas get only one eighth the representation of the cities in the National People's Congress. The Congress is largely a rubber stamp, but the peasants have a more difficult time joining the Communist Party too, the real locus of power. Once, to make the comparison, I noted that in a lacquerware factory in the southern city of Fuzhou, with 836 employees, there were ninety-three Party members, a ratio of more than one out of ten. But at the Huluzhen brigade outside the city, only fifteen of the 634 adult peasants belonged to the Party, less than one out of forty. Professor Lardy has calculated that from 1956 to 1978, while the consumption of grain per capita for China as a whole dropped slightly, it declined 5.9 percent in the countryside but rose 15.8 percent in the cities.* This was the result of a deliberate government decision to favor the urban areas.

The government's tilt in favor of the cities is obvious to Chinese. In the

---

*Lardy, "Food Consumption in the People's Republic of China," p. 19.

1950s, before Peking imposed tight restrictions on migration from the countryside through the household registration system, millions of peasants flooded into the cities. The great divide in China today, friends explained, is between those who have an "agricultural status" household registration and those with a "non-agricultural status" registration. Peasants, with a farm registration, depend on the erratic work-point earnings from their fields. But cadres at the commune level, the lowest group to be given the coveted non-farm registration, are paid a fixed salary regardless of the harvest. For many peasants the greatest success in life is to get a member of their family elevated to non-farm status, a kind of insurance policy. In turn, the government has devised countertactics to try to prevent this. Under the Communists' complex system of labels, people inherit their class backgrounds from their fathers—landlord, capitalist, poor peasant—but they get their household registrations from their mothers. For more men than women are assigned jobs as commune cadres, picking up non-farm registration, and when they die, their children revert to being peasants.

Another way to escape from the countryside is to go to work for a high-ranking cadre in the city as a maid. Bing, the daughter of the general who denounced her father during the Cultural Revolution, said her family had recruited an eighteen-year-old peasant girl from the village where her father had been born many years before. She was a shy, stocky youth who had never seen a bus or heard of airplanes and railroad trains until she came to Peking. Her father had died not long after she arrived in the capital, but she was consoled by a letter he wrote: "I feel very content, at least I managed to get one of my children a city household registration."

Most Western Sinologists have given Peking credit for not following Stalin's model of exploiting the peasants to spur China's economic growth. They have been impressed that the Communists set the grain tax on the peasants at a low, fixed level in the 1950s and as production has risen, the proportion paid in taxes has fallen, now perhaps an average of 3 to 8 percent of a team's annual income. The government also taxes the villages by requiring the peasants to sell additional amounts of their grain at a price set by the state. To benefit the peasants, this price has been raised several times in the past few years.

But as Peking has become more candid after Mao's death by publishing more economic data and letting a few foreign specialists do field research on communes, a different picture of the government's relations with the peasants has emerged. It suggests that Peking, like Moscow, has systematically squeezed the countryside, albeit in hidden fashion, to support industrialization.

Despite the recent increases in the state purchase price for grain, Professor

Lardy estimates that Chinese peasants are actually being paid the lowest amount of any villagers in Asia relative to the cost of the industrial products they must buy back from the cities, like tractors, chemical fertilizer, and electricity. The state charges $2,000 for a tiny 12-horsepower tractor, the size of a lawnmower, and $12,000 for a medium-sized 75-horsepower tractor, ensuring the factories that produce them a tidy profit. This difference between what the peasants get for their crops and what they must pay for manufactured goods amounts to a substantial indirect levy on the countryside. The reason the government has been reluctant to raise farm prices to a more realistic level is that it would hurt urban residents who have had to live with fixed wages for years and who the Communists evidently fear are more volatile and a greater threat to the regime. In the three decades of Communist rule, the cost of rice to urban consumers has never gone up. Most Chinese I knew in the cities treated stable rice prices as a matter of faith, a sacred obligation of the government. But to keep food prices down for these privileged city residents, the government has been forced to pay a subsidy of roughly $4.67 billion a year, a whopping 7 percent of total state revenue in the 1981 budget. The subsidy goes to the peasants, but even with it most peasants feel they are getting too little. As an indication of the real value of their grain, if they sell it in one of the rural free markets, they can still get 70 percent more than what the government pays.

To make the problem worse for the peasants, as China has begun to mechanize its farming, they must use more and more of the costly industrial inputs. In Hebei province, near Peking, an American scholar who was permitted to live on a commune there, Steven Butler, found that the ratio of peasants' costs to their gross income jumped from 25 to 30 percent in the early 1970s to 50 percent by 1980. "The cities are ripping off the countryside," Butler remarked. Farming costs have become so high, he estimated, that the peasants may actually get a negative return on their collectively planted grain crop. The key to their survival is in private sideline production where they can plant other crops or do other jobs with a good return on capital.

At the same time, the level of government investment in agriculture is actually much smaller than Western economists had believed. Farm investment comes from two sources—local profits the government allows the teams and brigades to retain for reinvestment and national appropriations. Recently published figures show that the total profits the government let the teams keep amounted to $4.2 billion in 1978, the latest year for which figures are available. That is only the same amount as in 1956, though the number of peasants climbed from 450 million to 800 million in those years. Put another way, it means that the teams can save only about $5 apiece for each peasant, the cost of a hoe, hardly enough to modernize agriculture. As for national appropriations, Peking has masked its actual amount of investment in agriculture in conflicting data, but Lardy estimates that it may have come to less than $3.3 billion in 1978. Added together with local investment, that would give a total investment in farming of only $7.3 billion. Since the real overall value of farm output in 1978 was $71.3 billion, that gives a rate of investment of only 10 percent. By comparison, in 1978 Peking reinvested the staggering total of 36.8 percent of its gross national product. That means that the great bulk of funds went to industry, a particularly lopsided figure remembering that 800 million Chinese, 80 percent of the population, are peasants.

Mao's successors have taken some measures to try to redress these imbalances. At a critical meeting in December 1978, the Third Plenum of the Eleventh Central Committee, where Deng Xiaoping asserted his predominance, the Party committed itself to a liberal new program to speed agricultural development. It promised to raise the purchase prices the peasants are paid for their crops, it sanctified the controversial private plots and free markets, and it offered the peasants much greater control over what crops they plant. In 1980 Peking took an even more controversial step by letting peasants in some of the poorer production teams farm their own land, abolishing the system of collective work points, and allowing the peasants to keep whatever they produced above a fixed quota. In many areas the initial results have been good. On the commune in Hebei where Steven Butler did research, he found the peasants there in the midst of what he described as an historic change. "They are no longer worried every day about where their next meal is going to come from," he said. The average grain ration has gone up from 330 pounds a year in the 1950s, the minimal subsistence level, to 550 pounds in 1980 with another 90 to 100 pounds from the peasants' private plots. Instead of raising only corn and sweet potatoes, as they did in the past, which the peasants regard as coarse, inferior food, they now plant wheat, a tastier product.

For the first time, Butler went on, "the peasants are beginning to think of buying things with their earnings—new houses, clothes, wristwatches, bicycles. Many of them have savings accounts in their local collective banks. It's the good life."

Most of the production teams he visited on the commune had purchased their own black-and-white television sets, which they set up on metal stands outdoors for everyone to watch. "It makes a huge difference in people's lives, having something to do in the evening, and they love it," Butler observed. "Some of the richer families were thinking of buying their own sets, but no one wants to be the first because they will be inundated with neighbors coming to watch." One prosperous team resolved the dilemma with a collective decision. They waited till every family in the team had enough money;

then they all went out and bought television sets simultaneously. In Butler's view, the people in his commune are ready for what economists call the take-off stage of sustained economic development which farmers in Japan, Taiwan, and South Korea have already moved into.

But despite the new prosperity of Butler's commune, some Western economists feel that Peking is still not going far enough to stimulate agriculture. In essence, Deng has tried for a cheap fix—to achieve an increase in farm output by letting the peasants till their own land, without making an expensive commitment of government investment for more fertilizer or improved irrigation facilities. In fact, since the reforms began, Peking's investment in agriculture has declined to an all-time low, and while farm output initially shot up because of the peasants' new enthusiasm, most economists feel it will eventually level off and stagnate, absent greater investment.

If Mao shortchanged the countryside, the peasants also outlasted the Chairman. The villages remain more traditional, more tied to their ancient customs and rhythms, and more centered around the family than the cities. This gives the peasants a certain autonomy, a kind of insulation from government dictates.

The very form of rural organization today is itself a compromise between what the Communists tried to impose from above, the commune, and the old system of villages, clans, and neighborhoods. Mao and the radicals long wanted to make the large commune what they called the basic accounting unit—the group that works together and shares its income. But in the Great Leap Forward this proved unworkable, and the Communists instead accepted the production team, which was based on the old small village, or a clan or a neighborhood of a larger village, as the basic unit. This meant that the team cadres were natives of the villages where they worked, and not only natives, but brothers, uncles, or cousins of the peasants. Having kinsmen in charge made collective farming acceptable to the Chinese peasant and reinforced his interest in the team's welfare. But it also gave the peasant leverage over local officials that city people don't have.

A trim, serious-minded woman in her late twenties with short pigtails who was sent to live in a village in Sichuan for six years recalled how the peasants took advantage of their natural connections with the team leaders. The legal minimum age for marriage for men was twenty-three and twenty-one for women, but every year several girls as young as sixteen or seventeen succeeded in getting married despite the restriction.

"They had to have a letter of introduction from the team leader to the brigade office before they could register their marriage," the woman said, "but everyone was related and the cadres didn't object." It was another example of the use of *guan-xi*, or "connections." Being related to the team leader or accountant also made it easier to get extra work points if someone was sick or to get your name on the list for the one bicycle team members were allowed to purchase every two years. In the city, such decisions are in the hands of the Party secretary of your office, factory, or school, the woman pointed out. City living requires more ingenuity to arrange things.

There was also less political pressure in the village, she remembered. Most of the families belonged to a single clan, and the team leader was always a member of that clan. The current team head, a hardworking, respected forty-nine-year-old man, was anxious to quit the post. He complained that he got no extra remuneration for the hours he spent on team chores and that his duties kept him from cultivating his private plot. Like team cadres throughout China, he was paid work points rather than a fixed state salary and had to work in the fields with the peasants. The team had political meetings only about twice a year—the peasants were too tired if meetings were called at night, after a hard day's work, and if they were held during the daytime, the peasants demanded work points to compensate them for time lost.

"Most times when the cadres did read out a document from Peking, the peasants didn't understand it anyway, unless it was directly about farm work," the woman said. She said that when Mao died, everyone was ordered to observe three minutes of silence. At the time, she had been assigned to brigade headquarters to make announcements over the loudspeaker system because as a native of Peking she had a proper accent.

"The militia were told to keep watch to make sure everyone obeyed the order for silence for the Chairman. But there was one old man who was selling tree ear fungus [a Chinese delicacy, like mushrooms] and he just kept right on selling. He didn't stand and close his eyes as required. When the militiaman demanded to know why he was behaving so badly, he asked, 'Who is Mao?' " She was stunned by this display of rural ignorance.

But it is in their marriage practices that the peasants remain most traditional and the old role of the family continues to predominate. When the Communists introduced their family law in 1950, they envisioned abolishing the old arranged marriage decided on by the parents for economic reasons and intended to replace it with free choice between young partners. But the confidential study prepared for the Women's Federation in 1980 on the condition of women in the countryside found that 75 percent of rural marriages are still arranged. For most peasants spend their entire time living and working in their own village, which is now also their team, and "opportunities to meet people from an outside village are small," the document reported. In villages with only one clan, there are still taboos about marrying a person with the same surname, and "there is an old-fashioned notion that for young people to bring up the matter of marriage independently is not correct. They must rely on an introduction." The study notes there has been one area of progress—in the past, many of these arranged marriages were blind, the couples never even met before their wedding. Now they may have one chance to eye each other in a village teahouse or the home of the prospective groom in the company of the matchmaker, with both partners having the right of refusal.

A young refugee in Hong Kong recalled how one of his cousins in Guangdong, Wang Guoying, had gotten married. When Wang was twenty-five years old, his parents hired a matchmaker who found a suitable bride for him in a nearby team. She was tall and strong, a good worker, so she would be as asset in earning work points, and her family was classified as poor peasants, a good class background, the two most important criteria to them. In an old peasant term, "the doors and the windows matched."

There was only one hitch. Her family wanted a high bride price for her, 1,000 yuan ($667), with a third in cash and the rest in food, clothes, and jewelry. That amounted to nearly two years' income for Wang's whole family. There was some bargaining, the amount was reduced slightly, and after the Wangs borrowed heavily from their local credit cooperative and pooled savings from relatives, the money was raised.

Such marriages by purchase, as the Communists call them, were prohibited by the family law, but friends told me they remain universal in the villages. Parish and Whyte conclude in their book about the countryside that expenditures by a bridegroom's family have actually increased on the average from about half a year's family income before Liberation to over a full year's earnings today.* One reason may be that since peasant women now work more in the fields than before 1949, their economic value has increased.

The refugee in Hong Kong related that their brigade Party secretary once called a meeting of the local cadres to read out a new directive from Peking inveighing against the feudal practice of buying brides. The refugee himself at the time was serving as a brigade financial officer, and so took part in the session.

"We laughed at the Party secretary," he remembered. "Everyone knew his own wife had cost his family 600 yuan [$400]. So some of us jeered at him, 'You should have gotten her free.'"

The Communists have largely succeeded in abolishing concubinage, another objective of the family law, but not entirely, as they have claimed. The report prepared for the Women's Federation found cases of women being sold as concubines in nineteen different provinces, ranging in age from fourteen to fifty. In a detailed investigation in several counties in Anhui province, the researchers discovered 22,339 women who had been sold

*Parish and Whyte, *Village and Family in Contemporary China*, pp. 188–89.

there. Curiously, 83 percent of them were from Sichuan, long reportedly a center of the trade because of its rural poverty. The report did not give details on how these women had been purchased, but it said, "Some of the women had been raped at some point and then sold to the rapist as his wife. Some had been sold many times."

Lihua related that in Gold Mountain some of her poorer neighbors still sold their children. There was a former wounded veteran of the Red Army who had eight children but whose wife had died and who had become lazy and unable to support his large family. Because of their impoverished condition, he couldn't purchase a bride for his oldest son, who was twenty-six. The father took care of that by arranging to have him "adopted" for a price by an elderly widow who had no son of her own to look after her in her advanced age. Then he sold his fourteen-year-old daughter to a family in a village ten miles away for 1,000 yuan ($667) and a fat pig. They wanted to ensure finding a wife for their son, who had a badly pockmarked face and a reputation as a lazy worker.

"The father was an uneducated man and really didn't care about his children's happiness," Lihua said. "When he had spent all the money from the fourteen-year-old, he went around the village asking who would like to buy his eleven-year-old daughter. No one did. She was too young and not very pretty." But eventually in another village he found a former landlord's family who had a son that was already thirty-two years old but couldn't find a wife because of his class label and age. The family agreed to purchase the young girl for 200 yuan ($133). "They put her to work in the kitchen," Lihua said. "When she reached eighteen, they would have a wedding ceremony."

Finally the father sold another son, who was only nine years old. He found an old couple who didn't have any children and wanted a son. The price was 50 yuan ($33). "When he left home, his father didn't give him anything, not even a set of extra clothes."

The Communists have also largely eliminated the Buddhist and Taoist priests and nuns, the geomancers and shamans, who lived in the countryside and said prayers at village festivals or chanted incantations at funerals. But as Lihua had told me about her life in Gold Mountain, the peasants continue to practice some of their folk religion underground. On a trip back to her village after I met her, she had consulted a blind fortune-teller who appeared in Gold Mountain. A hunched and grizzled man in his late fifties, he lived as an itinerant, wandering from village to village, stopping in the homes of whatever peasants would give him food and shelter. He had quickly earned a reputation for clairvoyance in Gold Mountain. A family who had not had a male heir for several generations and had just had a newborn male child brought their son to him to ask about his future. The fortune-teller told them the boy had a black spot behind his ear, a mark even his mother hadn't noticed. That meant his fate would be good, the fortune-teller prophesied. The parents were delighted. They gave the blind man eight yuan ($5), over a month's income for them.

In the cities, the Communists have made cremation mandatory because of the severe shortage of land and have succeeded in getting urban residents to simplify the elaborate, costly funerals which Chinese practiced for centuries, giving substance to the cult of the ancestors, China's native religion. In the countryside the government has also attempted to introduce cremation to save farmland; but here the Party's writ sits more lightly and the peasants have resisted these changes. In many villages, friends told me, the peasants still begin saving to buy coffins for themselves after they pass sixty, the number of years considered a normal life cycle.

A professor of English from Peking who was sent to labor in a village in Jiangxi, in central China, was assigned to live with a family in a small one-room mud hut. The floor was also mud and the roof leaked when it rained, but the grandmother in the family had already purchased a handsome camphor-wood coffin for 60 yuan ($40). She kept it stored in the family's single room, in readiness. When she died, her body was laid out for three days in front of a Buddhist altar that the family had kept hidden from the cadres during the Cultural Revolution. Little clay bowls were placed around her body, each labeled with the names of her favorite food. At night her sons and grandsons took turns "guarding the spirit," or standing in front of the body. Then for one night she was placed in the coffin, which was propped up on a sawhorse, and in keeping with local superstition her eldest son had to sleep under it.

If a person in the village died before reaching sixty, the professor said, the peasants called him a "short-life devil" and believed he had committed some misdeeds in this life or a previous one. His body was not honored inside the house. One peasant who was run over by a truck was left where he fell.

The village lay in a narrow valley topped by hills covered with fir trees, and the grandmother was buried on one of the hillsides. An elderly villager who was familiar with the ancient wisdom of *feng-shui,* the spirits of "the wind and the water," or geomancy, selected a favorable site for her grave. Several dozen peasants took part in the funeral procession, the close relatives dressed in white robes and white caps with strips of white paper over their shoes—white is the color of death. For seven days after her death, her close relatives were forbidden to eat meat, and her sons and daughters were not allowed to bathe or wash their hair for forty-nine days.

In early April, by our calendar, comes one of the most important traditional Chinese festivals, Qing Ming, when people are supposed to visit their family graves to "sweep" or clean them of weeds. The Communists do not give the peasants a holiday for Qing Ming, since it is regarded as a superstitious custom that interferes with work.

But I remember driving through the Fujian countryside on the day of Qing Ming and looking with astonishment as we passed hillside after hillside strewn with red, green, blue, and yellow paper flowers. They had been placed there to mark the low brick tombstones. Outside Quanzhou, which when Marco Polo visited China in the thirteenth century was one of the world's great ports, then known as Zaytun, a knot of a dozen peasants was tending a graveyard with hoes. One middle-aged woman, in loose black pants, was bent over a circular grave. She had just placed an offering of cooked rice in front of it and was kneeling in a posture of prayer, oblivious to the noisy traffic of trucks and buses on the road, a symbol of the hardy resistance the peasants had displayed to those parts of Mao's revolution which they didn't care for and the persistence of rural rhythms and traditions.

12. The Iron Rice Bowl

铁 饭 碗

INDUSTRY

"An Immortal said: 'In playing chess, there is no infallible way of winning, but there is an infallible way of not losing.' He was asked what this infallible way could be, and replied: 'It is not to play chess.' "
Feng Yulan, A History of Chinese Philosophy

Not long after I took up residence in Peking in June 1979, I got out an old pre-World War Two guidebook to the city and tried to retrace the site of the capital's ancient walls. Except for a short stretch around the Forbidden City and Zhongnanhai, where the country's leaders work, these magnificent barriers—forty feet high and sixty-two feet thick at the base—were torn down by the Communists in the 1950s as an obstruction to traffic and a sinful waste of space. Instead, I found, as I walked on an east–west line from the old Qian Men, or Front Gate, which still survives, the government had recently replaced the walls with a two-mile-long series of ten-story buff-colored apartment buildings. The concrete apartments, more than forty blocks in all, were a sparkling contrast to the shabbiness of most Chinese buildings, with their dingy exteriors badly in need of paint and cracked windows. The new buildings had large glass windows and small balconies, with space for shops on the ground floor. In a city where the average urban resident has only about three square yards of living space, this new project looked like a splendid attempt by the government to resolve one of its worst problems.

But as I walked farther, I began to sense something amiss. There were no children playing outside, no curtains in the windows, no laundry hanging out to dry, no sound of laughter or shouting reverberating from within. The apartments, in fact, were virtually empty.

"They are beautiful buildings," a taxi driver said to me over his shoulder a few days later as we drove along the avenue where the apartments stood, as mute as the tombs of the Ming emperors in the hills northwest of the city. "But whoever built them should be shot." Then he spit out the window in the universal gesture of contempt.

They had been completed over a year before, I learned from a dour, middle-aged man who worked in a photography shop nearby, but most people to whom they had been offered as new housing had refused to accept them. He himself had been assigned an apartment on the sixth floor of one of the buildings and had managed to stall for several months before his *danwei* ordered him to move in. The trouble with the buildings, he explained, was that they lacked adequate pressure to lift water above the third floor, there were no gas mains for the stoves, no elevators, and the heating system didn't work. He had to pump his water by hand with a makeshift device and he dreaded the coming of winter. The buildings were all supposed to be heated by hot water from a thermal power plant, but it was so far away that by the time the water arrived it was only 41 degrees fahrenheit and the radiators gave off no heat. The reason for the mess, he confided, was that there had been no coordination between the different government construction, engineering, and architectural agencies involved.

"Whoever arrived at the job first just set to work," he said, his tone a whisper so that other people in the shop couldn't hear. "That way, one group of workmen came to lay the foundations and put up the structures and walls before the water company came to install the pipes. No one cared about the results, because no one had overall responsibility."

He had clipped out an article from the *People's Daily* which chastised the construction industry for "anarchy." But, he added, the paper did not say anyone had been punished for wasting millions of yuan.

The apartment project symbolized for me both the achievements and blunders of Chinese industry. Before 1949 China's modern industrial sector was microscopic: a smattering of textile mills in Shanghai, a fledgling iron and steel industry in what was then called Manchuria, developed by the Japanese, and a skeletal railroad network linking only the major cities. But since the First Five-Year Plan in 1953, China's industrial production has grown at an average annual pace of 10 percent, one of the highest anywhere. China is now the world's leading producer of cotton textiles and tungsten; the second largest manufacturer of radios; the third biggest miner of coal; it ranks fifth in output of steel and tenth in oil. China manufactures its own computers, electron microscopes, nuclear missiles, and jet fighters.

These are impressive accomplishments, and during the four years I covered China from Hong Kong I regularly reported Peking's year-end claims of production increases in steel, oil, and chemical fertilizer as a measure of progress. But it wasn't until I lived in China that I realized these conventional indices of economic growth masked colossal waste, monumental miscalculations, an inefficient economic system, and bureaucratic bungling that China could ill afford. The rapid expansion of China's gross national product also obscured the lack of any real increase in living standards. Indeed, since the mid-1950s, the average amount of housing space has decreased, and until a sharp redirection of economic policy by Mao's successors starting in 1979, there was no significant improvement in the supply of consumer goods or food. Real wages in the cities fell from 1965 to the end of the decade of the 1970s. Chinese industry was much like the gigantic white-elephant apartment project in Peking—on the surface, the government had scored success, but somehow it didn't connect with people's livelihood.

A graying government economist, Lao Hu, offered an explanation of what went wrong. Tall and thin, erect and dignified, if a bit rigid in his bearing, he was courteous and formal in the manner of an old-fashioned upper-class Chinese. He spoke in quiet measured tones, always intense, thoughtful, and serious. He seldom smiled, but he retained an enthusiasm for his subject. One critical problem, as Lao Hu outlined it, was that in the early 1950s China had adopted the Stalinist model of intensive industrialization. Despite Peking's subsequent split with Moscow, the Russian system became Chinese orthodoxy.

"It was like shooting one's self in the foot," Lao Hu said. The Soviet model called for high forced savings, financed by keeping wages low, the cost of manufactured products expensive, and factory earnings high. There was no personal income tax, but the government siphoned off all the factories' profits to reinvest in the development of more industry, especially heavy industry like steel. These new heavy industrial plants produced glamorous annual gains in the gross national product which China's leaders could report with pride. But they also brought waste, imbalances, and inefficiency, he charged, because there was no attempt to measure the state's return on the capital it invested. Profit was considered a dirty capitalist word, and factory directors who worried about red ink were accused of "putting profits in command."

"It was a great blind rush to build as many factories as possible," Lao Hu went on. In the three decades of Communist rule, China constructed a grand total of 355,000 factories, with an investment equivalent to $213 billion, a staggering sum for a poor country like China. To achieve this the government reinvested an average of 30 percent of the country's gross national product each year, with the figure rising as high as 36.5 percent in 1978, leaving proportionately little for consumption. By comparison, total private investment in the United States in 1980 was 6.6 percent of America's GNP.

But in Peking's rush, it ignored the profitability of its new investments and their efficiency declined precipitously. In 1957 every $67 of assets (factories and their machinery) generated $23 in profits and taxes for the state. By 1976, the figure had fallen to $13.*

An American businessman with the Xerox Corporation, one of dozens to take up residence in the Peking Hotel in the late 1970s, recalled inspecting a number of factories managed by the Fourth Ministry of Machine Building, which produces electronic equipment for the armed forces. The ministry was interested in manufacturing an improved copying machine, and Xerox engineers were impressed by the quality of the research and workmanship they saw in the factories. But the Americans also found that the Chinese plants were greatly overequipped with machines, overstaffed, and were operating at only about 20 percent of capacity.

"One factory we visited was turning out only one hundred to two hundred copiers a year," the businessman related. "One of our own factories at home turns out that many in a single day."

On the day of his visit, the American noticed that many of the workers were idle, sitting in groups smoking, talking, or playing cards. The only ones working were constructing a new wing for the factory.

"I was amazed," the businessman added. "Here was this big factory with most of its workers and machines idle and they are expanding. What was the investment for? Finally I had an inspiration. They were just constructing a new plant because the workers didn't have anything else to do and the factory director had to use his allotted funds for the year or lose them. I asked the director if this was true, and he agreed with embarrassment it was."

A middle-aged factory worker with broad shoulders and a prominent scar on his right hand told me about another worker in his plant who had recently retired at the mandatory age of sixty. The factory gave a farewell party for him, but in the middle of drinking beer and eating small sweet cakes he began to cry. "Why are you crying, now your life will be easy?" his colleagues quizzed him.

"Yes," he replied. "But I have been a worker in this factory for twenty years, since they first started construction on it, and I have never done a day's work in the plant." The others knew what he meant. The factory was still under construction and had never opened because there was such competition for building materials that the plant could not get the supplies it needed. He had simply reported for work each day and then idled his time attending political study sessions, playing cards, or chatting with his friends.

His story was not unusual. Almost every Chinese I met had a favorite tale about a factory that was never finished or couldn't be used once it was built because some official had been too ambitious. In Urumqi, the capital of

*People's Daily, March 2, 1981, p. 5.

Xinjiang, the vast westernmost province of China that is as big as all of Western Europe or Alaska, my local guide joked about an oil refinery the government had constructed there at a cost equivalent to $140 million. The complex had been finished for over a year, but it was not in use. Xinjiang is the site of some of China's most promising new oil fields, but their output is shipped by railroad to another even larger refinery in Lanzhou, to the east, which would have to be shut down if the Urumqi plant was put on line.

This goof was small, however, compared to the blunders in building a $500 million addition to the steelworks at Wuhan, in central China, the country's second largest iron and steel complex, and the projected $13.3 billion Baoshan iron and steel mill near Shanghai designed to be the largest industrial undertaking since the founding of the People's Republic. When the Wuhan addition, which included five separate rolling, casting, and sheet mills built by Japanese and West German firms, was completed in 1978, it was supposed to manufacture three million tons of high-grade steel a year. But the Chinese builders had forgotten about electricity. When the plant was turned on, it drew more electric power than the entire surrounding province of Hubei could produce. Its operations had to be limited to one or two days a week.

The even larger Baoshan complex was to be the centerpiece of Peking's Four Modernizations program—the ambitious plan to modernize the country's agriculture, industry, science, and defense by the year 2000—a mammoth plant to turn out 6.7 million tons of steel a year with the most advanced technology imported from Japan, West Germany, and the United States. It was the kind of project that China's leaders once liked to show off as an example of how massive amounts of manpower and revolutionary spirit could produce an economic miracle. The Communists regarded it with such importance that for its ground-breaking ceremony a planeload of Politburo members had flown down to Shanghai to officiate. But when I visited the site, an hour's drive from Shanghai on the muddy banks of the broad Yangtze River, few workers were in sight and hardly a hammer blow could be heard. The girder skeletons destined to house two blast furnaces, a hot and a cold rolling mill, a tubing mill, cokers, converters, repair shops, and a power plant stood in various stages of noncompletion. The only activity was at a large wharf, still under construction. Although no official announcement had been made at the time of my trip, the project had been suspended. It was a victim of Peking's sharp retrenchment in 1980 and 1981 when the government finally began to recognize the effects of its overbuilding. The national budget for 1981 was slashed 13.4 percent, twice the size of President Reagan's precedent-making cuts in U.S. government spending the same year.

At Baoshan, a deputy director of the construction team admitted there had been a series of miscalculations. The Japanese blast furnaces proved too sophisticated for the low-grade ore China produces, so Peking had to buy higher-grade ore from Australia, which was too expensive. Then the location chosen for the steel mill was on swampy ground; it required 300,000 tons of steel supporting piles, some of which sank out of sight. The shallow Yangtze River estuary could not accommodate the 100,000-ton carriers bringing the ore from Australia, so the Chinese had to build a new port and storage facilities 130 miles to the south and transship the ore on smaller vessels. All of these unexpected expenses meant huge cost overruns. An official of the Ministry of Metallurgy admitted publicly that the real price for Baoshan might run to the equivalent of $27 billion, twice the original estimate, and an astronomical 40 percent of China's national budget for 1981 of $65 billion.

Lao Hu, the economist, suggested a historical reason for Peking's fascination with steel production as an index of national strength. "Many Chinese have long believed we were beaten by the imperialists starting in the nineteenth century because of our lack of steel," he said in a talk in his spacious apartment, a mark of his rank. "Mao himself put forward the slogan, 'Take steel as the key link.' But they turned this into a fixation with heavy industry." Over the last thirty years, he said, more than 50 percent of all government investment in construction has gone to heavy industry, with only 5 percent for the consumer-goods-producing light industry and 8 percent to agriculture. At the same time, he added, China's leaders had badly neglected other critical sectors—energy, transportation, and housing. "Last year we lost twenty-five percent of our potential industrial production because many factories didn't have enough electric power and had to accept brownouts." In 1980 the output of oil, coal, and natural gas actually decreased 2 percent because of the government's failure to put sufficient funds in new energy development and in 1981 fell further.

Paradoxically, part of the explanation for this incredible waste and inefficiency is central planning, the Soviet system of managing the economy by annual quotas rather than by profits and market forces. My friend Lao Hu saw it as another contagion China had picked up from the Soviets. In theory, he explained, central planning is very scientific: the state sets the target for each factory every year, then it delivers the necessary raw materials and workers, and the plant manager need only ensure that he meets his annual production quota.

"It is a command economy, like running an army, and it has strong appeal to men like Mao who came to power as generals," Lao Hu said. "The tragedy was that it did work remarkably well in the First Five-Year Plan," from 1953 to 1957, when the country was just recovering from decades of civil war and the Communists were full of energy and idealism. "But that was a one-time phenomenon," Lao Hu continued. The flaw, he said, is that the plan measures success by whether a factory turns out the correct number of radios or tractors according to a pre-set target, not by whether the products are actually sold or how much profit the factory earns.

As an example of what happens when the fetish for building factories is combined with central planning, Lao Hu suggested I look at the automotive industry. China has 130 car and truck plants, the largest number in the world. Indeed, twenty-eight of the twenty-nine provinces and independent municipalities into which China is divided each have at least one such factory —Tibet is the exception. But their total output is only 220,000 vehicles a year, putting China about twentieth in the world.

The biggest automobile factory in Peking manufactures jeeps, and I decided to ask for a tour of the plant. When I first called early in the month of December, a factory official apologized. They were sorry they would have to turn down my request. The plant had met its quota for the year in September, he explained, and it had been closed since then. The workers still reported each day, but only to maintain and repair the machinery. Perhaps I would like to apply again in January when the factory received its target for the next year and reopened.

I was intrigued. In January I renewed my request and this time was met by the head of the director's office, Wen Zhenxiang, a former army political commissar with a high forehead and longish hair that he combed straight back, much like Mao had. Wen was attired in a green cap, blue jacket with a gold pen in the left breast pocket, like cadres everywhere in China, and green army pants. The sickly sweet smell of a distillery a few blocks away hung over the sprawling brick factory.

Piles of parts waiting to be assembled lay scattered seemingly at random on the concrete floor: oil pans, radiator grills, headlights, drive shafts, crates of nuts and bolts. Two workers in their twenties were feeding metal panels for the jeeps' bodies into a 1,000-ton press, extracting their hands a split second before the machine crashed down, stamping the steel like a cookie cutter shaping dough. The workers, like those I observed elsewhere in Chinese factories, wore no protective goggles and had no device to shield their hands from the devouring press. The factory had only been a repair garage until 1958 and had been built up largely through the efforts of its own staff, Wen said. Over the years they had designed their own simple automated assembly line and automatic painting and drying shop in a model application of the dictum of self-reliance. Their jeep, though, remained unchanged, a copy of a Russian original, a boxy, no frills, four-door vehicle with a high running board, olive-drab paint, and an unsophisticated four-cylinder engine like those found in American cars in the late 1940s. The plant's production quota in 1980 was 15,000 jeeps, Wen said, or less than two for each of the factory's 9,700 workers. Could it produce more? I asked. Yes, he replied, it had a capacity of 30,000 vehicles a year. Then wouldn't it be more profitable to manufacture more instead of closing down for several months at the end of the year after they met their quota? I persisted. Wen chuckled at my question.

"We cannot produce at will, we must follow the task assigned us by the State Planning Commission. That is the path of socialism."

The planning commission also relieves the factory manager of responsibility for selling the jeeps—it issues certificates to the Machinery Equipment Agencies of each province and they in turn distribute the right to buy the vehicles to individual offices, factories, or communes. The customers must come to Peking themselves to collect their jeeps and are responsible for getting them home. Foreign customers might balk at that condition, except that for the Chinese cadres designated to make the pickups it means an all-expense-paid trip to Peking, a special treat.

The jeeps are not cheap. The selling price is equivalent to $9,333, high by American, Japanese, and European standards considering the quality of the vehicle. But the price, too, is fixed by the State Planning Commission, not the factory. Wen estimated the cost of production at $6,467, for a handsome profit of 44 percent per jeep. American automobile manufacturers mark up the price of their cars an average of only 15 percent; even the Cadillac never exceeded 25 percent. But when I congratulated Wen on the size of the margin, he again laughed at my ignorance. As a state-owned enterprise, the factory must turn over 95 percent of its profits to the government and retains only 5 percent. So neither the manager nor the workers have a vested interest in cutting costs or raising profits.

Under the rules of central planning, the director of the jeep factory lacked other types of authority which Western managers would take for granted. He cannot hire or fire a single worker, he can't raise an employee's salary, he can't purchase new machinery, and he can't redesign the model of the jeep. All these powers lie with the several layers of the bureaucracy above him to which he must report. The manager's lack of power added to the inefficiency.

An enterprising reporter from the *People's Daily* once interviewed the manager of the Heavy Machinery Plant in Shenyang, a major industrial center in the northeast, on the frustrations of his job. To build a new dormitory for some of the factory's 10,000 workers, he complained, he had to get permission from eleven separate government agencies and twenty-four official chops, or seals. In one three-month period, the manager was required to read 518 government documents and attend forty-eight meetings at offices outside the plant. First the national ministry in charge of the factory, the First Ministry of Machine Building, would hold a meeting, then the provincial agency would copy it, and next the city department involved would hold its own conference on the same topic. Each supervisory agency also bombarded the factory with inspection teams—quality inspection teams, financial rules inspection teams, production safety inspection teams, and family-planning inspection teams. On one day, when a reporter from the *People's Daily* was there, seven different inspection groups arrived at once and the factory's three reception rooms proved insufficient.

"Each team insisted its work was very important and demanded the leading comrade of the factory meet with it," the journalist wrote. "They wanted the director to mobilize the masses of workers in his plant to 'fight a people's war of annihilation' on their particular topic," a Maoist term borrowed from the Party's guerrilla days meaning an all-out effort. The problem, the director said, using a Chinese metaphor, was that he had "too many grandmothers."

John Bing, for many years the representative in Peking of Pullman Kellogg, a Texas-based company which constructed half a dozen large chemical fertilizer plants in China, once found himself in a discussion of American management practices with the director of one of the factories he had helped build. The Chinese official wanted to know how American managers raised productivity.

"I told him, we just concentrate on finding out what is wrong and then fix it," said Bing, a tall, slightly stooped sandy-haired man who had such affection for China that he gave up his retirement to come back to live and work in a small hotel-room office in Peking with his wife.

The Chinese cadre looked bemused. "I couldn't do that," he told Bing. "I have to spend ninety percent of my time dealing with personnel and political problems that have nothing to do with production."

By coincidence, I met an engineer and accountant from the American Motors Corporation, the makers of the U.S. Jeep, who were in Peking to negotiate a joint venture enterprise with the Capital Jeep factory. Under the proposed deal, A.M.C. would supply its technology to upgrade the Chinese jeep, whose antiquated engine gets poor gasoline mileage and can't meet most international standards for emission control. It took several years to complete the deal, and in the meantime the Americans got an unusual chance to inspect the Chinese factory. The men were surprised, they told me, by how overbuilt and underutilized it was. It should actually be producing 45,000 jeeps a year, triple its current output, they estimated.

"They have more equipment than they can use for years," the engineer commented. "In the machine shop, where maybe they need five lathes, they have twenty-five. They have all these forges and presses, too, which they may use only once or twice a month to make some small part they don't need in quantity. It's very uneconomical." In the United States, he said, a company would farm out such work to specialized subcontractors. The best way for the joint venture to make money, he joked, would be to sell off its excess machines to companies in the United States, where there is a market for used equipment.

There were two reasons the jeep factory felt it needed so much machinery, the accountant surmised after talks with Chinese cadres. One was the old Chinese Communist stress on self-sufficiency, dating to the Party's guerrilla days when each army band had to be self-contained. That was also why almost every province has its own car and truck assembly plants, regardless of the size of its population and road network. But there was a practical reason too. The jeep factory had found that if it didn't make all its own parts, like wire for its sparkplugs, and depended on deliveries from other factories under the state plan, the necessary materials tended not to arrive on time. The plan was constantly fouled up. So each ministry, each province, and each factory jealously guards its own turf, and they sometimes act more like warring nations than components of the same economy.

In a county in Shanxi province, in the west, the *People's Daily* related, such a conflict developed between a coal mine and an electric generating plant located next door to each other. "They are separated by only a wall, and all the coal produced in the mine is supposed to be consumed by the plant," the paper said. "According to the original design, only a conveyor belt is needed to move the coal from the mine to the generating plant. But the present situation is different." Because the mine comes under the Ministry of Coal and the plant under the Ministry of Electric Power, they refused to cooperate with each other. So the coal was first transported by truck to a railroad line four miles to the east. Then it was loaded on freight cars and shipped back to the power plant.

In Urumqi, the ramshackle capital of Xinjiang, built on an oasis between the perennially snow-capped Mountains of Heaven and the Dzungarian Desert, I came across an American sales manager for a company that makes giant trenchers to lay oil pipelines. His firm, Barber-Greene, had sold five of the $150,000 machines to China's Ministry of Petroleum the year before, plus $100,000 in spare parts. Two of the trenchers had been assigned to Xinjiang to help construct a new pipeline there. The American had flown out to Urumqi, a four-hour plane ride from Peking, to see how his equipment was performing. To his consternation, he could find only one of the two trenchers sent to Xinjiang.

Where was the other? he asked. It's not working, a cadre from the provincial office of the Ministry of Petroleum replied.

Why not, what went wrong? the American inquired.

"Oh, nothing's wrong with it. But we had to take it apart to get spare parts for the one that is working," the Chinese explained.

The American's perplexity deepened. "But why didn't you order up some of the $100,000 in spare parts you bought?" he asked.

"We don't know where they are," the Chinese answered. "And even if we did, we couldn't get them. They are in another province."

Such lack of concern with efficiency, by the standards of Western management, is not unusual. Although Mao's successors have condemned the leftists' attacks on "putting profits in command" and have called for more attention to the bottom line, 23 percent of China's state-owned factories operated at a loss in 1980, according to the State Statistical Bureau. Even though industrial production increased 8.4 percent that year, total profits from the country's factories dropped 1.3 percent, the bureau also reported. Since without an individual income tax the major source of the government's revenue is factory profits, this is a critical problem.

Lao Hu charged that devotion to central planning created a number of other practices antithetical to good cost accounting. "We have always tended to keep a lot of inventory and not turn it over very quickly," he said, "since no one is responsible for whether goods sell." Factories just produce to meet their quota; no one ever takes a market survey, he added.

A friend who was employed in a state corporation that handles electrical machinery estimated it had the equivalent of $400 million in stock in warehouses around China. But the government budget for 1981 to buy electrical machinery was only $200 million. So it would take two full years of purchases just to sell off their inventory, without any further production, he said. An official of the State Economic Commission, which oversees the economy, told delegates to the National People's Congress in 1980 that the total value of goods in warehouses in China is equal to a full year's income for all Chinese wage earners.

Poor quality, another trouble that has plagued Chinese industry, is also traceable to the plan, Lao Hu argued, for a factory's performance is measured only by the number of goods it produces, not their quality. A youthful Chinese who works in a Peking factory that makes components for computers told me the rejection rate for parts in his plant was over 50 percent. The New China News Agency once disclosed that a tractor factory in Canton had manufactured more than 7,000 tractors since it started in 1966, but not one of them met the specified quality standards. An article in the *People's Daily* lambasted a county farm-machinery plant in Jilin province, in the northeast, one of the rural small-scale industries which China's leaders have counted on to help mechanize the countryside. It turned out only fifty small hand-operated tractors a year, with a bad reputation for being too expensive and often breaking down. Nevertheless, the county Party secretary, to ensure the factory made a profit, forced the communes in the area to buy them. Some of the comrades in one commune rebelled and challenged the factory. They offered to buy as many tractors as the plant could drive to them. The plant picked out ten tractors; only three arrived.

During the four years I covered China from Hong Kong and dutifully reported Peking's annual year-end economic claims for *The New York Times,* I sometimes wondered how accurate the figures were which the government released. Western economists I talked with, from universities, the U.S. State Department, and the CIA, were reassuring. Almost all of them agreed that the Chinese data was reliable, though for the period from the Great Leap Forward in 1958 to the late 1970s it was often only fragmentary and expressed in percentages. Peking might assert, for instance, that the output of railway cars had met the yearly target. But that didn't say what the actual production was, or whether it had increased over the previous year. The Chinese didn't deliberately lie, the foreign specialists felt—they just issued their statistics selectively.

But a member of the State Statistical Bureau, the high-level agency responsible for gathering and collating data from every factory and commune across the country, essential to the centrally planned economy, presented a very different picture. During the Cultural Revolution, he said, the staff of the bureau in Peking had come under severe attack from the radicals because most of them were highly trained intellectuals. Many of the statisticians were packed off to labor in the countryside, and the number of employees in the office had been reduced from two hundred to a mere fourteen, to assemble data on hundreds of millions of people. Only in 1980, he related, had the State Statistical Bureau regained its pre-Cultural Revolution size, and their first task was to work out a new standard form for factories to report their production figures. Each factory had to turn in its statistics within three days after the end of every month.

How accurate had these reports been? I asked him. "After the chaos of the Cultural Revolution, we suspect a lot of factories just reported their planned targets as their output," he replied, "but we had no way to check on them." His bureau was only now establishing its own independent audit mechanism. The figures for agriculture were probably even more misleading, he added. Here again was an example of incalculable harm done to the country by the Cultural Revolution.

The worst problem had been created by the Communists' belief that the fastest way to spur an increase in grain production was to urge communes to concentrate on raising their yield per acre. This created a national mania for per unit yield, and at every commune I visited the cadres were always ready with a briefing on their own per unit output. But this also gave the cadres an easy way to doctor their achievements, for by reporting less land than they actually had, they could inflate the harvest per acre. So many teams and communes routinely did this, an official of the Ministry of State Farms and Land Reclamation told me, that Peking's estimates of the total amount of arable land in China had become unreliable. Using locally supplied figures, the government reckoned China had 250 million acres of cultivable land. But American satellite photographs given to the Chinese showed 350 million acres, a 40 percent discrepancy. This outright deceit was part of the breakdown in morality that followed years of political campaigns.

The most controversial figures Peking put out were for its population. Like a fat man sensitive about his weight, the Chinese estimates often seemed too low to foreign specialists. But China's leaders themselves were sometimes surprisingly candid about their own ignorance. In 1972, Li Xiannian, then the country's chief economic planner, was asked by a Japanese visitor about the size of China's population. The State Planning Commission uses a figure of less than 750 million people, Li responded; officials responsible for food go by the number of 800 million, and the Ministry of Commerce prefers 830 million. China is conducting a full-scale census in 1982, with the help of United Nations–provided computers, to clarify the mystery.

One morning when I was reading our daily intake of nearly a dozen Chinese newspapers with my assistant Lao Wu, he let out a loud cry of *"ai-ya,"* roughly, "my god." The story was about a team of peasants who had been working on their commune's fields in the suburbs of Peking. It was wintertime, and the peasants had built a fire to warm themselves. But when one farmer threw some of the burning brushwood into a nearby river, the stream caught fire and rapidly consumed a bridge and high-tension power lines. An investigation revealed the surface of the river was coated with oil discharged by five factories upstream.

The incident was one of a series of cases the Chinese press began to expose in 1980 as the Communists belatedly recognized that their industrial growth over the last thirty years had brought serious pollution. The government has not made public any studies of how foul the air and water have become, and in a country where political power is monopolized by the Communist Party there has been no popular movement to stop offending factories and cars. But to live in Peking in the winter is to be aware of the problem. For days at a time after Barbara and I moved into our new eleventh-floor apartment in one of the areas reserved for foreign diplomats and journalists, when we looked out the window in the morning all that was visible was a thick gray haze. It was like the effect of a white-out on skiers during a blinding snowstorm. The city below us disappeared.

A delegation from the U.S. Environmental Protection Agency that visited China confirmed our worst fears. One of the Americans had brought along a small instrument known as a "personal air quality monitor" which measures the number of particles in the air per million. The safe level is considered no higher than twenty-five or thirty, he told groups of Chinese. The highest level ever recorded in Washington was fifty.

But when he turned on the machine inside a classroom in Peking, it reached 120. In Wuhan, the heavy industrial center on the Yangtze River, the meter rose to 400, its highest point. Then the machine sputtered and broke.

For many years the Communists had insisted that pollution could occur only in capitalist countries where corrupt industrialists "make their enormous profits by rampantly discharging harmful substances into the environment at will and in complete disregard for the fate of the people," as the *People's Daily* once charged. As recently as 1972, a Chinese delegate to a United Nations environmental conference in Stockholm denounced the United States and other industrialized nations for causing the world's environmental troubles and demanded "compensation" for undeveloped countries, presumably including China. But Mao's more pragmatic successors have shown a greater ecological awareness and in 1980 enacted the first environmental protection law in China. How far China can or should now move to check pollution, however, poses a difficult dilemma for Peking. For the government owns the factories, and as Li Hongyuan, an official in charge of pollution control in Heilongjiang province, in the northeast, put it, "There is often a severe contradiction between production and protecting the environment."

A short, energetic man with an endless supply of facts and figures and an engaging passion for his job, Li took me to visit the Song Hua River, which flows through Harbin, the capital of Heilongjiang. The river has become contaminated, Li said, and virtually all the fish are gone from it. Fishermen who ate large quantities of aquatic products in recent years now show high amounts of mercury in their bodies. Some peasants who live downstream from factories that discharged chromium into the river have complained of vomiting, diarrhea, and stomach pains. Li's office has fined several of these factories and persuaded some of them to start cleaning up, but it may be too late to repair the long-term damage to the river.

Until the early part of this century, the land in Heilongjiang was virtually unsettled, a vast fertile prairie rimmed by lushly forested mountains. For China, overpopulated for centuries, it was a last frontier. But now the plains are peopled with peasants in mud-walled houses like the rest of the country, and the forests have been endangered by widespread felling of trees and by fires. Some Chinese scientists believe the destruction of the forests may account for a 50 percent drop in the province's rainfall since the early 1950s. As a result, in the past decade alone the average flow of water though the Song Hua River, which irrigates much of Heilongjiang, has fallen by half. In Harbin, an industrialized city of over two million people originally laid out by the Russians, the river now occupies only about half of its old course. "There is a medium linking the lord of the earth with the lord of heaven —that is vegetation, which evaporates moisture into the air and produces rainfall," said Chen Zhong, an official of the Ministry of State Farms and Land Reclamation. "But the lord of heaven is a merchant. He doesn't give if he isn't paid."

The offshore oil rig in the South China Sea, near Hainan Island, was on a high-priority project—it was running delicate tests with an air-pressure gun lowered down a well hole to try to confirm earlier seismic data about the presence of rich petroleum deposits in the area. So when an American engineer from a major U.S. oil company went aboard the rig he was astounded to find that the Chinese crewmen stopped drilling as lunchtime approached, turned off all their machinery, and then vanished for long midday naps, what the Chinese call *xiu-xi.*

It costs $50,000 a day to operate the platform, the American pointed out to the captain of the vessel. It is also technically dangerous to stop the drill —the equipment is more likely to get stuck. That's why foreign rig crews work twelve-hour shifts around the clock without resting. "You just can't interrupt the drilling," the American argued. But the captain was unpersuaded.

For since 1949 *xiu-xi* has become one of the most important and satisfying rituals of Chinese life. Few Chinese would consider doing anything else but sleep during their siesta, which lasts a full two hours in the winter, up to three hours in summer. Lunch is eaten on office time before 12 P.M.; shopping is accomplished during "tea" breaks in the morning and afternoon, which may last from fifteen minutes to a couple of hours. Workmen at a construction site outside our apartment building napped on heaps of gravel; I often drove past peasants dozing in the backs of donkey carts as they clattered down the street; office workers I knew slumbered on couches in their offices. At the *People's Daily* some offices come equipped with their own beds. When Jan Wong worked at the Foreign Languages Press, many of her fellow employees kept bedrolls on a shelf. At noontime they cleared all the books and papers off their desks, spread their blankets atop them, and nodded off.

So partial are Chinese to *xiu-xi* that nothing—even airplane travel—is allowed to interfere. On a CAAC flight from Canton to the old lakeside city of Hangzhou, about the distance from New York to Chicago, we put down at noon at a military airfield near the small provincial city of Nanchang. The stewardess explained it was time for lunch, and all the passengers trouped into an air force mess hall where we were fed steaming dishes of fried pork and peppers and bowls of hot soup. But after the meal we were still left waiting for another hour. The sky was a bright, cloudless blue, there was no problem with weather, and I passed the time watching several antiquated silver MIG-17's practice takeoffs and landings. When the crew finally reappeared, I quizzed the stewardess about the delay.

"The pilot had to have his *xiu-xi*," she answered.

Xiu-xi grows out of the ancient and natural rhythms of peasant life, rising early with the sun to labor hard in the fields, then taking a break during the heat of midday. But the Communists have enthusiastically embraced it as an accomplishment of socialism in an industrial society. It is even enshrined in China's constitution, Article 49: "The working people have the right to *xiu-xi*."

The siesta is only one of a number of comforts Communist rule has brought to urban Chinese as Peking has created an elaborate all-encompassing welfare state. There is free medical care, free public education, and heavily subsidized low-cost housing. Even the lowest paid factory workers get monthly coupons good for haircuts and trips to the public baths; most offices give out free movie tickets, and women get a small extra allowance to purchase paper for sanitary napkins.

But the centerpiece of the system is guaranteed lifetime employment, what the Chinese call the "iron rice bowl." In China, unless you commit a serious crime like robbery or murder, it is virtually impossible to be fired. At the huge Lanzhou Petrochemical complex in the west, the biggest of its kind in China, with 36,000 workers, a plant official told me they had never dismissed a single employee. And every worker has the right to pass on his post to one of his children, creating a system of inherited jobs.

"From my point of view, it is not good to fire workers, that would cause them troubles in their livelihood," remarked the cadre, Zhang Lianchang, a thin man with a pinched face who is the deputy head of the director's office. "That is not the socialist way. Before Liberation, workers were at the mercy of capitalists and could be laid off anytime, like you do in the United States. Lifetime employment is one of the great achievements of the revolution," he went on, sounding more like a Western union leader than an executive.

Such claims are not the hyperbole of propaganda. In 1981, when the government moved to close over 1,000 inefficient factories to cut its budget deficit, Chinese friends reported that the workers in these plants were still being paid. A tall, muscular young man with a pitted face whom I met during a stroll in the North Ocean Park said the tractor factory where he had worked for four years had been ordered to stop production. He was still drawing his regular salary. His biggest concern, he said, was what to do with his free time.

Socialism has brought other unique benefits to urban Chinese in their work life. Many people now take for granted that their *danwei* will supply them with what in the West would be considered personal property. Not long after arriving in Peking, I hired a driver for *The Times*'s office car, a necessity in

China to help with chores like paying bills, which is still done in person and not by mail. At the suggestion of Lao Wu, we asked the Diplomatic Services Bureau for an older man—they are much more reliable than youngsters these days, Lao Wu contended. The driver assigned to me turned out to be an affable, burly former peasant in his late forties, with a square jaw and a dry sense of humor. His surname was Shi, meaning stone, and because he was older than I, I addressed him as Lao Shi, a phrase that rhymes with the word for honest and upright, a description that fit him neatly.

But his good humor broke down on the first rainy morning. What was wrong? I inquired through Lao Wu, using a middleman in the Chinese fashion. The driver was unhappy, Lao Wu answered, because I had not bought an umbrella and thermos for the office car.

But he has an umbrella, I said, pointing to the black object standing dripping in a corner of the room. Yes, Lao Wu counseled patiently, but that is his own umbrella. After he arrives at the office, he should not be expected to have to use it.

This is part of the system of *bao-xiao,* or "putting it on the office expense account." Bing, the woman who denounced her father during the Cultural Revolution, told me that whenever she went to the airport to see off or greet a colleague she got a free meal at the airport restaurant. "You just tell the waiter you are on an official mission, and he marks it on the bill," she explained. "Then when you go back to your *danwei,* you can collect from them."

In Chinese eyes, these state-provided comforts help compensate for the continued low standard of living, the lack of individual choice in important decisions like education and jobs, and the frustrations of daily life, the standing in line to buy groceries and the overcrowded buses.

"If you are not overly ambitious and don't have any political troubles, life in China is pleasant, like living on a slow-moving conveyor belt," commented a balding professor at one of Peking's universities. "Everything is provided for you, you don't have to worry, and there is little pressure to make you hurry."

Not long before, his daughter, a woman in her mid-twenties, had managed to arrange a visit to Hong Kong on the pretext of seeing an uncle. The professor was afraid she might stay on in the British colony, as thousands of Chinese do each year, attracted by the bright lights, the job opportunities, and the much higher standard of living. But after two months she returned.

"It was too hectic, people have to work so hard," she told her father.

But some Chinese worry that the custom of *xiu-xi,* the iron rice bowl, and the welfare state mentality have eroded the old work ethic that made Chinese famous, the ability to *chi-ku,* or "eat bitterness." (The word "coolie" in English comes from a variant of this, *ku-li,* "bitter strength.")

"People in the cities don't work as hard as they used to," complained a talented surgeon who was trained before 1949. In his hospital, he said, many of the patients just come in to get medical excuses from work. They don't have to pay for the hospital visit, and simply by making a trip to the clinic they get a half day off from work. Some of them try to feign illness by tinkering with the thermometer or squeezing the blood-pressure apparatus.

"It's easy to tell that so many people are faking," the doctor continued. "On a day that is an official holiday, they suddenly vanish."

Our a-yi, whose surname was Wang, was a skilled practioner of life lived at the slow-motion pace of tai-ji, Chinese shadow boxing. Plump and middle-aged, with her hair worn short in the proletarian bowl-cut style, Wang a-yi had not gone past primary school, but she had a native shrewdness we soon learned to appreciate. When Barbara first asked her to iron some of our clothes, she requested that the ironing board be lowered and that we let her do the ironing sitting down. Barbara was incredulous—she had never seen anyone iron from a chair.

But Wang a-yi explained blithely, "Ironing is too hard to do standing up."

Then she pointed out she would need a special large cloth to spread on the floor; otherwise, with the board so low, the ironing would drag on the ground and get dirty. Of course, sitting down, she could not exert as much pressure on the iron, and in a full afternoon's work, accompanied by frequent sighs, she managed to iron three shirts, Barbara reckoned.

Since factory workers can't be fired, malingering on the job has become endemic in industry, and several foreign businessmen who had concluded deals with Chinese enterprises recounted their troubles with lazy employees. The owner of a large textile firm in Hong Kong I knew had decided to take advantage of Peking's new policy, starting in 1979, of allowing foreign companies to establish joint-venture factories in China to help China earn foreign currency and upgrade its technology. He had calculated in advance that the productivity of Chinese workers would probably be only one half of what it is among their cousins who labor across the border in Hong Kong, but with the lower wages in China, he was confident he could still earn a profit. To his chagrin, he said, he discovered that labor efficiency in the new plant in China was only one quarter of that in his factories in Hong Kong.*

In Shanghai, a Japanese businessman said, his company had furnished sophisticated new machinery to manufacture black-and-white television sets to a Chinese factory. The equipment enabled the plant to greatly speed up its production, but the Chinese workers rebelled. They claimed that since

*Hu Qiaomu, a senior adviser to Deng Xiaoping and head of the Academy of Social Sciences, once disclosed in a public report that labor productivity in Chinese factories did not increase between 1958 and 1978. That, Hu admitted, was a catastrophic problem that had undermined China's economic growth.

they were producing more, the machines made them work harder. Therefore, either they should be paid more or the machines should be slowed down. In the end, the Japanese agreed to change the machinery.

This is not to say that all Chinese are lazy. Lihua, the petitioner sent to the countryside, and my other Chinese friends were all conscientious and, with an objective to strive for, indefatigable. Chinese officials whom I watched accompany delegations of foreign dignitaries around the country inevitably exhausted their guests with their energy. But hard workers and those with initiative have become the exception, at least in the cities.

The system actually makes it hard to work hard. For students trying to study at Peking University, the library closes down for lunch from 11:30 A.M. to 2 P.M. It is open again from 2 P.M. to 5 P.M., but closed from 5 P.M. to 7:30 P.M. for dinner. In the evenings only the reading room is open and students cannot check out books because the staff has all gone home. The library is also closed on Thursday and Saturday afternoons so the students and staff can attend political study sessions. Lights in the school's dormitories are turned off at 11 P.M., and if students want to study late, they have to go outside and sit under the dim streetlamps. At Fudan University in Shanghai the administration became concerned that this practice was interfering with the students' sleep and turned off the streetlights too.

Goldbricking has been compounded by Peking's ideological difficulty in devising a wage system with built-in incentives. Mao held that the masses would work hardest out of revolutionary élan, not for material gain, and he abolished piece-rate wages, merit raises, and bonuses, the kinds of income that reward performance. It is no doubt true that in the 1950s and early 1960s, when many Chinese still ardently believed in communism, railroad workers and longshoremen were flattered to win a crimson banner identifying them as labor heroes. But in the two decades from the end of the 1950s to the late 1970s wages remained frozen across the country. Prices were also kept under careful check, but many Chinese felt a sense of genuine frustration and stagnation after years without a raise.

In the summer of 1975, the government had to dispatch 100,000 regular army troops to occupy eighteen factories in Hangzhou after a series of strikes at least partly connected with wage demands. Mao's more practical successors have pronounced his policy mistaken, the fallacy of "everyone eating from the same pot," and they have reinstituted the socialist principle of "to each according to his work," or, less grandly, material incentives. Peking's key reform has been to order factory managers to start paying bonuses again. In theory, to be effective, they should go to the best workers. But in more than twenty plants I visited they were given out to almost all the workers, with only small variations in amount, and tended to become part of the workers' regular pay package. For the Maoist ethic of egalitarianism still runs deep, and both cadres and workers seem ill at ease with a system that encourages differences. The result is that most workers still feel little motivation to excel.

"You get the same pay whether you work hard or not," observed Fuli, a worker in a musical instrument factory.

All the seven members of her workshop earn the same bonus, six yuan ($4) a month, she said, though the amount is supposedly based on a complex calculation that includes a worker's output, quality of labor, safety record, and attitude in political study sessions. "If you report for work regularly, you will get your bonus, and there is an upper limit on how much you can get for it," she added.

The tendency toward egalitarianism is reinforced by the public way in which the workers are paid. On pay day, once a month, Fuli related, one employee from her workshop goes to the factory office to collect the batch of envelopes containing their wages. Each person's name and salary is written on a slip glued to the envelope, so everyone knows what everyone else earns. But even without this overt tip-off, Fuli said, it is easy to tell what anyone makes. For over the years, pay raises have been granted almost entirely on seniority. "All you have to do is to look at a person's face to tell how much he earns," she advised.

In the late 1970s, after Mao's death, his pragmatic successors became increasingly aware of the inadequacy and waste of the Communists' fixation with heavy industry and rigid state planning. Starting in 1979, Deng Xiaoping introduced a two-pronged economic shake-up that was the most ambitious revision of Chinese industrial organization since the 1950s. The first part called for readjusting Peking's priorities: the government ordered curbs on investment in heavy industry and directed that more funds be channeled into the previously neglected sectors like energy, transportation, housing, consumer goods, and agriculture. This readjustment also meant lowering the rate of forced savings for reinvestment and funneling more of the country's national income to consumers in the form of higher wages. The second part of Deng's plan was intended to break out of the straitjacket of central planning by borrowing ideas of flexible market socialism from the innovative countries of Eastern Europe, Hungary, and Yugoslavia. Six thousand factories were given permission to experiment with a limited form of autonomy under which they could keep up to 20 percent of the profits they earned above their state quota. Managers in these factories were given new authority to reinvest their extra earnings as they chose, either in new plant and machinery or in higher wages for their employees. These managers were even given the unheard-of right to fix some prices—the most sacred power of all for central planners—alter their production quotas, and perhaps hire and fire a few workers. The experimental factories were also to be forced to take responsibility for selling their products; no longer would the state buy whatever they manufactured, regardless of the quality. In a final phase of the experiment, the factories would no longer automatically receive their accustomed annual operating funds from the People's Bank. Instead, they would have to apply to the bank and borrow the necessary funds in the form of loans, repayable with interest. The key word was profitability.

But in early 1981, amid considerable confusion, Peking suspended further implementation of the second half of its program, the structural reforms. The government had become nervous that the factories granted the new self-management rights often used them to raise their prices, contributing to inflation, or to build new plants, adding to the state's budget deficit of $11 billion. To the fiscally conservative Communists, both inflation and deficit financing are anathema. To counteract these problems, Peking ordered central planning and controls tightened again.

There was also another reason for Peking's suspension of its reforms, I heard from Chinese friends—resistance by factory managers and other bureaucrats who were unhappy with changing habits built up over the past thirty years. Both factory managers and workers alike were uncomfortable with the idea of firing a lazy or incompetent worker—it would break their iron rice bowl and might lead to retribution in the next political campaign. Then there was the problem of making a profit—it smacked of capitalism, and it was also much harder than simply fulfilling a quota. It required managers to curb expenses, monitor the quality of their products, make sure their goods sold, and raise labor productivity. Under the old system, too many people were doing nicely out of doing very little.

Under Deng's new policies, industrial output soared. But the Communists' failure to push through on the badly needed structural reforms raises serious doubts about how successful the regime will be in achieving its Four Modernizations program. The Four Modernizations has always been something of a hollow slogan, like "a chicken in every pot," without a clearly defined goal beyond Peking's oft-repeated phrase of making China into a "powerful modern socialist state by the year 2000." Perhaps the clearest definition of what it really will mean was given by Deng himself in an important speech to high-level officials in 1980. The target of the Four Modernizations, he said, is that by the end of the century China's per capita gross national product reach $1,000. "This represents a *xiao-kang* society," Deng added, using a classical Chinese term implying a peaceful era with a simple though sufficient standard of living. Deng's plan must have struck his audience as modest. In 1958 Mao had boasted that China would overtake Great Britain in industrial production and technology within fifteen years. When Deng spoke he knew that the per capita GNP of Hong Kong was already over $2,000 a year and that of Singapore, $3,000. That would leave China far short of its Asian neighbors and mean that it would probably not be a really powerful modern state, not a great power in military terms, certainly. Yet Deng's target is still ambitious. China's per capita GNP today is about $470 (he put it at only a little over $200 in another of those statistical inconsistencies). Can China achieve this?

Most foreign businessmen I talked with who had visited Chinese factories or spent months helping build new mines, ports, and plants were skeptical. To them it was critical that the Communists overhaul their management system.

"Chinese industry will continue to grow, it can't help but expand with all the reinvestment they pour into it," remarked an American engineer who has helped construct multimillion-dollar projects in several parts of China. "But it will be slow, and uneven, and wasteful," the engineer added.

He recalled an incident when his firm had just completed building a large chemical fertilizer factory. Everything looked wonderful. There was a big celebration for the opening, and the Chinese lined up a row of trucks to pick up the first production of fertilizer.

But the next day the plant manager summoned the American to his office. How could he shut the machinery down immediately? he inquired. The American was puzzled. The plant was running smoothly.

"Yes," the manager replied, "but we have run out of trucks. They belong to the local counties and communes and there is no way to tell when they will return to pick up more fertilizer."

The American was horrified. It would take several hours to shut off the equipment, then a week to restart production.

13. Follow the Leader

服从领导

THE ORGANIZATION

"Bureaucratism is an ulcer of countries which uphold proletarian dictatorship."

Red Flag

"Veteran revolutionaries only end up as monsters and ghosts."

Deng Xiaoping

Well before I arrived in China, I harbored a secret ambition—as a fanatic skier, I wanted to be the first foreigner to ski in China. I had seen photographs in one of Peking's glossy color magazines of Chinese skiers descending the piste, smiles pasted to their rosy faces; and shortly before I took up residence in Peking I was encouraged by an article released by the New China News Agency reporting that the China Travel Service had decided to allow foreigners to ski in China as part of its plan to expand the country's tourist industry. So my first December in Peking, I applied to the Information Department for permission to go to Heilongjiang (Black Dragon River), the province in the far northeast described in the articles about China's ski slopes. After a month's delay, the Information Department replied that I was mistaken. There was no skiing in China.

Thinking there might have been a misunderstanding, I reapplied, this time enclosing the pictures and copy of the news story. Four weeks later, they answered again—yes, there is skiing in China, but it is in an area closed to foreigners.

I was ready to accept defeat, but a few days later I spotted an American lawyer who represented U.S. business firms in China sauntering through the lobby of the Peking Hotel with skis on his shoulders. He and his wife had just been skiing for a week in Heilongjiang, they said, and while there had encountered a team of journalists from the American magazine *Ski*.

Armed with this fresh evidence, I approached the Information Department for the third time. After several more weeks passed, they finally conceded that yes, there is a place foreigners can ski, but they were very sorry it was now too late in the season—it was early March—and the snow had all melted. They would be happy to let me go to Heilongjiang to write about other subjects, but without my skis.

I decided to test their story. When I arrived in Harbin, the capital of Heilongjiang, it was 5 degrees below zero fahrenheit and my guide from the local Foreign Affairs Department said there was plenty of snow at the ski slope, a four-hour drive from the city. "You should have brought your skis," he suggested.

I had run into the Chinese bureaucracy. There was no way, I realized, I would get a straight answer from the Information Department about why they wouldn't let me go skiing. The Chinese invented bureaucracy over 2,000 years ago, and their capacity for it is endless. Avoiding responsibility has been raised to a national art form. The great early historian, Si-ma Qian, who lived from 145 to 90 B.C., had warned, "Do not take the lead in planning affairs, or you may be held responsible." In one of the red pavilions of the Forbidden City, where the Ming and Qing emperors kept their imperial seals, hangs a large inscription in gold letters on a blue background—*Wu-wei*, "Do nothing," or action through inaction. It is the old motto of the Taoist mystics; the key to merging with nature is not to strive. By this they did not mean complete inaction, rather, do only what is natural. "Do nothing, and nothing will not be done," the sage Lao Zi counseled. The favorite figure of the Taoists is water, which, though the softest of all things, wears away the hardest. The pavilion with its message was one of my favorite places to wander to get away from the hurly-burly of my office in the Peking Hotel. It seemed to explain the knack Chinese officials had for spontaneous inactivity.

In January 1979, shortly before Deng Xiaoping made his historic journey to the United States, *Time* magazine arranged an exclusive interview with him. It was a journalistic coup; Deng's picture would be on *Time*'s cover the day he arrived in Washington, and Hedley Donovan, *Time*'s editor in chief, flew in from New York along with Marsh Clark, the magazine's Hong Kong bureau chief. They were staying at the Peking Hotel, a five-minute drive from the Great Hall of the People where the meeting was to take place at 9 A.M. At 8:45 that morning the two men met an official from the Information Department who was to accompany them to the interview and went to the desk in the lobby that assigns taxis. But there weren't any cabs; Peking's taxi drivers were staging a go-slow strike to demand higher wages. Clark, anxious about being late, an unpardonable offense in China, especially when meeting the country's paramount leader, asked the official if they could use his Foreign Ministry car, which was parked out front, with the chauffeur sitting idly in the front seat.

No, the official replied tartly, that was impossible. Clark and Donovan were not guests of the state, therefore they couldn't drive in a government car. He was adamant.

Nine o'clock came and still no taxis appeared, Clark told me later. He was desperate. But the Information Department cadre wouldn't change his mind. Only at five minutes past nine did a cab finally arrive and they rushed down the Avenue of Eternal Tranquility. Deng was standing at the top of the marble steps of the Great Hall to greet them, a smile on his deeply furrowed face. Certainly he understood what it is like to deal with the 20 million cadres and 38 million members of the Communist Party who make up the heart of the bureaucracy.

Bureaucracy was so prevalent, I found, such a factor in people's daily lives, grinding them down with frustration, that it had spawned its own lexicon. In the past the Chinese had a special set of words to ease the pain of life. They all related to fate, to the vagaries of nature. When I lived on Taiwan, if something went wrong, friends would say, *"Suan-le-ba"* (Forget it), or *"Mei-yu fa-zi"* (There is nothing you can do about it). When the Communists came to power, they sought to overcome this passive, defeatist thinking; Mao's promise was that China had stood up. I noticed that in Peking people had stopped using the old phrases about fate. Instead they had been transmuted into a new vocabulary, the kinds of answers bureaucrats give when asked a question: "I must study the problem," "I will consider it," "I will get in touch with the responsible comrades," or the two most common replies, *"Bu fang-bian"* (It is not convenient), and *"Bu qing-chu,"* (I'm not too clear about it). They all meant the same thing; nothing would be done.

"The real problem in China is not the special privileges of the elite which everyone complains about," an outspoken scientist told me. "It's incompetence in the bureaucracy."

To prove his point, the scientist tipped me off to a big news story—a Chinese oil rig had collapsed in the Bohai Gulf off the coast of north China, and all seventy-two people aboard it had drowned. The tragedy had taken place eight months before, but not a word about it had appeared in the Chinese press, for the Minister of Petroleum, Song Zhenming, was a close personal friend and political follower of one of China's top officials, Kang Shien, a deputy prime minister. Song had served under Kang since Kang had been head of the Daqing oil field, the wonder child of Chinese industry, and each time Kang was promoted, he had brought Song, his subordinate, up with him. In Chinese terms, they had close *guan-xi,* connections, the cement of Chinese politics. Kang had helped stall off an investigation because it could reflect on him too. The scientist was furious about the cover-up, he said, offering me a crockery jar of yogurt in his living room, and he felt exposure would be good for China.

Indeed, a few weeks after I published an article about the disaster in *The New York Times,* the *People's Daily* followed up with its own detailed report. At 3:30 A.M. on November 25, 1979, the paper charged, a rig China had purchased from Japan for $25 million had capsized while it was being towed to a new drilling site. The skipper of the ship that was towing the rig did nothing to rescue the men in the water and did not transmit a distress signal. It took twelve hours, in fact, before the Ministry of Petroleum notified China's coast guard of the accident.

Song, the oil minister, said in his official report to the State Council, or cabinet, that the incident had been caused by unforeseen and exceptionally strong winds that reached gale force 11. Records of meteorological stations along the coast revealed they had correctly predicted a storm for that day, though the real winds were not nearly of such magnitude. According to the *People's Daily,* the oil-drilling platform had been bought from Japan seven years before, but no one had bothered to translate the operating and safety manuals for it. Top officials of the oil ministry had made a series of trips to Tokyo, presumably to ensure they knew how to work the rig, but they had not trained the workers aboard it, who had "a low education and technical standard," the paper asserted.

The month the accident occurred, the ministry was pushing to fulfill its annual quota for discovering new oil reserves. To meet its target, 20 million more tons of reserves had to be found in the shallow Bohai Gulf region by the end of the year. So on November 24, the day before the disaster, the director of the Ocean Petroleum Exploration Bureau, under the ministry, ordered the rig moved to a new site. Information on the impending storm was handed to him, but he simply ignored it, the paper said. He also over-ruled three protests from the rig's captain. The crew should apply the Party's old spirit of not being afraid of hardship or death, the official advised. Even so, the accident might have been averted if proper procedures had been followed. But the crew did not know they were supposed to pump the ballast water out of the rig to reduce its draft and make it more seaworthy before moving it. In the end, when the storm did blow up, the high waves just washed over and into the rig's cabin, making it turn turtle.

It was almost a textbook case of the troubles that plague China's bureau-cracy, which is responsible for running both the government and industry: lack of technical competence, arrogant officials who ignore advice from subordinates, factionalism, worship of state quotas, and the old guerrilla mentality that holds that sheer willpower can overcome any obstacle. There was even a scurrilous epilogue. When Song was promoted to be oil minister in Peking, he had brought with him his chauffeur of twenty years. His driver had the habit of cruising the streets at night in the minister's large Red Flag limousine looking for women to pick up. One woman later reported to the police that he had molested her in the back seat, a serious offense in puritanical China. But Song had interceded and gotten the charge dropped. A few months later the driver picked up another woman, near the Peking railway station, drove her to the suburbs, then raped and murdered her. This time he was tracked down and executed. Song was sacked for his role in the rig disaster, and Kang, his benefactor, was given a humiliating "big demerit."

Many Chinese now blame these bureaucratic troubles on their feudal past, the old love of hierarchy, obedience to authority, the lack of a scientific attitude, and the clannishness of factions in the imperial court. The Communists made a strategic error after 1949, an editor at the *People's Daily* confided to me.

"We thought the fundamental problem in China was capitalism," he said. "Actually, China was not yet industrialized and didn't have a large bourgeois class. The real problem was feudalism." This was a shorthand way of saying China was burdened by its past and not a "blank sheet of paper," as Mao had opined, on which anything could be written.

On one of my first trips to China, as a tourist, before the normalization of relations between the United States and China, I had an encounter that helped me realize just how ingrained the Chinese desire for authority is. At the railroad station across the border from Hong Kong, my guide from the China Travel Service greeted our group with the announcement that he had selected a leader from among our delegation. The group leader would be responsible for rounding us up each morning and evening, make sure we were on time for meals and bus rides, and pass on any complaints or suggestions we had to the Chinese. But in a case of mistaken identity, the Chinese had picked an eighteen-year-old American high school student who had come to China with his mother under protest. He didn't like China, and said so. His name was the same as that of his father, a U.S. diplomat, and the Chinese had calculated that a senior foreign service officer would be a suitable group leader. But no matter how many times the teen-ager tried to resign or we appealed for a change, the travel service guide declined.

"He is your leader, how can you change him?" the guide declared. "You must learn to follow the leader. That is what we Chinese do."

Behind this seemingly inexplicable incident, to us as Westerners, I discovered, was the instinctive Chinese penchant for authority. More than 2,000 years of imperial tradition have created in the collective unconscious the desire for a supreme, quasi-mystical leader. The collapse of the Qing dynasty and the abolition of the position of emperor in 1911 left a vacuum which Mao later shrewdly manipulated, building a personality cult for himself that verged on turning him into a deity.

The popular image of Mao in the West is that he was the great leveler, the crusader against bureaucracy and privilege. Wasn't it Mao who summoned the millions of Red Guards to humble Party cadres who had grown soft and fat with their years in power? An articulate, thoughtful historian who was trained in schools run by American missionaries before 1949 scoffed at this perception of the Chairman. Mao may have sensed that the Communists were slipping back into the old hierarchal and feudal ways of the imperial mandarins. But paradoxically Mao himself was no different. He lived in luxurious villas with servants, isolated from the common people, and he always demanded his own way. When he found he was outvoted in the Party Central Committee, he ignored the Party's normal procedures and went outside the Party to the Red Guards, to his wife, Jiang Qing, and then to the army. "There was nothing democratic about him," the professor contended. In fact, by his imperious ways, he unconsciously encouraged the old Chinese taste for separation between the leader and the masses. The Cultural Revolution for Mao was to overthrow his enemies in the Party, not authority itself, the professor added. When youthful rebels in Shanghai threatened to get out of control in early 1967 by establishing the so-called Shanghai Commune, modeled on the Paris Commune of a century before, Mao backtracked. Having heard that the rebels wanted to get rid of all "heads," Mao declared, "This is extreme anarchism, it is most reactionary. In reality there will always still be heads." Eventually in many factories and schools he called in the army to suppress Red Guard activity.

The professor saw irony in the Red Guards' almost mystical veneration of Mao and their ascription of "supernatural powers" and "magic" to the small red plastic-covered book of his quotations. "When we were supposedly attacking feudalism, bureaucracy, and all the bad old things, the Red Guards were out in the streets yelling *wan-sui* to Mao," literally, "10,000 years," or "eternal life." "That was what the mandarins and the people used to say for the Emperor," the professor related, pausing to shake his head in disbelief. "Even I myself was out in the streets shouting *wan-sui*. It was ridiculous."

The urge to be ruled by a strong leader remained in the countryside too. A wiry, thirty-two-year-old graduate student who had been sent to work in a village for nine years related the reaction of the peasant family where he was quartered in 1976 when Mao died. "That night they talked a lot, almost till dawn, they were very upset," he remembered. " 'The Emperor is dead, there is no one to replace him,' they kept saying. 'What will China do without an Emperor?' They really believed it, China must have an Emperor," the graduate student said.

Deng Xiaoping has proclaimed that Mao's deification of himself was a mistake and that there will be no more personality cults. There are no icons to Deng, no pictures of him in people's homes, no plaster busts of him in stores, as there were for Mao. But traces of the old Mao cult and the affinity the Chinese had for it remain strong. During a visit to a hilly tea-growing commune in Anhui, in central China, I noticed a red-painted sign prominently displayed over the entrance to the mill where the tea leaves are dried: "The great leader Chairman Mao came here on September 16, 1958." Another plaque announced, "It was here Chairman Mao gave his great instruction, 'Plant more tea bushes on the sides of mountains.'" Even his most banal utterances still conveyed apocalyptic force to some Chinese. After I inspected the mill, the commune Party secretary escorted me to a freshly painted yellow and white stucco meeting hall for a briefing on the commune's production figures. Above the doorway was an inscription: "The hall where Chairman Mao came to view the tea."

In the early part of the twentieth century, modern-minded young Chinese had tried to cast off filial piety as being outdated and an obstacle to China's progress. But the attitudes it inspired persisted—loyalty, respect for authority, self-discipline. These were ready-made for communism, and in the early 1950s, at least, as the psychiatrist Robert Lifton has put it, the Chinese became filial Communists.* The Cultural Revolution eventually undermined some of this discipline and replaced it with cynicism. Even so, I detected, the Chinese still have a far greater respect for the old virtues of loyalty and authority than Americans do.

The Communist revolution in China is often described as the triumph of the countryside over the cities. This usually refers to Mao's brilliant strategy of organizing peasant guerrillas in the villages and then using them to conquer the Nationalist-dominated urban areas. But I found the manner of the Communists' victory had a more far-reaching significance—it literally meant that when the Communists entered the cities in 1949 and found themselves governing the country, they took their peasant soldiers and installed them as Party secretaries and security chiefs in every office, factory, school, and hospital.

Fang Guanghua, a quiet, intense, twenty-six-year-old lathe operator with smooth skin, high cheekbones, and strong white teeth, explained what this meant in personal terms. For a year he had been going to night school six evenings a week, after finishing his shift in a truck factory, to brush up on his physics, chemistry, and math. He had been assigned to the plant after spending several years in the countryside and he desperately wanted to

*Robert Jay Lifton, *Thought Reform and the Psychology of Totalism* (New York: W. W. Norton and Co., 1961), p. 386.

further his education. It was the only way for him to get ahead and avoid a dreary life of working in a factory with little chance for promotion. His ambition was like that of Lingling, the bright sixteen-year-old high school student. He had actually passed the university entrance exam the year before, but his factory wouldn't let him go to college. Now he hoped to pass another test that would qualify him for China's new and highly popular television university. It was organized for workers like him, giving them screened lectures in the mornings, then live tutors in the afternoon. After a two-year program, he would get a degree and perhaps a better job as a technician or engineer. There was only one catch. He had to get approval to register for the exam from the Party secretary of the factory, a man named Ke. The Party secretary was the real boss of the plant; there was a professional factory manager, but he was a weak second. As everywhere in China, the Party forms a parallel system—to the government, to industry, to the universities, even to the army—and it is Party representatives placed within these organizations who exercise the real power. They in turn are responsible to the Party officials in the hierarchy above them, assuring strict central control.

Ke turned Fang down flatly. "Study is useless," he said. "Nothing you can learn will help the factory," and he refused Fang permission. Fang then tried asking the four other members of the factory Party committee. Each said no. Their opposition to his attempts to improve himself seemed at odds with the government's modernization program, and I was puzzled. But Fang understood, he told me, during a rendezvous in Jan Wong's apartment. Jan had originally met him when I sent her to cover a demonstration in front of Party headquarters at Zhongnanhai by disgruntled students and workers who were not being allowed to continue their schooling. Since Jan was ethnically Chinese and dressed in plain blue, like a native, she had been able to join the protestors and make friends with Fang.

Ke, Fang explained, was from a poor peasant family and had marched into the capital with the Red Army. By hard work and loyalty, he had made his way up the Party ladder to become boss of the factory, which had been a small shop to make rickshaws before Liberation. Ke had never attended school, Fang related, so at public meetings, when he was supposed to read out government documents, he had to call on a younger cadre to do it for him. Ke still retained some of the rough peasant ways of his boyhood. Once at a factory-wide gathering to issue handbooks on labor safety, he warned the employees not to use them as *hou-men-piao,* "back-door tickets," a euphemism for toilet paper. "The women workers thought he was very crude," Fang said.

The other members of the factory committee were former rickshaw pullers, part of the poorest urban class before 1949, and they couldn't read or write either. They had been with the factory since it was converted from making rickshaws to trucks and were very proud of their homemade accomplishments.

"They have a deep-seated distrust of intellectuals and get angry when they see me reading around the factory," Fang said. "But they are staunch Party members. They never question the Party's orders." During the campaign to criticize Deng in 1976, the second time he was purged, they energetically attacked him. After Deng was rehabilitated in 1977, they swung 180 degrees "without the slightest difficulty," Fang said.

Ke had never had any technical training, but he was a fanatic about keeping the factory clean. Recently he had shut down the plant for three days because it was due for inspection by the ministry which had jurisdiction over it. "We polished the same windows over and over to get it in perfect shape," Fang recalled. The reason Ke was so concerned about appearance is that he knew the higher-level cadres didn't know anything about production either and that neatness is what most impressed them, Fang added.

When Ke first became factory boss, he had still kept his wife, a peasant, in their home village. He had taken lumber from the plant and gotten some workers and one of the factory's trucks to help build himself a new home in the countryside. That offended Fang, but he was even angrier when Ke arranged through a back-door connection to get his wife's household registration moved to Peking. He then got her a job in the factory, and moved her and his children into a room in the plant, though the factory had no dormitories to offer its workers. Ke was finally forced to move them out only when one of his children had caused a serious accident by pulling a switch in the boiler room when a worker was inside a machine that feeds coal to the furnace.

Ke ate in the factory canteen with the workers in good proletarian style, Fang continued, but he had a weakness for presents. Anyone who wanted a promotion had to send him little gifts of eggs, chickens, or fruit. At the last Chinese New Year's, or Spring Festival as the Communists call it, eighty of the plant's four hundred workers had gone to his house with presents. Ke's petty corruption, his self-serving behavior, was another indication of how the Communists' early reputation for honesty and idealism had broken down after three decades in power.

Most studies of how China is run focus on a few top leaders like Mao, Zhou, and Deng, on their personalities, their foibles, their policy disputes. But as I traveled around the country, I was repeatedly impressed by the importance of the simple rural background of the bulk of the members of the Party and the bureaucracy, like Ke. He was not unusual in his peasant upbringing and lack of education. A study by the *Guangming Daily* revealed that only 22 percent of the Party secretaries and managers of China's factories have what it termed "technical knowledge." Hebei province, in north China, conceded in a radio broadcast that of its 700,000 cadres, only 227,000 had graduated from junior or senior high school. Then there was the Surgeon General of the People's Liberation Army, whom I met at a reception. He turned out not to be a trained physician but a former medic on the Long March in the 1930s. The Party secretaries of several university departments I visited were one-time political commissars in the army, not teachers.

When Mayor Ed Koch of New York came to Peking to establish a sister-city relationship with the Chinese capital, I had the unusual chance to sit at banquets next to three of Peking's deputy mayors. They all were born into peasant families in the same county in Shandong province, east of Peking, they told me in hesitant snatches of conversation; they had joined the Red Army as teen-agers, and they had marched victoriously into Peking in 1949. Now they were in charge of housing, finance, and industry for the city, though none had specialized training. They were all protégés of the mayor of Peking, a friend later explained, who came from their home region and had been their army commander.

Men like these had been revolutionaries in their youth, rebelling against the corrupt Kuomintang, but in power they have reverted to the inward-looking, conservative values of their rural homes: respectful of authority, suspicious of change, interested in their family's comfort, skeptical of the importance of technology, the intellect, and things Western, and, above all, xenophobic. For most, their only real training had come in the army, where they learned discipline and the thoughts of Chairman Mao. It is not surprising that, like other peasant revolutionaries in Chinese history who overthrew earlier dynasties, they re-created something of the old imperial state, with its pomp and privileges, once they rose to power. They were not prepared to run a modern state, and China suffered.

With their country accents and rough manners—even Deng keeps a spittoon by his feet during meetings with foreign heads of state and sometimes punctuates his sentences with an expectoration—these cadres are viewed by the more sophisticated natives of Peking and Shanghai as urban Americans would view hillbillies from Kentucky or Tennessee. Our friends the Wangs liked to tell jokes about the typical cadre.

"In a village the county authorities had announced they were going to form the militia and issue rifles," Li began one of his favorites stories. "It was a big event in a place where nothing ever happens and the peasants got very excited. But then days and weeks passed, and the county authorities were having trouble reaching a decision.

"Finally, after two years, a jeep came down to the village. An important-looking cadre got out and declared there would be a big meeting about forming the militia.

"At the meeting, he got up and began speaking slowly, 'I- am-the-county-

Party-secretary,' and with those words the audience burst into thunderous applause. It was a great honor to be visited by such a high cadre.

"But then the speaker added, 'That is, I was sent by the county Party secretary.' " Li told the story employing the thick dialect of Hunan province, where Mao and many other cadres came from.

" 'We have decided, about the guns, that one gun for each person,' and again there was a chorus of applause, 'is absolutely impossible.'

" 'We have reached the conclusion that one gun for every two people,' and there was still clapping, 'is not right.'

" 'So I want to announce the final decision of the county Party committee is, one gun for every three people,' which set off more applause. 'But they are wooden guns,' the cadre concluded."

A university diploma, of course, is not necessarily a qualification for leadership in any society. But it is striking how few of China's top leaders have any higher education. Of the twenty-six members of the Politburo, only one, Fang Yi, who oversees science, went to college, and his official biography does not say where or for how many years. Of the twelve men who make up the Secretariat of the Central Committee, which runs the Party apparatus, and the eighteen deputy prime ministers, who administer the government, only five have a college education. This means there is an enormous cultural gap between China's political leaders and the country's highly trained doctors, scientists, and professors, many of whom were educated at schools run by Western missionaries or in colleges in the United States, Europe, and Japan.

"We have very little common language," said an introspective, soft-spoken physicist in his fifties. "The cadres believe what Mao told his niece, Wang Hairong—'The more you learn, the more stupid you become.' They still see intellectuals as what Mao called us, 'the stinking ninth.' " (The ninth in a list of "bad elements" blackballed by the Communists.)

Not long before, he had applied for permission to do advanced research in the United States. The director of his institute, a scientist himself, had approved. But his application also had to go to the cadres in the institute's personnel department and security section, both former peasants and army political commissars. They vetoed it. The physicist says they had long distrusted him because he had spent two years studying in America and had come back in 1950 after the outbreak of the Korean War. He returned out of patriotism, he told me, but in the Cultural Revolution he was accused of being an American spy and arrested. He was later cleared of the charge; yet it remained in his dossier.

His older brother had also gone to the United States as a student before 1949 but had decided the political risks of returning to China were too great and had stayed on in America, where he had become a distinguished scientist.

The previous summer the Chinese Academy of Sciences had invited him to return to give a series of lectures, and he was accorded a hero's welcome. My acquaintance saw irony in this, but, instead of expressing bitterness, used it to make a significant point. China had been forced to pay a high price for the Communists' ignorance, incompetence, and distrust of intellectuals; several generations of talent were wasted, he charged.

"The reason China has not developed a powerful technocracy like the Soviet Union, with world-famous scientists and advanced military weapons, is because the Communists distrusted the intellectuals so much," he said. "They came from peasant families, they fought for years in the mountains. It was all they knew. After 1950 these men might have developed some expertise, but then Mao launched one political campaign after another. There was no time for education. Besides, Mao proclaimed it was better to be Red than to be expert," more important to be correct politically than to be educated and professional.

Chinese certainly are intelligent enough to produce great scientists, he added. "Look at Yang Chen-ning in the United States," one of three Chinese-Americans to win the Nobel Prize. China had succeeded in a few scientific fields where the government had felt urgency and concentrated its resources, my friend said, notably physics, with the production of nuclear weapons and ballistic missiles. In medicine Chinese doctors had also made pioneering advances in a few areas—burn care and limb transplants (in part because of the high rate of industrial accidents in China).

"But a lot of us were wasted," he went on. "Mao ordered us to be self-reliant, so instead of doing experiments, we spent our time making our own microscopes." For four years during the Cultural Revolution he had labored on a farm planting corn. After he returned to his institute, he found the supply of scientific journals from the outside world had been terminated as politically dangerous. For almost a decade he had worked on one project, he said, only to discover that another Chinese physicist had already done the same experiment in a separate research facility. "We weren't allowed to telephone or write each other for security reasons."

After Mao's death, Deng and his associates sought to correct some of these abuses. In a sharp departure from Maoist orthodoxy, Deng announced that henceforth intellectuals should be considered part of the working class, not members of the bourgeoisie, as they had been, because "science and technology are part of the productive forces." Deng lashed out at ideologues who still haggled over preserving Mao's sayings—"They sit on the pot, but they can't manage to shit," he exclaimed in a party meeting. In 1981 the Academy of Sciences officially elected a sixty-six-year-old chemist who had been trained in England and the United States, Lu Jiaxi, as its president, a move designed to show that scientists now are gaining more authority over their own work.

What was not said publicly, my friend pointed out, was that a veteran Communist and member of the Central Committee, Li Chang, remained as Party secretary of the academy, the key position, and also served as one of its three executive chairmen. The *People's Daily* disclosed in a survey of twenty-three institutes under the Academy of Sciences that only 25 percent of the officials in these organizations were really scientists. The rest were Party administrators and watchdogs. "A large number of college graduates who according to the original plans were to be assigned to scientific and technical work were instead appointed as buyers, sales workers, custodians, typists, cooks, etc.," the paper said in another article. "Some specializing in rocketry were assigned as doorkeepers. Remote-control specialists were turned into butchers. Mathematicians became bakers." At a national congress of the academy in 1981, Hu Yaobang, the new Party chairman, chastised the Party, charging that many comrades still did not trust intellectuals. The cadres feel "they are not docile, they think too much, and have too many views" of their own.

The predominance in the Party of older men from humble rural backgrounds makes it difficult to categorize the Chinese Communists with neat Western political labels like left or right. How to deal with this problem, how succinctly to identify the different Politburo factions for the readers of *The New York Times* was a never-ending conundrum for me. Mao and his cohorts, we journalists liked to write, were leftists, and, accepting Chinese terminology, Deng was a rightist. But this obscured as much as it clarified.

A young chemical engineer I met on a muggy summer afternoon when he was sending a telegram at the marble-floored cable office and I was filing a story to New York helped shake my tendency to oversimplify Chinese politics. After a brief, guarded talk at the cable office, he asked if he could meet me later at my hotel room. He had an uncle who was a senior official and often came to the hotel for a haircut, a carefully restricted privilege, and the engineer said it would be no problem for him to get past the hotel guards with his relative. A few days later he appeared, dressed in a loose, short-sleeved white shirt worn over gray pants and plastic sandals, standard summer garb for urban Chinese men.

Was I a leftist or a rightist? he wanted to know.

I said that in American political terms I considered myself a liberal, probably left of center.

"That's too bad," he said, obviously disappointed. "In China, we intellectuals don't like leftists. They are too conservative."

To a Westerner, where the political left has been associated with progressive and the right with conservative, the engineer's sentiment was a contradiction. But he went on to elucidate.

"In the Cultural Revolution, Mao and the Gang of Four called themselves leftists. They opposed individualism, freedom of speech, democracy; they preferred collective behavior and control and a closed door to the outside world." Now Deng Xiaoping is following a rightist policy, he continued, more moderate, more practical, with material incentives, more freedom of expression, and more open to trade and cultural contacts with the West.

The average cadre, like his uncle, he said, was nervous about Deng's experimental program. He had spent his entire career in the Party learning the Maoist catechism. "My uncle thinks that giving scientists like me the right to run our own institutes or travel abroad is an invitation to anarchy and the spread of capitalism," he said. We agreed that conservative might be a better word to describe these cadres, in the sense of resisting change, rather than as leftists, to avoid misunderstanding by foreigners.

Getting up from his chair to pace around the room, he wondered if I was aware of the central fact of Chinese politics—the importance of *guan-xi,* which are the real basis of all factions, not ideology. His uncle was from Sichuan, he said, the province where Deng was born, and had served in the army in Sichuan in the early 1950s when Deng was the senior army political commissar and Party secretary there before being promoted to Peking. That made his uncle part of the Sichuan *bang,* or Sichuan gang, currently the strongest faction in Peking. Another key member of the Sichuan group was Hu Yaobang, whom Deng installed as Party chairman in 1981. Hu had first met Deng in 1941 when, as a twenty-six-year-old army political commissar, he was assigned to work under Deng in the 18th Red Army group operating in the arid Taihang Mountains in the northwestern part of the country. The two men became practically inseparable. They served together in the army for eight years. They marched south into Sichuan in 1949 and helped set up the first Communist administration there. They were transferred simultaneously to Peking in 1952, and then, when Deng was purged in the Cultural Revolution as a capitalist roader, Hu was toppled along with him, labeled by the Red Guards as a member of Deng's "club." The pattern was repeated in 1976 when Deng was disgraced for the second time. It was probably not a coincidence, the engineer observed, that the two men share a striking physical resemblance—both are barely five feet tall.

Another leader with a Sichuan connection is the new Prime Minister, Zhao Ziyang. Deng had sent Zhao to Sichuan in 1975 as first Party secretary at a time when the vast province, with 100 million people, China's largest, was suffering from serious political infighting and an acute food shortage. Zhao's performance in transforming the province's bankrupt economy and then introducing some of Deng's pet economic reforms quickly won him Deng's favor.

As an example of how the factional system worked, the engineer said that recently his uncle had been having trouble in the ministry where he worked.

The minister belonged to a different clique—he had served in another army group during the civil war—and wanted to get rid of his uncle. His uncle had known Hu Yaobang since they both worked in Sichuan almost thirty years before, and though they didn't share the same political philosophy, his uncle had appealed to Hu to intercede on his behalf. After several months, Hu arranged a face-saving compromise: his uncle was transferred to another ministry but with a higher rank as deputy minister.

After a few months in China, I had made several Chinese friends and had become aware there was often a gap between the happy posture they assumed in public and the cynicism they expressed privately. But they were students, workers, and teachers, not Party members, and I was curious how cadres viewed communism after three decades of political campaigns, factional wrangles, and economic ups and downs.

That was when I met Mulan, a slight, frank woman whose pretty round face and large bright eyes concealed her forty-five years. I was walking down the Avenue of Eternal Tranquility on the eve of China's national day, October 1; in celebration, the government had strung clusters of lights in front of all the large offices lining the street, illuminating it like an amusement park. The broad sidewalks were jammed with hundreds of thousands of people, more I thought than live in some member states of the United Nations. Unexpectedly, I felt a tap on my arm and turned to see a woman smiling at me.

"How do you like our national day?" she asked, a careful, neutral gambit. Then she introduced herself and said she was an office worker who was trying to improve her English.

It wasn't until we had met several more times that I had the courage to ask if she was a Communist Party member. Mulan laughed. "It's no secret. Communist Party members are humans too. They are not monsters." Then she turned the question on me.

"Do you work for the CIA? I read that many American journalists are really CIA agents." I wasn't sure she believed my denial. But over a period of weeks she gradually unfolded the history of how she had come to join the Party and what she now felt about it.

"When I was young I was an activist—I always volunteered for everything, staying late in school to help clean the dormitory, speaking up at political study sessions, helping the slower students with their homework. That is the first thing they look for in selecting Party members.

"My family background was good too," she said. "My father was a poor tailor. That was the other thing they demanded in candidates." She was formally admitted to the Party when she was twenty, as a college student.

"Those were happier days, in the 1950s. I believed everything the Party said. I wanted to work to build up my country. We were very patriotic. It was the same as being a Communist. I remember being angry when I saw some foreign tourists aiming their cameras at people pulling carts. It was a shameful thing for China."

Mulan still was very disciplined in her personal life. She rose at 5:30 A.M. each day to jog, then went back to clean the tiny closet-size apartment she shared with her son and husband, and was in her office by 7:30. She was often still there till 9 or 10 P.M. taking care of extra work, I discovered when I called her on the phone.

During the Cultural Revolution, when the army was sent in to take over the ministry where she worked and restore order, she was selected to be one of the five leaders of the ministry, though she was only in her early thirties. That meant, she conceded, that she had been a radical and had been promoted like a "helicopter," in the Chinese expression, jumped over much more senior people. In 1970, when the cadres from her ministry were all sent to labor in the countryside, she remained one of the leaders.

"It was hard being a leader," she told me one day during a walk around the old Summer Palace just west of Peking. "You were supposed to set an example and to serve others. I had to be up at five A.M. when we were in the village, to get everyone out to the fields, then I had to pull carts all day loaded with bricks and bags of grain." One morning she was so sleepy she caught her hand in a threshing machine and severed the tendons in several of her fingers. At night, she said, when everyone else could rest, she had to go to meetings, often till midnight. "We examined people's cases, to determine if they were capitalist roaders or counterrevolutionaries, and we had to listen to people's grievances." Mulan had a four-year-old son—because of her schedule, she had to keep him in a nursery during the week and saw him only on Sundays.

"But I was happy. I believed I was helping my country," she recalled.

There were, however, the beginnings of doubt. "Something terrible happened. Some of the cadres put people accused of being counterrevolutionaries in bags and then slowly beat them to death. Every day I had to work side by side with these cadres and the families of the people who were tortured."

She also got into trouble when she turned down a man's petition to join the Party. "He had no qualifications, but he was very angry and later accused me behind my back of having an affair with another of the leaders. My husband was very upset."

After Mao's death and Deng's ascension, political power in her ministry shifted. Mulan found herself in the wrong faction, isolated, humbled, almost a pariah, though by then she had lost much of her interest in politics.

"The real power is at the top, too far away, what does it matter what we discuss in our meetings?" she said. "I used to put forward suggestions, but they were never acted on, so I've stopped being an activist." Instead, she related, she started finding excuses to skip political meetings or leave early. "I would say my job was very busy. If I couldn't leave, I just sat there and read the newspapers."

Mulan also detected a different spirit in the Party from what she knew in the 1950s—too many people were in it to get back-door privileges for their families. Her office handled large blocks of tickets for movies and plays, and every day dozens of people she barely knew called to ask her for some. "I finally had to put the phone on someone else's desk," she said. "In the old days, we talked about the Party with almost a mystical reverence, we referred to it just as the 'organization.' If you were a Party member, you spoke about leading 'the organization life.' But now the old spirit of sacrifice for the nation is gone."

Mulan hid her feelings. "I live a secret life now. No one knows. There is no room in our Communist society for human feelings. They think we should be made of wood. I can't discuss it with anyone in my *danwei,* that would be too dangerous." Only with a foreigner, who had no connection with the Party, would she share her inner turmoil. What she really wanted to do, she said, was to resign from the Party, but no one did that and she was afraid to go first. It would arouse intense suspicion.

One spring day, after a lengthy meeting she had to attend, Mulan was visibly depressed. Her usual smile had vanished, but she wanted to go for a walk. The Central Committee had just issued a major new set of guidelines for tightening Party discipline; all Communists would have to write confessions of their innermost thoughts; then they would have to undergo a screening by a review panel. If they passed, they would be issued Party cards, something the Chinese Communists had not done in many years. The purpose was to weed out those members whom Deng described in a confidential speech as "below standard." There had been only two million Party members in 1949 when the Communists came to power; now the Party had burgeoned to 38 million members, half of them recruited since the start of the Cultural Revolution in 1966. Deng wanted to retire some of the oldest members, now senile, and get rid of younger ones who had joined through their connections to the radicals. The program wasn't necessarily aimed at Mulan, but she was scared. We decided it was best not to see each other again.

From Mulan and other Chinese, I learned that the attitude of many people toward joining the Party had undergone a profound transformation since the 1950s. Instead of a calling, like the priesthood, it had come to be seen as the quickest, surest way to a better life.

"The first thing when you meet someone and they say they are a Party member, you wonder why," my friend Bing remarked. "What did they have to do to become a member? Sell their souls? Who did they have to turn in?" Among her girl friends, she said, "No one would want to marry a Party member now. They would worry about what kind of man he was."

It was only later that I learned her own husband was a Communist. She was candid about his reasons for joining. "If you are a Party member, there are lots of rewards. You get promoted faster, you are assigned more interesting and sensitive work in your job, and you have a better chance of being sent abroad." He had gotten a cushy job at CAAC, which enabled him to travel overseas, a rare privilege.

There are strategies for getting into the Party, she added. The easiest way for her husband to join was while he was in university, for the Party reserves a quota for new members in each college class. If you haven't been picked before you graduate, it is much harder later—offices have smaller quotas. For peasants the best hope is by joining the army first; the military has the largest of all quotas.

But for ambitious peasant youths who want to join there is also intense psychological pressure. For if a soldier doesn't get into the Party before his first tour of duty is up—three years in the army, four years in the air force, five years in the navy—he may be demobilized and will have lost his chance. Those who fail are sometimes resentful. Bing's father, a general, had told her that at a mustering-out banquet for a group of peasant soldiers, one disgruntled man who had not been accepted into the Party had stolen a hand grenade and hidden it under his bulky uniform jacket. He was sitting at a table with his regimental commander; when the officer rose to propose a farewell toast, the soldier pulled the pin, killing himself and a dozen others.

Admission to the Party is still not easy, Bing added. Her husband had to spend a year on probation, writing confessions nearly every day during that period to report everything he thought and did. "He had to put on a big show of being hardworking and making lots of sacrifices," she recalled. He also had to *pai-ma-pi,* "pat the horse's rump," or curry favor with his Party secretary.

A scholar in the Academy of Social Sciences, though not a Communist himself, deplored this new opportunism in the Party.

"The Party was built on the principle of selflessness," he said in a talk in his cramped fifth-floor walk-up apartment. "That was what enabled the Communists to beat the Kuomintang and to launch our industrialization in the 1950s. It was something all Chinese could be proud of."

The Party was still able to attract talented, capable people, but they no longer were willing to make the personal sacrifices, he said. His younger sister had recently been accepted for membership, but she had refused an assignment to Tibet after finishing college. In the old days no one would dare do that.

"In China, moral leadership has always been considered the basis of good government," he continued, pouring me a cup of steaming tea. "It is like Confucius said—'If a ruler himself is upright, all will go well without orders. But if he himself is not upright, even though he gives orders, they will not be obeyed.' "

This was what had happened in China after the Cultural Revolution—there had been a breakdown in moral authority. In the 1950s and early 1960s, one of the unique features of Chinese communism was Mao's mass line—he mobilized hundreds of millions of people for projects ranging from killing flies and sparrows to building giant dams with shovels and wheelbarrows. Voluntarily or not, everyone took part in weekly, sometimes daily, political study sessions, reading, memorizing, and reciting the latest editorial from the *People's Daily* or quotations from Chairman Mao. In those days, no one could afford to be labeled passive. Prudence dictated even opponents of the regime remain politically conscious. "If you didn't, your leader would make you wear tight shoes," the scholar from the Academy of Social Sciences related—he could make your life uncomfortable.

But by the late 1970s the malaise in the Party—the years of factional quarrels, the persecutions, the quest for special privileges, the twists and turns in the political line—had made popular participation increasingly formal, empty, and ritualistic. The masses retreated into indifference as their best defense.

On one of my early trips to China, in August 1977 to accompany Secretary of State Cyrus R. Vance, I happened to arrive in Canton from Hong Kong on the day the Eleventh Congress of the Chinese Communist Party ended. Rumors had circulated in Hong Kong that a high-level Party gathering was under way because the provincial Party leaders had vanished from public view for several weeks; but Peking had made no official announcement about the Congress, not even acknowledging its existence. Yet that afternoon in Canton, then a drab, crowded city of old buildings with peeling paint built along the muddy Pearl River, people were putting up red flags, colored lanterns, and large banners proclaiming, "Warmly welcome the victorious outcome of the Eleventh Party Congress." This was an important news story for me, and I asked my China Travel Service guide what the results of the congress were, who had been elected to the Politburo, and what decisions had been reached.

"I don't know anything about a Party congress," he said, looking me straight in the face. "There has been no announcement. You can listen to the news on the radio tonight."

Then how did the people know there was a congress and why were they so certain it was victorious? I persisted.

Without a flicker of emotion, he pointed to another red sign. It read,

"Long live the great, glorious and always correct Chinese Communist Party."
"That is how we know it was a success."

At my guide's suggestion, we decided to go to a downtown park that evening where a dance troupe was to perform to celebrate the Party meeting. At precisely 8 P.M., as the national news program began over loudspeakers strung through the park, thousands of firecrackers exploded and the band accompanying the dancers clanged their cymbals. It was impossible to hear a word of the news. Thousands of people were jammed into the park, but few of them seemed intent on hearing the tidings from Peking.

Peking's leaders are acutely aware of this growing disenchantment with their rule. Few Communist regimes have been as blunt about recognizing their own faults. The *People's Daily* in 1980 called it "a crisis of faith" in Marxism. The paper, which is distributed nationally with a circulation of 5.3 million, blamed it on distortions of Marxism by the Gang of Four and the appearance of "some new situations and new questions" for which Marxism does not yet have an answer. Among these, the paper said, is the problem of why capitalism has not yet collapsed, as Marx had predicted, and why most socialist countries are poorer than capitalist ones. These were questions most Chinese I knew were already asking among themselves.

The Party's theoretical journal, *Red Flag,* confessed in another 1980 article, "The Party's prestige is not high—this is a fact." Echoing Lord Acton's dictum that power tends to corrupt, *Red Flag* suggested there may be a "basic difference between a ruling party and an underground or nonruling party. What is the danger to a party after it has assumed power? The danger is that it will degenerate if it works carelessly. After it has assumed power, the party cannot order the masses and must not become the rulers and the ruling class of the old society." It is theoretically possible for a Communist party to degenerate into a fascist party, the journal added. "This is a very serious problem."

The Party seemed to hope that such candor would help recoup its declining prestige. In 1980 and 1981 the Communists also took several steps to try to return to their earlier, more democratic and popular ways. Peking called for an end to the system of lifetime tenure which allowed senile patriarchs to keep their posts in the Party, the government, or the army no matter how infirm or incompetent they became. It instituted limited local elections for people's congresses, the first since 1949. It promulgated China's first criminal code since Liberation to create a more equitable system of justice. And it installed a new team of leaders, including Hu as Party Chairman and Zhao Ziyang as Prime Minister. They succeeded the hapless Hua Guofeng, whose major claim to legitimacy was that a dying Mao had told him, "With you in charge, I'm at ease."

I met Zhao when I went to Sichuan in early 1980 to report on the industrial and agricultural reforms he had introduced there, giving factories more autonomy and peasants a greater say over what they planted. At the time he was only the Party boss of the province, though there were already rumors in Peking that Deng wanted to name him Prime Minister. Before making the trip, I had requested an interview with him, but ranking Chinese officials tend to avoid resident foreign journalists like the plague and I didn't expect to see him.

To my surprise, Zhao not only assented to the interview, he came over to my hotel himself and arrived without the usual retinue of aides. In person the sixty-three-year-old Zhao is unprepossessing. He has a medium build, receding gray hair—which he started to dye after his promotion to Peking—soft brown eyes, and a quiet voice. But part of his appeal is his low-key approach, his modesty, his avoidance of the grand visions and neat ideological solutions that got China into trouble in the past. Explaining his interest in experimenting with market forces and new forms of socialism borrowed from Hungary and Yugoslavia, he said, "In China, we have a saying—'When you cross the river, you grope for the stones.' But you must cross the river. You can't just jump over it. Sometimes things don't work and you have to start again."

But despite the Party's efforts, its reforms haven't rekindled the lost enthusiasm of its earlier years. An American graduate student at Peking University, whose Chinese roommate was a cautious, correct Party member and the daughter of a high cadre, recounted what happened after a campus meeting to distribute copies of the Party's new guidelines for discipline. It was an important document, but when her roommate came back to the dorm she unstapled it and used the pages to cover her books against Peking's dust. Paper is scarce and expensive in China, she explained; she didn't want to waste it.

An investigative team from the Propaganda Department of the Central Committee found that at the South China Teachers College in Hunan one third of the students didn't show up for a compulsory course on Marxism. Others sat in the classroom reading novels, writing letters, or doing their homework for other classes, according to an article in the *Guangming Daily*. The students complained that there wasn't much point in studying Marxism because the line always changed depending on who was in power. To add to the problem, most of the professors teaching the course on Marxism are of low quality, the paper reported. The better ones were purged in past campaigns and now most teachers are scared to deal with the subject.

Even among the country's leaders there is a ferment, an uncertainty, about what Marxism means for China. "We are having trouble defining what our system is," an official in Yunnan province, in the southwest, told an American diplomat visiting there. "We are trying a number of experiments. Those that work, we will call socialism. Those that don't, we will call capitalism."

Deng Xiaoping himself has defined Marxism simply as the principle of "seeking truth from facts." As a corollary to that, he has added, "Practice is the sole criterion of truth." Some older cadres I met abhorred this as reducing socialism to mere pragmatism.

Perhaps to help compensate for the reduced appeal of Marxism, Deng has dusted off the old nationalistic slogan of the reform-minded mandarins of the late nineteenth century who wanted to modernize China to catch up with the West. Their goal was to make China *fu-qiang,* or "rich and strong." In a 1980 meeting with a Rumanian delegation, Deng said concisely, "The purpose of socialism is to make the country rich and strong." At bottom, that is what most Chinese I knew really wanted out of communism.

The most volatile and sensitive issue for the Party has been what to do with the legacy of its Great Helmsman, Mao. For over two decades Mao was a demigod; his cult was China's secular religion. But many urban Chinese had long wearied of his incessant calls for class struggle and despised him for the chaos of the Cultural Revolution. At the large New China bookstore on Wangfujing Street, one of Peking's busiest shopping centers, the central counter opposite the glass front doorway is reserved for Mao's writings. But I noticed on several visits to the store that there were no clerks behind the counter and no customers anywhere around it. Instead, they were lined up to buy traditional Chinese novels or books on studying English and physics, two of the most popular subjects today since they are looked on as a way to get a better job or possibly earn a trip abroad.

A middle-aged college teacher told me that one morning, when she was disappointed with her students' performance on a test, she upbraided them by quoting a well-known essay of Mao's on the need for diligence. It involved a Canadian doctor, Norman Bethune, who had come to China in 1938 and had died serving the Red Army in its guerrilla bases. "We must all learn the spirit of absolute selflessness from Dr. Norman Bethune," Mao had written. But her students snickered.

"After class several of them came up to me," she recalled. " 'Teacher, you are really something, quoting Chairman Mao,' and they laughed."

In the middle of the vast Square of the Gate of Heavenly Peace, bigger than half a dozen football fields, sits Mao's last resting place. The mausoleum is a chunk of white marble, a neoclassical temple transplanted to China, looking more like the Lincoln Memorial in Washington than a traditional Chinese edifice. Only the roof, double-tiered and painted orange, in imitation of the imperial mustard-yellow tiles of the Forbidden City across the square, has a Chinese touch. In defiance of the laws of geomancy, the mausoleum faces north, a bad omen to some Chinese. Four members of the People's

Liberation Army, in long dark-green winter padded coats and fur caps with red stars, guarded the entrance the December day I paid my respects. Mao lies in an inner chamber with a floor of polished black marble, his body encased in a crystal sarcophagus. Only his head and upper chest are visible; the rest is draped with a Chinese Communist Party flag, red with a yellow hammer and sickle. Rumors after he died hinted the government had trouble preserving his body and had to call on the Vietnamese for help—they had earlier enshrined Ho Chi Minh. Mao's face looks very old and tired, the skin drawn and wrinkled, like a man who had an unhappy ending.

In Chinese fashion, visitors are admitted only in groups, not as individuals. You must come with your *danwei.* I was curious to check some facts about the construction of the memorial hall and asked a guard.

"I am a soldier," he replied. "I don't know."

Then I queried several other attendants in civilian dress; they also professed ignorance. They pointed me to a young, pigtailed woman at the entrance with padded shoes and a blue scarf over her head against the cold. She was the official greeter, they said. How long did it take to build the hall and when did it open? I asked, details I had read in the Chinese press several years before but had forgotten.

"I don't know," she said, too, turning away.

Unlike guides elsewhere, she had no briefing to give, and there were no signs or exhibits inside to recount Mao's exploits. The subject was too nettlesome. So the Chairman had become just another dead ancestor whose role was best left ambiguous.

Not long after I left China, the Central Committee issued a lengthy and carefully worded analysis of Mao's life. The document took over a year to prepare. Deng wanted to undercut once and for all those cadres who still harkened to Mao's calls for revolution. But he couldn't let the criticism go too far—if Mao had been wrong for so many years, wasn't the Communist Party itself in error? So the analysis was a compromise. "Comrade Mao Zedong was a great Marxist and a great proletarian revolutionary," it said; it was Mao who led the revolution to triumph in 1949. "It is true that he made gross mistakes during the Cultural Revolution"—he had become increasingly arbitrary, undemocratic, even irrational. "But if we judge his activities as a whole, his contributions to the Chinese revolution far outweigh his mistakes. His merits are primary and his errors secondary."

Yet I wondered how the older cadres, those who had served with Mao felt, whether they were saddened by his sharply reduced stature and this verdict. By lucky chance, on the night before I left China, a friend arranged for me to have dinner with a member of Mao's family. My friend specified we could meet only if I agreed not to divulge the man's identity—he lived a precarious existence—and I assented.

He turned out to be a dignified, reserved middle-aged man with a high forehead and swept-back hair reminiscent of Mao. Whenever he mentioned Mao, it was always as "the Chairman." He wanted to talk with me, he said, because he felt there was misunderstanding about Mao. Mao was not a conservative, he insisted, he was always open-minded. He loved to read books—when he went on tours of the provinces, the one thing he took with him were cartons of books, and his bed was always half covered with unread volumes.

"Let me give you an example," the relative said. "Even in his seventies he became interested in the United States, read about it, and this resulted in the invitation to Nixon to visit China.

"Many cadres now seek privileges for themselves, but the Chairman was always democratic. He lived very simply. Sometimes people did things for him which he didn't know about. Once when he went on a trip, they built a swimming pool in his garden. The Chairman loved to swim, but he was very mad.

"He told his children, 'Don't depend on me, don't depend on others, depend on yourselves.' He told us that when he died, he would leave all his money and possessions to the Party and the state.

"I remember once I went off to do labor on a commune," the relative continued, offering me some peanuts with his chopsticks. "When I came back I was very dirty with long hair and a beard. I was embarrassed about joining the family for dinner, but the Chairman said, 'Good, you look very good.' "

It was true, he added, that Mao and Jiang Qing, the Chairman's fourth wife, really had not gotten along, as the government claimed after Mao died and Miss Jiang was arrested as the ringleader of the Gang of Four. Their troubles started in Yanan in the 1940s, he asserted, and after the Communists' victory in 1949, they had not lived together in Peking as husband and wife.

"Mao didn't see her for long periods of time. At first it was his working schedule. He would work at night and sleep all day. They would have only one meal together a week, Saturday evening dinner. For him it was breakfast.

"Later they separated. When he was in Peking, she would go to the provinces. When he went on a tour, she would come back to the capital. Mao couldn't stand her, all her nagging and her ambitions. In his last years, sometimes he gave orders not to let her in the house. The guards kept her out."

When dinner was finished, Mao's relative wanted to ask me a question. Why, he pondered, was China so backward compared to Japan? One hundred years ago they had been at the same level. "Is it because socialism is not as good as capitalism?" he asked.

It was an awkward situation. I felt embarrassed to evaluate China's adoption of communism in front of a member of Mao's family. But then he answered for me.

"In theory, socialism is excellent," he said. "It provides for economic as well as political democracy. But in practice it has shown weaknesses. We let the state and the bureaucracy grow too strong and prevented the development of individual initiative. China needs to find some way to combine the two systems."

Would the Chairman feel that way? I asked.

"The Chairman was always prepared to learn," he answered.

14. A World Turned Upside Down

上 下 顛 倒

HONG AND WEIDONG

"Victorious, you are a king;
But vanquished, a bandit."
A Chinese adage

He was home on leave from the army. It was a hot August day, and Weidong ("Protect Mao") and another soldier from his regiment had been out drinking. They had consumed two bottles of *bai-jiu,* a potent Chinese version of white lightning with a burning, heavy taste of alcohol, when his companion suggested they look up a very pretty girl he knew named Hong ("Red").

She had a soft oval face, creamy white skin, liquid eyes, and long shiny black hair. Hong was bound to be at home, the friend said, because that was where she had been every day for the past five years since she had pretended to be sick in 1967 and had refused to "volunteer" to be resettled in the countryside like most of her high school classmates. Her teacher had come to her house repeatedly to urge her to go as her patriotic duty. Still she declined. She had also turned down an assignment from her neighborhood committee to work in the local collective laundry. It meant washing clothes by hand, often in cold water, even in the middle of Peking's long winters.

Hong was too proud and too angry to go along with the government's orders. Her father and mother were both professors, intellectuals by Chinese reckoning. They had come from prosperous merchant families, had gone to schools run by foreign missionaries before 1949, and spoke excellent English. Several of her parents' brothers and sisters had gone to college in the United States and Britain and stayed abroad after the Communists' victory. So when the Cultural Revolution broke out, her father was a prime target

—a bourgeois intellectual with "overseas relations," as the radicals put it. Just having a relative outside China was cause for suspicion by the Communists. Radicals in his college accused him of being a counterrevolutionary and put him in what was euphemistically called a "study class" for two years. It wasn't a prison, but he had to spend all his time reading Mao's works, writing confessions about his supposed dealings with foreign agents, and could come home only one day a month.

Hence when Weidong and his friend arrived at Hong's apartment in their army uniforms, red in the face and smelling of liquor, she pushed them out. She had no use for the Communist Party or the People's Liberation Army —especially, she thought, for a soldier who probably came from a family of high cadres, for Weidong was very tall for a Chinese, well over six feet, and only officials could afford to feed their children the milk and meat to help them grow that big.

But Weidong had been taken by her good looks and her coquettish pout when she rebuffed them. He was equally determined and headstrong. His father, in fact, was a former poor peasant who had joined the Red Army in its guerrilla days in Yanan in the 1930s and had risen to become a senior officer in the navy after its creation in 1949. Weidong was a star on the army's basketball team—tall, lean, rawboned, with large hands, an athlete's grace, and clean, handsome features. His voice was deep and resonant, with an air of authority. When he talked, everyone in the room listened. There was also something roguish about him, a boisterousness and bravado, and taken all together, he reminded me of a young Chinese John Wayne. Later I learned "the Duke" was his favorite movie star.

That evening, after it was dark, Weidong returned to Hong's apartment building, climbed over the brick fence around it, and snuck in a back window.

"Why wouldn't you let me in before?" he demanded to know.

Hong was startled. But an elderly woman neighbor, who was a member of the building's public security committee, had chanced to see Weidong slinking into the apartment. She had immediately summoned the police and they arrived within minutes.

"Who are you?" they began by questioning the tall soldier. When he revealed his identity, they called his father to check. Satisfied about his background, the police let Weidong go.

The next day he came back to Hong's to apologize. But she wasn't there. The police had taken her away, her mother said curtly. They gave no reason. For several more days, as long as his leave lasted, Weidong visited Hong's home to see if she had been released. She hadn't.

A month later, when he got another furlough, he came back again. By then, he learned, she had been officially arrested.* The accusation against her was that as the daughter of an intellectual with suspect "overseas relations" she had tried to seduce a soldier and the son of a general. In revolutionary China, where Mao ordained "take class struggle as the key link" and "put politics in command," the old notions of class had been reversed.

Weidong was contrite. He felt guilty about what he had done to Hong and tried to use his father's connections to get her released. He even went to a Peking court and confessed he was to blame. But it was a few months after Lin Biao, the Defense Minister and Mao's designated heir, had tried to assassinate the Chairman, and the police were jittery. Hong ended up spending a year in jail. When the Public Security Bureau finally let her out, she told me later, they warned her she had not been cleared of the charge against her. There just wasn't enough proof. The incident would remain in her dossier.

By now Weidong felt a deep attachment to her. She still had no job and he asked his father to help arrange employment for her. But his parents were suspicious of Hong's family and opposed to his seeing her again.

"They said I would become 'unreliable' in the Party's eyes if I had any relationship with her," Weidong said. "Since I was a boy I had dreamed of going to a military academy and becoming an officer like my father. I had good expectations of being promoted."** But when he continued to see Hong, his commanding officer told him his military career was finished and he was demobilized. The army officer in charge of assigning jobs to veterans made him a mechanic. It was a shocking loss of face for someone with the background and energy and talent of Weidong.

His only consolation was that the girl with the beautiful face had started to like him too. They took a trip hiking in the mountains west of Peking, just the two of them, and they fell in love. Unlike many young Chinese, who look on marriage as a way to enrich themselves, get a better job, or marry into a well-connected family, Hong and Weidong said theirs was a relationship based on real feeling. When he reached twenty-eight and she twenty-five, the legal minimum, they got married. For China, it was an uncommon match, the general's son and the professor's daughter.

I first met them at a party at a diplomat's house. It was Christmas, 1978, and the government had only recently begun its experiment in liberalizing the rules on freedom of expression and contact between Chinese and foreign-

*Chinese law makes a distinction between simple detention and formal arrest. In theory, the police can arrest a person only after they have filed charges against him and obtained a warrant from the prosecutor's office.

**In the Chinese armed forces, officers are selected from among the enlisted men rather than enrolled directly in officers schools from civilian life.

ers. Peking's Democracy Wall was jammed every day with avid readers. Hong had been invited to the reception by some foreign students she knew. But she was pessimistic about how long the era of greater openness would last.

"This is a very unusual opportunity," she confided to me at the end of the evening. "It is unlikely we will have the chance to meet again." She did give me her phone number, however, in a gesture of daring. I was in Peking for only a ten-day trip to mark the normalization of relations between the United States and China, and it wasn't until six months later that the government let *The New York Times* open its bureau and I returned to live full-time in the Chinese capital. One of the first things I did was to try calling Hong. The woman who answered asked me who I was. This presented a dilemma—I didn't want to get her in trouble by mentioning my name or *The Times*—so I said I was an American student from New York and hoped she would get the connection. Hong was not home, the woman then reported. After three more futile phone calls, I was ready to give up. But one day, as I walked out of the hotel at lunchtime, Hong and Weidong were standing on the sidewalk. They had guessed it was me, braved a call to the U.S. Embassy to ask where I was staying, and decided to wait outside the hotel, hoping to catch me.

Hong explained why she had not answered the phone. "The telephone is not in our apartment, but in the room of the people in the public security committee. They report to the police whenever there is a suspicious phone call, especially from a foreigner like you. The police came right over to ask me who you were. I was scared." Only officials have telephones of their own, she said, and all public phones are in shops, offices, or apartments of people who work for the police. It is one of the most basic mechanisms of government control.

Hong and Weidong were in a quandary, they told me. Her mother had arranged a trip to the United States for her where she would visit her mother's sister who lived in New York. The aunt hoped Hong would stay on and go to college in the United States. Mao's pragmatic successors, to increase the number of Chinese able to get a higher education, had instituted a new policy that permitted anyone with relatives overseas and the financial means to support themselves to go abroad to college. It was another turnabout. The Communists were once again recognizing the importance of education, and intellectuals were regaining some of their lost prestige. Suddenly millions of young Chinese dreamed of going to college and studying overseas. It was a marvelous opportunity for Hong.

But she was reluctant to go. Her mother, she admitted, had an ulterior motive. "She doesn't like Weidong—in fact, she hates him," Hong said. Her parents, like Weidong's, had been against their marriage. They didn't like cadres and particularly the children of high cadres, Hong added. Her mother was scheming to break them up.

Later, when I met her mother, a slender, well-preserved middle-aged woman with a brittle manner, I understood. "In 1966, in the Cultural Revolution, the Red Guards in our school came to our apartment and searched it for a whole day," her mother recounted. "They took all our furniture, my jewelry, all our books and records, many of which had been gotten from abroad. They left us with only one set of clothes. They made us carry our books and records down to the courtyard by the armloads. Then they held a bonfire on our campus. It lasted for three days.

"But it was very unfair. Later we learned that many of the most valuable books and records had been taken to warehouses around Peking. There the children of high cadres bought them back for fifteen cents a pound, not per record or book, but per pound.

"Before the Cultural Revolution, we Chinese lived under a great illusion. We believed the Communists could save China and make it prosperous and strong again. People were very idealistic and hardworking. Now people have seen through this, and they have suffered a terrible loss of faith. This is the key to understanding China today. The cadres have become concerned only with their own privileges, the factory workers are lazy, and the young people have lost ten years of schooling and don't have jobs. People have become selfish."

Her mother became more bitter as she spoke. "The great problem today is that there is no public morality. The old Confucian morality was destroyed, now the Communist morality is gone, too."

Although she detested Weidong because of his father's military rank, I found they had more in common than she realized. The Cultural Revolution had made Weidong cynical, too. With his dream of being an army officer shattered by his love for Hong and his role in life reduced to working as a mechanic, Weidong saw little future for himself or other Chinese of his generation.

"Young people now have no sense of purpose, we only *hun-xia-chu*," he said, using a popular expression meaning to muddle through from day to day. "If you give them a job, they will do it, but they won't put any energy into it." His only pleasure in life, apart from Hong, was going to watch American Western movies. Thanks to his father, he still had access to "internal" film shows.

I remarked that many young Americans are also lost and alienated. A surfeit of affluence—of growing up with everything the world has to offer, cars, television sets, comfortable houses—has left American young people without a sense of purpose, with nothing behind them to propel them forward.

"For Chinese, it is the opposite," Weidong commented. "We have something in front of us blocking our way. We can't get around it, the Party." The only hope he could see for China, he said one evening, was war with the Soviet Union. "Then all of China will be destroyed and we can start over."

It was an extraordinary statement for someone whose father was a veteran Communist general. How did his father feel? I asked.

"He is a very dedicated Party man, but he has lapsed into silence," Weidong replied. "When I go home, we don't talk anymore. My father has nothing to say. It is too dangerous for him to say what he thinks about what is happening." Deng Xiaoping had once declared in a confidential talk that China's generals could be divided into three groups, Weidong went on. One third supported Deng's modernization program, with its departures from Maoist orthodoxy, one third didn't care, and one third opposed it. His father was among the conservative third who preferred the old Maoist ways. He expected Deng would put pressure on him to retire, though he was only in his late sixties, still middle-aged in Chinese terms.

His father had bestowed one incalculable privilege on Weidong. Not long before, his father had moved into a large new house built especially for high-ranking generals and had left his comfortable old apartment to Weidong. It had two large bedrooms, a living room, and a toilet and kitchen of its own, far more space and amenities than the three square yards allotted to the average urban resident. On their own, Hong and Weidong would have had to apply to the city housing authority and might have had to wait three to five years for a tiny one-room apartment. On one wall was a black-bordered portrait of Zhou Enlai, modern China's one unblemished popular hero, a Communist with the moderation and subtlety and manners of a Confucian mandarin. On a bookcase was a white plaster bust of the Venus de Milo, covered with clear plastic to ward off the Peking dust. Weidong was an amateur artist, and idealized portraits he had painted of Hong and his father hung from other walls. A Chinese copy of Richard Nixon's book *My Six Crises* lay open on their double bed. Weidong had bought it in the special bookstore for high cadres with his father's identification card. Cartons filled with other books—*The Great Gatsby,* short stories of Mark Twain, traditional Chinese novels—were stacked in corners of the room. Given the political difficulties and shortage of books in China, they had assembled a sizable library.

Weidong was a natural leader. If he had not aroused the regime's suspicions, he might have gone far in the system. Whenever I dropped into their apartment in the evening, there were always three or four of his friends there —young men like him, about thirty, other sons of generals with whom he had grown up and gone to school. They enjoyed listening to him talk. One cold winter night, one of the visitors was a short, crew-cut, boyish-looking cadre in a green army jacket. Weidong introduced him without hesitation as head of the China Youth League branch at one of Peking's main colleges where he was responsible for recruiting new Party members and ensuring good classroom discipline. Was he as cynical as Weidong? I asked. Surely he believed in the Party and Marxism?

Weidong snorted. "He is a Party member, yes. But if he tells you he believes any of that stuff, I'll punch him in the face," and Weidong leapt off the bed where he was sitting and pretended to smack his friend, slamming his right fist into his left palm.

The young cadre laughed, too. "I'll tell you how I came to join the Party. I was in the army, and when it came time to be demobilized, my job assignment officer told me, 'If you join the Party, it will be a lot easier to get a good job. Right now we have some Party members who can't get decent jobs, so if you aren't in the Party, it will be even worse.' "

Does the Party still get good recruits? I asked. "Yes, some, but they join for the wrong reasons. We say they enter the organization but not its ideology. They want the material benefits." Many other people who should be in the Party, to strengthen it, don't want to join. "The hardest thing is, you have to curry favor with your Party secretary all the time. They always say, 'Please express your own opinion, the Party is very democratic.' But if you do, you are in trouble."

Another winter evening, there was a sharp knock on the door and Weidong ushered in a heavyset young man with a pockmarked face clad in a gray greatcoat with a tan scarf thrown around his neck. He was clutching a round bundle wrapped in copies of the *People's Daily*. Weidong introduced him by his nickname, Big China. Inside the package was a Ming dynasty landscape scroll; Big China was selling it on commission for a person he identified only as "the old man." He would not say more because by law all artistic works and antiques must be sold through a state agency so the government can reap the profit. Big China was a closet capitalist.

Weidong ordered the girl friend of another of his visitors to unroll the painting for him while he inspected it from a distance. "Put on your gloves, don't leave fingerprints," he commanded. It proved to be almost five yards long, a delicate depiction of mountains, rivers, and pavilions painted in pastel shades of green and brown. Weidong examined the style, the painter's signature, and several red seals stamped on it and then pronounced it was a sixteenth-century original.

How much? he asked Big China. Five thousand yuan ($3,333) was the answer. "Please give me some face," Weidong countered, the signal for bargaining. Finally they settled on 4,000 yuan ($2,667).

I was incredulous that Weidong could even consider buying it. His salary was only 48 yuan ($32) a month. "It's a great price," Weidong remarked.

"In a state shop, they would sell it to you foreigners for at least 30,000 yuan [$20,000]. But it's not for me, but for my father."

His father had been collecting Chinese art since 1949, when his Red Army division moved into the cities and he confiscated the holdings of several wealthy families. The art was better off in his father's possession, Weidong reasoned, because during the Cultural Revolution no Red Guards had dared to invade his home and destroy the paintings.

"The real power in China is the army, not the Party," Weidong added with a touch of pride. It was a comment I heard from other Chinese.

But in China even generals draw a limited salary, I interjected. The highest income I knew of was 400 yuan ($267) a month. That is true, Weidong agreed, but I was overlooking the host of other perquisites his father received: free housing, a car, driver, servant, orderly, food from military farms. Almost his entire salary went into the bank. "In China today, it's power, not money, that people want." Money by itself can not buy these other privileges.

Weidong's drifting, his marking time, came to an abrupt end a few months later when Hong became pregnant. The first I knew about it was when I stopped by to see them and Hong was holding a tiny tiger-striped kitten on her lap.

"Weidong gave it to me, so I could learn to take care of a baby," she ventured with a smile. In its way, it was still another of his boyish, daring gestures. Keeping cats and dogs is illegal in China's cities. They consume scarce food and the government believes they contribute to filth and disease.

"Having a cat is safer than a dog," Weidong said. "They stay inside where foreigners don't see them. Dogs go outside. What the government can't stand is if foreigners see their regulations aren't being obeyed."

But Weidong had become more serious: he was thinking about his career for the first time since his involvement with Hong had ruined his chance of becoming an army officer. Now he had a family to provide for. With his father's help, he had gotten a post as the lowest level cadre in a foreign trade corporation.

"All he thinks about now is business," Hong said. "He gets up early to go to work and is gone all day long. There isn't time to go to the movies so much anymore."

To her disgust, he was also thinking about joining the Party. "If I was in the Party, I could get promoted faster, get a little extra income, our family would be better off," Weidong said, running his hand over his brush-cut hair. "It's not that I don't care about China, I do, just as much as when I was young and an activist. But now I know what the Party really is." It would not be easy for him to get into the Party, but the atmosphere was more relaxed than in the early 1970s when his trouble with Hong occurred, and he hoped his father's rank and his many friends in the Party would help.

Hong disagreed with his plan. "I am an intellectual. I have always been apolitical. There is no way I can believe in the Party or Marxism. Politics is just the same as it has been since Confucius, a matter of manipulating people." With her stomach swelling, she was wearing one of her husband's large old army jackets—there are no ready-made maternity clothes in China.

Hong had gone out looking for books on child care but couldn't find any in the government bookshops. Pediatrics has only recently become a recognized branch of medicine in China, and most families always depended on folk wisdom passed on from generation to generation. But Hong had borrowed a volume from her father's college library that turned out to have been written by an American physician. Was the author any good? she asked me. It was Dr. Spock.

After their baby was born, I dropped by to see the new family, bringing a case of American disposable paper diapers, an invention they had never seen. Weidong had hired an *a-yi* for 20 yuan ($13) a month to help take care of the baby and wash the endless train of cloth diapers in their sink.

Hong, who had taken to wearing a hint of bright-red lipstick and darkening her eyebrows, in keeping with the gradual liberalization of the period, was enjoying being a mother. Before the baby was born, they had signed a pledge to have only one child. It was part of the government's stringent new campaign to reduce China's birth rate to zero by the year 2000. "There was a lot of pressure on us to sign from the neighborhood committee and our workplaces," Hong said. "They kept coming around to talk about it. We really couldn't refuse." Weidong was disappointed when their only baby turned out to be a girl; like most Chinese, he wanted a boy. But in exchange for their promise, Hong was granted six months of paid maternity leave from the ministry where she had finally gotten a job. She was employed as a translator. During the Cultural Revolution, when she stayed at home and had nothing to do, her parents taught her English so she would at least have some skill.

Now Hong wished she didn't have to go back to work. "If it was permitted, I'd just stay here after my leave is up and be a mother." It was a sentiment I heard from many Chinese women who face the opposite dilemma from American females. They don't confront a choice between career or family—they must work, by law.

Hong had also cut her long hair and gotten it permed, as many Chinese women began to do after the arrest of Jiang Qing. Mao's widow had demanded proletarian purity in hair styles as in everything else—only pigtails or the short, chopped, bowl cut were allowed. "I liked it long myself, but Weidong wanted me to get it curled, he said it looked more modern," Hong explained. On the bottom shelf of their bookcase, I noticed, was a set of plastic hair curlers, the ultimate bourgeois artifact, a sign of the changing times in China.

With a new career at stake, Weidong became more circumspect about our meeting. When I invited them over to our apartment for dinner, he took the precaution of first calling a friend who worked in the Public Security Bureau to see if I was on the list of foreigners being watched by the police. "We are very close, I can ask him anything," Weidong said. I had been on the list for a time, it transpired, but now I was off it. Weidong didn't offer any explanation, but I was safe.

We arranged the date for the meal over the phone. When I called his new office, another man answered and for a moment I hesitated. He began with the usual question, "Where are you?"

"I am an old friend of Weidong's from out of town," I responded, trying to hide the tremor in my voice.

I could hear him shout across the office, "There's a friend of yours from Shandong on the phone." I was both relieved and flattered. I had been mistaken for a Chinese. But Weidong laughed at me later. A Shandong accent is one of the worst in China, he said.

That evening, when Hong and Weidong came over, he played guns with Ethan, hiding in back of the sofa and popping out from behind a wall. "When you grow up, you should become a soldier," Weidong counseled him with nostaligia for his own lost dream.

Weidong had been under growing pressure from the city housing office to vacate the apartment his father had left him, he told me. "The other people in the building have been complaining. They say we have such a huge home for only the three of us when they have families of five or six living in a single room. They say it is only because I am the son of a high cadre that I can live like this. But I'm not going to move out. They can do what they want, they will have to throw me out." It sounded like his old bravado, but he was serious.

Eventually, the city government had given him a ten-day deadline. If he wasn't out, they would evict him. On the crucial day, Weidong stayed home from work. He had invited a group of a dozen friends over, "the biggest, meanest, toughest boys I could find."

At the appointed hour, a truck from the local housing office appeared with a cadre. But the official wasn't prepared for a fight and left. It was another lesson for me. In a totalitarian society, the Chinese Communists often relied on persuasion in dealing with their citizens. Mao had believed it was the most democratic and effective technique. But after the popular loss of faith in the Party in the Cultural Revolution, many people were no longer willing to cooperate; it often left the government paralyzed and impotent, an authoritarian country with an authority crisis.

"The people say we children of high cadres stink, with all our privileges," Weidong said. "But we don't have anywhere else to move to. I can't just put my family out in the cold." He, too, had become a survivor, battling the system and finally making it work for him.

PART

4

PERSUASIONS

—

15. Soldiers in the Grass

THE CONTROL APPARATUS

"The dictatorship of the proletariat is ravenous, more fearsome than the dictatorship of the bourgeoisie. In a bourgeois society, one can run when one violates the law, but when society is so tightly organized, where can one run to? There is no place to vent one's grief and no place to submit an appeal. . . . In our society, there is indeed the phenomenon that men are not treated as men."

Zhou Yang, Deputy Director of the Party Propaganda Department, 1966

Using the telephone in China, I learned on my first day in residence, requires a special technique—not in dialing the number, but in eliciting a response from the person you are trying to reach. I had just arrived in Peking and was calling the personnel office of the Diplomatic Services Bureau to inquire about hiring a Chinese assistant for *The New York Times*. The conversation went like this:

"Hello, is this the personnel office?"

"I'm not too clear," said a diffident voice.

"Is there anyone there who knows if this is the personnel office?" I tried again.

"They've just gone out," the voice answered. "What do you want?"

"I'm the new correspondent of *The New York Times* and want to hire an assistant. Who do I contact?"

"I'm not too clear," the voice said, retreating once more.

"Can I make an appointment to come over and talk to someone in your office about an assistant?" I said, trying a new tack.

"Please give me your phone number."

"Will someone call me back later?" I asked, my hopes by this time fading.

"I'm not too clear." With that, the voice hung up.

It was my first taste of the Chinese national mania for security and secrecy. Rule number one in making a telephone call, I learned, is never give out any information—it could be a state secret and get you in trouble. To the Communists, who fought their way to power as clandestine guerrillas, this originally had a useful purpose. But the lengths to which people go to avoid identifying themselves or divulging facts on the phone often reach comical proportions. When one Chinese calls another, the person answering the telephone always begins by saying *"wei,"* an all-purpose, neutral response. Even if you are calling an office, like the Information Department of the Foreign Ministry, the official government spokesman, the clerk who picks up the phone never answers by saying "This is the Information Department." It is up to the caller to guess whether he has dialed correctly.

But to add to the confusion, most times the person who initiated the call is also unwilling to identify himself. Instead of saying "This is Lao Wang calling" or "This is the Academy of Social Sciences," the caller will only say *"wei"* also. So neither party can be sure whom they are talking to until one finally relents and takes the daring step of giving out their organization or name. This sparring can consume several minutes. An exasperated American businessman told me that one slow afternoon he decided to play a game. He dialed numbers at random and said only *"wei,"* counting how many times the person answering would chime in with a *"wei"* of his own till he eventually gave up. The highest number of *"wei's"* he reached was thirty-four.

The same rule of discretion applies to important buildings. There is no sign in front of Zhongnanhai, the tall red-walled compound next to the Forbidden City where the top Party and government leaders work. There is no plaque to identify the drab yellow-brick building in the western suburbs of Peking that houses the Central Party School. In Shanghai, I noticed, there is not even a sign outside the imposing gothic Jinjiang Hotel, now largely reserved for foreign tourists. If you don't know what the building is already, it's none of your business.

Throughout China most offices, factories, schools, and even apartment buildings have walls around them and guards at the gates. Outside the new, whitewashed, walled compound of the *People's Daily,* two sentries of the People's Liberation Army stand guard with rifles. Everyone going both in and out must show a special work pass from the paper. There are uniformed guards now in the lobby of *The New York Times,* a result of recurrent bomb threats during the political turbulence of the late 1960s. But in China the reason for security is different. When I asked a tall, gaunt editor of the *People's Daily* why they needed so much protection, he replied, "Because it is one of the most secret places in China. Much of the information we handle is secret."

The Peking Hotel does not have a wall, but it does have its own company of army sentries who live in barracks near the hotel. Sometimes on Sunday mornings they woke me at 6 A.M. by practicing goose-step marching or the Chinese version of judo on the narrow street behind the hotel where my room faced. The shouts of fifty or sixty men yelling *"sha"* (kill) and stamping their feet in unison aren't conducive to sleep. When Jan Wong moved into her own new apartment building, her Chinese friends were delighted that it didn't have a fence or gatekeeper. That meant they could visit her without having to register and disclose their identity. Hoping this would be permanent, Jan asked the building manager if there were plans to erect a wall.

"Don't worry," he replied, misunderstanding her intention. "As soon as the two other high-rises in the compound are done we'll get on to building the wall and put in a gatekeeper. It will be very safe."

This passion for security sometimes reaches the point of being a danger itself, as I discovered when I often went out around midnight to file stories for my paper at the cable office, after the New China News Agency had finally released its daily bulletin. Late at night the employees in the Peking Hotel not only locked the fire exits and gradually shut off all the eight elevators, they also for a period began barricading the only internal stairway. I never found out why, but it was done with great care. The doors to the stairs were tied with rope and then tables and chairs piled in front of them. It was a good precaution against unauthorized entry, if someone managed to slip past the army sentries on the street and the Public Security Bureau guards at the door. But what about fires? Several times when I went to the movies or drama performances and decided to leave early, I found that all the doors had been padlocked, from the outside. Once when I protested to a guard, he reassured me that it was to keep people without tickets from crashing the show.

A professor at one of Peking's universities laughed when I recounted my complaints to him about these precautions. He invited me for a half-mile walk down the Avenue of Eternal Tranquility to the western wall of the old Forbidden City. There, running for several hundred yards, was a three-story building that looked like part of the palace, with the same madder-rose walls and mustard-yellow tiled roof. But my companion urged me to look closer. The windows on the west side of the building, which faced across the street to the Party and government headquarters in the Zhongnanhai compound, were only painted to look like windows; the whole edifice in fact was a facade. In 1973, the professor related, when the new seventeen-story wing of the Peking Hotel was completed, the Public Security Bureau discovered to its horror that a guest, looking west, could peer down across the Forbidden City and into the secret recesses of Zhongnanhai—if he had very strong binoculars. Wang Dongxing, then head of Mao's Praetorian Guard, a special army division known only by its numerical designation as the 8341 unit, devised the idea of putting up the fake palace building as a security screen. "It was outrageous," the professor lamented, "squandering millions of yuan on that hoax when satellites can look right down and take photos from the sky. It shows how well-informed some of our leaders are."

But such precautions are only the outer signs of an all-encompassing control apparatus, as intricate as the microscopic patterns etched on a silicon chip. Foreigners who visit China, including some experienced in traveling elsewhere in the Communist world, often come away saying proudly that they were able to walk wherever they wanted, poking down old lanes, looking into people's houses, without being followed. China really isn't a police state after all, they conclude. But an American who has lived in Peking since before 1949 scoffed at their naïveté. The control system operates the other way around, he explained, from the inside out, for the government has organized society as a security system as much as it is a social or economic system. It is built on three overlapping and mutually reinforcing components: the *danwei,* or workplace, the street committee, and the "small group" where political study sessions are held. "The Communists have created such a thorough organization, it is like radar, it picks you up wherever you go," the veteran American resident observed.

During a visit to the smog-bound industrial city of Wuhan on the Yangtze River, I looked up an American scholar who was doing research there at the Central China Normal Institute. To my surprise there was no gatehouse or guard at the school entrance—security is often more lax outside Peking—so I just drove in my taxi through the campus to the brick building on a hill where the American, Michael Gassiter, was living.

A few minutes after my arrival, the phone rang. I could hear a loud woman's voice ask, "Do you have a foreigner visiting you?" She did not identify herself, but when Gassiter answered in the affirmative, she probed further. "Is he an American reporter? We need to know."

It was Mrs. Zhou, said Gassiter, a specialist on China's 1911 Revolution. He recognized her voice. She was the cadre in the college security section assigned to watch him. I had not been overtly followed, but her intelligence was excellent. Everyone in the school, everyone who belonged to that *danwei,* was required to report to the security section when a stranger appeared on campus, and someone had glimpsed me arriving.

Gassiter was already accustomed to the constant monitoring of his daily activity. "If I go downtown to go shopping, the next day Mrs. Zhou will say to me, 'I suppose you went into town. I suppose you went to the department store. I suppose you bought two shirts.'"

Every Chinese, as discussed earlier, belongs to a *danwei* through his office, factory, school, or commune. Although technically a person's place of work, the *danwei* also often provides the housing where a Chinese lives, the school where his children get an education, clinics for when he gets sick, and ration cards for his rice, cooking oil, and soap. Before a Chinese can get married, he must get permission from the Party secretary of his *danwei;* if a couple want to get divorced, their *danwei* must first approve.

In a sealed envelope in the personnel section of each *danwei* is a confidential dossier for every employee. It contains not only the normal elements of biography—a person's education and work record—but also any political charges made against him by informers in the past and the Party's evaluation of the individual as an activist, for example, or a suspected counterrevolutionary. In addition, in keeping with the Communists' "bloodline" theory, the file lists the person's class background for three generations, whether his grandfather and father were landlords and capitalists or poor peasants and workers.

"Your dossier is strictly secret, only the cadres know what is in it," said a taciturn electrician in his early thirties. "You yourself can never find out." During the Cultural Revolution, though he himself was a Red Guard, he was labeled a Kuomintang agent and spent two years in jail. "Someone in another Red Guard faction must have made the charge against me, but I could never find out who or what it was," he said.

Before anyone can be transferred from one city to another, or from one job to another, he added, you must have a letter from your *danwei* confirming that your dossier has already been forwarded to your new unit. Your *danwei* also controls your right to travel. Before a Chinese can make a trip from his city or village that will take more than a day, he must get approval from the Party secretary of his *danwei,* like a soldier in a Western country getting a pass. He must come up with a concrete reason for needing leave, like a sick parent, because the only regular vacation time in China is six national holidays a year. To enforce this restriction, there are policemen at checkpoints on the main roads leading into Peking and other large cities who stop anyone they don't recognize. If a traveler wants to get a hotel room, he must first present a letter from his *danwei.* This is recorded and his name sent to the local police station.

It is difficult for foreigners to appreciate how much control this system gives the authorities over Chinese, but an American woman graduate student at Peking University related an incident that brought the totality of it home to her. It was soon after she arrived from her own college in the Midwest and she was shocked by the primitive living conditions on campus—running water only two hours a day, greasy, inedible food. So she had written a vivid description of her life to her husband, who was still back in the United States.

A few hours after she mailed the letter, the proctor in charge of foreign students at the school knocked on her door.

"May I talk with you?" he inquired politely. "Are you having any difficulty in China?" He then proceeded to quote her letter verbatim.

Not long after, another American student she knew received a letter from his girl friend in the United States. The letter was in good condition, except that the last page was in Danish. The proctor had made a mistake. "After that I knew what a *danwei* meant," the American woman said. "It's like a womb, you can never escape from it."

Chinese friends told me the Public Security Bureau maintains its own agents in the post office to open mail. China's original 1954 constitution guaranteed "privacy of correspondence," but this provision was dropped in the 1975 and 1978 revisions of the constitution. All letters I received mailed from inside China had been torn at the corners, opening a tiny slit through which an experienced operative could slip out the contents by first rolling it up with a round instrument like a pen, my acquaintances added.

Another part of the *danwei* organization in the universities is the "class monitor," a Party member whose job is to ensure political rectitude and discipline. When Jan Wong was at Peking University in the mid-1970s, the monitor assigned to her class in the history department was a former peasant in his late twenties, Pan Qingde (Qingde means "Celebration of Virtue"). With a square face, even white teeth, crew cut, and clean features, he reminded Jan of the movie stars typed to play the young hero in Chinese films. Pan stayed with her class for its entire three years on campus, sitting in on their courses and living in the dorm with the students, though he had his own private room. Some of her classmates liked to practice their English with Jan, but, she learned later, Pan had warned them, "I'm not against studying English, but the main thing we should do at school is engage in class struggle." At the time, Jan admitted, she had looked up to Pan as the Party leader in the class and entrusted him with confidences about her romance with Norman Shulman, an American who had lived in Peking since 1965. What she didn't know was that Pan suspected her of being a "secret agent" because she was an overseas Chinese and often spoke out frankly in political meetings. He had her Chinese roommate report every time Norman visited her and passed along the information to Norman's *danwei,* trying to stop their affair. When Jan and Norman decided to get married, Jan gave the invitations to their wedding party to Pan to hand out to her classmates. She felt wounded when not a single one of them showed up. It wasn't until four years later that one of her friends told her Pan had not distributed the cards.

If the *danwei* exercises control over Chinese in their workplaces, the street committee provides the government with a mechanism to watch them at home. In the five-story concrete building where my friends Hong and Wei-dong lived, the representative to the local street committee was a rotund, graying, illiterate woman in her fifties named Ma whose husband had been a poor waiter in a restaurant before 1949. Mrs. Ma was not a Party member, but she was energetic, shrewd, and had carefully cultivated good relations with the police by offering them a cup of tea or a cigarette whenever they happened to stop by the building. In time, at the annual meeting of all the adults in the building, Mrs. Ma was put forward by the neighborhood office, the lowest level of government, as the official candidate for street committee member. The ballot was not secret, and everyone knew whom they were supposed to vote for, Weidong related. Mrs. Ma won all the votes.

In action, Mrs. Ma was a cross between a building superintendent, police informant, social worker, and union-hall hiring boss. The powers of the street committee are not codified in law, for they are considered representatives of the "masses" rather than the police, but that only gives them more authority, Weidong said.

"Their most terrifying power is that they can search your house whenever they want," Weidong related. "The police are supposed to have a warrant, but the street committee cadres can come in when they please." Usually three or four members of the street committee, middle-aged women like Mrs. Ma, would just barge in without knocking after midnight when Hong and Wei-dong were asleep. "Their excuse is that they are here to inspect our *hu-kou,*" the household registration certificate. The street committee was checking for any people living in Peking illegally from the countryside, relatives of the family, perhaps, or rusticated youth who had snuck back into the capital. "I give them our certificates, but then they always look around the apartment and examine anything they are interested in.

"If we have friends over, even for dinner, Mrs. Ma may walk in and ask who they are," Hong interjected. "It is very humiliating. If you don't cooper-ate, she can call the police and they will come over and ask the same ques-tions." Once when Hong and Weidong quarreled late at night, Mrs. Ma stopped by the next day to chastise them for not resolving their domestic problems. "There is no way to be alone, she even watches what time we go to bed," Hong complained. "We are like caged animals."

Mrs. Ma also keeps a strict eye on the residents' neatness and sometimes reprimanded Hong for not washing the dishes or sweeping the floors. Often during the winter, when dusk falls early, Mrs. Ma and the other street committee cadres would hide in the unlighted entryways to the buildings to watch for strangers, Weidong cautioned me. He had seen her carrying a club. For me, it gave each of my nocturnal visits to their house an added and unwelcome sense of adventure. One evening, when walking through a dark field toward their apartment, I was accosted by two young men in ordinary blue workers' clothes. They demanded to know what my *danwei* was and what I was doing in the area. I offered the fiction that I was a foreign teacher on my way to visit the home of one of my students. Weidong explained that they were members of the local urban militia, another link in the security network.

The street committee cadres are not paid a regular salary, but they can count on small gifts of meat, vegetables, and rice from residents who want to keep on their good side. More important, their posts put them in position to help their families and friends, for it is the street committee that passes on recommendations about job assignments to the city labor department for unemployed young people in the neighborhood. It is also the street committee that advises the municipal housing office about which families need new quarters.

"Just look around and see whose children come back first from the countryside and get good jobs, and you'll know who the street committee people are," Weidong said.

In recent years the street committee has gained a further and extraordinary power—the right to decide which couples in the neighborhood may have children. This prerogative is part of the government's tough new birth-control campaign that aims to reduce China's rate of population increase to zero by the year 2000 by encouraging families to limit themselves to one child. Under the drive, each province and city has been awarded quotas for the number of babies they are allowed to sire per year, and the street committee then determines which families may use the quotas.

"We give first preference to couples without children," said Mrs. Tian, another energetic middle-aged woman street committee member I got to know. She took pride in her job and pointed out that she had helped establish a small cooperative for unemployed youngsters in her building making soles for shoes. She also made sure that elderly people in the building without children to support them got their small monthly welfare subsidies. But she took a firm attitude toward birth control.

"If a family already has one child, we ask them to wait at least four years before having another, or better, not to have a second baby. If a couple already has two children or more, we tell them not to have any more."

For those who agree to have only one baby there is a package of rewards: a monthly bonus of five yuan ($3.30) for each parent until the child reaches fourteen (or about 8 percent extra pay for an average urban worker), preference for their child in school enrollment, and, theoretically, the right to housing space normally allotted to a family of four.

Mrs. Tian was frank about how her street committee administered the program. "We assign a person to keep track of each woman's menstrual cycle. If someone misses her period and isn't scheduled to have a baby, we tell her to have an abortion. There isn't room for liberalism on such an issue."

The reason for this stringent program, the most ambitious family-limitation plan in history, is the dismal arithmetic of China's population figures. In A.D. 2, when China's first census was taken, there were 59.6 million people in the country; in 1840, 412 million, and in 1949, 540 million. In other words, it took about 4,000 years of recorded history for China to reach its first 500 million people. But in the past three decades, under Communist rule, the population has almost doubled to one billion, all in a country only slightly larger than the United States. In the early 1950s a respected economist, Ma Yinchu, warned that the country's population was expanding too fast and would interfere with China's economic growth. For his temerity in challenging the Marxist belief that more people mean more production, Ma was attacked and purged from his job as president of Peking University. (Only in 1979, at the age of ninety-eight, was he rehabilitated and named honorary chancellor of the school again.) With so many births since 1949, Peking calculates there are 20 million people a year reaching the marriageable age and that, even if everyone accepts the one-child family, the population will still climb to 1.2 billion by the turn of the century. After that, the government would like to see the total decline to 700 million before it gradually eases its restrictions.

Chinese government figures show that the I.U.D., or intrauterine device, is the most widely used method of birth control, accounting for 50 percent of all contraceptive practice. Sterilization is the next most common form, accounting for 30 percent, with female sterilizations outnumbering male sterilizations by ten to one nationwide, though the procedure for men is simpler to perform. China has also developed its own range of oral contraceptive pills, including a highly publicized experimental male pill made from a component of cotton seed oil, gossypol. The male pill was developed after an investigation of perplexing symptoms, including infertility and cardiac irregularities, which beset peasants in a cotton-growing area of Henan province, in north China.

Peking has not released national figures on the number of abortions a year, but in many communes I visited they outnumbered live births. Since Peking first instituted its serious birth-control campaign in the early 1970s, the rate of population increase has already fallen dramatically, especially in the cities. From its high point of 2.34 percent a year in 1971, the growth rate dropped to 1.2 percent in 1980. But that still fell short of the government's target of less than 1 percent a year. The real question remains whether the peasants, who make up 80 percent of the country, will accept having only one child when they know from experience that under China's economic system larger families tend to earn greater incomes. On a visit to the Xihong production brigade near Shanghai, I saw one technique the government is using to try to break this resistance. Pasted on a wall of the brigade's clinic was a large pink chart that displayed precisely how each local cadre was complying with the campaign. Of the brigade's twenty-nine officials (twenty-seven of them men), ten men had had vasectomies. Fourteen other cadres or their wives were using I.U.D.s or pills. Of the remaining five, three were too young to get married under China's policy of delayed wedlock, one had no children, and the other, a refractory type, had three children and wasn't taking any precautions. Aren't the cadres embarrassed by this public accounting of their private sexual decisions? I quizzed the brigade head. "Not at all," he replied with a diplomatic smile.

This constant exposure to public scrutiny and peer pressure makes life in China like living in an army barracks. I was reminded of this on my overnight train ride from Shanghai to Peking with Ding, the stocky drill sergeant conductor who tried her best to keep me comfortable and segregated from the Chinese passengers. The train was due to arrive in Peking at 6:10 A.M., much too early for my taste, but at 4:35 A.M. Comrade Ding used her passkey to open the door to my compartment and sound reveille.

"Time to get up," she said cheerfully, flipping on the light in the darkened room. "Wash your face." It was a clear command, but when I looked at my watch and saw the time, with still an hour and a half to go before we reached our destination, my decadent bourgeois body wanted to go back to sleep and I turned off the light.

Ten minutes later, when I failed to appear, Ding returned, opening the door again without a knock and switching on the light. "You'd better hurry, go to the toilet," she barked.

Why now? I implored her, rubbing my eyes. It isn't even 5 A.M. and we have well over an hour to go. "We will be locking the toilet at five thirty when we get close to Peking," she replied, closing off my line of retreat. "Here are your clothes"—and she reached up and took my shirt, pants, and sweater off the top bunk where I had put them.

This time I obeyed and stumbled down the corridor to the toilet. But it was locked. Comrade Ding rushed after me to open it.

"We keep it locked so the people in the next car won't use it," she explained. The adjoining coach was "hard berth," for the masses, jammed with triple-decker hard wooden bunk beds lining an open, smoke-filled corridor. I was traveling "soft berth," in a private compartment for four people with lace curtains and thick mattresses, the section reserved for cadres and foreigners.

By the time I had shaved and returned to my more opulent quarters, the loudspeakers started, to the stirring tune of "The East Is Red."

"Good morning," said a bright, soothing woman's voice from the black round box just above my head. "Today is Tuesday. We will now commen our broadcast. Our train will soon come to its final stop, our service personne are already starting to clean up the train for hygienic purposes. Everyone should go to the toilet, brush your teeth, and fold your blankets."

The radio announcer was like a combination of a disc jockey and catechist. Soon she began reading the morning's news and political lessons, quoting an editorial from the *People's Daily* on the need to work hard to increase grain production. "We must always remember that Chairman Mao taught us to 'take grain as the key link,' " she intoned. Generally I like listening to the news; it is my profession. But this was too early and I searched for a button to turn off the voice. There wasn't any. After the news, the announcer then recited the day's train schedule from Peking, for the benefit of connecting passengers. I stopped counting after the twentieth train. She also had useful advice on which way to walk when disembarking from the train and what the bus routes of the capital were.

Amid all her statistics, there was one she didn't rattle off that morning that kept popping into my head. A New China News Agency article I read when I first began working in Hong Kong in 1975 reported that there were 106 million loudspeakers in the Chinese countryside. They formed a network that gave the government direct access to 70 percent of all the homes of peasants. The article didn't say how many loudspeakers there are in the cities, but certainly a few million more would be a modest number. And judging from the peasants' homes I have sat in when the day's broadcast was beamed over the air, few of them had knobs that allow the listener the privilege of extinguishing the sound. China is a captive audience of hundreds of millions of people.

It has become commonplace among Sinologists to say that the Communists have combined the techniques of modern totalitarianism, like the loudspeaker network, with the traditional Chinese tendency toward conformity. Explanations repeated too often have a way of losing their force, which in this case would be too bad, because this one is still a cogent insight into how Peking's control apparatus works. There is no exact equivalent in Chinese for the word "conformity," for it is only a person doing what is expected, showing understanding of human relations and the *li,* the old laws of ritual and etiquette. Unlike the West, where we have glorified the individual, in China conformity enjoyed social approval. My friend Bing, the woman who as a teen-ager denounced her father, offered a series of Chinese aphorisms on the subject: " 'A tall tree will be crushed by the wind; a rock that sticks out on the riverbank will be washed by the current.' . . . That is what we were brought up on," she added, "not to show our talents. Instead you should be 'worn smooth like a cobblestone.' People are supposed to learn to have 'eight

329

faces polished like jade,' " meaning to be all things to all people. "Your expression should be unreadable."

It is this quiescent quality, this tendency toward compromise and conformity, which sometimes leads foreigners to think the Chinese are inscrutable. I remember on my tour of the United States with the group of Chinese journalists in 1972 a sweltering August afternoon when we stopped for gas on an interstate highway. While our car was parked at the gas pump, the three Chinese reporters announced they would go to the nearby Howard Johnson's restaurant and buy us ice-cream cones. Fifteen minutes later, when they hadn't returned, I went inside to find out what had happened. They were locked in a mutually uncomprehending discussion with the soda-fountain waitress. They had asked for ice-cream cones, but she had pointed to the board behind her listing all the available flavors. Which kind do you want? she asked. They couldn't bring themselves to express personal preferences. "Any flavor will do, just make them all the same," one of the newsmen finally said.

The great issue in Chinese philosophy has not been what is truth, or the difference between good and evil, but how the ruler should govern wisely and ensure that the people live harmoniously, accepting compromise and conformity. For Confucius the answer lay in education—he believed that everyone could be reformed through proper ethical schooling. "The cultivation of the person depends on rectifying the mind," he taught his disciples.

The Communists shrewdly exploited this tradition to try to transform the thinking of the nation and create a new socialist man. Their weapon was political study, which became another of their control mechanisms. Borrowing also from Lenin's ideas about small, tightly organized Party cells, the Communists in their cave headquarters in Yanan in the early 1940s worked out a technique to indoctrinate the thousands of disparate new adherents that were flocking to their cause: young nationalistic students, older intellectuals, poor illiterate peasants, and former warlord and Kuomintang troops. Everyone was divided into small groups, ten was a good number, and then spent several months undergoing intensive "thought reform," as the Communists called it. First came a period of study of assigned Party documents, then mutual criticism of their past attitudes and activities, and finally a time for submission and rebirth where each individual had to write and rewrite his personal confession until it was accepted by the Party. This process resembled a religious conversion, like our own revival meetings, but with added elements of physical isolation, psychotherapy, manipulation of a person's guilt, and often real terror. In the early 1950s, when the Communists had the whole country to govern, they applied this system to millions of other Chinese in special large "revolutionary" colleges they established.

By the time I arrived in China in the late 1970s, however, after the cataclysms of the Great Leap Forward and the Cultural Revolution, political study had become much less intensive, more formal, and often only a hollow ritual. As the psychiatrist Robert Lifton observed in his 1961 book on thought reform, it was subject to a law of diminishing conversions.* "Repeated attempts to reform the same man are more likely to increase his hostility . . . than to purge him of his 'incorrect' thoughts." The balance between genuine enthusiasm and coercion gradually shifted to the latter, Lifton concluded.

At Bing's college in Peking, the students now have only two hours of political study a week, which are held on Saturday afternoons in their *xiao-xu,* or "small groups," a permanent subdivision of their class. "In theory that is what we do," Bing told me on a warm Saturday noontime when we met for lunch, "but actually many of the students don't go at all anymore or are put to work cleaning up the dorm. If they have to go, some of my friends knit sweaters to kill the time." Only when there is an important new Central Committee document to be read out do people take a real interest, Bing added, since it is likely to contain major political or economic news that won't show up in the newspapers until much later, if at all.

At the end of each semester all the students must still write out a "summing up," a personal report card on their behavior. "In the past you had to be frank and describe your inner thoughts. They said everybody has three levels of consciousness. The first is the one you thought about yourself, your everyday feelings. The second level is the things you tell only your closest friends. The third is feelings you hide even from yourself, your unconscious. This is what you were supposed to report. It was very scary in those days.

"You were also supposed to be very hard on yourself, to tell about your failures," Bing continued. "It was a matter of loyalty to Chairman Mao and it was voluntary and sincere. But nowadays people just lie or emphasize their achievements.

"Last semester, for example, I wrote, 'I have been working very hard to study the thoughts of Chairman Mao.' That was not true, of course. Then I said, 'I took part in political study sessions very actively.' That was also not true. Finally I wrote, 'I studied very hard for my classes.' That was true.

"You have to read these out loud in front of your small group. The other students must comment on them, guided by the teacher, who is a Party member. In the past the others would be very critical of you, but no more. People are afraid that if they speak out, in the next campaign you will find something to use against them. That is our lesson from the Cultural Revolution."

*Robert Jay Lifton, *Thought Reform and the Psychology of Totalism* (New York: W. W. Norton and Co., 1961), p. 412.

If a student makes an error, he still has to write out a self-criticism, but this is used more for punishment now than as part of an effort to convert the sinner, as it was in the past. "One time when I lost my plastic college identification badge, I had to write a confession saying how inconsiderate it was because someone who was not a student could sneak onto campus," Bing said. With that, she picked up a copy of a book I had lent her, *The White Album* by Joan Didion, and announced, "I'm off to make revolution." I doubted she was headed for her Saturday afternoon political study session.

But the process still retains some of its rigor for Party members. Guo was a senior at Peking University who had been a factory worker before passing the college entrance exam and had a wife at home who was also a worker. At school he met and fell in love with a woman in his class who, like him, was a Party member. Unfortunately for Guo, one weekend his wife found a note from his girl friend that he had carelessly left in his pocket. She was furious and reported them to the college authorities. Their Party branch called a meeting where they both had to make self-criticisms, orally and in writing, and promise never to see each other again. An acquaintance at Peking University who told me about the affair said that if they hadn't confessed, they would have been expelled from school and their careers ruined.

Of all the examples of how the Communists control their people, the one that impressed and horrified me the most—perhaps because for much of my time in China I had to live apart from my family—was the casual, routine way Peking assigns husbands and wives to work in different parts of the country. The left-wing magazine *Cheng Ming* in Hong Kong once estimated that there are eight million people in China who have been forced to live separated from their spouses because of their jobs, two million of them cadres and six million ordinary workers and office employees. There is no official rationale for it, except that it is the way the labor offices have decided to assign people, for the convenience of the state.

Shen is a tall, thin, bespectacled man in his mid-forties with thinning hair and an anxious expression in the corners of his eyes. When I first met him, I thought he was a bachelor. He lived by himself in the dormitory of his scientific institute, with only a narrow bed and a trunk in which he kept his few possessions. Most days he also ate all his meals in the institute's mess hall. It took time for Shen to confide that he actually was married. Many years ago, in the late 1950s, he and his wife were students together at Qinghua University in Peking; they fell in love, and at graduation were wed. They had a total of one month living together. Then the state labor bureau assigned him to a post in the capital and her to a job in Shanghai. There was no appeal. He got to see her about three weeks a year, usually at Chinese New Year's, when they combined the three-day national holiday with the special two-week leave they were entitled to for working apart.

Even when his wife gave birth to a baby girl nine years ago, the government would not relent. They belonged to separate *danwei,* and neither unit would let them go, because of bureaucratic jealousy, Shen felt. His wife's troubles were compounded in 1975 when she criticized Jiang Qing in front of some office mates who informed on her. For that she was exiled to a village in the countryside outside Shanghai. In 1979 she was rehabilitated but still is confined to the village where she works as a peasant planting rice and raising her daughter.

Sometimes in the evenings Shen played with the children of neighbors outside his dorm, holding the babies on his lap or kicking a ball with young boys. "My prime is passing by," he said one such summer night, "and I'm still separated. My daughter knows me only as the man who visits once a year and brings presents. How many years does one have to live?"

In addition to couples like Shen and his wife, who were separated by their job assignments after graduation from college, there is also a large group of people from the countryside who were split up when the husbands became cadres and were promoted to work in the cities. Because of the government's tight restrictions on urban growth, they have not been allowed to bring their wives with them.

Sometimes, when I wandered down Wangfujing Street in Peking, or looked around outside the railroad station, or noticed the telephone poles near the Peking University campus, I saw small handwritten signs. At the top each had two horizontal arrows pointing in opposite directions. They are appeals to exchange jobs and housing from husbands and wives living in different cities.

"My family lives in Peking, but I work in a state-owned factory in Tianjin," one notice stuck on a telephone pole near the Peking Hotel read. "I have received permission from the leadership in my factory to transfer to Peking. Comrades wishing to return to Tianjin and work in a liquor factory should please contact me," and it gave the man's name and his plant's phone number.

The government's tardiness in resolving these problems of separated families struck me as more than mere bureaucratic rigidity. There was a certain callousness, much like the Party's attitude toward anything touching on sex, as if people could live for the revolution without love. When I reported on China from Hong Kong, I employed for a period a pretty young British-Chinese woman as my assistant, Lynn Kirkpatrick. She and her husband, Andrew, had studied for two years at Fudan University in Shanghai. Although they were married, the school forbade them to live together and assigned them to different crowded dormitories. When a British businessman in Shanghai allowed them to spend the night together at his home a few times, he was reprimanded by the local public security office.

The Public Security Ministry, which administers this vast control apparatus —the police, the security agents in each *danwei,* the street committees—is not as well known in the outside world as its Russian counterpart, the K.G.B. But many Chinese I knew referred to it as the *Ke Ge Bo,* Chinese for the initials K.G.B. The Public Security Ministry oversees both the regular blue-uniformed traffic policemen who work on city streets and plainclothes agents. Friends told me the ministry is divided into thirteen bureaus, with one especially delegated to monitor the activities of foreigners in China. While I was in Peking, this was the sixth bureau, but the ministry frequently switches the numerical designations for added security. The ministry also has its own armed troops, like companies and battalions of the People's Liberation Army, who guard some key Party organizations and prisons. But none of my Chinese acquaintances could estimate the total number of employees in the Public Security Ministry. The ministry's headquarters are located in a vast compound facing the Gate of Heavenly Peace and bordered by the Museum of Revolutionary History. Part of the ministry, including the courtroom where Jiang Qing and other members of the Gang of Four were tried in December 1980, occupies the old grounds of the pre-1949 British Legation. More than any other part of the regime, the Public Security Ministry is secretive about its operations, and a request I made to visit their offices was turned down. But Western diplomats in Peking say that from what little they know, the Chinese police don't make as much use of sophisticated electronic bugging devices as the Russians do. It may be because they don't have the advanced technology, or perhaps it's because the Chinese already have their own elaborate and dependable human intelligence-gathering network. In any case, the American Embassy in Peking has not found bugs planted in its walls or high-energy sensing devices aimed at it as has the U.S. mission in Moscow.

The factional quarrels of the Cultural Revolution took their toll in the Public Security Ministry as they did elsewhere. One head of the ministry, Li Zhen, disappeared in 1972 after reportedly being assassinated in the basement of his office. The real story of his demise is such a carefully held secret that even his wife and daughter have never been informed what happened to him after he left home in his chauffeur-driven Red Flag limousine that day, Chinese friends told me. Li was quietly succeeded by Hua Guofeng, though Hua's appointment to the post was not made public till three years later in 1975. In retrospect, it may well have been Hua's stewardship of the police post which helped him gain Mao's favor and be catapulted to the jobs of Prime Minister and Party Chairman in 1976 after Zhou Enlai and Mao died.

But Hua's connection with the ministry also meant that he ran the prisons where many of Mao's opponents, now China's leaders, were incarcerated.

The Public Security Ministry does not handle China's intelligence activities overseas—for that, there is an even more clandestine organization. On a crisp, sunny autumn afternoon, when Bing and I were driving to the Fragrant Hills, west of Peking, she called my attention to an unmarked drab gray concrete building just beyond the old Summer Palace. It was the Institute of International Relations, she said with a meaningful glance. The innocuous name meant nothing to me, I confessed. Bing looked triumphant.

"Top secret," she said with a grin. "It belongs to the Central Investigation Department.

"It's so secret that most Chinese don't even know about it," Bing explained. "It's like your CIA. They are in charge of spying on foreign countries. They send people abroad under cover as diplomats, cultural attachés, trade delegates, or journalists. The institute is where they train their recruits."

The Central Investigation Department is so important, she added, that it comes directly under the Party Central Committee, not the government. "If they want you, they can get you transferred from any *danwei*," Bing said with awe, the ultimate sign of bureaucratic clout in China. The husband of one of her friends at college worked for the Central Investigation Department in the Chinese Embassy in Paris and her friend consequently was the envy of all her classmates. "They think he must send her lots of good things, like French clothes, television sets, cassettes."

Given the immense power of the police in China, I was surprised that many Chinese had a casual, almost contemptuous attitude toward the uniformed policemen on duty on Peking's streets. Although the government has made efforts to instruct Chinese in traffic safety—creating reserved lanes for bicyclists, putting up billboards with rules for cars and pedestrians—traffic in China's cities is routinely chaotic. Pedestrians cross the street against red lights without even looking at the signals; cyclists cut into the fast automobile lanes without warning; cars operate by the rule of the horn—whoever honks loudest or drives fastest has the right of way. Several times I had to slam on my brakes in astonishment to avoid hitting people who were walking backward across busy streets because of an icy or dusty wind. This makes the Chinese very different from the self-disciplined Japanese. In Tokyo no one even steps off the curb until the light has turned green. "The Chinese have a rough edge, like animals in a jungle," a Japanese diplomat I had known in both Taiwan and Peking observed. "Just think what would have happened if it had been Japan that went Communist in 1949 instead of China."

335

Once on a cold winter afternoon, driving back to the Peking Hotel, I noticed a young policeman on his elevated traffic box hail a woman cyclist who was trying to cross the intersection. He was shouting at her for some apparent violation, but she wouldn't stop. So the policeman dismounted from his stand, grabbed her bike by the luggage rack on the back, and threw her off balance to the pavement. The woman was incensed. She jumped up, whacked the policeman on his shoulder, punched him in the chest, and then for good measure yanked off his stiff blue-cotton cap and hurled it across the street. In turn he took her by the arm and marched her over to a white-painted police sentry stand at the corner. She was a poor woman, in her late thirties, with tired eyes and rough skin. I noticed she was wearing a worn corduroy jacket, baggy blue-cotton pants, and thin cotton gloves, which had been crudely mended. Her cotton shoes were old and much too thin for that time of year. Several more police soon arrived and confiscated her bicycle, ordering her to report to a nearby police station to be questioned.

"But how can I get there if you have locked up my bike?" she protested. By this time a crowd of several hundred bystanders had gathered. There are few movies and plays to go to in Peking, and tickets are hard to come by anyway, so a crowd will gather to watch almost anything, especially a fight with a policeman. A teen-age boy stepped up to the woman, ignoring the police, and said, "Here, ride my bike to the station." His gesture was another sign of the breakdown in the Communists' prestige in the wake of the Cultural Revolution.

Yet despite such occasional acts of bravado, the ubiquity and intensity of the control apparatus have generated tremendous psychological pressures on the Chinese, creating mental strains that few Westerners can imagine. "People live under constant tension," remarked a dignified, taciturn engineer. "You always have to worry about someone you know betraying you," he explained, someone in your *danwei,* your street committee, or your political study group.

This pressure has been compounded by the years of political campaigns, the constant shifts in the official line, and the widespread political persecution, the engineer added. To try to minimize the dangers, he said, he follows one major precaution—he never talks about anything personal with people in his *danwei.* "For the next time a campaign comes up, the Party will order criticism meetings in your *danwei* and people will be compelled to say anything they know about you, whether they like you or not. So I make my friends with people outside my office."

The engineer and his wife both complained about suffering from what they called *shen-jing shuai-ro,* literally, "weakness of the nerves," or medically, neurasthenia, what Westerners identify as nervous tension, depression, and anxiety. Over time, I found, many of my Chinese friends talked about having *shen-jing shuai-ro*. Hua, the woman journalist who was arrested for talking with me about her sex life, said she suffered from constant headaches and insomnia. Often she slept only two or three hours a night, she said, and felt endlessly fatigued. When we went out to eat together, she said she had no appetite and only picked at her food. Miao, Mrs. Wang, also had headaches and couldn't sleep, and according to her husband, Li, was often irritable and listless. When he and I were alone, he diagnosed her problem as *shen-jing shuai-ro*. Some other Chinese I knew had nervous tics. Lao Wu, my conscientious assistant, had a habit of jiggling his foot. Whenever I put a difficult question to him or asked him to make a phone call to a government office that embarrassed him, the arc of his swing increased radically. Some Americans, of course, have nervous tics also, but it was the number of Chinese I encountered with habits like Lao Wu's which shocked me.

David Eisenberg, the young American doctor from the Harvard Medical School who was doing research at the Institute of Traditional Chinese Medicine in Peking, said that often when Chinese learned he was a physician they immediately began telling him about their cases of nervous tension. During a vacation trip to the old lakeside city of Hangzhou, south of Shanghai, Dr. Eisenberg related, he stopped to buy some cookies in a small shop.

"When the man behind the counter and I got to talking and he discovered I was a doctor, he said he had suffered from neurasthenia for a year. 'I've been to a traditional Chinese medicine doctor and to a Western-style doctor, but I can't sleep at night and I feel tired, nervous, and irritable all the time. Please give me some medicine.' "

In response, Dr. Eisenberg, a soft-spoken twenty-seven-year-old with curly blond hair and a neatly trimmed beard, asked the clerk if he had any problems in his personal life. It turned out he had been sent to Hangzhou over a year ago, far from his home. "I haven't seen my family in over a year, I can't ever see my girl friend again, and I hate my job," he told Dr. Eisenberg. "I wanted to study English, but when the Cultural Revolution came, I had to quit school. What future is there in selling cookies?"

Dr. Eisenberg himself was cautious in drawing conclusions from such random encounters, but he was very struck later when he spent a month observing how patients were treated in the acupuncture clinic of the traditional medicine hospital, the first American permitted actually to work in the hospital. Over a quarter of the one hundred patients he saw also complained about nervous tension.

"The patients themselves believed their problem had a purely physical origin," Dr. Eisenberg recounted. In part, he felt, this was because traditionally it was much more socially acceptable for Chinese to have physical rather than emotional sickness. Chinese have long felt a stigma in admitting to mental illness in the family.* But the Chinese doctors also encouraged this interpretation because they don't accept Freud's theory of the unconscious and therefore don't look into a patient's emotional background.

The government has added to the confusion by its own skittishness on the whole issue of mental health in China. Several Chinese doctors I talked with said the Communists officially insist that mental disorders have no biological basis and therefore are the result of social or ideological troubles—which the regime presumably should have resolved. In 1957, at a time when relations between Peking and Moscow were still close and China was under strong Soviet intellectual influence, the government abolished psychology as a field of study, branding it a "bogus bourgeois science." Most of China's small number of Western-trained psychologists were arrested and packed off to labor camps, a psychologist who earned his Ph.D. at Columbia University before 1949 told me. Psychiatrists were excepted, but most of China's medical schools stopped offering courses in the subject.

In his work at the acupuncture clinic, however, Dr. Eisenberg decided to try an experiment. While the Chinese doctors prescribed a course of treatment with needles for the headaches, insomnia, and fatigue, he inquired whether the patients had any emotional problems that might have triggered their symptoms.

"One young man said no, he didn't have any personal problems, but a few days ago his fiancée was stabbed to death by two guys," Dr. Eisenberg recalled. Among the other patients, some were depressed by their failure on the college entrance exam or by conflicts with the cadres in their *danwei* from whom they couldn't escape. Another man was catatonic. He couldn't speak or move and seemed numb. When Dr. Eisenberg asked a companion who had brought him into the clinic about his history, it turned out he had just been released after spending nine years in solitary confinement in prison.

In particular Dr. Eisenberg remembered an obese forty-five-year-old woman who came into the hospital sweating and breathing heavily. Her pants

*For instance, Chinese are still very reluctant to discuss the problem of mental retardation. In schools and nurseries I visited, whenever I asked how the teachers dealt with mentally retarded students, school officials denied there were any. The reason, I discovered, was that children with mental difficulties are usually kept at home and cared for by their families in the traditional style. The Communists have set up some special schools for the blind and a few factories where other handicapped people work, but I never found any facilities for the mentally retarded. A famous composer Jan Wong knew had a sixteen-year-old son, a tallish, bulky youth who talks in a thick low voice that is largely incomprehensible. When he was six, his parents sent him to first grade, not realizing his trouble. But he failed all his courses and the teachers refused to allow him to stay in school. Now he lives at home, where he can wash himself and do simple housework. When he was younger he loved to play with the children in the neighborhood, but now they laugh at him and he hides in his room when visitors come to the apartment.

were too short and her long gray woolen underwear hung down two inches below her cuffs. She complained that she was hysterical.

"Look at my mouth, it's crooked," she groaned. Only then did the Chinese physician in attendance and Dr. Eisenberg notice a strange overbite, her mouth twisting slightly to the right. When the woman talked or smoked, it went away, but when she was silent, there it was, like a comedian's grimace.

"I've had nervous tension for the past fifteen years, it started with the Gang of Four," the woman insisted. "Can't you give me some needles?"

While the Chinese doctor stuck needles in her, Dr. Eisenberg probed her personal life. She had not worked since 1965, after the birth of her fourth child, she said, since she was so busy at home taking care of her progeny. Her lack of employment was unusual for a Chinese woman. Then in 1966 her husband was packed off to the countryside to be a welder, separating him from the family, and had returned only a few months before. In the city, he couldn't find work.

"My two oldest children are big troublemakers," the woman went on. "Neither one has a job yet. I'd hoped they would get into university, but they just fight and get into mischief," she lamented. But when Dr. Eisenberg asked her if she saw any connection between these difficulties and her illness, she responded, "I don't see any relationship."

Until recently, China's psychiatric hospitals have been shrouded in almost as much secrecy as its nuclear test sites. There is no evidence that the Chinese systematically used their mental institutions as the Russians have done for dealing with troublesome political dissidents, but there have been reports of individual cases where the government did lock up political prisoners in mental clinics. During the Cultural Revolution, Red Guards found by accident a group of followers of Hu Feng—a prominent Marxist literary critic who had long been an outspoken opponent of Party intellectual policy—in a mental ward where they had been confined for several years. During my stay in Peking I saw a movie entitled *Dark Willows and Bright Flowers* about the conflict between youthful radicals and veteran cadres in the countryside. The heroine, who sides with the veteran cadres, is put into a mental hospital by a scheming leftist and tied to her bed. The villain's action did not produce any reaction from the audience, which suggested they were familiar with the practice.

But the main problem with China's mental hospitals, Chinese told me, was simply that there aren't enough of them. A balding engineer in Shanghai from a family that was affluent and middle-class before Liberation said that his brother had become chronically depressed and unable to work after he was sent to teach in a mountain village in 1958. His brother couldn't adjust to the rigors of rural life and had moved back to stay with his aged mother in the city, illegally. His symptoms grew progressively worse, but the large

Shanghai Psychiatric Hospital would not accept him for treatment. They were already overcrowded, and his condition was not considered severe enough. The hospital only took schizophrenics. He was a victim of depression, neurotic rather than psychotic. Eventually, the engineer said, he had arranged through a doctor he knew who treated members of the Politburo to get his brother into the hospital, using the back door.

Since Mao's death the regime has been more relaxed in its attitude toward the mental health question and has allowed a number of foreign delegations to visit the Shanghai hospital and another modern clinic in Peking. I toured the Shanghai hospital with Joseph A. Califano, then the U.S. Secretary of Health, Education and Welfare. It proved to be a pleasant rectangular compound of three-story concrete and brick buildings set around a garden in a suburb of the city. American doctors in the group thought its facilities and treatment compared favorably with large public hospitals in the United States. They were also interested that the Chinese staff used many of the same powerful new tranquilizers and other psychotropic drugs developed in the West in the past few decades. But they did note a major difference from American hospitals. The director, Dr. Xia Zhenyi, a slight, graying man trained in the United States, confirmed that 85 percent of the 1,000 inmates and 500 outpatients the hospital treats each day were schizophrenics, the most severe form of mental illness.

Talking as we scurried along the high-ceilinged corridors, Dr. Xia insisted China simply did not have the widespread problem of depression and other neuroses that exist in the West. "The incidence of mental disease in China is much lower than in America," he asserted. In China, he said, it occurs in only about seven people per thousand. But in the United States about 15 percent of the population suffer from some form of diagnosable mental disorder, according to the National Institute of Mental Health.

Shortly before I left China I met a woman psychologist in her late fifties who had been allowed to resume teaching her specialty again in 1978 after a twenty-year hiatus. Her books had all been burned years before, but her own spirit was still youthful, almost feisty, and she was deeply interested in the implications of psychology for China.

Did she agree with Dr. Xia that Chinese don't suffer from depression or had she noticed that many Chinese complained about nervous tension? I asked. Her dark eyes stared at me intently for a moment and I wondered if I had trespassed onto forbidden territory. But then she broke into a passionate discussion.

"After what we have gone through in the past thirty years, the whole country is depressed," she said, her eyes flashing. "Depression and anxiety are our psychological scars. I worry about this every day.

"But that is why we must find more positive things to say about our country and the Party. Otherwise we won't be able to cure ourselves and we will go around depressed. Try to be more cheery."

My friend Bing also saw depression and paranoia as the price China had to pay for the exigencies of the control system. "I talk about it sometimes with my very close friends," she said. "But you can talk only by stationing a guard at your mouth. You have to know exactly who you are talking to and the limits of what you can say to them."

China's condition, Bing suggested, was like a proverb that grew out of an incident in the late fourth century, a time of imperial disintegration in China, similar to the Dark Ages in Europe. A rebel named Fu Jian had gathered an army—said by Chinese historians to number a million men—to overthrow the state of Jin. The government commander had only 8,000 troops. But the usurper's soldiers mistook the moving grass and trees for advancing government forces and fled in terror. From the episode the Chinese have extracted a four-character phrase which has come to be a parable for paranoia and the fear of being surrounded by hostile spying eyes: *Cao-mu jie-bing,* or "In the grass, the trees, everything seems a soldier."

"That is the way it is for us," Bing said, "always soldiers in the grass."

16.

Lao Gai

THE CHINESE GULAG

"The Struggle . . . is a peculiarly Chinese invention, combining intimi-dation, humiliation, and sheer exhaustion. Briefly described, it is an intellectual gang-beating of one man by many, sometimes even thou-sands, in which the victim has no defense, even the truth."

Bao Ruo-wang, **Prisoner of Mao**

It began innocently enough. I was traveling in a delegation with the U.S. Secretary of Defense, Harold Brown, the first senior American military official to visit China since 1949, and our hosts from the Information Department wanted to be sure that when Brown left China via Shanghai, those of us who were resident correspondents in Peking would be able to get home. They were very solicitous and attentive to detail. For several days before the scheduled end of the trip, Lin Qingyun, an Information Department cadre of whom I was fond, asked how I planned on returning to Peking. A pleasant, boyish-looking man with a dark-brown complexion, Lin said he would buy a ticket for me, a great help in China where planes and trains are often booked weeks in advance. I said I intended to take the train, but I politely declined Lin's offer because I wanted discreetly to look up some Chinese friends in Shanghai and didn't know how long it would take to find them and arrange meetings. Then after we arrived in Shanghai and I had a chance to contact my friends, I went and bought my own train ticket for two days after the group was to leave.

But in the afternoon, a few hours after my purchase, as I was sitting at the large wooden desk in my hotel room rushing to finish a story for *The Times* on the significance of Brown's trip for Sino–U. S. relations, two officials from the Shanghai city government knocked on the door. They said they wanted to collect payment for the train ticket they had bought for me according to my request to Lin.

It was then I made a fatal mistake; I took a stand on principle. Perhaps because I was in a hurry to write my story and it was close to dinnertime, I reacted like a foreigner and refused to pay. I pointed out that I had not asked anyone to purchase the ticket for me. They replied courteously that I knew very well I had requested them to buy it, but if I didn't want the ticket, I could just pay the cancellation fee, six yuan ($4). I still refused. I felt I shouldn't have to pay for something I didn't order.

Later that evening, just as I returned to my room after dinner, an officer from the People's Liberation Army Foreign Affairs Department, Tang Yin-chu, who had accompanied the delegation, walked in. A square-jawed, crew-cut man with ramrod posture, Tang was visibly agitated.

"Why did you refuse to pay?" he demanded, his face flushed. I explained again that I had never asked for the ticket.

"But you did," he went on, calling my erstwhile friend Lin to the room to confront me. "You must recognize your error," they shouted at me in unison. My error? With that phrase I finally realized the seriousness of the situation. I was beginning to feel like the victim of a Chinese struggle session, a meeting where the target is surrounded by a group of his friends and colleagues and criticized, insulted, and screamed at, even slapped and spit on, till he is hopelessly confused and terrorized and confesses to whatever the charge against him. In real struggle sessions I had heard about, the process lasted anywhere from two or three hours to several days or even weeks. My plight was obviously not so severe, but it had many of the same elements.

Lin was transformed from the kindly man I knew. His face was red with anger, even with his dark skin, and he had assumed a mask of moral superiority.

"You are denying the facts," he lectured me. "I have proof. I have notes of our conversations and of all your phone calls. You cannot deny the facts." At least I had learned that my phone had been tapped.

"Mr. Lin, this seems to be a misunderstanding," I responded, trying to keep my temper and find a compromise.

"There are no misunderstandings in China, you are wrong," Lin replied, this time screaming. There was clearly no possibility of my proving my innocence. But I still hadn't learned there was no escape except total contrition.

"Mr. Lin, sometimes in the United States and China we do things differently," I tried a different tack. "In America people have to buy their own tickets, the government doesn't buy them for us."

"The problem is, you don't respect China," Lin returned to the attack.

"Secretary Brown has just completed a very important visit to China. It was to improve relations between our two countries. You don't want your mistake to harm those relations?" he asked. It was true the visit had been significant. Brown had disclosed that the Carter administration was prepared to sell China some nonlethal American military hardware. Lin was trying to manipulate my feelings of guilt, a common technique in struggle sessions.

Tang, who had taken off his green uniform jacket, joined the assault. "You are a bad element," he hissed, using a phrase usually reserved for reactionaries. "Of the forty correspondents on the trip, you are the only one who has given us trouble." Here was another of the standard techniques, isolating the victim.

Then Lin dredged up the past, the Chinese inquisitor's ultimate weapon. "You have had a bad attitude ever since you came to China. You caused trouble for the Information Department on your first visit to Peking."

I knew exactly what Lin was referring to, an incident that happened during a trip in August 1977, but Lin wasn't even in China then, he was stationed in the Chinese Embassy in Mexico. So he must have read about it in my dossier. In China, nothing is thrown away—not old bits of rag, twisted pieces of metal, scraps of paper, and especially not information. The earlier episode had occurred when I wanted to send a story to New York but discovered that the press card the Information Department had prepared for me listed the wrong filing address. The mistake had been inadvertently made by the State Department in Washington which passed on the wrong information to the Chinese. Instead of the telex number for *The Times* in New York, the State Department had provided my own incoming cable address in Hong Kong. When I pointed out the error to the Information Department officer accompanying me, he flew into a rage.

"China does not make mistakes," he pronounced categorically. "You are an imperialist trying to impose your will on the Chinese people." He was not mollified when an American diplomat admitted it was the State Department's fault and we discovered similar errors had been made on the press cards of the reporters for *The Washington Post, The Los Angeles Times,* and *Newsweek.*

By the time Lin recalled this past transgression from my dossier, I realized my cause was lost. "Mr. Lin, I will happily pay for the ticket, it is a small matter," I said, trying to sound conciliatory. But this wasn't enough; the guilty must confess fully. The Chinese are very formalistic. Even though the government has decided a person is guilty, he must confess to make it clear that justice has been done.

"I will not accept your money," Lin said, contempt showing on his face. "You must apologize and pay it to our hosts in Shanghai, whom you have offended."

By this time the discussion had dragged on for several hours, and it was after midnight. The two Shanghai officials who had originally come to see me that afternoon were asleep in rooms on a different floor of the hotel, billeted there for the duration of Brown's visit. I wasn't sure which they themselves preferred—sleep or a middle-of-the-night apology. But we marched together downstairs to their room, woke the two men, and after they pulled on their clothes, I handed over the money and apologized.

"You should draw conclusions from your behavior and improve your attitude," Lin chastised me as I started back for my room, exhausted, angry, and frightened.

It was only a minor encounter, I realized later, I suffered no harm, but it gave me a better appreciation for the accounts some Chinese acquaintances told of what it had been like to undergo a real struggle session. And millions of Chinese had been put through these pulverizing, humiliating, and terrifying experiences over the past three decades to purify them for the revolution. There were many targets: former landlords and capitalists, of course, but also professors, journalists, and lawyers, labeled as rightists, Christian ministers, even workers, peasants, and students who joined the wrong political faction.

A short, round-faced thirty-five-year-old former Red Guard with wavy hair and a high-pitched voice, Lo, recalled the two years he spent undergoing interrogation, much of it in struggle sessions. The questioning took place in a specially built prison run by the Public Security Ministry in a remote mountainous area in Jiangxi province, in central China. Lo was confined to a tiny mud hut by himself, with one guard stationed inside his cell and another just outside the door. Even at night a light was kept burning to monitor his activity. Lo was forbidden to talk with the guards, or with any of the other prisoners in the camp; hence for the entire two years, he said, the only words he heard were those of his inquisitors and other inmates when they shouted at him in struggle sessions.

Lo was accused of being a member of an ultra-radical group that seized control of the Foreign Ministry during the height of the Cultural Revolution. He didn't deny he had participated in the takeover, one of the most sensational Red Guard actions, but he claimed his group had followed direct orders from Jiang Qing. In 1972, when he was detained, she was still Mao's wife and at the height of her power. But Lin Biao, the Defense Minister and Mao's putative heir, had just died in a plane crash after trying to assassinate the Chairman, and the Public Security Ministry wanted Lo to admit that it was really Lin who gave the command to occupy the Foreign Ministry. The police were compiling a document for the Central Committee to use to discredit Lin.

Throughout his two years in the prison, the interrogators were always the same four men—two from the Public Security Ministry and two from the security section of the Foreign Ministry. They had accompanied him by train from Peking after his arrest.

"They would start every day at eight A.M., to twelve P.M., then from two P.M. to five P.M. and again in the evenings from eight P.M. to ten P.M.," Lo recalled. "They would never interrogate me when their stomachs were empty," he added with a laugh. He told me his story over a glass of beer in a small restaurant in Canton where we had met during a stopover I made in that southern city. Lo spoke dispassionately about his experience. The Chinese are a sober, unemotive people, and, like most Chinese I knew, he had a way of understating the horror of his misadventures.

"It was not fair questioning," Lo recalled. "They wanted to squeeze things out of me which just didn't happen. They wanted me to write a confession according to their version of events. It didn't do any good to deny it. Whenever I refused, they put me into a struggle session with other prisoners.

"Sometimes they held the struggle sessions in a pigsty," Lo went on. The guards would shove him down among the grunting animals. "They forced me to kneel on the dirt floor, with all the shit, and they held my head down so my nose practically was in the stuff. You weren't allowed to look up. Reactionaries aren't supposed to be proud. The police interrogators would say, 'Who ordered you to take over the Foreign Ministry?' When I said Jiang Qing, they would have everyone jump up and shout at me, 'You are slandering Chairman Mao.' Some of the other prisoners had to hit me and spit on me. If they didn't do it, the guards would criticize them for their bad attitude and they would be struggled with also.

"Actually, I was fortunate. They never beat me too badly. To get you to confess, the Communists prefer to use psychological pressure." But Lo recalled when he had taken part in a struggle session where the inmates beat a former leftist cadre from the Overseas Chinese Affairs Commission who refused to confess. "We pounded and kicked him so hard he spit blood. A few days later he died," Lo remembered.

While Lo was in the prison, he also related, three prisoners committed suicide. "They couldn't stand the pressure and humiliation. One slashed his wrists with some glass, another slit his throat, the third one hanged himself. They always announced it over the loudspeaker. The camp commander said, 'They died for fear their crimes would be discovered.' " Lo was anxious to know whether his father and mother had been affected by his arrest. But he never received any mail from home. Only after he was released did he learn that all his father's and mother's letters had been returned by the prison authorities.

As the inquisition wore on, the police promised Lo that if he admitted he had acted on Lin Biao's orders, they would release him immediately. But he declined. Finally they wrote out a confession for him.

"We had to rehearse it. First I had to memorize the whole thing, so there would be no mistakes when I spoke in front of the struggle session. They would tell me, 'This sentence you must say very sadly. This paragraph you must say with real emotion.' In some places they wrote 'pause' for the other prisoners to talk. In other places they wrote 'slogans' so people could shout at me. Once I couldn't remember what came next. The guards said I was trying to cover up; actually I just forgot. Eventually they gave me the paper so I could read it.

"The first time I was put in a struggle session, after fifteen minutes I felt numb, I was so scared. But eventually I got used to it. When they didn't beat me very hard, it was just like a pig going to market. Since my head was bowed and I couldn't see anybody, all there was was a lot of noise and shouting."

Finally one day the guards told him he would be released. "I never knew why. They told me, 'You are an enemy of the people, but your attitude is good.' "

Almost every Chinese I got to know during my twenty months in Peking had a tale of political persecution, many far worse than Lo's. From their stories it seemed as if a whole generation of Chinese (and 650 million of China's one billion people have been born since 1949) had known nothing but arbitrary accusations, violent swings in the political line, unjustified arrests, torture, and imprisonment. Few Chinese I knew felt free from the fear of physical or psychological abuse and a pervasive sense of injustice. There was Lihua, the girl who at the age of six was driven out of Peking and had to watch as her mother was beaten to death, and Bing, the thirteen-year-old who felt compelled to denounce her father, and Hong, who was thrown into jail because the drunken son of a general took a fancy to her. During a banquet in the provincial city of Hefei for Governor Harry Hughes of Maryland, I was seated next to a petite woman reporter from the New China News Agency, Zhang Wei. Her tiny frame, her short hair, an unlined face, and a perpetual girlish smile made her look much younger than her fifty years. Conversation with Chinese officials you haven't met before at formal dinners is often strained, so to try to find a safe beginning, I asked what her husband did.

"My husband is dead, he was a victim of the Gang of Four," she replied without elaboration, the smile never leaving the corners of her mouth. It was a simple statement of fact, a commonplace for China, shocking only to a foreigner.

At lunch one day in the Peking Hotel, an American businesswoman who was involved in bringing Chinese musical and theatrical groups to the United States invited me to join her and a woman pianist from the Peking Philharmonic Orchestra. The Chinese musician had a narrow, sad face and was silent for long periods of time. Before the Cultural Revolution, she explained, her husband was a leading violinist with the orchestra.

"But one day he made a mistake," she said in a flat voice. "During the Cultural Revolution the streets were a sea of red, all the shops were covered with red banners and their windows were filled with Mao's books. My husband was shopping with a friend. He remarked it was impossible to tell which store was a restaurant and which a barber shop." His friend then informed on him, and the police arrested him.

"When I tried to see him and find out what had happened, the police said, 'It is not good to ask,'" the pianist continued, putting down her chopsticks. "Later they came to see me. 'Your husband is a counterrevolutionary. You should divorce him. If you don't draw a clear line between yourselves, it will look like you support him in his crimes.' I had no choice. Usually it is very difficult to get a divorce, but my *danwei* approved immediately." Her husband ended up spending ten years in prison. After his release, he did not want to remarry her.

Across the room from us, eating at another table, I noticed, was China's leading pianist, Liu Shikun, a tall, gaunt man with brush-cut hair and black horn-rimmed spectacles. Liu had free access to the Peking Hotel because he had married a daughter of Ye Jianying, the octogenarian chairman of the National People's Congress. During the Cultural Revolution (from 1966 to 1969) Liu had originally been a leader of a virulently radical faction of Red Guards who paraded the leaders of the Peking city Party committee through the streets with placards around their necks. But later he became embroiled in a factional dispute with another leftist group, and they deliberately broke his hands. Playing Chopin, Mozart, and Beethoven on the piano, after all, was a bourgeois art. Then, for reasons never made clear, Liu was also thrown into prison for nine years. The only way he could practice his fingering exercises was on a bamboo shoulder pole, a fellow musician told me. Since the overthrow of the radicals in 1976, Liu has resumed his musical career.

There are statistics on the scale of persecution in China during the Cultural Revolution—since the arrest of the Gang of Four, the *People's Daily* has been a cornucopia of information. But the figures are contradictory, and fragmentary, and one could hardly expect the police and all the Red Guard groups to keep accurate records of how many people they arrested, tortured, or killed. So the numbers are only suggestive. The *People's Daily* once calculated that 100 million people were affected by the Cultural Revolution, one out of every nine Chinese at the time. Agence France Press, whose correspondents in Peking were among the best-informed and hardest-working I knew, reported in 1979 that a reliable Chinese source had told the agency that 400,000 people died as a result of the Cultural Revolution in the late 1960s.

During a tour of Fujian province, along the southeast coast, the Deputy Governor, Wen Fusan, told a group of us foreign newsmen that in the mountainous rural district where he worked during the Cultural Revolution, 1,700 people out of a population of two million had been beaten to death or committed suicide. If his district was average for China, that would mean more like 850,000 deaths nationwide. In a speech in 1980, Deng Xiaoping stated that 2.9 million people had been rehabilitated since the end of the Cultural Revolution, and "many more whose cases were not put on file," he added ambiguously. In one article, the *People's Daily* declared that 60 percent of all those accused of being counterrevolutionaries were falsely charged.

The official 20,000-word indictment against Jiang Qing, her cohorts in the Gang of Four, and the generals who participated in the plot to kill Mao with Lin Biao charged that they were personally responsible for wrongfully persecuting 750,000 people, 34,380 of whom died as a result, including six men who were mayors or deputy mayors of Peking and Shanghai. In the biggest single case mentioned in the indictment, over 346,000 cadres and others were falsely accused of belonging to a secret party in Inner Mongolia; 16,222 of them were killed. During the trial of the Gang of Four, the New China News Agency disclosed that a former Minister of Public Security, Xie Fuzhi, had instigated a wave of terror in Peking during late August and September 1966. In a forty-day period, "1,700 people were beaten to death, 33,600 households were searched and ransacked, and 85,000 people were driven out of the capital."* The list could go on and on. The indictment against the Gang of Four also accused them of persecuting 142,000 cadres and teachers under the Ministry of Education, 53,000 scientists and technicians in the Academy of Sciences, and over 500 of the 674 professors in China's medical schools, some of whom died as a consequence.

The Gang's trial itself produced graphic testimony of the terror of the times. The prosecution in the special high court set up to hear the case played parts of twenty tape recordings made at the interrogation of a sixty-seven-year-old professor, Zhang Zhongyi. Professor Zhang, who was already suffering from liver cancer, had been arrested because before 1949 he had taught at the now defunct Catholic-run Furen University in Peking. Wang Guangmei, the wife of Liu Shaoqi, China's head of state and Mao's chief target in the Cultural Revolution, had been a student in the school. The professor didn't know Miss Wang, the prosecution said, but Jiang Qing had organized a "special group" to gather material to prove she was an American spy and demanded that the team "squeeze" evidence out of Professor Zhang. Although he was confined to a hospital bed and had to be fed intravenously to keep him alive, Professor Zhang was interrogated twenty-one times dur-

*NCNA, December 23, 1980.

349

ing the twenty-seven days he was held, the last session alone lasting fifteen hours. After that, he died.

"People in the public gallery reacted with shock at the wailing of the aged professor during the interrogation," the New China News Agency said in its account of the trial. (I had to depend on the official Chinese reports of the trial because foreign journalists were not permitted to attend.) There were "moans and groans as the patient struggled to get up from the bed and was forced down again," the press agency reported, "orders to Professor Zhang to take medicine, shouts of 'Speak up, quickly,' and the confused answers of the dying man." Based in part on the professor's confession, Jiang Qing drew up a report labeling Miss Wang an agent of the U.S. Office of Strategic Services during World War Two. It was used to arrest her and Liu.

Political persecution under the Communists did not begin with the Cultural Revolution. In the land-reform campaign in 1949–51, in which land was redistributed to poor peasants, as many as three million former landlords, Kuomintang officials, and army and police officers were executed, according to one of the best-informed foreigners in China.* Mao himself gave a somewhat lower figure in a 1957 speech, reportedly stating that 800,000 "enemies of the people" were "liquidated" up to 1954.** In the "Campaign Against Counterrevolutionaries" in 1955–56, another four million people were investigated, documents circulated by Red Guards during the Cultural Revolution indicate. Then in the Anti-Rightist campaign in 1957–58, which followed the Communists' abortive experiment with more open expression in the Hundred Flowers period, several million students, teachers, scientists, writers, lawyers, and doctors—China's intellectuals—were sent to work in the countryside or sentenced to labor camps. Only in 1978, two years after Mao's death and the downfall of the Gang of Four, were the last 110,000 of these rightists released from the camps, a former prisoner told me in Peking. Many more died in prison, the ex-inmate said.

But where these earlier campaigns were aimed at particular groups, in the Cultural Revolution everyone became a potential target as the Party itself came under attack by its Chairman and the country was thrown into a madcap civil war. The slightest misstep could lead to arrest, imprisonment, or disgrace. A worker in a Peking chemical plant I met aboard a bus said that his father had been awarded three years in jail when he wrote a wall poster attacking the ousted chief of state, Liu. His father, who had only three years of schooling, had thought he was following instructions from his Party secre-

*Jacques Guillermaz, La Chine Populaire, 3rd ed. (Paris: Presses Universitaires de France, 1964), p. 47. General Guillermaz was French military attaché in China between 1937 and 1949 and again from 1964 to 1966.

**Roderick MacFarquhar, The Hundred Flowers Campaign and the Chinese Intellectuals (New York: Frederick Praeger, 1960), p. 270.

tary. But he accidently got one character wrong, and an alert cadre accused him of secretly slandering Chairman Mao.

A scientist related what he thought might have been the most absurd miscarriage of justice of the whole Cultural Revolution. Because Mao and Jiang Qing banned almost all literature except the Chairman's own works, a series of underground novels sprang up as popular entertainment. Some were serious autobiographical accounts of the sufferings of the period; others were merely serialized detective stories or pornographic romances told as oral epics. One thriller, entitled *Tales of the Plum Flower Society,* recounted a twenty-year effort to crack a Kuomintang spy network inside the Academy of Sciences. The chief Nationalist agent was a scientist named Peng Jiamu.

By coincidence, my acquaintance said, there existed a real scientist with the same name in the Institute of Optics and Precision Instruments in Changchun, in the northeast. The institute, one of China's most prestigious, had produced the country's first electron microscope in the 1950s and was a center of research for the defense industry. But in the Cultural Revolution a fanatic radical named Shan Guizhang was put in charge of the institute. He believed the character in the story was not just fictional but the real live Peng. As a result, 166 scientists in the institute were arrested as spies along with local accountants, policemen, workers, and even nursery attendants. A later dispatch by the New China News Agency, without giving any of the background of the incident, said Shan had "enforced fascist dictatorship" over the institute—"some of the people arrested were beaten to death, while others committed suicide." The scientists were slandered as "pigs, dogs, and devils with black hearts and rotten guts." Shan's proof that someone was a secret agent was that the accused either had a radio or camera at home or could speak a foreign language. Shan was rewarded by promotion to the provincial Party committee.

What made the persecutions of the Cultural Revolution more nightmarish for many Chinese than the earlier campaigns was the totality of it—it engulfed not only individuals but whole families; it divided each office, factory, and school into factions which are still contentious fifteen years later, and as happened in my brush with the authorities in Shanghai, the truth was a futile defense. Zheng Peidi, an English teacher at Peking University, slight, with delicate hands and a warm, likable smile, ran headlong into all these troubles.

"As we say in China, I have a very complicated family background," she told me with a self-effacing laugh. One of her mother's brothers was a Minister of Defense on Taiwan; another relative had been a dashing Communist movie producer in Shanghai in the 1930s who had introduced Jiang Qing into the Party and had an affair with her. "He could do everything, dance, ride, hunt, and they lived together," Peidi recounted. When she was an undergraduate at Peking University, she had mentioned her family connection to Jiang Qing to her roommates as student gossip. She graduated in 1962, was appointed a teacher at the school, and the story seemed forgotten.

But after the outbreak of the Cultural Revolution, Peidi found herself in a faction opposed to the one headed by the most prominent campus ultraleftist, Nieh Yuanzi, a woman cadre in the philosophy department. Nieh had composed the first wall poster in the Cultural Revolution, criticizing the university administration as revisionist, and Mao had ordered it published in the *People's Daily*. The Red Guards were looking for any excuse to attack Peidi's group, she recalled, and one of her former roommates informed on her. To the radicals, the story of her relative's affair with Jiang Qing was a malicious insult to China's leadership. Peidi was arrested and taken to what was called a "cowshed," a makeshift prison, in reality an old, small single-story classroom building that the Red Guards surrounded with coils of wire.

"There were twenty prisoners in my room, about two hundred in the whole building," Peidi remembered. "Most of them were famous older professors and the Party secretaries of their departments. I felt quite out of place." Like Lo, the former Red Guard, Peidi told her story with modesty, understating the terror and repulsion she felt.

"Actually, I was lucky," she said. "I was beaten only the day I arrived. They told me to confess the story was only a rumor, but when I said it was a fact, they accused me of slander and beat me." After that, she spent most of her time memorizing quotations from Chairman Mao.

"Every morning they would come into the room and make us recite a quotation by number—number thirty-five, number thirteen. I was young and my memory was good. So I could do it. I was also careful to keep my head bowed. But some of the older professors had studied in the United States and their Chinese wasn't very good. They couldn't memorize well enough to please the Red Guards. So they got beaten, with rubber whips, boards, bicycle chains. One professor was beaten every day till he died."

When Peidi was arrested in 1967, she had given birth to a son only a month before and was still nursing him. "The Red Guards said I couldn't see him anymore and gave me shots to stop my milk."

Her brother, an agricultural engineer, tried to visit her and complained that she was being treated inhumanely. He was locked up, too, for his insolence.

Meantime, her mother didn't know what had happened to Peidi. When she received an invitation from the Red Guards to see her daughter, she arrived only to be incarcerated in the building's cellar. The radicals tricked her into writing out a confession about the family connection with Jiang Qing by telling her Peidi had already admitted everything. When her mother, a "proud, old-fashioned intellectual," in Peidi's words, was sent back to her own office, she was put under what was called "supervision by the masses" and made to sweep the floors and clean the toilets for a year.

Nor did Peidi's father escape the dragnet. A prominent construction engineer, he was placed under house arrest. His driver recalled that once in the car he had complained that foreign can openers were better than Chinese can openers.

Peidi's husband was far away and couldn't help. He had been drafted into the army to work in Tibet as an English-language interpreter with Indian prisoners after China's 1962 border war with New Delhi. Only two years after her arrest was he able to get home leave and try to see her.

"The Red Guards wouldn't let him into the compound where we were kept," she recalled. "But he put on his army uniform and walked in. At the time the army enjoyed high prestige with the radicals because of Lin Biao." He managed to find her, but when a Red Guard became suspicious he whipped out a new single volume of Mao's quotations which had just been published by the army and wasn't yet available to civilians. He gave it to Peidi and said in a loud voice, "Here, see that you study this."

Only in 1971 was Peidi finally released, though she was also placed under "supervision" and made to live with the family of a politically reliable professor. "It was a very strange time," she told me one day sitting in the cafeteria in the lobby of the Peking Hotel. "None of my friends knew what crime I was supposed to have committed because the Red Guards wouldn't let me say what had happened."

Today many of the teachers and cadres who were involved in imprisoning her are still at Peking University. She has to work with them every day, and Peidi has learned to hide her feelings. Her only revenge was small. When she and her husband had a daughter several years ago, they named her Na, meaning "Silent."

Foreigners visiting Chinese offices, factories, and schools are usually unaware of how these factional divisions have persisted and how great a role personal vendettas play in everyday life. I displayed my own ignorance on my first trip to China in 1977. After eating lunch in a restaurant in Canton, I asked for the bill using the standard phrase I had been taught in Chinese textbooks and had heard in Taiwan, *suan-zhang,* or "settle the account." The pigtailed waitress stared at me angrily for a moment, then rebuked me sharply.

"We don't say that anymore in China, it isn't polite," she said.

What she meant, I learned, was that settling accounts with your friends and colleagues has become a serious national problem and so the old term for asking for the check has become an embarrassment.

China's leaders were not spared the terror. When Deng Xiaoping was purged the first time in the Cultural Revolution as a capitalist roader, he was sent to a rural cadre school in Jiangsu province, in central China, where he worked as a waiter, Chinese say. Liu Shaoqi, the disgraced head of state, was dispatched secretly to Kaifeng, the capital of Henan province, where he was kept under guard until he died of pneumonia in 1969. Two of his sons died of injuries or paralysis after being imprisoned or taken to struggle sessions, the Chinese press has since reported. Liu's widow, Wang Guangmei, a sophisticated, Western-educated woman who had been Jiang Qing's rival for the title of China's first lady, was confined to China's most top-secret prison, Qin Cheng Number One. Located inconspicuously near a verdant hotsprings resort once favored by the Empress Dowager Ci Xi in a suburb of Peking, it held about five hundred of China's leaders purged in the Cultural Revolution, including several who are now once again on the Politburo. Each was confined to a small cell by himself and forbidden to talk to other inmates; some prisoners went a decade without conversation. Every effort was made to ensure that no information leaked out about Qin Cheng. Until Mao's death and the downfall of the radicals, virtually no prisoners were ever released from it; inmates' families were not notified where they were; no visits were allowed, and prisoners were known to the guards only by numbers, never by their names.

I first learned about Qin Cheng from an exposé written by Wei Jingsheng, a former Red Guard and son of a high cadre turned dissident. His article was smuggled out of China in early 1979 by the wife of a French diplomat who had become close friends with Wei. She offered it to *The New York Times* bureau chief in Paris, Flora Lewis, who in turn passed it on to me. At almost the same time I reported Wei's account of the prison, he was arrested. The Chinese media have still never mentioned Qin Cheng by name, but the New China News Agency did once admit that there was a special prison outside Peking where thirty-four senior leaders were tortured to death, twenty maimed, and sixty went insane during the Cultural Revolution.

According to Wei and others, Qin Cheng had a series of peculiar regulations. Prisoners were required to sleep facing the glass-paneled door to their cells so the guards could keep watch over them. If an inmate turned over in his sleep, the guards would wake him. The Panchen Lama, the secondmost holy figure in Tibetan Buddhism after the exiled Dalai Lama, developed a swollen infected ear after sleeping on one side for over ten years. Only after he went berserk and tried to strangle his jailers when they woke him in the middle of the night was he permitted to turn over. Physical beatings were common, Wei contended; prisoners were kept on near-starvation rations, and some recalcitrant inmates were punished by being chained and left unable to move for so long their limbs were paralyzed. When Miss Wang was finally released in 1978, an inexplicable two years after the Gang of Four was arrested, her hair had started falling out, her back was bent double, and her hands and legs were palsied, mutual friends said.

One prisoner in Qin Cheng was a very bright and innovative woman theatrical director named Sun Weishi. Sun's father, an early Communist activist in the Shanghai underground, was killed in the 1930s and she was adopted by Zhou Enlai, who had no children of his own. Precisely why she was arrested is unclear—perhaps it was professional jealousy on the part of Jiang Qing, who fancied herself China's leading authority on drama. But Sun was thrown into Qin Cheng in March 1968 and died the following October after prolonged torture. Zhou, a truly popular figure among Chinese for his supposed efforts to moderate Mao's wilder policies during the Cultural Revolution, was unable or unwilling to save her.* When he found out she had died, he requested an autopsy, but when the medical personnel he sent to the prison arrived, Sun's body had been cremated and they couldn't even find the ashes. All the guards responsible for her death had already been transferred elsewhere. The man who told me about the incident was a friend of Sun's and a prisoner in Qin Cheng, an American, Sidney Rittenberg. A gregarious, charming native of Charleston, South Carolina, Sid first went to China as a Chinese interpreter with the U.S. Army in 1945. Sid's strong left-wing sympathies—he had helped organize southern textile-mill workers in the United States during the Depression—persuaded him to stay on in China after 1949, one of only about a dozen Americans to do so. His remarkable fluency in Chinese, his natural warmth, and his shrewd appreciation of the role of *guan-xi* in China made him a valuable conduit between Communist officialdom and the small community of maverick foreigners. But in the Cultural Revolution, Sid's usual enthusiasm and radical leanings got him in trouble. He was accused of participating in a faction that attacked Prime Minister Zhou and was kept in prison from 1968 to 1978.**

Qin Cheng is still in existence, Chinese friends said. Its most prominent inmate today is Jiang Qing. In his account of the prison, Wei had written, "We might ask the high cadres who have come out of Qin Cheng, When you suppressed the rights of others to express freely their political views, did you secure your own? When you persecuted others using political pretexts, did you foresee yourselves being subjected to the same kind of persecution?"

When they emerged from years of exile or prison after Mao's death and returned to power, Peking's current leaders like Deng Xiaoping clearly had a personal stake in preventing a recurrence of the trauma of the Cultural

*Zhou's ineffectiveness in protecting his own adopted daughter, of whom he was said to be very fond, raises questions about his real role in the Cultural Revolution. Most Chinese gloss over his crucial actions in 1966 when his votes with Mao in narrowly divided Party meetings enabled the Chairman to purge Liu and Deng and carry out the Cultural Revolution.

**Sid, a gifted raconteur, has been at work on his own memoirs about life in Communist China and Qin Cheng prison.

Revolution. They also knew that the persecutions of the past decade had shattered popular confidence in the Communist Party. So one of their first priorities was.to create a more equitable system of justice, or restore "socialist legality," in their own term. Hence in 1979 the Communists promulgated China's first criminal code since 1949. It promised that trials would be public; it prohibited the courts from using forced confessions as evidence; it gave defendants the right to a lawyer—the legal profession had been abolished in 1958—and it fixed strict limits on the time the police could detain suspects before bringing them to trial. Ominously, however, the new criminal code and a revised constitution passed in 1978 made no provision for judicial independence. Instead, the constitution reaffirmed that "the Communist Party of China is the core of leadership of the whole Chinese people" and that "citizens must support the leadership of the Communist Party." In other words, the Party is the law. And while China's tiny group of 2,000 lawyers was allowed to come out of the closet, the National People's Congress in 1980 passed regulations declaring them to be "state legal workers" who must "protect the interests of the state" as much as their clients. They should not act like their counterparts in the West and get bogged down in arguing against the prosecution. China's chief prosecutor gave an indication of how Peking regarded the new legal system when he disclosed in 1980 that 95 percent of all those arrested in the past year had been convicted. In essence, for those people who have been arrested and undergone police examination, by the time they get to trial innocence is no longer an issue. The question is, were the proper procedures followed to prevent arbitrary arrests, frame-ups, and torture. That was what the Chinese people hoped.

The trial of Jiang Qing, her cohorts in the Gang of Four, and five senior generals who had been associated with Lin Biao was to be the showpiece of the new legal system. The trial carried high risks—it couldn't help but look like personal vengeance and it would give Miss Jiang a political platform she had not had since her arrest in October 1976. But, friends said, Deng believed the trial would demonstrate to Chinese that he would not stoop to the low road the radicals had taken in dealing with their adversaries and he wanted to win back popular support from many disillusioned Chinese.

A few weeks before the trial began in November 1980, I accidentally encountered the general appointed deputy president of the special thirty-five-judge high court set up to hear the case, the most sensational in China's legal history. We were both at a reception in the Great Hall of the People for China's national day. The general, Wu Xiuquan, was a deputy chief of staff of the army and was considered China's leading authority on the Soviet military. He had studied in Moscow in the 1920s and had accompanied the Long March in the 1930s. His appearance was unmistakable, with an unusually capacious girth for a Chinese and a long jowly face that reminded me of an elderly basset hound. General Wu, who was seventy-one at the time, had no legal training, but he had been purged in 1967, another victim of the Cultural Revolution like most of the judges. When he spoke, I had noticed on previous occasions, he was cautious, with the circumspection of an old-fashioned mandarin, revealing as little as possible, often only chuckling at a questioner's probe.

But when I asked him if he thought Jiang Qing and the others were guilty of the charges against them—they were variously accused of persecuting large numbers of officials, plotting to seize state power, trying to kill Mao, and engineer an armed rebellion in Shanghai—he replied without hesitation, "They are guilty of terrible crimes."

Could they be sentenced to death then? I pressed him, conscious of a retinue of his aides in army green surrounding us. "They might be," General Wu said. "Ten years in prison is hardly enough punishment for such people."

It was an extraordinary moment. If the deputy chief judge was already convinced of the defendants' guilt, what kind of trial would it be? The answer came a few weeks later. It proved to be a trial disguised as Peking opera, a polished, professional performance complete with actors, costumes, court intrigues, and a well-written script, an utterly Chinese pageant. The signs of the trial as theater, as a morality play, were everywhere. The entire proceedings, a Chinese journalist told me, had actually gone through two rehearsals, the second reviewed on videotape by the Politburo. The Party wanted to be sure there would be no slips. The rehearsals explained why it took almost two months between the time the government announced the start of the trial and its commencement. Miss Jiang, the vitriolic, sixty-seven-year-old onetime movie actress, and Zhang Chunqiao, a former member of the Politburo Standing Committee and mayor of Shanghai, refused to confess as criminals are expected to. Instead, my journalist source informed me, Miss Jiang had tried to defend herself by saying she had only carried out the orders of her husband. "I was Chairman Mao's dog, whoever he told me to bite, I bit," she said in one of the dress rehearsals. Zhang simply remained silent, as he did later during the official trial. He evidently calculated he would not be allowed a legitimate chance to defend himself, that he had already been adjudged guilty, so the most honorable course was not to cooperate.

Otherwise the trial went as scheduled. In the large, converted auditorium at Number 1 Justice Road the other eight defendants pleaded guilty, some even adopting the language of the court and referring to themselves as counterrevolutionaries. Chen Boda, a frail, stooped seventy-six-year-old man who for many years had served as Mao's political secretary and ghost writer, admitted he had concocted an infamous editorial in the *People's Daily* entitled "Sweep Away All Monsters and Demons." "I don't oppose my own death by firing squad," said Chen, who had to hobble into the courtroom on crutches. "But that might be letting me off too lightly. Chopping off my head might be better." Wang Hongwen, the forty-five-year-old former Shanghai textile-mill security guard whom Mao catapulted to be third in the Party hierarchy behind only himself and Zhou Enlai, rushed to tell the court how he had collaborated with Miss Jiang in trying to block Deng's appointment in 1975 as first deputy prime minister.

The prosecutors and judges all sat together on a raised platform overlooking the defendants. The only visible difference between them was that the prosecutors were dressed in light-gray Mao suits, the judges in dark gray. At the end of each day's session, a prosecutor declared that the charge being heard had been proved, the presiding judge concurred, and the defendant involved was marched out with military precision by a blue-uniformed policeman. The defense attorneys for five of the ten defendants—the other five were said not to have requested counsel—were relegated to small tables in a corner of the room. At no point in the excerpts of the trial shown on the nightly television news—the footage was also edited by the Politburo—did a defense lawyer raise an objection, ask to cross-examine a government witness, or call a defense witness. Their only action was to plead for leniency because their clients had confessed.*

Enhancing the impression of a staged performance, the television cameras often showed the prosecutors, judges, and government witnesses reading from printed sheets. Private conversations and telephone calls between the accused that took place more than ten years in the past were quoted verbatim by the prosecutors, suggesting the Party has an elaborate tape-recording service that bugs its own leaders. Where witnesses were too old, or apparently uncooperative, and in two cases where they were actually already dead, their testimony was read for them by popular announcers from Peking Radio. One of the deceased was Mao's private secretary, Zhang Yufeng, a comely woman with whom he reportedly had a romantic involvement in his later years. She had committed suicide when she was arrested after Mao's death by Hua Guofeng, the new Party chairman, who feared she knew too much, Chinese said. It was as if ten years from now Richard Nixon was posthumously impeached for the Watergate scandal and Walter Cronkite read the testimony of the President's former aides like H. R. Haldeman and John Ehrlichman.

When the trial began, Chinese were excited by it the way Americans are by a presidential election. A dour middle-aged woman who ran the elevator in our apartment building and worked for the Ministry of Public Security

*Miss Jiang was originally assigned China's most prominent criminal lawyer, Ma Rongjie, on the order of the Ministry of Justice, I was told by a Chinese friend shortly before the trial began. But when I disclosed this in *The Times,* the party leadership was furious at the leak. Ma was taken off the case and placed under house arrest, he later told a mutual acquaintance. Miss Jiang ended up without an attorney.

asked if she could sneak in for a glimpse of the first night on television. But as Chinese watched the trial progress they rapidly grew skeptical and indifferent. On a Saturday evening during the middle of the six-week-long trial, we went to our friends the Wangs for dinner. At 7:30 P.M., when the daily coverage of the trial began, no one in the family moved to turn on their new television set which we had helped buy. Only at eight o'clock, when they expected an American-made series about the exploits of a squad of commandos during World War Two, *Garrison's Guerrillas,* did Li flick the switch. Father, mother, and daughter groaned loudly when they found the television station had delayed their program for extended news about the trial. To me, as a foreigner, it was a key day in the trial. A general was testifying how he had supposedly plotted in 1971 to blow up a train Mao was riding in with bombs, bazookas, and rockets.

"Everyone knows it was really Mao who gave the orders in the Cultural Revolution and it is he who should be on trial," Li explained when I asked about his lack of interest. Besides, he added, "the defendants look so pitiful, you almost begin to feel sorry for them." He personally detested Miss Jiang —she aroused a visceral distaste among many Chinese with her posturing, her arrogance, the dictatorship she had exercised over culture, and her own privileged life-style, complete with private villas, screenings of old Greta Garbo movies, and her wardrobe of Western dresses, all forbidden to the masses. But to Li and other Chinese the trial had come to look like another struggle session, the same unfair harassment which was all too familiar and which they wanted to see ended.

"No one can have illusions anymore about what socialist legality means," Li said sadly as we left that night. "It means more of the same, only more polite. They gave her a trial first. If Jiang Qing had won, she would have just thrown the others in prison." I thought about Li's comments as we drove home. With the trial the Communists had squandered an opportunity to show they were capable of dispensing justice and recoup some of the prestige they had forfeited with the persecutions of the Cultural Revolution.

When the verdict finally came—after a month's delay to allow the Politburo time to debate the sentence—it was almost an anticlimax. Jiang Qing and Zhang Chunqiao, the two who refused to confess, were sentenced to death, but with a two-year reprieve to see if they reformed. The two-year stay of execution is a Chinese Communist legal innovation. The other eight defendants were given prison terms ranging from sixteen years to life. Some Chinese considered the verdicts fair, since Mao was really to blame and it was time to exorcise the ghost of the Cultural Revolution. But other Chinese I knew grumbled; to them it was another example of the Communists' double standard—one set of rules for the masses, another for Party members. A thirty-year-old factory worker with a wispy mustache was especially bitter. "Punishments do not reach up to the lords," he said, quoting an ancient adage. His younger brother, who was still awaiting his job assignment after finishing high school two years before, had gotten into an altercation with some other neighborhood youths that led to a fight and the fatal stabbing of one of them. Exactly who was to blame was unclear, the worker contended. But his brother had been taken before a public rally in a sports stadium, with a howling crowd of 10,000 people as a jury, and convicted of murder. Then he was executed on the spot by a shot in the back of his head, the standard method of administering the death penalty in China.

It was one of about sixty executions I read about in the press or heard about from friends during 1980 and kept track of in a special file. The majority were for murder or rape, but some were for lesser offenses: a Peking bank cashier was executed for embezzling 125,000 yuan ($83,000); a nineteen-year-old in the northeast city of Harbin was sentenced to death for robbing a passenger on a bus and then assaulting a policeman who tried to arrest him. The real total of executions was undoubtedly much higher. During a visit to the coastal city of Xiamen, I spotted several printed posters announcing the execution of a man named Zhang Qingfu, a forty-one-year-old dock worker. Zhang had slashed a friend forty-three times with a vegetable cleaver when he refused to give Zhang a rowboat to escape to one of the small islands outside Xiamen harbor, still occupied by Nationalist troops from Taiwan.*

These executions are part of Peking's effort to stop what Chinese feel has been a growing crime wave since the Cultural Revolution. For years the Communists had boasted to visiting foreigners that they had virtually eliminated crime: reformed the prostitutes, rehabilitated the opium addicts, and improved society to the point where robbery, rape, and murder had disappeared. There was some truth to this—the Communists did put an end to the country's terrible drug addiction problem. But the credulous visitors never noticed that Chinese always carefully lock their bicycles, put broken shards of glass atop the walls around their buildings, and install iron bars in their first-floor windows. It would be equally misleading now to picture the increase in crime in recent years as being as serious as it is in some large American cities like New York, Atlanta, or Houston. But I was surprised by how daring some Chinese had become in defying the police. In quick succession in one winter month, a twenty-one-year-old unemployed man robbed Peking's largest department store of cameras, calculators, and cash worth 10,000 yuan ($6,670), two masked men stuck up a branch of the People's Bank in downtown Peking and shot a teller with a homemade zip gun, and another man tried to steal a fifteen-pound gold imperial seal dating from the

*The biggest island in the group is Quemoy.

sixteenth century from the hallowed Forbidden City before he triggered an electric alarm and was caught. The government has not published nationwide crime figures as it does for grain and steel production. But China's chief prosecutor did disclose that in the first half of 1980 the police had arrested 84,000 criminals, more than half of them for "grave crimes," probably murder and rape.

The prosecutor also confirmed that there has been an increase in white-collar crime. In the first six months of the year, he said, the police had uncovered 10,000 cases of corruption among officials. But, he admitted, "there is still great resistance in dealing with cases that involve state functionaries."

The problem, said a thoughtful historian in the Academy of Social Sciences, is the same as the problem with the Party as a whole. Since Liberation the Communists have gradually lost their revolutionary discipline and become more interested in their own comfort. But the Party also remains an elite—Party cadres run the police, the courts, and the prosecutors' offices. They form an old-boys network. Therefore, unless an official commits a political error like the Gang of Four and is purged, he enjoys a kind of diplomatic immunity from criminal punishment. As an example, he cited a scandal involving a senior army officer who was simultaneously deputy commander of the critical northeastern military region, responsible for China's main defense against the Soviet Union, and Party secretary of Luda, the naval port formerly known as Port Arthur. The officer, Liu Decai, misappropriated 34 million yuan ($23 million) by constructing a total of sixty-four unauthorized buildings for the pleasure of local cadres, including lavish clubs, theaters, guesthouses, and offices at a time when housing for the public was desperately short. Finally, after a series of complaints, the Cabinet and the Party Military Affairs Commission in Peking sent a special team to Luda to investigate. Liu was not arrested or taken to court, and his only punishment was to be removed from his official posts and have his salary cut. He was not even expelled from the Party. Only six lower-ranking cadres caught up in the scam were arrested, and their sentences were heavier the lower their rank. To the historian, it was merely another instance of the Communists' arbitrary justice.

But of all the stories I heard about arbitrary justice and unfair punishment, the most horrifying were those involving the Communists' system of labor camps. Western Sinologists have known about the existence of the camps for years, and a few former inmates, who were among the lucky ones to be released, have left chilling accounts.* But the Western press, Western intel-

*See, for example, Bao Ruo-wang, *Prisoner of Mao* (London: André Deutsch, 1975), and Lai Ying, *The Thirty-Sixth Way* (London: Constable, 1970).

lectuals—including specialists on China—and Western liberal political organizations have not displayed nearly as much interest in the workings of the Chinese labor camps as they have in the Soviet Gulag charted by Alexander Solzhenitsyn. If a Russian writer or artist is banished to Siberia, it is front-page news in Europe and the United States. This is particularly true if the victim is Jewish, given the sensitivities of the Jewish people to persecution and the number of Jews in the West who are descended from or related to the Jews in the Soviet Union. But if a Chinese dissident is exiled to Qinghai, Peking's equivalent of Siberia, the story is cut to a few paragraphs on an inside page or not printed at all. How many Westerners can name three imprisoned Chinese political activists? I sometimes felt there was a double standard—one for the Russians, who are Europeans, another for the Chinese, who are Asians and therefore not supposed to have the same feelings for human rights and life. Or perhaps we didn't want to believe that a country which had produced such a high level of civilization, with poetry and art that touched the sublime, could be so cruel.

Whatever the explanation, it was an old man of seventy, with snow-white hair and a bent back, who first gave me an eyewitness report of the Chinese Gulag. When I met him, through a relative, he was so emaciated that his skin was waxen, strangely transparent, as if you could see straight through to his bones and skull. His fingers were twisted and discolored, some of them reduced to stumpy digits, for he had just been released from a coal mine where he had worked scraping up chunks of black rock with his bare hands for the past twenty-one years. It was not an ordinary mine, but part of a large camp set behind barbed wire with 10,000 inmates, all sentenced to one form or another of what is called *laodong gaizhao,* or more commonly in its abbreviated form, *lao gai,* "reform through labor."

The mine where he worked is located near the city of Datong in Shanxi province, in the northwest. It is only one of hundreds of such labor-reform camps scattered throughout China that I gradually came to learn about from former prisoners like this old man. They are where most ordinary Chinese who fall afoul of the police are kept—plain criminals like thieves, political dissidents, former Kuomintang army officers, and religious leaders. There are regular jails in every city, juvenile reformatories, and a variety of detention centers for people not yet convicted. But 80 percent of all prisoners in China are assigned to the labor camps, the *People's Daily* disclosed in a rare article on the subject.

It is impossible to calculate the exact total of inmates in the camps. Estimates by former convicts range from several hundred thousand to several million. The government refuses to discuss the subject. Repeated requests for information I made to the Information Department of the Foreign Ministry, the Peking city government, the Public Security Ministry, and the Justice

Ministry were all turned down. An official of the Justice Ministry, which administers the courts, said his office had nothing to do with labor reform and it was handled entirely by the police. It was an inadvertent admission of what Chinese know—that many of the convicts sent to the labor camps are not tried at all in the Western sense but merely sentenced by the police. In 1979, despite the government's pledge to improve the legal system, the National People's Congress reissued a tough 1957 decree which gave the Public Security Ministry authority to sentence suspects to "reeducation through labor," or *lao jiao,* without having to go through the courts. On paper the government makes a distinction between this "reeducation through labor" and "reform through labor": the former is supposed to be lighter, noncriminal, with a maximum sentence of three or four years and the offenders convicted under it are to be kept separate from those prisoners given "reform through labor." But in practice, former inmates said, there is little difference.

Take the old man I met. His crime was that he was accused of being an American spy. In his student days he had attended a Presbyterian seminary in the United States, and in 1950, after the outbreak of the Korean War, he had returned to China. His motive was patriotism, he said sitting in his son's shoe-box-sized apartment. Then in 1957, at the time of the Hundred Flowers movement when Mao seemingly encouraged criticism of the Party, he suggested that Peking should improve its relations with the United States. Despite the Korean War, he argued at a political forum in his neighborhood, Americans liked China, and he asserted the United States would make a more dependable ally than the Soviet Union, then still regarded as China's "elder brother." But in a few months, as criticism of the Party grew out of control, Mao reversed directions and launched the Anti-Rightist campaign. The minister was arrested and confined to a cell four feet long, four feet wide, and about the same height. He could neither stand up nor lie down. It meant constant physical discomfort. His only activity over the next eighteen months was to write and rewrite his confession, or "autobiography," as his jailers called it. When the time finally came for what the police said was his trial, he was glad to at last have a sentence.

"The court was two policemen who had interrogated me and a woman in a police uniform whom they identified as the judge," the minister related. "I admitted I had spoken out in favor of better relations with America, but I denied I was a U.S. spy. I said they had no evidence for the charge. They just laughed contemptuously. There was no need for them to prove it, they said. I had been given my orders in America and they obviously couldn't go there to document it."

His sentence, read to him at the hearing, was ten years. He had the right to appeal, the judge told him, but when he did, the term was doubled. His appeal was proof that he still was not contrite, the police said. To a Westerner, the minister's trial and sentencing were a parody of the judicial process.

In the coal-mine camp where he was sent, the convicts worked from 6 A.M. to 6 P.M., seven days a week, with one day off every two weeks for political study sessions. In the early years he was there, the prisoners' rations were based on how many buckets of coal they chipped away each day. Beginners got only thirty-five pounds of food a month, barely enough to keep them alive. "We worked harder than anyone in a regular factory or mine in China," the minister recalled. "If you stopped even for a minute to smoke a cigarette or relieve yourself, you were in danger of failing to meet your daily quota. For the first few months, my hands were a bloody mess and my back and arms ached all the time, but there was no medical attention." The diet consisted of small pieces of steamed cornbread or cornmeal mush for breakfast, a watery soup or gruel with some vegetables for lunch, and more cornbread for dinner. The prisoners got meat only twice a month, little chunks of fat which they happily devoured since it was the only animal protein or oil they received. In the 1960s, the minister recalled, the guards assigned the prisoners themselves the task of calculating each man's output and food ration, a shrewd and sadistic tactic. It set each prisoner against the other. Later this was relaxed and every inmate except those sent to solitary confinement ate the same meager diet.

Despite these hardships, the minister told his story without rancor, almost with a sense of detachment which muted the monstrousness of the camps. "When I first arrived, the camp commandant gave us a lecture. He pointed to a group of coffins. 'The only way you will ever leave this place is in a box,' he warned us. For most of my friends, that was true, they died of starvation, disease, or exhaustion, or they committed suicide.

"What enabled me to survive was my faith in God and my easygoing nature. I tried not to feel sorry for myself."

Still, the minister's experience left its mark. When his son went to pick him up after he was released—he was too weak to travel on his own—the son brought his father a wristwatch as a present. Watches are still a luxury in China, but the minister wouldn't wear it. "He said it reminded him of the handcuffs he had to wear much of the time," his son said.

Several former inmates said that from what they had heard about conditions in the Russian Gulag, the Chinese police were less viciously brutal than their Soviet counterparts, more subtle, that they made more use of psychological controls like political study, confessions, and struggle sessions, and relied less on sheer physical terror. But the former prisoners also recalled moments of physical cruelty. A convict from Shanghai remembered being called out with his whole camp, 30,000 people, to watch the execution of a twenty-year-old woman. Her father had been arrested during the Cultural Revolution for remarks critical of Mao, but she loved her father deeply and was very hotheaded. She went to the police to protest. Eventually she, too, was sent to the labor camp for her "bad attitude." But she kept shouting at the guards that she and her father were innocent, and the authorities decreed she must be silenced. To make sure she wouldn't scream a reactionary slogan before her execution, two women guards held her down and cut out her tongue in front of the other prisoners. Then another policeman put a bullet through the back of her head, splattering blood and brains on the prisoners in the front row.

Each city and province maintains its own camp or set of camps. The Peking Public Security Bureau has a large labor farm east of the city called the Clear Stream Farm, with about 20,000 to 30,000 prisoners, and a group of labor-camp factories in the suburbs known as the New Capital Foundry, the New Capital Tile and Brick Works, the New Capital Steel Plant, and the New Capital Rubber Plant. The government is fussy about the nomenclature; it doesn't like to use the words "labor camp" or "prison."

The most extraordinary thing about these camps, several former prisoners said, was that unlike many regular civilian factories and farms, which are mismanaged and operate in the red, the labor-camp factories and farms all earn a profit. It is a tribute to the guards' ruthless exploitation of the convict laborers.

In addition, some of the biggest and most dreaded camps have been established in China's sparsely populated and rugged frontier regions, where, like their Russian equivalents, the convicts are put to work clearing the forests and swamps, planting the virgin land, or building roads and railways. The Peking police controlled one of these located in the far northeast on the Soviet border which was known for a nearby lake, Xing Kai Hu, or "The Lake of Emergent Enthusiasm." Temperatures at the camp, which once held 40,000 prisoners, fell to 40 degrees below zero fahrenheit in the winter and in summer the inmates were plagued with giant black flies and mosquitoes. The inmates' behavior in the frontier camps was less disciplined than in those around Peking, a former convict recalled, because the farther people were sent away from their homes, the less hope they had of returning and the less incentive they had to obey the rules. Being allowed to stay in the camps near the capital was regarded as a privilege, he said, and the inmates behaved better. At Xing Kai Hu, he added, some of the convicts tried to escape across the border to the Soviet Union. But the Russians didn't want them and sent them back alive in burlap bags.

West of Ningxia, in the far reaches of China, lies Qinghai province, an almost treeless, bitterly cold plateau of grasslands, salt lakes, and snow-covered mountains that was originally inhabited by Tibetans. What Chinese who have been there remember about Qinghai are the wind and the bleak loneliness, the howl of the wolves and the camel caravans of nomadic herdsmen, and, they say, one of the largest concentrations of labor camps. Until 1980 Qinghai was closed to foreigners. When a group of Australian journalists were finally taken to Xining, the provincial capital, they noticed a mud-walled prison that stretched for a mile on the drive in from the airport. That evening the deputy provincial governor hosted a press conference for the Australians, but when they quizzed him about the number of labor camps in his region, he terminated the meeting in embarrassment.

"No one goes to Qinghai voluntarily, you are sent," said Daniel Kelly, the son of an American missionary doctor and a Chinese nurse who spent twenty years in Chinese labor camps, three of them in Qinghai. "The whole province was built up as a penal colony, a Chinese Siberia, there were camps all over the place," Kelly recalled. He was arrested in 1958 as a seventeen-year-old for allegedly trying to escape to Macao, though he believes the government was angry at him because he refused to renounce his American citizenship and work for Chinese propaganda agencies. He was never tried or sentenced.

In Qinghai, Kelly was assigned to a camp southwest of Xining that was so large "you couldn't cover it in a day in a horse cart." He estimates that the camp, called by its Tibetan name of Tangemu, encompassed over five hundred square miles, with nine branch camps, each having its own substations scattered around the small mountain basins where farming was possible. "Each station had its own adobe walls," said Kelly, a slender serious-looking man with distinct Chinese features and prominent black eyebrows. "Some of the walls were huge, like medieval citadels, twenty feet high and ten feet thick at the bottom." Escape was hopeless. It was a three-hour drive to the nearest tiny town, and the surrounding region was a dry salt marsh. The only inhabitants were gophers. Occasionally an inmate would try to run away.

"After a few days a shepherd would come by and report a body in the bush," Kelly remembered. "Then the guards would go out on horseback and pick it up."

Kelly had been transported to Qinghai with a group of 1,800 other prisoners, all from Guangdong province, near Hong Kong, in 1959, the time of the Great Leap Forward.* But because of the terrible food shortages that followed the Great Leap, when his group was rounded up for transfer in 1962, only four hundred were still alive. The rest had starved to death, said Kelly, who because of his parents' medical background was assigned to work in the main camp hospital. It was a terrible survival ratio. From Qinghai, Kelly was later sent to four different camps near Peking and was released only in December 1978 after the normalization of Sino–U.S. relations. By

---

*His camp was run for prisoners from Guangdong and Jiangsu only. The other provinces had their own camps elsewhere in Qinghai.

chance I entered China from Hong Kong as he walked across the railroad bridge from the Chinese frontier post of Shenzhen in the other direction. He now lives in Plainfield, Indiana.

The overall number of prisoners in labor camps has probably fallen in the past few years, for two of the largest categories of convicts have either died off or were released in amnesties in the late 1970s—former Kuomintang army and police officers and the rightists arrested in 1957–58. But many of the camps are now being used to discipline the cynical generation of young people created by the Cultural Revolution, hoodlums, and dissidents. The *Peking Daily* reported while I was in Peking that a young woman who tricked passersby into paying for having their picture taken in front of the Gate of Heavenly Peace without any film in her camera had been sentenced to three years in the camps. The total of these new recruits is not small. A former teacher arrested as a rightist and sent to a labor camp in the remote desert in southern Xinjiang province, China's far west, recalled how all the 20,000 inmates there were rehabilitated together one day in 1978. As they left, they watched as another equally large group of younger prisoners were driven in to take their places in a convoy of trucks and jeeps guarded by soldiers with machine guns.

His group was an exception. Most inmates in the camps never return home, even after they have completed their sentences, Kelly and other Chinese said, for they stay on, or are kept on, as "long-term forced employees." The major difference is that they now are paid regular salaries and are permitted to marry and raise families.

"In our society, most of the prisoners can't face going back home," said the engineer who had been in Ningxia. "It would always be on your dossier. You couldn't get a decent job, and you'd have trouble finding a wife." In the camps, at least, he added, the men had friends and some had learned a trade so they could make a living. "For some other people, the guards just tell you that your wife has divorced you, or that they won't give you a residence permit to go back home. So you don't have a choice."

Many of the ethnic Chinese inhabitants of Qinghai now are former prisoners, said an ex-Red Guard who was banished there as servitude for his radical activities during the Cultural Revolution. All the workers in a shoe and hat factory in the ramshackle town of Gonghe, where he was sent, were freed prisoners.

"You could always tell who they were by their eyes," he explained. "You got the feeling they didn't have any confidence left. When they talked with you, they always bowed their heads."

Some former prisoners tell stories of great courage, sacrifice, or friendship among the inmates which helped sustain them. I heard of one incident from Yih Leefah, a quixotic, good-humored, sixty-six-year-old, Chinese-born

American citizen who served in the Marines in World War Two but was arrested when he returned to China to see his dying father in Shanghai in 1963. Yih, who had been a professor of fluid mechanics at the University of Iowa, was charged with being an American spy. As proof, the police cited his membership in Phi Beta Kappa. He was dispatched to White Grass Mountain, a camp in southern Anhui, in central China, where the Shanghai police kept 30,000 prisoners from China's largest city. Because he was an intellectual, the guards deliberately put him to tending the pigs, working in his bare feet in a brick pigsty. His job was to shovel out the excrement, mix it with straw, and then, after it had fermented into a rich stinking black mess of fertilizer, scoop it up into piles. Several times he contemplated suicide, Yih told me during a chance encounter in the Shanghai airport when he was on his way to the United States after he was released in 1979. But it was Monsignor Kong Pingmai, the Roman Catholic Bishop of Shanghai, who had been a prisoner since 1955, who dissuaded Yih, a Methodist.

"Bishop Kong kept on praying, morning and evening, while he was out working with the water buffaloes," recalled Yih, a matchstick of a man who talked at double speed. Some of the other prisoners informed on the bishop, a practice the guards encouraged, and he was taken before a struggle session.

"He stood calmly, his head down, showing no emotion while I had to insult him. I said, 'You old fool, why should you pray, if there is a god in heaven you would not be here.' Then he looked at me with very disappointed but loving eyes, like Jesus must have looked at Peter when Peter denied him three times after he had been arrested. I felt terrible."

A few days later, Yih chanced on Bishop Kong in the fields. The bishop said he forgave Yih and urged him not to give up his struggle for life. Bishop Kong, who is now in his late seventies, remains in prison, unrepentant by Communist standards, still swearing his allegiance to the Pope.

What struck me most in listening to the accounts of life in the labor camps, and all the struggle sessions and all the persecutions, was what a waste this suffering had been for China. Did the camps really make China any more revolutionary, Mao's goal, or more prosperous and modern, Deng's target?

An American diplomat I knew ran across a twenty-nine-year-old man in Chengdu, the capital of Sichuan, who had recently been released after spending eleven years in a labor camp in the hills in the northwest corner of the province. His crime had been to make a pun using Mao's name during the Cultural Revolution when he was a teen-ager. A friend tipped off the police, and he found himself bound hand and foot in a labor camp. For the first three years, the jailers had beaten him every day. The man extended his arms to show the diplomat the scars. Later he was allowed to take part in digging ditches, for which he was paid two yuan ($1.33) a month. He used the money to buy paper and stamps to write his family. During his entire eleven years in the camp, they were never permitted to visit him.

Then one day, as suddenly as he had been arrested, he was told he was free. The police gave him a certificate saying he was not guilty, but no money for the bus back to Chengdu, more than a day's ride. When he got home, the city labor office declined to help him find a job. It was not their responsibility that he had been mistakenly sent to labor reform. He met an attractive young woman, but when she discovered his past record, she stopped seeing him.

"There is no future for me," he said simply. "There is no future for China either when things like this can happen."

17. The American Agent

美 国 特 务

DR. BILL GAO

"A revolution is not the same as inviting people to dinner, or writing an essay, or painting a picture, or doing fancy needlework; it cannot be anything so restrained and magnanimous. A revolution is an uprising, an act of violence whereby one class overthrows another."

Mao Zedong

The first thing I noticed about Dr. Bill Gao was his flat, nasal American midwestern accent when he spoke English. We had been seated next to each other on an airplane flight from Peking to Shanghai by an unsuspecting CAAC ticket-counter clerk. As a matter of practice, I always tried to strike up conversations with Chinese near me in planes, trains, or restaurants, hoping to cross that invisible barrier of secrecy with which Chinese shield themselves from foreigners. Three times out of four I failed. Talk rarely went beyond the first few halting sentences.

But Bill—he liked to be called by his Americanized first name—needed no encouragement. He was a gentle, modest, and friendly man, tall and erect, with large hands like a lumberjack's, a strong square jaw, a shock of gray hair, and an avuncular manner. His eyes were warm and inviting. Without any prodding on my part, he disclosed that he had been born in Ann Arbor, Michigan, in 1923, while his father was studying engineering at the University of Michigan. The family had later returned to their home in Shanghai, where his father became a distinguished professor, and when Bill was twenty-three he had gone to medical school at Harvard, specializing in surgery. In 1949, with the Communists poised to conquer Shanghai, Bill had elected to return to his native country "to try to help build China up," he recalled. His background made him a member of that small pre-1949 Western-trained elite which staffed so many of China's hospitals, universities, and scientific institutes and was crucial to its modernization. In their education and professional interests, they had little in common with the Communist peasant revolutionaries who took charge of running the country, except their patriotism.

But Bill wasn't practicing surgery anymore, he said casually, without elaboration. There is no trace of rancor about him, no bitterness, so it took several visits to his home in Shanghai over a period of months before I learned why. I dropped by to see him whenever I was in the city, China's largest, with a population the government estimates at 11.4 million people.

After the outbreak of the Cultural Revolution in 1966, he eventually confided, Red Guards among the younger doctors and staff at his large city hospital had put up wall posters accusing him of being an "American secret agent." "They said I was a spy for you folks, it was ridiculous," Bill related, somehow laughing at the memory. The Red Guards' only evidence was his diploma from Harvard, which they confiscated during a search of his apartment, and several stickers on his old suitcases with the initials U.S.A. written on them. "That was the only English they knew, the letters U.S.A.," Bill added.

"I suppose I am too Western, too outspoken, but when they put up their wall posters, I put up mine, too, in response. I challenged them to produce real proof I was a spy."

It was a futile defense; it only deepened the suspicions against him. The young leftist doctors and cadres, working with radicals in the city administration, soon gained control of the hospital and stripped Bill of his posts as head of surgery and deputy hospital director. They also placed him under "supervision by the masses." It meant confinement in a hospital room, where he was not permitted to communicate with his wife, a nurse, and had to perform a daily round of chores, sweeping the floors and cleaning the toilets. He was also forbidden to see any more patients. From this menial position, he watched as more and more of his older colleagues, the best-trained and most competent doctors, came under attack, too, as capitalist roaders, reactionaries, or "ghosts, demons, and freaks."

"We became very sensitive to every nuance of our treatment," Bill remembered. "As long as they didn't kill you, it was all right. We could tell by the work they assigned you. If they just kept you sweeping the floors, you knew you were safe. But if they changed your work frequently, for example, made you a stevedore on the docks or put you to work cleaning windows on the outside of the tall buildings, you knew you were in trouble."

During this period, though he was held largely incommunicado, he began to pick up rumors about his parents. His father, he heard, had also been arrested as an American spy because of his years in the United States, and his mother was detained too. But no one would tell him precisely what had happened. They avoided his questions. It was only ten years later, long after the Cultural Revolution was over and the Gang of Four arrested, that he found out. His father, who was seventy years old at the time, had been kept in the basement of a classroom building on his campus; there he was interrogated every day for five months by his former students and colleagues turned leftists, subjected to struggle sessions, and, when he refused to confess his alleged crimes, beaten. Finally the beatings grew too violent and he died. Bill's mother was also beaten to death, but he had never been able to find out who was responsible. Despite Mao's successors' pledges to rectify the wrongs of the Cultural Revolution, there had not been an investigation into the incident. Many of the same faculty members and cadres who were at the school then are still there. So Bill thinks it will always remain a mystery.

"I was lucky myself, I didn't suffer as much as others," he said with his customary lack of self-pity. "I am still alive." I felt shriveled by his account and unable to speak. In a way, like the victims of the holocaust, Bill, his father, and his mother had all been persecuted because of their backgrounds, because they had lived and studied in the United States, not because of any crime they committed against China.

In his own case, Bill continued, after two years of "supervision," he was finally informed the evidence against him was not sufficient to arrest and convict him. But he was too dangerous to be allowed to stay in Shanghai. Therefore it was decided to exile him to Xinjiang, the vast, remote region of desert and mountains in China's far northwest that is largely inhabited by Turkish-speaking Moslem minority peoples. He was to work as a barefoot doctor, or paramedic, attached to a commune of Uighur peasants. It was the lowest, least dignified work the radicals could find for him. He was to dispense aspirin, help deliver an occasional baby, and bind up broken arms and legs with splints.

"I was willing to go, I like the peasants and I thought I could help," Bill told me over a meal of smoked duck and eels fried with red peppers that he and his wife had prepared. "At least they let me take my wife and two children with me."

But the difficulties were daunting. Recent Chinese settlers brought in by the army as part of its large Production and Construction Corps had seized the most fertile land in the region and pushed the Uighurs out to the edge of the desert where there was less water. "The Uighurs were terribly poor, but they were also very proud and hated the Chinese," Bill recounted. "At first when I set up my little medical operation in the village, the peasants would hide in their houses." The Uighurs were also very sensitive about the Chinese using their remaining wells.

"In my village, they would not let a Chinese come near their well. They felt the Chinese were dirty and they themselves were clean. The Chinese just left their buckets on the ground while filling them, but the Uighurs kept all their buckets hanging from pegs on a wall, so they wouldn't get mud on them and dirty the water when they dipped them down.

"Of course, when the wind blew, all the sand from the desert would just blow into the well anyway. But when you went to their village, you had to wait till they drew some water for you or there would be a fight."

In his spare time, of which he had a lot, Bill volunteered to go from village to village giving talks on elementary hygiene. The action was typical of his generous nature. "It was very simple stuff, I showed them how to brush their teeth, taught them not to use other people's handkerchiefs to blow their noses, and not to wipe their eyes with dirty cloths." The latter precaution was to try to curb the spread of trachoma, a contagious inflammation of the eyes that can lead to blindness and was chronic in the area. "For me, a skilled surgeon, teaching primary-school public health, it was a waste, but at least I was contributing something."

One day he and his wife and all the people in the village, a ramshackle collection of mud-walled buildings, were called out to attend a mass trial. Several policemen marched out an *ah-hong,* a Moslem holy man, into the main square in front of the crowd, perhaps 1,000 people.

"One policeman read out a document that accused the *ah-hong* of leading a rebellion against the government," Bill said. "But it was not really a trial. They just read out the charges, then the verdict, then shot him in front of us. It was all over in a few minutes."

After that relations between the Chinese and Uighurs grew even more tense. But a few days later when Bill went to the well to get some water, the peasants said to him, "You may draw water whenever you wish." He had become a friend.

In 1972, after three years of serving as a barefoot doctor, the provincial government transferred Bill to a large new industrial town founded by Chinese immigrants. He was assigned to the local hospital; it had eighty beds and sixty doctors, Bill remembers, all highly trained physicians like himself exiled for political reasons from the big cities on the east coast, Peking, Tianjin, and Shanghai. "With so many doctors, I performed three or four operations a month, an appendectomy, a cleft lip, an arm crushed in a factory accident, and the rest of the time was loafing. It was a terrible waste for all of us, and China."

Bill was a talented violinist. He had first met his future wife when he performed Beethoven's Ninth Symphony with an orchestra in Shanghai and she sang in the choir. But when the Red Guards had ransacked his home in Shanghai, they smashed his American-made violin and broke his cherished collection of records, all Bach, Mozart, and Beethoven. In Xinjiang, there were no violins for sale, so Bill had bought an accordion. Unfortunately the local stores were so poorly stocked they didn't have a manual to teach him how to play it, and it took him several years of experimenting to learn by himself.

His son and daughter had now finished junior high school, as far as they could go in the local education system. There was no senior high school, for Xinjiang does not receive as much government support as Peking and Shanghai, part of the government's surprising failure to press for full equality among different regions of the country. His son was assigned to be a construction worker with a road-building gang in the mountains; his daughter was made a peasant. Bill was afraid they would not be able to continue the family tradition of being intellectuals, a severe blow to him. By government regulation, every Chinese family had the right to keep one child home with them. It was a rule designed to mitigate the worst effects of the rustication policy. But this legal protection didn't apply to a suspected counterrevolutionary like Bill, a pariah.

"They didn't take our children away, that would be too impolite a word," he said with his usual restraint. "They just kept them away. We were considered such a bad influence."

He saw his son only once a month, when he came home for a bath, a change of clothes, and a good meal. He was always too tired to talk; he just collapsed. Bill's daughter made it home even less often, only once a year for a two-week visit. Oddly, however, Bill continued to draw his original hospital salary the entire time he was in Xinjiang, 120 yuan a month ($80), more than three years' income for the Uighur peasants in his area. "The Chinese are very rank-conscious," Bill explained. "They may attack you as a reactionary, but they wouldn't touch your rank or your corresponding salary."

When Mao died and then Jiang Qing was arrested in 1976, Bill hoped to be able to return to Shanghai. He had wasted too many years and he wanted to "pick up the knife again." He got his first encouragement when the old Party secretary of his hospital in Shanghai came all the way out to Xinjiang to see him, a week's journey by train. The Party secretary was a former peasant and a veteran of the Long March with no medical training, but he was a kind person and knew what a good surgeon Bill was.

"He told me Deng Xiaoping had declared that the intellectuals are now really members of the proletariat, the working class, not bourgeois as Mao said, and therefore things would be better for me if I came back," Bill told me. "I was flattered by the promotion."

So Bill took a trip to Shanghai to see for himself. "It was like a bucket of ice water poured on my head," Bill said. He could see that his own personal friends in the hospital, the older men, wanted him back, but many of the young leftist doctors and cadres promoted during the Cultural Revolution were still in key posts and they didn't want him. They were afraid he would try to "settle accounts" with them; they also knew he was a better surgeon and they might lose their jobs. Some of them had gone through medical school in the Cultural Revolution when classes were devoted to politics and were hardly qualified for the title of doctor. "They were good at shouting slogans but not much else," Bill asserted. The Cultural Revolution was not really over—it never would be. The internecine wrangles would go on. And China had missed a generation of doctors, a serious blow to the Communists' plan to expand the availability of medical care.

Bill now faced a difficult decision. "I was very apprehensive about going back to work there. It would be nice to be a surgeon again, to have my own ward, but that would mean having other doctors working under me and a secretary. I would have to get to know all the factional alliances, all the personal connections between these people. There would be administrative decisions to make and lots of potential for conflict."

So with some imagination Bill created what he called a "second-line job, out of the firing line." He applied his unusual command of English by offering to translate the English-language medical journals and textbooks which had accumulated in the hospital library. For years they had gathered dust while the hospital engaged in political battles and the doctors fell behind the staggering advances in the outside world in microsurgery, heart transplants, the use of computers, and bioengineering. In the past, the older doctors like Bill all knew a foreign language and could read the journals themselves. But because of the breakdown in China's educational system, the younger physicians knew only Chinese.

"It is a very safe job," Bill explained of his decision. "This way I can say I didn't write anything wrong. It is all in the journals, and you are the ones who ordered them from abroad."

He was almost apologetic about it. He had tried to make a comeback as best he could—he had even spent six months applying, pleading, and finally using a back-door connection to get permission to leave Xinjiang, where it turned out the local authorities now regarded him as valuable property. But the obstacles to resuming his old practice as a surgeon were overwhelming. So he had opted for survival. In the Chinese context, it was not unheroic.

"I am already over fifty. [He was fifty-seven when we met.] This hospital is the place I am going to work for the rest of my life. I can't afford to make any more mistakes, no business like the last time. In China, you can't just change jobs."

This reluctance to accept responsibility, to expose oneself to the vicissitudes of politics, was hurting Chinese science and medicine, Bill recognized. Another able doctor he knew, also trained abroad and a victim of the Cultural

Revolution, had been offered the post of the director of his hospital. He turned it down. "In that job he would have to make decisions about people every day. Some of them would get angry and would be waiting for revenge. You never know when the next campaign is coming, but it will. It's in the genes of this Communist Party. They can't help it."

Bill contrasted the pettiness, the cynicism, and the conservatism he saw around him with the happier, more optimistic, and idealistic days of the early 1950s when the Communists were fresh in power.

"At the time, I wasn't a Communist myself, but I believed in them. I saw how rotten the Kuomintang had been and how when the Communists entered Shanghai they changed things. Overnight they ended corruption and prostitution; they gave people work and they helped the poor. They were clean in those days, they practiced equality, there was a lot of hope.

"You weren't here then," he said to me, "you can't imagine how poor China was and how some people suffered. I remember one morning going to school in a rickshaw. The puller was very sick and weak. When I went home in the afternoon, he was lying in the street dead. I felt nauseous. I never took a rickshaw again."

We were sitting in the tiny one-room apartment where Bill and his wife were living after they returned from Xinjiang. Finding housing had been a serious problem. Their own apartment had been confiscated years ago and the hospital had no new housing to assign them. But in good Chinese fashion, Mrs. Gao's brother, who lived in Shanghai, had invited them to stay with him and his wife. There was space for only one double bed in the ten-by-twelve-foot room, so the families took turns sleeping on it. One night Bill and his wife used it while their in-laws slept on straw mats on the concrete floor; the next day they reversed the process. To make it even more cramped, they had to share their kitchen and a squat toilet with another family next door—the only separation was a blue cloth curtain. Every word was audible on both sides of the flimsy divider. Bill's only luxury was a miniature Japanese refrigerator which a cousin who fled to America in 1949 had given him when he returned a few months before on a visit. Whenever I arrived, Bill always had a cold bottle of beer or some watery Chinese ice cream ready in the ice box. He remembered what Americans liked from his years in the United States, and he was determined to be the gracious host no matter how humble his circumstances.

Resuming his account, Bill said that his first premonition of trouble came in 1952 when the Communists put all the doctors in his hospital into a thought-reform class, "what you Americans call brainwashing." It was part of the Communists' ambitious program to win personal conversions from all of China's intellectuals. Each individual's reform, his remolding, was to be part of the overall transformation of Chinese society. Just as the social evils of the past had to be eradicated, so did intellectuals have to cleanse their own personal sins in order to take part in the great renaissance. For doctors and scientists like Bill, it was an urgent task; his talents were badly needed by "the masses," yet his class background had so polluted him that until he was reformed he couldn't serve them.

For Bill, his thought-reform class consumed six painful months. "The Communist cadre who led our small group always said our task was to help the older doctors, to help them confess and carry out self-criticism. They were supposed to be the most poisoned by the bad old bourgeois thoughts they had.

"It was very hard for me. I was still relatively young then and some of the older doctors were my friends and teachers. I had great respect for them. I was brought up as a sort of Confucian, we believed in older people and teachers."

The final part of the course was the worst. Bill had to write out his own confession, first analyzing his class origin, going back three generations, then denouncing his father. It was a symbolic test to see if he was truly converted to the new Communist faith.

Bill penned an attack on his father, criticizing him for his slavish devotion to the United States and his bourgeois habit of liking Western food. But it was all false, Bill insists, extorted from him under pressure. "Thought reform was a fraud, it didn't work," Bill observed. "You always ended up pretending, not really telling what you thought." This laid the basis for much of China's current troubles, he believed, the cynicism, the deceitfulness, the easy reliance on the back door to get everything done.

"Because of all the thought-reform and criticism meetings, you could never even tell your wife what was on your mind. For the next time a campaign came along, the first thing the cadres would do was to turn to her and ask her to help you confess. So we hid our true feelings."

While we were talking, a ten-year-old boy with large, floppy ears and a crew cut knocked on the door. There would be a street committee meeting that evening at 7:30 P.M. in the large courtyard below and every family had to send one representative, he announced. I was afraid I might have been spotted coming into the building and gotten the Gaos in trouble, but they laughed and told me to relax. At 7:30 no one had yet shown up, and a middle-aged woman stood in the courtyard yelling, "The street committee meeting is starting, everyone hurry."

Mrs. Gao, a dainty, quiet woman with nervous eyes, picked up a small wooden stool, no bigger than a child's toy chair, and carried it downstairs to the open-air meeting. But fifteen minutes later she was back. "No one has come yet, they'll be lucky to get going at eight thirty," she reported.

At 8:30 she went again. Peering out from their third-floor window, I could see more than five hundred people gathered below. A squat and expansive matron with glasses was reading a document. When Mrs. Gao returned I asked what it was about, hoping it might be a new Central Committee directive with important political news. "I don't know what it was," she replied. "There were so many kids running around playing and shouting, I couldn't hear."

Here again was the result of Communist overkill. People had been required to attend so many meetings for so many years, to feign so much activism and fake so many confessions, that they tuned out.

On my last trip to Shanghai, I broached a delicate question to Bill. Had all the campaigns and persecutions of the past thirty years, particularly the greatest of all, the Cultural Revolution, caused any measurable increase in anxiety, depression, and mental illness? How had Chinese withstood all the tension?

"It's a question we doctors talk about often among ourselves," Bill answered. "But there have not been any scientific studies done, it's too sensitive an issue. In 1957 they abolished the whole profession of psychology and said all you needed to do to clear up a mentally disturbed person was to have them study Mao's works. It was nonsense."

Bill had a theory, however, based on his own experience and observation. "Contrary to what you might expect, there was no rise in mental illness during the Cultural Revolution," he suggested. "People either snapped all the way and committed suicide or they survived. It was something like what I've heard about the Jews in the concentration camps. There was very little you could do about it when they started attacking you—it was all arranged. So the main thing was to try and stay alive.

"In China, you also have to consider your family," Bill went on, now speaking more intensely. "It was knowing that I had to take care of my family that kept me going."

Some of his fellow doctors chose suicide instead, Bill recalled—over twenty physicians in his hospital from a total staff of three hundred killed themselves during the Cultural Revolution. "But if a person committed suicide, it was worse for his family. Then the Communists automatically considered you guilty. It was terrible. They would hold a ceremony, not to mourn the person but to formally condemn them."

But the strange thing was what happened when the pressure was lifted, after Mao died and the Gang of Four was arrested, Bill added. "It was then that the stress showed." Several of his friends were so happy they went out and drank so much alcohol they suffered brain hemorrhages. Another laughed so hard he became hysterical and couldn't stop laughing for weeks.

Bill's wife wouldn't talk for a month; she couldn't believe the radicals had really been toppled.

Settled in Shanghai, Bill and his wife were trying to put their lives back together. All their family memorabilia—their photo albums, their letters, their college yearbooks—had been burned by the Red Guards. But their friends had a surprise present for them. They had collected old pictures they had managed to keep of Bill, his wife, and his father and mother and assembled them in a new binder. There was even a fading snapshot of Bill as an infant sitting on his father's lap outside a rambling Victorian house in Ann Arbor. His father was sitting ramrod-straight, his hair parted neatly in the center, with an old-fashioned stiff high collar thrusting up his chin.

Bill's cousin in Chicago had arranged to pay for his daughter to make a trip to the United States and study English in a special program for foreigners. Since Bill was now legitimately living in Shanghai and no longer under a political cloud, the commune where his daughter had been sent agreed to let her leave. I gave her a letter of introduction to the U.S. Consulate in Shanghai to help her get an American entry visa.

A few weeks after she arrived in Chicago, Bill got his first letter from her. He was ecstatic. The letter was in English. "When she left China, she didn't speak a word of English," he said. "The English in her letter is terrible, really atrocious, but it's English." Another generation of the Gao family had survived; his daughter was on her way to becoming an intellectual, in Chinese terms, master of a foreign language and a higher education, not a peasant. For Bill, that was success.

PART
5

MESSAGES

—

18.   Little Road News

INFORMATION

"There are comrades without elementary notions of politics, and this brings them to entertain absurd ideas, such as the idea that we live in a time when critical journalism remains a necessity."
                                                                    Mao Zedong

In early January 1980, Chinese cadres in offices attached to the Central Committee were called in to be briefed on an important document. There were elderly white-haired veterans of the Long March now in the Military Affairs Commission, cautious operatives from the public security apparatus, and the heads of China's media, the *People's Daily,* the New China News Agency, and Peking Radio and Television. The directive was classified "secret" and the officials were not permitted to take notes on the briefing, but what they heard startled them. It portended a watershed in Chinese politics. At the next session of the National People's Congress, more than half a year away, they were told, the then Party boss of Sichuan province, Zhao Ziyang, would be named Prime Minister. At the time the Prime Minister was Hua Guofeng, the man picked for the job by Mao Zedong himself, and the cadres who attended the briefing must have known Hua would not voluntarily surrender his post.

It was almost as if a select group of Americans in Washington had been told in the spring of 1980 that Jimmy Carter would step down as President in favor of Ronald Reagan the next November. In the United States, the news would have been banner headlines on the front pages of all the newspapers the next day, but not a word about the impending switch in Peking appeared in the Chinese press. Nevertheless, over the next eight months, news of the change was slowly and deliberately spread through similar briefings and documents, moving out from officials under the Central Committee to government ministries in the capital, then to provincial Party headquarters, to army commands, and finally in ever-widening ripples to middle- and lower-level cadres.

I first heard about the possibility of Zhao becoming Prime Minister only a few days after the original briefing from a journalist acquaintance who worked as an aide to a senior figure in the Party Propaganda Department. He mentioned it casually, and I had no idea what the source of his information was, so I reported it only as a rumor in *The New York Times.* I did journey down to Sichuan to interview Zhao. He, of course, denied the story and said he had no desire to give up working in the provinces where he had spent his whole career. Little did I realize how the news was being fed to China's officials. By the time the National People's Congress eventually met that September, there was hardly a Chinese with any interest in politics who didn't know. But the *People's Daily* and other papers did not mention it until the NPC had made Zhao's appointment official by a formal vote. The last place news appears in China is in the papers or on radio and television.

The episode offered me an insight into the vast hidden communications network in China. Westerners numbed by reading endless articles in the *People's Daily,* the Party's flagship paper, about heroic factory workers and stalwart peasants churning out more tons of steel and grain are inclined to dismiss China's media as mere propaganda tools. That is a misunderstanding of how the system functions, I came to learn. For there is a separate, semi-clandestine information belt that carries accurate news about the inner workings of the Politburo, the real state of China's economy, and international affairs which never shows up in the country's public press. In fact, Chinese are often at least as well informed about what is happening in Peking as Americans are about politics in Washington.

Peking's leaders prefer their classified approach to the news, rather than using newspapers and radio and television, because it fits into their belief that information is power, the power to shape people's minds. Having risen to success as guerrillas, operating for several decades before 1949 in an environment where secrecy was essential for survival, the Communists are chary about disclosing anything, no matter how trivial.

During the time that the news about Zhao's elevation was being spread around China, Mayor Ed Koch of New York arrived in Peking to establish a sister-city relationship with the Chinese capital. The visit was more of a chamber of commerce promotional gimmick than a serious diplomatic mission, and Koch himself admitted he had come partly because he hadn't had a vacation in over a year and had always wanted to see China. But in keeping with the niceties of protocol, the Chinese arranged for Koch to be received in the Great Hall of the People, like other distinguished visitors, by Li

Xiannian, a vice chairman of the Party. What questions should I put to Li? Koch asked me and some of the other journalists accompanying him. There were strong rumors that an important meeting of the Central Committee was under way in Peking—several Chinese had told me about it and convoys of Red Flag limousines had been spotted outside the Great Hall. Why not ask Li what the gathering was about? I suggested. Good idea, Koch responded, and the next day, when he walked in the polished marble entryway to the Great Hall, Koch popped the question.

"There's no meeting," Li said curtly, stopping the discussion dead.

Three days later the *People's Daily* reported there had indeed been a week-long Central Committee meeting and it had voted on a series of key decisions. One was to rehabilitate Liu Shaoqi, the former head of state vilified and purged in the Cultural Revolution as China's main capitalist roader. Another was to promote Zhao to the Standing Committee of the Politburo, a clue to his rising star. Li's misleading response to Koch reflected the contrasting styles of American and Chinese politicians. Both recognize the value of news as a tool; but where American politicians dispense it, to keep themselves in the public eye, Chinese hoard it.

The government goes to extraordinary lengths to try to encase its workings in secrecy. In 1980, upset by a number of foreign press reports on developments inside the Politburo, Peking pointedly republished a draconian set of "Regulations on Guarding State Secrets" first issued in 1951. The law is a detailed document enumerating fifteen categories of information that must not be revealed: anything about the armed forces and national defense, about foreign affairs, the police and state economic planning, but also about culture, public health, the ethnic minorities, warehouses, and even weather forecasts. The law then lists a sixteenth article covering "all state affairs which have not yet been decided upon, or which have been decided upon but have not yet been made public." For good measure a seventeenth article specifies the law also includes "all other state affairs which should be kept secret." Newspapers and radio stations "are not permitted to touch on state secrets," the law warns, and it provides for a government censor. "Before publications are published, they must be examined by the personnel in charge of guarding state secrets." To ensure that no one misunderstood the decree's intent, the *People's Daily* printed an editorial to accompany the text of the regulations. "In a situation where class struggle still exists at home and abroad, our enemies have never ceased to steal secret information from us," the paper charged. "A small number of counterrevolutionaries and other bad people at home and the hegemonists and other reactionaries abroad are always prying about our secrets."

My friend Bing told me that, shortly after the law was reissued, her school called a political study session to go over the regulations. The cadre in charge of her group summarized the message by saying that people should feel free to discuss only that information which had already been published in the newspapers. That was the way they could be sure something was not a secret.

"But what about my name?" a student asked flippantly. "My name has never been in the press. Is it a state secret?"

This fetish for secrecy means that Chinese must do without some everyday information that Westerners take for granted. Whenever I arrive in a new city, one of the first things I do is purchase a map so I can learn my way around. In Peking I bought a copy of the standard three-color street and bus-route map which the government publishes in Chinese. But our friends the Wangs laughed at me. It is not really accurate, they confided. The angles and dimensions of the streets and the locations of some important buildings have been distorted to foil Western intelligence. That helped me make sense of an incident I remembered from the time in 1972 when I escorted the first group of Chinese journalists around the United States. On our first afternoon in the car, we had stopped for gas on the New Jersey Turnpike. The three Chinese sauntered into the gas station to look around. One of them spotted a rack of road maps. He carefully unfolded a map of New Jersey and, as casually as he could, asked whether it was for sale. I explained the maps were free; you could take as many as you like. The three Chinese hesitated for a minute, then pounced on the rack like hungry wolves. They took several copies of each state that were available, New Jersey, New York, and Pennsylvania. Every time after that when we stopped for gas, the journalists made a ritual of stuffing a satchel full of maps. I could envision the award they would receive on their return to China for this intelligence coup.

Even something as ordinary as a telephone directory presents a problem in China. When I first arrived in Peking in 1979, the only telephone book available to foreigners was a thin red-covered booklet published for $25 by Julie Munro, the wife of Ross Munro, a former correspondent for the Toronto *Globe and Mail* who had been expelled from China in late 1977 after a series of tough articles on human rights. She had painstakingly assembled the telephone numbers of foreign embassies, journalists, hotels, restaurants, and the main government foreign-trade corporations to meet the need of Western residents to communicate in Peking. It was only after I had been in China for half a year that a friend told me there was a Chinese telephone book but it was supposed to be kept secret from foreigners. It was 190 pages long, my friend said, and was issued to offices by special subscription through the post office. An individual could not just walk in and buy one. As a favor, my friend one day smuggled out her office's copy of the bright-orange-covered telephone book to show me. It had been published in 1975, four years before, and not updated since, I noticed. On the back were eleven important numbers in bold print, among them the police, the fire department, the long-distance operator, directory assistance, and time and weather information.

But the telephone book contained odd lacunae. All the listings were for offices, there were none for individuals. Not many Chinese have phones in their homes, it is true, but the omission helped me understand why Chinese are always nervous about losing the little pocket-size personal phone-number booklets they must carry with them. The government phone directory gave nine numbers for the tiny non-Communist "patriotic parties" that have been allowed to survive as a token of democracy—but there was no indication which number belonged to which party. My friend speculated it was a ploy to prevent people from getting in touch with these largely moribund organizations.

In 1980, as part of its effort to become more open, and perhaps to compete commercially with Julie Munro's successful directory, the government for the first time issued a public phone book. About thirty pages give the numbers of public telephone kiosks, but it still did not list private phone numbers or people's addresses. The first number in the book is that of the Standing Committee of the National People's Congress, followed by the Supreme People's Procurate, relatively powerless organizations. The Communist Party Central Committee is included under the heading "Partisan Organizations." But for the nation's most puissant and important body constituting a complete shadow government that matches the entire structure of government ministries, the directory gave only two numbers—one for the reception center for petitions from "the masses," the other the United Front Work Department.

The numbers of the other Central Committee departments are strictly confidential, as I discovered when reports began to circulate in late 1980 that Hua Guofeng had suddenly been forced to resign as Party Chairman. For several weeks the government itself was in confusion. When I called the Information Department of the Foreign Ministry, the official spokesman, and asked who was Party Chairman, the cadre who answered said, "I don't know." With this uncertainty, I tried to think of other official sources who might be better placed to know what had happened. China had close relations with Yugoslavia and presumably would want to keep the Yugoslav Communist Party informed about something as important as a switch in Party Chairman. So I asked Lao Wu, my assistant, to try calling the International Liaison Department of the Central Committee, which deals with foreign Communist parties. Lao Wu had worked in the Yugoslav Embassy before being transferred to *The Times* office, and I was sure he would know the number. But he refused to tell me. "That number is *bu-dui-wai,"* he said, "not open to foreigners."

Communication is much easier for senior officials. Politburo members have their own special telephone exchange—all their phone numbers begin with the prefix 39, Bing told me. There is also a separate exchange for the army, with its own lines, operators, and switching equipment, she added. This is quite a privilege, because telephones are not only hard to get in Peking—there is an installation fee of 1,900 yuan ($1,267) and a year's waiting list —but service is erratic. Phones often emit strange buzzing and clicking noises, and it can take several minutes to get a dial tone, signs, most foreigners assume, that someone else is listening.

During the visit to China by the U.S. Secretary of Defense, Harold Brown, when he was being feted at the Great Hall of the People, he ordered an American diplomat to send an urgent message back to Washington for him. The diplomat was uncertain how to proceed and asked a liaison officer from the People's Liberation Army for help. He was immediately taken to a central communications room inside the bowels of the Great Hall that had a bank of red phones and a list of the numbers for members of the Politburo and editors of the *People's Daily* and the New China News Agency, the latter presumably so the leadership could check on important articles or editorials. When the American picked up the phone, he noticed the connection was marvelously clear, unlike anything he had ever heard in China before. (There is also a secret underground passageway wide enough for cars between the Great Hall and Zhongnanhai, where China's leaders have their offices, so they can attend meetings in the Great Hall without showing themselves in the streets, friends said.)

The special telephones are only the tip of the iceberg of China's huge inner communications network. Like everything else in China, information is not a matter of money, but of connections. The higher an official's rank, the better informed he can be, for information, like consumer goods, is rationed out by title. The principle is to keep the leaders well informed without contaminating the minds of the masses.

The heart of this hidden network is a system of classified documents. Each Party, government, and army unit distributes its own, including the State Council and the various ministries. But because of its source, the most important are those issued by the Central Committee. It was one of the keys to Mao's power that he commanded the right to read and approve each of these Central Committee papers before it was sent.* The Central Committee documents are used for a variety of purposes, Chinese told me. They can transmit authoritative directives which must be followed punctiliously. They may be designed to start discussions on a new experimental policy—the Communists

*For a detailed and perceptive description of this document system, see Kenneth Lieberthal, *Central Documents and Politburo Politics in China* (Ann Arbor: The University of Michigan Press, 1978).

often try out a program in a limited area of the country before instituting it nationwide. Or they might simply be to keep local cadres informed of events in Peking, like the document about Zhao's promotion. The Central Committee documents are not sent through the post office but are delivered by a special courier, and each paper is numbered to forestall leaks. Each document also contains one of three levels of security classification: secret, institutional secret, or absolutely secret. The latter must be returned by the reader. A notation at the top specifies how widely the document may be circulated within the receiving office or province. Despite the extraordinary shifts in power in Peking since 1949, the document system has remained largely unchanged.

Many high-level organizations in Peking have a document room where cadres with the proper clearance can peruse the directives. Central Committee directives are also read out at what are called "transmission" meetings. Usually the process is divided into steps. First the cadres are read the actual document; later, if the document is not too highly classified, "the masses" are informed about its content in general terms, without the text, at their weekly political study sessions in factories, schools, and offices. Only after this transmission has taken place will references to the document begin to surface in the newspapers. People who are under political suspicion are not allowed to attend these meetings. Nor are those Chinese who have regular contact with foreigners, like interpreters for the embassies and foreign correspondents or guides for the China Travel Service. That way, they can't accidentally let slip some state secret.

A pert, vibrant woman I knew who worked for the Central Broadcasting Station was told she could no longer listen to documents because she had become overly friendly with a European colleague hired by the station to help with some of its foreign-language broadcasts. She was disconsolate; she knew it meant she was in political trouble, and it cut her off from the most interesting source of news.

Complementing this classified stream of documents is a hierarchy of *neibu*, literally "internal," or restricted, publications which go far beyond what is available in the open media. There are four layers of these internal bulletins, Chinese told me: the narrower and more high-level the circulation, the more complete, candid, and interesting the contents. At the bottom comes a four-page tabloid-sized paper called *Reference News*, which reprints articles from the foreign press about international events and carries some dispatches by Western journalists in Peking about domestic Chinese developments. Its circulation of over 10 million is nearly double that of the Party paper, the *People's Daily*, an indication of the value Chinese readers place on the two papers, and Chinese claim it is the most widely read paper in the world.

Reference News, I found, enables Chinese to be more knowledgeable about the outside world than foreigners realize. The day the vote on China's seat was coming up at the United Nations in 1971, after Peking had been excluded by American opposition since 1949, the Chinese people knew about it from *Reference News,* though the story had not appeared in the *People's Daily.* During the Watergate crisis, when President Nixon was under daily assault, the *People's Daily* spared him embarrassment by not mentioning it, since he was considered a "friend" of China for reopening Sino–U.S. relations after more than two decades of hostility. But *Reference News* kept the Chinese public informed, friends recalled.

Any Chinese can subscribe to *Reference News* for only 50 cents a month ($0.33). But though its content is drawn exclusively from articles written by foreigners, foreigners in China may not legally buy or read it. Often when I stopped by the service counter on the third floor of the Peking Hotel to pick up my laundry or buy a cold drink, the room attendants would be glued to the day's edition of *Reference News.* But as soon as they realized my presence, they would quickly tuck it out of sight under a stack of other papers. One reason for this secrecy is that *Reference News,* which is put out by the New China News Agency, doesn't pay the Western and Japanese wire services and newspapers for the material of theirs it prints, violating international copyright laws. Another is that Peking's leaders occasionally use it to float stories they don't want to confirm officially by printing in the government press. When I reported in early 1980 that Zhao might replace Hua as Prime Minister, *Reference News* carried an excerpt from my story on its front page, my friend Weidong informed me, presenting me with a copy of the paper. Its appearance in *Reference News* was a clue to politically conscious Chinese. An editor at the New China News Agency jokingly told me later that Chinese newsmen referred to this practice of using Western correspondents' stories about China as "turning exports into imports."

At the next level above *Reference News* comes *Reference Material,* a much richer and more detailed digest of foreign news articles that is printed twice a day, averaging a hundred pages in the morning and fifty in the afternoon. It is available only to Party members and cadres through their *danwei,* not to individuals, and is printed in large characters to help the fading eyesight of elderly officials.

"It is too thick to read all the way through, if you did, you wouldn't do your job," Weidong remarked. Now that he had become a cadre himself, he often took a copy to his political study meetings to avert boredom.

At a still more rarefied level is a group of publications known as *nei-can,* "internal reference," which are distributed only to officials above grade 12 on the ladder of twenty-four ranks, equivalent to deputy cabinet ministers. Each ministry puts out its own *nei-can* bulletin, a compendium of unvarnished reports about its area of responsibility—agriculture, industry, the railways, crime. But the most widely read *nei-can* are those published by the *People's Daily* and the New China News Agency. Wandering through the long corridors of the *People's Daily* and the huge compound of the New China News Agency, I often wondered what their staffs did all day. The *People's Daily* has 600 reporters to put out an eight-page paper (*The New York Times* has an editorial staff of 475 people to publish a daily paper averaging over eighty pages), and the New China News Agency has 3,000 reporters and editors in its Peking office, a total of 6,000 nationwide, to put out a few thousand words of copy a day. The explanation, a reporter at the *People's Daily* told me, was that many of them are assigned to *Reference News* and *Reference Material*, while the most trusted newsmen are detailed to work on *nei-can*. Here they can actually employ their talents as reporters, for they are empowered to investigate sensitive problems that receive scant coverage in the open media: official corruption, labor strikes, friction between Chinese and the ethnic minorities, rural hunger, police brutality, and the unequal treatment of women.

"Before Liberation there was a saying in China that reporters are uncrowned kings," the journalist friend added. "It isn't quite true anymore, but when a correspondent from the *People's Daily* or the New China News Agency shows up at a factory, the plant Party secretary has to be very polite and helpful. Otherwise he knows he may get in trouble."

As an example of a story published by the *People's Daily* version of *nei-can,* titled "Current Information," he mentioned an incident in Henan province in which the county Party authorities had been lax in implementing the government's birth-control campaign. When the local cadres realized there were 3,000 more women pregnant than their quota for the year permitted, they suddenly ordered a "clean out the stomachs" movement. All 3,000 women were ordered to undergo immediate abortions, including one expectant mother almost nine months along. Some of the women fled into hiding; when the cadres came around to find them, children in the neighborhood organized themselves into an antigovernment militia to warn the pregnant women and help them escape. "It was a shocking story, just like during our war against the Nationalists and the Japanese, only now the Communists were the enemy," the reporter said.

Finally, I learned, there is a special digest called *Cable News,* only for members of the Central Committee and the commanders of the large military regions. It provides them with a highly informative bulletin of major Chinese and international news flashes, like the daily briefing the U.S. President gets each morning from his national security adviser.

But if the Communists have devised a careful system to ration information according to rank, what intrigued me even more was how ingeniously the Chinese people have tapped into this with their own widespread grapevine dubbed *Xiao-dao xiao-xi,* or "little road news." Just as the Chinese use their connections, or *guan-xi*, in back-door deals to arrange a better apartment or a coveted job, they can call on their circle of relatives, friends, and colleagues to learn about Central Committee documents or intrigues in the Politburo. With a sense of triumphant self-satisfaction, a balding bespectacled scholar in the Academy of Social Sciences recalled that he had first learned of the arrest of Jiang Qing and her cohorts in the Gang of Four on Thursday, October 7, 1976, less than twenty-four hours after they were detained in the greatest secrecy. He had a niece who worked in the special army hospital in Peking for senior generals, and as soon as she heard the astounding news from one of her patients, she had rushed to tell him. The government did not publicly confirm the arrests for a week. Whenever there were Central Committee meetings, the scholar added, he read daily bulletins of their activities, virtual transcripts, lent him by a friend whose father was a Politburo member.

With the breakdown of Party discipline after the Cultural Revolution, children of high cadres have become notorious gossips, and I noticed with amusement that the press often complained about their loquacity. "Influenced by liberalism, some people pose as well-informed sources and are fond of spreading rumors," the *Worker's Daily* charged in one outburst. "Some allow their family members and children to read secret documents at will and reveal secrets to them. These children of high cadres then pass on the secrets to their friends. Consequently, a strange phenomenon has recently occurred. Party secrets have come back to us from outside the Party and state secrets have come back from abroad."

In January 1980, when Deng Xiaoping gave a major speech in the Great Hall of the People to 20,000 officials calling for the abolition of the right to put up wall posters, I learned about it the next day from another young reporter at the *People's Daily*. His father had been in the select audience and had recounted the contents to him when he returned home. I had been in China only a half year at the time and was still wary about the quality of such information. From two years of reporting in South Vietnam during the war I had become distrustful of all street rumors. But in China, I came to realize, "little road news" was uncannily accurate. When excerpts of Deng's speech were later made public, they squared exactly with what I had been told. The reason the grapevine was so reliable, Chinese friends suggested, was precisely because it was based on the government's own secret communications network rather than the public media, which the people disdained as propaganda.

Most Chinese take it for granted that journalists are servants of their government. When the *People's Daily* and the New China News Agency sent their first correspondents to Washington in 1979, they traveled on official government passports and took up residence in the Chinese Embassy, like other officials. Chinese I met usually assumed I lived in the U.S. Embassy and were baffled when I told them I had a room in the Peking Hotel. "But why don't you live in the embassy where the facilities are better?" they asked, since they did not believe my explanation that *The New York Times* is not part of the American government.

A senior editor at the *People's Daily* made no effort to disguise the political purpose the regular press is expected to play in China. On a sun-dappled early fall morning, with the leaves just starting to turn from mottled green to russet, I went for a formal interview to the old, drab, five-story concrete headquarters of the *People's Daily* around the corner from the Peking Hotel.*
A People's Liberation Army guard with a fixed bayonet stood athwart the stairs leading to the front door. Inside, the building was a stark contrast to an American newspaper—instead of a large central newsroom, crowded with desks, reporters, typewriters, and computer terminals, with a hum of activity and cries of "copy," the building was quiet, the pace slow, and the space divided into a series of separate and unmarked offices with closed doors.

"The *People's Daily* is the organ of the Chinese Communist Party," explained An Gang, a deputy editor in chief. Youthful-looking and cherubic, with a rosy complexion and a full head of black hair though he was a veteran of the Long March, An put the paper's main purpose succinctly. "It is to propagate Marxism–Leninism–Mao Zedong thought."

To a Western reader, that is a prescription for dullness. There are no racy inside stories about how the country's leaders live, no sensational murders, no features on the latest fashion in clothes or trends in sexual appetites, no photos of bathing beauties, no tips on how to decorate your home or cook a gourmet meal. Some embarrassing subjects are ignored entirely. When a devastating earthquake obliterated the industrial city of Tangshan in north China in 1976 and severely shook Peking and Tianjin, one of the greatest natural disasters of recent centuries, the press gave no details. Only more than two years later, in a small box at the bottom of page four, did the *People's Daily* disclose that the quake had killed 242,000 people and seriously injured another 164,000. Instead, the *People's Daily*'s prose tends to be bombastic and self-righteous, with endless long-winded stories about model workers in the Daqing oil field laboring in subzero temperatures or peasants in south China exceeding their rice production quota. The result is a picture of a China ceaselessly advancing toward a brighter future. But since most Chinese are keenly aware of problems like unemployment, inflation, and persecution, the *People's Daily* tends to increase popular cynicism, adding to the credibility gap rather than making converts to socialism.

*The paper has since moved to an elaborate, new, walled compound on the outskirts of the city which encompasses its editorial offices, printing plant, living quarters, and schools.

One of the young reporters I knew at the *People's Daily,* whose father was a cadre, complained privately that all the articles were written by committee. If he was assigned to cover, say, a meeting between Deng Xiaoping and an American senator, after he wrote a draft of the story, it would be passed to another reporter who checked the facts and often rewrote it to get the political nuances correct. Then it went to the editor of his section, from there to the editor in charge of domestic news, and then to the deputy editor in charge of putting out the paper that day. There was a progress sheet attached to the story, and every reporter and editor who worked on it had to sign his name before it could be printed. In theory, my friend said, that was to make sure everyone took responsibility; in fact, it was a way to finesse responsibility if anything went wrong. No one person could be blamed.

My friend was also frustrated by a lack of a sense of timeliness. "Most of the stories we write don't have a date on them," he told me during a long drive around Peking. "That way, we can store them up, and on a day when there is a political meeting in the office, we can dump them in the paper." Walking past the paper's office early in the evening, the time when Western papers are at their busiest on deadline, I was surprised to see all the lights turned off and the front door shut. "Everyone goes home very promptly at five thirty," my friend related. "We usually have the paper laid out early in the morning for the next day, since we don't print much spot news. Sometimes after an event happens, a leader gives a speech or makes an appearance, it takes us two or three days to get the story into the paper." This leisurely pace is accentuated by the paper's delivery system. Newspapers in China are not distributed by delivery boys—shades of private enterprise—but by the post office, which brings the *People's Daily* around after 10 A.M., too late for breakfast reading but just in time to be consumed in the office instead of working.

Another young reporter I met, who worked for the English-language monthly magazine *Women of China,* recounted the instructions given her by the editor, Shen Yier. A vigorous sixty-five-year-old woman with a plain face and short, trimmed hair who had worked in the Communists' wartime cave headquarters at Yanan, Shen took a strict view of a journalist's duties. "All clues for a story must come from official papers, magazines, government broadcasts, and speeches by Party leaders," Shen cautioned her employees. "We don't print anything the Party has not said."

Shen personally assigned each story for the magazine, which was designed to advertise the achievements of Chinese women under communism to readers abroad. Then after an article was drafted, she read it, made revisions, and forwarded it to the English-language section to be translated. When the English-language version came back, she again read and revised it and signed her name before sending it to the printers. The reporters jokingly referred to her as "Marxist Grandma," partly out of respect. For they knew she was a conscientious old-fashioned cadre: she declined to use the office car, always riding the crowded public bus, and she and her husband, the head of China's largest publishing house, had pledged to leave all their savings to the Party, not to their children. But her fussy editing annoyed the more energetic members of her staff. One time in a story about a Rumanian women's delegation that visited the Great Wall, she found the sentence "Once we are standing here on the Great Wall, we are like heroines." Shen was displeased and phoned the magazine's English-language specialist, a scholarly sixty-year-old who had graduated from the Columbia School of Journalism.

"You must omit the word 'like,' " she said sternly. "You should bear in mind that the Rumanian Party is our brother Party and their people are a great people. We shouldn't underestimate their heroism and cater to the likings of the bourgeoisie. So make it read, 'Once we are standing here on the Great Wall, we are heroines.' "

But in spite of its reputation for fustian prose and somnolent subject matter, the Chinese press bore careful reading and often contained valuable insights into Peking politics. They would usually be buried obscurely, like clues in a detective novel. In 1973, when Deng Xiaoping first returned to public view after being purged in the Cultural Revolution as China's number two capitalist roader, his rehabilitation was signaled by his appearance at a banquet for Prince Norodom Sihanouk of Cambodia. In reporting the festivities, the *People's Daily* merely included Deng's name in the middle of the guest list, without comment. It was as if the Cultural Revolution had never happened.

Oddly, I also noticed, in one of the most secretive societies in the world, China's leaders often argued their most private political quarrels out in the pages of the press. When Deng was trying to remove Hua as Party Chairman and Prime Minister from 1978 to 1981, he repeatedly assured visiting foreign heads of state that he and Hua had no differences. But the Chinese press, in a series of vague and menacing articles, spoke of a serious conflict between those conservative officials who still clung to "whatever" Mao had said and other more progressive types who followed Deng's motto of "practice is the sole criterion of truth." Chinese readers could draw the proper conclusion. Hua had been picked by Mao and was the target of the stories. The reason for the oblique approach was that Deng did not want to destroy China's prized unity by attacking Hua head on. Instead, these indirect forays effectively warned away Hua's supporters and undermined his position.

Contrary to what many people think in the West, the *People's Daily* also does provide a safety valve for minor popular grievances against the government—letters to the editor. These are a big business. The *People's Daily* gets an average of 2,000 letters a day from readers, An, the editor, said, and the paper maintains a staff of eighty employees, "the Masses Work Department," just to handle them. Some of the letters are printed in the paper itself, others are forwarded to the government ministries the readers are complaining about, and some are printed in a classified bulletin that is circulated to the Cabinet and Central Committee. The most common criticisms are about inflation and corruption, An said. But unlike papers such as *The New York Times,* which see their duty done when a letter is printed, An continued, the *People's Daily* often assigns a reporter to check out the complaint.

"For example, in yesterday's paper some local officials in Hebei province wrote a letter to criticize the provincial Party committee for waste on their public tree-planting day. The problem was, the provincial officials took part for only two hours, but they used a hundred cars. It was an extravagance. We got in touch with the provincial Bureau of Forestry, which had arranged the occasion, and gave them a chance to reply to the letter. They wrote that they had worked hard and planted two thousand *mou* [330 acres] of trees," An went on. "Actually, that would take that bunch of cadres a whole year to do, so their answer was bad, they were lying. We printed both letters and we'll continue to follow up the story."

Such letters clearly provide Peking with a useful barometer of popular opinion. But how much real influence they have is another question. At the time of my interview with An, I was having trouble getting a New China News Agency teleprinter for *The Times* office, as were several other newly arrived American correspondents. We had all made repeated applications to the press agency, to the Information Department, and to the Ministry of Telecommunications, but each disclaimed responsibility and said we should try the other agencies. Without the news ticker, we had to wait twenty-four hours to get a printed text of the previous day's report by the New China News Agency, putting us at a competitive disadvantage with the other resident correspondents. It was a daily frustration, but no one would give us an explanation why we couldn't have the machines. When I mentioned this to An, he suggested I write a letter to the *People's Daily* which he would ensure got printed in their special bulletin and sent to the Central Committee. It still took a year to get the teleprinter.

But since Mao's death and Deng's ascendancy, the Chinese press has taken a number of steps to improve its coverage and try to increase its credibility. Several times while I was in Peking the *People's Daily* confessed that it had published false and misleading stories, like a dispatch from a commune in the east China province of Jiangsu where the peasants supposedly had discovered a way to manufacture celluloid from wheat straw. In fact, the paper admitted, all they had done was perform a few tests in a bottle. Even more serious, another time the paper admitted in a major front-page story that it had contributed to the disastrous Great Leap Forward in 1958 by spreading a "premature Communist wind" and had helped perpetuate the Cultural Revolution by making many "false accusations" against good officials. Several of my Chinese friends gave the paper credit for its newfound candor, but they were skeptical that the *People's Daily* could avoid similar fabrications in the future.

In the past few years, Mao's successors have also allowed the Chinese press to print more investigative articles. Chinese reporters had been writing these kinds of stories all along, but in the past they had appeared only in the limited "internal reference" publications for high-level officials. Some of the most shocking revelations have been about industrial accidents, a subject the press previously ignored. For China is officially a workers' state, a dictatorship of the proletariat, and only capitalists are supposed to exploit their workers with dangerous factory conditions. But in one case reported in the *People's Daily,* the Party leaders of a coal mine in Jilin province, in the northeast, realized in late 1979 that they were still more than 100,000 tons short of their annual production quota. To make up the difference, they held a series of "oath-taking rallies" among the miners, offered them large bonuses, and began what they called a "high output battle" in an unexploited though dangerous pit. The mine's gas inspector and the deputy chief engineer soon protested that an excessive concentration of gas was developing. But their warnings were ignored and the engineer was criticized for shirking his duty. A few days later an explosion occurred in which fifty-two miners were killed and six badly injured.

These investigative stories usually follow a pattern. They focus only on individual factories, directors, or ministries, I noticed. There have been no articles about the incidence of black lung disease among China's coal miners nationwide, though a doctor I met who worked in a coal-mining town said the problem was endemic and crippled most of the older miners. The purpose of this investigative journalism is not to question the sagacity of the Communist leadership but to show that it cares and is on top of the situation. The discovery of a few minor blemishes only proves that the Party is doing its job and is, as the thousands of billboards around China proclaim, "Great, glorious, and always correct."

Even so, this kind of journalism has aroused resistance from more conservative cadres, Yuan Xianlu, the former foreign editor of the *People's Daily,* told me, and therefore the press must tread carefully. Yuan confided that before another paper, the *China Youth News,* ran a sensational story in which a youthful cook accused the Minister of Commerce, Wang Lei, of entertaining his friends in Peking's most expensive restaurant without paying his bills, the paper first sought clearance from the Party Propaganda Department. "On a story like that, we can't afford to be wrong," said Yuan, a thin, angular man with a soft voice and pleasant manner. But Yuan, who has since been made one of the *People's Daily*'s correspondents in Washington, believes the press's courage shows it is improving. "Where there is a little hope, there is a beginning, a start toward more democracy."

China established its first television station only in 1958 and until 1979 there were less than five million television sets in the whole country of a billion people. But now suddenly Chinese are becoming as addicted to television as Americans and Japanese, at least in urban areas where the ownership of sets is concentrated. When a Peking television station aired its first American program, a lightweight science-fiction series about a man who can swim like a fish, *The Man From Atlantis,* so many people stayed home to watch it on Saturday nights that the usual jammed movie theaters were empty and the number of crimes in Peking dropped, a journalist from the television studio told me with astonishment. I was curious why the Communists selected such an improbable program as their first regular foreign series. It had no redeeming social message, and it showed Americans in wealthy, glamorous, and adventuresome settings, nothing to discourage envy of the capitalist way of life. The reason, the journalist explained, was that the government television station operates on a small budget—it carries only minimal advertising—and *The Man From Atlantis* was the cheapest series China could buy from Hollywood.

Chinese television was full of surprises. In 1980 the government took the liberal step of adding ten minutes of international news, picked up by satellite from Viznews in Britain and ABC in the United States, to its regular half-hour evening national news broadcast. Before, the evening news had been largely a turgid rehash of stories from the *People's Daily,* plus some dreary homemade features on the latest improvement in machine tool production. But now, in living color, without censorship, Chinese could watch the Pope touring Africa, Ronald Reagan winning the U.S. presidential election, political terrorism in Italy, and even stock-car races in North Carolina and surfing in Hawaii. After thirty years of almost total isolation from the outside world, the Chinese were being fed a rich, confusing diet of exotic new images. Television, it seemed to me, was likely to have a number of unintended side effects on China. For the Communists it could be a useful new propaganda tool. But it also tended to break down the old stratified system of rationed information; it gave Chinese a much better appreciation of how wide a political and economic gap separated them from the United States, Western Europe, and Japan; and it bred a desire for more consumer goods, particularly television sets. In 1981, Chinese factories upped their production of television sets to 2.5 million and the government imported another one million sets from Japan, ten times the number sold only three years before.

Television has also spawned one of China's first celebrities, the petite, charming teacher of a three-mornings-a-week class in English on Peking's educational television station, one of three channels in the capital. There are no Nielsen ratings in China yet, but the language class is considered the most popular program in China. In a bizarre and happy twist of fate, the hostess is Zheng Peidi, the woman professor from Peking University who was incarcerated during the Cultural Revolution because one of her relatives had an affair with Jiang Qing during the 1930s.

"Now wherever I go, I am recognized," Zheng told me with embarrassment, folding her tiny hands in her lap. "When I get on the bus, even when it is horribly crowded, people stand up to give me their seats. Often people gather in crowds to ask for my autograph." She gets an average of thirty letters a week from fans, and her husband is kept busy hauling back the gifts she receives from the post office: a 100-pound sack of potatoes from Heilongjiang in the northeast, bags of rice from the south, a crate of oranges from Zhejiang, the best in China, and packets of expensive tea. "The people are so kind, they write notes saying, 'We know you can't get oranges in Peking.' " Unfortunately, she added with a laugh, "My butcher doesn't study English, he is always rude and gives me the fatty cuts of pork."

Zheng has also authored a best seller—an English textbook that has sold 1.6 million copies and would sell more except for the severe paper shortage in China which limits the printing of all books, papers, and magazines. In keeping with past egalitarian practice, she gets only 1.50 yuan ($1) an hour for her television broadcasts, in addition to her regular university salary of 60 yuan ($40) a month. And she gets no royalties from the book. But there are emotional rewards. After she sent an autographed copy of her book to a soldier on the Soviet border who couldn't find one for sale in his remote region, he wrote back in exultation, "Tomorrow at the riflery competition I'll fire in the air as a salute to you, Zheng Peidi." It was the kind of guileless comment that makes Chinese often seem so good-natured despite the decades of turmoil and privation they have had to endure.

If television threatens to break down the government's system of controlled access to information, China's libraries have preserved it in its pristine form. The library at Peking University is one of the newest and most impressive buildings on its tree-shaded campus, a modern concrete and glass structure guarded by a three-story-tall white-stone statue of Chairman Mao, one of the last surviving icons of the Cultural Revolution. Inside, the library houses three million volumes, the second largest collection of books in China, after the Peking National Library near the Forbidden City; but there is no central card catalogue. Instead, I learned on a tour of the building, each department has its own individual catalogue scattered among a labyrinth of corridors and small rooms, most without identifying signs. The division serves a purpose. A student may borrow books only in the field in which he or she is majoring. A math student cannot take out books from the English-language section, not even a volume of Shakespeare's plays or Mark Twain's stories; a history major is barred from the philosophy department, though he may need a book on Plato or Confucius. There are other quirks, too, to discourage inquisitiveness. When I looked up Trotsky in the history department catalogue, the card said see Lev Bronstein, his original name. When I checked Bronstein, the card recommended trying under Trotsky. The stratagem was deliberate, a thirty-year-old major in library science said later, because the Chinese Communists still admire Stalin and view Trotsky as an apostate.

After you have found the number of the book you want, you take it to the main charge-out counter, a clamorous room crowded with knots of students shouting to get the attention of the few clerks, who are dressed in long beige smocks to protect them against dust. The library stacks themselves are closed except to a few privileged professors and library science majors, so students are totally dependent on the clerks, like supplicants.

"At least half the time, they take your slip, walk into the stacks, go only a few steps, and without ever leaving the main aisle check off *mei-you* (we don't have it)," the student studying library science related. One problem, she added, is that most of the clerks are former peasants or factory workers with only a primary school education. During the Cultural Revolution when the university was closed, a factory was set up in some of its classroom buildings; but in 1972 when the school reopened, the factory was shut down and the workers were given the option of transferring to the library, a soft job.

Angela Zito, a brilliant American graduate student from the University of Chicago who was writing her doctoral dissertation on Chinese philosophy, recalled a run-in with one of these clerks. Zito had requested a copy of *The Book of Rites,* one of the ancient Chinese classics, like the Old Testament in the West. But the clerk, a young woman dressed in old patched blue trousers and a faded jacket with printer's oversleeves, said the library didn't have the book. It didn't exist. Zito was perturbed and asked if she knew what the book was. No, the clerk said grumpily, she didn't know and she didn't care. It was the kind of contempt for learning that Mao had fostered with his statements that the more books you read, the more stupid you become.

Still, Zito and other students told me, the Peking University library is one of the best in China. Undergraduates are given five cards to borrow books, meaning they can check out five books at any one time. At other colleges I visited, like Yunnan University in the southwest, the students were restricted to a total of three books a semester. At the Shanghai Teachers College the students can take out six books a semester, but two of them must be in

Marxism–Leninism. The Peking University library also has several reading rooms with seats for 1,000 people. The trouble is, there are 8,000 students on the campus. Because the students live in small crowded dormitory cubicles of four to twelve people stacked on bunk beds, it is almost impossible for them to study in their rooms and there is tremendous competition for the reading-room seats. Students often line up at 6:30 A.M. for the 7:30 A.M. opening.

To further limit access to information that might poison young minds, in all the libraries I visited the foreign-language periodicals, the dictionaries, and the encyclopedias were kept in reference rooms reserved for teachers and graduate students. Once during a tour of the Shanghai Teachers College library with an American governmental delegation, we were led into the reference room of the foreign-languages department. The scene looked like that in any American library—there were several dozen undergraduates busily examining copies of *Time* magazine, *The New Yorker, Le Monde,* and *The New York Times.* I was surprised to see them there and asked the short, rumpled-looking boy who was thumbing through *The Times* if he came there often.

"Oh, no," he answered in a whisper. "This room is only for our teachers. They let us in here today just because of your visit."

But the worst problem in many libraries, students told me, was the damage caused by the Cultural Revolution. With the universities closed and education under attack, most libraries had to stop buying books and periodicals from 1966 to the late 1970s. At some schools, like Fudan in Shanghai, Red Guards vandalized the stacks, burning books or scattering them all over the campus. "Our catalogue is intact," a librarian at Fudan said in sadness, "but we don't know where most of our books are." In 1980 the Peking Cultural Relics Bureau reported it had recently returned to their original private owners 2.1 million copies of ancient Chinese books, weighing 314 tons, confiscated during the Cultural Revolution. They were part of millions more volumes that had been labeled as "old culture" and were carted off to paper plants, garbage dumps, and warehouses around the city. In one paper plant alone, the Cultural Relics Bureau disclosed, it had found 2,000 tons of valuable books that were being turned into pulp, but it was too late to stop much of the destruction.

Chinese science has also had to pay the price for the Communists' mania for secrecy and the ignorance of some senior Party leaders. In only a few cases, Chinese scientists told me, have they really been able to put together the facilities and talent they need free from political interference, like the large rocket and jet-fighter center outside Xian where China's ICBM was developed. Even it faced difficulties. A physicist from the rocket center told an American diplomat that its staff had trouble learning about research elsewhere in China because the government did not allow scientists to publish their findings in journals, write to each other, or meet in conferences. "Some professor at Qinghua University may have just made an important discovery in metals technology that would allow us to build a higher-performance airframe for our fighters, but we'll be lucky to find out about it," the physicist lamented.

The most curious case is the hold a Chinese-American scientist, Dr. Niu Man-chang, has had over Chinese biology, much like the infamous Trofim Lysenko in the Soviet Union under Stalin and Khrushchev. Just as Lysenko asserted that characteristics acquired from the environment can be transmitted in the evolutionary process, reversing the findings of modern Mendelian genetics, so Niu has convinced China's leaders that he can alter characteristics through the use of RNA, ribonuclei acid, in a controversial form of bioengineering. Niu was a little-known professor at Temple University in Philadelphia whose experiments with goldfish were largely discredited by the American scientific community until he began coming to China in 1972 after Nixon's pioneering visit. But Niu carefully cultivated contacts with Peking's officials in the traditional Chinese way. He came back to work in Chinese laboratories for six-month stretches, winning a reputation as a patriot, and he helped secure a large grant from the Rockefeller Foundation in New York to build a new Institute of Developmental Biology in Peking. Soon he was on good terms with Deng and Fang Yi, the Politburo member who heads the State Science and Technology Commission, friends said. What added to Niu's appeal was that the leaders of China's Institute of Genetics had been trained by Russians in the early 1950s and were still under the influence of Lysenko, since they had been cut off from the outside scientific world in the 1960s and 1970s. Hence Niu's theory was politically welcome to them. In his experiments with goldfish, Niu contended that by injecting RNA into the fishes' eggs he could alter not only their characteristics but that of their descendants. Niu claimed he achieved this because the injected RNA affects the structure of the fishes' DNA, or deoxyribonucleic acid, containing the basic genetic code of life. As an example of what miracles his research may produce, other Chinese biologists working with him say they have created rice with the protein content of soybeans by injecting RNA from soybeans into the ovaries of rice. The Chinese press has trumpeted this as a possible cure for the world's food problems.

To publicize his findings, Niu helped organize an international conference on RNA in Peking in 1980. But American scientists I talked to afterward said they were shocked by the presentations of Niu and his followers. Walter Gilbert, a Nobel Prize laureate and professor of microbiology at Harvard, said Niu's work smacked of "alchemy."

"What we found when we looked at their papers was that their experiments were entirely uncontrolled and were not doing what the people claimed they were doing," Gilbert said. He speculated that either Niu and his followers were intentionally misinterpreting the data or the laboratory technicians were sloppy.

If Niu's work was correct, Gilbert added, it would overturn one of the most basic tenets of contemporary biology, which holds that it is DNA that determines the form of life, not RNA. DNA is synthesized into RNA before being in turn synthesized into protein. Gilbert said that several Chinese biologists he met, who had not been invited to the conference, came up to him to thank him and other American scientists for publicly challenging Niu. Because of Niu's political position, they didn't dare, they explained, and many Chinese biologists had been ordered by the Academy of Sciences to assist him.

Many times Americans, aware of Peking's hold over information, have asked me if the government censored my dispatches from China. The answer is no, the Information Department never made an overt attempt to influence what I wrote, and the clerks at the cable office and the international telephone operators were unfailingly cooperative in helping me file my stories, no matter how late the hour. I owe them deep gratitude.

But the answer is also no because censorship in China is both more subtle and more pervasive than merely tinkering with a foreign correspondent's copy. It is designed to be so all-encompassing that it blots out facts of life that Deng and the Politburo do not want to exist.

I was reminded of this when the Chinese press in 1980 suddenly discovered that the country's long-time model agricultural unit, Dazhai, was a fraud. Since Mao first sainted Dazhai in 1963, proclaiming with his ultimate wisdom, "In agriculture, learn from Dazhai," millions of Chinese pilgrims had trouped to the small production brigade of eighty-three families on 250 acres of stony, arid land in Shanxi province, in the northwest. All across the country, China's peasants had dutifully copied Mao's words in bold characters written on every available wall, "In agriculture, learn from Dazhai." Dazhai was to China what apple pie and motherhood are to America—the symbol of its most sacred virtues, in this case, hard work, self-reliance, and cooperative living. Dazhai's peasants had even voluntarily given up their private plots to devote themselves to the common good. Or so the People's Daily and China's other papers had said in thousands of panegyrics.

But that was Mao's version of Dazhai. Now Deng saw it differently. Hua Guofeng, his colorless but stubborn opponent, had embraced Dazhai and called for all of China to turn itself into imitations of the shrine. Further, one of Hua's few remaining supporters was the former Party secretary of Dazhai, a peasant turned Politburo member, Chen Yonggui. So for Deng, Dazhai became a totem of all that was wrong with the Maoist way and a handy target with which to dishonor Hua. The *People's Daily* confessed that Dazhai hadn't really relied on its own efforts to terrace its rocky hills and dig its irrigation ditches; the truth was that Dazhai had accepted millions of yuan in government subsidies and help from battalions of army laborers. Dazhai's ever-increasing grain production figures were fake, too, a lie by the local authorities; its output had actually gone down year by year. Not only that, Chen, the Politburo member who wore a peasant's checkered cloth around his head, had persecuted 141 people to death during the Cultural Revolution and his son was a "spoiled brat and good-for-nothing moral degenerate," the paper added. The son had divorced his wife to marry another man's fiancée and raped a number of farm workers. One conscientious peasant who wrote to Mao and Hua about all these misdoings was beaten and imprisoned. Now all those millions of signs, "In agriculture, learn from Dazhai," would have to be painted over.

This kind of comprehensive censorship, of "turning black into white and white into black," to use a popular Communist slogan, is tireless work, requiring endless attention to detail. At a photographic exhibition on the life of Zhou Enlai in the huge, Stalinesque, sandstone Museum of History, one of the pictures showed the Party leadership attending his funeral in January 1976. In the solemn rank of mourners there were four blank spaces, gaps in the line. Once, I guessed, these had been Jiang Qing and the Gang of Four. Chinese visitors had noticed the holes, you could tell, because the glass covering the photo was smudged with fingerprints where they had pointed out the missing faces to their friends.

Museums present a tricky problem in China, and they often tend to be closed. In Shanghai, each time I visited the city I tried to get into the elegant black-brick mansion where the Chinese Communist Party held its first congress in 1921 and the home of Lu Xun, China's greatest twentieth-century writer. Both were now public museums, but each time I went, they were shuttered. In Peking, courtesy of the visit by Harold Brown, the U.S. Defense Secretary, I managed to make it into the Military Museum, but only one of its two wings was open, that commemorating the Red Army before 1949. The other, covering the history of the People's Liberation Army since 1949, its fighting in the Korean War, and its border skirmishes with India and Vietnam, was off limits. Why the difference? I asked my guide, a stunningly handsome woman in green army fatigues with high cheekbones, large almond eyes, short thick braids, and a saucy turned-up nose.

"We have not yet come to a conclusion about certain things," she replied with a straight face. Translated, it meant that it was difficult to decide what to say about Lin Biao, the former Defense Minister and military hero who had tried to assassinate Mao in 1971.

Later, driving back to the hotel, I asked my driver, Lao Shi, what he thought about Marshal Lin. "I don't know what to think myself, I just know what the newspapers tell me," he answered.

What was striking about these incidents, the debunking of Dazhai and the closed museums, was that the Party's monopoly of the means of communications makes it very difficult for Chinese to know what to think about anything. Accustomed to an ever-shifting political line, people tend to become cynical and apathetic.

"We are a nation where the government controls not only the present, but the past," my friend Bing remarked sagely. She had been given an essay of George Orwell's by one of her foreign teachers, "Looking Back on the Spanish War," and she quoted a passage she thought applied to China: "If the leader says of such and such an event 'It never happened'—well, it never happened. If he says that two and two are five, well, two and two are five. This prospect frightens me much more than bombs."

19. To Rebel Is Justified

造反有理

DISSENT

"Some people have the following view: it is revolutionary if we act in accordance with the will of the leaders in power and counterrevolutionary to oppose the will of the people in power. I cannot agree with this debasing of the concept of revolution."

Wei Jingsheng

It seems an old story now—Peking's Democracy Wall is already covered with billboards advertising water pumps, fork lifts, and machine tools. But one bitterly cold winter evening, a few weeks before an irritated government ordered the posters ripped down from that two hundred-yard stretch of yellow-gray brick wall in front of a bus station on the Avenue of Eternal Tranquility, I remember setting out for the home of an activist, Liu Qing, a thirty-six-year-old factory technician. The previous afternoon, a Sunday, he had been at the wall distributing copies of the transcript of the trial of China's best-known dissident, Wei Jingsheng, when a phalanx of fifty policemen arrived and arrested several customers and a teen-ager helping Liu count change. Liu himself melted into the crowd and escaped. The Public Security Ministry was angry that Liu had gotten hold of the text of the trial and published it, even though the government officially described it as a public proceeding.

I had found Liu's address in the back of the underground magazine he helped edit, *The April Fifth Forum,* where he daringly printed it so people who shared his ideas could contact him. But that Monday night it was hard to locate his house down a labyrinth of narrow mud-paved alleys in an old quarter of the city. There were no streetlights and no numbers on the doors. As I walked in the pitch black, each compound of traditional tile-roofed courtyards looked the same. The darkness did serve a useful purpose—it was easier for me to escape notice as a foreigner, dressed in a fur cap and a borrowed Chinese long blue overcoat. At one corner I almost bumped into a man drawing water from an outdoor common spigot. The encounter did not lessen my anxiety. After a few wrong guesses, I finally stumbled into Liu's tiny one-room apartment. Three men and a woman, all in their twenties, were sitting on low stools and Liu's bed debating what had happened to him. In an act of idealism, he had gone to a police station after the arrests to plead for the release of the innocent bystanders and confess that he was the man the police really wanted. That was twenty-four hours before, and he still had not returned.

The four people in the apartment were startled when I took off my cap and coat to see I was a foreigner. I was the first Western journalist they had met, and I could have been a danger to them, given the rules about contact with foreigners; but being Chinese, they were hospitable and gave me a stool to sit on. The first thing I noticed was how cold it was in the room. There was a small cast-iron stove in the center of the concrete floor heating a tea kettle, but it did not radiate much warmth, and in a corner of the room was a basin of water frozen into a block of ice. When I took my hands out of my gloves, it was difficult to write notes. My breath showed in tiny puffs. A pile of trash had been swept, or pushed, under the bed; Liu was a man with a mission, too busy for housekeeping. The one bare fluorescent bulb, dangling from a wire in the ceiling, cast a dim light, adding to the conspiratorial atmosphere.

There was a knock at the door. One of the men moved to answer it and asked in a whisper, "Who is it?" "We are people from Yunnan," came the reply, a province 2,000 miles to the southwest. They had read Liu's journal and had come all the way by train to visit him. It was a remarkable feat. Travel is expensive in China, and they either had had to get permission from their *danwei* Party committee or, more likely, had forged travel orders, an act that could land them in jail. I was astonished by these visitors; it showed that dissent in China was not limited to a coterie of malcontents in Peking. Indeed, as I was to discover, dissent was spread throughout the country and took many forms.

As the evening wore on, more and more young people arrived to fill the cramped room, about eight feet by ten feet. Most were factory workers, young people in their twenties or early thirties. Few of them had more than a high school education. But in their spare time they had been laboriously using a primitive mimeograph machine to print *The April Fifth Forum* and then sell the copies at Democracy Wall. The old wooden-frame machine sat on a bench. Each page had to be copied by hand on a cloth matrix. Then a sheet of paper was placed beneath and an inked cylinder roller over the matrix, printing the magazine one page at a time. Still they had managed to churn out 1,000 copies a month of the fifty- to sixty-page journal. There was an intensity in their conversation, an earnestness, and an innocence which reminded me of my own college days.

"What we need is democracy and freedom of speech," said Lu Lin, a stocky twenty-four-year-old press operator in an electric machine factory whom I had met before. "We also need more science." The juxtaposition of democracy and science was striking, because those were precisely the slogans of China's great nationalistic revival of the early part of the century, the May Fourth movement. It was named after the date in 1919 of a student demonstration in Peking against Japanese colonial occupation of parts of China and warlord rule. The movement had led to an upsurge of political activity by intellectuals and indirectly to the founding of the Communist Party in 1921.

Over and over again in talking with the young activists who took part in writing posters or printing underground journals for Democracy Wall I heard these echoes of the May Fourth period—it was as if the intervening sixty years had never occurred. China's political discourse runs on a strong historical track, and the workers who were responsible for Democracy Wall saw themselves as the descendants of that earlier movement. To them as Chinese the connection was made even more explicit by a historical and linguistic coincidence. For the Chinese term for May Four is *Wu Si*, or "Five Four," the month and the day. But the activists in Liu's house had taken their name from another more recent popular demonstration, the commemoration of Zhou Enlai on April 5, 1976, by 100,000 people in the Square of the Gate of Heavenly Peace which turned into a protest against the radicals and Mao. In Chinese, April Five is written *Si Wu*, "Four Five."

In listening to Lu and the others talk that night, I sensed they were grappling with the same questions and using the same language their predecessors had six decades before: how to bring about more democracy in China and how to modernize their country. There was one fundamental difference. Where for the young people of the 1920s Marxism was new and exciting, the latest and best panacea, it was now old and tarnished.

"Before, I used to believe in Marxism," said Lu, a dark-skinned man with a mustache. "But that was forced on me and I was blind. I didn't understand what it meant. Now I can see Marxism has not brought China any benefits." He did not want outright capitalism either; capitalism exploits the working class, he was convinced. But China should borrow more of the techniques of capitalism which make the Western nations and Japan more advanced than China, like democracy.

Most important to Lu was his commitment to China. "I believe the Chinese people are great, that they are intelligent and hardworking and our country should not be in this backward and tragic state." Here again was a theme redolent of the May Fourth era and of all modern Chinese patriots, including Mao and Deng.

Lu spoke slowly, almost awkwardly, not with the style and polish of college-educated Chinese I knew. Both his father and mother were factory workers, and he had gone only through junior high school. As with many young Chinese, his first political interest came in the Cultural Revolution when he heard older students shouting one of Mao's dictums: "To rebel is justified." Mao the revolutionary had unintentionally fostered a spirit of skepticism among young people about the Communist Party and Marxism. But it was the demonstration on April 5, 1976, which the radicals crushed with the urban militia, that triggered Lu's own political activity. He had been in the square facing the Gate of Heavenly Peace that day and was infuriated when he saw the militiamen beat people who had come to honor Zhou Enlai. "The people are not masters of their own country, there is no democracy," he charged.

As we were talking, Liu Qing's younger brother arrived. He had been at the main public reception center of the Peking Public Security Bureau for seven hours trying to find out about Liu's fate. The police were not helpful. In a Kafkaesque scene, they had first met his questions with silence, then a police officer had asked him to register, and next they had escorted him to a dark empty room.

"We repeated the process each hour, each time with another policeman," the brother told the group gathered in the apartment. He was smoking cheap cigarettes, lighting one after another in his nervousness. "They would never say anything, just stare at me, then make me register and lead me to another room." Finally one policeman broke the silence.

"We have been ordered to detain your brother, he is a counterrevolutionary."

Why, the brother asked, is it counterrevolutionary to print transcripts of the trial of Wei Jingsheng when the government itself declared it a public trial? (Despite the government's pronouncement, only specially selected spectators had been invited to attend, and even Wei's family were excluded.) "The trial was public," the policeman replied, "but Wei was a counterrevolutionary and therefore the transcript is a state secret." His double-speak brought laughs from the audience in the apartment.

It was approaching midnight, and I needed to go back to the Peking Hotel to file a story about the day's events for the paper. If I stayed longer, I would be too tired to write and would miss my deadline. Liu's brother put on his coat and escorted me with a flashlight back through the alleyways to the main street where I had parked my car. It was a Chinese gesture of courtesy. But I knew that I and the other foreign correspondents in Peking also represented one of the few resources these young dissidents had. *The April Fifth Forum* had a core of at most twenty-five people who put it out. Chinese friends estimated there were no more than twenty similar underground publications in Peking and perhaps another dozen in other Chinese cities during the period from late 1978 to early 1980 while they were allowed to exist. On any given day a few thousand people who had the time and the nerve might read the posters on Democracy Wall. But my story about Liu's arrest, and that by Victoria Graham of the Associated Press, who had also stopped by the apartment that night, would be picked up by the BBC and the Voice of America and broadcast back to China. Since Mao's death, the government had allowed Chinese to listen to foreign radio broadcasts without interference. The new policy was designed partly to help Chinese improve their foreign-language skills after a decade of stunted education. But it was also a sign of a genuinely more liberal approach by Deng Xiaoping and his colleagues. So millions of Chinese would hear the next morning about Liu's detention from their shortwave sets. I knew how intently people listened. If a story of mine was mentioned on the Voice of America, the next day I often got calls congratulating me from Chinese friends. This made foreign journalists participants in what Chinese called the democracy movement and angered the government, which saw our actions as outside interference. We could argue, justifiably, that we were only doing reporting we would do in the United States or Europe. But I understood their complaint. In China, the press is supposed to play a different role.

There was a tragic denouement to Liu's story. In the fall of 1981, after I had left China, he managed to smuggle out a 196-page manuscript describing his nightmarish odyssey from his first day in the police station till he was sent to a labor-reform camp. That first afternoon at the Public Security Bureau station, Liu wrote, when the police had detained him, he had bravely challenged them: "Without legal procedures, to arrest people is against the law."

"But they replied simply, 'This is the office of the dictatorship.' "

For six months, Liu said, he was kept in solitary confinement in a small unheated cell in Peking's main detention center with only a single thin blanket against the winter cold. He began to realize the harsh conditions were affecting his health. "One day I saw a great pile of hairs on my blanket. I walked over to the mirror on the door and saw I was bald on top. My left side was swollen and painful, possibly because of the coldness and dampness of the room and my habit of curling up for long hours in a corner to try to keep warm. My already severe nearsightedness deteriorated even further."

Liu was repeatedly interrogated by a white-haired policeman about his contacts with other dissidents, and one day when he refused a guard's order to bow his head and cup his hands over his crotch, he was beaten until he was black and blue. The guards then handcuffed his hands behind his back and covered his face with a cloth mask that impaired his breathing.

On July 21, 1980, more than eight months after his original detention, two guards entered Liu's cell and ordered him to get ready to leave. He was to serve a three-year sentence of "reeducation through labor" at a camp in Shanxi province, in western China, known as the Lotus Flower Temple. He had never been formally indicted or tried. What happened to Liu after his manuscript reached the outside world can only be surmised.

Liu's arrest had come on November 11, 1979. The democracy movement did not have much more time. On December 1, the *Peking Daily* reported that the city government had decided to close Democracy Wall. Then on January 16, 1980, Deng gave an important speech in which he insisted that the right to put up wall posters be stripped from China's constitution. It was being abused by a "handful of reactionaries with ulterior motives" to undermine China's "stability and unity," two of Deng's favorite words, and threaten his plans for economic development. Deng's speech contrasted with the position he had espoused only a little over a year earlier, at the start of Democracy Wall in November 1978, when he told a visiting Japanese politician that the appearance of the wall posters "is a normal thing and shows the stable situation in our country. To write big character posters is allowed by our country's constitution. We have no right to deny this or criticize the masses for making use of democracy and putting up big character posters. If the masses feel some anger, we must let them express it."

What went wrong? Had Deng miscalculated, as Mao did in the Hundred Flowers period, and believed that if he allowed people to speak out they would support him? Or was it just a political maneuver? In November 1978 Deng was preparing for a key party conference, the Third Plenum of the Eleventh Central Committee, in Communist terminology, where he scored a significant victory over Hua Guofeng and other conservatives who wanted to hew closer to Mao's old policies. At the beginning the posters had been largely aimed at these conservatives and had been useful to Deng. But after the Third Plenum, Deng himself began to become a target of some of the writers who complained he was not going far enough in allowing freedom of speech. There was still a third possibility that some thoughtful Chinese suggested. Deng was genuinely concerned that Democracy Wall had gotten out of hand and might turn into another chaotic movement like the Cultural Revolution. He also had not yet really finished off the conservatives—Hua remained Party Chairman and Prime Minister—and he had to stage a tactical retreat to prevent many of the old hard liners in the middle and lower levels of the bureaucracy from siding with Hua.

I happened to arrive in China on a tourist visa in December 1978 near the beginning of the movement. The first posters I saw were in the People's Square in downtown Shanghai pasted over three sides of an empty building. A crowd of 10,000 people was surging excitedly, almost euphorically, around the building, like surf breaking on a sandy beach, carrying me from one spot to another. Every time I tried to get close enough to read a poster, I would be swept off in another direction. The emotion of the crowd was contagious, and I, too, felt a thrill at seeing all these pent-up sentiments suddenly and daringly displayed in public. Some of the posters were only small single sheets of paper torn from a school notebook, others were written on old newspaper pages, and some were on pink or yellow paper over ten feet high. The largest poster was assembled on twenty-nine pages of white paper, each fifteen feet tall, and was titled "Human Rights and Democracy." "Society without human rights is a fearful society," it began. "Only with respect for human rights can we achieve real modernization for the people."

Human rights was a new term for China; it was borrowed from the West. But contrary to what some Maoist sympathizers have written, while the Chinese tradition subordinated the individual to the group, it did contain strong injunctions about good morality. To Confucius, the most important virtue was benevolence, *ren,* sometimes translated as "human heartedness." It was an essential quality for any ruler. Human rights and respect for the individual might not be the same in China as in the West, but it is condescending and incorrect to conclude that China lacked a humanist tradition.

As I was scanning the giant poster, a man in his early twenties grabbed my arm and pulled me toward a later page of the broadside. "Are you an American?" he asked with a smile. When I replied yes, he pointed toward the page. "Then you should read that." The phrases seemed oddly familiar, as if I had heard them before, but it took me several minutes to translate the Chinese back into its original English. It was the Declaration of Independence:

"We hold these Truths to be self-evident, that all Men are created equal, that they are endowed by their Creator with certain unalienable Rights, that among these are Life, Liberty, and the Pursuit of Happiness . . .

"In 1776 in the American Revolution," the poster went on, "the Declaration of Independence for the first time in the history of mankind spoke about people's right to live as human beings. We ought to have these rights too, not to be the emperor's slaves."

A few days later, when I reached Peking, diplomats and journalists in the capital were talking about a brilliant new poster by a man named Wei Jingsheng, "The Fifth Modernization." Wei was the most articulate, outspoken, and forceful of the new writers who had suddenly made their appearance in the past month. The Four Modernizations was Deng's catchphrase for his development program: they were agriculture, industry, science, and national defense. All involved the economy. But Wei argued that without a fifth modernization, democracy, China would not advance.

"People should have democracy. If they ask for democracy, they are only asking for something they rightfully own. Anyone refusing to give them democracy is a shameless bandit no better than a capitalist who robs workers of their money earned with their sweat and blood."

Wei attributed China's current backwardness to Mao's "autocracy" and "the socialist road." "We can see that victory for democracy has always brought along with it the most favorable conditions and the greatest speed for social development. On this point, American history has supplied the most forceful evidence."

I never met Wei. My tourist visa soon expired and I didn't return to Peking until June 1979 to open *The Times*'s bureau. Wei was arrested that March. But I learned more about him from Chinese acquaintances. If Lu Lin represented one ingredient of the democracy movement, the young factory workers from humble backgrounds, Wei represented its other source, disillusioned offspring of Communist Party officials. His father was a deputy director of the State Capital Construction Commission and a close aide to Chen Yun, a powerful Politburo member. When Wei was twelve years old, his father began to make him memorize Mao's writings. He had to learn a page a day or got no dinner. His mother, also a Party cadre, tried a softer approach. She recalled for him personal stories from before Liberation in which only the Communists had helped China's poor and oppressed. Wei often cited this upbringing to explain his development. His father's rigidity taught him to question Party dogma. His mother's kindness led him to concern for all those Chinese still poor or persecuted.

The Cultural Revolution was another formative influence on Wei. He was sixteen when the Cultural Revolution began in 1966 and soon joined a Red Guard faction composed of other children of high cadres. This gave him an unusual opportunity to travel to remote parts of the countryside, where, he later wrote, he witnessed a naked young woman begging for food at a railroad station and people his own age exiled for life to state farms in the far western parts of China. At one point he was arrested and spent four months in jail for his factional activities. His disillusionment with communism dated from this period, he told friends, when he concluded that the Cultural Revolution was not designed to end bureaucracy, as Mao had preached, but merely to help Mao get rid of his personal enemies. Wei had later enlisted in the army, and when he was demobilized was made an electrician at the Peking zoo, not an inspiring job for a man of his talent and energy.

At his one-day trial in October 1979, Wei acted as his own defense counsel. The prosecutor charged that articles Wei had written for the magazine *Tansuo,* or "Explorations," were counterrevolutionary because they "agitated for the overthrow of the dictatorship of the proletariat." But Wei took issue with the prosecutor's view of what constitutes being a revolutionary and a counterrevolutionary. He said he could not agree with the presumption that criticizing a government in power is automatically counterrevolutionary. That would "debase" the idea of revolution. And as for trying to overthrow the dictatorship of the proletariat, Wei boldly denounced the need for dictatorship.

"We find that governments organized under the form of dictatorship, . . . such as the Soviet Union, Vietnam, and China before the Gang of Four was smashed, have without exception degenerated into kinds of fascist governments with a minority of the leading class exercising dictatorship over the broad masses of the working people.

"The fate of Marxism," Wei continued, "is like that of many schools of thought. Its revolutionary essence was emasculated after its second and third generations. Some of its ideals have been used by rulers as the pretext for enslaving people."*

I was standing outside the modern two-story concrete courthouse while Wei's trial took place. The police had barred all his friends and foreign newsmen from entering. Conveniently, the court reached its verdict, without needing to take a break to deliberate, at 5:30 P.M., the end of the regular working day. Wei was sentenced to fifteen years in prison. By the time I got back to my office, the New China News Agency English-language ticker already had a full account of the trial. It was a record-breaking performance. Normally the agency requires several hours, sometimes even days, to report on a breaking news story to make sure all the political nuances are correct. To translate the story from Chinese into English alone takes several hours. The press agency's speed gave the strong impression that the trial and verdict had been rehearsed.

Not long afterward I went to see another editor of *The April Fifth Forum*, Xu Wenli. A calm, cheerful man of thirty-six with a receding hairline and a delicate build, Xu was deeply disturbed by the sentence.

"It is killing the chicken to scare the monkey," he remarked, using a Chinese adage for a warning. Most of the other underground journals which had sprouted with Democracy Wall had now stopped publishing, and Xu was in a quandary. He considered himself a moderate, not a firebrand like Wei. "The socialist system has many good points," he liked to say, and he had scrupulously given a copy of each issue of his magazine to his boss in the Railroad Ministry where he, too, worked as an electrician. In his small apartment there were pictures of Zhou and Mao on the walls. But he wasn't sure whether he should keep publishing. So he had gone to the Public Security Ministry to ask if it was acceptable. He got no reply.

"They have a policy, they know the limits, but they won't tell us," he said afterward. His nine-year-old daughter, who had painted her fingernails red

*It was these excerpts that Liu Qing's group had gotten hold of and printed that aroused the police.

to match the ribbon in her hair and her dress, wandered into the room and climbed into her father's lap.

"We can see which way the wind is blowing," Xu commented, and he, too, made the painful decision to stop printing in January 1980. I dropped in to check on Xu every few months after that, wondering if the police would move against him, hoping they wouldn't. The last time I saw him was in January 1981, shortly before I left China. A few of the former editors still gathered in his room once or twice a week to chat, and he corresponded with the editors of several defunct magazines in other cities. But otherwise he had abandoned his political activities and he was sad.

"As a Chinese, I don't want disorder," he said, sitting on a bamboo chair. "But the government should learn from the recent events in Poland that man does not live by material things alone. He needs more political freedom also."

Four months later, after I had returned to the United States, Xu was arrested on unspecified charges. I remembered his last words: "The democracy movement will go through a very difficult period now, a low tide. But it won't die. Among the intellectuals and young people the democratic idea has been started. It will continue to exist."

For all the resemblances between these young dissidents and their counterparts in the Soviet Union, there was one profound difference: they did not include any prominent writers, artists, or scientists, any members of China's intellectual establishment. There was no Chinese version of Solzhenitsyn, no Andrei Sakharov, the pioneer of the Soviet hydrogen bomb turned opponent, or Boris Pasternak, or Zhores Medvedev, the dissident biologist. China's intellectuals, who took such pride in their centuries of literacy and leadership, were disconcertingly quiet. It was not because of a lack of tradition of dissent. The Confucian code decreed that a good mandarin must speak out when the government deviated from proper ethical conduct. Unlike the West, this right to opposition was not guaranteed by law, but it was assumed to be part of an intellectual's responsibility.* So at first I was puzzled.

"We intellectuals don't bother to go to Democracy Wall," a Columbia-trained economist, Tan, told me when I asked about this reticence. "The educational level of those people putting up posters is very low, even Wei Jingsheng is not really interesting," Tan added. "They don't represent the mainstream of Chinese thinking. You journalists make too much fuss over Wei," he chided me, sounding like a government spokesman.

If I hadn't known Tan well, I would have interpreted his attitude as condescension or indifference. But Tan did care deeply about both democ-

*For an excellent discussion of the intellectuals' role in Communist China, see Merle Goldman, *China's Intellectuals, Advise and Dissent* (Cambridge: Harvard University Press, 1981).

racy and China, and he was not snobbish. He was a kindly man with graying hair, reserved and courtly in his demeanor, cautious in his choice of words, but warm and affectionate with his friends and family. He was so erudite that his colleagues, other professors, nicknamed him "Doctor." He had been at Columbia when the Korean War broke out in 1950 and elected to return to China rather than stay in the United States and accept an attractive teaching job. For this act of patriotism, he had been labeled a rightist in 1957 and was arrested again in the Cultural Revolution—the police regarded him as a security risk.

Why then did senior Chinese intellectuals not become involved in the democracy movement? Was it because they were afraid of being arrested again or losing their comfortable salaries and apartments? I pressed Tan. No, he replied slowly, it was that I didn't yet understand Chinese politics. In China intellectuals worked inside the system, not outside it; they aligned themselves with factional groups at the center of power in Peking, just as they had in the imperial court. Actually, he asserted, some intellectuals today were very influential, right at the top with Deng himself, and were guiding him toward more liberal political and economic policies. It was dissent from within.

"Deng has his own brain trust made up of some of the freest-thinking people in China," Tan said. It was these people who had helped Deng formulate three critical documents on reforming industry, science, and the Party in 1975 when he made his first comeback from political purgatory. The radicals had labeled the documents the "Three Poisonous Weeds" and used them to disgrace Deng a second time in 1976. But when Deng returned triumphantly after Mao's death, the documents formed the basis of his plans for shifting China's priority from class struggle to economic growth and putting consumer goods ahead of steel production.

Deng's brain trust, Tan continued, was not composed of professors at universities, purely academic types; instead they were Party intellectuals, men who occupied administrative jobs in Party institutes or organizations. That gave them a deceptive face to the outside world. When they gave public talks or received foreign delegations, they often took a conservative line, criticizing dissidents like Wei. They had to for tactical reasons, to protect themselves against attacks from hard-line bureaucrats. But in private they were far more liberal and democratic, Tan assured me. Foremost among these men was Hu Qiaomu, the son of a wealthy land-owning family who studied physics at Qinghua University and is the author of the only authorized history of the Chinese Communist Party. Deng named Hu president of the newly created Academy of Social Sciences in 1978. Other key members of Deng's inner circle of intellectual advisers, Tan said, were Feng Wenbin, the Director of the Higher Party School, Wang Roshui, an editor of the

People's Daily, and Deng Liqun, a deputy president of the Academy of Social Sciences. Several of these men had actively encouraged their children to take part in the democracy movement, including Deng (no relation to Deng Xiaoping), whose daughter helped organize the first unofficial exhibit of photography in a Peking park in 1979, Tan disclosed.

These men had also grown skeptical of Marxism. They frequently took trips to the United States, Japan, Hungary, and Yugoslavia to study other models of development and, among themselves, discussed whether China should turn toward market socialism or capitalism. One of them, Li Shenzhi, the director of the newly established Institute of the United States, told another friend of mine, "Nothing still holds true now, not a single element of Marxist theory." It was a breathtaking statement. Li was a graduate of Yenching University, the prestigious American missionary-run school in Peking and a longtime ghost writer for Zhou Enlai.

Deng's brain trust played an important political role, too, helping him in his battle to oust Hua Guofeng as Party Chairman and Prime Minister. Since Hua had been Mao's choice as his successor, Deng had to move against him indirectly, in traditional style, disguising his attack as an abstract intellectual debate, using historical allegories and esoteric aphorisms, Tan explained. That preserved the appearance of amity and the legitimacy of the regime. In this contest, Deng's intellectual advisers provided the ammunition by publishing a series of articles criticizing unnamed conservatives who still held steadfastly to "whatever" Mao had said. To Chinese readers, attuned to reading between the lines, the message was clear.

Although Tan was not a member of the Party, the existence of relatively liberal intellectuals around Deng made him optimistic for the future. It also helped explain why he did not become a critic himself and why China was unlikely to produce a Solzhenitsyn or a Sakharov.

"I'm a patriot, not a dissident," Tan said one afternoon sitting on a couch in his spacious living room. He had his own telephone, a mark of high status and good *guan-xi.* "I can see many faults," Tan went on. "But I'm not a dissident because I believe the present system is the best we can have, there is no viable alternative to Deng." Patriotism and preserving China's unity were so important to him that he would not risk criticism of the government. "It would be traitorous of me to jeopardize our modernization."

Tan did admit, however, that the combination of tight government control and this tug of patriotism had combined to stifle most Chinese literary and artistic creativity. "It is true that our best writers did all their great work before 1949," he conceded, like Ding Ling, the woman writer known for her outspoken views on the need for artistic freedom, Cao Yu, the country's most famous playwright, and Ba Jin and Mao Dun, China's leading novelists. None of them had produced work after Liberation to match the quality and force and honesty of their writings in the 1930s; none certainly could be compared in stature to Pasternak or Solzhenitsyn. Some had gotten entangled in Party literary quarrels or the persecutions of the Cultural Revolution and had been sent to prison, but with Deng's ascendancy, they now drew comfortable salaries from the official writers' association, along with homes and cars, and they kept a discreet silence.

If China has not produced a Solzhenitsyn or a Sakharov, great writers and scientists turned dissidents, neither has it been plagued by a series of famous defectors like the Soviet Union, dancers like Mikhail Baryshnikov or diplomats like Arkady Shevchenko, the Soviet Under Secretary-General at the United Nations. Indeed, despite an explosion in the number of Chinese officials, scientists, and theatrical groups traveling abroad in the past few years, there have been only two or three minor incidents of defections involving younger and unknown people. This, too, puzzled me, for China's intellectuals, artists, and even many officials bore deep grudges at their treatment over the past three decades and had more than sufficient reason to seek exile abroad.

An accidental encounter helped explain this to me. One of the very few prominent Chinese to defect was Fou Tsong, a musical prodigy and China's top pianist who had sought refuge in England in 1957 during a concert tour. But in 1979 he quietly returned to China and was staying in the Peking Hotel, where my assistant Jan Wong spotted him. It would be hard to imagine Baryshnikov going back to dance in Moscow, but arrangements had been made for Fou to come back and give a series of concerts and teach master classes for young Chinese pianists. When I went to his room to try to interview him, he was practicing on an old Baldwin grand piano, the words Cincinnati, U.S.A., still faintly imprinted on it. It had been his piano as a boy in Shanghai, he said, and now after his absence of twenty years and much rancor on both sides, the Central Conservatory of Music had found the piano and brought it to him in Peking as a gesture of reconciliation.

"It was with anguish that I left," he said of his defection. "But if I hadn't, it would have been the end for both my father and me." His father had come under attack as a rightist, and Fou feared that when he returned from his tour abroad the Communists were going to pit the two men against each other. "I would have had to attack him and he would have had to attack me. They were going to squeeze us at each other like two tubes of toothpaste." His father was a professor and China's leading translator of French literature. Later, in the Cultural Revolution, both his father and mother committed suicide. Fou did not want to talk about it. "It's an old story, like many others. It's only the theme and variations that are different," he added in the clipped tones of Oxford English he had acquired in his home abroad. He was dressed in a black turtle-neck sweater and gray slacks, and with his long hair flopping over his ears and a pipe stuck in his mouth he looked much more the emigré artist than a native Chinese. Chopin scores were stacked on the piano, along with a bowl of tangerines some Chinese admirers had sent as a present.

Why had he come back? "I have too much feeling for China to stay away," Fou answered. It was that instinctive sense of patriotism that Chinese have, the inescapable pride at being a member of the world's oldest and largest and arguably greatest civilization. Defection was not a glorious act by a noble individual asserting his right to artistic freedom but a traitorous insult to China.

Still, Fou did not intend to settle down permanently in China; when his concert tour was up, he went back to London. "If I was here to stay, I couldn't do and say some of the things I have," Fou said. He was a realist who saw that the Party still exercised rigid control over culture. But he hoped to come back for future visits, if the authorities agreed.

"The ironic thing for me is that the Chinese people are very kind, they have a Mozartian quality, a natural charm," Fou said. "They still smile no matter how hard life is, no matter how oppressed they are. This fools foreigners who think China is different from the Soviet Union. I always have to argue with naïve foreigners about this."

Paradoxically, where nationalism may constrain older and more prominent Chinese from defecting, young Chinese—those who have known nothing but years of political campaigns and a sluggish economy—have regularly escaped in far greater numbers than East Germans or Russians. These escapes, largely unnoticed in the West, have been across the one accessible border, into Hong Kong.

From 1975 to 1980, 460,000 Chinese made it into Hong Kong, constituting almost 10 percent of the tiny British colony's 5.08 million people and straining its already overcrowded housing and schools. Some of these were legal immigrants—people with valid exit visas from China who were able to get out because they had relatives living in Hong Kong or elsewhere in Southeast Asia. But most have been illegals. To escape, the refugees must often walk for several days to get to the heavily guarded special border zone on the Chinese side. Then they must swim for several hours across shark-infested waters or climb over the double walls of barbed wire along the rugged, hilly twenty-five-mile land border. Each morning there are fresh scraps of bloodied clothing snagged in the coils of wire. Cardboard cartons flattened on top of the fences show where people have clambered over. Finally the refugees have to evade patrols of British and Gurkha mercenary soldiers on the Hong Kong side.

Despite the large number who have managed to flee, these escapes are risky. In 1979, 320 bodies of escapees were found in the ocean or on the beaches of Hong Kong's numerous islands. The rubber tires or inflated plastic bags they used to help them swim proved insufficient. I remember one poignant incident in which a man who had lost part of his leg to a shark was rounded up by a British patrol after finally making it ashore and shipped back to China. Because of these physical difficulties, the Hong Kong government estimates that 80 percent of those who escape are young men between 18 and 26 who live in the counties of Guangdong province adjacent to the colony, largely peasants or city school graduates sent down to the countryside.

When I interviewed a number of these refugees, they offered several reasons for leaving. For some it was simply the poverty of life on their commune and the much higher standard of living in Hong Kong. For others, it was the lack of individual choice over schooling, jobs, and housing. But for all of them, Hong Kong's streets looked paved with gold. One refugee, a sturdily built twenty-five-year-old man with a short neck and powerful arms like a boxer, said he had tried four times before escaping successfully—once he was caught by Chinese soldiers, twice by Hong Kong patrols. Each time he was taken to a detention center at the border town of Shenzhen and then to a prison in Canton that the refugees called "Eat Four Ounces" because of its meager diet.

"It was worth it," he said. "Now I send money back each month to my parents in our village and they have bought a television set." He himself had made a trip back, legally, protected by his new Hong Kong identity card. "The cadres were happy to see me," he related. To them he represented a valuable source of foreign currency earnings.

But finally in November 1980, after the number of illegal refugees rose to as high as five hundred a night, the Hong Kong government moved to turn off the flow. It declared an end to its liberal "touch base" policy under which any escapee who made it past the actual border or coastal area into urban Hong Kong was allowed to stay. The flood was reduced to a trickle. For Hong Kong the new restrictions were a matter of economic survival. But I wondered what would happen if the West German government refused to accept escapees from East Berlin or the United States turned down a request for asylum by a Russian scientist. Do we have a double standard, one for exiled Europeans, another for Chinese peasants?

Young Chinese in other parts of the country do not enjoy the geographical advantage of those in Guangdong, and escape for them is impossible. But I was surprised at how open young people could become about their criticism of the regime. The government itself unwittingly provided an opportunity for this dissent in 1980 when it began experimenting with the first free, if limited, elections in China since 1949. The move was part of Deng Xiao-ping's plan to relax the Stalinist political controls of the past decade and try to rekindle popular enthusiasm for the Communists. Deng also envisioned the elections as a way to make incompetent, senile, or conservative cadres more accountable. The elections were held for district people's congresses in the cities and county people's congresses in the countryside. For the first time Peking required that the ballots be secret and that there be more than one candidate for each seat. In theory the winning candidates were to have some authority to oversee local government, though the Party remained the supreme organ of power. The local congresses were also to pick delegates to city and provincial congresses, and they in turn would select representatives to the National People's Congress. In the past, Chinese friends joked, delegates to the NPC had only two rights: to raise their hands to vote yes and to applaud the speeches of Communist leaders. But at a session of the NPC in September 1980 the official press gave prominent coverage to sharply framed questions by deputies who quizzed cabinet ministers about scandals like the expensive Baoshan Steel Mill in Shanghai and the offshore oil rig that sank, drowning seventy-two people. In most places the elections to the local people's congresses were lackluster affairs, guided carefully by Party cadres. But some university students were encouraged by the press accounts about the NPC and took their own elections seriously.

One evening I received a surprise telephone call from Judy Shapiro, an American woman teaching English at the Hunan Normal College in Chang-sha, in central southern China. A native of New York and a graduate of Princeton, Shapiro had married one of her students, Liang Heng, one of the first Americans to wed a Chinese since 1949.* I didn't know Shapiro or her husband, but she wanted to report that eighty students at her college had gone on a hunger strike and another 5,000 had joined them in a sit-in demonstration at the provincial Party headquarters in Changsha. They were protesting Party interference in the election for deputies from the college to the local congress. Four of the students on the hunger strike had already fainted from lack of food, she related, her words rushing out faster than I could grasp the unusual situation. Many of the protestors were shouting "Down with bureaucracy, down with feudalism, long live democracy," Shapiro added. Students from several other schools in the city had joined the demonstration and they planned to start boycotting their classes the next day.

The conflict had begun when Liang, her husband, a non-Communist candidate, had gotten up to introduce himself and make an unplanned campaign speech before an outdoor movie show. He was afraid that otherwise the election would not attract any interest, like those held in many offices and

---

*Liang, with Shapiro's help, went on to write a remarkable autobiography, Son of the Revolution (New York: Knopf, 1983).

factories. Liang had startled his fellow students and faculty members by admitting he did not believe in Marxism.

Not all the students supported Liang, Shapiro admitted. Some wall posters had appeared asking whether the college should pick a representative who didn't believe in socialism, and some students had snickered at her—"We don't need foreigners interfering in our affairs."

But in a preliminary election Liang was among the top vote getters and qualified for a run-off contest. It was then the local authorities tried to rig the election by putting pressure on Liang to withdraw and adding several new candidates of their own. The resulting student revolt was stopped only when the Central Committee in Peking agreed to investigate the students' complaints.

At Peking University, which has a long tradition of activism dating to the May Fourth movement, some of the student candidates were equally outspoken. An American graduate student I knew recounted attending a campaign rally by a twenty-six-year-old former Red Guard named Fang Zhiyuan. The meeting was held in a classroom with seats for two hundred, but over five hundred spectators had packed the hall, sitting on the floor and spilling out the double doors. One of the first questions put to Fang, passed up on a sheet of folded paper, was whether he considered China a socialist country.

No, he replied, holding a microphone and rummaging through a stack of other written questions. The written form provided the safety of anonymity. "I think, domestically speaking, Russia and China are similar and Russia isn't socialist either," Fang explained. His candor brought applause.

"I don't think that what we have now in China is what Marx called socialism," he went on. Public ownership of the means of production, or machines and factories, doesn't constitute socialism by itself, Fang said, taking issue with the government's usual definition of socialism. "To say something is truly publicly owned, we must see if the leaders represent the interests of the people.

"To have this, you need a system, and that system is democracy," Fang concluded. The audience exploded with approval.

For the students the election provided an outlet for their concern with China's direction, just as putting up posters on Democracy Wall did for the activists of the democracy movement. But some other Chinese have found expression for their discontent with the Communist regime in a quieter, more personal form—religion.

When Communist guerrillas took over Long Bow village in 1947 in Shanxi province, in western China, one of their major targets was the local Catholic church, a gothic brick structure built by Dutch Franciscan fathers at the turn of the century. It had a tall square tower that stood proudly, arrogantly some thought, high above the peasants' mud houses, and many of its parishioners were associated with the defeated Kuomintang. The Communists chased away the priest, closed the church, and persecuted the worshipers. William Hinton, the American writer who described the Communist victory in Long Bow in his classic book, *Fanshen,* thought the Church was on its way to extinction. "All the power of the Church and all its efforts to convert Long Bow to Catholicism failed in the end," Hinton wrote.* He calculated that most of the converts were only "rice Christians," Chinese who were attracted to the Church because of its wealth and privileged position, protected by the Western imperial powers.

But in 1980 when he returned to Long Bow, Hinton found many peasant homes had printed pictures of Mary and Jesus on their walls, along with the stock portraits of Marx and Mao. On Sundays a group of 150 families, about the same number of Catholics as in 1947, had also started to hold mass again. They gathered in the loft of the house of a carpenter, a man whose father had been a lay preacher before Liberation.

"There are so many people the crowd spills out into his courtyard," Hinton told me with incredulity. "I didn't want to ask them where they got the pictures of Mary and Jesus," since presumably they were either smuggled into China or printed illegally. "It is mighty quiet in the village on Sundays now," Hinton added, tossing back a lock of white hair that fell in his ruddy face. "The peasants would rather go to the service than out to the fields to work."

The reemergence of the villagers' Catholic faith is only part of a broad if cautious revival of religion in China in the years since Mao's death.** It has taken place not only among Catholics and Protestants, but also among China's other religions as well, Buddhism, Islam, and Taoism. Mao's more pragmatic successors have encouraged this rebirth by lifting some of the stifling restrictions placed on religion during the Cultural Revolution. Deng and his associates have recognized the need to mobilize all possible support for their modernization program. Some Chinese and diplomats I knew were skeptical at first that Peking's more tolerant policy was merely a well-contrived showpiece to attract foreign backing for China, particularly from the Arab states in the Middle East and the Buddhist countries in Southeast Asia. But as I traveled around China, I sensed that there were deeper forces at work, forces the government didn't control, and that this renaissance was an outpouring of profound human feelings, another form of dissent.

By chance, along with a group of other foreign correspondents escorted

*William Hinton, *Fanshen, A Documentary of Revolution in a Chinese Village* (New York: Random House, 1966), p. 67.
**In 1949 there were roughly three million Catholics and 700,000 Protestants in all of China, a tiny minority of the population.

by the Information Department, I happened to be in the southern coastal port of Fuzhou on Good Friday. Fuzhou had been a center of American and British Protestant missionary activity in the late nineteenth and early twentieth centuries when it was a treaty port, one of the Chinese cities where the foreign powers had arrogated extralegal powers for themselves from the weak Manchu, warlord, and Kuomintang regimes. There had been a total of twenty-four Protestant and four Roman Catholic churches in Fuzhou before 1949, most with small congregations of a few hundred people. In the 1950s the Protestant churches were gradually forced to close down and unify in one remaining "patriotic" nondenominational church guided by Peking. The Catholic cathedrals were also compelled to merge and forswear their allegiance to the Pope as a foreign power. Then in the Cultural Revolution all Christian churches in China were shuttered except for one Protestant and one Catholic church in Peking reserved largely for the foreign diplomatic community. But the officials in Fuzhou told us they had recently permitted a Protestant church to reopen in accord with the government's new more liberal policy and, after repeated entreaties, they let us visit it.

It proved to be an old gray-stone building down a narrow alley that had been built by American Methodist missionaries in 1938 and was known as the Flower Lane Church. The inside had been freshly painted a cool lime green and white by the parishioners to cover up the traces of vandalism by Red Guards. For the past dozen years, the church had served as a warehouse. At the front a tall, elderly man with thinning hair was practicing for the Easter service on an old tinny piano. In a full rich tenor voice that filled the hall, he intoned in Chinese, "Christ the Lord Is Risen Today." Our guides from the Information Department in Peking and local officials from Fuzhou were standing there with us, and I had to pinch myself to be sure the scene was real.

Upstairs in the vestry we met the chief pastor, Bishop Moses P. Xie, an Anglican. A warm, gentle man of seventy-seven, he spoke English with the high church accent he had acquired in his early training in Britain. He had already picked out the psalm with which he would begin his Easter sermon, from St. Matthew:

> And, behold, there was a great earthquake: for the angel of the Lord descended from heaven, and came and rolled back the stone from the door, and sat upon it. His countenance was like lightning, and his raiment white as snow. And for fear of him the keepers did shake, and became as dead men. And the angel answered and said unto the women, 'Fear not ye: for I know that ye seek Jesus, which was crucified. He is not here: for he is risen, as he said. Come, see the place where the Lord lay.'

Bishop Xie said he expected 2,000 worshipers for the morning service, another 2,000 in the afternoon. Since the church had reopened a few months before, people began coming for the nine o'clock service at 7 A.M.

"If you don't come early, you can't get a seat," the bishop said with a twinkle in his eye. "Then they stay after the service is over, to read the Bible and practice singing some more. After thirteen years, one service is not enough."

There are actually more Protestants in Fuzhou now than in 1949, he insisted. His claim was seconded by five other ministers sitting with us who had banded together, as required by the government, to open the one nondenominational "patriotic" church which had no links to foreign organizations.

How did he account for the increased number of parishioners after all the persecutions of the Cultural Revolution and the government's restrictions on religion? I asked.

"The people are thirsty for something spiritual," he explained. Then, as if to answer our doubts about his claims, he added, "Before Liberation, we used to have a half-hour sermon. Now, if you preach for only half an hour, the people wouldn't be satisfied." But the bishop was careful to add that he does not preach anything against the government. "We are very clear about that."

During the Cultural Revolution Bishop Xie had all his vestments and religious books burned by Red Guards, and he was sent to work first in a factory and then in a village. His superior, the former Anglican Bishop of Fuzhou, was tortured to death.

The Christian faith had survived by going underground, he recounted. "Quite a number of people had services in their families secretly. They would preach to their friends and relatives. I think they did an even better job than we did."

Although he and the other five ministers who now share duties in the church are older men, in their sixties and seventies, he said one third of the congregation is composed of young people with another third drawn from the middle-aged. There is no Sunday school, because the government has forbidden the pastors to try to convert people under eighteen. (The 1978 constitution guarantees that the people "enjoy freedom to believe in religion and freedom not to believe in religion," but a further clause adds that they may only "propagate atheism.") Yet the ministers said they can now baptize adults who wish to become Christians, they have officiated at some weddings and funerals, and they planned to send a few students to the newly reopened Protestant Theological Seminary in Nanjing, one of the most significant concessions by the government. Without it, the Protestant Church would eventually wither away.

As another indication of the Church's strength, the bishop said the congregation had raised enough money to pay its six ministers a monthly salary of 70 yuan ($47) apiece, better than average in China. Some of the funds come from rent on church properties which have been returned by the government, some from English classes the pastors teach in the church, and the rest from Sunday collections. At the back of the church was a blackboard that recorded that on the previous Sunday the worshipers had contributed 267 yuan ($180) to the collection box, a munificent sum of money given the low wages Chinese earn. They had also donated ration coupons for twelve pounds of rice which the church will give to the poor, the bishop said.

The church's main problem, Bishop Xie related, was that all their Bibles and hymnals had been destroyed by Red Guards. He was waiting for a shipment from Shanghai where the government had allowed a printing house to reissue copies of the Bible for the first time in over a decade. Some of these treasured books had already made their way into the hands of Chinese I knew. The *a-yi,* or maid, who worked for Hong and Weidong, had made a special trip to Shanghai to purchase one. A middle-aged woman with a stout figure, buck teeth, and short bowl-cut hair, she was always reading her Bible aloud around the house, Hong told me. Neither Hong nor Weidong had any religious predisposition, but their *a-yi* often tried to persuade them of the superiority of her faith.

"Do you know why there are so many rich Americans?" she asked Hong. "It's because they believe in Christianity."

China's own folk religion, an eclectic amalgam of Buddhism, Taoism, ancestor worship, and popular superstition, also has proved more resilient than outsiders realize. During the 1950s, and then particularly during the Cultural Revolution, most Buddhist and Taoist temples and monasteries were closed and their priests and nuns defrocked. But Susan Wilf, a Harvard graduate student who taught in Peking and married a Chinese, recalled what she saw when she spent her honeymoon climbing Mount Taishan in Shandong province, east of the capital. It is one of China's traditional five sacred peaks, like Mecca or Jerusalem to Moslems and Christians. As she walked, she encountered hundreds of peasant women making the trek to the top. They had come by train from villages throughout north China and climbed all night to reach the summit on the anniversary of the local goddess. Some of the women, whose feet had been bound as youngsters, burned paper offerings and incense or brought food and bowed before an image of the goddess in a temple atop the mountain. Until a few months before, such celebrations were illegal.

A Peking office worker who went home at New Year's to visit her family in the central province of Anhui said the peasants there had become excited by a prophesy about a miraculous stone animal. The animal, a Qilin, a Chinese mythical beast with the head of a lion, is one of several that stands guard outside the tomb of the mother of the founder of the Ming dynasty.

"The peasants believe the animal has come alive and is very powerful medicine," the woman said. So many peasants had chipped away at the animal's legs to get shavings to eat that the Qilin was toppling over.

Local officials made no move to stop the cannibalization of the stone animal. But Peking has become concerned that some forms of religious expression are going too far and either reviving what the Communists see as the evils of the old pre-1949 society or challenging their rule. In Jiangsu province, near the city of Nanjing in central China, the police arrested a witch and a warlock after they put two six-year-old boys to death during an exorcism, a provincial broadcast revealed. The witch beat the boys with branches, poured boiling water over them, and then set fire to one and strangled the other. The rites, which started with a dance of incantation, were supposed to heal a paralyzed woman by ridding her of ghosts that had come back to haunt her.

If religion has provided an outlet for long-pent-up and proscribed feelings among China's Christians, Buddhists, and Taoists, it is an even more volatile and important issue to many of the country's ethnic minorities who inhabit much of the vast western parts of the country. Sitting in Peking it is easy to forget that there are fifty-five identifiable separate minority peoples in China, making China a more heterogeneous society than the countries of Western Europe, Japan, or even the United States. They account for only 56 million people, 6 percent of the total population. But they occupy over half of China's land area, and their significance is magnified because they live along the critical inner Asian frontiers with the Soviet Union, Mongolia, Afghanistan, Pakistan, India, Burma, and Vietnam.

In theory the Communists have recognized the cultural, religious, and ethnic diversity of these non-Chinese peoples by declaring the areas where they live "autonomous regions" rather than regular provinces. Thus Xinjiang, 8 of whose 12 million inhabitants are Turkish-speaking Moslem peoples, including Uighurs, Kazakhs, and Kirghiz, closely related to the natives of the Soviet Central Asian republics across the border, is called the Xinjiang Autonomous Region. But in practice the Communists have kept political control tightly in the hands of Chinese officials and soldiers sent to settle the frontier areas. To the Chinese their presence is civilizing; to the ethnic minorities it is colonial.

In Urumqi, the nondescript modern capital of Xinjiang built on the north side of the snowcapped Mountains of Heaven, the sun does not rise in the summer till 8 A.M. and office hours don't start till 10 A.M.; the lunch break begins at 2 P.M. For though Urumqi is over 1,500 miles west of Peking, as far as Denver from New York or London from Moscow, the Communists have decreed that Urumqi must operate by Peking time, ignoring the meridians of the earth. All of China does.

"We tried to use local time, but it wasn't convenient," explained my guide, Wang Guorong, a Chinese, or Han, as they are called in Xinjiang, after the name of the early dynasty. I told Wang, an eager boyish man with crew-cut hair and a desire to please, that in the United States we overcome the problem of the 3,000-mile distance from New York to California by having four time zones. But he was dubious. "It would cause confusion with the railroad and airplane schedules," he insisted.

Wang had been assigned to Xinjiang from his home near Peking, one of four million Han settlers dispatched to the province in the past thirty years. In 1949, when the Communists marched into Xinjiang, only 6 percent of the population were Chinese; now the proportion is up to 42 percent. Despite Mao's successors' proclaimed policy of being more respectful of the minorities' rights and giving them greater political power, the Party boss of Xinjiang is a Chinese. So is the army commander and six of the eight provincial Party secretaries. Only 40 percent of the 400,000 Party members in Xinjiang are minorities, most of them working at the lowest village level.

The Chinese presence has brought prosperity to parts of Xinjiang, the Chinese proudly point out. Where there was only the terrible red rock desert of Central Asia, nomadic herdsmen and ranges of mountains over 20,000 feet, now there are oil wells, railroads, and dozens of factories. In Turfan, an oasis city on the ancient silk route where Marco Polo rested on his way to China, Wang and a local Chinese official took me to see Zora Han, a heavyset forty-year-old Uighur woman with a deeply wrinkled face and skin parched brown by the desert sun. She, her husband, and her grown daughter earn an average of 275 yuan ($183) a year apiece planting wheat and cotton for their commune, she said. That is more than three times the national average. The family makes another 525 yuan ($350) a year—a prodigious amount in China—by growing green seedless grapes in the shaded courtyard of their mud-walled home. She picked a large bunch from a trellis, washed them with water drawn from an irrigation ditch that flows gurgling by their house, and handed them to me. I had never tasted sweeter grapes, I admitted. Outside, men perched astride slow-footed donkeys trotted past on their way to the large free market where the authorities allow the Uighurs to sell their produce.

Conversation was awkward because Mrs. Han, who was dressed in a black skirt and stockings with a green scarf over her head, very distinct from the blue trousers of Chinese women, spoke only a few words of Chinese. My Chinese escorts, both of whom had been in Xinjiang for over ten years, spoke no Uighur at all. Finally a twelve-year-old neighbor, a Uighur girl who was watching from the doorway, helped translate. She was learning Chinese in school, she said. She had to—all her classes were in Chinese, for the benefit of the Han students.

This ready Chinese assumption of cultural superiority, not unlike Americans' treatment of the Indians, has kept relations between the Han immigrants and native Moslems tense. In 1980 several hundred civilians and soldiers were killed during a fight in Aksu, another oasis city west of Turfan. A Peking actor who was in the town at the time filming a movie said he and his colleagues had to hide for several days inside a building while angry Uighurs roamed the streets shouting death to all Chinese. To quell the disturbance, the government had to call in an army division, some of 300,000 troops Peking keeps stationed in Xinjiang, partly to defend against the Soviet Union and partly to assure local order. A Uighur student in Peking said the incident was only one of several that year, often involving gun battles and then the execution of the suspected rebel ringleaders. The situation grew so tense that Deng Xiaoping himself paid a quiet visit to Xinjiang to investigate.

Many of the disputes arise from the government's attempt to control religion. Virtually all the mosques in China were closed during the Cultural Revolution and Peking began to allow some of them to reopen only in 1980. At the main mosque in Urumqi, a simple edifice devoid of any religious decoration, the *ah-hong,* or "religious leader," Abdullah Haji Imam, said he had been kept under house arrest during the Cultural Revolution.

"The Red Guards burned my copies of the Koran and called me a monster and a demon," he related, speaking in heavily accented Chinese. A tall, proud man with a patriarchal gray beard, flashing dark eyes, and a strong aquiline nose, he was clad in a black clerical robe and a white turban. He could have been in Iran or Saudi Arabia. In fact, he said, he had been on a pilgrimage to Mecca in 1958; but then, aware of the Chinese officials with me, he hastily added that he had also met Mao. I wondered if the two events were of equal significance to him. He drew his salary not from the mosque but from the United Front Department of the Party, he related, the agency responsible for the Communists' ties with non-Communists. It was Friday, the Moslem holy day, and he asked to be excused to prepare himself for prayers. Old men and young boys with white-, green-, and red-embroidered skullcaps were drifting into the unlit mosque. There were few men between the ages of twenty and fifty, I noticed. It was because they are at work, the *ah-hong* explained. Friday is not a holiday in Xinjiang—only Sunday, the Chinese official day off.

As the Communists have sharply reduced the powers of the Moslem clergy in Xinjiang, so they have transformed the once-all-powerful Lamaist theocracy that long ruled neighboring Tibet into little more than a museum piece. Since the Chinese assumed full control over Tibet after an abortive Tibetan uprising in 1959, the number of Buddhist monasteries has been cut from 2,464 to 10, Chinese officials told me during a week's tour of "the roof of the world." Some, like the Gadan monastery, once the third largest in Tibet with nearly 10,000 monks, simply disappeared during the Cultural Revolution, the officials added without explanation. Their fate was suggested by what I found when I went to look for a famous temple on Medicine King Hill in the center of Lhasa, the capital. It had been razed and its site is now occupied by a company of the People's Liberation Army. The only traces were several red, green, and orange frescoes of Buddha in a cave partway up the rocky promontory; each had had its face gouged out, its stomach disemboweled, and was then smeared with lime. The damage was done by Red Guards who poured into Lhasa from China, a Tibetan teen-ager confided on an impromptu tour of the hillside. As recently as 1979, a Chinese archaeologist told me, large numbers of precious bronze statues looted from temples in Tibet had been transported to Peking by truck where they were melted down for copper. The practice was stopped only after a high-ranking Communist leader who liked antiques intervened. The remaining objects are being kept in a warehouse outside Peking by a so-called waste-collecting company, the archaeologist added. He said no decision had been made on what to do with them.

At the same time, the number of lamas, or monks, has shrunk from 110,000, about one fifth of Tibet's pre-1959 male population, to about 2,000, the Chinese officials who hosted me in Lhasa disclosed. They were "not too clear" about what had happened to the monks. Some, they said, were returned to being peasants and herdsmen. But others, according to Tibetans I met in Peking, had been executed or sent to labor-reform camps.

Several of the surviving monks professed they now believe socialism is a better faith than Tibetan Buddhism, a rich mixture of the benevolent teachings of Buddha and Tibet's own primitive nature worship cult, Bon.

"In the final analysis materialism will triumph over religion, because Marxism–Leninism–Mao Zedong thought is true and scientific," remarked Gandunjiacuo, a fragile, aging monk in a thick crimson wool robe in the Drepung monastery. Before the 1959 revolt when the Dalai Lama, the supreme pontiff of the Tibetan church and state, fled to India, the Drepung was the largest monastery in the land with up to 15,000 lamas and ownership of estates with 25,000 serfs. Now it is a ghost town, albeit a majestic layered complex of terraces, balconies, and tiled roofs built on a cliff overlooking the brown, sere Lhasa Valley, 11,800 feet above sea level. To reach its main halls, which the Chinese were now repainting in preparation for the arrival of foreign tourists, a visitor must walk up steep overgrown cobbled paths between old stone barracks where the monks once lived. Today most of them are vacant with the windows boarded. Before the advent of the Chinese, the monasteries, along with a small noble class, governed Tibet through a religious-secular hierarchy like Europe's political system in the Middle Ages.

It is a strange, lonely place, full of memories and not much future. Gandunjiacuo, who said he studied Mao's works every week, insisted Buddhism would die out. There have been no young men admitted to the church since 1959, he disclosed. To become a lama, an acolyte must study sutras with a living buddha, and the government does not permit anyone to hold that title anymore. "The masses have raised their consciousness and have not asked anyone to read scriptures," was the way another monk put it to me and a group of journalists from Peking.

Shortly before our arrival the government had reopened the Drepung and two other major holy places which had been closed since the start of the Cultural Revolution. They were the Potala, the magnificent 1,000-room palace upon a fortress upon a hill where the Dalai Lama resided, and the Jokhang, the golden-roofed temple built in 652 to commemorate the arrival of a Tang dynasty princess who brought Buddhism to Tibet. They had been placed under the Chinese-run Bureau for the Preservation of Cultural Relics, and stern-faced Chinese cadres in blue Mao tunics opened and closed the gates for our arrival and departure.

After a few days in Lhasa, I was inclined to accept a prophesy made in the fifth century B.C. by Sakyamuni, Buddha himself. He forecast that in 2,500 years, the present century, the faith he preached would die out. In Tibet, at first glance, that seemed to be coming true.

That was certainly the impression our Chinese hosts wanted to give. The Chinese presence is formidable. The First Party Secretary of Tibet is a Chinese, an army officer, and every few miles in the countryside there is a mud-walled Chinese fort with its garrison, looking like a French Foreign Legion outpost in *Beau Geste.* Only 120,000 of Tibet's 1.78 million people are Chinese, but they account for 53 percent of the cadres and many of the teachers, doctors, factory workers, and even bus and truck drivers. Although Lhasa is located eight hundred miles away from the nearest Chinese city, in Sichuan, separated by four mountain ranges each taller than the Rockies, the city awakens every morning to the strains of "The East Is Red" over loud-speakers in Chinese.

Tibetans and Chinese differ about the history of their relations. Tibetans argue that they were an independent nation with their own language, literature, and civilization and were never really occupied by China. Peking asserts Tibet "is an inalienable part of China." No effort is spared to reinforce this point.

In a fresco in the Potala honoring the thirteenth Dalai Lama, there is a scene that looks like His Holiness riding in a gold encrusted 1930s Packard sedan. The Dalai Lama, resplendent in an orange silk robe and high, yellow conical hat, is beaming graciously to a welcoming crowd. Our guide in the Potala, a pigtailed woman in her twenties, made a special point of showing us the mural. She said it depicted the thirteenth Dalai Lama's trip to Peking in 1908 to pay homage to the Chinese Empress Dowager, Ci Xi, and the boy emperor who was soon to be deposed by the Revolution of 1911.

The guide was not conscious of the drawing's anachronism. Indeed, it is a small point easily lost in the magnificence of the chamber, which also contains a fifty-foot-high stupa—a dome-shaped Buddhist shrine—coated with 270 pounds of gold and a miniature pagoda made from 250,000 pearls. The whole room, including the ceiling and pillars, is swathed in silk brocade.

But the guide used the fresco for a history lesson. It proved that Tibetans had always recognized China's suzerainty, she said. In the hall of the fifth Dalai Lama, she again pointed to a fresco showing a visit to Peking, this one in 1652. Score another point for China.

But did the Dalai Lama ever visit another country? a French newsman asked. No, the guide replied flatly. Then what, he pressed her, was a drawing that looked like the Dalai Lama on a pilgrimage to India, the homeland of the Buddha? "I don't know, I'm not a Buddhist," the guide responded, her temper rising.

But aren't you a Tibetan? she was asked. No, she confessed, she was a Chinese, from central China, and she didn't speak or read Tibetan. It was like having a German give the tour of the French forts at Verdun or a Japanese guide Americans around Pearl Harbor.

It was only after we had been in Lhasa for several days that I realized my mental picture of a moribund religion being inexorably squeezed out of existence was askew. The Jokhang, the most sacred of all the temples to Tibetans themselves, was open only three mornings a week to the public, and we had been taken there on a day when it was closed. So several of us decided to go back on our own when Tibetans could get in. To our surprise, the small square in an old section of the city around the temple was jammed with people; they formed a long line waiting to go inside. There were people from all over the high plateau of Chinese central Asia, pilgrims in grimy black robes, silver daggers at their belts, with high canvas boots and carrying chalices laden with yak butter for offerings. It looked like a picture in a medieval tapestry.

As the faithful entered the richly decorated inner chamber of the Jokhang, many fell to the floor, prostrating themselves before a statue of Guanyin, the goddess of mercy, or a gold-encrusted carving of Sakyamuni. One young man, with his face burned nearly black by the sun, which pierces the thin atmosphere at Tibet's altitude, kowtowed repeatedly for a full ten minutes. In an elaborate ritual, first he raised his hands over his head, then he folded them in a gesture of prayer before his face, dropped to his knees, and finally flung himself on the cement floor, hands and arms outstretched.

As he chanted an incantation, a boy about ten years old performed the same ritual beside him. Nearby an elderly woman, with a shaven head and a red blouse under her worn woolen robe, rubbed her wooden prayer beads before dropping to the floor. Along the walls of the temple other worshipers were pouring yak butter into open lamps. Some stuck coins or paper money at sacred spots with globs of melted butter.

It was a young Chinese cadre who helped me comprehend this fervor, the vitality of the Tibetan faith despite the government's destruction of the church organization. The cadre had been sent to Tibet from his home in Peking eight years before to work as an administrator in a small county seat. He and his wife, who was also from Peking, worried about the effect of the high altitude and the poor diet of wheat and barley on their children. So when his wife became pregnant, she went back to Peking to give birth and left her son and daughter with their grandparents. They saw their children only once every two years, when they got home leave. They yearned to be allowed to return to their home in the Chinese capital, but they had never been given any date for the end of their term of duty in Tibet. Yet the cadre said he felt more sorry for the Tibetans around him.

Despite government subsidies, grain production in his county had not increased since the Cultural Revolution; and the number of cattle, which produce milk for the butter that forms a mainstay of the Tibetan diet, had declined year after year. For the local Chinese officials had ordered the Tibetans to plant wheat, a Chinese crop, rather than barley, which the Tibetans eat. And the government had placed strict limits on the number of cattle the peasants could raise privately, equating prosperity with capitalism.

"The people's stomachs are never full," the cadre told me during a talk in Peking while he was on leave. "It is no wonder the Tibetans have no love for the Communist Party and put their faith in Lamaism." From the few Tibetans he had gotten to know, he learned that each family still selected one male member to secretly be a monk, in keeping with tradition, and that the Tibetans themselves still picked living buddhas.

When a delegation of exiled Tibetans, including the Dalai Lama's sister, visited his county town in 1980, the local people lined the streets to greet them. The visit had been arranged by Peking as a gesture of reconciliation to the Tibetans, with hopes it might entice the Dalai Lama himself to return from India. But the local people used it to make a point of their own. They prostrated themselves in front of the visitors and stuck out their tongues, the Tibetan sign of welcome.

"When the delegation passed, the people stuffed money into their pockets and begged to be rubbed on the head, which would ensure them a place in paradise," the cadre recalled. The people even deliberately jostled Chinese officials escorting the guests in the streets. It was a rude shock to the Chinese. The behavior of the Tibetans, like the activism of the young dissidents in

Peking and the Christians in Fuzhou, suggested there is still a range of deep human feelings in China, an inner center of resistance to political controls and enforced ideology, that even thirty years of Communist rule have not obliterated.

20. Serving the Workers and Peasants

为 工 农 服 务

WANG KEPING

"The statesman hates the writer because the writer sows the seeds of dissent. What the statesman dreams of is to be able to prevent people from thinking, and thus he always accuses the artists and writers of upsetting his orderly state."

Lu Xun

The floor of Wang Keping's fourth-floor walk-up apartment is littered with wood chips, the sign of his adopted trade, sculpture. To do his carving, he sits on a wood plank spread over two sawhorses—at night it doubles as his bed. He has only a few rough tools: a knife or two, and an awl he fashioned himself. It is always dark in Wang's six-by-ten-foot cubicle—the one small window doesn't seem to have the capacity for light—so when he works, he keeps on the single bare forty-watt bulb, suspended from the ceiling by a wire. Outside, on a tiny balcony, are several cabbages and a bowl with scraps of meat left over from a previous meal—Wang's refrigerator in Peking's long cold winter.

But clustered in rank upon rank on the walls above his head, jammed onto shelves, and stuck in corners around the room are the brooding, bitter, powerful works that have made Wang an important symbolic figure for many young Chinese. He is China's best-known dissident artist. On one shelf is a primitive, distorted gargoyle of a head titled "The Silence." One of its eyes is blinded, slashed in geometrical patterns, "so he gets only a one-sided view," Wang explained during a visit to his home. The nose has no nostrils with which to smell, and the mouth is plugged up with a cylinder, so he cannot speak. "This is our average bad cadre, he symbolizes our lack of freedom to speak what is in our hearts," Wang added. On another shelf is a satirical bust of Jiang Qing shaped from a toy wooden gun Wang found on the street. The stock is carved to look like a woman's skirt, the barrel is an extension of her arm, which she is using as a cudgel to beat people. "Mao always said, 'Political power grows out of the barrel of a gun,' " Wang added with a smirk.

Short, friendly, and ingratiating, with a soft, almost whispery voice and plain, homely features, Wang in person doesn't suggest the anger and brazen political challenge implicit in his carvings. I had to strain to hear his words.

Carefully concealed under his workbench-bed, hidden behind old rags, is his own favorite, a large totemic figure of Mao as Buddha, with one slanted eye closed in repose and the other slyly opened "to see who is praying and making their devotions to him." The resemblance to the late Chairman is striking; no one could miss the point. "It stands for the deification of the Communist Party and our worship of idols during the Cultural Revolution," Wang elaborated. His works are not subtle and sophisticated, at least by contemporary Western aesthetic standards; they are more crude and home-spun. Wang had only begun to sculpt in 1978, I later learned. But his carvings are provocative and moving, the invention of some minor form of genius.

Wang keeps the Mao icon secreted because he lives with uncertainty about how the police and the Party authorities who govern China's art world intend to deal with him. To compound the problem, Wang is not only irreverent and censorious in his sculpture, he is not, by the government's calculation, even an artist. By definition, artists in China must belong to one of the state art associations, an official *danwei,* like the Peking Art Academy or the Peking Creative Society. The older, more senior artists were accepted as members on the basis of their recognized work before 1949; the younger artists, with few exceptions, have had to go through a state art school, study formally, and pass academic exams. There is an advantage to this official sponsorship— these artists draw a regular salary and are provided with housing by the art associations, like other government employees. No airless garrets or worry-ing about where the next meal will come from for them. In return, these official artists are expected to teach in an art institute or commune or factory study class and to produce paintings to decorate hotels or perhaps sell in expensive shops to foreigners to earn hard currency.

They are also expected to conform to the Party's aesthetic canon. This was laid down, with breathtaking clarity, by Mao himself in 1942 in a series of talks on art and literature at Yanan. "Art for art's sake, art which transcends class or party, art which stands as a bystander to, or independent of, politics, does not in actual fact exist," Mao intoned. "In the world of today, all culture or literature and art belong to some one definite class, some one definite party." In China, Mao explained, that meant artists and writers must serve the workers and peasants. "Our literature and art are first and foremost for the workers, peasants, and soldiers." It also meant that artists would have to be reeducated. "The science of Marxism–Leninism is a required course, not excepting artists and writers." Mao was impatient with any art that did not glorify and idealize the workingman or that found fault with the Communist Party. "We cannot love our enemies or social evils; our aim is to eliminate both. How can our artists and writers fail to understand this commonsense view?"

The problem was, how should China's artists create the new national revolutionary art after 1949 that the Party wanted? The Communists were uncomfortable with China's traditional ink-wash landscapes, a relic of the feudal aristocracy, they thought. But they also condemned modern Western painting, virtually everything European and American since 1890, as "bourgeois formalism." Abstract art they abhorred as empty, form devoid of content, a morally neutral statement. Nudes were offensive to their revolutionary puritanism. One safe solution, China's post-Liberation artists found, was to churn out banal propaganda posters of clean, healthy, smiling pink-cheeked soldiers; another was to embellish an old landscape of mountains and mist and plum blossoms with a tractor cultivating the fields or a hydro-electric plant and high-tension power lines. China's great artistic tradition was muffled.

But Wang did not fit this mold. He had not attended an official art academy; he actually worked for Peking Central Television as a scriptwriter, and he had taken up sculpting as a hobby. In the fall of 1979, encouraged by Democracy Wall and the Party's temporarily more liberal line toward literature and art, he and a group of twenty-two other amateur artists decided to organize their own exhibition. It was a daring step. There had been very few art shows of any kind since the Cultural Revolution began in 1966. A few years before the radicals had taken works by China's most honored traditional painters and held an exhibit of "black art." Since 1949 no one had ever tried to open a display of his own work without clearance by the government art association. But when they could not get official permission, Wang and his friends went ahead anyway and set out 150 of their paintings and carvings on the sidewalk outside the Peking Fine Arts Museum for two sunny days in September. Each time the police broke up the exhibit and tried to confiscate their works, claiming they were "upsetting social order." But to their surprise, the group, who styled themselves "the Stars," had an unknown ally in the Art Museum who helped them take their paintings inside before the police could grab them.

Wang was never sure who authorized it—he speculated it must have been a sympathizer high in the Party—but after two months of negotiations with the Ministry of Culture, his group finally received permission to hold a formal show in the North Ocean Park behind the Forbidden City. Wang was ecstatic. The site lent for their exhibition was a lovely Qing dynasty courtyard, set around a frozen pond, which encompassed a series of small one-story pavilions decorated with flaming red, green, and blue prancing dragons and frolicking cats, all connected by covered walkways. It was late November and the temperature had already dropped close to zero, driven down by boreal gusts from Siberia, and none of the old buildings where the art was hung was heated. But that didn't discourage thousands of people from coming to see the show each day.

When I arrived, Wang was sitting on a balustrade over the pond, the reflected glare off the ice of the noonday sun in the azure sky giving the only warmth. He was also basking in the glow of sudden new glory. His fiercely provocative sculpture, though an unusual medium in China, had struck an instantaneous response. As I approached, a middle-aged man in a quilted black jacket and black scarf stopped to ask Wang for his autograph. As if in apology for the intrusion, he explained, "I used to be an artist, too, until they labeled me a counterrevolutionary for my sketches and locked me up for three years."

He came from the coal-mining city of Fushun in the northeast, the man said, where he and his friends had put out a private journal in which they published photographs of their paintings. There was no text, only the photographs and the titles of the works. The magazine circulated among a few art connoisseurs in the city. They had gotten through twelve issues before the "Counterattack the Right Deviationist Wind" campaign in early 1976 struck, the radical-inspired movement to dump Deng Xiaoping a second time. The amateur artist had been imprisoned and beaten. Now at last he had been freed and had come down to Peking to see Wang's show.

In traditional Chinese practice, the exhibitors had set out a large book and sheets of paper for comments by visitors at the gateway. The show included paintings in a variety of styles which had all been officially attacked as decadent—imitations of French Impressionists, haunting abstract canvases, and a sprinkling of nudes. But it was Wang's grotesque carvings that had stolen the show. A number of young Chinese stood beside them, tracing their blatantly political shapes in copy books.

"Wang Keping, we congratulate you on your daring," one visitor had written in an elegant calligraphic appreciation. "Compared with you, the professional sculptors of China are like walking corpses." Another guest commented, "Have the Chinese people gone numb? No, I have seen that the Chinese people's spirit is still alive. This is the best art exhibit since Liberation." The *People's Daily* and the other major government papers studiously ignored the exhibition.

One of the carvings on display, in dark brown wood that could almost have been African, was of a misshapen, mindless man with mouth agape, his two arms protruding to the side. In one hand is a little red piece of plastic, the infamous Little Red Book of Mao's quotations which millions of Red Guards memorized and embraced as their hymnal during the Cultural Revolution. In the other hand is a miniature knife, a symbol of the destruction the Red Guards wrought. The work is titled "Hold High," shorthand for the radicals' rallying cry, "Hold high the great banner of Chairman Mao."

The sculpture is an ironic personal indictment, for in 1967, fresh out of high school, Wang had been a self-righteous Red Guard and helped loot a Roman Catholic church in his home town of Tianjin. "I burned paintings like these and smashed statues," Wang recalled, still sitting on the balustrade, his long, unkempt hair protruding from beneath a gray worker's cap. "I believed Chairman Mao was our savior."

Wang was born in 1949, the same year the People's Republic was established, he recounted, and his father, a high-level Communist writer and army officer, had named him in commemoration of the Communists' triumph. His given name, Keping, means "Conquer Peking." His mother was a Party member, too, an actress in a military drama troupe, and his sister was in the navy. The sunny living room of their apartment—where Wang had his bedroom-studio—was decorated with pictures of his parents with Mao and Zhou Enlai. I was always amused that among the photos was one of his sister posed coquettishly on the bow of a rowboat, hand on her chin, with her legs showing under a short skirt, like some cheesecake snapshot from the 1940s.

Wang's transformation from fanatic votary to disillusioned skeptic had followed the path of so many young Chinese. Watching the endless factional wars among his Red Guard colleagues, the beatings, burnings, and arrests, he had come to question the purpose of the Cultural Revolution. Then at a critical juncture in his thinking, he had been shipped off to a state farm in Heilongjiang province, in the frozen northeast, part of Mao's rustication program to continue the Red Guards' revolutionary education at the hands of the peasants.

"It was terrible, worse than hell," Wang remembered. "Ten of us slept in one tiny room, all piled next to each other on one bed like dried persimmons, all squashed flat and wrinkled. And the lice, whew," he added, pursing his lips. He reached under his blue ski parka to squeeze an imaginary louse. It was an ignoble end to Wang's vision of revolution.

He had come to sculpture accidentally. Bored with his job as a writer, one day he picked up a piece of wood that had broken off a chair. "I didn't know how to carve, but as a scriptwriter I had been influenced by the French theater of the absurd, especially Beckett's *Waiting for Godot* and Ionesco's *The Bald Soprano*. So I decided to try to carve a kind of theater of the absurd in wood."

Finding wood to sculpt was a tough problem. China has such a huge population and its forests have been depleted for so many centuries that there is a chronic shortage of timber. In Peking lumber is not for sale to individuals, not even by ration coupons. But in China there is always the back door. Wang began dropping by a small factory that supplied kindling to people with wood-burning stoves.

"They are supposed to break up old pieces of wood into kindling, but sometimes the wood is too hard, or too big, or they are too lazy, and they don't chop it up," Wang recounted. "I made friends with them, chatted them up. Whenever I stopped in, I gave them a few presents—liquor, cigarettes, movie tickets. They began giving me wood." It was a modest supply, and the wood was knotted, gnarled, and rough, but that served to make his heretical carvings all the more disfigured.

His parents were originally opposed to his sculpting; good Party members, they were shocked by his unorthodox art. "They said I was wasting my time and would get in trouble," Wang told me. Only after his exhibit, when they read all the flattering comments, did they realize Wang wasn't mad. "They didn't say it, but they were secretly proud of me, I think."

Despite the exhibition, Wang lived in a kind of political minefield—he could never be certain when one misstep might lead to a confrontation with the authorities. So we arranged to rendezvous with conspiratorial precaution. I had recently come back from Hong Kong with two thick books on modern sculpture for Wang. At the show he had surprised me by saying he had never heard of Henry Moore, Brancusi, or Giacometti; the most recent Western sculptor he knew was Rodin, whose safe "realistic" works are reproduced in Chinese art books. Like other Chinese writers and artists, he lived isolated from the rest of the twentieth century. To meet Wang to deliver the books, I had to first drop him a note—he didn't have a telephone. Then, when he called from a public phone booth, without identifying himself, we agreed on the spot where we had last seen each other, the pavilion in the park, not mentioning the place over the phone for security reasons.

To be as inconspicuous as possible, we made our way from the pavilion to a quiet enclosure of artificial hills, rock gardens, and a covered promenade around a small pond. In imperial times, the emperor and his consorts must have played there, imagining the earth mounds to be mountains and the pond an ocean. In the distance skaters glided over the frozen surface of the park's main lake in the pale gray light of a Peking winter afternoon.

Wang was the first to notice something was wrong. "Police," he said simply, twisting his head slightly to the right. There they were, standing on one of the little man-made peaks, two men in bright-blue uniforms with high fur caps decorated with red stars. Did he want to leave? I asked. No, he replied.

"As the saying goes, a dead pig doesn't care about being scalded." He had already been spotted, it was too late.

From their perch on the hill, the two policemen, one tall and thin, the other short and round, descended to the stone bench where we were sitting, Wang, myself, and Jan Wong. I was half frozen by the bitter cold and a raging wind, but the sight of the police made me even chillier. They walked directly up in front of us, eyed the three of us, and I felt certain we were about to be arrested as spies. I had the two books in an Air France airlines bag at my feet, what must have looked to their suspicious eyes like proof of our evil intent. But instead of detaining us, the two officers sat down on our bench, one on either side of us, close enough so our legs and shoulders were touching and I could smell the garlic on their breaths.

I felt intimidated, but Wang kept his courage, he had lived with the system and still chose to challenge it. Wang generated a steady conversation about modern art, the virtues of form as content, the integrity of the artist, the names of famous museums in Europe and America. Finally, after fifteen minutes, the two policemen got up and left, walking away without a word.

On our way out of the park, I saw they had stopped at the little booth near the entrance where a middle-aged woman bundled in layers of padded clothing sold penny admission tickets. So she had tipped the police off that a Chinese and a foreigner were together in the park, I realized.

I offered Wang a ride in our car. The police didn't seem to have a vehicle, and we could drop him off where they couldn't follow him. But he declined.

"If they want to get you, they will," he said.

What reason would they give? I asked.

"They don't need a reason. After they arrest you, they will make up a reason. Reasons are very easy to come by. Besides, in our society, to have contact with a foreigner is one of the worst crimes." Wang knew, because after his show several agents from the Public Security Ministry had come to see him to ask why he had talked to foreign journalists. "They told me not to do it again, if I knew what was good for me."

Wang's hope, what kept him going, was a belief that Mao's successors hadn't yet entirely made up their minds about what kind of art was acceptable.

"Our new leaders have made their ideas about economics clear, but they have not yet decided about art and culture," he said during another encounter. "Many of them are still afraid of Western influences, thinking they are bad for China and immoral. The leaders have been isolated for such a long time that many of them are not very cultivated. But as living standards go up, there will be an effect on art and culture too. The best way to develop art is not to pay official attention to it at all."

I wondered if he was too sanguine. Deng's program for China is the Four Modernizations, four and no more: agriculture, industry, science, and defense. All are material. There are none for politics, social life, leisure-time recreation, or culture. That is not accidental. The term "the Four Modernizations" reflects Deng's own interests.

During his triumphal tour of the United States in early 1979, Deng was escorted one evening in Washington to a gala reception at the soaring new wing of the National Gallery of Art. It was designed by I. M. Pei, the Shanghai-born architect who is the best-known contemporary Chinese artistic figure in the world. (Why has China itself not produced contemporary artists of international stature? Wang once asked rhetorically, suggesting the reason lay with the government, not the race.) Pei, short, bouncy, and gracious, was eager to show Deng around the building. But Deng staggered his hosts by skipping the tour and leaving abruptly after he gave a prepared speech. I was standing next to an official of the Information Department, Yao Wei, a crew-cut, boyish-looking man in his fifties who had been educated at a school run by American missionaries and spoke English with a deceptively American accent. He always impressed foreigners who met him as being thoroughly Westernized. What did he think of Pei's creation? I asked.

At first Yao didn't respond. He hadn't really looked around, he confessed. Then when I pressed him further, he finally said, "What a queer building. If this is modern art, it is one modernization we don't need."

The Communists' selective interest in the West is not new. It goes back to the nineteenth century when the first Chinese reformers, seeking to modernize the old Central Kingdom in the face of incursions by the industrialized Western powers, pondered over what course to adopt. They hit on a formula that translates as "Western learning for practical use, Chinese learning for the essence." It meant China should copy the West's science and technology, its machines and gunboats, but somehow preserve its own philosophy and culture intact. China's leaders today, like their forebears, still have difficulty grasping that industrialization carries its own new values.

But Peking has fought to insulate itself against the contagion of most of the cultural developments of the twentieth century: atonal music, modern dance, stream-of-consciousness prose, abstract art. Several American and European orchestras visiting China have been asked not to perform any twentieth-century music. In 1981 the Communists vigorously sought to remove thirteen abstract paintings from the first show of American art in China since 1949. They backed down only at the last minute when U.S. officials threatened to cancel the whole exhibition if the paintings were taken out and scrap a Sino–U.S. cultural exchange agreement for the year. Even then, as a face-saving protest, the Chinese delayed the opening ceremony for an hour, holding up a speech by the U.S. Chief Justice, Warren E. Burger, who had flown to China in part to dedicate the exhibit. Among the canvases the Chinese objected to were Jackson Pollock's "Abstract Number 10" and works by Franz Kline and Helen Frankenthaler.

Wang himself had been subjected to this kind of dogmatism. He had once talked with officials from the Peking Art Academy about becoming a member; they said they could accept him only if he gave up his heretical work.

"They told me the workers, peasants, and soldiers can't understand my art, so it doesn't serve the masses," Wang related. "They accused me of being a slave of the West. I answered that they aren't workers, peasants, or soldiers themselves, so how do they know what the masses want."

Wang was not alone in playing this cat-and-mouse game with the authorities, searching for new modes of cultural expression before being suppressed. Many other artists and writers labor in silence and obscurity. Wang introduced me to one, a tall, reticent painter with a high forehead and finely chiseled features. He was a factory worker by trade but took up painting in his spare time. For several years he had lived in the far southwest of China, on the border with Laos, a region of tropical rain forests, towering jungle-covered mountains, and verdant valleys inhabited by the Dai ethnic minority, cousins of the Thais. For him, it was like Gauguin's journey to Tahiti. He came away with a mystical vision of this primitive land that he transformed into shimmering silvery-blue canvases, the colors of the rain forest. In his scroll paintings, which he unrolled for me, the people were engaged in some ancient ritual, the women eloquently slender, with bare breasts, long black hair cascading to their waists, and their narrow hips outlined in batik wrap skirts. His figures were all seated amid the forest, along with giant cranes whose own elongated legs and narrow frames mirrored those of the women.

His work was a blend of Chinese and Western sensibilities, of Chinese ink-wash colors and Western perspective, and I was enraptured. I asked if he had ever tried to sell any of his paintings. He had taken one, he said, to Rong Bao Zhai, the fancy shop on Wangfujing Street near the Peking Hotel which sells contemporary Chinese art to foreigners at inflated prices. They turned him down. "No one would understand it," the shop clerks told him. "Try sticking to landscape painting."

Another time I met an industrial designer who wanted to be a poet. From somewhere he had acquired an old leather jacket and he had let his hair grow long over his collar, still a rebellious act in China. It gave him the desired Bohemian effect. But his verse was too blasphemous, in subject matter and its free-wheeling style, to be accepted by the Party's cultural czars and win him a job as an established writer. So he had to settle for his factory post. He belonged to an informal group who called themselves the *tui-fei-pai,* literally the "decadent school," China's Beat poets. One evening he recited a verse he had titled "Mad Dog":

"After enduring cruelties,
I don't think of myself as a human being.
It is as if I had become a mad dog,
wandering around without purpose in the human world.
I am not yet really a mad dog;
if I were, I could jump over a wall when I am desperate.
Now all I can do is bear things in silence.
If I was really a mad dog,
Then I could free myself from this invisible chain and lock.
Then I would not hesitate
To give up my so-called human life."

Despite all his artistic trials, Wang considered himself better off than some Western artists, for he had a regular job that paid him an average wage, by Chinese standards. It was even better than that, Wang said, because he didn't have to go to work. The only time he reported to his office in the Central Broadcasting Station was on the fifth of each month to pick up his salary.

But didn't his absenteeism get him in trouble? I asked.

"It doesn't matter," Wang replied with a sly smile. "Under socialism, they can't fire you, that's one of the virtues of our system."

Of the five writers in his section, who were supposed to produce two-hour plays for evening television, none reported for work. "I'm actually considered the most productive," Wang went on. "At least last year I wrote one play. Some of them in twenty years haven't turned in a single manuscript for radio or television. They have good relations with the leaders of the office, so it doesn't matter.

"They don't use our plays anyway, they're not politically safe," he added. "The leaders prefer to use stories from the *People's Daily* or government magazines, that way they can't get in trouble. They have never used a single word I have written. When I submit a manuscript, about ten cadres have to read it. First one reads it, he gives it to another, who gives it to another, and so on."

It was beginning to sound as if Wang's idea for a theater of the absurd in wood grew out of his experience in the office. Here was a government that prided itself on ensuring that every worker had a job—how different from the evil ways of capitalism. But then in a mad burlesque of policy-making, the regime didn't care what happened in the office.

Wang laughed at my consternation. He had saved the choicest morsel for last. "Anyhow, even if I did go to work, I couldn't work, because there isn't an office anymore," he said with delectation. "The broadcasting station ran out of housing for the staff a long time ago, so they converted our office into a dorm. My leader even told me to stay home."

Wang's situation was not much different from that of workers assigned to factories that had never opened because of delays in construction or that had been closed down by Peking because of shortages of electricity and raw materials. They all still drew their pay. No one complained. It was the government's way of keeping people happy.

In the fall of 1980, not long before I left China, the country's most beloved movie actor died, Zhao Dan. He had starred in more than sixty films since the 1930s, and Chinese liked to compare him with Clark Gable. Zhao Dan was also a Communist, and as an indication of the esteem even the Party leadership held for him, he was visited in the hospital by no less than Deng, the new Prime Minister, Zhao Ziyang, and the then still Party Chairman, Hua Guofeng. Perhaps emboldened by these callers, Zhao Dan penned a deathbed appeal to the Party to relax its grip over literature and art.

"The Party can lead in formulating national economic planning and implementing agricultural and industrial policy," he wrote. "However, why should the Party tell us how to farm, how to make a stool, how to cut trousers or how to fry vegetables? Why should they instruct writers how to write, or actors how to act? Literature and art are the business of writers and artists. If the Party controls literature and art too tightly, there will be no hope for literature and art, they will be finished."

It was intoxicating language for China. What made it even more astonishing was that the *People's Daily* printed the text; that seemed to give it the Party's imprimatur. A few weeks later I paid a final call on Wang. I suggested he might have been encouraged by the movie star's plea and the *People's Daily*'s action. Wang eyed me with disdain, like a teacher chastising a schoolboy who forgot his lesson. Didn't I know what had happened? Wang asked. The Politburo was furious about the article. The *People's Daily* had acted on its own authority, without checking with the Party leadership. Now the paper's liberal editors had been forced to make a self-criticism. Things were getting tighter again, Wang sensed; Deng had told a Party meeting that there had been too much "bourgeois liberalism" in culture. Wang was desolate. He knew he would have to draw his carapace around him again, like an armadillo's hide, to toughen himself for the harder Party line.

Before I left, Wang had a present to give me. It was an old Qing dynasty vase, in yellow and famille rose, emblazoned with dragons and flowers. But the gaudy glaze was chipped and there was a jagged piece missing from the vessel's narrow mouth. Wang had scavenged it in the Cultural Revolution.

"It is broken, I know," he said, handing it to me with both hands, a Chinese gesture of politeness. "Consider it a symbol of our broken culture."

Still Alive in the Bitter Sea

依舊苦海餘生

EPILOGUE

"We do not fear spilling blood, and we do not fear international reaction."
Deng Xiaoping, April 25, 1989

"Lies written in ink cannot obscure a truth written in blood. This is not the conclusion of an incident, but a new beginning."
Lu Xun, on the massacre of anti-government demonstrators by Nationalist troops in 1926

I called with trepidation.

It was early July, only a month after the People's Liberation Army massacred hundreds of civilians in Peking, and boyish-looking soldiers in their tan summer uniforms were still patrolling the capital's broad streets, their AK-47 assault rifles at the ready. I had returned to China, after an absence of eight years, and I was deeply curious about what had happened to my old Chinese friends. Some had kept in touch by writing letters, often having the missives delivered courtesy of other Americans they had met, rather than trusting the Chinese post office. Others had managed to get coveted passports and had traveled to the United States.

Still, I hesitated before dialing Tang. The Chinese government had denounced my book, and I didn't want to get Tang in trouble, especially with Peking under martial law. He had written a few months earlier to report that he had gotten a job as an official in one of the new Army-owned companies exporting Chinese weapons to the Middle East and Southeast Asia. It was a cushy position, arranged by his father, a retired general. With the job came a spacious apartment and a telephone at home, still something of a luxury for Chinese. Fortunately, when I called, Tang recognized my voice. It was my accent in Chinese, he joked, which made me sound like someone from Shandong province—in other words, like a country bumpkin. He suggested we meet at the usual place, if I remembered it.

The spot was an intersection a few blocks north of the Peking Hotel, where I had lived during most of my time in China. Tang, a tall, big-boned forty-year-old with a strong chin, used to pedal his bicycle to our encounters, the normal means of transportation for Chinese in those days. But this time I almost missed him, for he arrived in a shiny new Jeep Cherokee. The Jeep was an emblem of the extraordinary economic changes that had taken place in China over the past decade, since Deng Xiaoping began his reforms in 1979. The vehicle, which belonged to his office, was symbolic in other ways too. It was produced in a Peking factory jointly owned by the Chrysler Corporation and a Chinese state enterprise. This new form of ownership, a joint venture with foreign investment, was another of Deng's heretical breaks with the Maoist past. When I had visited the old, purely Chinese-owned plant almost ten years earlier, it was a model of inefficiency, with piles of parts scattered on the concrete floor. Then it manufactured only a 1950s-style Soviet jeep and was so badly run that it could turn out only two vehicles a year for each of the factory's 9,700 workers.

Tang suggested dinner in one of the privately owned restaurants that had sprung up as another of Deng's reform measures, allowing the revival of private enterprise. Under Mao, individual businesses had been shuttered as "tails of capitalism," and the state-run eateries were inevitably dirty and crowded, with inedible food and surly service. But our meal of sautéed eggplant in spicy brown sauce and "returned to the pot" pork arrived promptly, served by a smiling waitress.

Tang looked prosperous, an exemplar of all the stories I had read about China's recent economic growth. When I had last seen him, in 1981, he still wore baggy blue proletarian pants and plastic sandals. Now he had on a pair of well-tailored beige slacks and leather Topsiders, the American yachting shoes which had suddenly become a status symbol among fashion-conscious young Chinese. His career had clearly taken a turn for the better. When I had known him, he was reduced to being a mechanic. His education had been cut short by the Cultural Revolution when his father came under attack as a capitalist-roader and Tang had been shipped off to the countryside. Now his political fortunes had been reversed.

But Tang was as despondent as he had been ten years earlier. Why was he so morose, I asked?

"It's true things are better on the surface, there are more goods for sale in the stores," Tang replied in a low voice, his eyes fixed on the plastic tabletop. "But you have to look deeper. You foreigners saw Kentucky Fried Chicken in Peking and you thought China was going capitalist and democratic," he said,

447

referring to the branch of the American fast food company that had opened on the side of Tiananmen Square. "But the massacre shows some things did not change. The reforms only covered up the real troubles in China."

Tang had not participated in any of the pro-democracy demonstrations. He had shrewdly calculated early on that the students did not have the Army on their side. But like almost everyone in Peking, he was enraged by the killings that began on the night of June 3. "Not since I was born under what we used to call the Red Sun has the People's Army shot people in Peking," he said. "China is like a mad dog that sinks its fangs into its own tail. Our leaders have gone crazy."

In the modern high-rise apartment building where he lived, he related, a compound reserved for high cadres or their relatives, a sixty-eight-year-old woman had been shot to death in her living room. "She had gone to the window to open it, and when she did, a soldier in the street just opened fire."

He also had a twenty-five-year-old cousin who had been shot when he went out with his camera to take pictures that first night. "His family was frantic," Tang said. "They had no idea what had happened to him. The next day they went to the hospital and found his name on a list of the dead, but they couldn't find his body. Maybe it was all a terrible mistake, they thought. Finally, the other day, a clerk in the hospital uncovered the body. He found it underneath a pile of other corpses. Because my cousin was one of the first to die, the other bodies had been shoved on top of him and he had been overlooked."

Tang paused. There was more to the story. His cousin was to have started work on a Ph.D. in the fall in America. His wife had won a scholarship to go abroad also, and because she was pregnant, had had an abortion so she could continue her studies too. Now she was being questioned by the police. Since she was the widow of a "hooligan," as all demonstrators were called, her passport would probably be revoked, Tang said.

Tang himself had been required to attend political study sessions in his office since the crackdown a month earlier. It was an old technique the Communists had largely abandoned with Deng's reforms ten years before. But now every day, Tang said, the ritual was the same. In the morning he and his colleagues had to read a speech by Deng justifying the massacre. Then in the afternoon they each had to "express their opinions," being careful to parrot back Deng's words. "It's just like the Cultural Revolution again," he said.

"This Communist Party wants to control everything," Tang continued. "It's all they are good at. If they say the students are counterrevolutionaries, then you must say they are counterrevolutionaries. If they say no one was killed, then no one was killed." It reminded me of a passage from George Orwell that another friend, Bing, had quoted to me in 1981. "If the leader says of such and such an event, 'It never happened'—well, it never happened. If he says that two and two are five, well, two and two are five. This prospect frightens me much more than bombs."

By now it was getting late. Tang was worried that soldiers might stop his Jeep on the way home, as they often did at night in the first month after the killings. When we stepped outside in the hot summer night, we could see a crimson banner hung from the third-floor window of the building opposite the restaurant. It was the first propaganda slogan I had seen publicly displayed on my trip. In earlier years, with the onset of a political campaign, walls throughout China would have been festooned with banners and posters like the graffiti that erupted in New York's subways. "Resolutely oppose bourgeois liberalism," the solitary banner proclaimed, the Communists' code word for creeping Western influence. It was bourgeois liberalism that Deng blamed for the democracy movement.

Tang looked at the words for a moment, then said softly, *"Fang-pi."* This literally means "break wind," or "fart." In Chinese it had the force of absolute rejection.

Here was a man who should have been grateful to the Communists. His father had risen to be a general in the People's Liberation Army, and he himself now had a good job, a large apartment, and access to a car. His job, selling weapons abroad, had even allowed him to travel to Hong Kong several times, a rare privilege. But Tang was as disillusioned with the Party as he and other Chinese I had known were after the Cultural Revolution, before the recent decade of affluence. Despite all the economic improvements in his life, Tang was still a cynic.

Before climbing into his Jeep, Tang had one last thought. "The Chinese people love China," he said, quoting the popular writer Bai Hua, "but China does not love the Chinese people."

As I traveled around China in the summer of 1989, much of what I found was like my talk with Tang. There had been profound economic changes, which I had not anticipated even a few years before. Indeed, China had just enjoyed its best, most properous, and most stable decade since the Opium War of 1840–42, when British gunboats forced the old Central Kingdom to open to the outside world. But these changes kept bumping up against a harsher reality—the repressive system the Communists had constructed to ensure their power. That system was now slowly being undermined, partly by the economic progress and partly by the continued spread of the disenchantment with the Communists that began in the Cultural Revolution. Yet the security system was still there. It was as if China was moving in two directions at once, like a country straddling two giant tectonic plates that slowly grind against each other. Pressure kept building up along the fault line, and from time to time the result was eruptions: Democracy Wall in 1979, the student protests in late 1986, and now a political earthquake in Tiananmen Square.

The economic changes that Deng had initiated in 1979—by allowing a return to private family farming in the countryside, by permitting the revival of private enterprise, and by trying to introduce the profit motive in industry—had come so fast that they had knocked many knowledgeable foreigners, and even Chinese, off-balance. An American banker who had been doing business in China since the mid-1970s confided to me after the June massacre, "Things were so much better, I really did believe change was inexorable." The government had relaxed to the point that the banker found himself being invited to play tennis on Sunday mornings with several members of the Politburo at an exclusive new tennis club. The senior Party leaders did not even try to hide the fact that they were bringing attractive young women with them in their chauffeur-driven black Mercedes limousines. The women, clearly not their wives, sat politely and watched the tennis.

The banker also had generals from the People's Liberation Army coming to his Peking office to offer deals. They wanted to turn parts of their bases or airfields into hotels, office buildings, or golf courses, the banker said. "They just wanted to get in on the money. It was all so overwhelming, I forgot where I was living. We were lulled into believing it was working."

China has always been so big that it exerted its own gravity, enchanting and baffling foreigners. Deng's reforms were just the latest in a series of beguilements. Certainly the statistics alone were amazing. After years of stagnation, in the decade from 1979 to 1988 China's gross national product doubled. Average per capita income rose from perhaps $400 a year, in real terms, to $1,200 a year, a huge gain for a poor country.* Foreign trade quintupled to $102 billion in 1988. In a reversal of Mao's policy of self-reliance and keeping China shuttered against the outside world, foreign investors were welcomed—and 5,000 foreign companies signed investment deals. The number of television sets, one of the best measures of a family's standard of living in China, soared from 3 million in 1979 to 130 million in 1988. One in ten families in Shanghai acquired a video cassette recorder. All this was accompanied by the greatest demographic shift in China's history. After centuries of being an overwhelmingly rural society, the share of the population living in the cities exploded from 20 percent in 1979 to 45 percent in 1988, according to United Nations figures. By the year 2000, the

*China's per capita income has long been a subject of dispute. The World Bank put it at $305 in 1988, but that was almost the same figure used ten years earlier, before the decade of enormous growth. Instead, I have adopted the estimates of Nicholas Lardy, now a professor of economics at the University of Washington, who has factored in the real purchasing power of China's currency.

U.S. Bureau of the Census projected, more than half of China's 1.1 billion people will live in urban areas.

In keeping with these economic changes, the Communists even loosened the control system, at least on the surface. On my return, I was surprised to find city maps readily for sale. In the past maps were kept secret, part of the government's fetish for security. But with a flood of foreign tourists, providing badly needed dollars to help fund China's modernization program, maps had been declassified. Similarly, at the large hotels, where ordinary Chinese in the past had been stopped by security guards, making business and friendship difficult, people were now free to enter.

Nor did Chinese any longer need special permission to travel from one city to another, one of the most stringent of the old control mechanisms. In fact, under the new dispensation, security personnel at airports and train stations had become almost comically relaxed. When I entered China by train, arriving at the Canton railway station from Hong Kong, I was nervous that the immigration authorities might be on the watch for me. But the two border control officers who took my passport barely glanced at my name before stamping it. Then customs officials simply waved me through without an inspection. There was still an X-ray machine, like those used for security checks in airports, where passengers were directed to place their bags on a conveyor belt. But as I crossed to the other side to collect my bag, I noticed no one was stationed behind the machine to watch the monitor. It had become a sham procedure.

Jerome A. Cohen, a former professor at Harvard Law School who largely pioneered the field of Chinese legal studies in the United States, was convinced China was finally developing a modern legal system. After years in which China's handful of lawyers were either powerless or imprisoned, the country suddenly swarmed with a million people working in the legal system, Cohen found. They included students in new law schools, employees in a vastly expanded network of courts and legal advisers to government agencies. During the 1980s, Peking passed a new criminal law, new commercial codes and regulations to cover the joint venture foreign investments, which was good business for American lawyers like Cohen, who resigned from Harvard to work for the large New York law firm of Paul, Weiss, Rifkind, Wharton & Garrison, based in Hong Kong. This spring, shortly before the massacre, China even passed a landmark new law giving its citizens the right to appeal in court against government decisions involving taxes, fines, and the police. It was an almost unthinkable advance, at least on paper.

Chinese themselves sometimes found the speed of change hard to comprehend. Wang Keping, my friend the dissident sculptor, had married a Frenchwoman and moved to Paris after I left China in 1981. At the time, given the Communists' all-encompassing and rigid control over art, it was the only way for him to pursue his career. But early this spring Wang had returned to Peking and went to an avant-garde art show. Just a decade before he had daringly helped organize China's first unofficial art exhibition, when such action could lead to swift arrest.

While he was walking through the new show, at the Peking Fine Arts Museum, pandemonium suddenly broke out. "I heard shots," Wang related later. "Then a whole bunch of police came running."

But this was performance art. The shots had been fired by the artist, Xiao Lu, who had fired two pellets into her work, a pair of phone booths. Another artist tossed condoms on the floor. A third sat half naked on eggs.

Wang, now forty years old and a successful sculptor in France, was stunned by what he found. "Lots of bureaucrats who know nothing about art are organizing vulgar exhibits to make money," he said. At a radical chic party in the living room of a Swedish diplomat, Wang look bemused at the sight of a twenty-five-year-old self-styled "Tibetan" artist, who was wandering around in jungle fatigues and boots, his shoulder-length hair gathered in a ponytail. Wang still wore his old plain blue Chinese worker's jacket with a Mandarin collar and buttons of knotted cloth. The other artist, Cao Yong, was not really a Tibetan, but found that his assumed identity was a useful ploy to help sell his surrealistic oils of Tibetan monks in red and yellow silk robes sitting on a mound of naked women. To ensure the success of a one-man show at a private gallery, Cao had to bribe a crew from China's government-owned television network 500 yuan, the equivalent of $135. "If we don't get publicity, how can this gallery work?" the owner of the shop later complained.

Wang's surprise at the vitality, and crassness, of the Chinese art scene underscored an important point about the economic reforms. They seemed to have unleashed a new materialism that stood in sharp contrast to the virtues Mao had preached: selflessness, simplicity, and working for the common good rather than for profit. It was as if Maoism, China's ideology, had been replaced by its antithesis, an unvarnished commercialism. After all the years of hardship, poverty, and sacrifice, making money suddenly supplanted the Communist Party as the source of legitimacy. Deng himself had sanctified the new doctrine, writing in an edition of his *Selected Works* published in 1983, that China's goal was to "make some people rich first, so as to lead all the people to wealth." Someone in the Party propaganda department then put this into a simple slogan: "To get rich is glorious."

Even at the time of the Tiananmen killings this new materialism was everywhere. When I boarded the train from Hong Kong to Canton, I noticed the passenger cars were still the familiar green and yellow carriages that had carried me across the border many times in past years. But the Chinese "service personnel," the conductors and waitresses, had a new task. From the moment I sat down, they cruised the aisles like hungry salesmen, purveying an odd assortment of Remy Martin cognac, Winston cigarettes, Ritz crackers, and Chinese apples. The front of the car bore a warning against smoking. But next to the admonition was a large color ad for Marlboro cigarettes, complete with the usual cowboy lassoing a brown stallion in front of a snowcapped mountain range. Over the train's loudspeakers came another sign of the changes. Even though Peking was under martial law, there were no more of the political messages I was accustomed to hearing. Instead came the voice of Stevie Wonder singing, "I just called to say I love you."

Under Mao, one of the asperities of Chinese life had been a severe shortage of consumer goods and services. But Deng had permitted a revival of private enterprise, and abruptly there was an explosion of new goods and shops. In Shanghai, on crowded and fashionable Nanjing Road, I started to make a survey, then gave up because there were so many new restaurants, bookstores, and dance halls. One magazine kiosk carried a series of publications unthinkable a few years earlier, with titles like *Modern Movies, World Television, Furniture and Life,* and *Better Life,* the latter complete with dozens of pictures of Western fashion models and patterns with directions on how to make the dresses they were displaying. The latest edition of a periodical called *World Screen* carried the famous nude centerfold picture of Marilyn Monroe draped against a red rug. An electronics store was selling Japanese-made color television sets and video games with names like Star Wars. The imported games cost $100 to $200 apiece, several months' wages for the average Chinese. Next door a pharmacy was selling a popular new perfume named Poison. "When the mysterious purple appears before your eyes, you seem to see . . . Poison," an ad read. In the ad, standing beside a bottle of the magic elixir was a semi-nude woman, her left arm barely hiding her breasts.

The drugstore carried a whole array of other temptations. There were electric body massagers, a Super Effective Hair Regenerating Cream, and bottles of Beauty brand breast enlargement cream. "It relies on the most up-to-date scientific techniques of the 1980s and will enlarge your breasts without needles, without pills, and without any painful side effects," an ad proclaimed. Accompanying photographs showed before and after shots of a long-haired young Chinese woman who miraculously went from being flat-chested to a voluptuous D cup. In another display window the store had cartons of what was delicately described in English as "Erectile Apparatus of Penis." It promised "family happiness" or your money back.

All this new interest in the human body, in sex, and in beauty seemed particularly subversive of the old puritanical Maoist order. Mao had been an evangelist of selflessness. "Serve the people" was his credo. Now young

453

Chinese were striving for self-expression, even self-glorification, and turning it into a commercial operation.

As I walked back out onto the sidewalk, a slender man in his early twenties approached me, smiling. "Change money?" he suggested. It was an old invitation that any foreigner living in Asia has heard hundreds or thousands of times, from Korea and Vietnam to India and Afghanistan. But in Communist China it was startling, the very essence of capitalism, profiteering on the difference between the official exchange rate of 3.7 renminbi to the American dollar, and the black market rate, about 6.8 renminbi to $1.00.

I told the stranger that I had no dollars with me, which was true. But it did not deter him.

"That's okay," he said happily. "I'll change any amount. Would you like to change a thousand dollars?"

When I repeated my situation, he still pressed on. "Never mind, it's not important," he said. "Which hotel are you staying in? You can go back to your hotel and get some dollars. I'll meet you there."

No amount of demurrals would dissuade my new companion. He began following me down the street, pressing his case, until I finally hailed a passing taxi. I admired his gumption; it bespoke a new sense of motivation stirring in Chinese after years of apathy induced by too many political campaigns and too little attention to the economy. But the encounter also left me vaguely uneasy.

That evening I had made an appointment with another young man whom I had met in a Shanghai restaurant. He was a twenty-nine-year-old engineer named Huang, with a quizzical grin, a quick wit, and an astounding knowledge about the United States. Huang had gleaned it, he said, from listening to the Voice of America every day and buying used copies of *Time* magazine in a secondhand bookstore. The magazines had been left behind by tourists in their hotels and sold by the roomboys. Huang wanted me to see the latest and best entertainment in Shanghai, of which he was immensely proud.

We drove by taxi to a large three-story European-style villa in what, before 1949, had been the International Settlement. On the ground floor was a new privately owned bar, on the second floor a privately run restaurant, and on the third a large nightclub with the English name of the Esen Music Club. Nothing that I had seen in China before prepared me for what lay inside. When my eyes adjusted to the dim red and yellow lights flashing from the black-painted ceiling, I saw a vast room with perhaps twenty-five tables covered with red-checked cloths and tastefully decorated with candles and bud vases, each containing fresh irises or peonies. A red carpet covered the floor. Along one wall, Chinese customers reclined on low red imitation-leather couches. In a corner of the room a huge air conditioner kept the club not only cool, but cold, an unheard-of luxury in steamy Shanghai, whose climate is like that of New Orleans. In another corner was a small raised dance floor with mirrored walls. But the centerpiece, on which all eyes focused, were two 27-inch video monitors playing Chinese pop music videos from a very expensive digital machine.

For this was a Chinese copy of a Japanese karaoke club, a type of nightclub wildly popular in Japan and Taiwan, where patrons watch their favorite crooners on video and then get up, take a microphone, and sing along in front of the rest of the audience. The menu proved to be a list of 300 video selections the club had stocked, from which we were free to pick songs we wanted played and would then sing to. A bevy of waitresses dressed in short black skirts with white lacy satin blouses and red-checked aprons hovered over us, waiting to take our orders for drinks. I had never seen such prompt and courteous service in China before. But I had never seen such prices either. A beer was $5; the cover charge was more than $10 apiece. Our tab, before we were finished, was nearly $50, about Huang's monthly salary. With this much money at stake, decor and service promptly improved.

The patrons were all private entrepreneurs, Huang told me, the new class of businessmen spawned by the reforms. Only they could afford these prices. One tall young man was wearing a powder-blue polo shirt and very short khaki shorts, with a beeper tucked conspicuously in his belt. He also had on a pair of fresh white Adidas sneakers. Another guest, a portly man in his early forties, was attired in a white polo shirt and Levi jeans, with the label showing, held up by bright yellow suspenders. They were China's yuppies.

At one point two men in their early twenties got up together to sing. One was short and stubby, with a huge mound of frizzed hair, looking like a Maori warrior, though clad in a brown Western business suit. The other resembled a gangster in an old Chinese movie, dressed in a blousy black shirt with a low mandarin collar, black pants, and black high-heeled leather shoes. His hair was pomaded and slicked back, making him handsome in a menacing way. They were two of Shanghai's leading pop singers, Huang said, part of a new youth culture, enjoying a kind of busman's holiday. They had become millionaires in Chinese terms by making cassette recordings that sold hundreds of thousands of copies. The song they had picked to sing in front of us, "I Am a Bad Boy," came from Taiwan.

As the video rolled, showing a Chinese teenager in a black motorcycle jacket cruising the streets of Taipei on a red motorcycle, the two men began to sing.

"I am a bad boy, a bad boy," they wailed.

"I have gone beyond this age of the eighties, this age of yours."

"I have gone into my own time, where I do what I want."

Here, on the video, the cyclist stopped to pick up a pretty girl smoking a cigarette, and then put her on the back of his machine.

"Don't misunderstand me," the song continued. "I am not a well-behaved child," the kind prized by centuries of Chinese families.

"I am a really bad boy."

What would Mao have thought about all this, I asked Huang when the song stopped. "In Shanghai today people say old Mao was just a peasant," Huang replied.

But is this the new China, the direction China is headed? I persisted. "I don't know," Huang said, barely audible above the start of another video. "Something is wrong with our society, we have become so materialistic and so escapist."

Huang himself had a deeply pessimistic view of China. His goal, the overriding joy and frustration of his life, was to go to the United States to continue his engineering studies. This was why he spent so much time listening to the Voice of America and reading *Time* magazine, to improve his English. But two years earlier, when he was a graduate student, his college had held a competitive exam to pick one student to receive a fellowship to go to the United States. Ten students had been selected to take the test, including Huang and the son of a senior city Party official who was generally considered lazy and got poor grades. "I got the highest grade on the test, but the high official used his connections to make his son the winner," Huang said. "We ordinary people have no power over our own lives.

"The present is not good," Huang concluded. "The past was no good. There is no future." It was the kind of despair I had heard so often in the aftermath of the Cultural Revolution. Now it was possible for some Chinese to make money, and they concentrated their energies on this pursuit of affluence. But the sense of alienation persisted.

Even many students at Peking University, before the start of the demonstrations this spring, appeared materialistic, self-indulgent, and cut off from the patriotic concerns that had motivated generations of their predecessors. With deliberate irony, they caricatured themselves as either the Ma faction, meaning Marxist but with a pun on mah-jongg, which they played instead of attending classes, or the Tuo faction, meaning Trotskyist, but with a pun on TOEFL, the Test of English as a Foreign Language, for which they were cramming to go abroad. There was also the splinter Tiao faction, meaning those who liked to attend dances and spent their time dating, something new for Chinese students.

Cai Jinqing, then a junior chemistry major at Peking University, was a self-professed member of the Tuo faction, a grind who wanted to follow her three older brothers to graduate school in America. "A lot of the teachers expressed disappointment with us," said Cai, who became one of the leaders in Tiananmen Square and eventually was able to escape to the United States, where she was given a scholarship by Wellesley College.

"My chemistry lab instructor used to say, 'Oh, how I wish you were like the students in 1978 and 1979,' at the time of the Democracy Wall movement," an earlier outbreak of dissent. "He thought we were lazy and just interested in ourselves," added Cai, a trim, purposeful twenty-year-old who radiated the old Confucian virtues of modesty and sincerity.

Some of her best friends organized a fashion show at Peking University late in the winter as a way to make money. "It became very, very important to make money," Cai recalled. "People were going to fewer classes this spring semester. They wanted money to go to more discos or parties. Since they had no hope for the future, they were living only for the present."

"Some of the students put up ads on bulletin boards around the campus where there used to be revolutionary slogans," she said. "They would go out and buy clothes from a factory, or get some American cigarettes, and then go round the dorm selling them." The joke on campus was that China would have been better off if England had colonized all of China after the Opium War, not just taken Hong Kong. That way all Chinese would be as prosperous as their cousins in the British colony.

The new materialism and hedonism popped up in the most unexpected places. On a tour of the Temple of Heaven, the fifteenth-century compound of sky-blue and red ocher painted temples where the emperor came at the winter solstice to pray for good harvests, I noticed two teenage girls seated beside a Japanese-made boom box. They were freelancing—selling tickets for a privately staged exhibit of nude photographs. It was being held in a pavilion inside the temple compound. Curiosity naturally got the better of me. I paid the exorbitant, for China, price of 75¢ and walked in. There on the old walls were quantities of breasts, thighs, and buttocks in poses that looked as if they had come from *Playboy*. Standing beside me examining the pictures were three soldiers from the People's Liberation Army. With hesitation, they acknowledged they were part of the troops brought in to Peking to put down the demonstrators and happened to be bivouacked in another quarter of the temple compound. It was, in Chairman Mao's terms, an exquisite contradiction. The exhibit was surely an example of bourgeois liberalism, the contagion the Army had come to eradicate. Yet the pornography show was going on under their noses, and they obviously enjoyed it.

With the new commercialism have also come some of the problems more familiar in capitalist societies, or in China before Liberation in 1949. My old assistant Jan Wong, who in 1988 returned to China as the correspondent for the *Toronto Globe and Mail,* came out of the Peking Hotel one day to find her car stolen. It was one of five hundred reported stolen in the capital in 1988. In Xian, the ancient capital of China in the country's midwest, Jan stumbled on an opium den. The Communists had taken great pride in wiping out drug addiction, a scourge of old China, after 1949. But Jan found the opium den down a narrow dirt alley; its customers, mostly young people, included prostitutes, flight attendants, and even police.

Prostitution was another of those social evils that the Communists claimed to have eliminated, though as I had discovered when I first lived in Peking in 1979, it had begun to reappear after the chaos of the Cultural Revolution. Now, ten years later, with all the emphasis on making money and the continued erosion of popular belief in the Communists, prostitution was becoming commonplace. On my first day back in Peking, I was sitting in the lobby lounge of the Jianguo Hotel, a carbon copy of the Holiday Inn in Palo Alto, when I spotted a West German businessman I had known years before. He was walking across the lobby with two fashionably attired young Chinese women: one was tall, slender, and reserved, with long straight black hair to her waist; the other was short and curvaceous, with a bouffant hairdo and tiny, heavily made-up eyes. They were both wearing miniskirts, a far cry from the shapeless Maoist clothing of the past.

My acquaintance took them to the door to get a taxi, then returned to talk about his adventure. He had met the two women in the lobby only an hour before, he said, while they were having coffee at an adjoining table. It was a Sunday, and they had proposed going bowling at the Lido Hotel, another of the foreign-designed and -run hotels that had sprung up since my time in Peking, complete with a fully automated twenty-lane bowling alley. The German assented to their proposal, and said he had to go to his room first to change his clothes.

That is fine, the women said, we will come up with you.

My acquaintance, still intrigued by their boldness, entranced by their looks, and not yet skeptical about their motive, agreed.

But when they got to his room, he said, the taller of the two, Wen Qian, said she was tired and needed to rest before going bowling. She then lay down on one of the two beds in the room. The other woman, Li Hui, suggested in polite Chinese fashion that the German lie down himself on the other bed, "to get some rest." But when he did so, she promptly snuggled in beside him, pulling up her white cotton blouse and putting his hand on her ample breast. For modesty, Wen Qian had turned her back on the couple.

By now, the German was suspicious and somewhat concerned, because under Chinese law prostitution is illegal, and a number of foreign businessmen had been fined or detained for several days after being caught with prostitutes in their hotel rooms. Some foreigners had been fined simply for sleeping with Chinese women, without any exchange of money. But Li Hui said not to worry. Taking him by the hand, she led him to the bathroom.

"There are no hidden microphones here," she said reassuringly.

She then shed her blouse and skirt and climbed awkwardly on the sink, spreading her legs. "Now, if you want to come, it will cost you $100 in American dollars," Li Hui announced, grabbing at the German's pants.

He was tempted; she was very pretty, but it was too dangerous, the businessman decided. There were still soldiers on guard near the hotel enforcing martial law. He felt ridiculous, but sheepishly told the women to leave. Li Hui was not deterred. "I can come back tomorrow night if you want," she suggested. It turned out she was an elementary school teacher who was moonlighting.

"The work is really boring," Li Hui said. "You have to use your brain all the time. Besides, most of the other teachers are much older than I am and are very conservative. They don't like my clothes." But the worst problem, she said, was the pay. She was earning the equivalent of only $30 a month. By contrast, from her new sideline she often made $200 or $300 on a weekend. "To get rich is glorious, old Deng said so himself," Li Hui said, and she chuckled.

In a sense, Li Hui was only another private entrepreneur taking advantage of Deng's reforms, a small, unpleasant side effect of China's economic progress. But the reforms and the new materialism created a major opportunity for a far more corrosive by-product—corruption. "China used to have a small 'back door,' " said Weidong, another of my old Chinese friends whom I had looked up again. He was referring to the well-established practice of "taking the back door," the nationwide system of informal exchange, or the counter-economy, that had grown up to circumvent the rigidities and shortages created by the Communist bureaucracy. But, Weidong explained with disgust, "the small back door has turned into a big front door, corruption."

Practically everything Weidong wanted to do now required paying a bribe or kickback. Recently, an inspector from the Peking city electric company had demanded a payoff; otherwise he would shut off the electricity to Weidong's apartment. When he went to the railroad station to get a seat on the train to Shanghai, Weidong discovered he would have to bribe the ticket seller. Most troublesome, Weidong said, was that thieves had broken into an apartment owned by one of his cousins and stolen his television set. When his relative went to the authorities to report the incident, the police refused to act until they had been given a payoff.

Growing public outrage about the spread of official corruption has led to periodic announcements of government crackdowns. *The China Daily,* the government's new English-language newspaper, reported, for example, that the Shanghai authorities had received 15,000 complaints about bribery and embezzlement, resulting in 450 arrests, during an anti-corruption drive in 1989. In China's biggest scandal during the 1980s, the government discovered that local officials on Hainan Island in the South China Sea had misused their authority to import $1 billion worth of Toyota cars and vans, which they then resold at big markups to officials elsewhere in China.

An American investment banker recalled how the requests for bribes had gradually escalated during the decade of reform and growing prosperity. In the late 1970s, when he signed his first deal with China, the banker said, he had been asked for a Cross gold pen. Several years later, he was asked by a Chinese official for a Japanese-made color television set. Next it was a Mercedes-Benz sedan. Then a senior official of a foreign trade corporation had requested that the banker arrange and pay for his son's graduate study at the Massachusetts Institute of Technology. By 1989, the demands had spiraled out of control, the banker thought.

In one recent case, he had just completed all the paperwork for a $55 million joint venture investment with a Chinese ministry when the official in charge said there was a minor hang-up. The translation of the documents needed to be checked. The banker readily agreed. But then the official said, "We will need to hire a special translation service." The banker was still prepared to consent until the official said the service would cost 3 percent of the total value of the deal, or $1.6 million. That was clearly exorbitant. But the American was truly stunned when the Chinese official calmly explained that the funds should be deposited into his personal bank account in Singapore. "It was just like doing business in Indonesia," the banker concluded, a country with the reputation of being the most corrupt in Asia.

Despite the occasional public announcements of crackdowns on corruption, my friend Weidong was skeptical that the Communists were making a real effort to stamp it out. For the worst form of corruption, the kind that had really burgeoned in the 1980s, was nepotism. Nepotism drew on the old use of *guan-xi,* or the network of personal connections, to benefit an official's family members. And nowhere were *guan-xi* more exploited than by the top leaders of the Party.

During the 1980s, under China's new open door policy, virtually every member of the Politburo had managed to send a son or daughter to the West to school, a highly coveted privilege. Jiang Zemin, the new General Secretary of the Communist Party, picked in June 1989 after the ouster of Zhao Ziyang, had a son who was studying electrical engineering at Drexel University in Philadelphia. Li Peng, the Prime Minister, had a son studying nuclear energy in Toronto. Qiao Shi, the third-ranking member of the Politburo, who was in charge of security, had a daughter doing postdoctoral work at the Baylor College of Medicine in Houston.

Many of the new generation of leaders who emerged in the 1980s were themselves offspring of Communist Party patriarchs, it turned out. Mr. Li, the Prime Minister, was a foster son of the late Zhou Enlai. A son of Liu Shaoqi, the former president of China who was attacked by Mao as the major target of the Cultural Revolution, had become a deputy governor of Hunan province. A son of Ye Jianning, one of the marshals of the Red Army and a key Party elder after the Cultural Revolution, was serving as governor of Guangdong province in the south, China's most affluent region. Li Ruihuan, a former carpenter who was named to the Politburo after the June 4th massacre, was a son-in-law of Wan Li, another member of the Politburo. Still another member of the Politburo, Li Tieying, was the son of Deng Xiaoping's former wife. The list was endless.

Nepotism, I learned on my return to China, had become so rampant that diplomats and scholars analyzing the power struggle in Peking must now pay as much attention to an official's family lineage as to the more conventional factors like his factional allegiances and his ideological predilections.

This was one of the biggest changes in Chinese politics over the past decade. In traditional China, where the family was all-important, taking precedence over the individual and often the state, such use of family connections was common. But after the Communists' triumph in 1949, it came to be believed by Chinese and foreign specialists alike that Mao's insistence on egalitarianism had stamped out nepotism. It was only after Mao's death in 1976 and then China's opening to the outside world under Deng that it became clear many Communist officials had been carefully grooming their children for power. The old saying "Dragons give birth to dragons and phoenixes to phoenixes" still applied. One of the leaders' first steps was to send some of their offspring to universities in the Soviet Union in the early 1950s, when relations between Peking and Moscow were close. Both Jiang, the new Party chief, and Li, the Prime Minister, studied engineering there at the time. In the past few years, the Party leaders have switched and send their children to the West, mostly to the United States.

The shrewdest Party leaders installed their children in a variety of posts, making some of them army officers, placing others in government jobs, and often putting the younger ones in some of the new foreign trade corporations where there are opportunities for travel abroad and earning large profits in dollars. Wang Zhen, for instance, China's vice-president and a veteran army commander, has one son who is a political commissar in the Chengdu military region in southwest China, another son who works for a government company that imports computers, and a third son who runs a firm called Ocean Helicopters. The company has an exclusive contract to provide transport to the crews working on the foreign-owned offshore oil rigs drilling in the South China Sea.

Perhaps the most dramatic example of how government in China has become a family affair is that of Deng Xiaoping's clan. Deng's eldest son, Deng Bufang, was crippled during the Cultural Revolution after being

461

pushed from his dorm room at Peking University by Red Guards. In public, he lives an exemplary life as head of the China Fund for the Handicapped. But he has also been involved with the Kang Hua corporation, a large new government trading company that has been charged in the Chinese press with making hundreds of millions of dollars in illicit profits. The company specialized in a Chinese form of arbitrage—buying such rationed raw materials as coal at the low official fixed price and then reselling them on the free market for four or five times as much. Kang Hua owed its success to well-placed people like Deng Bufang who could get access to raw materials at the cheap state price.

Mr. Deng's second son, Deng Zhifang, is a physicist who got a Ph.D. from the University of Rochester. But he now works for the China International Trust and Investment Corporation, or Citic, a combination investment bank and trading company that is the biggest of the new government firms. This has meant frequent trips to Hong Kong and other overseas spots, a luxury beyond the reach of ordinary Chinese.

Mr. Deng's oldest daughter, Deng Lin, is a painter. In 1988 she held an exhibition in Shenzhen, the new city of one million people that has sprouted just across the border from Hong Kong. The New China News Agency, which serves as Peking's unofficial embassy in the British colony, sent invitations to many of Hong Kong's wealthiest businessmen "requesting" that they buy some of her paintings to ensure the show's success. "It was all very polite, there was no threat," said a lawyer who got one of the invitations. "But the message was clear. Everyone knows who will be running Hong Kong after 1997," he added, referring to the date when the colony is scheduled to revert to China's control. The lawyer himself bought one of Miss Deng's works for $50,000.

The Dengs' fourth child, Deng Nan, a daughter, is also a physicist. After the June killings, she began appearing at her father's side, apparently to help with his poor hearing. Her husband, named He Ping, is a former army officer and military attaché at the Chinese embassy in Washington. He is now president of a subsidiary of Citic with the innocuous name of Poly Technologies. But Poly Technologies happens to be China's main arms dealer and helped make China the world's fourth largest supplier of weapons to developing nations, with sales of $4.8 billion in 1987, according to a congressional report.

When the Reagan administration complained about China's sale of anti-ship missiles to Iran, which threatened American ships, and its shipment of CSS-2 intermediate-range ballistic missiles to Saudi Arabia, which threatened Israel, officials in Peking disclaimed responsibility. An American diplomat who sat in on the talks said the Chinese insisted the arms dealers were simply freelancing.

"What can you do, it's the kids," a senior Chinese official told the irate Americans, who were led by Secretary of State George Shultz. Until President Bush imposed a ban on American military sales to China after the killings in Peking, he was also negotiating with American companies to buy helicopters and artillery shells, said businessmen involved in the proposed sales.

He Ping and Deng Nan have a daughter who was a student at the Jing Shan high school in Peking, a special school largely reserved for the offspring of high officials. By chance, there were several American exchange students from Newton North High School in Boston at Jing Shan during the pro-democracy demonstrations in the spring of 1989. One of the Americans remembered the young Miss Deng as a very bright student who enjoyed virtual diplomatic immunity in the school. "In English class she was allowed to sleep through class or do her math homework, the teacher didn't dare say anything," the American said. When the protests began in Tiananmen Square, only a few blocks away, the Chinese students at the school split into two factions, with the children of senior officials denouncing the demonstrators. Miss Deng herself had a simple remedy, the American recalled. "She said the police ought to chop off their heads."

This desire by China's first families to hold on to power may be one reason why the Communists were willing to kill unarmed demonstrators in Peking, said Su Shaozhi, the former head of the Institute of Marxism-Leninism-Mao Zedong Thought in the Chinese Academy of Social Sciences. In the view of Su, a respected sixty-six-year-old former editor of the *People's Daily,* the massacre resulted from "a confrontation between the noble families and commoners." To Su, the "princes' faction," the younger generation, "are more cruel, more greedy and more cynical than their parents, because they grew up believing they were special, or 'born Red.' " Moreover, Su told me, the princes had fewer scruples than their parents because they didn't believe in Marxism. It was a reversion to a traditional pattern of "Oriental despotism," said Su.

To underscore the importance of nepotism as an issue, Su pointed out that initially, when the student protestors were only calling for democracy, they did not draw large crowds. But when the students began criticizing the Party for corruption and nepotism, they struck an immediate responsive cord from workers and office employees throughout Peking. It soon became one of the major rallying cries of the movement. At the same time, the nepotism charge also represented a serious threat to the Communist leaders, Su said. In a secret speech in late May, as the protests escalated out of the government's control, Yang Shangkun, China's president and executive secretary of the powerful Party Military Commission, told the Politburo: "There is no way for us to retreat. To retreat means our downfall." Su believed Yang meant

the words literally. He and his family's power was threatened. Not coinciden-
tally, Yang had helped make his brother chief political commissar of the
People's Liberation Army, while the commander of the 27th Army, which
did much of the shooting in Peking, was widely rumored to be Yang's
nephew. "The massacre was purely personal politics for the noble families,"
Su said. "They were fighting for their survival."

Su himself was a fascinating example of another important change in China
in the past decade—the emergence for the first time since 1949 of high-level
dissidents and defectors. In sharp contrast to the Soviet Union, China had
never produced critics such as Andrei Sakharov, Natan Sharansky, or Aleksandr Solzhenitsyn. There was not even a word in Chinese for dissident, I
noticed, and there had not been a single senior intellectual who defected to
the West despite the horrors of the Anti-Rightist campaign in 1957, the
Great Leap Forward, or the Cultural Revolution.

In large measure this grew out of the Confucian tradition in which government officials were drawn from the country's scholar class through a system
of examinations. This bound intellectuals to the state and meant that writers
were more comfortable working within the system, not outside it. For a
Chinese intellectual, there was no higher calling than to become a court
official. Deng Xiaoping and his hand-picked successors, first Hu Yaobang
and then Zhao Ziyang, as Party General Secretaries, had sought to perpetuate this practice. They set up brain trusts, research institutes, to enlist the best
and brightest Chinese in the reform cause.

But in the 1980s, as China opened to the outside world and discontent with
the Communist Party spread, some intellectuals began challenging the
Party's authority. Su was one of these. An ethnic Manchu, a descendant of
the nomadic tribes that founded the Qing dynasty, Su had a shock of black
hair, narrow slits for eyes, and a soft, full face. In the late 1970s, as Deng
was pondering how to launch China on its reform course, Su had been
dispatched to Eastern Europe as part of a study mission to see what China
might learn from the then-fledgling experiments in Yugoslavia and Hungary.
He was also entrusted with the prestigious job as head of the Institute of
Marxism-Leninism, one of the research agencies. Based on what he had
observed in Hungary, Su formulated the heretical notion that economic
reform cannot succeed without political reform. "The crux of the matter lies
in carrying out inner party democracy," he wrote. The Communist Party, in
his view, had become an obstacle to progress because it preserved China's
feudal reverence for authority. The Communist Party had simply substituted
itself for the old imperial system.

Other intellectuals were developing their own unorthodox and subversive
ideas. In February and March of 1989, two groups of high-ranking scholars,

writers and scientists drew up petitions calling for the release of Wei Jing-sheng, the imprisoned hero of the Democracy Wall period ten years before. Although the petitions failed to free Wei or other political prisoners, they marked the first time China's intellectuals as a group had publicly opposed the leadership on such a sensitive issue. The petitions reportedly infuriated Deng, who had personally ordered Wei arrested. More significantly, they also helped encourage students at Peking's universities and thereby played a critical role in helping start the democracy movement.

Although it was the students who launched the demonstrations, many intellectuals were sympathetic. At the Institute of Marxism-Leninism, for example, out of the entire staff of seventy-five, only one person agreed with a secret speech by Deng on April 25 calling for a crackdown, using blood-shed if necessary, Su told me. A text of Deng's talk had been circulated around the institute. Moreover, Su said, as the demonstrations gathered in size and momentum in mid-May, with up to a million people filling Tianan-men Square, more and more intellectuals and even officials began to join the marchers. According to one confidential Party document Su read, 80 percent of all the organizations that make up the central government and Party machinery had personnel who participated in the protests, including the Party Propaganda Department, the Party Organization Department, the *People's Daily,* the Foreign Ministry, and the Ministry of Public Security.

After the crackdown finally did occur, Su rapidly calculated he was in danger and drove out to Peking's airport. Fortunately, he had a standing invitation to be a visiting scholar at Marquette University in Wisconsin, and so had a Chinese passport and an American visa. He grabbed a seat on the first available plane, which happened to be flying to Helsinki. His defection would have been unthinkable in the past, a betrayal of all that being a good Chinese meant. But to Su, the Party died in Tiananmen Square. "As an organization, the Party has totally discredited itself among Chinese," said the man who was head of the Institute of Marxism-Leninism.

Liu Binyan, China's most widely read and respected writer, underwent a similar transformation in the 1980s. A tall sixty-three-year-old with a digni-fied manner, a silver mane of hair, and a handsome, craggy face, Liu had been a loyal Party member since his youth in the early 1940s. His father had lost his job with the railroad during the Japanese invasion of Manchuria, and Liu developed a lifelong concern with social justice. Assigned to be a reporter by the new Communist government in the early 1950s, Liu pursued his interest by pioneering a new style of journalism which came to be called literary reportage, or *baogao wenxue,* a hybrid of investigative fact-based journalism and fiction, not unlike the New Journalism of the late 1960s in the United States. In 1956, when Mao initiated the Hundred Flowers Move-ment, seeming to invite free intellectual debate, Liu took the Party at its word and wrote a story contrasting two symbolic figures: a young, idealistic, and courageous engineer working on a bridge construction site, and an older Communist bureaucrat who out of fear of making a mistake and being criticized does nothing when a flood hits.

Unfortunately for Liu, Mao soon reversed course, moving to silence his critics in the Anti-Rightist campaign in 1957, and the Chairman personally singled out Liu as an example. He would spend most of the next twenty-two years living in exile in the remote countryside, in penury and in disgrace. But still a faithful Communist, Liu did not complain. "My first reaction was that naturally my thought must be incorrect," Liu told me. "How could the Party and Chairman Mao be wrong? I was so embarrassed that when I was walking down the street and saw a friend, I would try to avoid them." It did not help that Liu's friends and colleagues joined in the attacks on him.

Finally, after his rehabilitation in 1979, Liu published his most famous work, "People or Monsters." It reported the true story of a corrupt cashier who used her post as a springboard to become a powerful and abusive official. "The Communist Party regulated everything, but it would not regulate the Communist Party," Liu concluded in a sentiment that made him an instant national hero. Bushels of mail arrived at his new office in the *People's Daily* from Chinese who described similar experiences in their towns and villages. Liu still insisted he was a good Party member. "I am not a dissident," he told a Hong Kong journalist. He believed in reform from within. But as the Communists seemed to loosen their hold over art and literature in the 1980s, Liu became ever bolder and even began to travel around the country denouncing Party malfeasance and advocating freedom of the press. For his temerity, in January 1987, after the series of student protests at the time, he was disgraced again and expelled from the Party.

But Liu was more stunned by the difference in reaction by ordinary Chinese this time, compared to his pariah status in earlier years when he was under attack. On the very day he was stripped of his Party membership, he happened to be returning from a trip and landed at the Peking airport. "A young man with an older woman came over to me as I was waiting for my luggage," Liu recalled. "He asked if I was Liu Binyan. When I said yes, he said he was a diplomat stationed in a Chinese embassy in Europe. Then he said, 'This is my mother. We want you to know we admire you. We hope you win the Nobel prize.' "

That night, twenty-seven people showed up at his apartment to make sure he knew he had public sympathy. Later, the letters began to arrive. Five young workers from the industrial city of Wuhan wrote to ask if he was in jail. They assumed that if he was, he would have lost his salary, and so they offered to send him 50 renminbi a month, a month's wages for one of them. Another worker from Changsha in Sichuan sent his life's savings, 200 renminbi. He also proposed that Liu come and stay in his house. "It is a small house and my roof leaks, but it is a very quiet place," the man said. There were even offers of shelter from the mayor of a city, and the tender of a seaside villa at the resort of Beidaihe by an army general.

Eventually, under the weight of Chinese opinion and world pressure, the government let Liu travel to the United States to accept a Nieman fellowship at Harvard. Unintentionally, he had become another dissident and another defector.

Su and Liu, now living in exile in America, offered their insights into why the pro-democracy demonstrations in 1989 had gathered such sudden popularity. The roots, Liu said, sitting in an apartment in Cambridge, near the Harvard campus, lay back in the Cultural Revolution. The cruelties and hardships inflicted on an estimated 100 million Chinese during that period began the process of public discontent with the Party. Moreover, when Mao, the Great Helmsman, told Red Guards that "to rebel is justified," one of the major slogans of the Cultural Revolution, he gave legitimacy to a new questioning of Party authority. "Only Mao could undermine the Party," Liu said.

On the more immediate causes, Su believed that once the students began their public protests, they unconsciously touched a nerve of disenchantment throughout China. "Millions of Chinese suddenly found other people shared their feelings," Su said.

Professors were frustrated by the slow pace of political reform, compared to the economic changes, which meant that there continued to be restrictions on what they could publish. Workers, on fixed wages, were upset by inflation, running at 30 percent a year. Inflation was a real shock for Chinese, because for years the Communists had prided themselves on maintaining absolutely stable prices. They remembered that galloping inflation had helped defeat the Nationalists in the late 1940s. When I lived in Peking, the government still used to distribute pamphlets in tourists' hotel rooms with the title, "Why China Has No Inflation." Students, in turn, were annoyed by their atrocious living conditions. I was surprised to learn that at Peking University, the country's most prestigious institute of higher learning, the students still had to carry their own metal bowls to the cafeteria to fetch their meals, then take the food back to their tiny, cramped dormitory rooms to eat because there were no tables or chairs in the dining room. This had been the practice ten years earlier, before the decade of economic growth, and its continuation now grew out of the Communists' miserly spending on education. In fact, the government still invested barely more than 1 percent of the country's gross national product in education, placing China virtually last in the world in its support for schooling, trailed only by Haiti. Some intellectuals believed this was a deliberate policy, to keep people ignorant.

Young people were discouraged at being assigned to dead-end jobs, with little chance for advancement. Everyone was furious about corruption and nepotism. Many people I talked to were beginning to ask tough questions. "The Chinese people are not lazy or stupid. Why are we so backward compared to Japan, South Korea, and Taiwan?" a taxi driver in Canton remarked.

The demonstrations were given further impetus by an unusual confluence of events. The death on April 15 of Hu Yaobang, posthumously sainted as the chief apostle of liberalization, provided an initial rallying point. Then came May 4, the seventieth anniversary of the great student movement of early twentieth-century China, a date freighted with significance for history-conscious Chinese students who wanted to uphold the tradition of their predecessors. On May 15, with the protests building, Mikhail Gorbachev, the champion of *glasnost*, arrived for the first Sino-Soviet summit in thirty years. Equally important, he brought with him the world press and television, so that for the first time internal conflict in China was seen live around the globe. The Communist leadership itself contributed to the demonstrators' success by remaining deadlocked for weeks over how to react.

Encamped in the vast hundred-acre open space of Tiananmen Square, the symbolic heartland of the country and the capital, the students and their newfound allies among workers, housewives, and government employees became giddy with success. "We were intoxicated," said Cai Jinqing, the junior from Peking University. "We finally had something to belong to, something good. It was as if we were part of history." Cai, a heretofore studious chemistry major, found herself helping broadcast announcements for the hunger strikers from a commandeered bus being used as the students' headquarters. When her voice gave out, she was put in charge of stamping passes for anyone wishing to gain admission to the area of the square roped off for the hunger strikers. In keeping with ancient Chinese custom, she used a chop, or seal, signifying authority. She also interpreted into English at several press conferences held by the de facto student leaders.

On May 19, with bus service canceled, Cai's mother walked for four hours from the family's apartment in the eastern part of the capital to reach Tiananmen Square. She had heard a rumor, correctly it turned out, that martial law would be declared the next day, and she wanted to warn her daughter. While not a member of the Communist Party, the mother had long been a loyal believer in the government. She felt indebted to the Party for giving her a job, though she had never gone to school, and she was grateful that her four children had all attended Peking University.

"But my mother was so moved by what she saw in the square that she stayed for hours and decided to support the students," Cai said. Her mother too had caught the feeling that after so many years of depression and failure, China was doing something right. It had launched the biggest nonviolent

468

demonstrations for democracy in history. People were proud. Cai and others later told how they had never seen Chinese be so polite. They smiled at each other. When two bicyclists collided, they apologized. Even pickpockets declared a holiday.

The students, who initially had rather limited demands—that the government declare they were patriotic and provide some greater freedom of speech—soon became more militant. They began attacking Prime Minister Li Peng and Deng Xiaoping by name, a dangerous insult in a country where the conventions of saving face still determine much behavior. One student poster read:

> *The lower levels obey the upper levels.*
> *The upper levels obey the Party Central Committee.*
> *The Party Central Committee obeys Deng Xiaoping.*
> *Deng Xiaoping follows his whim.*

The students had forgotten about the control system. "We were naive," Cai said later, having managed to get to Boston.

A week after the massacre, Chinese television broadcast segments of a street interview done by ABC News in Peking following the army's assault. A man was shown being interviewed, his voice rising with anger and his arms imitating the motion of a machine gun as he described a scene of carnage inflicted by the soldiers. "Tanks and armored personnel carriers rolled over students, squashing them into jam, and the soldiers shot at them and hit them with clubs," the man was shown telling an American reporter. "When students fainted, the troops killed them. After they died, the troops fired one more bullet into them. They also used bayonets. They were too cruel." During the Chinese rebroadcast of the interview, a caption on the bottom of the screen identified the man as "someone spreading rumors about the cleanup of Tiananmen Square." When the man finished speaking, the Chinese news announcer appealed to the public to turn him in.

Two nights later the national news reported that the man, now identified as Xiao Bin, a forty-two-year-old unemployed factory worker, had been turned in one hour after the initial broadcast. In police custody, Xiao retracted his earlier claims. "I never saw anything," Xiao said on Chinese television, looking haggard and terrified. "I apologize for bringing great harm to the Party and the country." He confessed he was a counterrevolutionary.

Driving around Peking a few weeks later, I asked a taxi driver what made someone turn in Xiao. The driver, whose surname was Lin, scoffed at my ignorance. In China no one can escape because of the *danwei,* the work unit that every Chinese belongs to, whether it is his factory, office, or school. I had encountered the power of the unit system before and had written about it, but with all the economic changes, hadn't the unit lost some of its authority? I asked. Not really, Lin insisted. It still formed the bedrock of the Communists' control system, so deeply embedded in society that the unit was like a form of internal radar, picking people up wherever they went.

In Lin's case, his unit, the taxi company, not only provided his job and set his bonus, but also assigned him his housing, in an apartment building filled with other employees of the taxi company. "It guarantees you nosy neighbors," said Lin, a slight twenty-nine-year-old with a wispy mustache. The unit also was responsible for providing Lin his ration coupons for rice, pork, and cooking oil. When Lin got married, he had been required to get permission from the Party secretary of his unit. Now Lin and his wife wanted to have a child, and under the Communists' one-child-per-family policy, designed to limit China's population, they had applied to the unit. Last year, because the unit had not yet overused its annual quota for births, they had received clearance. Unfortunately, the couple had not conceived within the year and they lost their place on the list. Now they had to wait a full year before reapplying.

"It is really *lihai,*" Lin said, using a word that translates as tough. "If you have a child without permission, not only can they fire you, but your child will be a black child. He won't get a household registration permit, so he won't be able to get coupons for rice and pork and he will have a very hard time getting into school."

Someone in the taxi company had donated 1,000 renminbi, or $270, to the students from the organization's funds. Now there was a full-scale investigation to discover who had done it and who was sympathetic to the protestors, Lin related. It meant that every day he had to attend political study classes with other people from his unit and was being asked to report on his friends and neighbors.

As we were driving, an old Soviet-style green jeep passed us, weaving dangerously across several lanes of traffic. The vehicle had a white license plate beginning with two red letters. That meant it belonged to the Ministry of Public Security, Lin pointed out. "They can't drive very well, but they can control you," he said with a mixture of contempt, fear, and anger.

At its heart, China is still a vast network of *danwei*s, or units, each like a feudal domain controlled by its Communist Party secretary. Although organizations such as the taxi company or a factory appeared to be business enterprises, they are organized more for social control over the populace and for the personal power of their leaders than for making a profit. Any time a local official can expand his enterprise, adding more workers and more investment, it represents a gain in power for him. An American architect who had worked on the design of the Jinling Hotel in Nanjing recalled how it accidentally became the tallest building in China when it opened in 1983, towering thirty-seven stories over the old southern capital of China. The architect's original plan was for two eighteen-story towers, already daring and monumental by Chinese standards. But the provincial governor, after examining models of the proposed hotel for several days, called the architect into his office. The governor then picked up one of the model towers and placed it on top of the other. "This is how we would like it," he dictated. Having China's first skyscraper enhanced his prestige.

With society organized around the unit, profit sometimes seemed to be an afterthought. Local officials had so much power that they were virtually able to compel the branches of the Bank of China to loan them money for any new favorite project. The banks, by contrast, had little power to collect on the loans, and so in effect they began printing money. In 1988 China's money supply grew 50 percent faster than its gross national product, a sure formula for inflation. There was so much overstaffing that many factories had only 20 percent of their work force actually working. Despite the decade of reforms and economic growth, I was surprised to find that one fifth of all China's state-owned factories were actually operating at a loss, according to the New China News Agency. This was particularly serious in a country where almost all tax revenue came from the profits of the large state-owned enterprises. To bail out the losers, the government had to provide subsidies that amounted to a fifth of the total national budget in 1988, the State Statistical Bureau reported. To try to make the economy more efficient and more market-oriented, the reformers in Peking had finally won passage of a bankruptcy law in 1987 through the National People's Congress. It would have required factories to operate at a profit or go bankrupt, and was hailed as a centerpiece of the reforms. But as far as I could learn, the law had never been implemented and no factory had actually been closed. For in addition to threatening the lifelong job security of factory workers, the new law also endangered the duchies of the Party's faithful organization men. This was the real sin of the reformers like Zhao Ziyang, who was putatively purged for his leniency in the face of the pro-democracy demonstrations.

While many foreigners looked at the economic growth of the 1980s and saw inexorable movement toward capitalism and even democracy, officials in the Public Security Ministry saw other opportunities. They installed hidden cameras in the high-ceilinged dining room of the Peking Hotel, where they would eventually record a luncheon meeting of Wuer Kaixi, one of the students leaders, with some foreign journalists. They put other miniature cameras on traffic lights, ostensibly to observe traffic, but also handy for photographing all activities in Tiananmen Square. At the Xiang Shan Hotel, designed by I. M. Pei and set in a lovely Peking suburban park, Chinese officials kept up a running battle with one of the American contractors over how many wires to install in the rooms. "They kept asking to put in four more wires than we needed," the American recounted. "When I asked why, they just said, 'They will be needed in the future.' Of course I knew what they wanted them for. Microphones."

China's security services also found new chances in the burgeoning academic exchanges between China and American universities. At a center set up at Nanjing University by Johns Hopkins University, China's military intelligence agency, the Central Investigation Department, infiltrated four young officers as students. In theory, they were at the center to learn English; in practice, their duty was to spy on the American teachers and students and to improve their English in preparation for being dispatched to serve as spies under diplomatic cover in China's embassy or consulates in the United States. All this might have remained secret, but one of the "students," Xu Meihong, a pert, twenty-six-year-old first lieutenant with sparkling eyes and broad cheekbones, fell in love with her American professor, Larry Engelmann. Engelmann was incredulous, but Xu showed him a picture of herself in her PLA uniform. Then she revealed that all the mail to and from the American teachers was opened and all their phone calls were tapped. She knew, she said, "Because I am the person in charge of doing it." She and the three other "students" had been assigned to the Hopkins Center by their own training agency, innocuously named the Nanjing Institute for International Relations, which came under the Central Investigation Department.

Unfortunately, Xu's affair with Engelmann was uncovered. She was arrested and charged with "male-female difficulties." To make her situation worse, the Chinese had found what they thought was incriminating evidence in Engelmann's room. He was writing a book on the fall of Saigon in 1975 and had brought with him three boxes of declassified CIA documents about the end of the Vietnam war. They were clearly marked declassified, but their very existence suggested Engelmann was more than just a visiting history professor from San Jose State University, his regular job. Under Chinese prodding, the Hopkins authorities asked Engelmann to hurriedly leave China. He departed, but felt his American academic colleagues had caved in to Chinese pressure without a proper hearing.

The clearest evidence, however, of the continued power of the Communists' control apparatus was the government's Orwellian attempt to rewrite the events in Tiananmen Square. Within a week of the massacre, China's newspapers and television outlets proclaimed that what had been watched around the world, live, had never taken place. Instead of a bloody crackdown, it became a heroic, largely peaceful operation aimed at "quelling the turmoil brought about by a very small number of hooligans." The government's chief spokesman, Yuan Mu, held a press conference to report that at most three hundred people were killed, almost all soldiers. An army commander at the press conference said that "not a single student was killed."

It would be easy to write off such claims as mere lies. But they were too brazen. It seemed to me that something else was at work here, something involving the old Chinese penchant for make-believe and the importance Chinese have attached to the li, or the Confucian rites. Confucius held that it was very important to observe the proper ritual, particularly the outer form of something, and that if the form was correct, things would follow their proper course. He also believed that words carried an almost magical power of their own. I recalled the story from the third century B.C., when a scheming prime minister wished to determine who among his courtiers were really faithful to him. So when a deer was presented in court, he pretended it was a horse. Those who insisted it was a deer were executed. There was a more modern example of this playacting, about the way Chinese can conjure reality out of illusion with the right words. Chiang Kai-shek, after all, claimed that Taipei was the capital of "Free China" after he fled the mainland in 1949, and for thirty years we accepted the fiction.

But the problem for the Communists now is that what has worked for them in the past has lost its potency. As the psychiatrist Robert Lifton observed in his 1961 book on thought reform, it is subject to a law of diminishing conversions.* Or as Liu Binyan, the writer put it to me, "The distance between what the Party wants to do and its ability to do it is getting greater and greater. The trouble is, Deng still lives in the illusions of the 1950s. He still believes the Party enjoys high prestige and authority. This leads him to make mistakes." In the past Deng would never have had to call in the army, because it would have been sufficient to mobilize the Party apparatus to get the students off the streets, Liu said. But the Party was becoming a discredited shell, "a great rotting tree," in Liu's words, and all that was left to Deng were the security organs, the secret police, and the army.

At the epicenter of the tragedy of Tiananmen was Deng Xiaoping, now at eighty-five an increasingly fragile patriarch. Deng was the man who had set the reforms in motion, who more than anyone else was responsible for China's economic growth in the 1980s. He should have been a hero, perhaps a more significant figure than Mao himself in Chinese history. Deng came out of that long line of great Chinese statesmen who, since the Opium War in the nineteenth century exposed the country's weakness, had sought to make China "rich and strong" again, or *fu-qiang.*

But Deng was never the liberal that many Americans thought he was. It was true he was a pragmatist—he had taken Mao's dictum "Put politics in command" and reversed it with his own simple edict, "Seek truth from

*Robert Jay Lifton, *Thought Reform and the Psychology of Totalism* (New York: Norton, 1961), p. 412.

facts." Instead of trying, like Mao, to remake human nature, Deng was shrewd enough to harness human nature as he found it. He wanted to use individual interest and greed to spur the economy. Deng's policies grew out of China's reality after the disaster of the Cultural Revolution in the late 1970s, as he regained his freedom and then was restored to power. Looking around the world, Deng saw that orthodox Communism had failed, long before Gorbachev recognized this in the Soviet Union. Deng was strongly influenced by what he found in China's neighbors, Japan, South Korea, Hong Kong, and Taiwan, Chinese officials told me. He had to wonder who had won World War II and who had won the Chinese civil war, these officials said.

Deng discerned what might be termed an Asian model of modernization. It combined economic entrepreneurship with tight political control, the formula that had worked so successfully from Seoul to Singapore. To implement the formula in China, Deng came up with two basic policies: opening China to the outside world and market-oriented economic reforms. He recognized that the Party itself needed some overhauling—aging, uneducated cadres would have to be retired and a better legal system be established. But Deng's policies made no provision for real political change, and he did not see that economic growth might inevitably produce a yearning for greater democracy.

Deng was blunt about the need for the Party to keep power to itself. In 1979 he enunciated what came to be called the Four Cardinal Principles: everyone must uphold socialism, the people's democratic dictatorship, the leadership of the Communist Party, and Marxism-Leninism. In 1986, faced with a round of student protests, Deng told Party leaders, "We can't do without the means of the dictatorship of the proletariat. Not only must we talk about it, we must use the means of dictatorship." Or as he told a Yugoslav visitor, "The greatest advantage of the socialist system is that when the central leadership makes a decision, it is promptly implemented without interference from any other quarter. We don't have to go through a lot of repetitive discussion and consultation, with one branch of the government holding up another." Deng, after all, was the Secretary General of the Party during the Anti-Rightist campaign in 1957 when hundreds of thousands of intellectuals were imprisoned or shipped off to exile in remote villages. Deng's tragedy was that he had raised expectations—that he had created such successful economic change that it gave rise to demand for political changes—but that at the crucial moment he was not prepared to share political power.

As I traveled around China in the summer of 1989 I found there were many Chinese who agreed with Deng, who shared his hybrid amalgam of progressive economics and tough politics. They were older Chinese, some of the peasantry, and many members of the army who instinctively craved stability. Because these Chinese tended to be more conservative, because they were not as interested in the Western world and did not speak English or want to go abroad to study, they did not have as much contact with foreigners in China as the liberals did. What had happened, it seemed to me, was that many diplomats and China specialists had gotten caught in a circular flow of information. They tended to talk with the Chinese who wanted to talk with them, and those were the Western-looking liberals. We simply didn't know the conservatives. This left us unprepared for the crackdown.

Walking in a park beside the muddy brown waters of the Pearl River in Canton, I encountered one of these men, what might be called a Dengist. He was a retired general in the People's Liberation Army, a diminutive sixty-eight-year-old just over five feet tall, with an unlined face, a shock of thick white hair cut short in military fashion, and an animated way of speaking.

Holding up his thumb in an old Chinese gesture of approbation, he said, "Deng Xiaoping is the best.

"Without Deng, China would still be poor. If the student movement had continued, China would have fallen into chaos."

Like Deng, the general saw himself as pragmatic, prepared to be flexible to achieve economic modernization, but ready to be ruthless to preserve order. He had been born into a poor peasant family in a village lost in the vast forest of far northeast Heilongjiang province and had never been to school before joining the Red Army guerrillas as a twenty-year-old. But even though his only education had been in the thoughts of Chairman Mao, the general did not regard himself as an arch conservative.

"There is no conflict between Marxism and capitalism," he said with surprising equanimity. "They are just two religions, like Buddhism and Christianity. What's the difference?

"I speak frankly because I never went to school," he said, insisting he was still a simple peasant at heart.

The key to the modern world, the general said, sounding like his hero, Deng, is science. "Look at World War II. I was just a foot soldier with a single-shot rifle. All I could do was go pow, pow, pow," he said, punctuating his remarks by pointing his folding fan like a gun at an imaginary enemy. "But then the United States developed the atomic bomb and dropped two on Japan. That ended the war fast."

So now China must follow the path of more contact with the outside world and economic innovation, the general insisted. "To go back would be to return to the poverty we experienced in the Cultural Revolution," he said as ferryboats chugged across the river in the background. In those days, he said, Jiang Qing, Mao's wife, was so enraptured with radicalism that "she would say a tree was good if it had no leaves. She wanted everyone to be poor."

The general had nothing but praise for Deng's economic initiatives. He pointed to the nearby White Swan Hotel, a modern 34-story hostelry complete with swimming pool, tennis courts, and two nightclubs built by a Hong Kong Chinese businessman. Instead of seeing it as a Trojan horse for Western influence, as some conservatives do, the general fondly recalled that two years before, Deng and his wife stayed in the hotel.

Still, the general was not sympathetic to the students. "Their goals may have been good, but their tactics were bad. No country can afford chaos," he said, echoing an ancient Chinese fear about the division of the nation. "Just look around," he added. "The countries that are doing well have a stable society, like the United States, West Germany, and Japan. In the end, the students got what they deserved."

He was skeptical of the government's claim that few students had been killed, since like many people in Canton he had watched American television pictures of the events rebroadcast from Hong Kong. But he believed the army had been provoked. "If you are a soldier, and you are just standing there and people throw rocks at you, what can you do?" he asked.

At this moment of crisis, the general said, it was a good thing that the Party elders, the hard-line oligarchs who had officially retired from their leadership posts, had come out to assert power and back Deng. "They made the revolution," the general said. "Who cares about their titles?" He did not mind that the oligarchs' reemergence undermined one of Deng's most prized reforms—establishing a more orderly political process.

It was this Gang of Elders, as some Chinese called them, who seemed to have been the real winners in the crackdown. They included such venerables as Chen Yun, the eighty-five-year-old long-time economic czar, Li Xiannian, another eighty-five-year-old who had been president of China, and Peng Zhen, eighty-eight, a former head of the National People's Congress. Although each of them had initially supported Deng's reforms, they had come to feel that the changes went too far too fast. They preferred the safe old methods of orthodox Soviet-style central planning. They had also been pushed into retirement by Deng, as part of his effort to modernize the Party by promoting younger, better-educated leaders. But they had quietly fought back behind the scenes—first helping oust Deng's protégé, Hu Yaobang, as General Secretary of the Party in 1987, then zeroing in on Zhao Ziyang, Hu's replacement. By the fall of 1988, well before the democracy movement, Zhao was in trouble, taking the blame for China's inflation, and the conservatives were staging a major comeback. In fact, by some accounts, Zhao ended up siding with the students only as a desperate, last-minute attempt to outmaneuver the hard-liners by assuming a populist mantle. But Zhao's conciliatory stance toward the protestors infuriated Deng, his patron, and doomed him to being purged also.

For Deng, however, the crackdown was not a victory. He had been forced to jettison both of his handpicked successors, Hu and Zhao, and after the massacre he had to compromise on a new candidate to be General Secretary, Jiang Zemin. Jiang was a sixty-three-year-old former mayor of Shanghai with a soft, full face and a reputation as a leading member of the "wind faction," meaning that like a weathervane he swung with the prevailing currents. In his first news conference broadcast nationwide on television, Jiang insisted that the massacre in Tiananmen was not a "tragedy." Chinese who examined Jiang's career noted that he had close connections to two of the oligarchs, Chen Yun and Li Xiannian, but none to Deng.

Like the new Prime Minister, Li Peng, Jiang had been trained as an engineer in the Soviet Union in the 1950s and had risen through the ranks of the industrial ministries. Neither of them had any experience in directing political organizations, in Party propaganda work, or in the army. In this they were typical of the new generation of Chinese leaders in the late 1980s—they were bureaucratic technocrats. In fact, the change in the makeup of the top Party posts had been so swift that where in 1980 there was only one member of the Politburo who had been to college, by 1989, 40 percent of the members of the Central Committee were engineers. Among central government ministers, 70 percent were either engineers or former factory managers, with half of the provincial governors having similar backgrounds.

The influx of so many highly educated officials is certainly important for China as it tries to modernize. But, said Hong Yung Lee, a research associate at the East-West Center of the University of Hawaii who compiled these figures, it does not mean the new leaders will be more democratic than their predecessors. As a group, he suggested, "They hate uncertainty, they like central planning, and they are still Leninists who crave control." If Mao was like Stalin, and Deng China's Khrushchev, then Jiang Zemin and Li Peng may be Peking's Brezhnev, with China in for a period of retrenchment or stagnation. This was a thought expressed by some marchers in Tiananmen Square who carried a sign reading, "Our Gorbachev is still in school. All we have now is a bunch of Brezhnevs."

But any predictions about China's future are fraught with peril. Despite China's decade of openness, we may know less today about the real inner workings of the Party leadership than at any time since Mao's death in 1976. Then his handpicked successor, Hua Guofeng, lasted only two years. Clearly Deng's death will set off a major political struggle between the conservatives and the surviving liberals, who are supported by most Chinese intellectuals, journalists, students, and private entrepreneurs. This represents a minority of Chinese, albeit a vocal and insistent group. A key unknown is the loyalty of the army, which had been undergoing its own modernization program. More and more officers are younger and better educated also, with interest in modernizing their weapons and keeping China's links to the West. But many Chinese fear that the army has become the private preserve of the Yang family, headed by Yang Shangkun, the country's eighty-two-year-old president, who is also first vice chairman of the Party's powerful Military Commission. Yang's younger brother, Yang Baibing, sixty-nine, is the army's chief political commissar as well as head of the Military Commission's secretariat, giving him day-to-day authority over the armed forces. With all this continued intrigue and so little knowledge, it sometimes seemed that there is still a Forbidden City at the heart of China, as my friend Angela Terzani wrote in her book *Chinese Days.*

Whoever emerges supreme after Deng will inherit a series of daunting problems. China's population passed 1.1 billion in 1989 and is growing by 15.7 million people a year, well beyond Peking's goal. This means that Peking must feed 22 percent of the world's population on 7 percent of its arable land. Worse, China is losing 1 percent of its own arable land every year now because of the spread of the cities, the growth of rural factories, and environmental destruction. The age-old gap between the living standards of the villages and the cities had started to narrow at the beginning of the 1980s, with the return to private family farming, a cheap fix for Peking. But the difference has increased again as the Communists neglected agriculture and government investment in farming has fallen to its lowest level since 1949. On the other side of the ledger, government subsidies to city dwellers, to keep them quiescent, rose to $8.6 billion in 1988, 12 percent of the national budget. These subsidies include keeping the price of rice and housing low, providing free education and health benefits, and guaranteeing generous pension plans.

There were also some signs that Peking was simply too weak to deal with new economic troubles. From 1978 to 1988, for example, government revenue from taxes fell from being 37 percent of national income to only 19 percent, largely through inefficiency or corruption. That drop would make Ronald Reagan happy. But it has crimped vital new spending for education, roads, harbors, power plants, and modern industry.

With the hard-liners in charge after the June crackdown, there has been a movement back to more central planning and a slowdown in the rate of industrial growth. This may help by reducing inflation. But the ongoing policy struggle in Peking also sends mixed messages to the provinces which can result in confusion or paralysis.

This panoply of economic dangers suggests that the next erruption in China may not come from students, but from the country's factory workers, a threat Deng has long warned about. "Everywhere the world is changing for the better, except here in China," a thirty-one-year-old lathe operator remarked while eating fried dumplings at a sidewalk food stand on the Avenue of Eternal Tranquility. He and his colleagues had taken part in the democracy demonstrations only towards the end, he said, because they had no real connection to the students. But now he was furious about the killings, about inflation, and about corruption, which allowed his boss's wife to be on the factory payroll. "Next time we will be better prepared," he said.

As I talked to more and more Chinese, the key to the country's future seemed to lie in whether the economic changes would finally force political changes. The evidence on this was contradictory. Certainly the number of liberals at the top of the regime had been reduced by the events of 1989, despite a decade of growth. But there were hints some economic changes were eroding the old control apparatus at the bottom. At the forty-three-story Hilton Hotel in Shanghai, the manager, Heinz Schwander, a Swiss, had refused the government's demand after the crackdown that the hotel's 1,400 Chinese employees be required to attend political study sessions. The Shanghai city government considered the Hilton a danwei, a unit; but Schwander contended that the hotel was 100 percent foreign-owned and therefore not a work unit of the government. In the end, a compromise was worked out, and Schwander agreed to post a speech by Deng in the employees' cafeteria. But no one was compelled to read it.

The Hilton, a gleaming confection of glass and marble, with a five-story atrium and several full-time orchestras, was actually a quiet base for subversion. Working there was so popular that the hotel had to rent the Shanghai stadium for four days to interview prospective employees. Virtually all of them took the job in hopes of getting abroad, said Onie Chu, the public relations manager. Indeed, of the first 150 college graduates the Hilton had hired when it opened in 1987, all but 30 had already found ways to leave China.

In Peking after the massacre, one of the student leaders, Shen Tong, a twenty-year-old biology major at Peking University, was able to escape with help from sympathetic police officers and officials from CAAC, China's airline. They purchased a ticket for him to Tokyo, without entering his name in the computerized reservation system, then escorted him through customs and immigration. Shen, now a student at Brandeis University, told me other friends had arranged a fallback escape plan just in case. For $550, they had contracted with a group of Chinese underworld operatives to smuggle him out by fishing boat to the Portuguese colony of Macau. Shen was only one of more than a dozen student leaders wanted by the regime who managed to flee abroad. Such escapes, with the connivance of officials, were utterly unimaginable in the past.

A professor at Peking University put it best. He was depressed by the killings, but he was optimistic for the long run. "It was the Cultural Revolution that destroyed Maoism," he said. "It will be the reaction against the Tiananmen massacre that will end communism. Deng gave us so much, and we dreamed a better dream." He envisioned a long, slow process that could take years. He was only sure of the outcome. The situation reminded him of a Chinese aphorism: "When a bird gets too big, it breaks its cage."

Index

ABC News, 398, 469
abortions, 208, 227–28, 327
Academy of Sciences, 291–92
Academy of Social Sciences, 275n, 416
  Institute of Marxism-Leninism-Mao Zedong Thought of, 463–65
adultery, 160–61, 229–31
Agence France Press, 348
agricultural development and production, 14, 106, 118, 165–66, 236–38, 241, 244–53, 268–70, 478
All-China Women's Federation, 166, 167, 168–69, 176
An Gang, 393, 396
Anti-Rightist campaign, 5, 350, 363, 464, 466
April Fifth Forum, 406–10, 414–15
arms sales, 462–63
art, artists, 186–87, 311–12, 435–45, 451–52
athletes, policy toward, 79–80

Babaoshan Cemetery, 88
"back door," *see* countereconomy
Bai Hua, 449
Ba Jin, 80–81, 417
Bank of China, 471
baogao wenxue reporting style, 465
bao-jia system, 41
Bao Ruo-wang, 342, 361n
bathing facilities, 109, 132
BBC, 410
Bethune, Norman, 301
bicycles, 101
Bing, John, 266
birth control, 15, 141, 208, 227–28, 313, 326–28, 391, 470
Book of Rites, The, 164
bookstores, special, 71
Booz, Elizabeth, 107
Brown, Harold, 26, 342, 344, 388
Buchwald, Art, 132

Buddhism, 120, 255, 256, 423, 429–33
bureaucracy:
  authority and, 284–86
  incompetency of, 280–83
  Party and, 286–92
Bureau of the Census, U.S., 451
Burger, Warren E., 442
Bush, George, 463
Butler, Steven, 165, 250, 251
Butterfield, Barbara, xiv, xx, 16–17, 45, 47, 162–63, 205
Butterfield, Ethan, xiv, 23, 45, 205, 206, 207, 209
Butterfield, Fox, Chinese name of (Bao Defu), 89
Butterfield, Sarah, 204, 205, 206
"buyers," 97–98

Cable News, 391
cadres, description of, 67
Cai Jinqing, 456–457, 468–69
Califano, Joseph A., 27–28, 340
Campaign Against Counterrevolutionaries, 350
Canton, treaty port of, 26
Cao Yiou, 169–70
Cao Yong, 452
Cao Yu, 417
"caps," political, 5, 58–59
car ownership, 75–76
Carter, Jimmy, xiv, 29, 134
Catcher in the Rye, The (Salinger), 211
Catholicism, 422–24
Central Broadcasting Station, 86, 389, 444
Chandler, Laura, 204–5
Chen Boda, 357–58
Chen Daying, 32
Cheng Ming, 239, 332
Chen Muhua, 83–84, 168, 172
Chen Ping, 196
Chen Yi, 156
Chen Yun, 53, 219, 231–32, 476–77

Chiang Kai-shek, 7, 57, 473
child care, public, 172, 203–4,
    208–11, 219
children, 203–11
    attitude toward, 206–8, 210, 211,
        229
    behavior of, 203–4, 209–11
    rearing practices and, 204–6, 208,
        313
    sale of, 255
    see also education; youth
China, People's Republic of:
    as "Chinese" vs. "Communist,"
        61–62, 69–70, 87, 175, 217, 273,
        330
    constitution of, 165, 324, 356
    demography of, xix, 14, 15, 16,
        141, 181, 196, 197, 220, 237–39,
        247, 270, 327, 450–51, 478
    egalitarian rhetoric and practice in,
        64–88, 100, 101, 164–65, 168,
        176–77, 199, 244, 276–77
    fate of revolution in, 6, 8, 19–20,
        70, 88, 181, 201–2, 225, 298,
        309
    geography of, 14, 239
    historical national character of,
        12–13, 24–26, 41–42, 44, 48–49,
        52, 56–57, 61–63, 69, 72,
        133–34, 164, 196, 207–8, 217,
        252, 281, 284–86, 289, 298, 329,
        408, 412, 415
    minority peoples in, 240, 372–73,
        427–34, 443
    Westerners' view of, 6–7, 26
    Western influences and, 37–38,
        441–43
    xenophobia in, 24–25, 289
China Daily, 459
China Democratic League, 163
China Fund for the Handicapped, 462
China International Trust and
    Investment Corporation (Citic),
    462
China Reconstructs, 179
China Travel Service, xvii, 3, 66
China Youth League, 201
China Youth News, 142–43, 157, 397
Chinese Days (Terzani), 478
Chinese Music Association, 186–87
Chinese People's Association for
    Friendship with Foreign Countries,
    175
Chin Shi Huang, 12

Cho Lin, 169
Chong Wen Men market, 103
chop (seal), 62, 99
Christianity, 7–8, 202, 422–26
Church, Frank, 53–54
cigarettes, 81, 86, 95, 153
Clark, Marsh, 281–82
Classic for Girls, 164
Coale, Ansley J., 242n
Cohen, Jerome A., 451
Coming Alive, China After Mao
    (Garside), 34
commercialism, 453–57
communes, 27–28, 116, 165–66, 170,
    219, 238, 240–52
communications system, 383–405
    classified documents in, 388–92
    libraries and, 399–401
    museums and, 404–5
    public vs. semi-clandestine, 384,
        388, 389, 391
    shortwave broadcasts and, 410
    telephones and, 308, 319–20,
        386–88
    television and, 37, 398–99
    Xiao-dao xiao-xi in, 391–92
    see also newspapers and journals;
        specific publications
Communist Party, 7, 181, 200, 356,
    457
    artistic conformity and, 186–87,
        436–37, 445
    attempted modernization of, 474,
        476
    bureaucracy and, 286–92
    bureaucratic technocrats in, 477
    Central Investigation Department of,
        335, 472
    control by, 122–23, 124, 249, 308,
        322, 328, 329, 334, 344, 364,
        376–77, 470–75
    corruption in, 11, 361, 460–64,
        466, 468
    cult of Mao and, 301–4
    democracy movement and, 464,
        467–69
    disaffection from, 138, 181–82, 201,
        295–301, 310–12, 458
    education levels in, 290–92
    factions in, 292–94
    foreigners as viewed by, 26
    headquarters of, 62
    History Department of, xvii–xviii
    intellectuals in, 416–18, 464

loyal supporters of, 218, 228
marriage policy in, 154–55
Marxism and, 62, 68, 69, 164, 299, 300–301, 327, 408, 414, 417, 422
Military Affairs Commission of, 169, 478
military personnel in, 76–77, 297
news stories on, 383–85, 387, 390, 393
Organization Department of, 465
peasants in, 248, 287, 288–90, 292, 297
persecutions by, *see* political persecutions and repression
prerogatives of officials of, 8–9, 38, 67, 70–78, 83–87, 155–58, 189, 288, 296–97, 359, 361, 392, 460–63
Propaganda Department of, 187, 384, 465
repressive system created by, xix, 449, 451–52
secrecy imposed by, 383–91, 392, 405
self-evaluation in, 299, 302
Tiananmen Square demonstrations and, xvii–xviii, 448, 463–65, 473, 476
United Front Department of, 429
veneration for age in, 219–20
women in, 168–69
concubinage, 135, 254–55
Confucian code, 49, 52, 61, 69, 126, 164, 175, 206, 207, 329–30, 412, 415
Confucius, 7, 23, 39, 52, 56–57, 69, 217, 235, 298, 473
consumerism, 37, 102–5, 277, 398
control, techniques of, 122–23, 124, 249, 308, 322, 328, 329, 334, 344, 364, 376–77, 470–75
cost-of-living index, 79
"Counterattack the Right Deviationist Wind" campaign, 438
countereconomy, 11–12, 92–112
corruption and, 97, 99, 112, 459–60
foreign trade and, 96–98
guan-xi and, 94–96
imposters and, 92
private enterprise and, 104–5, 109
rationing and, 100–101, 102, 108
"squeeze" and, 99

crime, 11, 50–51, 109, 158–60, 299, 360–61
1979 code on, 356
sex and, 140, 144, 145, 146, 157–60, 161, 284, 458–59
youth and, 180–81, 184, 191
Cui Xinfeng, 91–92
Cultural Revolution, 29, 46, 51, 57, 58, 62, 68, 77, 78, 84, 126, 269, 447, 464, 474–75, 480
breakdown in authority and, 84, 149, 151, 286, 361, 392
depredations of, xix, 5, 6, 17–20, 70, 81, 113–22, 221, 309, 348–56, 372, 375, 378, 401, 425, 430
Mao and, 5, 6, 17–20, 77, 183–85, 188–89, 196, 197, 223, 224, 285, 292–93, 355, 461
pro-democracy demonstrations and, 467
public alienation after, 449, 456, 458
younger generation affected by, 126, 181–85, 188–89, 194, 196, 197, 201, 212–13, 221–25, 309–10, 331, 409, 413, 439

dai-mao-zi custom, 58–59
Dalai Lama, 430–32, 433
dancing, 187–88
danwei system, 40–42, 322, 323–24, 469–70, 479
Dark Willows and Bright Flowers, 339
Davis-Friedman, Deborah, 218
Dazhai, 403–4
Declaration of Independence, U.S., 412
defectors, 418–20, 464–67
democracy movement, 20, 32, 46, 86, 114, 307, 410–18, 437, 465–67, 476
intellectuals and, 415–18, 464–65
Tiananmen Square demonstrations and, xvii–xix, 448–50, 456, 463–65, 468–70, 473, 475–77, 479
Democracy Wall, 37, 308, 406–8, 410, 411, 415, 450, 457, 465
Deng Bufang, 461–62
Deng Lin, 462
Deng Liqun, 417
Deng Meisheng, 170
Deng Nan, 462–63

Deng Qin, 177–78
Deng Xiaoping, 38, 53, 67, 72, 169, 219, 246, 275n, 280, 285, 301, 349, 445, 446, 464, 480
  changes from Mao's policies by, 20, 37, 101–2, 111, 242, 277–79, 291–93, 310, 355–56, 403–4, 410–11, 416–17, 421, 423, 442, 447, 473–74
  economic policy of, xix, 101–2, 111, 242, 277–79, 447–48, 450, 452, 453, 459, 464, 473–76, 479
  foreign policy of, 36–37
  Four Cardinal Principles of, 474–75
  future of freedom and, 20, 37, 411
  Hua Guofeng and, 395, 403–4, 411, 417
  nepotism practiced by, 461–62
  purges of, 353
  Tiananmen Square demonstrations and, xviii, 448–49, 465, 469, 473, 476–77
  U.S. visit of, 29, 37, 49–50, 177, 281–82, 442
Deng Yingchao, 168
Deng Zhifang, 462
Didion, Joan, 332
diet, statistics on, 106–7, 118, 238–39, 243
Ding Ling, 417
Diplomatic Services Bureau, 24, 33–34
diplomats, foreign, 34, 93
dissidents, 20, 114, 115, 126, 138, 305–12, 362–69, 406–34
  artists as, 435–45, 451–52
  defectors and, 418–20, 464–67
  intellectuals and, 415–18, 464–65
  religion and, 422–34
  see also political persecutions and repression
divorce, 142, 161, 167, 173–76, 231
Dolfin, John, 62–63
Donovan, Hedley, 281–82
dress style and code, 78, 124, 131, 194–95, 206–7, 443
drivers, privileges of, 77–78, 95
drug addiction, 360, 457–58
duty labor, 125

"East Is Red, The," 221, 224
economy, 13–14, 467
  counter ("taking the back door"), see countereconomy

foreign currency and, 35, 97, 275
foreign trade and, 37, 96–98, 450
housing and, see housing conditions
inefficiencies in, 260–69, 471
materialism and, 453–59
present condition of, 9, 15, 99–100, 278–79, 450, 478–79
private enterprise and, 104–5, 109, 190, 219, 244, 251
reforms in, xix, 101–2, 111, 242, 277–79, 293, 300, 447–48, 450, 452, 453, 459, 464, 471, 473–76
reports on, 269–70
welfare state mentality and, 273–77
see also agricultural development and production; consumerism; industry; standard of living
education, 15, 18–19, 68, 79, 86–87, 121, 166, 180, 188, 195–202, 247–48, 399–401
  government spending on, 467, 478
  history courses in, 200
  reforms in, 196–201, 308
  statistics on, 196–97, 199
  status and, 197–200, 287
  see also students, Chinese
Eisenberg, David, 43, 147, 214, 337–39
elections, 421–22
Engelmann, Larry, 472
entertainment, entertainers, 454–56
Esen Music Club, 454
ethnic minorities, dissent and, 427–34
executions, 360

"face," concept of, 60–61
factory workers, 478–79
Fairbank, John K., xiii–xiv, xv, 60
Family (Ba Jin), 80
family relationships, 49–51, 69, 126, 165, 169, 173–77, 211–13, 217–19, 253–55, 332–34
  breakdown of, 221–25, 228–29
  see also children; marriage
Fang Guanghua, 286–88
Fang Yi, 73, 290
Fang Zhiyuan, 422
Fanshen (Hinton), 235, 423
Feighon, Lee, xvii–xviii
Feng Wenbin, 416–17
Feng Yulan, 258
fish supply, 104, 243
Five-Year Plans, 259, 263
Fleming, Peggy, 53

food:
  price stabilization and, 250
  shopping for, 13
  shortages of, 15, 100–101, 105–8,
    116–17, 118, 238–39, 242, 243,
    247
  see also agricultural development and
    production
foreigners:
  attitudes toward, 23–38, 49, 237
  double-price policy for, 35–36, 89
  nationalism and, 24–25
  quarantine of, 29–31
  romantic involvements with, 31–33
  as spy suspects, 34
  surveillance of, 33–35, 471–72
Foreign Languages Press, 180, 181
Foreign Ministry, 465
foreign trade, 37, 96–98, 450
Four Cardinal Principles, 474–75
Four Modernizations program, 262,
    278, 412, 442
Fou Tsong, 418
Freud, Sigmund, 139, 338
friendship, Chinese sense of, 47–48
Friendship Store, 31, 32, 47, 98
fuel, shortage of, 109, 110
Fu Jian, 341
funerals, 256

ganbu (cadre), 67
Gandunjiacuo, 430–31
Gang of Elders, 476
Gang of Four, 5, 84, 156, 292–93,
    349, 356–59
Gao, Bill, 370–79
Garside, Roger, 34
Gassiter, Michael, 322
generation gap, 212–13, 228–29
Gilbert, Walter, 402–3
glasnost, 468
Golden Lotus, The, 71, 134–35
Goldman, Merle, 415n
Gorbachev, Mikhail, 468, 474, 477
Graham, Victoria, 410
grain production, 14, 106, 236–37,
    238, 241, 244–46, 249
Great Britain, 25–26, 449, 457
Great Hall of the People, 25, 26, 29,
    66, 188, 219, 388
Great Leap Forward, 6, 51, 116, 242,
    244–45, 464
grocery shopping, time spent in, 103
group, primacy of, 13

guai, concept of, 207
Guangming Daily, 197
guan-xi relationships, 44, 48–49,
    94–96, 149, 211, 252, 392, 460
guesthouses, 82–83
Guillermaz, Jacques, 350n

Han, Zora, 428
handicapped, 338n
He Ping, 462–63
He Zizhen, 155
Hilton Hotel, 479
Hinton, William, 235, 423
homosexuality, 145–46
Hong Kong, 185, 274, 419–20
Hong Songdao, 174–75
Hong Yung Lee, 477
hostmanship, 26–29, 31, 45
household registration certificates,
    122–23, 124, 249
housing conditions, 29–30, 45, 64,
    72–73, 78–79, 82–83, 110–12,
    124–25, 147, 219, 258–59, 310
Hsu, Francis L. K., 207–8
Hua Guofeng, 9, 26, 53, 67, 156,
    169, 242, 299, 334–35, 411, 477
  ousting of, 383, 387, 395, 403–4,
    417
Huang Hua, 38, 182
Huang Zhou, 73
Hu Feng, 339
Hughes, Harry, 82
Hundred Flowers Campaign, 5, 6,
    363, 465–66
Hu Qiaomu, 275n, 416
Hu Yaobang, xviii, 292, 293, 294,
    299, 464, 468, 476–77

industry, 79, 97, 166, 247
  agricultural production and, 249–50,
    252, 268
  bungling in, 260–69, 279, 282–83
  central planning and, 263–68, 277
  corruption and, 460
  foreign companies concerned in,
    261, 262–63, 266, 267, 275, 279,
    447–48, 451, 460
  heavy vs. consumer goods, 99–100,
    101–2, 277, 278
  pollution and, 270–72
  present condition of, 9, 15, 99–100,
    258–79, 471
  productivity in, 272–77, 278
inflation, 467, 476

information, management of, 72,
319–22, 370, 383–405
Information Department, 54, 55, 116,
280–82, 403
Institute for Traditional Chinese
Medicine, 147
Institute of International Relations, 335
Institute of the United States, 417
intellectuals, 439, 440, 477
democracy movement and, 415–18,
464–65
persecution of, 18, 19, 113–14, 197,
269, 290–92, 350–51, 374,
376–77
International Club, 86
International Settlement, 454
intimacy, lack of, 43
Iran, 462

Jiang Hua, 193
Jiang Qing, 5, 72, 122, 155, 156, 168,
169, 303, 345, 349, 351–52, 355,
476
trial of, 356–59
Jianguo Hotel, 458
Jiang Zemin, 460–61, 477
Jing Shan, 463
Jinjiang Hotel, 42
Jinling Hotel, 471
job assignments, 86, 87, 96, 97, 169,
189–91, 198, 215–16, 218–19,
249, 273, 332
Johns Hopkins University, Nanjing
Center of, 472

Kang Hua, 462
Kang Keli, 190–91
Kang Keqing, 166, 168–69
Kang Sheng, 169
Kang Shien, 282, 284
Kates, George, 60, 203
Kelly, Daniel, 366–67
Kennedy, John F., xiii
Kentucky Fried Chicken, 447–48
Kirkpatrick, Lynn and Andrew, 333–34
kissing, 32–33, 132–33, 137
Kissinger, Henry, 66
Koch, Ed, 29, 289, 384–85
Kong Pingmai, 368
Korean War, 363, 404

labels, political, 5, 18, 19, 59, 113,
115, 125, 129, 137, 151, 224,
249

labor camps, 361–69, 411
Lai Ying, 361n
land reform campaign, 6, 58–59, 235,
350
Lao She, 18
Lao Wu, see Wu Qianwei
Lardy, Nicholas, 241, 244–45, 247n,
248, 250, 251, 450n
League of Left-Wing Writers, 187
legal system, 451
Lei Feng, 182
Lei Jieqiong, 40–41
Lennon, John, 25
Lewis, Flora, 354
li, concept of, 52–53, 55, 60–61
Liang Heng, 421–22
Liao Mosha, 18
Li Bo, 246
Li Chang, 292
Lido Hotel, 458
Lieberthal, Kenneth, 388n
life expectancy, 16, 220, 241
Lifton, Robert Jay, 211, 286, 331, 473
Li Guyi, 187, 194
Li Hongyuan, 271
Li Hui, 458–59
Li Jianzhi, 204
Lin Biao, 155, 156, 157, 221, 345,
349, 356, 405
Lin Like, 156–57
Lin Qingyun, 342–345
Li Peng, 460–61, 469, 477
Li Rentang, 86
Li Ruihuan, 461
Li Shenzhi, 417
literature, 80, 187, 351, 417–18,
443–45
love and sex in, 71, 134–35, 145
Li Tieying, 461
"little road news," 391–92
Liu Binyan, 465–67, 473
Liu Decai, 361
Liu Guanghua, 185–86
Liu Qing, 406–11
Liu Shaoqi, 38, 169, 200, 349, 354,
385, 460–61
Liu Shikun, 85, 348
Li Xiannian, 53, 270, 384–85, 476–77
Li Yizhe (pen name), 20
Li Zhen, 334
Long Bow village, 235–37, 239, 423
Long March, xiii, 65, 67
loudspeakers, 329
love:

marriage and, 130–31, 132, 134,
137–39, 141–42, 144, 307
romantic, 133–34, 136–37, 139,
142–43
and sex in literature, 71, 134–35,
145
Lu Hong, 183
Lu Jiaxi, 291
Lu Lin, 408–9
Lu Xun, 24, 404, 435, 446
Lysenko, Trofim, 402

Macartney, Earl of, 25
MacFarquhar, Roderick, 350n
MacLaine, Shirley, 29
Ma faction, 456
Malraux, André, 172, 179
Mandarin, 246
Mao Dun, 417
Mao Zedong, 12, 156, 181, 200, 241,
263, 388, 408, 413, 436–37, 457,
465–66, 475–77
aphorisms of, 71, 172, 179, 183,
284, 291, 370, 383, 409, 439
cult of, 285–86, 301–4, 399, 436
Cultural Revolution and, 5, 6,
17–20, 77, 183–85, 188–89, 196,
197, 223, 224, 285, 292–93, 355,
461
Deng Xiaoping's policies vs., 20, 37,
101–2, 111, 242, 277–79,
291–93, 310, 355–56, 403–4,
410–11, 416–17, 421, 423, 442,
447, 473–74
economic policy of, 447, 450, 452,
453
foreign policy of, xiii, 36
Great Leap Forward and, 6, 51, 116,
242, 244–45
new youth culture and, 456
personal life of, 155, 156, 285, 303
privileges accorded to, 67, 72,
82–83
pro-democracy demonstrations and,
467
selflessness of, 453–54
Ma Rongjie, 358n
marriage, 51, 59, 96, 154–55, 167,
176, 229–31, 253–55
"live-in" vs., 147
love and, 130–31, 132, 134,
137–39, 141–42, 144, 307
maltreatment in, 167–68
matchmakers and, 149–51, 254

policies on, 32–33, 41, 141, 147,
150, 154–55, 213, 252–54
see also divorce
Marxism, 62, 68, 69, 164, 202, 299,
300–301, 327, 408, 414, 417,
422, 463, 475
masturbation, 143–44
materialism, 453–59
May Fourth movement, 181, 408
Ma Yinchu, 327
May Seventh Cadre School, 68
medicine and health care, 18, 79, 81,
94–95, 162–63, 241, 248, 375
Mencius, 134, 229
menstruation, 171
mental health, 336–41, 378–79
middle age, conditions met in, 215–17
military, 157, 160, 307, 310
rank in, 67, 78
status of, 76–77, 312
Military Museum, 404–5
missionaries, xiv, 7, 368, 424–26
mobility, social, 213–16
see also education; job assignments;
rank
Mosher, Maggie, 147–48
Moslems, Chinese, 240, 372–73, 423,
429
movies, movie industry, 72, 75, 86,
93, 309, 445
Munro, Julie and Ross, 386
music, pop, 186–87, 188, 195, 455–56

Nadelson, Carol C., 159
names, significance of, 57–58
Nanjing University, Johns Hopkins
Center at, 472
National Day (October 1st), 72
Nationalities Palace, 32
National People's Congress (NPC),
248, 421, 471, 476
nepotism, 84–87, 460–64, 468
New China News Agency, 9, 17, 43,
50, 196, 354, 390, 391, 462, 471
New Journalism, 465
newspapers and journals, 453
censorship and, 403–4
improvements in, 396–98
investigative stories in, 397, 465–66
journalists in, 391, 392–95
letters to editor and, 395–96
political role of, 393–95
underground, 406–10, 413, 414–15,
438

487

newspapers and journals (*cont'd*)
see also communications system;
specific newspapers
New York Times, The, xiv, xv, xix, 6,
24, 61, 74, 283, 308, 320, 358*n*,
391
Nieh Yuanzi, 352
1984 (Orwell), 188
Niu Man-chang, 402–3
Nixon, Richard, 42, 44, 71, 303, 390

Ocean Helicopters, 461
official exchange rate, 9*n*, 454
old age, benefits of, 217–20
Onie Chu, 479
opera, Chinese, 56
Opium War, 26, 36, 449, 457, 473
Orwell, George, 188, 405, 448

Pan American World Airways, 25
Panchen Lama, 354
Pan Qingde, 324
paper, shortage of, 71, 399
Parish, William L., 239, 254
Parks, Michael, 171
Passages (Sheehy), 13, 214, 215*n*, 230
patriotism, 24–25, 417, 419
peasants, 235–57
   in Communist Party, 248, 287,
      288–90, 292, 297
   industrialization and, 249–50, 252,
      268
   standard of living of, 116–19,
      237–38, 240, 243, 250–52
   see also communes; rural life
Pei, I. M., 442, 471
Peking Art Academy, 436, 443
Peking City Food Supply Place, 70–71
Peking Cultural Relics Bureau, 401
Peking Evening News, 91
Peking Exhibition Hall, 89
Peking Fine Arts Museum, 452
Peking First Infectious Diseases
   Hospital, 162–63
Peking Foreign Languages Institute,
   18, 109
Peking Hotel, 8, 39, 40–41, 61, 81,
   321, 447, 457, 471
Peking Second Foreign Languages
   Institute, 32
Peking University, xviii, 15, 166, 202,
   400, 422, 456–57
Peng Jiamu, 351
Peng Zhen, 85, 476

"People or Monsters" (Liu Binyan),
   466
People's Daily, 6, 17, 37, 84, 152, 193,
   196, 261*n*, 265, 283, 299, 320,
   348, 384, 391, 393–94, 445, 463,
   465–66
People's Liberation Army, 9, 64, 334,
   450
   Foreign Affairs Department of, 343
   in Tiananmen Square massacre, xviii,
      446, 448–49, 457, 464, 469
People's University, xvii–xviii, 77
petitioners, 114, 122–23
pets, 312
physicians, 374–77, 378
Piccus, Robert, 83
Pike, Adrian, 239
Ping-Pong diplomacy, 29
pinyin system, xv
playacting, 56–57, 473
political persecutions and repression,
   5–6, 17–20, 30–31, 41, 113–22,
   125, 129, 140, 151, 155, 158,
   221, 305–7, 335, 344–59,
   373–74, 409, 413–14, 416, 441
political study, "small group," 322,
   330–32
Poly Technologies, 462
pregnancies, pre-marital, 147, 227
prisons and reformatories, 145, 335,
   354–55, 362
privacy, lack of, 42, 49
private enterprise, 104–5, 109, 190,
   219, 244, 251
production teams, 242, 252–53
prostitution, 135, 151–54, 185,
   458–59
psychiatry, 338–41, 378–79
Public Security ministry, 3, 8, 9–10,
   30, 40, 90–91, 98, 324, 334–35,
   345, 363, 414, 465, 470–71
puritanism, 135–46, 155, 156, 453

Qiao Shi, 460
Qi Mingzong, 54–56
Qin Cheng Number One, 354–55
Qinghai, 362, 365–66
Quemoy-Matsu crisis, xiii

rank, 8–9, 249
   cadre and, 67
   privileges of, 64–88, 100, 107, 118,
      137, 155–58, 160, 180, 199, 284,
      288, 310, 374, 382, 392

rigidities of, 216
structure of, 66–69, 189
rape, 157–60
rationing system, 100–101, 102, 108
rank and, 70, 78, 81
Reagan, Ronald, 12, 262, 462, 478
Red Flag, 280, 299
Red Flag cars, 75–76
Red Guards, 18, 19, 20, 58, 71, 183,
  285, 339, 439
see also Cultural Revolution
Red Guerrillas, 239
Red Star Over China (Snow), xiii
Reference Material, 390, 391
Reference News, 389–90, 391
"Regulations on Guarding State
  Secrets," 385–86
Reischauer, Edwin O., xiii
religion, xiv, 7–8, 202, 240, 372–73
  dissent and, 422–34
  folk, 120–21, 255–57, 426–27
renao, preference for, 43
Rich, John, 107–8
Rickshaw Boy (Lao She), 18
Rittenberg, Sidney, 355
Ritter, Martha, 211
ritual, 52–56, 60–61, 473
RNA research, 402–3
Roderick, John, 145
Rong Bao Zhai, 443
Rosenthal, A. M., 145
Rubin, Jerry, 6
Rumania, 395
rural life, 27–28, 116–21, 165–66,
  170, 196, 219, 235–57
  backwardness of, 240, 245–48,
    253–57, 327
  mismanagement and, 241, 242–43
  modern improvements in, 235–37,
    241, 250–52
  urban life vs., 16, 241, 245–52, 286
  violence in, 119–20
  see also agricultural development and
    production; communes; peasants
Russians, The (Smith), 12
rustication program, 12, 18, 119, 157,
  182–85, 188–90, 305

Schell, Orville, 153
Schultz, George, 463
Schwander, Heinz, 479
science, secrecy and, 401–3
Scott, Sir Peter, 179
Scott-Stokes, Henry, 61

secrecy, prevalence of, 72, 319–22,
  370, 383–405, 409
security, xiv, 3–4, 9–10, 320–41
  classified documents and, 388–92
  organizations concerned in, 322,
    323–27, 330–32
  peer pressure in, 328–29
  police in, 326, 334–36
  precautions taken for, 72, 308,
    319–22, 370, 383–405
  separation of families in, 332–34
  spy suspects and, 34, 371–74
  strains caused by, 336–41
  surveillance in, 33–35, 322, 323–32,
    471–72
Selected Works (Deng Xiaoping), 452
self-criticism, 331–32, 377, 445
self-help meetings, 5
Senate Foreign Relations Committee,
  U.S., 42
servants, rank and, 65, 77–78, 249
service industry, 99
sexual mores, 71, 131–161, 284, 453
  changes in, 146–61, 226, 458–59
Shanghai, commercialism in, 453–57
Shanghai Communiqué, 42
Shan Guizhang, 351
Shapiro, Judy, 421–22
Sheehy, Gail, 13, 214, 215, 230
Shen Tong, 479
Shen Yier, 394–95
Shen Zhongling, 193
Shephard, Joan, 50
shop clerks, 95, 103–4
Shulman, Norman, 108, 111–12, 324
Sichuan *bang,* 293–94
Sichuan cooking, 105–6
Si-ma Qian, 281
slogans, 57, 301, 408
Smith, Hedrick, 12
Snow, Edgar, xiii
Socialist Education Campaign, 161
Solzhenitsyn, Aleksandr, 415, 418, 464
Song Mingchao, 184–85
Song Zhenming, 282–84
Southern Daily, 192
Soviet Union, China vs., 12, 26, 142,
  194, 229, 240, 244, 249, 260,
  263, 310, 330, 338, 362, 363,
  402, 415, 418, 422
Sports of China, 136
Stalin, Joseph, 6, 400
standard of living, 15, 45–47, 101–12,
  274, 428, 433

standard of living (*cont'd*)
  of privileged, 64–88
  in rural areas, 116–19, 237–52
State Statistical Bureau, 269–70, 471
street committees, 9, 322, 325–27
  birth control and, 326–28
struggle sessions, 344–47
students, Chinese, 189, 194–202, 300,
    331–32, 421–22, 477
  in democracy movement, 465–67
  living conditions of, 77, 106–7, 109,
    110, 467
  materialism and self-indulgence of,
    456–57
  overseas, 34, 38, 195, 308, 456,
    460–63
  in Tiananmen Square
    demonstrations, xvii–xix, 448,
    465, 468–70, 473, 475–77, 479
students, foreign, in China, 33, 43
Sui, Yolanda, 85–86
suicide, 167, 198, 224, 378
Sun Weishi, 355
Sun Yat-sen, Madame, 73–75, 85, 86,
    168
Su Shaozhi, 463–65, 467
Swiss bank accounts, 96

Taiwan, xiii, 57, 473
Tales of the Plum Flower Society, 351
Tang, Nancy, 156
Tang Yinchu, 343–44
Tansuo, 413
Taoism, 255, 281, 423
technology, education and, 197, 198,
    200
telephones, control and, 308, 319–20,
    386–88
television, effects of, 37, 398–99
Temple of Heaven, 457
Teng, Teresa, 187
Terzani, Angela, 478
thought reform, 331, 376–77, 473
Three Character Classic, 121
Three Gates Theater, 72
Tiananmen Square:
  attempt to rewrite events in, 472–73
  massacre in, xviii, 446, 448, 450,
    451, 452, 457, 462–64, 469, 472,
    477, 479–80
  pro-democracy demonstrations in,
    xvii–xix, 448–50, 456, 463–65,
    468–70, 473, 475–77, 479
  security surveillance in, 471

Tiao faction, 456
Tibet, 54, 96, 429–34
Time, 281, 454, 456
titles, importance of, 58–59, 69
toasts, banquet, 53–54
Torch, 191
Toronto Globe and Mail, 457
tourists, tourism, 33, 280
  relaxing of restrictions on, 451,
    452–53
travel, travel facilities, 98, 328
  rank and, 80, 82, 85
  relaxing of restrictions on, 451,
    452–53
trial goods system, 12
tribute system, 25–26, 56
Tunghsiang, 193
Tuo faction, 456
Twenty-four Examples of Filial Piety, The,
    208, 211

Uighurs, 372–73, 428–29
Ulanhu, 73
United States:
  children of Party elite at schools in,
    38, 460–63
  Deng Xiaoping's visit to, 29, 37,
    49–50, 177, 281–82, 442
  normalization of relations between
    China and, xiv, 26, 38, 42, 308,
    342
  Taiwan Nationalists and, xiii, 57,
    473
urban life, rural life vs., 16, 241,
    245–52, 286

values, Chinese vs. Western, 42–44,
    47–53, 172–73, 177, 200, 204–5,
    207–8, 214–15, 217, 229
Vance, Cyrus R., 298
Vietnam, 187
Vietnam war, xiv, 472
*Village and Family in Contemporary
    China* (Parish and Whyte), 239,
    254n
Viznews, 398
Voice of America, 410, 454, 456

Walker, Sue, 16–17
Walker, Tony, 34
wall posters, policies on, 392, 411–12
  see also Democracy Wall
Wang Chaoqi, 163
Wang Dongxing, 53, 168, 322

Wang family, 44–48, 49, 51–52,
    149–51, 170–71, 187–88, 205
Wang Guangmei, 169, 349–50, 354
Wang Guorong, 428
Wang Guoying, 254
Wang Hairong, 156, 179
Wang Hongwen, 358
Wang Jinhung, 237
Wang Keping, xiv, 435–45, 451–52
Wang Meng, 77
Wang Roshui, 416–17
Wang Yonghe, 192
Wang Zhen, 461
Wan Li, 461
Wei Jingfeng, 174–75
Wei Jingsheng, 86, 354, 406, 409,
    412–14, 415, 465
Welch, Holmes, 56
Wen Fusan, 349
Wen Qian, 458
Wen Zhenxiang, 264–65
White Album, The (Didion), 332
Whyte, Martin King, 40, 239, 254
Wilf, Susan, 32, 141, 426
Witke, Roxanne, 155
women, 162–78
    discrimination against, 163, 165–66,
        170
    postrevolutionary, 230, 313
    prominence achieved by, 163,
        168–69
    rights of, 165, 175
    traditional attitudes toward, 164,
        165, 166–67, 174, 214
    as workers, 164, 165–66, 170–73
Women of China, 394–95
Wong, Jan, xv, 33–34, 108, 111–12,
    115, 160, 177, 212, 287, 321,
    324, 457–58
wood, shortage of, 108, 440
Woodcock, Leonard, 40
Workers' Daily, 133
Wuer Kaixi, 471
Wu Qianwei (Lao Wu), 24, 33,
    60–61, 172, 206, 337
wu-wei tradition, 281
Wu Xiuquan, 356–57

Xiang Shan Hotel, 471–72
Xiao Bin, 469
Xiao Lu, 452
Xiao Yan, 51
Xia Zhenyi, 340
Xie, Moses P., 424–26

Xie Fuzhi, 349
Xinjiang Autonomous Region, 427–29
Xiong twins, 159–60
xiu-xi tradition, 272–73
Xu Meihong, 472
Xu Wenli, 414–15

Yang Baibing, 478
Yang Chen-ning, 291
Yang Fuguo, 155
Yang Guidi, 132
Yang Kaihui, 155
Yang Shangkun, 463–64, 478
Yang Wanhua, 136–40
Yan Youmin, 53–54
Yan Ziyang, 157
Yao Wei, 442
Years That Were Fat, The (Kates), 60,
    203
Ye Jianying, 53, 84–85, 219–20,
    461
Ye Xiangzhen, 85
Ye Xiangzhi, 43
Yih Leefah, 367–68
yin-yang principle, 164
You Can Get There From Here
    (MacLaine), 29
youth:
    accommodations by, 312–15
    alienation of, 179–202, 212–13,
        225, 228–29, 309–12, 468
    counterculture of, 185–88, 193,
        194–95, 435–45
    Cultural Revolution and, *see* Cultural
        Revolution
    generation gap and, 212–13, 228–29
    as political activists, 421–22
    pop culture of, 455–56
    problems of adolescents, 211–13
    as students, *see* education; students,
        Chinese
    unemployed, 189–90
Yuan Mu, 472–73
Yuan Xianlu, 397–98
Yugoslavia, 387

Zhang Chunqiao, 357, 359
Zhang Guangdou, 37–38
Zhang Junshi, 199
Zhang Kaichi, 106
Zhang Lianchang, 273
Zhang Longqian, 92
Zhang Nanxiang, 73
Zhang Wei, 347–48

Zhang Yufeng, 156, 358
Zhang Zhongyi, 349–50
Zhao Dan, 445
Zhao Ziyang, 293, 299, 300, 383–84,
    385, 460, 464, 471, 476–77
Zheng Peidi, 351–53, 399

Zhou Enlai, 45, 67, 81, 156, 310,
    355, 408, 417, 460
Zhou Yang, 187, 319
Zhuang Zedong, 80
Zhu De, 67, 168
Zito, Angela, 400